CW01574589

THE COMPLETE RESULTS & LINE-UPS OF THE COPA LIBERTADORES 2006-2011

Dirk Karsdorp and Romeo Ionescu

British Library Cataloguing in Publication Data
A catalogue record for this book is available from the British Library

ISBN: 978-1-86223-229-7

Copyright © 2012, SOCCER BOOKS LIMITED (01472 696226)
72 St. Peter's Avenue, Cleethorpes, N.E. Lincolnshire, DN35 8HU, England
Web site www.soccer-books.co.uk
e-mail info@soccer-books.co.uk

All rights are reserved. No part of this publication may be reproduced, stored in a retrieval system or transmitted, in any form or by any means, electronic, mechanical, photocopying, recording, or otherwise, without the prior written permission of Soccer Books Limited.

Printed in the UK by 4Edge Ltd.

FOREWORD

In 1948, the first tournament for the champion clubs of South America (named *Campeonato Sudamericano de Campeones* – the South American Championship of Champions), was held in Santiago, Chile. The tournament took place following many years of preparation by a number of South American football administrators and the Chilean club, Colo-Colo hosted this first competition. Colo-Colo, the reigning Chilean champions, played in a round-robin competition along with the Champion clubs of Argentina, Bolivia, Brazil, Ecuador, Peru and Uruguay, but it was the Brazilian champions, Vasco da Gama, who lifted the trophy, finishing undefeated with a record of four victories and two draws. This tournament has since been recognised as a precursor of the Copa Libertadores by the Confederación Sudamericana de Fútbol, the South American Football Federation more commonly known as CONMEBOL.

Although this first competition was considered a success, it was not until 1960 that CONMEBOL themselves initiated a new continental competition for the Champion clubs of their member countries, a move possibly influenced by the success of UEFA's European Champions Clubs' Cup. This new competition was perhaps unsurprisingly named the *Copa Campeones de América* (American Champions Cup) and it remains one of the most prestigious club competitions in world football to this day.

Initially, each country entered just one club in the *Copa Campeones*, generally their League Champions, though Brazil entered their national cup winners as there was no national league in the country at that time. However, from 1966 onwards, the competition was renamed the *Copa Libertadores de América* (American Liberators Cup) in honour of the revered heroes of the South American wars of independence. Together with this change in name came a change in format as the competition was expanded and each country now entered teams with the exception of the nation of the current holders of the trophy, who did not enter the competition until the second round (semi-final stage).

Over the years the actual format of the *Copa Libertadores* has varied with the teams being split into groups of varying sizes and the top team in each group progressing to the next round (often a further group stage). However, the format changed markedly in 1988 with the top three teams in each group joining the reigning champions in a second round of 16 clubs. The second round onwards was then played out as a classical knock-out tournament with the aggregate score of home and away ties deciding progression, with the final also being decided over two matches.

The next major change to the competition came in 1998 when Mexican teams were invited to enter the tournament for the first time – despite the fact that Mexico is a member of the CONCACAF federation! Two Mexican teams competed in a preliminary round with two teams from Venezuela, the two winners of this stage progressing to the group stage of the competition proper.

A further change in format came in 2000 when the number of entrants in the competition proper was increased to 32 teams (taken from the 11 countries represented). These 32 teams were split into 8 groups of 4 teams with the top two in each group qualifying for the second round knock-out stage. This format remains to this day although, with up to 40 teams entering in recent years, a preliminary knock-out round is now played to decide some of the entrants in the group stage.

I have endeavoured to make the contents of this book as accurate as possible but often, checking two different sources leads to different information for the same match. In cases such as this, I have used what I consider to be the most trustworthy information which I could find.

Dirk Karsdorp and Romeo Ionescu

2006

FIRST STAGE

NACIONAL ASUNCIÓN – UNIVERSITARIO DE LIMA 2-2 (0-0)
Defensores del Chaco, Asunción, 24.01.2006
Referee: Sergio Fabián Pezzota (ARG), Attendance: 3.000
NACIONAL: Miguel Cárdenas, Julio César Irrazábal, Ángel Marcelo Martínez (87 Pánfilo Ramón Escobar), Enrique Gabriel Meza, Fábio Ramón Ramos, Glacinei Martins "INCA", Troadio Daniel Barreto, Mauro Milciades Monges (77 Rodrigo Fabián Cantero), Carlos Alberto González (61 Cristian Bogado), Oscar René Cardozo, Heber Alberto Arriola. DT: Carlos Jara Saguier
UNIVERSITARIO: Juan Ángel Flores, Jhoel Alexander Herrera, Luis Alberto Guadalupe, Germán Martín Centurión, José Alberto Moisela, José Antonio Pereda (75 José Adolfo Mendoza), Gregorio Abel Bernales, Luis Alberto Hernández, Arnaldo Daniel Alonso (75 Paolo Freddy Maldonado), Piero Fernando Alva, Víctor Alonso Rosell (46 Gastón Maximiliano Sangoy). DT: Juan Amador Sánchez
Goals: Germán Martín Centurión (62 own goal), José Alberto Moisela (66 own goal) /
José Alberto Moisela (64), Gastón Maximiliano Sangoy (90+3).

UNIVERSITARIO DE LIMA – NACIONAL ASUNCIÓN 0-0
Monumental, Lima, 31.01.2006
Referee: Carlos Eduardo López (COL)
UNIVERSITARIO: Juan Ángel Flores, Luis Alberto Guadalupe, Germán Martín Centurión, José Alberto Moisela, Jhoel Alexander Herrera, José Antonio Pereda (53 Marco Antonio Ruiz), Gregorio Abel Bernales (46 José Adolfo Mendoza), Arnaldo Daniel Alonso, Luis Alberto Hernández, Piero Fernando Alva, Gastón Maximiliano Sangoy (73 Víctor Alonso Rosell). DT: Juan Amador Sánchez
NACIONAL: Miguel Cárdenas, Julio César Irrazábal, Ángel Marcelo Martínez, Pánfilo Ramón Escobar, Troadio Daniel Barreto, Glacinei Martins "INCA", Mauro Milciades Monges (53 Cristian Bogado), Fábio Ramón Ramos (73 Ariel Gregorio Bogado), Carlos Alberto González, Oscar René Cardozo, Heber Alberto Arriola (77 Fabio Escobar). DT: Carlos Jara Saguier
Sent off: Herrera (38) , Cárdenas (90+2)

COLO COLO SANTIAGO – CD GUADALAJARA 1-3 (0-2)
Monumental, Santiago, 24.01.2006
Referee: Roberto Carlos Silvera (URU)
COLO COLO: Claudio Andrés Bravo, Moisés Fermin Villarroel (71 Fernando Andrés Meneses), David Andrés Henríquez, Miguel Augusto Riffo, Andrés Felipe González, Héctor Arturo Sanhueza, José Luis Jerez, Matias Ariel Fernández, Jorge Luis Valdivia, Humberto Andrés Suazo (84 Braulio Antonio Leal), Héctor Raúl Mancilla (58 Gonzalo Antonio Fierro). DT: Claudio Borghi
GUADALAJARA: Oswaldo Javier Sánchez, Francisco Javier Rodríguez, Héctor Reynoso, Carlos Arnoldo Salcido, Diego Alfonso Martínez (55 Jorge Armando Barrera), Manuel Bernardo Sol, Gonzalo Pineda, Ramón Morales, Sergio Alejandro Santana (83 Manuel Alejandro Vela), Omar Bravo (75 Edwin Alejandro Borboa), Alberto Medina. DT: Hans Westerhoff
Goals: Matias Ariel Fernández (49) / Omar Bravo (35, 52), Ramón Morales (45+1 penalty).

CD GUADALAJARA – COLO COLO SANTIAGO 5-3 (3-1)
Jalisco, Guadalajara, 31.01.2006
Referee: Gustavo Alonso Brand (VEN)
GUADALAJARA: Oswaldo Javier Sánchez, Francisco Javier Rodríguez, Héctor Reynoso (64 Jhonny García), Carlos Arnoldo Salcido, Diego Alfonso Martínez (72 Jorge Armando Barrera), Manuel Bernardo Sol, Gonzalo Pineda, Ramón Morales, Sergio Alejandro Santana (54 Adolfo Bautista), Omar Bravo, Alberto Medina. DT: Hans Westerhoff

COLO COLO: Claudio Andrés Bravo, Andrés Felipe González, Celso Rafael Ayala, David Andrés Henríquez, Luis Arturo Mena (68 Miguel Ángel Aceval), Héctor Arturo Sanhueza, José Luis Jerez, Matias Ariel Fernández (86 Fernando Andrés Meneses), Jorge Luis Valdivia, Humberto Andrés Suazo, Héctor Raúl Mancilla (46 Gonzalo Antonio Fierro). DT: Claudio Borghi
Sent off: Pineda (71)
Goals: Alberto Medina (24, 78), Sergio Alejandro Santana (34), Francisco Javier Rodríguez (36), Adolfo Bautista (81) / Humberto Andrés Suazo (39, 67, 76).

PALMEIRAS – DEPORTIVO TÁCHIRA FC 2-0 (1-0)
Palestra Itália, São Paulo, 25.01.2006
Referee: Ricardo Grance (PAR), Attendance: 30.000
PALMEIRAS: MARCOS Roberto Silveira Reis, PAULO César BAIER, DANIEL da Silva, Carlos Alberto Gamarra, LÚCIO Carlos Cajueiro Souza, Márcio Glad "MARCINHO GUERREIRO", EDMUNDO Alves de Souza Neto (46 REINALDO José Zacarias da Silva), Carlos Rodrigues CORRÊA (46 Sergio Alejandro GIOINO), Ricardo Souza Silva "RICARDINHO" (67 CRISTIAN Martins Cabral), Márcio Miranda Rocha da Silva "MARCINHO", WASHINGTON Luiz Mascarenhas Silva. DT: Emerson Leão
DEPORTIVO TÁCHIRA: José Leonardo Morales, Pedro Boada, Grendy Perozo, Gregory Evans Lancken (35 Darwin Valbuena, 62 Evelio Hernández), Edixon Cuevas, Javier Villafraz, Jhon Ospina, Jhonny José González (87 Francisco Javier Campos), Gerson Chacón, Alexander Rondón, Juan García. DT: Manuel Plasencia
Goals: Márcio Miranda Rocha da Silva "MARCINHO" (19), Carlos Alberto Gamarra (49).

DEPORTIVO TÁCHIRA FC – PALMEIRAS 2-4 (0-2)
Olímpico de Pueblo Nuevo, San Cristóbal, 1.02.2006
Referee: Óscar Julián Ruiz (COL)
DEPORTIVO TÁCHIRA: José Leonardo Morales, Gerson Chacón, Pedro Boada, Grendy Perozo, Edixon Cuevas (74 Evelio Hernández), Javier Villafraz (64 Jesús Márquez), Jhon Ospina, Marlon Fernández, Jhonny José González, Juan García, Alexander Rondón. DT: Manuel Plasencia
PALMEIRAS: MARCOS Roberto Silveira Reis, PAULO César BAIER (60 ALCEU Rodrigues Simoni Filho), DANIEL da Silva, Carlos Alberto Gamarra, LÚCIO Carlos Cajueiro Souza, Márcio Glad "MARCINHO GUERREIRO", Carlos Rodrigues CORRÊA, Márcio Miranda Rocha da Silva "MARCINHO" (77 LEONARDO Fabiano da SILVA e Silva), Ricardo Souza Silva "RICARDINHO" (70 CRISTIAN Martins Cabral), EDMUNDO Alves de Souza Neto, WASHINGTON Luiz Mascarenhas Silva. DT: Emerson Leão
Goals: Juan García (69), Jhonny José González (73) / WASHINGTON Luiz Mascarenhas Silva (13, 45), EDMUNDO Alves de Souza Neto (60), Márcio Miranda Rocha da Silva "MARCINHO" (73).

RIVER PLATE – ORIENTE PETROLERO 6-0 (4-0)
Antonio V. Liberti 'Monumental', Buenos Aires, 26.01.2006
Referee: Rubén Marcos Selman, Attendance: 44.000
RIVER PLATE: Juan Pablo Carrizo, Paulo Andrés Ferrari, Julio César Cáceres, Danilo Telmo Gerlo, Lucas Armando Mareque, Jonathan Santana, Óscar Adrián Ahumada (46 Andrés San Martín), Jairo Leonard Patiño, Marcelo Daniel Gallardo (70 Víctor Eduardo Zapata), Daniel Gastón Montenegro (59 Luciano Gabriel Figueroa), Ernesto Antonio Farías. DT: Daniel Passarella
ORIENTE PETROLERO: Sergio Daniel Galarza, Miguel Ángel Hoyos, Juan Doyle Vaca, Oscar Alcides Espínola, Luis Alberto Gutiérrez, Percy Limbert Pizarro, Carlos Alberto Durán, Eduardo Melgar, Nelson Omar Agoglia (48 Rolando Campos), Uriel Pérez (46 Federico Antonio Astudillo), Juan Carlos Arce. DT: Carlos Amodeo
Sent off : Melgar (67)
Goals: Jonathan Santana (20), Daniel Gastón Montenegro (37), Marcelo Daniel Gallardo (39 penalty, 57 penalty), Ernesto Antonio Farías (43), Andrés San Martín (46).

ORIENTE PETROLERO – RIVER PLATE 0-2 (0-2)
Ramón Tahuichi, Santa Cruz, 2.02.2006
Referee: Sálvio Spínola Fagundes (BRA), Attendance: 20.000
ORIENTE PETROLERO: Sergio Daniel Galarza, Miguel Ángel Hoyos, Oscar Alcides Espínola, Juan Doyle Vaca, Luis Alberto Gutiérrez (46 Luis Javier Méndez), Rolando Campos (78 Carlos Alberto Durán), Richard Sandro Uriona, MAURÍCIO da Silva Duarte, Juan Carlos Arce, Federico Antonio Astudillo (82 Uriel Pérez), Martín Adrián Palavicini. DT: Víctor Hugo Antelo
RIVER PLATE: Juan Pablo Carrizo, Cristián Andrés Álvarez, Leonardo José Talamonti, Danilo Telmo Gerlo, Federico Hernán Domínguez, Diego Armando Barrado, Andrés San Martín, Juan Carlos Toja, Marcelo Daniel Gallardo (64 Lucas Andrés Pusineri), Luciano Gabriel Figueroa (83 Gonzalo Daniel Abán), Gustavo Andrés Oberman (56 Lucas Armando Mareque). DT: Daniel Passarella
Sent off: Domínguez (52)
Goals: Juan Carlos Toja (15), Juan Doyle Vaca (23 own goal).

DEPORTIVO CUENCA – GOIÁS EC 1-1 (0-1)
Alejandro Serrano Aguilar, Cuenca, 26.01.2006
Referee: Víctor Hugo Rivera (PER)
DEPORTIVO CUENCA: Javier Hernán Klimowicz, Enrique Roberto Gámez, Julio Marcelo Fleitas, Jorge Enrique Parra, Marcelo Cristian Bohórquez, Lorvelis Salomón Mina (83 Raúl Esteban Alvarado), Carlos Enrique Gutiérrez, Hólger Eduardo Matamoros, Omar Alfredo Guerra, Carlos Gregorio Quiñónez, Wálter Richard Calderón (34 Washington Stalin España). DT: Diego Barragán
GOIÁS: HARLEI de Menezes Silva, LEONARDO Devanir de Paula, CLÉBER Rezende de Oliveira, José JADÍLSON dos Santos Silva, ROGÉRIO CORRÊA de Oliveira, FABIANO Cézar Viegas, JÚLIO César dos SANTOS, CLÉBER "GAÚCHO" Nelson de Andrade Raphaelli (87 Cícero VÍTOR dos Santos Junior), JÉFFERSON "FEIJÃO" Marques da Conceição (71 Romero Mendonça Sobrinho "ROMERITO"), Raimundo NONATO de Lima Ribeiro (78 WELLITON Soares de Morais), DANILO PORTUGAL Bueno Ferreira. DT: Eugenio Machado Souto "Geninho"
Goals: Hólger Eduardo Matamoros (57) / ROGÉRIO CORRÊA de Oliveira (14).

GOIÁS EC – DEPORTIVO CUENCA 3-0 (1-0)
Serra Dourada, Goiania, 1.02.2006
Referee: Martín Vázquez (URU), Attendance: 10.000
GOIÁS: HARLEI de Menezes Silva, CLÉBER Rezende de Oliveira (84 Cícero VÍTOR dos Santos Junior), ROGÉRIO CORRÊA de Oliveira, LEONARDO Devanir de Paula, FABIANO Cézar Viegas, JÚLIO César dos SANTOS, José JADÍLSON dos Santos Silva, DANILO PORTUGAL Bueno Ferreira, JULIANO Gomes Soares (89 Mário JARDEL de Almeida Ribeiro), Romero Mendonça Sobrinho "ROMERITO", Raimundo NONATO de Lima Ribeiro (69 WELLITON Soares de Morais). DT: Eugenio Machado Souto "Geninho"
DEPORTIVO CUENCA: Javier Hernán Klimowicz, Enrique Roberto Gámez, Jorge Enrique Parra, Julio Marcelo Fleitas, Marcelo Cristian Bohórquez, Carlos Enrique Gutiérrez, Lorvelis Salomón Mina, Hólger Eduardo Matamoros (70 Camilo David Hurtado), Raúl Esteban Alvarado (46 Washington Stalin España), Omar Alfredo Guerra, Carlos Gregorio Quiñónez (82 Juan Pablo Romero). DT: Diego Barragán
Sent off: Parra (78)
Goals: José JADÍLSON dos Santos Silva (29), Romero Mendonça Sobrinho "ROMERITO" (75, 81 penalty).

DEFENSOR SPORTING – INDEPENDIENTE SANTA FE 2-2 (0-1)
Parque Central, Montevideo, 27.01.2006
Referee: Héber Roberto Lopes (BRA), Attendance: 10.000
DEFENSOR SPORTING: Juan Guillermo Castillo, Ignacio Ithurralde, Nelson Eusebio Semperena, Williams Guillermo Martínez, Victorio Maximiliano Pereira, Álvaro Rafael González, Carlos Richard Díaz, Fernando Jorge Fajardo (46 Pablo Di Fiori), Andrés Nicolás Olivera, Mauro Adrián Vila (68 Álvaro Damián Navarro), Danilo Javier Peinado (46 Román Marcelo Cuello). DT: Jorge Da Silva

INDEPENDIENTE: Luis Enrique Martínez, Pablo César Pachón, Álvaro Francisco Nájera, Nelson Artigas Olveira, Edgar Francisco Delgado, Gabriel Enrique Gómez, Juan Carlos Ramírez, Carlos Alberto Ortiz, Luis Daniel Gamarra (65 David Fernando Montoya), Leider Calimenio Preciado (87 Jairo Andrés Suárez), Diego Leandro Armani (77 Luis Alfredo Yánez). DT: Germán González
Andrés Nicolás Olivera missed a penalty in the 88th minute
Goals: Andrés Nicolás Olivera (86), Ignacio Ithurralde (90) / Nelson Artigas Olveira (35), Leider Calimenio Preciado (81).

INDEPENDIENTE SANTA FE – DEFENSOR SPORTING 0-0
Nemesio Camacho, Bogotá, 2.02.2006
Referee: Mauricio Javier Reinoso (ECU), Attendance: 30.000
INDEPENDIENTE: Luis Enrique Martínez, Pablo César Pachón, Álvaro Francisco Nájera, Nelson Artigas Olveira, Edgar Francisco Delgado, Gabriel Enrique Gómez, Carlos Alberto Ortiz, Juan Carlos Ramírez (11 Jairo Andrés Suárez), Luis Daniel Gamarra (61 Luis Alfredo Yánez), Diego Leandro Armani (65 David Fernando Montoya), Leider Calimenio Preciado. DT: Germán González
DEFENSOR SPORTING: Juan Guillermo Castillo, Ignacio Ithurralde, Antonio Adolfo Esmerode, Andrés Lamas, Álvaro Rafael González, Carlos Richard Díaz (66 Pablo Di Fiori), Victorio Maximiliano Pereira (86 Diego Alejandro De Souza), Diego Ismael Ferreira, Román Marcelo Cuello, Andrés Nicolás Olivera (61 Danilo Javier Peinado), Fernando Jorge Fajardo. DT: Jorge Da Silva
Sent off: Thurralde (67)

SECOND PHASE

GROUP 1

CIENCIANO – CD GUADALAJARA 0-1 (0-0)
Inca Gracilaso de la Vega, Cusco, 8.02.2006
Referee: José Patricio Carpio (ECU)
CIENCIANO: Oscar Manuel Ibáñez, Giuliano Santiago Portilla, Jahir Butrón, Miguel Ángel Villalta, Miguel Ángel Huertas, Paolo Giancarlo De La Haza, Jean Franco Ferrari, Julio César García (74 Miguel Ángel Torres), Hilden Salas (74 Luis Alberto Ramírez), Miguel Ángel Mostto, Roberto Enrique Silva (66 Douglas Junior Ross). DT: Wilmar Valencia
GUADALAJARA: Oswaldo Javier Sánchez, Francisco Javier Rodríguez, Héctor Reynoso, Carlos Arnoldo Salcido, Diego Alfonso Martínez, Manuel Bernardo Sol, Ramón Morales, Sergio Alejandro Santana, Adolfo Bautista (82 Edwin Alejandro Borboa), Alberto Medina (80 Manuel Alejandro Vela), Omar Bravo. DT: Hans Westerhoff
Goal: Ramón Morales (90+1).

CARACAS FC – SÃO PAULO FC 1-2 (0-1)
Brígido Iriarte, Caracas, 1.03.2006
Referee: Albert Duarte (COL), Attendance: 2.450
CARACAS: Javier Eduardo Toyo, Weymar Franck Olivares (65 Jorge Francisco Casanova), Oswaldo Augusto Vizcarrondo, José Manuel Rey, Enrique Andrés Rouga, Luis Enrique Vera, Edgar Hernán Jiménez, Jorge Alberto Rojas (72 Pedro Javier De Pablos), César Eduardo González, Alejandro Abraham Guerra, Wilson Alberto Carpintero (69 Jorge Horacio Serna). DT: Noel Sanvicente
SÃO PAULO: João BOSCO de Freitas Chaves, ANDRÉ Gonçalves DIAS, ALEX Bruno Costa Fernandes, EDCARLOS Conceição Santos, Jenilson Angelo de Souza "JÚNIOR", Carlos Luciano da Silva "MINEIRO", JOSUÉ de Oliveira, DANILO Gabriel de Andrade (90+1 José RAMALHO de Freitas), Williamis de SOUZA Silva, ALEX DIAS de Almeida (57 THIAGO Ribeiro Cardoso), José ALOÍSIO da Silva. DT: Muricy Ramalho
Goals: José Manuel Rey (72 penalty) / DANILO Gabriel de Andrade (35), José ALOÍSIO da Silva (62).

CD GUADALAJARA – CARACAS FC 1-1 (0-0)
Jalisco, Guadalajara, 7.03.2006
Referee: Víctor Hugo Rivera (PER), Attendance: 13.072
GUADALAJARA: Oswaldo Javier Sánchez, Francisco Javier Rodríguez, Héctor Reynoso, Carlos Arnoldo Salcido, Diego Alfonso Martínez, Manuel Bernardo Sol, Gonzalo Pineda (46 Alberto Medina), Ramón Morales, Adolfo Bautista (46 Edwin Alejandro Borboa), Sergio Alejandro Santana (66 Jhonny García), Omar Bravo. DT: Hans Westerhoff
CARACAS: Javier Eduardo Toyo, Weymar Franck Olivares (73 Jorge Francisco Casanova), Oswaldo Augusto Vizcarrondo, José Manuel Rey, Enrique Andrés Rouga, Luis Enrique Vera, Edgar Hernán Jiménez (61 Jorge Horacio Serna), Jorge Alberto Rojas, César Eduardo González (75 Pedro Javier De Pablos), Alejandro Abraham Guerra, Wilson Alberto Carpintero. DT: Noel Sanvicente
Goals: Sergio Alejandro Santana (57) / Wilson Alberto Carpintero (75).

SÃO PAULO FC – CIENCIANO 4-1 (2-1)
Cícero Pompeu de Toledo "Morumbí", São Paulo, 8.03.2006
Referee: Martín Vázquez (URU)
SÃO PAULO: ROGÉRIO CENI, José Fábio Alves Azevedo "FABÃO" (34 EDCARLOS Conceição Santos), Diego Alfredo Lugano, ANDRÉ Gonçalves DIAS, Williamis de SOUZA Silva, Carlos Luciano da Silva "MINEIRO", JOSUÉ de Oliveira, DANILO Gabriel de Andrade, Jenilson Angelo de Souza "JÚNIOR" (68 RICHARLYSON Barbosa Felisbino), ALEX DIAS de Almeida (64 THIAGO Ribeiro Cardoso), José ALOÍSIO da Silva. DT: Muricy Ramalho
CIENCIANO: Oscar Manuel Ibáñez, Miguel Ángel Huertas (46 Jahir Butrón), Carlos María Lugo, Miguel Ángel Villalta, Guillermo Alejandro Guizasola, Jean Franco Ferrari, Juan Carlos Bazalar, Paolo Giancarlo De La Haza (62 Miguel Ángel Mostto), Julio César García, Hilden Salas (74 Miguel Ángel Torres), Roberto Enrique Silva. DT: Wilmar Valencia
Goals: José Fábio Alves Azevedo "FABÃO" (2), ALEX DIAS de Almeida (20), THIAGO Ribeiro Cardoso (66), Williamis de SOUZA Silva (77) / Roberto Enrique Silva (30).

CIENCIANO – CARACAS FC 2-1 (1-0)
Inca Gracilaso de la Vega, Cusco, 14.03.2006
Referee: Iván Igor Gamboa (BOL)
CIENCIANO: Oscar Manuel Ibáñez, Miguel Ángel Huertas, Miguel Ángel Villalta, Carlos María Lugo, Giuliano Santiago Portilla, Jean Franco Ferrari, Juan Carlos Bazalar (72 Luis Alberto Ramírez), Paolo Giancarlo De La Haza (46 Miguel Ángel Mostto), Hilden Salas (59 Miguel Ángel Torres), Roberto Enrique Silva, Julio César García. DT: Wilmar Valencia
CARACAS: Javier Eduardo Toyo, Weymar Franck Olivares (46 Jorge Horacio Serna), Oswaldo Augusto Vizcarrondo, José Manuel Rey, Enrique Andrés Rouga, Edgar Hernán Jiménez (82 Ronald Alejandro Vargas), Luis Enrique Vera, Jorge Alberto Rojas, César Eduardo González (71 Jorge Francisco Casanova), Alejandro Abraham Guerra, Wilson Alberto Carpintero. DT: Noel Sanvicente
Goals: Julio César García (11), Roberto Enrique Silva (74) / Jorge Horacio Serna (53).

CD GUADALAJARA – SÃO PAULO FC 2-1 (1-1)
Jalisco, Guadalajara, 21.03.2006
Referee: Rubén Marcos Selman (CHI), Attendance: 21.512
GUADALAJARA: Oswaldo Javier Sánchez, Francisco Javier Rodríguez, Héctor Reynoso, Carlos Arnoldo Salcido, Diego Alfonso Martínez, Patricio Gabriel Araujo, Gonzalo Pineda, Ramón Morales (22 Jorge Armando Barrera), Sergio Alejandro Santana (63 Alberto Medina), Adolfo Bautista (82 Jhonny García), Omar Bravo. DT: José Manuel De La Torre
SÃO PAULO: ROGÉRIO CENI, ANDRÉ Gonçalves DIAS, Carlos Luciano da Silva "MINEIRO", Diego Alfredo Lugano, José Fábio Alves Azevedo "FABÃO" (80 LEANDRO Lessa Azevedo), RICHARLYSON Barbosa Felisbino, JOSUÉ de Oliveira, Williamis de SOUZA Silva, THIAGO Ribeiro Cardoso, DANILO Gabriel de Andrade, José ALOÍSIO da Silva (82 ALEX DIAS de Almeida). DT: Muricy Ramalho
Goals: Adolfo Bautista (39), Omar Bravo (68) / DANILO Gabriel de Andrade (25).

CARACAS FC – CIENCIANO 4-0 (1-0)
Brígido Iriarte, Caracas, 28.03.2006
Referee: Alberto Duque (COL)
CARACAS: Javier Eduardo Toyo, Weymar Franck Olivares, Oswaldo Augusto Vizcarrondo, José Manuel Rey, Enrique Andrés Rouga, Luis Enrique Vera, Edgar Hernán Jiménez, César Eduardo González (77 Alejandro Abraham Guerra), Jorge Alberto Rojas (85 Giovanny Leonardo Pérez), Wilson Alberto Carpintero, Jorge Horacio Serna (86 Pedro Javier De Pablos). DT: Noel Sanvicente
CIENCIANO: Oscar Manuel Ibáñez, Miguel Ángel Huertas, Miguel Ángel Villalta, Carlos María Lugo, Jean Franco Ferrari, Juan Carlos Bazalar (46 Carlos Oswaldo Fernández), Paolo Giancarlo De La Haza, Julio César García, Giuliano Santiago Portilla, Roberto Enrique Silva, Miguel Ángel Mostto. DT: Wilmar Valencia
Sent off : Portilla (90)
Goals: Jorge Horacio Serna (44), José Manuel Rey (57), Jorge Alberto Rojas (59, 75).

SÃO PAULO FC – CD GUADALAJARA 1-2 (1-1)
Cícero Pompeu de Toledo "Morumbí", São Paulo, 5.04.2006
Referee: Daniel Orlando Giménez (ARG), Attendance: 44.648
SÃO PAULO: ROGÉRIO CENI, José Fábio Alves Azevedo "FABÃO", EDCARLOS Conceição Santos (82 Francisco de LIMA Aparecido), Diego Alfredo Lugano (60 RICHARLYSON Barbosa Felisbino), Jenilson Angelo de Souza "JÚNIOR", Carlos Luciano da Silva "MINEIRO", JOSUÉ de Oliveira, DANILO Gabriel de Andrade, LEANDRO Lessa Azevedo (71 ALEX DIAS de Almeida), José ALOÍSIO da Silva, THIAGO Ribeiro Cardoso. DT: Muricy Ramalho
GUADALAJARA: Oswaldo Javier Sánchez, Francisco Javier Rodríguez, Héctor Reynoso, Carlos Arnoldo Salcido, Diego Alfonso Martínez, Patricio Gabriel Araujo, Gonzalo Pineda, Ramón Morales (69 Alberto Medina), Sergio Alejandro Santana (67 Jorge Armando Barrera), Adolfo Bautista (81 Jhonny García), Omar Bravo. DT: José Manuel De La Torre
Sent off: Bravo (72)
Goals: José ALOÍSIO da Silva (30) / Sergio Alejandro Santana (44), Diego Alfonso Martínez (80).

CARACAS FC – CD GUADALAJARA 0-0
Brígido Iriarte, Caracas, 12.04.2006
Referee: Samuel Haro (ECU), Attendance: 5.000
CARACAS: Javier Eduardo Toyo, Weymar Franck Olivares (76 Jorge Francisco Casanova), Oswaldo Augusto Vizcarrondo, José Manuel Rey, Enrique Andrés Rouga, Luis Enrique Vera, Edgar Hernán Jiménez (67 Alejandro Abraham Guerra), César Eduardo González, Jorge Alberto Rojas, Wilson Alberto Carpintero (83 Ever Espinoza), Jorge Horacio Serna. DT: Noel Sanvicente
GUADALAJARA: Alfredo Talavera, Christian Michel Armas, Jhonny García, Héctor Reynoso, Jorge Armando Barrera (71 José Jonny Magallón), Diego Alfonso Martínez, Patricio Gabriel Araujo, Manuel Alejandro Vela (79 Edgar Iván Solís), Sergio Alejandro Santana, Edwin Alejandro Borboa (49 Alberto Medina), Adolfo Bautista. DT: José Manuel De La Torre

CIENCIANO – SÃO PAULO FC 0-2 (0-2)
Inca Gracilaso de la Vega, Cusco, 12.04.2006,
Referee: Carlos Manuel Torres (PAR)
CIENCIANO: Oscar Manuel Ibáñez, Carlos María Lugo, Miguel Ángel Villalta, Jorge Martín Araujo (46 Hilden Salas), Paolo Giancarlo De La Haza, Jean Franco Ferrari, Juan Carlos Bazalar, Carlos Oswaldo Fernández, Miguel Ángel Torres (29 Roberto Enrique Silva), Douglas Junior Ross, Miguel Ángel Mostto (74 César Camilo Ccahuantico). DT: Julio César Uribe
SÃO PAULO: ROGÉRIO CENI, ANDRÉ Gonçalves DIAS, José Fábio Alves Azevedo "FABÃO", Diego Alfredo Lugano, Jenilson Angelo de Souza "JÚNIOR" (83 RICHARLYSON Barbosa Felisbino), Carlos Luciano da Silva "MINEIRO", JOSUÉ de Oliveira (77 José RAMALHO de Freitas), DANILO Gabriel de Andrade, Williamis de SOUZA Silva, José ALOÍSIO da Silva (83 ALEX DIAS de Almeida), THIAGO Ribeiro Cardoso. DT: Muricy Ramalho
Sent off: Ferrari (72)
Goals: José ALOÍSIO da Silva (21), Carlos Luciano da Silva "MINEIRO" (42).

CD GUADALAJARA – CIENCIANO 0-0
Jalisco, Guadalajara, 20.04.2006
Referee: René Marcelo Ortubé (BOL)
GUADALAJARA: Alfredo Talavera, Héctor Reynoso, Jhonny García, Christian Michel Armas, Diego Alfonso Martínez, Manuel Bernardo Sol (67 José Jonny Magallón), Patricio Gabriel Araujo, Manuel Alejandro Vela (72 Edgar Iván Solís), Alberto Medina, Adolfo Bautista, Edwin Alejandro Borboa (54 Sergio Alejandro Santana). DT: José Manuel De La Torre
CIENCIANO: Oscar Manuel Ibáñez, Miguel Ángel Huertas, Carlos María Lugo, Miguel Ángel Villalta, Giuliano Santiago Portilla, César Camilo Ccahuantico, Luis Alberto Ramírez (67 Miguel Ángel Torres), Hilden Salas, Julio César García, Roberto Enrique Silva (60 Miguel Ángel Mostto), Juan Ramón Rodríguez (60 Douglas Junior Ross). DT: Julio César Uribe

SÃO PAULO FC – CARACAS FC 2-0 (0-0)
Cícero Pompeu de Toledo "Morumbi", São Paulo, 20.04.2006
Referee: Jorge Luis Larrionda (URU), Attendance: 21.854
SÃO PAULO: ROGÉRIO CENI, ANDRÉ Gonçalves DIAS, José Fábio Alves Azevedo "FABÃO" (55 ALEX DIAS de Almeida), Diego Alfredo Lugano, Jenilson Angelo de Souza "JÚNIOR", Carlos Luciano da Silva "MINEIRO", JOSUÉ de Oliveira, Williamis de SOUZA Silva, DANILO Gabriel de Andrade, José ALOÍSIO da Silva (83 LEANDRO Lessa Azevedo), THIAGO Ribeiro Cardoso (90+2 RODRIGO FABRI). DT: Muricy Ramalho
CARACAS: Javier Eduardo Toyo, Daniel José Godoy, Jaime Andrés Bustamante, Oswaldo Augusto Vizcarrondo, Edder Alfonso Pérez, Luis Enrique Vera, Pedro Javier De Pablos, Giovanny Leonardo Pérez, Jorge Francisco Casanova (54 Enrique Andrés Rouga), Ronald Alejandro Vargas (67 Jorge Horacio Serna), Alejandro Abraham Guerra (63 Jorge Alberto Rojas). DT: Noel Sanvicente
Sent off: Bustamante (50)
Goals: DANILO Gabriel de Andrade (57), ROGÉRIO CENI (90+2 penalty).

1	SÃO PAULO FC	6	4	0	2	12	6	12
2	CD GUADALAJARA	6	3	3	0	6	3	12
3	Caracas FC	6	1	2	3	7	7	5
4	Cienciano	6	1	1	4	3	12	4

GROUP 2

BOLÍVAR LA PAZ – ESTUDIANTES DE LA PLATA 1-0 (0-0)
Hernando Siles, La Paz, 7.02.2006
Referee: Carlos Manuel Torres (PAR), Attendance: 25.000
BOLÍVAR: Joel Fernando Zayas, Aldo Andrés Mores, Óscar Carmelo Sánchez, ANDRÉS Felipe DE SOUZA, Luis Aníbal Torrico (71 Ricardo Balderas), Daner Jesús Pachi, Carmelo Angulo, Leonel Reyes, Limberg Gutiérrez, Miguel Mercado (46 Luis Gatty Ribeiro), José Martín Menacho. DT: Carlos Aragonés
ESTUDIANTES: Martín Horacio Herrera, Pablo Sebastián Álvarez, Fernando Ortiz, Agustín Alayes, Jorge Martín Núñez, Marcos Agustín Gelabert (78 Horacio Ramón Cardozo), Juan Augusto Huerta, Rodrigo Braña, Juan Elías Cominges, José Ernesto Sosa (69 Marcelo Adrián Carrusca), José Luis Calderón (61 Pablo Ariel Lugüercio). DT: Jorge Burruchaga
Goal: Limberg Gutiérrez (83).

SPORTING CRISTAL – INDEPENDIENTE SANTA FE 1-2 (1-0)
Nacional, Lima, 9.02.2006
Referee: Gustavo Alonso Brand (VEN)
SPORTING CRISTAL: Erick Guillermo Delgado, Amilton Jair Prado, Norberto Carlos Araujo, Alberto Júnior Rodríguez, Carlos Alberto Marczuk, Rainer Torres (74 David Soria), Carlos Alberto Zegarra, Henry Edson Quinteros, Jorge Antonio Soto (70 Carlos Augusto Lobatón), Gustavo Enrique Vassallo, Sergio William Leal. DT: José Guillermo Del Solar

INDEPENDIENTE: Luis Enrique Martínez, Pablo César Pachón, Nelson Artigas Olveira, Álvaro Francisco Nájera, Edgar Francisco Delgado, Gabriel Enrique Gómez, Carlos Alberto Ortiz, David Fernando Montoya, Luis Daniel Gamarra (41 Jairo Andrés Suárez), Diego Leandro Armani (46 Luis Alfredo Yánez), Leider Calimenio Preciado (76 John Alexander Cano). DT: Germán González
Sent off: Suárez (69)
Goals: Jorge Antonio Soto (38) / Luis Alfredo Yánez (62), David Fernando Montoya (89).

INDEPENDIENTE SANTA FE – BOLÍVAR LA PAZ 2-2 (0-1)
Nemesio Camacho, Bogotá, 15.02.2006
Referee: Manuel Alejandro Garay (PER), Attendance: 13.000
INDEPENDIENTE: Luis Enrique Martínez, Pablo César Pachón, Nelson Artigas Olveira, Álvaro Francisco Nájera, Edgar Francisco Delgado, John Alexander Cano (46 Carlos Daniel Hidalgo), Gabriel Enrique Gómez, Carlos Alberto Ortiz, David Fernando Montoya, Luis Alfredo Yánez, Leider Calimenio Preciado. DT: Germán González
BOLÍVAR: Joel Fernando Zayas, Luis Aníbal Torrico, Óscar Carmelo Sánchez, Aldo Andrés Mores, ANDRÉS Felipe DE SOUZA, José Luis Almaraz (87 Luis Gatty Ribeiro), Daner Jesús Pachi (79 Getulio Joaquín Vaca), Leonel Reyes, Carmelo Angulo, Limberg Gutiérrez, José Martín Menacho (84 Miguel Ángel Cuéllar). DT: Carlos Aragonés
Sent off: Delgado (90) / Angulo (88)
Goals: Leider Calimenio Preciado (53 penalty), David Fernando Montoya (54) / Limberg Gutiérrez (44), José Martín Menacho (47).

ESTUDIANTES DE LA PLATA – SPORTING CRISTAL 4-3 (0-3)
Centenario, Quilmes, 21.02.2006
Referee: Roberto Carlos Silvera (URU), Attendance: 16.146
ESTUDIANTES: Martín Horacio Herrera, Juan Daniel Cáceres, Agustín Alayes, Jorge Martín Núñez, Carlos Luciano Araujo (46 José Ernesto Sosa), Marcelo Adrián Carrusca (66 Pablo Ariel Lugüercio), Horacio Ramón Cardozo, Gastón Rubén Esmerado, Diego Alberto Galván (46 Juan Elías Cominges), José Luis Calderón, Hugo Mariano Pavone. DT: Jorge Burruchaga
SPORTING CRISTAL: Erick Guillermo Delgado, Amilton Jair Prado, Norberto Carlos Araujo, Alberto Júnior Rodríguez, Wálter Ricardo Vílchez, Carlos Alberto Marczuk, Rainer Torres, Carlos Alberto Zegarra, Jorge Antonio Soto (70 David Soria), Henry Edson Quinteros (90 César Carlos Casas), Sergio William Leal (82 Gustavo Enrique Vassallo). DT: José Guillermo Del Solar
Goals: José Luis Calderón (55 penalty, 65), Hugo Mariano Pavone (79), Pablo Ariel Lugüercio (90) / Jorge Antonio Soto (17 penalty, 37), Amilton Jair Prado (32).

SPORTING CRISTAL – BOLÍVAR LA PAZ 2-1 (0-0)
Nacional, Lima, 8.03.2006
Referee: Leonardo GACIBA da Silva (BRA)
SPORTING CRISTAL: Erick Guillermo Delgado, Amilton Jair Prado, Norberto Carlos Araujo, Alberto Júnior Rodríguez, Carlos Alberto Marczuk, Rainer Torres, Carlos Alberto Zegarra (46 David Soria), Sergio William Leal (70 Carlos Augusto Lobatón), Jorge Antonio Soto (85 César Carlos Casas), Henry Edson Quinteros, Gustavo Enrique Vassallo. DT: José Guillermo Del Solar
BOLÍVAR: Joel Fernando Zayas, Luis Gatty Ribeiro, Óscar Carmelo Sánchez (72 Ovidio Guatía), ANDRÉS Felipe DE SOUZA, Aldo Andrés Mores, José Luis Almaraz (25 Carlos Oswaldo Camacho), Leonel Reyes, Raúl Justiniano (69 Miguel Ángel Cuéllar), Daner Jesús Pachi, Limberg Gutiérrez, José Martín Menacho. DT: Carlos Aragonés
Goals: Gustavo Enrique Vassallo (52), Rainer Torres (82) / Daner Jesús Pachi (79).

INDEPENDIENTE SANTA FE – ESTUDIANTES DE LA PLATA 3-1 (1-1)
Nemesio Camacho, Bogotá, 9.03.2006
Referee: Carlos Eugênio Simón (BRA)
INDEPENDIENTE: Luis Enrique Martínez, Jairo Andrés Suárez, Álvaro Francisco Nájera, John Freddy Tierradentro, César Antonio Fawcett, Gabriel Enrique Gómez, Juan Carlos Ramírez, José

Largacha (68 Carlos Daniel Hidalgo), David Fernando Montoya (89 Fabián Camilo Díaz), Mario Efrain Gómez (82 Raúl Esneider Marín), Luis Alfredo Yánez. DT: Ricardo Gareca
ESTUDIANTES: Martín Horacio Herrera, Pablo Sebastián Álvarez (74 Juan Elías Cominges), Agustín Alayes, Juan Daniel Cáceres, Jorge Martín Núñez, Gastón Rubén Esmerado, Horacio Ramón Cardozo, Marcos Agustín Gelabert (78 Diego Alberto Galván), Marcelo Adrián Carrusca (82 José Ernesto Sosa), José Luis Calderón, Hugo Mariano Pavone. DT: Jorge Burruchaga
Goals: David Fernando Montoya (33), Gabriel Enrique Gómez (66), Luis Alfredo Yánez (89) / Hugo Mariano Pavone (23).

BOLÍVAR LA PAZ – SPORTING CRISTAL 1-2 (0-1)
Hernando Siles, La Paz, 15.03.2006
Referee: Samuel Haro (ECU)
BOLÍVAR: Joel Fernando Zayas, Luis Gatty Ribeiro, Óscar Carmelo Sánchez, Aldo Andrés Mores, ANDRÉS Felipe DE SOUZA, Daner Jesús Pachi, Leonel Reyes, Carmelo Angulo, Getulio Joaquín Vaca (46 Miguel Ángel Cuéllar), Limberg Gutiérrez, José Martín Menacho (74 Miguel Mercado). DT: Carlos Aragonés
SPORTING CRISTAL: Erick Guillermo Delgado, Alberto Júnior Rodríguez, Amilton Jair Prado, Norberto Carlos Araujo, Wálter Ricardo Vílchez, Carlos Alberto Marczuk (46 William Medardo Chiroque, 68 Henry Juan Colán), Rainer Torres, Jorge Antonio Soto (84 César Carlos Casas), Carlos Alberto Zegarra, Henry Edson Quinteros, Sergio William Leal. DT: José Guillermo Del Solar
Goals: José Martín Menacho (58) / Sergio William Leal (20), Henry Edson Quinteros (89).

ESTUDIANTES DE LA PLATA – INDEPENDIENTE SANTA FE 1-0 (0-0)
Centenario, Quilmes, 21.03.2006
Referee: Héber Roberto Lopes (BRA), Attendance: 21.000
ESTUDIANTES: Martín Horacio Herrera, Marcos Alberto Angeleri, Agustín Alayes, Juan Daniel Cáceres, José María Basanta (65 Jorge Martín Núñez), José Ernesto Sosa (65 Pablo Ariel Lugüercio), Horacio Ramón Cardozo (79 Diego Alberto Galván), Juan Augusto Huerta, Juan Elías Cominges, Hugo Mariano Pavone, José Luis Calderón. DT: Jorge Burruchaga
INDEPENDIENTE: Luis Enrique Martínez, Pablo César Pachón (89 Mario Efrain Gómez), Álvaro Francisco Nájera, John Freddy Tierradentro (56 Nelson Artigas Olveira), César Antonio Fawcett, Gabriel Enrique Gómez, Juan Carlos Ramírez, Jairo Andrés Suárez, David Fernando Montoya, José Largacha (65 Carlos Daniel Hidalgo), Luis Alfredo Yánez. DT: Ricardo Gareca
Goal: Pablo Ariel Lugüercio (87).

BOLÍVAR LA PAZ – INDEPENDIENTE SANTA FE 1-0 (0-0)
Hernando Siles, La Paz, 28.03.2006
Referee: Wilson De Souza (BRA), Attendance: 6.993
BOLÍVAR: Joel Fernando Zayas, Luis Gatty Ribeiro, ANDRÉS Felipe DE SOUZA, Óscar Carmelo Sánchez, Aldo Andrés Mores (46 Luis Aníbal Torrico, 79 Carlos Oswaldo Camacho), Daner Jesús Pachi, Leonel Reyes, Carmelo Angulo, Getulio Joaquín Vaca, Limberg Gutiérrez, José Martín Menacho (46 Miguel Ángel Cuéllar). DT: Carlos Aragonés
INDEPENDIENTE: Luis Enrique Martínez, Pablo César Pachón, Nelson Artigas Olveira, Álvaro Francisco Nájera, César Antonio Fawcett, Juan Carlos Ramírez, Gabriel Enrique Gómez, Mario Efrain Gómez, Jairo Andrés Suárez (85 Fabián Camilo Díaz), Carlos Daniel Hidalgo (58 David Fernando Montoya), José Largacha (65 Luis Alfredo Yánez). DT: Ricardo Gareca
Goal: Carmelo Angulo (71).

SPORTING CRISTAL – ESTUDIANTES DE LA PLATA 2-2 (1-1)
Nacional, Lima, 4.04.2006
Referee: Jorge Luis Larrionda (URU), Attendance: 40.000
SPORTING CRISTAL: Erick Guillermo Delgado, Amilton Jair Prado, Norberto Carlos Araujo, Alberto Júnior Rodríguez, Wálter Ricardo Vílchez, Rainer Torres, Carlos Alberto Zegarra (57 Gustavo Enrique Vassallo), Henry Edson Quinteros, Jorge Antonio Soto, Carlos Augusto Lobatón (67 William Medardo Chiroque), Sergio William Leal (81 Carlos Alberto Marczuk). DT: José Guillermo Del Solar

ESTUDIANTES: Martín Horacio Herrera, Marcos Alberto Angeleri (84 Pablo Ariel Lugüercio), Agustín Alayes, Juan Daniel Cáceres, Jorge Martín Núñez, Marcos Agustín Gelabert (82 José Ernesto Sosa), Horacio Ramón Cardozo (82 Diego Alberto Galván), Rodrigo Braña, Juan Augusto Huerta, José Luis Calderón, Hugo Mariano Pavone. DT: Jorge Burruchaga
Goals: Jorge Antonio Soto (20 penalty), William Medardo Chiroque (75) /
Hugo Mariano Pavone (34), José Luis Calderón (88).

INDEPENDIENTE SANTA FE – SPORTING CRISTAL 2-1 (2-0)
Nemesio Camacho, Bogotá, 13.04.2006
Referee: Mauricio Javier Reinoso (ECU)
INDEPENDIENTE: Luis Enrique Martínez, Jairo Andrés Suárez, Álvaro Francisco Nájera, John Freddy Tierradentro, Edgar Francisco Delgado, César Antonio Fawcett, Gabriel Enrique Gómez (88 Fabián Camilo Díaz), Juan Carlos Ramírez, David Fernando Montoya (80 Pablo César Pachón), Luis Alfredo Yánez (73 José Largacha), Leider Calimenio Preciado. DT: Ricardo Gareca
SPORTING CRISTAL: Erick Guillermo Delgado, Amilton Jair Prado, Norberto Carlos Araujo, Alberto Júnior Rodríguez, Wálter Ricardo Vílchez, Rainer Torres, Carlos Alberto Zegarra, Henry Edson Quinteros, Henry Juan Colán (19 Gustavo Enrique Vassallo), Jorge Antonio Soto (71 Luis Alberto Bonnet), Sergio William Leal. DT: José Guillermo Del Solar
Goals: Jairo Andrés Suárez (7), Luis Alfredo Yánez (40) / Luis Alberto Bonnet (90).

ESTUDIANTES DE LA PLATA – BOLÍVAR LA PAZ 2-1 (1-1)
Centenario, Quilmes, 13.04.2006
Referee: Carlos Eugênio Simón (BRA), Attendance: 25.000
ESTUDIANTES: Martín Horacio Herrera, Marcos Alberto Angeleri, Juan Daniel Cáceres, Agustín Alayes, Jorge Martín Núñez (72 Pablo Ariel Lugüercio), Rodrigo Braña (63 Marcelo Adrián Carrusca), Marcos Agustín Gelabert, Juan Augusto Huerta, José Ernesto Sosa (68 Diego Alberto Galván), Hugo Mariano Pavone, José Luis Calderón. DT: Jorge Burruchaga
BOLÍVAR: Joel Fernando Zayas, Luis Aníbal Torrico, ANDRÉS Felipe DE SOUZA, Óscar Carmelo Sánchez, Aldo Andrés Mores, Carlos Oswaldo Camacho (90 Luis Gatty Ribeiro), Leonel Reyes, Carmelo Angulo, Miguel Ángel Cuéllar, Limberg Gutiérrez (65 Miguel Mercado), José Martín Menacho (68 Daner Jesús Pachi). DT: Carlos Aragonés
Goals: Hugo Mariano Pavone (38, 90+1) / Miguel Ángel Cuéllar (25).

1	INDEPENDIENTE S.TA FE	6	3	1	2	9	7	10
2	ESTUDIANTES	6	3	1	2	10	10	10
3	Sporting Cristal	6	2	1	3	11	12	7
4	Bolívar	6	2	1	3	7	8	7

GROUP 3

THE STRONGEST LA PAZ – NEWELL'S OLD BOYS 3-2 (1-1)
Hernando Siles, La Paz, 9.02.2006
Referee: Rubén Marcos Selman (CHI), Attendance: 15.000
THE STRONGEST: Ever Alexis Caballero, Juan Carlos Paz, Alejandro Damián Mena, Rosauro Rivero, Ronald Gutiérrez (84 Sergio Antonio Jáuregui), Gustavo Daniel Britos, Wilder Arévalo, Sandro COELHO Leite, Julio César Rico Baldivieso, Líder Paz (87 Sergio Enrique Fernández), Diego Aroldo Cabrera (58 Róger Suárez). DT: Víctor Barrientos
NEWELL'S OLD BOYS: Justo Wilmar Villar, Germán David Ré, Nicolás Federico Spolli, Germán Ricardo Rivera, Mauro Emiliano Cejas (72 Gustavo Ariel Rodas), Ariel Hernán Zapata, Hugo Roberto Colace, Marcelo Alejandro Penta (78 Oscar Adrián Lucero), Gastón Damián Aguirre, Héctor Damián Steinert, Iván Emiliano Borghello (56 Lucio Darío Cereseto). DT: Nery Pumpido
Goals: Gustavo Daniel Britos (34), Julio César Rico Baldivieso (60), Róger Suárez (82) /
Hugo Roberto Colace (43), Héctor Damián Steinert (82).

UNIÓN ESPAÑOLA – GOIÁS EC 0-2 (0-1)
Santa Laura, Santiago, 14.02.2006
Referee: Carlos Manuel Torres (PAR), Attendance: 8.000
UNIÓN ESPAÑOLA: Julio César Gaona, Sebastián Miguel Miranda, Juan Pablo Toro, Clarence Williams Acuña, Alexis Patricio Norambuena, Francisco Ulises ROJAS (73 Matías Leonardo Vidangossy), Joel Antonio Reyes, Emerson Pereira, José Luis Sierra (46 Luis Jara), Héctor Santiago Tapia (57 Francis Ricardo Ferrero), Manuel Alejandro Neira. DT: Fernando Carvalho
GOIÁS: HARLEI de Menezes Silva, Cícero VÍTOR dos Santos Junior, ROGÉRIO CORRÊA de Oliveira (82 ALDO César da Silva), LEONARDO Devanir de Paula, FABIANO Cézar Viegas (90 RAFAEL DIAS do Nascimento), JÚLIO César dos SANTOS, José JADÍLSON dos Santos Silva, DANILO PORTUGAL Bueno Ferreira, JULIANO Gomes Soares (46 Raimundo NONATO de Lima Ribeiro), Romero Mendonça Sobrinho "ROMERITO", WELLITON Soares de Morais. DT: Eugenio Machado Souto "Geninho"
Goals: DANILO PORTUGAL Bueno Ferreira (20), FABIANO Cézar Viegas (85).

NEWELL'S OLD BOYS – UNIÓN ESPAÑOLA 2-0 (0-0)
Coloso del Parque, Rosario, 21.02.2006
Referee: Wilson De Souza (BRA), Attendance: 21.015
NEWELL'S OLD BOYS: Justo Wilmar Villar, Gastón Damián Aguirre, Nicolás Federico Spolli, Germán David Ré, Diego Antonio Gavilán, Claudio Daniel Husaín (44 Mauro Emiliano Cejas), Hugo Roberto Colace, Marcelo Alejandro Penta (46 Héctor Damián Steinert), Fernando Daniel Belluschi, Ariel Arnaldo Ortega, Ignacio Martín Scocco (84 Gustavo Ariel Rodas). DT: Nery Pumpido
UNIÓN ESPAÑOLA: Julio César Gaona, Sebastián Miguel Miranda, Juan Pablo Toro, Adán Jonathan Vergara, Francisco Ulises Rojas, Clarence Williams Acuña (60 José Luis Sierra), Emerson Pereira, Joel Antonio Reyes, Luis Jara (79 Matías Leonardo Vidangossy), Manuel Alejandro Neira, Héctor Santiago Tapia (79 Francis Ricardo Ferrero). DT: Fernando Carvalho
Goals: Ignacio Martín Scocco (49, 65).

GOIÁS EC – THE STRONGEST LA PAZ 2-0 (2-0)
Serra Dourada, Goiania, 22.02.2006
Referee: Carlos Amarilla (PAR)
GOIÁS: HARLEI de Menezes Silva, Cícero VÍTOR dos Santos Junior, ROGÉRIO CORRÊA de Oliveira, LEONARDO Devanir de Paula, FABIANO Cézar Viegas (89 CLÉBER "GAÚCHO" Nelson de Andrade Raphaelli), José JADÍLSON dos Santos Silva, DANILO PORTUGAL Bueno Ferreira, JÚLIO César dos SANTOS, Raimundo NONATO de Lima Ribeiro (69 Marcos André Batista Santos "VAMPETA"), Romero Mendonça Sobrinho "ROMERITO" (87 JÉFFERSON "FEIJÃO" Marques da Conceição), WELLITON Soares de Morais. DT: Eugenio Machado Souto "Geninho"
THE STRONGEST: Ever Alexis Caballero, Juan Carlos Paz, Alejandro Damián Mena, Rosauro Rivero (46 Sergio Antonio Jáuregui), Ronald Gutiérrez, Wilder Arévalo, Edson Marcelo Zenteno, Sandro COELHO Leite (71 Sergio Enrique Fernández), Líder Paz, Julio César Rico Baldivieso, Róger Suárez (46 Diego Aroldo Cabrera). DT: Víctor Barrientos
Goals: Raimundo NONATO de Lima Ribeiro (16), Romero Mendonça Sobrinho "ROMERITO" (33).

UNIÓN ESPAÑOLA – THE STRONGEST LA PAZ 1-0 (0-0)
Santa Laura, Santiago, 28.02.2006
Referee: Samuel Haro (ECU)
UNIÓN ESPAÑOLA: Jaime Alejandro Bravo, Sebastián Miguel Miranda, Adán Jonathan Vergara, Juan Pablo Toro, Francisco Ulises Rojas, Joel Antonio Reyes, Emerson Pereira, José Luis Sierra, Luis Jara (87 Raúl Patricio Arenas), Cristián Montecinos (79 Matías Leonardo Vidangossy), Manuel Alejandro Neira. DT: Fernando Carvalho
THE STRONGEST: Ever Alexis Caballero, Alejandro Damián Mena, Juan Carlos Paz, Sergio Antonio Jáuregui, Ronald Gutiérrez, Wilder Arévalo, Gustavo Daniel Britos (75 Róger Suárez), Sandro COELHO Leite, Diego Aroldo Cabrera (65 Sergio Enrique Fernández), Julio César Rico Baldivieso, Líder Paz. DT: Víctor Barrientos Sent off: Mena (85)
Goal: Emerson Pereira (65).

GOIÁS EC – NEWELL'S OLD BOYS 3-0 (2-0)
Serra Dourada, Goiania, 15.03.2006
Referee: Roberto Carlos Silvera (URU)
GOIÁS: HARLEI de Menezes Silva, JÚLIO César dos SANTOS, ROGÉRIO CORRÊA de Oliveira, LEONARDO Devanir de Paula, FABIANO Cézar Viegas (90+7 Marcos André Batista Santos "VAMPETA"), CLÉBER Rezende de Oliveira, DANILO PORTUGAL Bueno Ferreira, Romero Mendonça Sobrinho "ROMERITO", José JADÍLSON dos Santos Silva, WELLITON Soares de Morais (90+5 CLÉBER "GAÚCHO" Nelson de Andrade Raphaelli), Rodrigo de SOUZA Cardoso (74 Raimundo NONATO de Lima Ribeiro). DT: Eugenio Machado Souto "Geninho"
NEWELL'S OLD BOYS: Justo Wilmar Villar, Diego Antonio Gavilán, Gastón Damián Aguirre, Nicolás Federico Spolli, Germán David Ré, Fernando Daniel Belluschi (83 Adrián Maximilliano Peralta), Claudio Daniel Husaín (46 Hugo Roberto Colace), Ariel Hernán Zapata, Oscar Adrián Lucero (46 Mauro Emiliano Cejas), Ariel Arnaldo Ortega, Ignacio Martín Scocco. DT: Nery Pumpido
Sent off: Aguirre (78)
Goals: WELLITON Soares de Morais (18, 19), Romero Mendonça Sobrinho "ROMERITO" (80 penalty).

NEWELL'S OLD BOYS – GOIÁS EC 0-0
Coloso del Parque, Rosario, 22.03.2006
Referee: Martín Vázquez (URU), Attendance: 35.000
NEWELL'S OLD BOYS: Justo Wilmar Villar, Diego Antonio Gavilán (67 Adrián Maximilliano Peralta), Germán David Ré, Nicolás Federico Spolli, Germán Ricardo Rivera, Mauro Emiliano Cejas, Claudio Daniel Husaín (67 Hugo Roberto Colace), Ariel Hernán Zapata, Fernando Daniel Belluschi, Ariel Arnaldo Ortega (75 Lucio Darío Cereseto), Ignacio Martín Scocco. DT: Nery Pumpido
GOIÁS: HARLEI de Menezes Silva, LEONARDO Devanir de Paula, JÚLIO César dos SANTOS, ROGÉRIO CORRÊA de Oliveira, José JADÍLSON dos Santos Silva, FABIANO Cézar Viegas, CLÉBER Rezende de Oliveira, DANILO PORTUGAL Bueno Ferreira, Marcos André Batista Santos "VAMPETA" (70 CLÉBER "GAÚCHO" Nelson de Andrade Raphaelli), Rodrigo de SOUZA Cardoso (90+2 ALDO César da Silva), WELLITON Soares de Morais (70 Raimundo NONATO de Lima Ribeiro). DT: Eugenio Machado Souto "Geninho"
Sent off: Scocco (90+3) / Ferreira (90+1), Danilo Portugal (90+1), Aldo (90+3)

THE STRONGEST LA PAZ – UNIÓN ESPAÑOLA 0-1 (0-0)
Hernando Siles, La Paz, 29.03.2006
Referee: Leonardo GACIBA da Silva (BRA), Attendance: 6.618
THE STRONGEST: Ever Alexis Caballero, Ronald Gutiérrez (60 Zackary Flores), Juan Carlos Paz, Sergio Antonio Jáuregui, Juan Carlos Sánchez, Gustavo Daniel Britos (64 Jaime Cardozo), Wilder Arévalo, Luis Héctor Cristaldo, Julio César Rico Baldivieso (73 Sandro COELHO Leite), Líder Paz, Diego Aroldo Cabrera. DT: Sergio Luna
UNIÓN ESPAÑOLA: Julio César Gaona, Alexis Patricio Norambuena, Pedro Antonio Reyes, Adán Jonathan Vergara, Omar Jesus Riquelme, Joel Antonio Reyes, Emerson Pereira (55 Luis Jara), Juan Pablo Toro, José Luis Sierra (55 Gonzalo Andrés Villagra), Héctor Santiago Tapia, Manuel Alejandro Neira (64 Matías Leonardo Vidangossy). DT: Fernando Carvalho
Goal: Héctor Santiago Tapia (90).

THE STRONGEST LA PAZ – GOIÁS EC 1-0 (0-0)
Hernando Siles, La Paz, 5.04.2006
Referee: Víctor Hugo Rivera (PER), Attendance: 6.533
THE STRONGEST: Ever Alexis Caballero, Pedro Adrián Rocabado (58 Ronald Gutiérrez), Alejandro Damián Mena, Sandro COELHO Leite, Sergio Antonio Jáuregui, Zackary Flores (79 Gustavo Daniel Britos), Wilder Arévalo, Luis Héctor Cristaldo, Jaime Cardozo, Diego Aroldo Cabrera (70 Sergio Enrique Fernández), Líder Paz. DT: Sergio Luna
GOIÁS: HARLEI de Menezes Silva, Cícero VÍTOR dos Santos Junior, ROGÉRIO CORRÊA de Oliveira (82 JULIANO Gomes Soares), LEONARDO Devanir de Paula, JÚLIO César dos SANTOS, José JADÍLSON dos Santos Silva, FABIANO Cézar Viegas (66 RAFAEL DIAS do Nascimento),

CLÉBER "GAÚCHO" Nelson de Andrade Raphaelli, Marcos André Batista Santos "VAMPETA" (75 JORGE Luis Pereira MUTT), Raimundo NONATO de Lima Ribeiro, WELLITON Soares de Morais.
DT: Eugenio Machado Souto "Geninho"
Sent off: Leonardo (82)
Goal: Ronald Gutiérrez (72).

UNIÓN ESPAÑOLA – NEWELL'S OLD BOYS 1-1 (1-0)
Santa Laura, Santiago, 11.04.2006
Referee: Carlos Amarilla (PAR), Attendance: 6.980
UNIÓN ESPAÑOLA: Julio César Gaona, Sebastián Miguel Miranda, Pedro Antonio Reyes, Adán Jonathan Vergara, Francisco Ulises Rojas, Joel Antonio Reyes (76 Gonzalo Andrés Villagra), Emerson Pereira (53 Juan Pablo Toro), José Luis Sierra, Luis Jara (65 Matías Leonardo Vidangossy), Héctor Santiago Tapia, Manuel Alejandro Neira. DT: Fernando Carvalho
NEWELL'S OLD BOYS: Justo Wilmar Villar, Diego Antonio Gavilán, Nicolás Federico Spolli, Germán David Ré, Lautaro Roque Formica, Fernando Daniel Belluschi, Claudio Daniel Husaín, Ariel Hernán Zapata (77 Gustavo Ariel Rodas), Adrián Maximilliano Peralta, Mauro Emiliano Cejas, Lucio Darío Cereseto (58 Héctor Damián Steinert). DT: Nery Pumpido
Sent off: Spolli (28)
Goals: José Luis Sierra (25) / Héctor Damián Steinert (86).

NEWELL'S OLD BOYS – THE STRONGEST LA PAZ 2-0 (1-0)
Coloso del Parque, Rosario, 19.04.2006
Referee: Carlos Manuel Torres (PAR), Attendance: 35.000
NEWELL'S OLD BOYS: Justo Wilmar Villar, Diego Antonio Gavilán, Gastón Damián Aguirre, Germán David Ré, Fernando Daniel Belluschi, Ariel Hernán Zapata (77 Hugo Roberto Colace), Claudio Daniel Husaín, Adrián Maximilliano Peralta (77 Oscar Adrián Lucero), Mauro Emiliano Cejas (64 Gustavo Ariel Rodas), Ariel Arnaldo Ortega, Héctor Damián Steinert. DT: Nery Pumpido
THE STRONGEST: Ever Alexis Caballero, Alejandro Damián Mena, Sandro COELHO Leite, Sergio Antonio Jáuregui, Pedro Adrián Rocabado, Ronald Gutiérrez (24 Edson Marcelo Zenteno), Wilder Arévalo, Luis Héctor Cristaldo, Zackary Flores (71 Jaime Cardozo), Líder Paz, Diego Aroldo Cabrera (74 Adrián Cuéllar). DT: Sergio Luna
Goals: Ariel Hernán Zapata (8), Héctor Damián Steinert (52).

GOIÁS EC – UNIÓN ESPAÑOLA 0-0
Serra Dourada, Goiania, 19.04.2006
Referee: Olivier Humberto Viera (URU)
GOIÁS: HARLEI de Menezes Silva, JÚLIO César dos SANTOS, LEYRIELTON Moura de Morais, ROGÉRIO CORRÊA de Oliveira, FABIANO Cézar Viegas, José JADÍLSON dos Santos Silva, DANILO PORTUGAL Bueno Ferreira, CLÉBER "GAÚCHO" Nelson de Andrade Raphaelli (80 Marcos André Batista Santos "VAMPETA"), Romero Mendonça Sobrinho "ROMERITO" (46 JULIANO Gomes Soares), Rodrigo de SOUZA Cardoso (66 Raimundo NONATO de Lima Ribeiro), WELLITON Soares de Morais. DT: Eugenio Machado Souto "Geninho"
UNIÓN ESPAÑOLA: Julio César Gaona, Sebastián Miguel Miranda, Pedro Antonio Reyes, Adán Jonathan Vergara, Alexis Patricio Norambuena, Clarence Williams Acuña (72 Luis Jara), Juan Pablo Toro, Gonzalo Andrés Villagra, José Luis Sierra, Héctor Santiago Tapia (82 Cristián Montecinos), Manuel Alejandro Neira. DT: Fernando Carvalho

1	GOIÁS EC	6	3	2	1	7	1	11
2	NEWELL'S OLD BOYS	6	2	2	2	7	7	8
3	Unión Española	6	2	2	2	3	5	8
4	The Strongest	6	2	0	4	4	8	6

GROUP 4

UNIVERSIDAD CATÓLICA – UANL 3-2 (2-1)
San Carlos de Apoquindo, Santiago, 8.02.2006
Referee: Paulo César De Oliveira (BRA), Attendance: 12.000
UNIVERSIDAD CATÓLICA: José Maria Buljubasich, Jaime Rubilar, Mauricio Zenteno, Facundo Jorge Imboden, José Pedro Fuenzalida (80 Alejandro Osorio), Jorge Andrés Ormeño, Eros Roque Pérez, Francisco Arrué (80 Miguel Ponce), Darío Leonardo Conca, Eduardo Javier Rubio (81 Luis Núñez), Jorge Roberto Quinteros. DT: Jorge Pellicer
UANL: Rogelio Rodríguez, Luis Ángel García (46 Javier Saavedra), Emilio Damián Martínez, JULIO CÉSAR Santos Correia, Juan Nazario Montano, Enrique Escudero (46 Sixto Raimundo Peralta), Argemiro Veiga, Jesús Alejandro Palacios (75 José Luis Mendoza), Carlos Adrián Morales, Sebastián Ignacio González, Jesús Aldo De Nigris. DT: Ricardo Ferreti
Goals: José Pedro Fuenzalida (5), Jorge Roberto Quinteros (7, 68) / Sebastián Ignacio González (1), Jesús Aldo De Nigris (74).

DEPORTIVO CALI – CORINTHIANS PAULISTA 0-1 (0-0)
Pascual Guerrero, Cali, 15.02.2006
Referee: Horacio Marcelo Elizondo (ARG), Attendance: 15.000
DEPORTIVO CALI: Juan Pablo Ramírez, Freddy Andrés Hurtado, Nelson Enrique Rivas, Darío Raúl Caballero, Jair Benítez, Hernando Patiño, Óscar Díaz, Álvaro José Domínguez, Ricardo Manuel Ciciliano (78 Gustavo Eliseo Morínigo), Habynson Escobar (61 Armando José Carrillo), Blas Antonio Miguel Pérez (78 José Hermes Mera). DT: Pedro Sarmiento
CORINTHIANS: MARCELO dos Santos Marinho, DYEGO Rocha COELHO (90+1 EDUARDO "RATINHO" Filho Correia Piller), Ebert William Amâncio "BETÃO", WESCLEY Pina Gonçalves, GUSTAVO NERY de Sá da Silva, MARCELO Mendonça de MATTOS, BRUNO OCTÁVIO Jovanelli, CARLOS ALBERTO Gomes de Jesus (70 RAFAEL Martiniano de Miranda MOURA), Ricardo Luis Pozzi Rodrigues "RICARDINHO", Carlos Alberto Tévez, NILMAR Honorato da Silva (81 RÓGER Galera Flores). DT: Antônio Lopes
Sent off: Rivas (63)
Goal: Ricardo Luis Pozzi Rodrigues "RICARDINHO" (79).

UANL – DEPORTIVO CALI 5-4 (2-3)
Universitario, Monterrey, 21.02.2006
Referee: Leonardo GACIBA da Silva (BRA)
UANL: Rogelio Rodríguez, Javier Saavedra, Emilio Damián Martínez, JULIO CÉSAR Santos Correia, Gabriel Omar Briceño, Carlos Adrián Morales, Juan Nazario Montano, Argemiro Veiga (85 Jesús Alejandro Palacios), Wálter Nicolás Gaitán (85 Sixto Raimundo Peralta), Jesús Aldo De Nigris, Sebastián Ignacio González. DT: Ricardo Ferreti
DEPORTIVO CALI: Juan Pablo Ramírez, Freddy Andrés Hurtado, Darío Raúl Caballero, José Hermes Mera, Jair Benítez, Óscar Díaz, Hernando Patiño (77 Anthony David Tapia), Ricardo Manuel Ciciliano (60 Habynson Escobar), Álvaro José Domínguez, Armando José Carrillo (46 Jorge Henrique López), Blas Antonio Miguel Pérez. DT: Pedro Sarmiento
Goals: Jesús Aldo De Nigris (20), JULIO CÉSAR Santos Correia (39), Carlos Adrián Morales (49), Wálter Nicolás Gaitán (56, 80) /
Álvaro José Domínguez (12, 90 penalty), Armando José Carrillo (16, 41).

CORINTHIANS PAULISTA – UNIVERSIDAD CATÓLICA 2-2 (1-0)
Paulo Machado de Carvalho "Pacaembú", São Paulo, 22.02.2006
Referee: Héctor Walter Baldassi (ARG)
CORINTHIANS: MARCELO dos Santos Marinho, DYEGO Rocha COELHO, Ebert William Amâncio "BETÃO", WESCLEY Pina Gonçalves, GUSTAVO NERY de Sá da Silva, MARCELO Mendonça de MATTOS, ROSINEI Adolfo Nascimento (59 CARLOS ALBERTO Gomes de Jesus), Ricardo Luis Pozzi Rodrigues "RICARDINHO", RÓGER Galera Flores (78 RAFAEL Martiniano de Miranda MOURA), NILMAR Honorato da Silva, Carlos Alberto Tévez. DT: Antônio Lopes

UNIVERSIDAD CATÓLICA: José Maria Buljubasich, Jaime Rubilar, Mauricio Zenteno (16 Claudio Muñoz), Facundo Jorge Imboden, José Pedro Fuenzalida (80 Alejandro Osorio), Jorge Andrés Ormeño, Eros Roque Pérez, Darío Leonardo Conca, Francisco Arrué, Luis Ignacio Quinteros (72 Luis Núñez), Jorge Roberto Quinteros. DT: Jorge Pellicer Sent off: Arrué (87)
Goals: RÓGER Galera Flores (21), NILMAR Honorato da Silva (61) /
Jorge Roberto Quinteros (52, 63).

UANL – CORINTHIANS PAULISTA 2-0 (0-0)
Universitario, Monterrey, 9.03.2006
Referee: Carlos Luis Chandía (CHI), Attendance: 27.500
UANL: Edgar Adolfo Hernández, Javier Saavedra (60 Luis Ángel García), Emilio Damián Martínez, JULIO CÉSAR Santos Correia, Gabriel Omar Briceño, Juan Nazario Montano (61 Sixto Raimundo Peralta), Argemiro Veiga, Wálter Nicolás Gaitán, Jesús Aldo De Nigris, Sebastián Ignacio González, Carlos Adrián Morales (82 Jesús Alejandro Palacios). DT: Ricardo Ferreti
CORINTHIANS: Johnny Christián Herrera, Ebert William Amâncio "BETÃO", MARCUS VINÍCIUS Cesário, Javier Alejandro Mascherano, GUSTAVO NERY de Sá da Silva, WENDEL Raúl Gonçalves Gomes (59 ROSINEI Adolfo Nascimento), MARCELO Mendonça de MATTOS, Ricardo Luis Pozzi Rodrigues "RICARDINHO", RÓGER Galera Flores (46 CARLOS ALBERTO Gomes de Jesus), Carlos Alberto Tévez (76 RENATO Eduardo de Oliveira Ribeiro), NILMAR Honorato da Silva. DT: Antônio Lopes
Sent off: Marcelo Mattos (51)
Goals: Emilio Damián Martínez (53), Sixto Raimundo Peralta (88).

UNIVERSIDAD CATÓLICA – DEPORTIVO CALI 2-1 (2-1)
San Carlos de Apoquindo, Santiago, 21.03.2006
Referee: Víctor Hugo Rivera (PER), Attendance: 11.875
UNIVERSIDAD CATÓLICA: José Maria Buljubasich, Claudio Muñoz, Mauricio Zenteno, Jaime Rubilar, José Pedro Fuenzalida (75 Diego Rosende), Jorge Andrés Ormeño, Alejandro Osorio, Miguel Ponce (46 Nicolás Núñez), Darío Leonardo Conca, Eduardo Javier Rubio (67 Luis Núñez), Jorge Roberto Quinteros. DT: Jorge Pellicer
DEPORTIVO CALI: David González, Jair Benítez, José Hermes Mera, Darío Raúl Caballero, Freddy Andrés Hurtado, Diego Fernando Valdés, Hernando Patiño, Jarol Herrera (80 Habynson Escobar), Álvaro José Domínguez (82 Ricardo Manuel Ciciliano), Blas Antonio Miguel Pérez, Armando José Carrillo (46 Óscar Díaz). DT: Pedro Sarmiento
Sent off: Patiño (45)
Goals: Jorge Andrés Ormeño (25, 43) / Diego Fernando Valdés (34).

CORINTHIANS PAULISTA – UANL 1-0 (1-0)
Paulo Machado de Carvalho "Pacaembú", São Paulo, 22.03.2006
Referee: Carlos Manuel Torres (PAR)
CORINTHIANS: MARCELO dos Santos Marinho, DYEGO Rocha COELHO (77 EDUARDO "RATINHO" Filho Correia Piller), Ebert William Amâncio "BETÃO", MARCUS VINÍCIUS Cesário, GUSTAVO NERY de Sá da Silva (84 RUBENS Rodrigues dos Santos JÚNIOR), Javier Alejandro Mascherano, Anderson Conceição XAVIER, Ricardo Luis Pozzi Rodrigues "RICARDINHO", RÓGER Galera Flores (66 RENATO Eduardo de Oliveira Ribeiro), Carlos Alberto Tévez, NILMAR Honorato da Silva. DT: Ademar Braga
UANL: Edgar Adolfo Hernández, Luis Ángel García (58 Enrique Escudero), Emilio Damián Martínez, Juan Nazario Montano, Luis Rolando Ramírez, Javier Saavedra, Argemiro Veiga, Jesús Alejandro Palacios (58 Emmanuel Cerda), José Luis Mendoza, Carlos Alberto Ramírez, Néstor Andrés Silvera. DT: Ricardo Ferreti
Carlos Alberto Tévez missed a penalty
Goal: Carlos Alberto Tévez (27).

DEPORTIVO CALI – UNIVERSIDAD CATÓLICA 2-3 (1-1)
Pascual Guerrero, Cali, 30.03.2006
Referee: Samuel Haro (ECU), Attendance: 3.000
DEPORTIVO CALI: David González, Freddy Andrés Hurtado, Darío Raúl Caballero, José Hermes Mera, Juan Geovanni García, Óscar Díaz, Diego Fernando Valdés (60 Gustavo Eliseo Morínigo), Jarol Herrera, Álvaro José Domínguez (46 Habynson Escobar), Blas Antonio Miguel Pérez, Armando José Carrillo (46 Ricardo Manuel Ciciliano). DT: Pedro Sarmiento
UNIVERSIDAD CATÓLICA: José Maria Buljubasich, Jaime Rubilar, Mauricio Zenteno, Facundo Jorge Imboden, José Pedro Fuenzalida (58 Alejandro Osorio), Jorge Andrés Ormeño, Francisco Arrué (76 Nicolás Núñez), Miguel Ponce, Darío Leonardo Conca, Eduardo Javier Rubio (79 Luis Núñez), Jorge Roberto Quinteros. DT: Jorge Pellicer
Goals: Jarol Herrera (14), Blas Antonio Miguel Pérez (81) /
Jorge Roberto Quinteros (30), Miguel Ponce (50), Darío Leonardo Conca (90+2).

UNIVERSIDAD CATÓLICA – CORINTHIANS PAULISTA 2-3 (2-2)
San Carlos de Apoquindo, Santiago, 6.04.2006
Referee: Roberto Carlos Silvera (URU), Attendance: 17.578
UNIVERSIDAD CATÓLICA: José Maria Buljubasich, Jaime Rubilar (74 Luis Núñez), Mauricio Zenteno, Facundo Jorge Imboden, José Pedro Fuenzalida (61 Nicolás Núñez), Jorge Andrés Ormeño, Miguel Ponce (65 Eros Roque Pérez), Francisco Arrué, Darío Leonardo Conca, Eduardo Javier Rubio, Jorge Roberto Quinteros. DT: Jorge Pellicer
CORINTHIANS: Johnny Christián Herrera, DYEGO Rocha COELHO, Ebert William Amâncio "BETÃO", WENDEL Raúl Gonçalves Gomes, GUSTAVO NERY de Sá da Silva, MARCELO Mendonça de MATTOS, Javier Alejandro Mascherano, Ricardo Luis Pozzi Rodrigues "RICARDINHO" (77 Anderson Conceição XAVIER), CARLOS ALBERTO Gomes de Jesus (85 RENATO Eduardo de Oliveira Ribeiro), Carlos Alberto Tévez, NILMAR Honorato da Silva (75 RUBENS Rodrigues dos Santos JÚNIOR). DT: Ademar Braga
Sent off: Wendel (57), Gustavo Nery (73)
Goals: Francisco Arrué (2, 38) / Carlos Alberto Tévez (23), NILMAR Honorato da Silva (37, 60).

DEPORTIVO CALI – UANL 2-2 (1-1)
Pascual Guerrero, Cali, 11.04.2006
Referee: Juan Carlos Paniagua (BOL)
DEPORTIVO CALI: David González, Jarol Herrera, Darío Raúl Caballero, Nelson Enrique Rivas, Jair Benítez, Hernando Patiño, Diego Fernando Valdés (82 Rolan De La Cruz), Gustavo Eliseo Morínigo (76 Jámison Olave), Álvaro José Domínguez, Habynson Escobar (53 Armando José Carrillo), Blas Antonio Miguel Pérez. DT: Pedro Sarmiento
UANL: Edgar Adolfo Hernández, Javier Saavedra (85 Luis Rolando Ramírez), Sidney Balderas, JULIO CÉSAR Santos Correia, Gabriel Omar Briceño, Wálter Nicolás Gaitán, Carlos Adrián Morales, Juan Nazario Montano (46 Enrique Escudero), Sixto Raimundo Peralta, Argemiro Veiga, Sebastián Ignacio González (87 Jesús Aldo De Nigris). DT: Ricardo Ferreti
Goals: Gustavo Eliseo Morínigo (41), Blas Antonio Miguel Pérez (52) /
Sebastián Ignacio González (16, 48).

UANL – UNIVERSIDAD CATÓLICA 1-0 (0-0)
Universitario, Monterrey, 19.04.2006
Referee: Daniel Orlando Giménez (ARG)
UANL: Edgar Adolfo Hernández, Javier Saavedra, Emilio Damián Martínez, JULIO CÉSAR Santos Correia, Gabriel Omar Briceño, Carlos Adrián Morales (67 José Luis Mendoza), Juan Nazario Montano, Sixto Raimundo Peralta (62 Argemiro Veiga), Wálter Nicolás Gaitán, Sebastián Ignacio González, Jesús Aldo De Nigris (79 Carlos Alberto Ramírez). DT: Ricardo Ferreti

UNIVERSIDAD CATÓLICA: José Maria Buljubasich, Jaime Rubilar (61 Claudio Muñoz), Mauricio Zenteno, Facundo Jorge Imboden, José Pedro Fuenzalida, Jorge Andrés Ormeño, Miguel Ponce (61 Eros Roque Pérez), Alejandro Osorio, Darío Leonardo Conca, Eduardo Javier Rubio (76 Luis Ignacio Quinteros), Jorge Roberto Quinteros. DT: Jorge Pellicer Sent off: Briceño (84)
Wálter Nicolás Gaitán missed a penalty in the 27th minute
Goal: Carlos Alberto Ramírez (90+1).

CORINTHIANS PAULISTA – DEPORTIVO CALI 3-0 (2-0)
Paulo Machado de Carvalho "Pacaembú", São Paulo, 19.04.2006
Referee: Manuel Alejandro Garay (PER), Attendance: 33.918
CORINTHIANS: Johnny Christián Herrera, DYEGO Rocha COELHO, Ebert William Amâncio "BETÃO", MARCUS VINÍCIUS Cesário, RUBENS Rodrigues dos Santos JÚNIOR, MARCELO Mendonça de MATTOS (62 Anderson Conceição XAVIER), Javier Alejandro Mascherano, CARLOS ALBERTO Gomes de Jesus, Ricardo Luis Pozzi Rodrigues "RICARDINHO" (66 RÓGER Galera Flores), Carlos Alberto Tévez (71 RENATO Eduardo de Oliveira Ribeiro), NILMAR Honorato da Silva. DT: Ademar Braga
DEPORTIVO CALI: David González, Jámison Olave, Darío Raúl Caballero, Nelson Enrique Rivas, Jair Benítez, Hernando Patiño, Diego Fernando Valdés, Rolan De La Cruz (82 Habynson Escobar), Jarol Herrera, Gustavo Eliseo Morínigo (89 Anthony David Tapia), Blas Antonio Miguel Pérez (86 Iván Rodrigo Trujillo). DT: Pedro Sarmiento Sent off: Caballero (43)
Goals: MARCUS VINÍCIUS Cesário (6), Carlos Alberto Tévez (28), NILMAR Honorato da Silva (81).

1	CORINTHIANS	6	4	1	1	10	6	13
2	UANL	6	3	1	2	12	10	10
3	Universidad Católica	6	3	1	2	12	11	10
4	Deportivo Cali	6	0	1	5	9	16	1

GROUP 5

ROCHA FC – UNIVERSITARIO DE LIMA 0-0
Domingo Burgueño Miguel "Campus Municipal", Maldonado, 7.02.2006
Referee: Enrique Osses (CHI), Attendance: 8.000
ROCHA: Álvaro Marcelo García, Nelson Matías González (78 Álvaro Fernando Becerra), Diego Roberto Sosa, Diego Alberto Bonelli, Diego Ciz, Pablo Gabriel Esquivel (60 Ruben Darío Rodríguez), Herley Martín González, Luis Alejandro Maguregui, Juan Marcelo Segales, Héber Alfonso Caro (83 Leonardo Maldonado), José Pedro Cardoso. DT: Luis González
UNIVERSITARIO: Juan Ángel Flores, José Adolfo Mendoza, Luis Alberto Guadalupe, Germán Martín Centurión, José Alberto Moisela, Luis Alberto Hernández, Gregorio Abel Bernales (88 Marco Antonio Ruiz), José Antonio Pereda, Arnaldo Daniel Alonso (90 Luis Daniel Benito Hernández), Piero Fernando Alva, Gastón Maximiliano Sangoy (79 Víctor Alonso Rosell). DT: Juan Amador Sánchez

LIGA DEP. UNIVERSITARIA – VÉLEZ SARSFIELD 1-3 (0-1)
La Casa Blanca, Quito, 7.02.2006
Referee: Óscar Julián Ruiz (COL)
LDU: Cristian Rafael Mora, Néicer Reasco, Carlos Alberto Espínola, Giovanny Patricio Espinoza, Alfonso Andrés Obregón, Paul Vicente Ambrossi, Patricio Javier Urrutia (67 Diego Marcelo Ceballos), Édison Vicente Méndez, Roberto Carlos Palacios, Agustín Javier Delgado, Elkin Antonio Murillo (75 Moisés Antonio Candelario). DT: Juan Carlos Oblitas
VÉLEZ SARSFIELD: Gastón Alejandro Sessa, Santiago Andrés Ladino, Hernán Darío Pellerano, Maximiliano Pellegrino, Marcelo Hernán Bustamante, Maximiliano Andrés Bustos, Leandro Daniel Somoza, Ariel Esteban Broggi, Leandro Gracián (75 Sergio Román Sena), Lucas Martín Castromán (80 Claudio Marcelo Enría), Rolando David Zárate (89 Mauro Matías Zárate). DT: Miguel Ángel Russo
Roberto Carlos Palacios missed a penalty in the 72nd minute
Goals: Patricio Javier Urrutia (55) /
Leandro Daniel Somoza (36), Leandro Gracián (65), Rolando David Zárate (84).

VÉLEZ SARSFIELD – ROCHA FC 3-0 (1-0)
José Amalfitani, Buenos Aires, 14.02.2006
Referee: René Marcelo Ortubé (BOL), Attendance: 17.000
VÉLEZ SARSFIELD: Gastón Alejandro Sessa, Fabián Alberto Cubero, Maximiliano Pellegrino, Hernán Darío Pellerano, Ariel Esteban Broggi, Maximiliano Andrés Bustos, Leandro Daniel Somoza, Emanuel Adrián Centurión (79 Sergio Román Sena), Leandro Gracián (83 Ramón Darío Ocampo), Rolando David Zárate, Lucas Martín Castromán (86 Claudio Marcelo Enría). DT: Miguel Ángel Russo
ROCHA: Álvaro Marcelo García, Diego Roberto Sosa (77 Leonardo Maldonado), Diego Alberto Bonelli, Nelson Matías González, Diego Ciz, Álvaro Fernando Becerra (68 Cristiano Araujo), Herley Martín González, Luis Alejandro Maguregui, Héber Alfonso Caro (68 Andrés Delgado), Juan Marcelo Segales, José Pedro Cardoso. DT: Luis González
Goals: Emanuel Adrián Centurión (34), Leandro Gracián (75), Lucas Martín Castromán (83).

UNIVERSITARIO DE LIMA – LIGA DEP. UNIVERSITARIA 1-2 (1-1)
Monumental, Lima, 16.02.2006
Referee: Pablo Antonio Pozo (CHI), Attendance: 35.000
UNIVERSITARIO: Juan Ángel Flores, Luis Alberto Guadalupe, Germán Martín Centurión, José Alberto Moisela, José Adolfo Mendoza (72 Jhoel Alexander Herrera), José Antonio Pereda, Luis Alberto Hernández (81 Alex Segundo Magallanes), Arnaldo Daniel Alonso, Paolo Freddy Maldonado (62 Mauricio Mendoza), Piero Fernando Alva, Gastón Maximiliano Sangoy. DT: Juan Amador Sánchez
LDU: Cristian Rafael Mora, Néicer Reasco, Carlos Alberto Espínola, Giovanny Patricio Espinoza, Paul Vicente Ambrossi, Patricio Javier Urrutia, Alfonso Andrés Obregón, Édison Vicente Méndez, Roberto Carlos Palacios, Agustín Javier Delgado (90+2 Diego Marcelo Ceballos), Elkin Antonio Murillo (73 Enrique Daniel Vera). DT: Juan Carlos Oblitas
Goals: Gastón Maximiliano Sangoy (23) / Agustín Javier Delgado (12, 51).

UNIVERSITARIO DE LIMA – VÉLEZ SARSFIELD 0-1 (0-0)
Monumental, Lima, 7.03.2006
Referee: Wilson De Souza (BRA), Attendance: 5.204
UNIVERSITARIO: José Aurelio Carvallo, Luis Alberto Guadalupe, Germán Martín Centurión, José Alberto Moisela (82 Mauricio Mendoza), Luis Daniel Benito Hernández, Marco Antonio Ruiz, Miguel Ángel Cevasco, José Adolfo Mendoza (76 José Antonio Pereda), Rafael Nazareno Maceratesi (65 Gastón Maximiliano Sangoy), Piero Fernando Alva, Arnaldo Daniel Alonso. DT: Juan Amador Sánchez
VÉLEZ SARSFIELD: Sebastián Darío Peratta , Fabián Alberto Cubero, Maximiliano Pellegrino (69 Mariano Esteban Uglessich), Hernán Darío Pellerano, Ariel Esteban Broggi, Maximiliano Andrés Bustos, Leandro Daniel Somoza, Emanuel Adrián Centurión (41 Marcelo Hernán Bustamante), Leandro Gracián, Rolando David Zárate, Lucas Martín Castromán (90 Sergio Román Sena). DT: Miguel Ángel Russo
Goal: Leandro Gracián (71).

ROCHA FC – LIGA DEP. UNIVERSITARIA 3-2 (2-1)
Domingo Burgueño Miguel "Campus Municipal", Maldonado, 7.03.2006
Referee: Ricardo Grance (PAR), Attendance: 1.850
ROCHA: Oscar Andrés Lemos, Nelson Matías González, Diego Roberto Sosa, Diego Alberto Bonelli, Diego Ciz, Pablo Gabriel Esquivel (90 Pablo Martín Seijas), Herley Martín González, Álvaro Fernando Becerra (60 Leonardo Maldonado), Héber Alfonso Caro, Juan Marcelo Segales, José Pedro Cardoso (82 Martín Larrosa). DT: Luis González
LDU: Cristian Rafael Mora, Néicer Reasco, Giovanny Patricio Espinoza, Carlos Alberto Espínola, Paul Vicente Ambrossi, Alfonso Andrés Obregón (77 Wálter Ramiro Iza), Patricio Javier Urrutia, Édison Vicente Méndez (65 Diego Marcelo Ceballos), Roberto Carlos Palacios (89 Moisés Antonio Candelario), Elkin Antonio Murillo, Agustín Javier Delgado. DT: Juan Carlos Oblitas
Goals: José Pedro Cardoso (7), Juan Marcelo Segales (28), José Pedro Cardoso (81) /
Agustín Javier Delgado (16), Patricio Javier Urrutia (82).

VÉLEZ SARSFIELD – UNIVERSITARIO DE LIMA 4-3 (3-3)
José Amalfitani, Buenos Aires, 14.03.2006
Referee: Ricardo Grance (PAR)
VÉLEZ SARSFIELD: Sebastián Darío Peratta, Santiago Andrés Ladino, Hernán Darío Pellerano, Walter Óscar Alcaráz, Marcelo Hernán Bustamante (85 Carlos Andrés Soto), Sergio Román Sena, Leandro Daniel Somoza, Damián Ariel Escudero (88 Ariel Esteban Broggi), Ramón Darío Ocampo, Lucas Martín Castromán (82 Rolando David Zárate), Mauro Matías Zárate. DT: Miguel Ángel Russo
UNIVERSITARIO: José Aurelio Carvallo, Germán Martín Centurión, Luis Daniel Benito Hernández , Percy Lozada, Marco Antonio Ruiz, Miguel Ángel Cevasco (46 Jhoel Alexander Herrera), Arnaldo Daniel Alonso (77 Víctor Alonso Rosell), Piero Fernando Alva, José Alberto Moisela, Rafael Nazareno Maceratesi (79 Mauricio Mendoza), Gastón Maximiliano Sangoy. DT: Juan Amador Sánchez
Sent off: Ocampo (43)
Goals: Marcelo Hernán Bustamante (5), Damián Ariel Escudero (42, 87), Mauro Matías Zárate (45) / Rafael Nazareno Maceratesi (1), Gastón Maximiliano Sangoy (7), Germán Martín Centurión (23).

LIGA DEP. UNIVERSITARIA – ROCHA FC 5-0 (2-0)
La Casa Blanca, Quito, 16.03.2006
Referee: Gustavo Alonso Brand (VEN), Attendance: 10.000
LDU: Cristian Rafael Mora, Néicer Reasco, Carlos Alberto Espínola, Giovanny Patricio Espinoza, Paul Vicente Ambrossi, Patricio Javier Urrutia, Enrique Daniel Vera, Édison Vicente Méndez (79 Moisés Antonio Candelario), Roberto Carlos Palacios (86 Diego Marcelo Ceballos), Elkin Antonio Murillo (66 Wálter Ramiro Iza), Agustín Javier Delgado. DT: Juan Carlos Oblitas
ROCHA: Oscar Andrés Lemos, Nelson Matías González, Diego Roberto Sosa, Diego Alberto Bonelli (60 Pablo Martín Seijas), Diego Ciz (24 Darwin Norberto Noguéz), Herley Martín González, Pablo Gabriel Esquivel, Luis Jesús Toscanini (50 Cristiano Araujo), Héber Alfonso Caro, Juan Marcelo Segales, José Pedro Cardoso. DT: Luis González
Goals: Elkin Antonio Murillo (13), Patricio Javier Urrutia (25, 61), Édison Vicente Méndez (64), Moisés Antonio Candelario (65).

LIGA DEP. UNIVERSITARIA – UNIVERSITARIO DE LIMA 4-0 (2-0)
La Casa Blanca, Quito, 6.04.2006
Referee: Albert Duarte (COL), Attendance: 10.000
LDU: Cristian Rafael Mora, Néicer Reasco, Carlos Alberto Espínola, Giovanny Patricio Espinoza, Paul Vicente Ambrossi, Enrique Daniel Vera, Patricio Javier Urrutia, Édison Vicente Méndez (75 Moisés Antonio Candelario), Roberto Carlos Palacios (69 Jairo Rolando Campos), Elkin Antonio Murillo (62 Joffre David Guerrón), Agustín Javier Delgado. DT: Juan Carlos Oblitas
UNIVERSITARIO: Juan Ángel Flores, José Adolfo Mendoza, Marco Antonio Ruiz, Luis Daniel Benito Hernández, José Alberto Moisela, José Antonio Pereda (75 Gregorio Abel Bernales), Miguel Ángel Cevasco, Alex Segundo Magallanes, Piero Fernando Alva, Arnaldo Daniel Alonso (39 Paolo Freddy Maldonado), Gastón Maximiliano Sangoy. DT: Jorge Amado Nunes
Sent off: Espinoza (67) / Alva (67)
Goals: Agustín Javier Delgado (28), Enrique Daniel Vera (40), Édison Vicente Méndez (51), Joffre David Guerrón (81).

ROCHA FC – VÉLEZ SARSFIELD 0-5 (0-3)
Domingo Burgueño Miguel "Campus Municipal", Maldonado, 11.04.2006
Referee: Rubén Marcos Selman (CHI)
ROCHA: Oscar Andrés Lemos, Nelson Matías González, Diego Roberto Sosa, Diego Alberto Bonelli, Diego Ciz (70 Darwin Norberto Noguéz), Herley Martín González, Álvaro Fernando Becerra, Luis Alejandro Maguregui (49 Leonardo Maldonado), Héber Alfonso Caro, Juan Marcelo Segales, José Pedro Cardoso (35 Ruben Darío Rodríguez). DT: Luis González

VÉLEZ SARSFIELD: Gastón Alejandro Sessa, Fabián Alberto Cubero, Hernán Darío Pellerano (69 Santiago Andrés Ladino), Walter Óscar Alcaráz, Marcelo Hernán Bustamante, Sergio Román Sena, Maximiliano Andrés Bustos (57 Maximiliano Pellegrino), Ariel Esteban Broggi, Emanuel Adrián Centurión (66 Pablo Martín Batalla), Sebastián Adolfo Ereros, Mauro Matías Zárate. DT: Miguel Ángel Russo
Goals: Sebastián Adolfo Ereros (1, 33, 71), Mauro Matías Zárate (9), Marcelo Hernán Bustamante (56).

UNIVERSITARIO DE LIMA – ROCHA FC 1-1 (0-0)
Monumental, Lima, 18.04.2006
Referee: Alberto Duque (COL), Attendance: 3.500
UNIVERSITARIO: José Aurelio Carvallo, Luis Alberto Guadalupe, Germán Martín Centurión, Percy Lozada (70 Luis Daniel Benito Hernández), Willy Alexander Rivas, Jhoel Alexander Herrera, Gregorio Abel Bernales, Paolo Freddy Maldonado, Arnaldo Daniel Alonso (53 Alex Segundo Magallanes), Mauricio Mendoza, Víctor Alonso Rosell (46 Gastón Maximiliano Sangoy). DT: Jorge Amado Nunes
ROCHA: Damián Diego Magarzo, Diego Roberto Sosa, Diego Alberto Bonelli, Cristiano Araujo, Darwin Norberto Noguéz, Pablo Gabriel Esquivel, Álvaro Fernando Becerra, Ruben Darío Rodríguez (65 Herley Martín González), Héber Alfonso Caro (81 Martín Larrosa), Luis Jesús Toscanini (65 Luis Alejandro Maguregui), José Pedro Cardoso. DT: Luis González
Goals: Alex Segundo Magallanes (63) / José Pedro Cardoso (76).

VÉLEZ SARSFIELD – LIGA DEP. UNIVERSITARIA 2-2 (0-1)
José Amalfitani, Buenos Aires, 18.04.2006
Referee: Carlos Amarilla (PAR), Attendance: 16.000
VÉLEZ SARSFIELD: Sebastián Darío Peratta, Santiago Andrés Ladino, Maximiliano Pellegrino, Walter Óscar Alcaráz, Carlos Andrés Soto, Sergio Román Sena, Fabián Alberto Cubero, Emanuel Adrián Centurión (85 Damián Ariel Escudero), Ramón Darío Ocampo (82 Pablo Martín Batalla), Mauro Matías Zárate, Sebastián Adolfo Ereros. DT: Miguel Ángel Russo
LDU: Cristian Rafael Mora, Néicer Reasco, Carlos Alberto Espínola, Rolando Santiago Jácome, Juan Keli Guerrón, Enrique Daniel Vera, Roberto Carlos Palacios (90 Joffre David Guerrón), Pedro Sebastián Larrea (46 Elkin Antonio Murillo), Patricio Javier Urrutia, Édison Vicente Méndez, Agustín Javier Delgado. DT: Juan Carlos Oblitas
Goals: Sebastián Adolfo Ereros (55), Emanuel Adrián Centurión (59 penalty) /
Patricio Javier Urrutia (30), Roberto Carlos Palacios (57).

1	VÉLEZ SARSFIELD	6	5	1	0	18	6	16
2	LDU QUITO	6	3	1	2	16	9	10
3	Rocha FC	6	1	2	3	4	16	5
4	Universitario de Lima	6	0	2	4	5	12	2

GROUP 6

NACIONAL MONTEVIDEO – UNAM 2-0 (1-0)
Parque Central, Montevideo, 8.02.2006
Referee: Héctor Walter Baldassi (ARG), Attendance: 18.000
NACIONAL: Jorge Rodrigo Bava, Diego Jaume, Mauricio Bernardo Victorino, Ignacio Ramon Paniagua, Mauren Franco (86 Marcelo Adrián Mansilla), Marco Eduardo Vanzini, Agustín Viana, Rodrigo Sebastián Vázquez, Juan Angel Albín (81 Jorge Orlando Brítez), Andrés Leonardo Márquez, Gonzalo Castro (66 José Luis Garcés). DT: Martín Lasarte
UNAM: Victor Odin Patiño, Darío Anastacio Verón, Marco Antonio Palacios (62 LEANDRO AUGUSTO Oldoni Stachelski), Raúl Alberto Salinas, Israel Castro, Héctor Alfredo Moreno, Cesáreo Victorino, Franz Eric Torres (46 Ismael Iñíguez), Julio César Pinheiro, Joaquín Botero (46 Paulo Marcel Pereira Merabet "ROMA"), Bruno Marioni. DT: Miguel España
Sent off: Verón (72)
Goals: Gonzalo Castro (16, 62 penalty).

UNIÓN ATLÉTICO MARACAIBO – INTERNACIONAL 1-1 (0-0)
José Encarnación Romero, Maracaibo, 16.02.2006
Referee: Pedro Senatore Ramos (ECU), Attendance: 30.000
UA MARACIABO: Gilberto Angelucci, Elvis Alfonso Martínez (55 Rubén Ramón Yori), Lucas Alfredo Bovaglio, Juan José Fuenmayor, Pedro Alfonso Fernández, Andreé Aníbal González, Guillermo Fabián Beraza, Gamadiel Adrián García (75 Darío Damián Figueroa), Héctor Augusto González, Giancarlo Gregorio Maldonado, Cristian Alfonso Cásseres (85 Diony José Guerra). DT: Carlos Maldonado
INTERNACIONAL: CLEMER Melo da Silva, Marcos Venâncio de Albuquerque "CEARÁ", Fabián Guedes "BOLÍVAR", FABIANO ELLER dos Santos, RUBENS Vanderlei Tavares CARDOSO, Edimo Ferreira Campos "EDINHO", Fábio de Jesús "FABINHO", Paulo César Fonseca do Nascimento "TINGA" (78 JORGE WAGNER Góes Conceição), Pedro IARLEY Lima Dantas (83 Cleiton Eduardo Vicente "PERDIGÃO"), MICHEL Neves Dias (69 Carlos ADRIANO de Souza Vieira), Fernando Lúcio da Costa "FERNANDÃO". DT: Abel Braga
Goals: Giancarlo Gregorio Maldonado (88) / Marcos Venâncio de Albuquerque "CEARÁ" (48).

UNAM – UNIÓN ATLÉTICO MARACAIBO 0-1 (0-1)
Olímpico Universitario, México City, 22.02.2006
Referee: Héber Roberto Lopes (BRA)
UNAM: Sergio Arturo Bernal, Héctor Alfredo Moreno, Joaquín Beltrán, Raúl Alberto Salinas, José Luis López, Gerardo Gabriel Galindo, LEANDRO AUGUSTO Oldoni Stachelski, Cesáreo Victorino (46 José David Toledo), Franz Eric Torres (46 Paulo Marcel Pereira Merabet "ROMA"), Ismael Iñíguez (70 Marco Antonio Palacios), Bruno Marioni. DT: Miguel España
UA MARACIABO: Gilberto Angelucci, Renier Alexander Rodríguez (73 Rubén Ramón Yori), Lucas Alfredo Bovaglio, Juan José Fuenmayor, Héctor Augusto González, Pedro Alfonso Fernández, Andreé Aníbal González, Guillermo Fabián Beraza, Darío Damián Figueroa, Rafael Castellín (71 Giancarlo Gregorio Maldonado), Cristian Alfonso Cásseres (63 Gamadiel Adrián García). DT: Carlos Maldonado
Goal: Rafael Castellín (39).

INTERNACIONAL – NACIONAL MONTEVIDEO 3-0 (2-0)
Beira-Rio, Porto Alegre, 23.02.2006
Referee: Horacio Marcelo Elizondo (ARG), Attendance: 31.170
INTERNACIONAL: CLEMER Melo da Silva, Marcos Venâncio de Albuquerque "CEARÁ", Fabián Guedes "BOLÍVAR", FABIANO ELLER dos Santos, RUBENS Vanderlei Tavares CARDOSO, Fábio de Jesús "FABINHO", Cleiton Eduardo Vicente "PERDIGÃO", Paulo César Fonseca do Nascimento "TINGA" (82 Carlos ADRIANO de Souza Vieira), Pedro IARLEY Lima Dantas (84 JORGE WAGNER Góes Conceição), MICHEL Neves Dias (70 José Márcio da Costa "MOSSORÓ"), Fernando Lúcio da Costa "FERNANDÃO". DT: Abel Braga
NACIONAL: Jorge Rodrigo Bava, Ignacio Ramon Paniagua, Diego Jaume, Mauricio Bernardo Victorino, Daniel Leites, Marco Eduardo Vanzini, Jorge Orlando Brítez, Jorge Andrés Martínez (72 Marcelo Adrián Mansilla), Juan Angel Albín (57 Mauren Franco), José Luis Garcés, Gonzalo Castro. DT: Martín Lasarte
Sent off: Jaume (62)
Goals: MICHEL Neves Dias (20), Fernando Lúcio da Costa "FERNANDÃO" (22), RUBENS Vanderlei Tavares CARDOSO (89).

UNAM – INTERNACIONAL 1-2 (1-0)
Olímpico Universitario, México City, 8.03.2006
Referee: Rubén Marcos Selman (CHI)
UNAM: Sergio Arturo Bernal, Joaquín Beltrán, Israel Castro, Héctor Alfredo Moreno, Gerardo Gabriel Galindo, Franz Eric Torres (46 Fernando Morales), LEANDRO AUGUSTO Oldoni Stachelski (72 Marco Antonio Palacios), Cesáreo Victorino, José Luis López, Paulo Marcel Pereira Merabet "ROMA" (77 Joaquín Botero), Bruno Marioni. DT: Miguel España

INTERNACIONAL: CLEMER Melo da Silva, Fabián Guedes "BOLÍVAR", FABIANO ELLER dos Santos, MICHEL Neves Dias (62 José Márcio da Costa "MOSSORÓ"), Fábio de Jesús "FABINHO", RUBENS Vanderlei Tavares CARDOSO (75 JORGE WAGNER Góes Conceição), Paulo César Fonseca do Nascimento "TINGA", Marcos Venâncio de Albuquerque "CEARÁ", Edimo Ferreira Campos "EDINHO" (62 Wason Libardo Rentería), Pedro IARLEY Lima Dantas, Fernando Lúcio da Costa "FERNANDÃO". DT: Abel Braga
Goals: José Luis López (43) /
Wason Libardo Rentería (63), Fernando Lúcio da Costa "FERNANDÃO" (80).

NACIONAL MONTEVIDEO – UNIÓN ATLÉTICO MARACAIBO 0-0
Parque Central, Montevideo, 9.03.2006
Referee: Carlos Manuel Torres (PAR), Attendance: 11.009
NACIONAL: Jorge Rodrigo Bava, Mauricio Bernardo Victorino, José Ignacio Pallas (57 Daniel Leites), Mauren Franco (78 Carlos Alberto Juárez), Marco Eduardo Vanzini, Ignacio Ramon Paniagua, Agustín Viana, Jorge Andrés Martínez, Juan Angel Albín, José Luis Garcés (62 Andrés Leonardo Márquez), Gonzalo Castro. DT: Martín Lasarte
UA MARACIABO: Gilberto Angelucci, Renier Alexander Rodríguez, José Francisco González, Héctor Augusto González, Lucas Alfredo Bovaglio, Pedro Alfonso Fernández, Andreé Aníbal González, Guillermo Fabián Beraza, Darío Damián Figueroa (80 Gamadiel Adrián García), Rafael Castellín (58 Giancarlo Gregorio Maldonado), Cristian Alfonso Cásseres. DT: Carlos Maldonado
Sent off: Rodríguez (90)

UNIÓN ATLÉTICO MARACAIBO – NACIONAL MONTEVIDEO 2-3 (1-0)
José Encarnación Romero, Maracaibo, 16.03.2006
Referee: Héctor Walter Baldassi (ARG), Attendance: 30.000
UA MARACIABO: Gilberto Angelucci, Elvis Alfonso Martínez, José Francisco González, Lucas Alfredo Bovaglio, Héctor Augusto González, Pedro Alfonso Fernández (81 Vicente Antonio Suanno), Andreé Aníbal González, Guillermo Fabián Beraza, Darío Damián Figueroa (64 Giancarlo Gregorio Maldonado), Rafael Castellín (72 Diony José Guerra), Cristian Alfonso Cásseres. DT: Carlos Maldonado
NACIONAL: Jorge Rodrigo Bava, Diego Jaume, Mauricio Bernardo Victorino, Ignacio Ramon Paniagua (38 Andrés Leonardo Márquez), Daniel Leites, Marco Eduardo Vanzini (84 Jorge Orlando Brítez), Agustín Viana, Rodrigo Sebastián Vázquez, Jorge Andrés Martínez (46 Juan Angel Albín), José Luis Garcés, Gonzalo Castro. DT: Martín Lasarte
Sent off: Garcés (36)
Goals: Cristian Alfonso Cásseres (2), Giancarlo Gregorio Maldonado (90+1) /
Rodrigo Sebastián Vázquez (57), Gonzalo Castro (67), Juan Angel Albín (87).

INTERNACIONAL – UNAM 3-2 (1-2)
Beira-Rio, Porto Alegre, 22.03.2006
Referee: Sergio Fabián Pezzota (ARG), Attendance: 37.593
INTERNACIONAL: CLEMER Melo da Silva, Marcos Venâncio de Albuquerque "CEARÁ", Fabián Guedes "BOLÍVAR", FABIANO ELLER dos Santos, RUBENS Vanderlei Tavares CARDOSO, Fábio de Jesús "FABINHO", Cleiton Eduardo Vicente "PERDIGÃO" (46 José Márcio da Costa "MOSSORÓ"), Paulo César Fonseca do Nascimento "TINGA", MICHEL Neves Dias (67 Carlos ADRIANO de Souza Vieira), Pedro IARLEY Lima Dantas (46 Wason Libardo Rentería), Fernando Lúcio da Costa "FERNANDÃO". DT: Abel Braga
UNAM: Sergio Arturo Bernal, Héctor Alfredo Moreno, Raúl Alberto Salinas, Israel Castro, Fernando Morales (82 Efrain Velarde), Gerardo Gabriel Galindo, Fernando Espinosa, Marco Antonio Palacios, Joaquín Botero (72 Luis Ricardo Rosas), Paulo Marcel Pereira Merabet "ROMA" (69 Gerardo Hernández), Bruno Marioni. DT: Miguel España
Sent off: Castro (85)
Goals: MICHEL Neves Dias (37), Fernando Lúcio da Costa "FERNANDÃO" (52),
Carlos ADRIANO de Souza Vieira (76) / Gerardo Gabriel Galindo (4), Joaquín Botero (35).

UNIÓN ATLÉTICO MARACAIBO – UNAM 3-0 (0-0)
José Encarnación Romero, Maracaibo, 30.03.2006
Referee: Albert Duarte (COL), Attendance: 28.515
UA MARACIABO: Gilberto Angelucci, Rubén Ramón Yori, Juan José Fuenmayor, Lucas Alfredo Bovaglio, Elvis Alfonso Martínez, Pedro Alfonso Fernández, Andreé Aníbal González, Guillermo Fabián Beraza, Darío Damián Figueroa (90 Vicente Antonio Suanno), Giancarlo Gregorio Maldonado (78 Rafael Castellín), Cristian Alfonso Cásseres (81 Héctor Augusto González). DT: Carlos Maldonado
UNAM: Sergio Arturo Bernal, Joaquín Beltrán, Darío Anastacio Verón, Marco Antonio Palacios, Fernando Morales (68 Julio César Pinheiro), Gerardo Gabriel Galindo, Cesáreo Victorino, José Luis López (65 Bruno Marioni), Paulo Marcel Pereira Merabet "ROMA", Joaquín Botero (46 LEANDRO AUGUSTO Oldoni Stachelski), Gerardo Hernández. DT: Miguel España
Guillermo Fabián Beraza missed a penalty in the 15th minute
Goals: Cristian Alfonso Cásseres (50), Giancarlo Gregorio Maldonado (77), Rafael Castellín (90).

NACIONAL MONTEVIDEO – INTERNACIONAL 0-0
Parque Central, Montevideo, 4.04.2006
Referee: Carlos Amarilla (PAR), Attendance: 7.525
NACIONAL: Jorge Rodrigo Bava, Mauricio Bernardo Victorino, Diego Jaume, Daniel Leites, Rodrigo Sebastián Vázquez, Marco Eduardo Vanzini, Agustín Viana, Javier Omar Delgado (56 Juan Angel Albín), Andrés Leonardo Márquez (75 Jorge Andrés Martínez), Carlos Alberto Juárez (65 Luis Alberto Suárez), Gonzalo Castro. DT: Martín Lasarte
INTERNACIONAL: CLEMER Melo da Silva, Marcos Venâncio de Albuquerque "CEARÁ", Fabián Guedes "BOLÍVAR", FABIANO ELLER dos Santos, RUBENS Vanderlei Tavares CARDOSO, Fábio de Jesús "FABINHO", Paulo César Fonseca do Nascimento "TINGA", Carlos ADRIANO de Souza Vieira, MICHEL Neves Dias (46 José Márcio da Costa "MOSSORÓ"), Wason Libardo Rentería (77 RAFAEL Augusto SÓBIS), Pedro IARLEY Lima Dantas (77 JORGE WAGNER Góes Conceição). DT: Abel Braga

UNAM – NACIONAL MONTEVIDEO 1-1 (0-0)
Olímpico Universitario, México City, 18.04.2006
Referee: Horacio Marcelo Elizondo (ARG)
UNAM: Sergio Arturo Bernal, Joaquín Beltrán, Darío Anastacio Verón, Marco Antonio Palacios, Israel Castro, Efrain Velarde (60 José David Toledo), Cesáreo Victorino (60 Fernando Morales), José Luis López, LEANDRO AUGUSTO Oldoni Stachelski, Ismael Iñíguez (81 Gerardo Hernández), Bruno Marioni. DT: Guillermo Vázquez
NACIONAL: Jorge Rodrigo Bava, Diego Jaume, Mauricio Bernardo Victorino, Daniel Leites, Marco Eduardo Vanzini, Agustín Viana, Rodrigo Sebastián Vázquez, Javier Omar Delgado (74 Jorge Andrés Martínez), Juan Angel Albín (46 Jorge Orlando Brítez), Andrés Leonardo Márquez, Gonzalo Castro (88 Marcelo Adrián Mansilla). DT: Martín Lasarte
Sent off: Verón (54)
Goals: Daniel Leites (66 own goal) / Jorge Andrés Martínez (79).

INTERNACIONAL – UNIÓN ATLÉTICO MARACAIBO 4-0 (1-0)
Beira-Rio, Porto Alegre, 18.04.2006
Referee: Carlos Luis Chandía (CHI), Attendance: 17.001
INTERNACIONAL: CLEMER Melo da Silva, ELDER da Silva GRANJA, Fabián Guedes "BOLÍVAR", FABIANO ELLER dos Santos, JORGE WAGNER Góes Conceição, Edimo Ferreira Campos "EDINHO", Cleiton Eduardo Vicente "PERDIGÃO", Paulo César Fonseca do Nascimento "TINGA" (37 Pedro IARLEY Lima Dantas), Carlos ADRIANO de Souza Vieira (79 MICHEL Neves Dias), RAFAEL Augusto SÓBIS (78 Wason Libardo Rentería), Fernando Lúcio da Costa "FERNANDÃO". DT: Abel Braga

UA MARACIABO: Gilberto Angelucci, Rubén Ramón Yori, Juan José Fuenmayor, Lucas Alfredo Bovaglio, Elvis Alfonso Martínez, Pedro Alfonso Fernández, Andreé Aníbal González, Darío Damián Figueroa (63 Héctor Augusto González), Guillermo Fabián Beraza, Rafael Castellín (59 Giancarlo Gregorio Maldonado), Cristian Alfonso Cásseres (81 Gamadiel Adrián García). DT: Carlos Maldonado
Sent off: González (90)
Goals: Carlos ADRIANO de Souza Vieira (35), Fabián Guedes "BOLÍVAR" (77), MICHEL Neves Dias (82), Wason Libardo Rentería (85).

1	INTERNACIONAL	6	4	2	0	13	4	14
2	NACIONAL M	6	2	3	1	6	6	9
3	UA Maracaibo	6	2	2	2	7	8	8
4	UNAM	6	0	1	5	4	12	1

GROUP 7

ATLÉTICO NACIONAL – ROSARIO CENTRAL 1-0 (1-0)
Atanasio Girardot, Medellín, 9.02.2006
Referee: Wilson De Souza (BRA), Attendance: 45.000
ATLÉTICO NACIONAL: Andrés David Saldarriaga, Humberto Antonio Mendoza, Luciano Vera, Vladimir Marín (82 Gerardo Alberto Bedoya), Carlos Alberto Díaz (21 Juan Carlos Mosquera), Luis Felipe Chará, José Antonio Amaya, Andrés Felipe Casañas, Hugo Alberto Morales, Víctor Hugo Aristizábal, Jairo Oliver Rambal (54 Héctor Hugo Hurtado). DT: Santiago Escobar
ROSARIO CENTRAL: Juan Marcelo Ojeda, Gabriel Alejandro Loeschbor, Ricardo Ariel Moreira, Cristián Carlos Villagra, Diego Agustín Cálgaro (70 Ángel Fabián Di María), Ronald Raldes, Andrés Alejandro Díaz, Eduardo Germán Coudet, José Alfredo Castillo, Pablo Ernesto Vitti (60 Marco Gastón Rubén), Juan Eduardo Eluchans (61 Hernán Fabián Encina). DT: Ángel Zof
Sent off: Díaz (84)
Goal: Carlos Alberto Díaz (14).

CERRO PORTEÑO – PALMEIRAS 0-0
Gral. Pablo Rojas, Asunción, 15.02.2006
Referee: Martín Vázquez (URU), Attendance: 15.000
CERRO PORTEÑO: Diego Daniel Barreto, Pedro Juan Benítez, José Ricardo Devaca, Fidel Amado Pérez, Walter Milciades Fretes, Edgar Daniel González, Mario Darío Grana, Ernesto Rubén Cristaldo, Carlos Daniel Genes (46 Pablo Junior Giménez), Erwin Lorenzo Ávalos (65 Alejandro Damián Da Silva), Jorge Daniel Achucarro. DT: Gustavo Costas
PALMEIRAS: SÉRGIO Luis de Araújo, PAULO César BAIER, VALDOMIRO Duarte de Macedo (46 Ricardo Souza Silva "RICARDINHO"), DANIEL da Silva (14 LEONARDO Fabiano da SILVA e Silva), Carlos Alberto Gamarra, LÚCIO Carlos Cajueiro Souza, Márcio Glad "MARCINHO GUERREIRO", Carlos Rodrigues CORRÊA, Márcio Miranda Rocha da Silva "MARCINHO", ENÍLTON Menezes de Miranda (67 WASHINGTON Luiz Mascarenhas Silva), EDMUNDO Alves de Souza Neto. DT: Emerson Leão

ROSARIO CENTRAL – CERRO PORTEÑO 0-2 (0-1)
Gigante de Arroyito, Rosario, 23.02.2006
Referee: Sálvio Spínola Fagundes (BRA), Attendance: 19.503
ROSARIO CENTRAL: Cristián Darío Álvarez, Juan Fernando Grabowski, Ronald Raldes, Ramiro Fernando Fassi, Ricardo Ariel Moreira (46 Diego Agustín Cálgaro), Eduardo Germán Coudet, Leonardo Luis Borzani, Germán Ezequiel Rivarola, Pablo Ernesto Vitti (56 Emiliano Gabriel Vecchio), Germán Ariel Alemanno (65 Emilio José Zelaya), Marco Gastón Rubén. DT: Ángel Zof
CERRO PORTEÑO: Diego Daniel Barreto, Pedro Juan Benítez, Carlos Alberto Báez, José Ricardo Devaca, Ernesto Rubén Cristaldo, Walter Milciades Fretes, Edgar Daniel González, Mario Darío Grana, José Domingo Salcedo, Jorge Daniel Achucarro (8 Pablo Junior Giménez), Erwin Lorenzo Ávalos (79 Roberto Ovelar). DT: Gustavo Costas
Goals: Erwin Lorenzo Ávalos (45), Leonardo Luis Borzani (56 own goal).

PALMEIRAS – ATLÉTICO NACIONAL 3-2 (2-1)
Palestra Italia, São Paulo, 2.03.2006
Referee: Jorge Luis Larrionda (URU)
PALMEIRAS: SÉRGIO Luis de Araújo, PAULO César BAIER, DOUGLAS Roberto dos Santos (75 VALDOMIRO Duarte de Macedo), LEONARDO Fabiano da SILVA e Silva, MÁRCIO "CARECA" Ferreira, Márcio Glad "MARCINHO GUERREIRO", Carlos Rodrigues CORRÊA, Ricardo Souza Silva "RICARDINHO" (85 ALCEU Rodrigues Simoni Filho), Márcio Miranda Rocha da Silva "MARCINHO", EDMUNDO Alves de Souza Neto, ENÍLTON Menezes de Miranda (37 WASHINGTON Luiz Mascarenhas Silva). DT: Emerson Leão
ATLÉTICO NACIONAL: Andrés David Saldarriaga, Carlos Alberto Díaz, Humberto Antonio Mendoza, Oscar Enrique Passo, Vladimir Marín, Andrés Felipe Casañas (80 Cristian Camilo Marrugo), José Antonio Amaya, Luis Felipe Chará, Aldo Leao Ramírez (81 Héctor Hugo Hurtado), Víctor Hugo Aristizábal, MARCELO Silva RAMOS. DT: Santiago Escobar
Sent off: Passo (89)
Víctor Hugo ARISTIZÁBAL Posada missed a penalty in the 53rd minute
Goals: Márcio Miranda Rocha da Silva "MARCINHO" (18), EDMUNDO Alves de Souza Neto (35 penalty), DOUGLAS Roberto dos Santos (71) /
MARCELO Silva RAMOS (31), Víctor Hugo Aristizábal (73).

CERRO PORTEÑO – ATLÉTICO NACIONAL 1-5 (1-4)
Gral. Pablo Rojas, Asunción, 14.03.2006
Referee: Daniel Orlando Giménez (ARG)
CERRO PORTEÑO: Hilario Bernardo Navarro, Pedro Juan Benítez, Carlos Alberto Báez, José Ricardo Devaca, Ernesto Rubén Cristaldo (31 Pablo Junior Giménez, 72 Juan Antonio Cardozo), Walter Milciades Fretes, Edgar Daniel González (58 Pablo Daniel Escobar), Mario Darío Grana, José Domingo Salcedo, Jorge Daniel Achucarro, Erwin Lorenzo Ávalos. DT: Gustavo Costas
ATLÉTICO NACIONAL: Breiner Clemente Castillo, Carlos Alberto Díaz, Hugo Emilio Soto, Luciano Vera, Gerardo Alberto Bedoya, José Antonio Amaya, Luis Felipe Chará, Vladimir Marín, Aldo Leao Ramírez, Víctor Hugo Aristizábal (62 MARCELO Silva RAMOS), Sergio Alejandro Galván (71 Juan Carlos Mosquera). DT: Carlos Navarrete
Sent off: Báez (75) / Ramírez (56), Bedoya (64)
Goals: Walter Milciades Fretes (39) /
Vladimir Marín (18, 74), Sergio Alejandro Galván (26), Víctor Hugo Aristizábal (27, 45)

PALMEIRAS – ROSARIO CENTRAL 0-0
Palestra Italia, São Paulo, 15.03.2006
Referee: Carlos Manuel Torres (PAR)
PALMEIRAS: SÉRGIO Luis de Araújo, DOUGLAS Roberto dos Santos (46 ALCEU Rodrigues Simoni Filho), DANIEL da Silva, Carlos Alberto Gamarra, PAULO César BAIER (46 Ricardo Souza Silva "RICARDINHO"), Márcio Glad "MARCINHO GUERREIRO", Carlos Rodrigues CORRÊA, Márcio Miranda Rocha da Silva "MARCINHO", LÚCIO Carlos Cajueiro Souza, EDMUNDO Alves de Souza Neto, ENÍLTON Menezes de Miranda (55 WASHINGTON Luiz Mascarenhas Silva). DT: Emerson Leão
ROSARIO CENTRAL: Hernán Claudio Castellano, Ricardo Ariel Moreira, Ronald Raldes, Ramiro Fernando Fassi, Cristián Carlos Villagra, Hernán Fabián Encina (75 Eduardo Germán Coudet), Damián Andrés Ledesma (79 Juan Fernando Grabowski), Leonardo Luis Borzani, Juan Eduardo Eluchans, Pablo Ernesto Vitti (69 Emilio José Zelaya), Marco Gastón Rubén. DT: Leonardo Astrada

ROSARIO CENTRAL – PALMEIRAS 2-2 (1-1)
Gigante de Arroyito, Rosario, 23.03.2006
Referee: Roberto Carlos Silvera (URU), Attendance: 35.000
ROSARIO CENTRAL: Hernán Claudio Castellano, Cristián Carlos Villagra (63 Ricardo Ariel Moreira), Ronald Raldes, Ramiro Fernando Fassi, Germán Ezequiel Rivarola, Eduardo Germán Coudet (75 Ángel Fabián Di María), Leonardo Luis Borzani, Damián Andrés Ledesma, Juan Eduardo Eluchans (68 Hernán Fabián Encina), Pablo Ernesto Vitti, Marco Gastón Rubén. DT: Leonardo Astrada

PALMEIRAS: SÉRGIO Luis de Araújo, DANIEL da Silva, Carlos Alberto Gamarra, LEONARDO Fabiano da SILVA e Silva, PAULO César BAIER (76 ALCEU Rodrigues Simoni Filho), Márcio Glad "MARCINHO GUERREIRO", Carlos Rodrigues CORRÊA, LÚCIO Carlos Cajueiro Souza, Márcio Miranda Rocha da Silva "MARCINHO", EDMUNDO Alves de Souza Neto (64 ENÍLTON Menezes de Miranda), WASHINGTON Luiz Mascarenhas Silva. DT: Emerson Leão
Goals: Marco Gastón Rubén (6), Damián Andrés Ledesma (89) /
WASHINGTON Luiz Mascarenhas Silva (18, 88).

ATLÉTICO NACIONAL – CERRO PORTEÑO 2-2 (0-1)
Atanasio Girardot, Medellín, 23.03.2006
Referee: Mauricio Javier Reinoso (ECU), Attendance: 35.000
ATLÉTICO NACIONAL: Breiner Clemente Castillo, Oscar Enrique Passo, Luciano Vera (37 Juan Carlos Mosquera), Humberto Antonio Mendoza, Hugo Emilio Soto (66 Jairo Oliver Rambal), Cristian Camilo Marrugo, Luis Felipe Chará, Héctor Hugo Hurtado (56 MARCELO Silva RAMOS), Vladimir Marín, Sergio Alejandro Galván, Víctor Hugo Aristizábal. DT: Carlos Navarrete
CERRO PORTEÑO: Diego Daniel Barreto, Fidel Amado Pérez, Pedro Juan Benítez, José Ricardo Devaca, Ernesto Rubén Cristaldo, Edgar Daniel González, Mario Darío Grana, Walter Milciades Fretes (68 Pedro Richar Irala), José Domingo Salcedo, Jorge Daniel Achucarro (64 Pablo Junior Giménez), Erwin Lorenzo Ávalos (83 Roberto Ovelar). DT: Gustavo Costas
Goals: Fidel Amado Pérez (75 own goal), Vladimir Marín (90) /
José Domingo Salcedo (29), Erwin Lorenzo Ávalos (78).

ATLÉTICO NACIONAL – PALMEIRAS 1-2 (0-2)
Atanasio Girardot, Medellín, 4.04.2006
Referee: Carlos Luis Chandía (CHI), Attendance: 45.000
ATLÉTICO NACIONAL: Breiner Clemente Castillo, Hugo Emilio Soto (85 Jairo Oliver Rambal), Carlos Alberto Díaz, Humberto Antonio Mendoza, Gerardo Alberto Bedoya, José Antonio "Ringo" Amaya, Cristian Camilo Marrugo (51 Luis Felipe Chará), Vladimir Marín (75 MARCELO Silva RAMOS), Aldo Leao Ramírez, Sergio Alejandro Galván, Víctor Hugo Aristizábal. DT: Carlos Navarrete
PALMEIRAS: SÉRGIO Luis de Araújo, DANIEL da Silva , Carlos Alberto Gamarra, LÚCIO Carlos Cajueiro Souza, Antônio Cleílson da Silva Feitosa "AMARAL", Márcio Glad "MARCINHO GUERREIRO", LEONARDO Fabiano da SILVA e Silva, Carlos Rodrigues CORRÊA, PAULO César BAIER, Márcio Miranda Rocha da Silva "MARCINHO" (86 ENÍLTON Menezes de Miranda), WASHINGTON Luiz Mascarenhas Silva. DT: Emerson Leão
Goals: Carlos Alberto Díaz (90+3) /
Carlos Rodrigues CORRÊA (13), LEONARDO Fabiano da SILVA e Silva (24).

CERRO PORTEÑO – ROSARIO CENTRAL 1-3 (0-1)
Defensores del Chaco, Asunción, 6.04.2006
Referee: Rubén Marcos Selman (CHI), Attendance: 8.000
CERRO PORTEÑO: Diego Daniel Barreto, Carlos Alberto Báez, Pedro Juan Benítez (68 Jorge Daniel Achucarro), José Ricardo Devaca, Fidel Amado Pérez, Walter Milciades Fretes (35 Pablo Daniel Escobar), Edgar Daniel González, Mario Darío Grana, José Domingo Salcedo, Pablo Junior Giménez, Erwin Lorenzo Ávalos. DT: Gustavo Costas
ROSARIO CENTRAL: Cristián Darío Álvarez, Gabriel Alejandro Loeschbor, Ronald Raldes, Ricardo Ariel Moreira, Cristián Carlos Villagra, Hernán Fabián Encina (75 Leonardo Luis Borzani), Damián Andrés Ledesma, Emiliano Gabriel Vecchio (60 Andrés Alejandro Díaz), Juan Eduardo Eluchans (69 Ángel Fabián Di María), Pablo Ernesto Vitti, Marco Gastón Rubén. DT: Leonardo Astrada
Pablo Ernesto Vitti missed a penalty in the 64th minute
Goals: José Domingo Salcedo (49) / Marco Gastón Rubén (43, 72), Hernán Fabián Encina (75).

ROSARIO CENTRAL – ATLÉTICO NACIONAL 1-2 (0-2)
Gigante de Arroyito, Rosario, 13.04.2006
Referee: Jorge Luis Larrionda (URU), Attendance: 23.289
ROSARIO CENTRAL: Cristián Darío Álvarez, Ricardo Ariel Moreira, Ronald Raldes, Ramiro Fernando Fassi, Germán Ezequiel Rivarola (43 Cristián Carlos Villagra), Eduardo Germán Coudet (57 Emiliano Gabriel Vecchio), Leonardo Luis Borzani, Juan Eduardo Eluchans (46 Ángel Fabián Di María), Hernán Fabián Encina, Pablo Ernesto Vitti, Marco Gastón Rubén. DT: Leonardo Astrada
ATLÉTICO NACIONAL: Andrés David Saldarriaga, Hugo Emilio Soto, Carlos Alberto Díaz, Humberto Antonio Mendoza, Gerardo Alberto Bedoya, Luis Felipe Chará, José Antonio Amaya, Vladimir Marín, Aldo Leao Ramírez (89 Héctor Hugo Hurtado), Sergio Alejandro Galván (81 Cristian Camilo Marrugo), Víctor Hugo Aristizábal. DT: Carlos Navarrete
Sent off: Raldes (77) / Aristizábal (77)
Goals: Cristián Carlos Villagra (75) / Víctor Hugo Aristizábal (31), Vladimir Marín (45+2).

PALMEIRAS – CERRO PORTEÑO 2-3 (0-0)
Palestra Italia, São Paulo, 13.04.2006
Referee: René Marcelo Ortubé (BOL)
PALMEIRAS: SÉRGIO Luis de Araújo, PAULO César BAIER, DOUGLAS Roberto dos Santos, DANIEL da Silva (37 LEONARDO Fabiano da SILVA e Silva), LÚCIO Carlos Cajueiro Souza, Márcio Glad "MARCINHO GUERREIRO", Carlos Rodrigues CORRÊA, Márcio Miranda Rocha da Silva "MARCINHO", Ricardo Souza Silva "RICARDINHO" (60 ENÍLTON Menezes de Miranda), EDMUNDO Alves de Souza Neto (46 ALCEU Rodrigues Simoni Filho), WASHINGTON Luiz Mascarenhas Silva. DT: Emerson Leão
CERRO PORTEÑO: Diego Daniel Barreto, Juan Antonio Cardozo, Carlos Alberto Báez, José Ricardo Devaca, Fidel Amado Pérez, Mario Darío Grana, Edgar Daniel González (73 Esteban Javier Ramírez), José Domingo Salcedo, Ernesto Rubén Cristaldo, Pablo Junior Giménez (55 Jorge Daniel Achucarro), Erwin Lorenzo Ávalos (89 Nelson David Cabrera). DT: Gustavo Costas
Sent off: Douglas (45) / Báez (45)
Márcio Miranda Rocha da Silva "MARCINHO" missed a penalty in the 89th minute
Goals: Márcio Miranda Rocha da Silva "MARCINHO" (70, 89) /
José Domingo Salcedo (55), Erwin Lorenzo Ávalos (61, 83).

1	ATLÉTICO NACIONAL	6	3	1	2	13	9	10
2	PALMEIRAS	6	2	3	1	9	8	9
3	Cerro Porteño	6	2	2	2	9	12	8
4	Rosario Central	6	1	2	3	6	8	5

GROUP 8

EL NACIONAL – PAULISTA FC 1-1 (0-0)
Olímpico Atahualpa, Quito, 14.02.2006
Referee: Albert Duarte (COL), Attendance: 6.918
EL NACIONAL: Oswaldo Johvani Ibarra, Omar Andrés De Jesús, Jorge Daniel Guagua, Carlos Ernesto Castro, Erik Rolando De Jesús, Segundo Alejandro Castillo, Mario David Quiróz, Wálter Orlando Ayoví (46 Christian Rogelio Benítez), Cristian Rolando Lara, Ebelio Agustín Ordóñez (46 Gustavo Omar Figueroa), Félix Alexander Borja. DT: Ever Almeida
PAULISTA: RAFAEL Wihby Bracalli, LUCAS da Silva, Valdemar Cirino Andalécio Junior "DEMA", REVER Humberto Alves de Araújo (69 NIVALDO Batista Santana), Ricardo Sales Alves do Santos "BOSCO", GLEYDSON Marcelino Freire, Carlos Rafael do AMARAL, WILSON Rodrigues Fonseca (46 FÁBIO VIDAL), Luis Alberto de Souza "BETO", León Darío Muñóz, JEAN CARLOS da Conceição (66 ABRAÃO Lincoln Martins). DT: Wagner Mancini
Goals: Félix Alexander Borja (68) / ABRAÃO Lincoln Martins (81).

LIBERTAD ASUNCIÓN – RIVER PLATE 2-0 (0-0)
Defensores del Chaco, Asunción, 16.02.2006
Referee: Jorge Luis Larrionda (URU), Attendance: 10.000
LIBERTAD: Aldo Antonio Bobadilla, Edgar Gabriel Balbuena, Pedro Alcides Sarabia, Deivis Barone, Martín Emilio Hidalgo, Javier Alejandro Villarreal (82 Edgar Arnulfo Robles), Cristian Miguel Riveros, Pablo Horacio Guiñazú, Carlos Bonet, Nelson David Romero (75 Pablo Sebastián Garnier), Hernán Rodrigo López (87 Roberto Carlos Gamarra). DT: Gerardo Martino
RIVER PLATE: Germán Darío Lux, Paulo Andrés Ferrari, Julio César Cáceres, Leonardo José Talamonti, Cristián Andrés Álvarez, Lucas Andrés Pusineri (59 Jairo Leonard Patiño), Óscar Adrián Ahumada, Juan Carlos Toja, Marcelo Daniel Gallardo (61 Gonzalo Daniel Abán), Daniel Gastón Montenegro, Ernesto Antonio Farías (77 Luciano Gabriel Figueroa). DT: Daniel Passarella
Sent off: Toja (76)
Goals: Deivis Barone (60), Roberto Carlos Gamarra (88).

PAULISTA FC – LIBERTAD ASUNCIÓN 0-0
Dr. Jaime Pinheiro de Ulhoa Cintra, Jundiaí, 2.03.2006 Referee: Rubén Marcos Selman (CHI)
PAULISTA: RAFAEL Wihby Bracalli, Ricardo Sales Alves do Santos "BOSCO", REVER Humberto Alves de Araújo, Valdemar Cirino Andalécio Junior "DEMA", FÁBIO VIDAL, GLEYDSON Marcelino Freire (46 JEAN CARLOS da Conceição), Carlos Rafael do AMARAL, Jorge SAMMIR Cruz Campos, WILSON Rodrigues Fonseca (69 Luis Alberto de Souza "BETO"), WESLEY Brasília Almeida (67 ABRAÃO Lincoln Martins), León Darío Muñóz. DT: Wagner Mancini
LIBERTAD: Aldo Antonio Bobadilla, Raúl Hernán Damiani, Edgar Gabriel Balbuena, Pedro Alcides Sarabia, Ricardo Julián Martínez, Víctor Javier Cáceres, Javier Alejandro Villarreal, Carlos Bonet (80 Edgar Arnulfo Robles), Hernán Rodrigo López (90 Roberto Carlos Gamarra), Pablo Horacio Guiñazú, Nelson David Romero (77 Pablo Sebastián Garnier). DT: Gerardo Martino

RIVER PLATE – EL NACIONAL 4-3 (1-2)
Antonio V. Liberti, Buenos Aires, 8.03.2006
Referee: Óscar Julián Ruiz (COL), Attendance: 15.957
RIVER PLATE: Germán Darío Lux, Paulo Andrés Ferrari, Julio César Cáceres, Leonardo José Talamonti (46 Christian Alberto Tula), Lucas Armando Mareque, Jonathan Santana, Óscar Adrián Ahumada, Gonzalo Daniel Abán (54 Gustavo Andrés Oberman), Marcelo Daniel Gallardo, Daniel Gastón Montenegro (82 Víctor Eduardo Zapata), Ernesto Antonio Farías. DT: Daniel Passarella
EL NACIONAL: Oswaldo Johvani Ibarra, Renán Calle, Carlos Ernesto Castro, Jorge Daniel Guagua, Jhon Patricio Cagua (83 Wálter Orlando Ayoví), Omar Andrés De Jesús, Mario David Quiróz, Segundo Alejandro Castillo, Carlos Ramón Hidalgo, Cristian Rolando Lara (83 Christian Rogelio Benítez), Félix Alexander Borja. DT: Ever Almeida
Sent off: Oberman (89)
Goals: Ernesto Antonio Farías (4), Jonathan Santana (68), Daniel Gastón Montenegro (79), Marcelo Daniel Gallardo (82) / Cristian Rolando Lara (30), Félix Alexander Borja (38, 50).

RIVER PLATE – PAULISTA FC 4-1 (2-1)
Antonio V. Liberti, Buenos Aires, 16.03.2006
Referee: Carlos Luis Chandía (CHI), Attendance: 42.000
RIVER PLATE: Germán Darío Lux, Paulo Andrés Ferrari, Julio César Cáceres, Christian Alberto Tula, Federico Hernán Domínguez, Jonathan Santana, Óscar Adrián Ahumada (87 Lucas Armando Mareque), Víctor Eduardo Zapata (66 René Martín Lima), Jairo Leonard Patiño (46 Lucas Andrés Pusineri), Daniel Gastón Montenegro, Gonzalo Daniel Abán. DT: Daniel Passarella
PAULISTA: RAFAEL Wihby Bracalli, Ricardo Sales Alves do Santos "BOSCO" (77 Luis Alberto de Souza "BETO"), REVER Humberto Alves de Araújo, Valdemar Cirino Andalécio Junior "DEMA", FÁBIO VIDAL, GLEYDSON Marcelino Freire (60 LUCAS da Silva), Carlos Rafael do AMARAL, JAÍLSON Alexandre Alves do Santos (66 WESLEY Brasília Almeida), WILSON Rodrigues Fonseca, ABRAÃO Lincoln Martins, León Darío Muñóz. DT: Wagner Mancini
Goals: Jonathan Santana (10), Daniel Gastón Montenegro (13, 51), Gonzalo Daniel Abán (82) / León Darío Muñóz (28 penalty).

LIBERTAD ASUNCIÓN – EL NACIONAL 4-1 (1-1)
Defensores del Chaco, Asunción, 23.03.2006
Referee: Héctor Walter Baldassi (ARG)
LIBERTAD: Aldo Antonio Bobadilla, Raúl Hernán Damiani (63 Edgar Gabriel Balbuena), Pedro Alcides Sarabia, Martín Emilio Hidalgo, Ricardo Julián Martínez, Cristian Miguel Riveros, Nelson David Romero (65 Pablo Sebastián Garnier), Javier Alejandro Villarreal, Hernán Rodrigo López (74 Roberto Carlos Gamarra), Pablo Horacio Guiñazú, Carlos Bonet. DT: Gerardo Martino
EL NACIONAL: Oswaldo Johvani Ibarra, Omar Andrés De Jesús, Carlos Ernesto Castro, Jorge Daniel Guagua, Jhon Patricio Cagua, Mario David Quiróz, Carlos Ramón Hidalgo (46 Danny Alejandro Vera), Segundo Alejandro Castillo, Christian Rogelio Benítez (73 Wálter Orlando Ayoví), Cristian Rolando Lara (64 Kléber Manuel Chalá), Félix Alexander Borja. DT: Ever Almeida Sent off: Chalá (82)
Goals: Ricardo Julián Martínez (5), Cristian Miguel Riveros (60), Javier Alejandro Villarreal (69), Hernán Rodrigo López (71) / Félix Alexander Borja (19).

EL NACIONAL – LIBERTAD ASUNCIÓN 1-1 (1-0)
Olímpico Atahualpa, Quito, 30.03.2006
Referee: Carlos Luis Chandía (CHI), Attendance: 3.000
EL NACIONAL: Robinson Geovanny Sánchez, Pedro Ángel Quiñónez (46 Omar Andrés De Jesús), Carlos Ernesto Castro, Jorge Daniel Guagua, Pavel Cipriano Caicedo (46 Erik Rolando De Jesús), Mario David Quiróz, Segundo Alejandro Castillo, Cristian Rolando Lara, Christian Rogelio Benítez, Ebelio Agustín Ordóñez (63 Wálter Orlando Ayoví), Félix Alexander Borja. DT: Ever Almeida
LIBERTAD: Aldo Antonio Bobadilla, Edgar Gabriel Balbuena, Pedro Alcides Sarabia, Martín Emilio Hidalgo (68 Edgar Arnulfo Robles), Ricardo Julián Martínez, Cristian Miguel Riveros, Nelson David Romero (54 Osvaldo David Martínez), Javier Alejandro Villarreal (74 Roberto Carlos Gamarra), Hernán Rodrigo López, Pablo Horacio Guiñazú, Carlos Bonet. DT: Gerardo Martino
Goals: Félix Alexander Borja (11) / Ricardo Julián Martínez (86).

PAULISTA FC – RIVER PLATE 2-1 (2-1)
Dr. Jaime Pinheiro de Ulhoa Cintra, Jundiaí, 5.04.2006
Referee: Carlos Manuel Torres (PAR)
PAULISTA: RAFAEL Wihby Bracalli, LUCAS da Silva, REVER Humberto Alves de Araújo, Valdemar Cirino Andalécio Junior "DEMA", Luis Alberto de Souza "BETO", GLEYDSON Marcelino Freire, Carlos Rafael do AMARAL, WILSON Rodrigues Fonseca, JAÍLSON Alexandre Alves do Santos (72 JEAN CARLOS da Conceição), DOUGLAS Marques dos Santos, León Darío Muñóz (76 Ricardo Sales Alves do Santos "BOSCO"). DT: Wagner Mancini
RIVER PLATE: Germán Darío Lux, Cristián Andrés Álvarez, Julio César Cáceres, Christian Alberto Tula, Lucas Armando Mareque, Lucas Andrés Pusineri (62 Víctor Eduardo Zapata), Óscar Adrián Ahumada, Andrés San Martín, Jairo Leonard Patiño (73 Daniel Gastón Montenegro), Gonzalo Daniel Abán (62 Ernesto Antonio Farías), Gustavo Andrés Oberman. DT: Daniel Passarella
Goals: Carlos Rafael do AMARAL (6), JAÍLSON Alexandre Alves do Santos (17) / Jairo Leonard Patiño (18).

LIBERTAD ASUNCIÓN – PAULISTA FC 1-0 (1-0)
Defensores del Chaco, Asunción, 12.04.2006
Referee: Óscar Julián Ruiz (COL), Attendance: 1.033
LIBERTAD: Aldo Antonio Bobadilla, Edgar Gabriel Balbuena, Pedro Alcides Sarabia, Martín Emilio Hidalgo, Ricardo Julián Martínez, Cristian Miguel Riveros, Nelson David Romero (60 Pablo Sebastián Garnier), Javier Alejandro Villarreal, Hernán Rodrigo López (85 Roberto Carlos Gamarra), Pablo Horacio Guiñazú, Carlos Bonet (90+1 Edgar Arnulfo Robles). DT: Gerardo Martino
PAULISTA: RAFAEL Wihby Bracalli, LUCAS da Silva, REVER Humberto Alves de Araújo, Valdemar Cirino Andalécio Junior "DEMA", Luis Alberto de Souza "BETO" (69 FÁBIO VIDAL), GLEYDSON Marcelino Freire, Carlos Rafael do AMARAL, WILSON Rodrigues Fonseca, JAÍLSON Alexandre Alves do Santos, DOUGLAS Marques dos Santos (55 JEAN CARLOS da Conceição), León Darío Muñóz (73 LUIZ HENRIQUE de Oliveira). DT: Wagner Mancini
Goal: Martín Emilio Hidalgo (19).

EL NACIONAL – RIVER PLATE 2-0 (2-0)
Olímpico Atahualpa, Quito, 12.04.2006
Referee: Carlos Luis Chandía (CHI)
EL NACIONAL: Oswaldo Johvani Ibarra, Carlos Ernesto Castro, Jorge Daniel Guagua, Pavel Cipriano Caicedo, Segundo Alejandro Castillo, Omar Andrés De Jesús, Mario David Quiróz, Cristian Rolando Lara (65 Christian Rogelio Benítez), Wálter Orlando Ayoví (90 Manuel Antonio Cotera), Kléber Manuel Chalá (82 Carlos Ramón Hidalgo), Félix Alexander Borja. DT: Ever Almeida
RIVER PLATE: Germán Darío Lux, Cristián Andrés Álvarez, Leonardo José Talamonti, Danilo Telmo Gerlo, Christian Alberto Tula, Jairo Leonard Patiño, Andrés San Martín, René Martín Lima, Juan Carlos Toja (63 Jonathan Santana), Gonzalo Daniel Abán, Gustavo Andrés Oberman. DT: Daniel Passarella
Goals: Danilo Telmo Gerlo (11 own goal), Mario David Quiróz (38 penalty).

RIVER PLATE – LIBERTAD ASUNCIÓN 1-0 (0-0)
Antonio V. Liberti, Buenos Aires, 20.04.2006
Referee: Carlos Eugênio Simón (BRA), Attendance: 22.000
RIVER PLATE: Germán Darío Lux, Paulo Andrés Ferrari, Julio César Cáceres, Danilo Telmo Gerlo, Lucas Armando Mareque, Jonathan Santana (59 Gustavo Andrés Oberman), Óscar Adrián Ahumada, Víctor Eduardo Zapata, Jairo Leonard Patiño (59 Marcelo Daniel Gallardo), Daniel Gastón Montenegro (87 Lucas Andrés Pusineri), Ernesto Antonio Farías. DT: Daniel Passarella
LIBERTAD: Aldo Antonio Bobadilla, Raúl Hernán Damiani, Pedro Alcides Sarabia, Edgar Gabriel Balbuena, Martín Emilio Hidalgo, Javier Alejandro Villarreal, Carlos Bonet, Cristian Miguel Riveros, Pablo Horacio Guiñazú (58 Osvaldo David Martínez), Pablo Sebastián Garnier (75 Edgar Arnulfo Robles), Roberto Carlos Gamarra (70 Nelson David Romero). DT: Gerardo Martino
Goal: Víctor Eduardo Zapata (68).

PAULISTA FC – EL NACIONAL 0-0
Dr. Jaime Pinheiro de Ulhoa Cintra, Jundiaí, 20.04.2006
Referee: Rubén Marcos Selman (CHI)
PAULISTA: RAFAEL Wihby Bracalli, LUCAS da Silva, REVER Humberto Alves de Araújo, Valdemar Cirino Andalécio Junior "DEMA", FÁBIO VIDAL, Luis Alberto de Souza "BETO" (74 ABRAÃO Lincoln Martins), GLEYDSON Marcelino Freire, Carlos Rafael do AMARAL, WILSON Rodrigues Fonseca, JAÍLSON Alexandre Alves do Santos (80 NIVALDO Batista Santana), León Darío Muñóz (60 JEAN CARLOS da Conceição). DT: Wagner Mancini
EL NACIONAL: Oswaldo Johvani Ibarra, Carlos Ernesto Castro, Jorge Daniel Guagua, Pavel Cipriano Caicedo, Segundo Alejandro Castillo, Carlos Ramón Hidalgo (75 Gustavo Omar Figueroa), Omar Andrés De Jesús, Mario David Quiróz, Cristian Rolando Lara (83 Manuel Antonio Cotera), Christian Rogelio Benítez, Félix Alexander Borja. DT: Ever Almeida

1	LIBERTAD ASUNCIÓN	6	3	2	1	8	3	11
2	RIVER PLATE	6	3	0	3	10	10	9
3	El Nacional	6	1	3	2	8	10	6
4	Paulista FC	6	1	3	2	4	7	6

ROUND OF 16

ESTUDIANTES DE LA PLATA – GOIÁS EC 2-0 (0-0)
Centenario, Quilmes, 25.04.2006
Referee: Carlos Luis Chandía (CHI), Attendance: 18.776
ESTUDIANTES: Martín Horacio Herrera, Marcos Alberto Angeleri, Agustín Alayes, Juan Daniel Cáceres, Jorge Martín Núñez (71 Pablo Ariel Lugüercio), Marcos Agustín Gelabert (75 Diego Alberto Galván), Rodrigo Braña (64 Marcelo Adrián Carrusca), Juan Augusto Huerta, José Ernesto Sosa, Hugo Mariano Pavone, José Luis Calderón. DT: Jorge Burruchaga
GOIÁS: HARLEI de Menezes Silva, LEONARDO Devanir de Paula, JÚLIO César dos SANTOS, ROGÉRIO CORRÊA de Oliveira, José JADÍLSON dos Santos Silva (89 ALDO César da Silva), FABIANO Cézar Viegas, CLÉBER Rezende de Oliveira, DANILO PORTUGAL Bueno Ferreira, Marcos André Batista Santos "VAMPETA" (75 CLÉBER "GAÚCHO" Nelson de Andrade Raphaelli), Rodrigo de SOUZA Cardoso, Roniéliton Pereira Santos "RONI" (77 Raimundo NONATO de Lima Ribeiro). DT: Eugenio Machado Souto "Geninho"
Sent off: Souza (70), Leonardo (89)
Goals: Diego Alberto Galván (80), José Luis Calderón (90+1 penalty).

GOIÁS EC – ESTUDIANTES DE LA PLATA 3-1 (0-0)
Serra Dourada, Goiánia, 4.05.2006
Referee: Óscar Julián Ruiz (COL), Attendance: 17.895
GOIÁS: HARLEI de Menezes Silva, Cícero VÍTOR dos Santos Junior (75 JULIANO Gomes Soares), ROGÉRIO CORRÊA de Oliveira, FABIANO Cézar Viegas, JÚLIO César dos SANTOS, José JADÍLSON dos Santos Silva, DANILO PORTUGAL Bueno Ferreira (80 LEYRIELTON Moura de Morais), Raimundo NONATO de Lima Ribeiro, Roniéliton Pereira Santos "RONI", Romero Mendonça Sobrinho "ROMERITO", WELLITON Soares de Morais. DT: Eugenio Machado Souto "Geninho"
ESTUDIANTES: Martín Horacio Herrera, Marcos Alberto Angeleri, Agustín Alayes, Juan Daniel Cáceres, Jorge Martín Núñez, Rodrigo Braña, Juan Augusto Huerta, Marcos Agustín Gelabert (73 Horacio Ramón Cardozo), José Ernesto Sosa (80 Marcelo Adrián Carrusca), José Luis Calderón (88 Diego Alberto Galván), Hugo Mariano Pavone. DT: Jorge Burruchaga
Goals: Cícero VÍTOR dos Santos Junior (51), Raimundo NONATO de Lima Ribeiro (65), JULIANO Gomes Soares (90+1) / José Luis Calderón (76).

LIGA DEP. UNIVERSITARIA – ATLÉTICO NACIONAL 4-0 (2-0)
La Casa Blanca, Quito, 25.04.2006
Referee: Víctor Hugo Rivera (PER), Attendance: 11.303
LDU: Cristian Rafael Mora, Néicer Reasco, Carlos Alberto Espínola, Giovanny Patricio Espinoza, Paul Vicente Ambrossi, Enrique Daniel Vera, Patricio Javier Urrutia, Édison Vicente Méndez (90 Joffre David Guerrón), Elkin Antonio Murillo (74 Moisés Antonio Candelario), Roberto Carlos Palacios (85 Alfonso Andrés Obregón), Agustín Javier Delgado. DT: Juan Carlos Oblitas
ATLÉTICO NACIONAL: Andrés David Saldarriaga, Hugo Emilio Soto, Carlos Alberto Díaz, Humberto Antonio Mendoza, Gerardo Alberto Bedoya, Luis Felipe Chará, José Antonio Amaya, Vladimir Marín, Aldo Leao Ramírez (10 Cristian Camilo Marrugo), MARCELO Silva RAMOS (50 Óscar Marino Echeverry), Sergio Alejandro Galván (78 Héctor Hugo Hurtado). DT: David Ospina
Goals: Elkin Antonio Murillo (10, 13), Enrique Daniel Vera (63), Moisés Antonio Candelario (75).

ATLÉTICO NACIONAL – LIGA DEP. UNIVERSITARIA 0-1 (0-1)
Atanasio Girardot, Medellín, 2.05.2006
Referee: Sálvio Spínola Fagundes (BRA), Attendance: 10.000
ATLÉTICO NACIONAL: David Ospina, Hugo Emilio Soto, Carlos Alberto Díaz, Humberto Antonio Mendoza, Oscar Enrique Passo (53 Luis Felipe Chará), José Antonio Amaya, Andrés Felipe Casañas (53 Óscar Marino Echeverry), Vladimir Marín, Héctor Hugo Hurtado (71 Jairo Oliver Rambal), Víctor Hugo Aristizábal, Sergio Alejandro Galván. DT: Carlos Navarrete

LDU: Cristian Rafael Mora, Néicer Reasco, Carlos Alberto Espínola, Giovanny Patricio Espinoza, Paul Vicente Ambrossi, Enrique Daniel Vera, Alfonso Andrés Obregón, Patricio Javier Urrutia, Édison Vicente Méndez (79 Moisés Antonio Candelario), Roberto Carlos Palacios (71 Elkin Antonio Murillo), Agustín Javier Delgado (84 Ariel José Graziani). DT: Juan Carlos Oblitas
Sent off: Amaya (86), Marín (88) / Obregón (86)
Goal: Édison Vicente Méndez (40).

RIVER PLATE – CORINTHIANS PAULISTA 3-2 (2-1)
Antonio V. Liberti, Buenos Aires, 26.04.2006
Referee: Carlos Amarilla (PAR), Attendance: 38.910
RIVER PLATE: Germán Darío Lux, Danilo Telmo Gerlo, Julio César Cáceres, Leonardo José Talamonti, Paulo Andrés Ferrari, Jonathan Santana, Óscar Adrián Ahumada, Federico Hernán Domínguez, Marcelo Daniel Gallardo (83 Jairo Leonard Patiño), Gonzalo Daniel Abán (77 Gonzalo Gerardo Higuaín), Ernesto Antonio Farías (86 Christian Alberto Tula). DT: Daniel Passarella
CORINTHIANS: SILVIO LUIZ de Oliveira de Paula, DYEGO Rocha COELHO (86 EDUARDO "RATINHO" Filho Correia Piller), Ebert William Amâncio "BETÃO", MARCUS VINÍCIUS Cesário, RUBENS Rodrigues dos Santos JÚNIOR, Javier Alejandro Mascherano, MARCELO Mendonça de MATTOS, CARLOS ALBERTO Gomes de Jesus, Ricardo Luis Pozzi Rodrigues "RICARDINHO" (88 RÓGER Galera Flores), Carlos Alberto Tévez, NILMAR Honorato da Silva (68 Anderson Conceição XAVIER). DT: Ademar Braga
Sent off: Talamonti (85) / Mascherano (66)
Goals: Ernesto Antonio Farías (25), Paulo Andrés Ferrari (30), Jonathan Santana (80) / Carlos Alberto Tévez (15), Anderson Conceição Xavier (90+2).

CORINTHIANS PAULISTA – RIVER PLATE 1-3 (1-0)
Paulo Machado de Carvalho "Pacaembú", São Paulo, 4.05.2006
Referee: Carlos Luis Chandía (CHI), Attendance: 32.089
CORINTHIANS: SILVIO LUIZ de Oliveira de Paula, DYEGO Rocha COELHO (78 EDUARDO "RATINHO" Filho Correia Piller), MARCUS VINÍCIUS Cesário, Ebert William Amâncio "BETÃO", RUBENS Rodrigues dos Santos JÚNIOR, MARCELO Mendonça de MATTOS, Anderson Conceição XAVIER (65 RÓGER Galera Flores), Ricardo Luis Pozzi Rodrigues "RICARDINHO", CARLOS ALBERTO Gomes de Jesus (76 RAFAEL Martiniano de Miranda MOURA), Carlos Alberto Tévez, NILMAR Honorato da Silva. DT: Ademar Braga
RIVER PLATE: Germán Darío Lux, Danilo Telmo Gerlo, Julio César Cáceres, Christian Alberto Tula, Paulo Andrés Ferrari, Jonathan Santana, Óscar Adrián Ahumada, Federico Hernán Domínguez, Marcelo Daniel Gallardo, Gonzalo Daniel Abán (65 Gonzalo Gerardo Higuaín), Ernesto Antonio Farías. DT: Daniel Passarella
Goals: NILMAR Honorato da Silva (39) /
DYEGO Rocha COELHO (56 own goal), Gonzalo Gerardo Higuaín (71, 81).

CD GUADALAJARA – INDEPENDIENTE SANTA FE 3-0 (1-0)
Jalisco, Guadalajara, 26.04.2006
Referee: Olivier Humberto Viera (URU), Attendance: 5.000
GUADALAJARA: Alfredo Talavera, Diego Alfonso Martínez, Héctor Reynoso, Patricio Gabriel Araujo, Jhonny García, Christian Michel Armas (36 Alberto Medina), Omar Alejandro Esparza, Juan Pablo Rodríguez (73 Manuel Bernardo Sol), Adolfo Bautista, Edwin Alejandro Borboa (80 Marco Antonio Parra), Sergio Alejandro Santana. DT: José Manuel De La Torre
INDEPENDIENTE: Luis Enrique Martínez, Pablo César Pachón, John Freddy Tierradentro, Jairo Andrés Suárez, César Antonio Fawcett (59 Edgar Francisco Delgado), Gabriel Enrique Gómez (73 Carlos Alberto Ortiz), David Fernando Montoya, Juan Carlos Ramírez, Leider Calimenio Preciado (66 José Largacha), Álvaro Francisco Nájera, Luis Alfredo Yánez. DT: Ricardo Gareca
Sent off: Yánez (58)
Goals: Omar Alejandro Esparza (45), Edwin Alejandro Borboa (51), Alberto Medina (80).

INDEPENDIENTE SANTA FE – CD GUADALAJARA 3-1 (1-1)
Nemesio Camacho, Bogotá, 2.05.2006
Referee: Rubén Marcos Selman (CHI)
INDEPENDIENTE: Luis Enrique Martínez, Jairo Andrés Suárez, John Freddy Tierradentro, Álvaro Francisco Nájera, Edgar Francisco Delgado, Gabriel Enrique Gómez, Juan Carlos Ramírez (46 José Largacha), Carlos Alberto Ortiz (69 Carlos Daniel Hidalgo), César Antonio Fawcett (22 Mario Efrain Gómez), David Fernando Montoya, Leider Calimenio Preciado. DT: Ricardo Gareca
GUADALAJARA: Oswaldo Javier Sánchez, Diego Alfonso Martínez, Héctor Reynoso, Jhonny García, Christian Michel Armas, Omar Alejandro Esparza, Jorge Armando Barrera, Juan Pablo Rodríguez (61 Manuel Bernardo Sol), Adolfo Bautista (81 Edwin Alejandro Borboa), Sergio Alejandro Santana (46 Manuel Alejandro Vela), José Jonny Magallón. DT: José Manuel De La Torre
Goals: Leider Calimenio Preciado (36), José Largacha (50), David Fernando Montoya (87 penalty) / Héctor Reynoso (9).

PALMEIRAS – SÃO PAULO FC 1-1 (1-1)
Palestra Italia, São Paulo, 26.04.2006
Referee: Carlos Eugênio Simón (BRA)
PALMEIRAS: SÉRGIO Luis de Araújo, PAULO César BAIER, DANIEL da Silva (27 THIAGO GOMES Antequeira), Carlos Alberto Gamarra, MÁRCIO "CARECA" Ferreira (81 REINALDO José Zacarias da Silva), Márcio Glad "MARCINHO GUERREIRO", Carlos Rodrigues CORRÊA, WENDEL Santana Pereira Santos, Márcio Miranda Rocha da Silva "MARCINHO", WASHINGTON Luiz Mascarenhas Silva (62 Oswaldo Giroldo Júnior "JUNINHO PAULISTA"), EDMUNDO Alves de Souza Neto. DT: Marcelo Villar
SÃO PAULO: ROGÉRIO CENI, José Fábio Alves Azevedo "FABÃO", Diego Alfredo Lugano, ANDRÉ Gonçalves DIAS, Williamis de SOUZA Silva, Carlos Luciano da Silva "MINEIRO", JOSUÉ de Oliveira, DANILO Gabriel de Andrade, Jenilson Angelo de Souza "JÚNIOR", José ALOÍSIO da Silva, THIAGO Ribeiro Cardoso (76 LEANDRO Lessa Azevedo). DT: Muricy Ramalho
Goals: EDMUNDO Alves de Souza Neto (36 penalty) / José ALOÍSIO da Silva (23).

SÃO PAULO FC – PALMEIRAS 2-1 (1-0)
Cícero Pompeu de Toledo "Morumbí", São Paulo, 3.05.2006
Referee: Wilson De Souza (BRA), Attendance: 55.080
SÃO PAULO: ROGÉRIO CENI, José Fábio Alves Azevedo "FABÃO", Diego Alfredo Lugano, ANDRÉ Gonçalves DIAS, Williamis de SOUZA Silva, JOSUÉ de Oliveira, Carlos Luciano da Silva "MINEIRO", DANILO Gabriel de Andrade, Jenilson Angelo de Souza "JÚNIOR" (89 EDCARLOS Conceição Santos), LEANDRO Lessa Azevedo, José ALOÍSIO da Silva (76 THIAGO Ribeiro Cardoso). DT: Muricy Ramalho
PALMEIRAS: SÉRGIO Luis de Araújo, PAULO César BAIER, THIAGO GOMES Antequeira, Carlos Alberto Gamarra, LÚCIO Carlos Cajueiro Souza, Márcio Glad "MARCINHO GUERREIRO", Carlos Rodrigues CORRÊA, WENDEL Santana Pereira Santos (76 Ricardo Souza Silva "RICARDINHO"), Márcio Miranda Rocha da Silva "MARCINHO" (18 CRISTIAN Martins Cabral, 88 LEONARDO Fabiano da SILVA e Silva), EDMUNDO Alves de Souza Neto, WASHINGTON Luiz Mascarenhas Silva. DT: Marcelo Villar
Sent off: Leandro (68) / Paulo Baier (90+2), Thiago Gomes (90+3), Marcinho Guerreiro (90+3)
Goals: José ALOÍSIO da Silva (13), ROGÉRIO CENI (86 penalty) /
WASHINGTON Luiz Mascarenhas Silva (56).

NEWELL'S OLD BOYS – VÉLEZ SARSFIELD 2-4 (1-1)
Colose del Parque, Rosario, 27.04.2006
Referee: Horacio Marcelo Elizondo (ARG), Attendance: 20.640
NEWELL'S OLD BOYS: Justo Wilmar Villar, Diego Antonio Gavilán (46 Mauro Emiliano Cejas), Gastón Damián Aguirre, Nicolás Federico Spolli, Germán David Ré, Fernando Daniel Belluschi, Claudio Daniel Husaín, Ariel Hernán Zapata (75 Héctor Damián Steinert), Adrián Maximilliano Peralta, Ariel Arnaldo Ortega, Ignacio Martín Scocco. DT: Nery Pumpido

VÉLEZ SARSFIELD: Gastón Alejandro Sessa, Fabián Alberto Cubero, Maximiliano Pellegrino, Hernán Darío Pellerano, Marcelo Hernán Bustamante, Maximiliano Andrés Bustos, Leandro Daniel Somoza, Ariel Esteban Broggi (65 Sergio Román Sena), Leandro Gracián (90 Ramón Darío Ocampo), Sebastián Adolfo Ereros (76 Emmanuel Gaspar Fernándes), Mauro Matías Zárate. DT: Miguel Ángel Russo
Sent off: Zárate (56)
Goals: Nicolás Federico Spolli (32), Ignacio Martín Scocco (53) / Mauro Matías Zárate (16), Leandro Daniel Somoza (51 penalty, 66 penalty), Sebastián Adolfo Ereros (52)

VÉLEZ SARSFIELD – NEWELL'S OLD BOYS 2-2 (0-0)
José Amalfitani, Buenos Aires, 3.05.2006
Referee: Daniel Orlando Giménez (ARG), Attendance: 14.270
VÉLEZ SARSFIELD: Gastón Alejandro Sessa, Fabián Alberto Cubero, Maximiliano Pellegrino, Hernán Darío Pellerano, Marcelo Hernán Bustamante, Maximiliano Andrés Bustos, Leandro Daniel Somoza, Ariel Esteban Broggi (78 Sergio Román Sena), Leandro Gracián (86 Ramón Darío Ocampo), Sebastián Adolfo Ereros (70 Emmanuel Gaspar Fernándes), Lucas Martín Castromán. DT: Miguel Ángel Russo
NEWELL'S OLD BOYS: Justo Wilmar Villar, Nicolás Federico Spolli, Miguel Ángel Torrén, Germán David Ré, Claudio Daniel Husaín, Fernando Daniel Belluschi, Ariel Hernán Zapata (55 Hugo Roberto Colace), Adrián Maximilliano Peralta, Ariel Arnaldo Ortega (78 Gustavo Ariel Rodas), Héctor Damián Steinert, Ignacio Martín Scocco. DT: Nery Pumpido
Sent off: Husain (63)
Goals: Leandro Daniel Somoza (76 penalty), Ramón Darío Ocampo (90+2) /
Ignacio Martín Scocco (53), Hugo Roberto Colace (84).

NACIONAL MONTEVIDEO – INTERNACIONAL 1-2 (1-1)
Parque Central, Montevideo, 27.04.2006
Referee: Óscar Julián Ruiz (COL), Attendance: 10.221
NACIONAL: Jorge Rodrigo Bava, Diego Jaume, Mauricio Bernardo Victorino, José Ignacio Pallas, Marco Eduardo Vanzini, Agustín Viana (62 Jorge Andrés Martínez), Rodrigo Sebastián Vázquez (72 Luis Alberto Suárez), Jorge Orlando Brítez, Juan Angel Albín, Andrés Leonardo Márquez (62 Carlos Alberto Juárez), Gonzalo Castro. DT: Martín Lasarte
INTERNACIONAL: CLEMER Melo da Silva, Fabián Guedes "BOLÍVAR", Edimo Ferreira Campos "EDINHO", FABIANO ELLER dos Santos, ELDER da Silva GRANJA, Fábio de Jesús "FABINHO", ALEX Raphael Meschini (80 EDIGLÉ Quaresma Farías), JORGE WAGNER Góes Conceição, Carlos ADRIANO de Souza Vieira (65 MICHEL Neves Dias), Fernando Lúcio da Costa "FERNANDÃO", RAFAEL Augusto SÓBIS (46 Wason Libardo Rentería). DT: Abel Braga
Sent off: Rentería (75), Edigle (82)
Goals: Marco Eduardo Vanzini (29) /
JORGE WAGNER Góes Conceição (45), Wason Libardo Rentería (64).

INTERNACIONAL – NACIONAL MONTEVIDEO 0-0
Beira-Rio, Porto Alegre, 3.05.2006
Referee: Carlos Manuel Torres (PAR), Attendance: 26.225
INTERNACIONAL: CLEMER Melo da Silva, ELDER da Silva GRANJA, Fabián Guedes "BOLÍVAR", FABIANO ELLER dos Santos, JORGE WAGNER Góes Conceição, Fábio de Jesús "FABINHO", Edimo Ferreira Campos "EDINHO", Carlos ADRIANO de Souza Vieira (83 MICHEL Neves Dias), ALEX Raphael Meschini (83 Cleiton Eduardo Vicente "PERDIGÃO"), José Márcio da Costa "MOSSORÓ" (59 Pedro IARLEY Lima Dantas), Fernando Lúcio da Costa "FERNANDÃO". DT: Abel Braga
NACIONAL: Jorge Rodrigo Bava, Diego Jaume, Mauricio Bernardo Victorino, José Ignacio Pallas, Rodrigo Sebastián Vázquez, Marco Eduardo Vanzini, Jorge Orlando Brítez (79 Andrés Leonardo Márquez), Juan Angel Albín, Agustín Viana, Luis Alberto Suárez (73 Jorge Andrés Martínez), Gonzalo Castro. DT: Martín Lasarte

UANL – LIBERTAD ASUNCIÓN 0-0
Universitario, Monterrey, 27.04.2006
Referee: Jorge Luis Larrionda (URU)
UANL: Edgar Adolfo Hernández, Javier Saavedra, Emilio Damián Martínez, JULIO CÉSAR Santos Correia, Sidney Balderas, Enrique Escudero, Juan Nazario Montano, Sixto Raimundo Peralta (46 Wálter Nicolás Gaitán), Carlos Adrián Morales (21 Jesús Alejandro Palacios), Alfredo David Moreno, Ariel Maximiliano López (58 Sebastián Ignacio González). DT: Ricardo Ferretti
LIBERTAD: Aldo Antonio Bobadilla, Edgar Gabriel Balbuena, Pedro Alcides Sarabia, Ricardo Julián Martínez, Martín Emilio Hidalgo, Cristian Miguel Riveros, Javier Alejandro Villarreal, Pablo Horacio Guiñazú (83 Edgar Arnulfo Robles), Hernán Rodrigo López (88 Pablo Sebastián Garnier), Roberto Carlos Gamarra (59 Nelson David Romero), Carlos Bonet. DT: Gerardo Martino

LIBERTAD ASUNCIÓN – UANL 0-0, 5-3 penalties
Defensores del Chaco, Asunción, 4.05.2006
Referee: Horacio Marcelo Elizondo (ARG), Attendance: 5.000
LIBERTAD: Aldo Antonio Bobadilla, Edgar Gabriel Balbuena, Pedro Alcides Sarabia, Ricardo Julián Martínez (31 Raúl Hernán Damiani), Carlos Bonet, Martín Emilio Hidalgo, Javier Alejandro Villarreal (66 Edgar Arnulfo Robles), Cristian Miguel Riveros, Pablo Horacio Guiñazú (73 Osvaldo David Martínez), Roberto Carlos Gamarra, Hernán Rodrigo López. DT: Gerardo Martino
UANL: Edgar Adolfo Hernández, Javier Saavedra, Emilio Damián Martínez, JULIO CÉSAR Santos Correia, Sidney Balderas, Gabriel Omar Briceño, Sixto Raimundo Peralta, Argemiro Veiga (81 Jesús Alejandro Palacios), Juan Nazario Montano, Wálter Nicolás Gaitán (90 Sebastián Ignacio González), Alfredo David Moreno. DT: Ricardo Ferretti
Penalties: 1-0 Roberto Carlos Gamarra, 1-1 Sixto Raimundo Peralta, 2-1 Hernán Rodrigo López, 2-2 Alfredo David Moreno, 3-2 Pedro Alcides Sarabia, 3-3 Javier Saavedra, 4-3 Edgar Arnulfo Robles, * Emilio Damián Martínez, 5-3 Martín Emilio Hidalgo

QUARTER-FINALS

CD GUADALAJARA – VÉLEZ SARSFIELD 0-0
Jalisco, Guadalajara, 9.05.2006
Referee: Carlos Luis Chandía (CHI), Attendance: 15.504
GUADALAJARA: Luis Ernesto Michel, Héctor Reynoso, Jhonny García, Christian Michel Armas, Jorge Armando Barrera, Diego Alfonso Martínez (60 Alberto Medina), Juan Pablo Rodríguez, Edgar Iván Solís, José Jonny Magallón, Sergio Alejandro Santana (67 Edwin Alejandro Borboa), Adolfo Bautista. DT: José Manuel De La Torre
VÉLEZ SARSFIELD: Gastón Alejandro Sessa, Fabián Alberto Cubero, Maximiliano Pellegrino, Hernán Darío Pellerano, Marcelo Hernán Bustamante (62 Sergio Román Sena), Maximiliano Andrés Bustos, Leandro Daniel Somoza, Ariel Esteban Broggi, Leandro Gracián, Sebastián Adolfo Ereros (75 Emmanuel Gaspar Fernándes), Mauro Matías Zárate. DT: Miguel Ángel Russo

VÉLEZ SARSFIELD – CD GUADALAJARA 1-2 (0-1)
José Amalfitani, Buenos Aires, 20.07.2006
Referee: Carlos Manuel Torres (PAR)
VÉLEZ SARSFIELD: Gastón Alejandro Sessa, Fabián Alberto Cubero, Maximiliano Pellegrino, Hernán Darío Pellerano, Marcelo Hernán Bustamante, Maximiliano Andrés Bustos, Leandro Daniel Somoza, Damián Ariel Escudero, Ramón Darío Ocampo (56 Pablo Martín Batalla), Sebastián Adolfo Ereros (56 Emmanuel Gaspar Fernándes), Mauro Matías Zárate. DT: Miguel Ángel Russo
GUADALAJARA: Oswaldo Javier Sánchez, Héctor Reynoso, José Jonny Magallón, Diego Alfonso Martínez, Francisco Javier Rodríguez, Juan Pablo Rodríguez (74 Sergio Alejandro Santana), Patricio Gabriel Araujo, Gonzalo Pineda (60 Edgar Iván Solís), Ramón Morales, Adolfo Bautista, Omar Bravo (68 Omar Alejandro Esparza). DT: José Manuel De La Torre
Sent off: Martínez (65)
Goals: Pablo Martín Batalla (82) / Ramón Morales (27 penalty), Adolfo Bautista (73).

LIGA DEP. UNIVERSITARIA – INTERNACIONAL 2-1 (0-1)
La Casa Blanca, Quito, 10.05.2006
Referee: Horacio Marcelo Elizondo (ARG), Attendance: 16.016
LDU: Cristian Rafael Mora, Néicer Reasco, Carlos Alberto Espínola, Giovanny Patricio Espinoza, Paul Vicente Ambrossi, Enrique Daniel Vera, Patricio Javier Urrutia (81 Moisés Antonio Candelario), Édison Vicente Méndez, Roberto Carlos Palacios (65 Ariel José Graziani), Agustín Javier Delgado, Elkin Antonio Murillo (72 Joffre David Guerrón). DT: Juan Carlos Oblitas
INTERNACIONAL: MARCELO Boeck, ELDER da Silva GRANJA, Fabián Guedes "BOLÍVAR", FABIANO ELLER dos Santos, ALEX Raphael Meschini (74 RUBENS Vanderlei Tavares CARDOSO), Fábio de Jesús "FABINHO", Edimo Ferreira Campos "EDINHO", Cleiton Eduardo Vicente "PERDIGÃO" (61 Marcos Venâncio de Albuquerque "CEARÁ"), MICHEL Neves Dias, JORGE WAGNER Góes Conceição, Fernando Lúcio da Costa "FERNANDÃO" (68 Wason Libardo Rentería). DT: Abel Braga
Goals: Agustín Javier Delgado (58), Ariel José Graziani (84) /
JORGE WAGNER Góes Conceição (25).

INTERNACIONAL – LIGA DEP. UNIVERSITARIA 2-0 (0-0)
Beira-Rio, Porto Alegre, 19.07.2006
Referee: Jorge Luis Larrionda (URU), Attendance: 34.664
INTERNACIONAL: CLEMER Melo da Silva, ELDER da Silva GRANJA, Fabián Guedes "BOLÍVAR", FABIANO ELLER dos Santos, ALEX Raphael Meschini (89 Cleiton Eduardo Vicente "PERDIGÃO"), Fábio de Jesús "FABINHO", Edimo Ferreira Campos "EDINHO", Paulo César Fonseca do Nascimento "TINGA" (57 Carlos ADRIANO de Souza Vieira), JORGE WAGNER Góes Conceição, Fernando Lúcio da Costa "FERNANDÃO", RAFAEL Augusto SÓBIS (83 Wason Libardo Rentería). DT: Abel Braga
LDU: Cristian Rafael Mora, Néicer Reasco, Carlos Alberto Espínola, Giovanny Patricio Espinoza, Paul Vicente Ambrossi, Enrique Daniel Vera (83 Moisés Antonio Candelario), Patricio Javier Urrutia, Alfonso Andrés Obregón (64 Elkin Antonio Murillo), Édison Vicente Méndez (86 Ariel José Graziani), Roberto Carlos Palacios, Agustín Javier Delgado. DT: Juan Carlos Oblitas
Goals: RAFAEL Augusto SÓBIS (52), Wason Libardo Rentería (87).

ESTUDIANTES DE LA PLATA – SÃO PAULO FC 1-0 (0-0)
Centenario, Quilmes, 10.05.2006
Referee: Rubén Marcos Selman (CHI), Attendance: 21.677
ESTUDIANTES: Martín Horacio Herrera, Pablo Sebastián Álvarez, Agustín Alayes, Juan Daniel Cáceres, Jorge Martín Núñez (65 Marcelo Adrián Carrusca), Rodrigo Braña, Juan Augusto Huerta (65 Pablo Ariel Lugüercio), Marcos Agustín Gelabert (77 Diego Alberto Galván), José Ernesto Sosa, Hugo Mariano Pavone, José Luis Calderón. DT: Jorge Burruchaga
SÃO PAULO: ROGÉRIO CENI, ANDRÉ Gonçalves DIAS, José Fábio Alves Azevedo "FABÃO", Diego Alfredo Lugano, Williamis de SOUZA Silva, JOSUÉ de Oliveira, Carlos Luciano da Silva "MINEIRO", Jenilson Angelo de Souza "JÚNIOR", DANILO Gabriel de Andrade, ALEX DIAS de Almeida (55 LENÍLSON Batista de Souza, 76 EDCARLOS Conceição Santos), José ALOÍSIO da Silva. DT: Muricy Ramalho
Sent off: Pavone (4) / André Dias (4), Lugano (73)
Goal: Agustín Alayes (86).

SÃO PAULO FC – ESTUDIANTES DE LA PLATA 1-0 (0-0), 4-3 penalties
Cícero Pompeu de Toledo "Morumbi", São Paulo, 19.07.2006
Referee: Carlos Luis Chandía (CHI), Attendance: 66.056
SÃO PAULO: ROGÉRIO CENI, José Fábio Alves Azevedo "FABÃO", ALEX Bruno Costa Fernandes, EDCARLOS Conceição Santos, Williamis de SOUZA Silva, Carlos Luciano da Silva "MINEIRO", JOSUÉ de Oliveira, Jenilson Angelo de Souza "JÚNIOR", DANILO Gabriel de Andrade, LEANDRO Lessa Azevedo (72 THIAGO Ribeiro Cardoso), RICARDO de OLIVEIRA. DT: Muricy Ramalho

ESTUDIANTES: Martín Horacio Herrera, Pablo Sebastián Álvarez, Marcos Alberto Angeleri, Agustín Alayes, Fernando Ortiz, Diego Alberto Galván (67 Juan Elías Cominges), Rodrigo Braña, Juan Augusto Huerta (89 Horacio Ramón Cardozo), José Ernesto Sosa (79 Marcelo Adrián Carrusca), Pablo Ariel Lugüercio, José Luis Calderón. DT: Jorge Burruchaga
Goal: EDCARLOS Conceição Santos (44).
Penalties: 1-0 RICARDO de OLIVEIRA, 1-1 José Luis Calderón, 2-1 ROGÉRIO CENI, 2-2 Juan Elias Cominges, 3-2 José Fábio Alves Azevedo "FABÃO", 3-3 Pablo Ariel Lugüercio, * DANILO Gabriel de Andrade, * Agustín Alayes, 4-3 Jenilson Angelo de Souza "JÚNIOR", * Marcelo Adrián Carrusca

RIVER PLATE – LIBERTAD 2-2 (0-1)
Antonio V. Liberti, Buenos Aires, 11.05.2006
Referee: Carlos Eugênio Simón (BRA), Attendance: 58.000
RIVER PLATE: Germán Darío Lux, Julio César Cáceres (74 Daniel Gastón Montenegro), Leonardo José Talamonti, Danilo Telmo Gerlo, Paulo Andrés Ferrari, Jonathan Santana (46 Lucas Andrés Pusineri), Óscar Adrián Ahumada, Federico Hernán Domínguez (61 Víctor Eduardo Zapata), Marcelo Daniel Gallardo, Gonzalo Gerardo Higuaín, Ernesto Antonio Farías. DT: Daniel Passarella
LIBERTAD: Aldo Antonio Bobadilla, Raúl Hernán Damiani, Pedro Alcides Sarabia, Edgar Gabriel Balbuena, Martín Emilio Hidalgo, Carlos Bonet, Cristian Miguel Riveros, Javier Alejandro Villarreal, Pablo Horacio Guiñazú (79 Edgar Arnulfo Robles), Roberto Carlos Gamarra (36 Nelson David Romero, 90+2 Pablo Sebastián Garnier), Hernán Rodrigo López. DT: Gerardo Martino
Sent off: Pusineri (87)
Goals: Daniel Gastón Montenegro (76), Ernesto Antonio Farías (81) / Carlos Bonet (38, 77).

LIBERTAD ASUNCIÓN – RIVER PLATE 3-1 (2-0)
Defensores del Chaco, Asunción, 18.07.2006
Referee: Rubén Marcos Selman (CHI)
LIBERTAD: Aldo Antonio Bobadilla, Carlos Bonet, Pedro Alcides Sarabia, Edgar Gabriel Balbuena, Martín Emilio Hidalgo, Sergio Daniel Aquino (79 Edgar Arnulfo Robles), Javier Alejandro Villarreal, Cristian Miguel Riveros, Pablo Horacio Guiñazú, Roberto Carlos Gamarra (67 Nelson David Romero), Hernán Rodrigo López. DT: Gerardo Martino
RIVER PLATE: Germán Darío Lux, Eduardo Nicolás Tuzzio, Julio César Cáceres, Danilo Telmo Gerlo, Paulo Andrés Ferrari, Óscar Adrián Ahumada, Víctor Eduardo Zapata, Federico Hernán Domínguez (46 Augusto Matías Fernández), Marcelo Daniel Gallardo, Gonzalo Gerardo Higuaín, Gonzalo Daniel Abán (46 Ernesto Antonio Farías). DT: Daniel Passarella
Sent off: Gallardo (62)
Goals: Hernán Rodrigo López (16), Sergio Daniel Aquino (40), Cristian Miguel Riveros (47) / Ernesto Antonio Farías (76).

SEMI-FINALS

CD GUADALAJARA – SÃO PAULO FC 0-1 (0-0)
Jalisco, Guadalajara, 26.07.2006
Referee: Jorge Luis Larrionda (URU), Attendance: 47.440
GUADALAJARA: Oswaldo Javier Sánchez, Héctor Reynoso, José Jonny Magallón, Patricio Gabriel Araujo, Francisco Javier Rodríguez, Juan Pablo Rodríguez (63 Sergio Alejandro Santana), Gonzalo Pineda (70 Sergio Gabriel Ávila), Ramón Morales (87 Alberto Medina), Omar Alejandro Esparza, Adolfo Bautista, Omar Bravo. DT: José Manuel De La Torre
SÃO PAULO: ROGÉRIO CENI, José Fábio Alves Azevedo "FABÃO", Diego Alfredo Lugano, EDCARLOS Conceição Santos, Williamis de SOUZA Silva, Jenilson Angelo de Souza "JÚNIOR", Carlos Luciano da Silva "MINEIRO", JOSUÉ de Oliveira, LEANDRO Lessa Azevedo (74 LENÍLSON Batista de Souza), DANILO Gabriel de Andrade (86 RICHARLYSON Barbosa Felisbino), RICARDO de OLIVEIRA (61 José ALOÍSIO da Silva). DT: Muricy Ramalho
Goal: ROGÉRIO CENI (84 penalty).

SÃO PAULO FC – CD GUADALAJARA 3-0 (2-0)
Cícero Pompeu de Toledo "Morumbí", São Paulo, 2.08.2006
Referee: Daniel Orlando Giménez (ARG), Attendance: 66.750
SÃO PAULO: ROGÉRIO CENI, José Fábio Alves Azevedo "FABÃO", Diego Alfredo Lugano, EDCARLOS Conceição Santos, Williamis de SOUZA Silva, Jenilson Angelo de Souza "JÚNIOR" (75 RICHARLYSON Barbosa Felisbino), Carlos Luciano da Silva "MINEIRO", JOSUÉ de Oliveira, LEANDRO Lessa Azevedo, DANILO Gabriel de Andrade (57 LENÍLSON Batista de Souza), RICARDO de OLIVEIRA (80 José ALOÍSIO da Silva). DT: Muricy Ramalho
GUADALAJARA: Oswaldo Javier Sánchez, Héctor Reynoso, José Jonny Magallón, Patricio Gabriel Araujo, Francisco Javier Rodríguez, Juan Pablo Rodríguez, Sergio Alejandro Santana (78 José Antonio Patlán), Diego Alfonso Martínez, Ramón Morales (46 Alberto Medina), Adolfo Bautista, Omar Bravo. DT: José Manuel De La Torre
Sent off: Reynoso (73)
Ramón Morales missed a penalty in the 27th minute
Goals: LEANDRO Lessa Azevedo (32), Carlos Luciano da Silva "MINEIRO" (39), RICARDO de OLIVEIRA (47).

LIBERTAD ASUNCIÓN – INTERNACIONAL 0-0
Defensores del Chaco, Asunción, 27.07.2006
Referee: Héctor Walter Baldassi (ARG), Attendance: 20.000
LIBERTAD: Horacio Javier González, Carlos Bonet, Pedro Alcides Sarabia, Edgar Gabriel Balbuena, Martín Emilio Hidalgo, Sergio Daniel Aquino (74 Juan Eduardo Samudio), Javier Alejandro Villarreal, Cristian Miguel Riveros, Pablo Horacio Guiñazú, Roberto Carlos Gamarra (54 Nelson David Romero, 87 Víctor Javier Cáceres), Hernán Rodrigo López. DT: Gerardo Martino
INTERNACIONAL: CLEMER Melo da Silva, Marcos Antônio de Lima "ÍNDIO", Fabián Guedes "BOLÍVAR", FABIANO ELLER dos Santos, Fábio de Jesús "FABINHO", Edimo Ferreira Campos "EDINHO" (77 WELLINGTON MONTEIRO), JORGE WAGNER Góes Conceição, ALEX Raphael Meschini (68 Pedro IARLEY Lima Dantas), Marcos Venâncio de Albuquerque "CEARÁ", Fernando Lúcio da Costa "FERNANDÃO", RAFAEL Augusto SÓBIS (86 Wason Libardo Rentería). DT: Abel Braga

INTERNACIONAL – LIBERTAD ASUNCIÓN 2-0 (0-0)
Beira-Rio, Porto Alegre, 3.08.2006
Referee: Óscar Julián Ruiz (COL), Attendance: 44.064
INTERNACIONAL: CLEMER Melo da Silva, Marcos Antônio de Lima "ÍNDIO" (73 WELLINGTON MONTEIRO), Fabián Guedes "BOLÍVAR", FABIANO ELLER dos Santos, Fábio de Jesús "FABINHO" (61 Wason Libardo Rentería), Edimo Ferreira Campos "EDINHO", Marcos Venâncio de Albuquerque "CEARÁ", ALEX Raphael Meschini (90 Cleiton Eduardo Vicente "PERDIGÃO"), JORGE WAGNER Góes Conceição, Fernando Lúcio da Costa "FERNANDÃO", RAFAEL Augusto SÓBIS. DT: Abel Braga
LIBERTAD: Horacio Javier González, Carlos Bonet, Pedro Alcides Sarabia, Víctor Javier Cáceres, Martín Emilio Hidalgo (70 Nelson David Romero), Edgar Gabriel Balbuena, Javier Alejandro Villarreal (85 Sergio Daniel Aquino), Cristian Miguel Riveros, Pablo Horacio Guiñazú, Roberto Carlos Gamarra (73 Juan Eduardo Samudio), Hernán Rodrigo López. DT: Gerardo Martino
Goals: ALEX Raphael Meschini (62), Fernando Lúcio da Costa "FERNANDÃO" (68).

FINALS

SÃO PAULO FC – INTERNACIONAL PORTO ALEGRE 1-2 (0-0)
Cícero Pompeu de Toledo "Morumbi", São Paulo, 9.08.2006
Referee: Jorge Luis Larrionda (URU), Attendance: 71.456
SÃO PAULO: ROGÉRIO CENI, José Fábio Alves Azevedo "FABÃO", Diego Alfredo Lugano, EDCARLOS Conceição Santos (76 José ALOÍSIO da Silva), Williamis de SOUZA Silva, Carlos Luciano da Silva "MINEIRO", JOSUÉ de Oliveira, DANILO Gabriel de Andrade (63 LENÍLSON Batista de Souza), Jenilson Angelo de Souza "JÚNIOR", RICARDO de OLIVEIRA, LEANDRO Lessa Azevedo (86 RICHARLYSON Barbosa Felisbino). DT: Muricy Ramalho
INTERNACIONAL: CLEMER Melo da Silva, Marcos Venâncio de Albuquerque "CEARÁ" (56 WELLINGTON MONTEIRO), Fabián Guedes "BOLÍVAR", FABIANO ELLER dos Santos, JORGE WAGNER Góes Conceição, Edimo Ferreira Campos "EDINHO", Fábio de Jesús "FABINHO", Paulo César Fonseca do Nascimento "TINGA", ALEX Raphael Meschini (74 Marcos Antônio de Lima "ÍNDIO"), RAFAEL Augusto SÓBIS (78 MICHEL Neves Dias), Fernando Lúcio da Costa "FERNANDÃO". DT: Abel Braga
Sent off: Josué (9) / Fabinho (38)
Goals: EDCARLOS Conceição Santos (75) / RAFAEL Augusto SÓBIS (53, 61).

INTERNACIONAL PORTO ALEGRE – SÃO PAULO FC 2-2 (1-0)
Beira-Rio, Porto Alegre, 16.08.2006
Referee: Horacio Marcelo Elizondo (ARG), Attendance: 55.000
INTERNACIONAL: CLEMER Melo da Silva, Marcos Antônio de Lima "ÍNDIO", Fabián Guedes "BOLÍVAR", FABIANO ELLER dos Santos, Marcos Venâncio de Albuquerque "CEARÁ", Edimo Ferreira Campos "EDINHO" , Paulo César Fonseca do Nascimento "TINGA", ALEX Raphael Meschini (78 MICHEL Neves Dias), JORGE WAGNER Góes Conceição, Fernando Lúcio da Costa "FERNANDÃO", RAFAEL Augusto SÓBIS (82 EDIGLÉ Quaresma Farías). DT: Abel Braga
SÃO PAULO: ROGÉRIO CENI, José Fábio Alves Azevedo "FABÃO", Diego Alfredo Lugano, EDCARLOS Conceição Santos (70 ALEX DIAS de Almeida), Williamis de SOUZA Silva, Carlos Luciano da Silva "MINEIRO", RICHARLYSON Barbosa Felisbino (58 THIAGO Ribeiro Cardoso), DANILO Gabriel de Andrade (58 LENÍLSON Batista de Souza), Jenilson Angelo de Souza "JÚNIOR", José ALOÍSIO da Silva, LEANDRO Lessa Azevedo. DT: Muricy Ramalho
Sent off: Tinga (66)
Goals: Fernando Lúcio da Costa "FERNANDÃO" (29), Paulo César Fonseca do Nascimento "TINGA" (66) / José Fábio Alves Azevedo "FABÃO" (50), LENÍLSON Batista de Souza (85).

2007

FIRST STAGE

CF AMÉRICA – SPORTING CRISTAL 5-0 (2-0)
Nemesio Díez, Toluca, 24.01.2007
Referee: Rubén Marcos Selman (CHI), Attendance: 13.138
CF AMÉRICA: Francisco Guillermo Ochoa, Ismael de Jesús Rodríguez, José Antonio Castro, Óscar Adrián Rojas, Duilio César Davino, Diego Alberto Cervantes, Germán Villa, Alejandro Argüello (64 Juan Carlos Mosqueda), Salvador Cabañas, Cuauhtémoc Bravo Blanco, Nelson Rafael Cuevas (87 Ignacio Torres). DT: Luis Fernando Tena
SPORTING CRISTAL: Erick Guillermo Delgado, Ramiro Fernando Fassi, César Miguel Rebosio, Miguel Ángel Villalta, José Adolfo Mendoza, Amilton Jair Prado, Jesús Martín Álvarez, Édison Hipólito Chará (57 Carlos Augusto Lobatón), Juan Elías Cominges, Luis Daniel Benito Hernández (72 Damián Ísmodes), Carlos Alberto Orejuela (81 Luis Alberto Bonnet). DT: Jorge Sampaoli
Goals: Óscar Adrián Rojas (20), Salvador Cabañas (42, 66, 81), Cuauhtémoc Bravo Blanco (48).

SPORTING CRISTAL – CF AMÉRICA 2-1 (0-0)
Nacional, Lima, 31.01.2007, Referee: Jorge Hernán Hoyos (COL)
SPORTING CRISTAL: Erick Guillermo Delgado, Amilton Jair Prado, Miguel Ángel Villalta, César Miguel Rebosio, Ramiro Fernando Fassi, Jesús Martín Álvarez (46 Rainer Torres), José Adolfo Mendoza, Carlos Augusto Lobatón (73 Jorge Antonio Soto), Damián Ísmodes, Carlos Alberto Orejuela, Luis Alberto Bonnet (73 Gabriel Ramón García). DT: Jorge Sampaoli
CF AMÉRICA: Francisco Guillermo Ochoa, Ismael de Jesús Rodríguez, Óscar Adrián Rojas, Diego Alberto Cervantes, Raúl Alberto Salinas (55 Carlos Jesús Infante), Ricardo Francisco Rojas, Germán Villa, Alejandro Argüello, Salvador Cabañas, Cuauhtémoc Bravo Blanco (68 Juan Carlos Mosqueda), Nelson Rafael Cuevas (30 Luis Fernando Saritama). DT: Luis Fernando Tena
Amilton Jair Prado missed a penalty in the 59th minute
Goals: Miguel Ángel Villalta (77), César Miguel Rebosio (79) / Luis Fernando Saritama (84).

VÉLEZ SARSFIELD – DANUBIO FC 3-0 (1-0)
José Amalfitani, Buenos Aires, 30.01.2007, Referee: Héber Roberto Lopes (BRA), Attendance: 15.000
VÉLEZ SARSFIELD: Gastón Alejandro Sessa, Hernán Darío Pellerano, Maximiliano Pellegrino, Mario Méndez, Marcelo Hernán Bustamante (46 Ariel Esteban Broggi), Emiliano Ramiro Papa, Lucas Martín Castromán (36 Javier Sebastián Robles), Maximiliano Andrés Bustos, Iván Diego Moreno y Fabianesi (73 Damián Ariel Escudero), Gustavo Alberto Balvorín, Mauro Matías Zárate. DT: Ricardo La Volpe
DANUBIO: Néstor Esteban Conde, Jorge Adrián García (81 Álvaro Daniel Noble), Sergio Gonzalo Rodríguez, JADSON Viera Castro, Damián Alejandro Malrecauffe, Raúl Freddy Ferro, Pablo Martín Lima, MARCOS "TORA" Juliano Vidal da Silva (50 Deley Yesid Mena), Ignacio María González, Hamilton Ricard, Carlos Javier Grossmüller. DT: Gustavo Matosas
Sent off: Ricard (39)
Goals: Mauro Matías Zárate (13), Gustavo Alberto Balvorín (48), Maximiliano Pellegrino (75).

DANUBIO FC – VÉLEZ SARSFIELD 1-2 (1-1)
Parque Central, Montevideo, 6.02.2007, Referee: Carlos Luis Chandía (CHI), Attendance: 2.000
DANUBIO: Néstor Esteban Conde, Damián Alejandro Malrecauffe, JADSON Viera Castro, Sergio Gonzalo Rodríguez, Leonardo Daniel Abelenda (60 Deley Yesid Mena), Wálter Alejandro Gargano, Jorge Adrián García, Pablo Martín Lima, Ignacio María González, Cristhian Ricardo Stuani (69 Willians Omar Peralta), Carlos Javier Grossmüller (86 Raúl Freddy Ferro). DT: Gustavo Matosas

VÉLEZ SARSFIELD: Gastón Alejandro Sessa, Hernán Darío Pellerano, Maximiliano Pellegrino, Marcelo Hernán Bustamante, Mario Méndez, Maximiliano Andrés Bustos, Emiliano Ramiro Papa (75 Mariano Esteban Uglessich), Javier Sebastián Robles (46 Ariel Esteban Broggi), Iván Diego Moreno y Fabianesi, Lucas Martín Castromán, Mauro Matías Zárate (78 Ramón Dario Ocampo). DT: Ricardo La Volpe
Sent off: González (57)
Goals: Cristhian Ricardo Stuani (45) /
Lucas Martín Castromán (38), Iván Diego Moreno y Fabianesi (75).

DEPORTIVO TÁCHIRA – DEPORTES TOLIMA 1-2 (1-1)
José 'Pachencho' Romero, Maracaibo, 30.01.2007
Referee: Manuel Alejandro Garay (PER), Attendance: 250
DEPORTIVO TÁCHIRA: Giancarlos Martínez, Pedro Luis Boada, Gregory Evans Lancken (86 Edgar Fernando Pérez), Grendy Adrián Perozo, Gerson Armando Chacón, José Javier Villafraz (80 Marlon Antonio Fernández), Edixon Vladimir Cuevas (46 Diego Alejandro Guerrero), Francisco Javier Campos, Dickson Ruberth Morán, Alexander Rondón, Jhonny José González. DT: Manuel Plasencia
DEPORTES TOLIMA: Agustín Julio, Gerardo Enrique Vallejo, Hilario Cuenú, Yesid Martínez, Ricardo Adolfo Álvarez, Hernando Patiño, Franklin Emir González, Juan Carlos Escobar (74 Andrés Camilo Ramírez), Yulián José Anchico, Jhon Jairo Charría (87 Darío Alberto Bustos), Jorge Isaacs Perlaza (59 César Augusto Rivas). DT: Jaime De la Pava
Goals: Dickson Ruberth Morán (37) / Jorge Isaacs Perlaza (44), Jhon Jairo Charría (75 penalty).

DEPORTES TOLIMA – DEPORTIVO TÁCHIRA 2-0 (1-0)
Manuel Murillo Toro, Ibagué, 8.02.2007, Referee: José Patricio Carpio (ECU)
DEPORTES TOLIMA: Agustín Julio, Gerardo Enrique Vallejo (35 Franklin Emir González), Hilario Cuenú, Yesid Martínez (64 Nicolás Nahuel Ayr), Jesús Brahman Sinisterra, Hernando Patiño, Juan Carlos Escobar, Yulián José Anchico, Jhon Jairo Charría, Jorge Isaacs Perlaza, Gustavo Humberto Savoia (69 Diego Emilio Cochas). DT: Jaime De la Pava
DEPORTIVO TÁCHIRA: Giancarlos Martínez, Gerson Armando Chacón, Pedro Luis Boada, Grendy Adrián Perozo, Gregory Evans Lancken, José Javier Villafraz, Diego Alejandro Guerrero, Marlon Antonio Fernández (82 Francisco Javier Campos), Edgar Fernando Pérez (80 Jhonny José González), Yeferson José Velazco (56 Anderson Arias), Dickson Ruberth Morán. DT: Manuel Plasencia
Goals: Gustavo Humberto Savoia (19), Jorge Isaacs Perlaza (67).

BLOOMING – SANTOS FC 0-1 (0-0)
Ramón 'Tahuichi' Aguilera, Santa Cruz, 31.01.2007
Referee: Líber Tabare Prudente (URU), Attendance: 11.901
BLOOMING: Yadín Salazar, Sergio Antonio Jáuregui, Carlos Venderlei Dos Santos "DECARLO" (60 Cristian David Wernly), Jorge Antonio Ortíz, Germán Méndez, Jesús Alejandro Gómez, ALEXANDRE de Oliveira da Silva, Joselito Vaca, Juan Eduardo Fierro (46 Limberg Méndez), DIMAS Roberto da Silva, Diego Orlando Suárez (53 ALEX Rodrigo DA ROSA Domelles). DT: Alvaro Peña
SANTOS: FÁBIO COSTA, ADAÍLTON José dos Santos Filho, KLÉBER de Carvalho Corrêa, PEDRO Alves da Silva, ANTÔNIO CARLOS Zago, RODRIGO Ribeiro SOUTO, Claudio Andrés del Transito Maldonado (82 Cristiano Espíndola de ÁVALOS), José "ZÉ" ROBERTO da Silva Júnior, CLÉBER SANTANA Loureiro, FABIANO Vieira Soares (62 MARCOS AURÉLIO de Oliveira Lima), RODRIGO "TIUÍ" Bonifácio da Rocha (71 RODRIGO Barbosa TABATA). DT: Vanderley Luxemburgo
CLÉBER SANTANA Loureiro missed a penalty in the 75th minute
Goal: PEDRO Alves da Silva (48).

SANTOS FC – BLOOMING 5-0 (3-0)
Urbano Caldeira, Santos, 7.02.2007, Referee: Sergio Fabián Pezzotta (ARG), Attendance: 11.005
SANTOS: FÁBIO COSTA, ADAÍLTON José dos Santos Filho, KLÉBER de Carvalho Corrêa (78 Carlos Andrade Souza "CARLINHOS"), PEDRO Alves da Silva, ANTÔNIO CARLOS Zago, RODRIGO Ribeiro SOUTO (46 Pedro Paulo de Oliveira "PEDRINHO"), Claudio Andrés del Transito Maldonado, José "ZÉ" ROBERTO da Silva Júnior, CLÉBER SANTANA Loureiro (62 RODRIGO Barbosa TABATA), MARCOS AURÉLIO de Oliveira Lima, RODRIGO "TIUÍ" Bonifácio da Rocha. DT: Vanderley Luxemburgo
BLOOMING: Yadín Salazar, Jorge Antonio Ortíz, Sergio Antonio Jáuregui, Carlos Venderlei Dos Santos "DECARLO", Germán Méndez, Limberg Méndez (40 Carlos Suárez), ALEXANDRE de Oliveira da Silva, Carmelo Angulo, Getulio Joaquín Vaca (40 ALEX Rodrigo DA ROSA Domelles), DIMAS Roberto da Silva (63 Jesús Alejandro Gómez), Diego Orlando Suárez. DT: Alvaro Peña
Goals: CLÉBER SANTANA Loureiro (2, 28), RODRIGO "TIUÍ" Bonifácio da Rocha (36, 83), MARCOS AURÉLIO de Oliveira Lima (76).

COBRELOA CALAMA – PARANÁ CLUBE 0-2 (0-1)
Municipal, Calama, 1.02.2007 Referee: René Marcelo Ortubé (BOL), Attendance: 9.765
COBRELOA: Fernando Javier Hurtado, Víctor Alexis Osorio (68 José Luis Arias), Cristián Felipe Olguín, Luis Alberto Fuentes, Rodrigo Antonio Pérez (68 Leandro Javier Delgado), Juan Luis González, Rodrigo Martín Mannara, Cristian Alejandro Ríos (68 Charles Mariano Aránguiz), José Luis Díaz, Esteban Efraín Paredes, Lucas Ramón Barrios. DT: Gustavo Huerta
PARANÁ: FLÁVIO Emidio dos Santos Vieira, ADERALDO Ferreira André, DANIEL MARQUES da Silva, Anderson da Silva de Jesús "NEGUETE", ANDRÉ LUIZ de Oliveira Regatieri, Valberto Amorim Santos "BETO", Emerson Bueno dos Santos "GOIANO", EGÍDIO de Araújo Pereira Júnior (70 JOÃO VITOR da Silva), José GERSON Ramos, DINELSON dos Santos Lima (70 Clennyson Silva do Nascimento "XAVES"), HENRIQUE Dias Carvalho (70 JOSIEL da Rocha).
Goals: HENRIQUE Dias Carvalho (15), JOSIEL da Rocha (88).

PARANÁ CLUBE – COBRELOA CALAMA 1-1 (0-0)
Durival de Britto e Silva, Curitiba, 7.02.2007, Referee: Antonio Javier Arias (PAR), Attendance: 14.953
PARANÁ: FLÁVIO Emidio dos Santos Vieira, DANIEL MARQUES da Silva, Anderson da Silva de Jesús "NEGUETE", ANDRÉ LUIZ de Oliveira Regatieri, Valberto Amorim Santos "BETO", Emerson Bueno dos Santos "GOIANO", EGÍDIO de Araújo Pereira Júnior, José GERSON Ramos (74 JOELSON dos Santos Silva), DINELSON dos Santos Lima (65 Clennyson Silva do Nascimento "XAVES"), HENRIQUE Dias Carvalho, JOSIEL da Rocha (71 Rodrigo LIMA dos Santos). DT: Armelino Donizetti Quagliato 'Zetti"
COBRELOA: Fernando Javier Hurtado, Víctor Alexis Osorio, Luis Alberto Fuentes, Cristián Felipe Olguín, Rodrigo Antonio Pérez, Juan Luis González, Cristian Alejandro Ríos (59 Jean Andre Emanuel Beausejour), José Luis Díaz, Esteban Efraín Paredes (63 Charles Mariano Aránguiz), Rodrigo Martín Mannara, Lucas Ramón Barrios. DT: Gustavo Huerta
Sent off: Goiano (28) / Osorio (61)
Goals: Rodrigo LIMA dos Santos (75) / Rodrigo Martín Mannara (89).

TACUARY FC – LIGA DEP. UNIVERSITARIA 1-1 (1-0)
Defensores del Chaco, Asunción, 1.02.2007
Referee: Sálvio Spínola Fagundes (BRA), Attendance: 1.316
TACUARY FC: Anthony Domingo Silva, Celso Pablo González (64 Lorenzo Raúl Silva), Gregor Alcides Aguayo, Ángel Marcelo Martínez (75 Luis Fernando Páez), Patrocinio Samudio, Ignacio Ramón Paniagua, Fidencio Oviedo, David Raúl Villalba, Hugo Américo Luzardi, Víctor Hugo Ortiz (70 Emilio Hernán Ibarra), Gilberto Ramón Palacios. DT: Oscar Paulin
LDU: Cristian Rafael Mora, Arlín Segundo Ayoví, Jairo Rolando Campos, Norberto Carlos Araujo, Enrique Daniel Vera, Patricio Javier Urrutia, Pedro Sebastián Larrea (76 Alfonso Andrés Obregón), Paul Vicente Ambrossi, Cristian Rolando Lara (83 Luis Alberto Bolaños), Joffre David Guerrón (90+2 Franklin Agustín Salas), Luis Miguel Escalada. DT: Edgardo Bauza
Goals: David Raúl Villalba (38) / Patricio Javier Urrutia (64).

LIGA DEP. UNIVERSITARIA – TACUARY FC 3-0 (1-0)
La Casa Blanca, Quito, 6.02.2007, Referee: Martín Vázquez (URU), Attendance: 11.686
LDU: Cristian Rafael Mora, Arlín Segundo Ayoví, Jairo Rolando Campos, Norberto Carlos Araujo, Paul Vicente Ambrossi, Enrique Daniel Vera, Alfonso Andrés Obregón (67 Pedro Sebastián Larrea), Patricio Javier Urrutia, Cristian Rolando Lara, Joffre David Guerrón (72 Franklin Agustín Salas), Luis Miguel Escalada (77 José Nicolás Vizcarra). DT: Edgardo Bauza
TACUARY: Anthony Domingo Silva, Ignacio Ramón Paniagua, Luciano Vera, Gregor Alcides Aguayo, Patrocinio Samudio (56 Luis Fernando Páez), Fidencio Oviedo, David Raúl Villalba (66 Víctor Hugo Ortiz), Lorenzo Raúl Silva, Hugo Américo Luzardi (77 Gustavo Sanabria), Emilio Hernán Ibarra, Gilberto Ramón Palacios. DT: Oscar Paulin
Goals: Joffre David Guerrón (24), Patrocinio Samudio (54 own goal), Paul Vicente Ambrossi (70).

SECOND PHASE

GROUP 1

EL NACIONAL – CF AMÉRICA 1-2 (1-1)
Olímpico Atahualpa, Quito, 20.02.2007, Referee: Albert Duarte (COL), Attendance: 6.246
EL NACIONAL: Oswaldo Johvani Ibarra, Érik Rolando De Jesús, Omar Andrés De Jesús, Carlos Ernesto Castro, Pavel Cipriano Caicedo, Jhon Patricio Cagua (46 Mario David Quiroz), Wellington Eduardo Sánchez (53 Ebelio Agustín Ordóñez), Carlos Ramón Hidalgo, Christian Rogelio Benítez, Jaime Iván Kaviedes (83 Wálter Orlando Ayoví), Wálter Richard Calderón. DT: Ever Hugo Almeida
CF AMÉRICA: Francisco Guillermo Ochoa, Ismael de Jesús Rodríguez, José Antonio Castro, Diego Alberto Cervantes, Rodrigo Iñigo (46 Raúl Alberto Salinas), Germán Villa, Alejandro Argüello, Juan Carlos Mosqueda (59 Ignacio Torres), Luis Fernando Saritama (46 Nelson Rafael Cuevas), Raúl Alvin Mendoza, Santiago Fernández. DT: Luis Fernando Tena
Sent off: Hidalgo (76)
Goals: Christian Rogelio Benítez (27) / Santiago Fernández (41), Germán Villa (46).

LIBERTAD ASUNCIÓN – CA BANFIELD 1-0 (0-0)
Defensores del Chaco, Asunción, 20.02.2007, Referee: Héber Roberto Lopes (BRA), Attendance: 1.457
LIBERTAD: Jorge Rodrigo Bava, Carlos Bonet, Pedro Alcides Sarabia, Pedro Juan Benítez, Édgar Gabriel Balbuena (66 Édgar Benítez), Sergio Daniel Aquino (72 Osvaldo David Martínez), Cristian Miguel Riveros, Pablo Horacio Guiñazú, Vladimir Marín, Freddy José Bareiro (71 Nelson David Romero), Hernán Rodrigo López. DT: Sergio Markarian
BANFIELD: Cristian David Lucchetti, Julián Edgardo Maidana, Ricardo Hernán Pagés (68 Marcos Adrián Galarza), Julio Eduardo Barraza, Javier Alejandro Villarreal, Javier Estebán Sanguinetti, Daniel Eduardo Quinteros, José Manuel Chatruc (68 Gastón Ezequiel Schmidt), Darío Cvitanich, Martín Ezequiel Andrizzi, Pablo Ernesto Vitti (58 Josemir Lujambio). DT: Patricio Hernández
Goal: Cristian Miguel Riveros (85).

CA BANFIELD – EL NACIONAL 4-1 (3-1)
Florencio Sola, Banfield, 27.02.2007, Referee: Leonardo Gaciba (BRA), Attendance: 5.773
BANFIELD: Cristian David Lucchetti, Julián Edgardo Maidana, Ricardo Hernán Pagés (73 Carlos Alberto Galván), Julio Eduardo Barraza, Javier Alejandro Villarreal, Javier Estebán Sanguinetti, José Manuel Chatruc (69 Roberto Hernán Salvatierra), Daniel Eduardo Quinteros, Darío Cvitanich, Martín Ezequiel Andrizzi, Josemir Lujambio (44 Pablo Ernesto Vitti). DT: Patricio Hernández
EL NACIONAL: Oswaldo Johvani Ibarra, Omar Andrés De Jesús, Carlos Ernesto Castro, Pavel Cipriano Caicedo, Érik Rolando De Jesús, Wellington Eduardo Sánchez, Santiago Damián Morales (53 Gustavo Omar Figueroa), Pedro Ángel Quiñónez, Wálter Orlando Ayoví (46 Mario David Quiroz), Jaime Iván Kaviedes, Wálter Richard Calderón. DT: Ever Hugo Almeida
Sent off: Quiñónez (85)
Goals: Darío Cvitanich (8), Martín Ezequiel Andrizzi (24, 29), Cristian David Lucchetti (65 penalty) / Wálter Richard Calderón (22),

CF AMÉRICA – LIBERTAD ASUNCIÓN 1-4 (1-3)
Azteca, México City, 1.03.2007, Referee: Roberto Carlos Silvera (URU)
CF AMÉRICA: Armando Navarrete, Duilio César Davino, Diego Alberto Cervantes (29 Nelson Rafael Cuevas, 54 Ignacio Torres), Carlos Jesús Infante, Ricardo Francisco Rojas, Juan Carlos Mosqueda, Fabián Peña (46 Luis Fernando Saritama), Alejandro Argüello, Raúl Alvin Mendoza, Salvador Cabañas, Santiago Fernández. DT: Luis Fernando Tena
LIBERTAD: Jorge Rodrigo Bava, Carlos Bonet, Pedro Alcides Sarabia, Pedro Juan Benítez, Édgar Gabriel Balbuena, Sergio Daniel Aquino (78 Nelson David Romero), Cristian Miguel Riveros, Pablo Horacio Guiñazú, Vladimir Marín (89 Édgar Benítez), Osvaldo David Martínez (74 Wilson Osmar Pittoni), Hernán Rodrigo López. DT: Sergio Markarian
Goals: Nelson Rafael Cuevas (41) / Sergio Daniel Aquino (3), Pedro Juan Benítez (20, 79), Hernán Rodrigo López (45+1).

EL NACIONAL – LIBERTAD ASUNCIÓN 1-1 (0-0)
Olímpico Atahualpa, Quito, 6.03.2007, Referee: Óscar Julián Ruiz (COL), Attendance: 3.000
EL NACIONAL: Oswaldo Johvani Ibarra, Omar Andrés De Jesús, Carlos Ernesto Castro, Pavel Cipriano Caicedo, Érik Rolando De Jesús, Carlos Ramón Hidalgo, Mario David Quiroz, Wellington Eduardo Sánchez (42 Wálter Orlando Ayoví), Jaime Iván Kaviedes (64 Gustavo Omar Figueroa), Christian Rogelio Benítez, Wálter Richard Calderón. DT: Ever Hugo Almeida
LIBERTAD: Jorge Rodrigo Bava, Carlos Bonet, Pedro Alcides Sarabia, Pedro Juan Benítez, Édgar Gabriel Balbuena, Sergio Daniel Aquino (82 Edgar Arnulfo Robles), Cristian Miguel Riveros, Pablo Horacio Guiñazú, Vladimir Marín (63 Nelson David Romero), Osvaldo David Martínez (76 Édgar Benítez), Hernán Rodrigo López. DT: Sergio Markarian
Sent off: Caicedo (81)
Goals: Wálter Richard Calderón (68) / Hernán Rodrigo López (78).

CF AMÉRICA – CA BANFIELD 4-0 (2-0)
Azteca, México City, 7.03.2007, Referee: Carlos Luis Chandía (CHI), Attendance: 14.000
CF AMÉRICA: Francisco Guillermo Ochoa, Ricardo Francisco Rojas (56 Raúl Alvin Mendoza), Duilio César Davino, Óscar Adrián Rojas, Ismael de Jesús Rodríguez, José Antonio Castro, Juan Carlos Mosqueda (70 Santiago Fernández), Germán Villa, Alejandro Argüello (75 Ignacio Torres), Cuauhtémoc Bravo Blanco, Salvador Cabañas. DT: Luis Fernando Tena
BANFIELD: Cristian David Lucchetti, Julián Edgardo Maidana, Ricardo Hernán Pagés, Julio Eduardo Barraza, Javier Alejandro Villarreal, Javier Estebán Sanguinetti, José Manuel Chatruc (63 Pablo Ernesto Vitti), Daniel Eduardo Quinteros, Darío Cvitanich, Ángel Alejandro Morales (53 Gastón Ezequiel Schmidt), Martín Ezequiel Andrizzi (46 Guillermo Adolfo Esteban). DT: Patricio Hernández
Goals: Óscar Adrián Rojas (20), Salvador Cabañas (23, 48), Juan Carlos Mosqueda (52).

CA BANFIELD – CF AMÉRICA 3-1 (2-0)
Florencio Sola, Banfield, 21.03.2007, Referee: Ricardo Grance (PAR), Attendance: 4.903
BANFIELD: Cristian David Lucchetti, Julio Eduardo Barraza, Carlos Alberto Galván, Javier Estebán Sanguinetti, Gastón Ezequiel Schmidt, José Manuel Chatruc (63 Ángel Alejandro Morales), Javier Alejandro Villarreal, Daniel Eduardo Quinteros, Martín Ezequiel Andrizzi (84 Roberto Hernán Salvatierra), Darío Cvitanich, Josemir Lujambio (46 Cristian Pedro Bardaro). DT: Pablo Sánchez & Hernán Lisi
CF AMÉRICA: Francisco Guillermo Ochoa, Ricardo Francisco Rojas, Diego Alberto Cervantes, Ismael de Jesús Rodríguez (26 Raúl Alberto Salinas), José Antonio Castro, Alejandro Argüello (46 Daniel Rubén Bilos), Juan Carlos Mosqueda (73 Santiago Fernández), Óscar Adrián Rojas, Germán Villa, Luis Fernando Saritama, Salvador Cabañas. DT: Luis Fernando Tena
Goals: Josemir Lujambio (24, 39), Darío Cvitanich (70) / Salvador Cabañas (89).

LIBERTAD ASUNCIÓN – EL NACIONAL 1-0 (1-0)
Defensores del Chaco, Asunción, 22.03.2007
Referee: Héctor Walter Baldassi (ARG), Attendance: 2.000
LIBERTAD: Jorge Rodrigo Bava, Carlos Bonet, Pedro Alcides Sarabia, Pedro Juan Benítez, Édgar Gabriel Balbuena, Sergio Daniel Aquino (87 Wilson Osmar Pittoni), Cristian Miguel Riveros, Pablo Horacio Guiñazú, Osvaldo David Martínez (82 Vladimir Marín), Hernán Rodrigo López, Freddy José Bareiro (68 Nelson David Romero). DT: Sergio Markarian
EL NACIONAL: Rixon Javier Corozo, Willian Ángelis Cuero (79 Luis Armando Checa), Omar Andrés De Jesús, Carlos Ernesto Castro, Jhon Patricio Cagua, Érik Rolando De Jesús, Mario David Quiroz (46 Wálter Richard Calderón), Carlos Ramón Hidalgo, Pedro Ángel Quiñónez, Wálter Orlando Ayoví (77 Jaime Iván Kaviedes), Christian Rogelio Benítez. DT: Ever Hugo Almeida
Goal: Carlos Bonet (10).

EL NACIONAL – CA BANFIELD 0-1 (0-0)
Olímpico Atahualpa, Quito, 3.04.2007, Referee: José Hernando Buitrago (COL)
EL NACIONAL: Rixon Javier Corozo, Omar Andrés De Jesús (80 Jhon Stalin Minda), Carlos Ernesto Castro, Pavel Cipriano Caicedo, Jhon Patricio Cagua, Wálter Orlando Ayoví, Mario David Quiroz (46 Ebelio Agustín Ordóñez), Pedro Ángel Quiñónez, Wellington Eduardo Sánchez, Wálter Richard Calderón, Jaime Iván Kaviedes. DT: Ever Hugo Almeida
BANFIELD: Cristian David Lucchetti, Julio Eduardo Barraza, Carlos Alberto Galván, Javier Estebán Sanguinetti, Luciano Civelli, José Manuel Chatruc (60 Pablo Ernesto Vitti), Daniel Eduardo Quinteros, Javier Alejandro Villarreal, Martín Ezequiel Andrizzi, Josemir Lujambio (83 Fabián Ernesto Santana), Darío Cvitanich (88 Ángel Alejandro Morales). DT: Pablo Sánchez & Hernán Lisi
Goal: Daniel Eduardo Quinteros (79).

LIBERTAD ASUNCIÓN – CF AMÉRICA 1-2 (1-0)
Defensores del Chaco, Asunción, 11.04.2007, Referee: Jorge Luis Larrionda (URU), Attendance: 3.000
LIBERTAD: Jorge Rodrigo Bava, Carlos Bonet, Pedro Alcides Sarabia (17 Deivis Barone), Ricardo Julián Martínez, Édgar Gabriel Balbuena, Sergio Daniel Aquino (82 Vladimir Marín), Víctor Javier Cáceres, Pablo Horacio Guiñazú, Osvaldo David Martínez, Édgar Benítez (58 Wilson Osmar Pittoni), Hernán Rodrigo López. DT: Sergio Markarian
CF AMÉRICA: Armando Navarrete, Rodrigo Iñigo, Carlos Jesús Infante (46 Nelson Rafael Cuevas), Raúl Alberto Salinas, Ismael de Jesús Rodríguez, Raúl Alvin Mendoza, Fabián Peña, Luis Fernando Saritama (46 Salvador Cabañas), Ignacio Torres, Daniel Rubén Bilos, Santiago Fernández (80 Ricardo Francisco Rojas). DT: Luis Fernando Tena
Sent off: Guiñazu (44) / Bilos (84)
Goals: Hernán Rodrigo López (7 penalty) / Salvador Cabañas (63, 75).

CF AMÉRICA – EL NACIONAL 2-1 (1-1)
Azteca, México City, 18.04.2007, Referee: Manuel Candelario Andarcia (VEN)
CF AMÉRICA: Francisco Guillermo Ochoa, José Antonio Castro, Duilio César Davino, Ismael de Jesús Rodríguez, Ricardo Francisco Rojas, Alejandro Argüello, Raúl Alvin Mendoza, Germán Villa, Salvador Cabañas, Santiago Fernández (87 Ignacio Torres), Cuauhtémoc Bravo Blanco. DT: Luis Fernando Tena
EL NACIONAL: Oswaldo Johvani Ibarra, Omar Andrés De Jesús, Carlos Ernesto Castro, Pavel Cipriano Caicedo, Jhon Patricio Cagua, Wálter Orlando Ayoví, Bolívar Efrén Gómez, Pedro Ángel Quiñónez, Jhon Stalin Minda (71 Santiago Damián Morales), Christian Rogelio Benítez, Jaime Iván Kaviedes (71 Ebelio Agustín Ordóñez). DT: Ever Hugo Almeida
Goals: Salvador Cabañas (30), Santiago Fernández (67) / Wálter Orlando Ayoví (17).

CA BANFIELD – LIBERTAD ASUNCIÓN 0-1 (0-0)
Florencio Sola, Banfield, 18.04.2007, Referee: Carlos Eugênio Simón (BRA), Attendance: 6.570
BANFIELD: Cristian David Lucchetti, Roberto Hernán Salvatierra (61 Cristian Pedro Bardaro), Carlos Alberto Galván, Javier Estebán Sanguinetti, Luciano Civelli (85 Ángel Alejandro Morales), José Manuel Chatruc, Javier Alejandro Villarreal, Daniel Eduardo Quinteros, Martín Ezequiel Andrizzi (76 Pablo Ernesto Vitti), Darío Cvitanich, Josemir Lujambio. DT: Pablo Sánchez & Hernán Lisi
LIBERTAD: Horacio Javier González, Ricardo Julián Martínez, Pedro Alcides Sarabia, Deivis Barone (46 Edgar Arnulfo Robles), Carlos Bonet, Sergio Daniel Aquino, Víctor Javier Cáceres, Édgar Gabriel Balbuena, Osvaldo David Martínez (85 Raúl Hernán Damiani), Hernán Rodrigo López, Roberto Carlos Gamarra (46 Vladimir Marín). DT: Sergio Markarian
Josemir Lujambio missed a penalty in the 35th minute
Goal: Vladimir Marín (55).

1	LIBERTAD ASUNCIÓN	6	4	1	1	9	4	13
2	CF AMÉRICA	6	4	0	2	12	10	12
3	CA Banfield	6	3	0	3	8	8	9
4	El Nacional	6	0	1	5	4	11	1

GROUP 2

AUDAX ITALIANO – SÃO PAULO FC 0-0
San Carlos de Apoquindo, Santiago, 14.02.2007
Referee: Roberto Carlos Silvera (URU), Attendance: 3.413
AUDAX ITALIANO: Nicolás Miroslav Peric, Boris Alexis Rieloff, Jorge Antonio Carrasco, Juan Claudio González, Roberto Andrés Cereceda, Carlos Alberto Garrido, Diego Scotti, Miguel Ángel Romero, Carlos Andrés Villanueva, Rodolfo Antonio Moya (75 Fabián Ariel Orellana), Franco Matías Di Santo (75 Leonardo Andrés Medina). DT: Raúl Toro
SÃO PAULO: ROGÉRIO CENI, ALEX Sandro da SILVA, ANDRÉ Gonçalves DIAS, João MIRANDA de Souza Filho, Néicer Reasco, FREDSON Câmara Pereira, JOSUÉ de Oliviera, José JADÍLSON dos Santos Silva, LENILSON Batista de Souza (58 HUGO Assis do Nascimento), ALOÍSIO José da Silva, LEANDRO Lessa Azevedo. DT: Muricy Ramalho

ALIANZA LIMA – NECAXA 1-2 (0-2)
Alejandro Villanueva, Lima, 20.02.2007, Referee: Iván Igor Gamboa (BOL)
ALIANZA: George Patrick Forsyth (43 Francisco Pizarro), Guillermo Sandro Salas, Santiago Roberto Salazar, Augusto Jesús Poroso, Jorge Jair Yglesias, Juan José Jayo, Marko Gustavo Ciurlizza, Carlos Alberto Zegarra (75 Alexander Gustavo Sánchez), Martín Ricardo Ligüera, Renzo Émerson Benavides (66 Johan Joussep Sotil), Flavio Francisco Maestri. DT: Gerardo Pelusso
NECAXA: Alexandro Álvarez, Pablo Javier Quattrocchi, Joaquín Beltrán, Luis Omar Hernández, Osvaldo Lucas, Horacio Javier Cervantes, EVERALDO Vergne de Assis BARBOSA, Gerardo Gabriel Galindo, Juan Manuel Salgueiro (84 Héctor Horacio Giménez), Alfredo David Moreno (73 Julio Javier Marchant), KLÉBER João BOAS Pereira (85 Aarón Padilla). DT: José Luis Trejo
Goals: Martín Ricardo Ligüera (57) / Alfredo David Moreno (17), Juan Manuel Salgueiro (32).

NECAXA – AUDAX ITALIANO 2-0 (1-0)
Victoria, Aguascalientes, 28.02.2007, Referee: Martín Vázquez (URU)
NECAXA: Alexandro Álvarez, Pablo Javier Quattrocchi, Salvador Cabrera (46 Aarón Padilla), Luis Omar Hernández, EVERALDO Vergne de Assis BARBOSA, Horacio Javier Cervantes, Osvaldo Lucas (56 Frankie Oviedo), Jaime Ruiz (82 Fernando Morales), Mario Pérez, KLÉBER João BOAS Pereira, Alfredo David Moreno. DT: José Luis Trejo
AUDAX ITALIANO: Nicolás Miroslav Peric, Juan Claudio González, Boris Alexis Rieloff, Roberto Andrés Cereceda, Jorge Antonio Carrasco, César Elías Santis (67 Fabián Ariel Orellana), Miguel Ángel Romero, Carlos Alberto Garrido, Diego Scotti, Carlos Andrés Villanueva (77 Leonardo Andrés Medina), Rodolfo Antonio Moya (80 Franco Matías Di Santo). DT: Raúl Toro
Goals: KLÉBER João BOAS Pereira (8), Aarón Padilla (69).

SÃO PAULO FC – ALIANZA LIMA 4-0 (1-0)
Cícero Pompeu de Toledo 'Morumbí', São Paulo, 28.02.2007, Referee: Sergio Fabián Pezzotta (ARG)
SÃO PAULO: ROGÉRIO CENI, ANDRÉ Gonçalves DIAS, Ilson Pereira Dias Júnior "ILSINHO", ALEX Sandro da SILVA (84 EDCARLOS Conceição Santos), João MIRANDA de Souza Filho, José JADÍLSON dos Santos Silva (82 Jenilson Angelo de Souza "JÚNIOR"), JOSUÉ de Oliviera, Williamis de SOUZA Silva (90 FREDSON Câmara Pereira), HUGO Assis do Nascimento, LEANDRO Lessa Azevedo, ALOÍSIO José da Silva. DT: Muricy Ramalho
ALIANZA: George Patrick Forsyth, Guillermo Sandro Salas, Augusto Jesús Poroso, Ismael Enrique Alvarado, Jorge Jair Yglesias, Marko Gustavo Ciurlizza, César Junior Viza, Jhoel Alexander Herrera, Carlos Alberto Zegarra (62 Luis Alberto Hernández), Martín Ricardo Ligüera (82 Johan Joussep Sotil), Roberto Enrique Silva (62 Flavio Francisco Maestri). DT: Gerardo Pelusso
Goals: ALEX Sandro da SILVA (14, 77), LEANDRO Lessa Azevedo (57), Jenilson Angelo de Souza "JÚNIOR" (87).

ALIANZA LIMA – AUDAX ITALIANO 1-3 (0-1)
Alejandro Villanueva, Lima, 13.03.2007, Referee: Mauricio Javier Reinoso (ECU)
ALIANZA: Joel Ademir Pinto, Guillermo Sandro Salas, Augusto Jesús Poroso, Ernesto Seiko Arakaki, Jhoel Alexander Herrera, Marko Gustavo Ciurlizza, Juan José Jayo (19 Erick Omar Torres), Alexander Gustavo Sánchez, Martín Ricardo Ligüera, Aldo Italo Olcese (59 César Junior Viza), Flavio Francisco Maestri (66 Roberto Enrique Silva). DT: Gerardo Pelusso
AUDAX ITALIANO: Nicolás Miroslav Peric, Boris Alexis Rieloff, Jorge Antonio Carrasco, Juan Claudio González, Roberto Andrés Cereceda, Carlos Alberto Garrido, Miguel Ángel Romero, Braulio Antonio Leal, Carlos Andrés Villanueva (77 César Elías Santis), Leonardo Andrés Medina (61 Franco Matías Di Santo), Rodolfo Antonio Moya (90+2 Enzo Carlo Cabrera). DT: Raúl Toro
Goals: Roberto Enrique Silva (67) / Carlos Andrés Villanueva (44), Roberto Andrés Cereceda (81), Rodolfo Antonio Moya (88).

NECAXA – SÃO PAULO FC 2-1 (0-1)
Victoria, Aguascalientes, 21.03.2007, Referee: Sergio Fabián Pezzotta (ARG)
NECAXA: Alexandro Álvarez, Pablo Javier Quattrocchi, Joaquín Beltrán, Horacio Javier Cervantes, Osvaldo Lucas, Luis Omar Hernández (37 Mario Pérez), Gerardo Gabriel Galindo, EVERALDO Vergne de Assis BARBOSA, Juan Manuel Salgueiro (79 Jaime Ruiz), KLÉBER João BOAS Pereira, Alfredo David Moreno (87 Héctor Horacio Giménez). DT: José Luis Trejo
SÃO PAULO: ROGÉRIO CENI, Ilson Pereira Dias Júnior "ILSINHO", ANDRÉ Gonçalves DIAS (19 EDCARLOS Conceição Santos, 75 MARCEL Augusto Ortolan), João MIRANDA de Souza Filho, JOSUÉ de Oliviera, LEANDRO Lessa Azevedo, Williamis de SOUZA Silva, ALOÍSIO José da Silva, ALEX Sandro da SILVA, José JADÍLSON dos Santos Silva, LENILSON Batista de Souza. DT: Muricy Ramalho
Alexandro Álvarez saved a penalty taken by ROGÉRIO CENI in the 41st minute.
Goals: KLÉBER João BOAS Pereira (61), Juan Manuel Salgueiro (68) /
José JADÍLSON dos Santos Silva (40).

AUDAX ITALIANO – ALIANZA LIMA 1-0 (1-0)
Nacional, Santiago, 27.03.2007, Referee: Juan Carlos Paniagua (BOL), Attendance: 1.606
AUDAX ITALIANO: Nicolás Miroslav Peric, Enzo Carlo Cabrera, Jorge Antonio Carrasco, Juan Claudio González, Roberto Andrés Cereceda, Braulio Antonio Leal, Carlos Alberto Garrido, Miguel Ángel Romero, Carlos Andrés Villanueva (63 César Elías Santis), Franco Matías Di Santo, Rodolfo Antonio Moya. DT: Raúl Toro
ALIANZA: Joel Ademir Pinto, Guillermo Sandro Salas, Santiago Roberto Salazar, Ernesto Seiko Arakaki, Jorge Jair Yglesias, Marko Gustavo Ciurlizza, Luis Alberto Hernández (79 Carlos Alberto Zegarra), César Junior Viza (73 Johan Joussep Sotil), Martín Ricardo Ligüera, Douglas Junior Ross, Roberto Enrique Silva (46 Renzo Émerson Benavides). DT: Gerardo Pelusso
Goal: Rodolfo Antonio Moya (26).

SÃO PAULO FC – NECAXA 3-0 (1-0)
Cícero Pompeu de Toledo 'Morumbí', São Paulo, 4.04.2007, Referee: Héctor Walter Baldassi (ARG), Attendance: 30.992
SÃO PAULO: ROGÉRIO CENI, Ilson Pereira Dias Júnior "ILSINHO" (70 Néicer Reasco), ALEX Sandro da SILVA, João MIRANDA de Souza Filho, José JADÍLSON dos Santos Silva (77 Jenilson Angelo de Souza "JÚNIOR"), JOSUÉ de Oliviera, RICHARLYSON Barbosa Felisbino, Williamis de SOUZA Silva, HUGO Assis do Nascimento, LEANDRO Lessa Azevedo, ALOÍSIO José da Silva (84 Humberlito BORGES Teixeira). DT: Muricy Ramalho
NECAXA: Alexandro Álvarez, Pablo Javier Quattrocchi, Joaquín Beltrán, Horacio Javier Cervantes, Osvaldo Lucas, Gerardo Gabriel Galindo, Luis Omar Hernández (54 Juan Manuel Salgueiro), EVERALDO Vergne de Assis BARBOSA, Jaime Ruiz (74 Mario Pérez), Héctor Horacio Giménez (77 Julio Javier Marchant), KLÉBER João BOAS Pereira. DT: José Luis Trejo
Sent off: Cervantes (61)
Goals: Williamis de SOUZA Silva (11), João MIRANDA de Souza Filho (57), HUGO Assis do Nascimento (73).

AUDAX ITALIANO – NECAXA 2-1 (1-0)
David Arellano, Santiago, 11.04.2007, Referee: Gabriel Favale (ARG), Attendance: 7.000
AUDAX ITALIANO: Nicolás Miroslav Peric, Boris Alexis Rieloff, Eladio Felipe Rivera, Juan Claudio González, Roberto Andrés Cereceda, Carlos Alberto Garrido, Braulio Antonio Leal, Miguel Ángel Romero, Carlos Andrés Villanueva (86 Leonardo Andrés Medina), Rodolfo Antonio Moya, Franco Matías Di Santo (86 Fabián Ariel Orellana). DT: Raúl Toro
NECAXA: Alexandro Álvarez, Pablo Javier Quattrocchi, Joaquín Beltrán, Víctor Manuel Gutiérrez (80 Osvaldo Lucas), Juan Manuel Salgueiro, EVERALDO Vergne de Assis BARBOSA, Gerardo Gabriel Galindo, Luis Omar Hernández, Mario Pérez (46 Jaime Ruiz), Héctor Horacio Giménez (75 Julio Javier Marchant), KLÉBER João BOAS Pereira. DT: José Luis Trejo
Goals: Rodolfo Antonio Moya (23), Miguel Ángel Romero (62) / Juan Manuel Salgueiro (53).

ALIANZA LIMA – SÃO PAULO FC 0-1 (0-1)
Alejandro Villanueva, Lima, 18.04.2007, Referee: Alfredo Stalin Intriago (ECU), Attendance: 288
ALIANZA: George Patrick Forsyth, Jhoel Alexander Herrera, Ernesto Seiko Arakaki, Santiago Roberto Salazar, Jorge Jair Yglesias, Marko Gustavo Ciurlizza, Ismael Enrique Alvarado, Juan José Jayo (83 César Junior Viza), Martín Ricardo Ligüera (73 Aldo Italo Olcese), Roberto Enrique Silva (65 Renzo Émerson Benavides), Douglas Junior Ross. DT: Gerardo Pelusso
SÃO PAULO: ROGÉRIO CENI, João MIRANDA de Souza Filho, ALEX Sandro da SILVA, ANDRÉ Gonçalves DIAS, Jenilson Angelo de Souza "JÚNIOR", JOSUÉ de Oliviera, JORGE WAGNER Góes Conceição, Néicer Reasco, Williamis de SOUZA Silva, Humberlito BORGES Teixeira, ALOÍSIO José da Silva (77 LENILSON Batista de Souza). DT: Muricy Ramalho
Goal: Humberlito BORGES Teixeira (45+1).

NECAXA SA – ALIANZA LIMA 2-0 (1-0)
Victoria, Aguascalientes, 25.04.2007, Referee: Enrique Osses (CHI)
NECAXA: Alexandro Álvarez, Pablo Javier Quattrocchi, Joaquín Beltrán, Horacio Javier Cervantes, Juan Manuel Salgueiro (72 Fernando Morales), EVERALDO Vergne de Assis BARBOSA, Gerardo Gabriel Galindo, KLÉBER João BOAS Pereira, Héctor Horacio Giménez (63 Alfredo David Moreno), Jaime Ruiz, Julio Javier Marchant (85 Luis Omar Hernández). DT: José Luis Trejo
ALIANZA: Joel Ademir Pinto, Jhoel Alexander Herrera, Ernesto Seiko Arakaki, Santiago Roberto Salazar, Jorge Jair Yglesias, Juan José Jayo, Carlos Alberto Zegarra, Luis Alberto Hernández (61 Aldo Italo Olcese), César Junior Viza, Douglas Junior Ross (76 Johan Joussep Sotil), Renzo Émerson Benavides (65 Roberto Enrique Silva). DT: Gerardo Pelusso
Goals: KLÉBER João BOAS Pereira (7), Juan Manuel Salgueiro (48).

SÃO PAULO FC – AUDAX ITALIANO 2-2 (1-0)
Cícero Pompeu de Toledo 'Morumbí', São Paulo, 25.04.2007
Referee: Carlos Amarilla (PAR), Attendance: 20.795
SÃO PAULO: ROGÉRIO CENI, Ilson Pereira Dias Júnior "ILSINHO", ALEX Sandro da SILVA, João MIRANDA de Souza Filho, Jenilson Angelo de Souza "JÚNIOR", JOSUÉ de Oliviera, RICHARLYSON Barbosa Felisbino, Williamis de SOUZA Silva, HUGO Assis do Nascimento (83 JORGE WAGNER Góes Conceição), LEANDRO Lessa Azevedo, ALOÍSIO José da Silva (85 MARCEL Augusto Ortolan). DT: Muricy Ramalho
AUDAX ITALIANO: Nicolás Miroslav Peric, Boris Alexis Rieloff (46 Enzo Carlo Cabrera), Juan Claudio González, Eladio Felipe Rivera (46 Franco Matías Di Santo), César Elías Santis (46 Braulio Antonio Leal), Carlos Alberto Garrido, Diego Scotti, Roberto Andrés Cereceda, Carlos Andrés Villanueva, Miguel Ángel Romero, Rodolfo Antonio Moya. DT: Raúl Toro
Goals: RICHARLYSON Barbosa Felisbino (6), ALOÍSIO José da Silva (67) /
Franco Matías Di Santo (59), Rodolfo Antonio Moya (71).

1	NECAXA	6	4	0	2	9	7	12
2	SÃO PAULO FC	6	3	2	1	11	4	11
3	Audax Italiano	6	3	2	1	8	6	11
4	Alianza Lima	6	0	0	6	2	13	0

GROUP 3

CÚCUTA DEPORTIVO – DEPORTES TOLIMA 0-0
General Santander, Cúcuta, 13.02.2007, Referee: Jorge Hernán Hoyos (COL), Attendance: 15.412
CÚCUTA: Róbinson Zapata, Rubén Darío Bustos, Wálter José Moreno, Julián Hurtado, Joe Louis Raguá, Nélson Alfonso Flores (73 Roberto Carlos Bobadilla), Charles Castro (83 Lin Carlos Henry), Macnelly Torres, David Camilo Córdoba (73 Alexander Del Castillo), Blas Antonio Miguel Pérez, Víctor Javier Cortés. DT: Jorge Luis Bernal
DEPORTES TOLIMA: Agustín Julio, Hilario Cuenú, Yesid Martínez, Jesús Brahman Sinisterra, Hernando Patiño, Franklin Emir González, Yulián José Anchico, Juan Carlos Escobar, Jhon Jairo Charría, Jorge Isaacs Perlaza (61 Nicolás Nahuel Ayr, 77 Darío Alberto Bustos), Gustavo Humberto Savoia (73 César Augusto Rivas). DT: Jaime de la Pava
Sent off: Martínez (58)

CERRO PORTEÑO – GRÊMIO FOOTBALL 0-1 (0-0)
Gral. Pablo Rojas, Asunción, 15.02.2007, Referee: Héctor Walter Baldassi (ARG), Attendance: 10.000
CERRO PORTEÑO: Hilario Bernardo Navarro, Lorgio Álvarez, RODRIGO Barbosa Rodrigues COSTA, Fidel Amado Pérez, Jorge Martín Núñez (82 Ernesto Rubén Cristaldo), Jorge Orlando Brítez (73 Pablo Junior Giménez), Édgar Daniel González, José Domingo Salcedo, Gustavo Eliseo Morínigo (58 Eder Ricardo Godoy), César Augusto Ramírez, Alejandro Damián Da Silva. DT: Gustavo Costas
GRÊMIO: Diego Sebastián Saja, PATRICIO Antônio Boques, WILLIAM Machado de Oliveira, Rolando Carlos Schiavi, Wender Coelho da Silva "TECO", LUCAS Pezzini Leiva (90+3 SANDRO "GOIANO" Gomes Luz), EDMÍLSON Carlos Abel, DIEGO de SOUZA Andrade, CARLOS EDUARDO Marques (69 RAMÓN Rodrigo de Freitas), Ânderson Simas Luciano "TCHECO", Moacir Bastos "TUTA" (21 DOUGLAS de Oliveira). DT: Mano Menezes
Diego Sebastián SAJA saved a penalty taken by César Augusto RAMÍREZ Caje in the 89th minute.
Goal: LUCAS Pezzini Leiva (52).

GRÊMIO FOOTBALL – CÚCUTA DEPORTIVO 0-0
Olímpico Monumental, Porto Alegre, 27.02.2007
Referee: Pablo Antonio Pozo (CHI), Attendance: 36.373
GRÊMIO: Diego Sebastián Saja, PATRICIO Antônio Boques, WILLIAM Machado de Oliveira, Rolando Carlos Schiavi, LÚCIO Carlos Cajueiro Souza, LUCAS Pezzini Leiva, DIEGO de SOUZA Andrade (85 ALOÍSIO dos Santos), RAMÓN Rodrigo de Freitas (66 SANDRO "GOIANO" Gomes Luz), Ânderson Simas Luciano "TCHECO", CARLOS EDUARDO Marques, DOUGLAS de Oliveira (64 EVERTON Santos). DT: Mano Menezes
CÚCUTA: Róbinson Zapata, Rubén Darío Bustos (78 Braynner Yesid García), Julián Hurtado, Wálter José Moreno, Joe Louis Raguá, Charles Castro, Nélson Alfonso Flores, Dúmar Ricardo Rueda (46 Alexander Del Castillo), Macnelly Torres, Víctor Javier Cortés (73 Juan Manuel Martínez), Blas Antonio Miguel Pérez. DT: Jorge Luis Bernal

DEPORTES TOLIMA – CERRO PORTEÑO 1-0 (0-0)
Manuel Murillo Toro, Ibagué, 7.03.2007, Referee: Víctor Hugo Rivera (PER), Attendance: 6.110
DEPORTES TOLIMA: Agustín Julio, Gerardo Enrique Vallejo, Hilario Cuenú, Roller Cambindo, Jesús Brahman Sinisterra, Hernando Patiño, Juan Carlos Escobar, Yulián José Anchico, Jhon Jairo Charría (83 Franklin Emir González), Jorge Isaacs Perlaza (76 César Augusto Rivas), Gustavo Humberto Savoia (61 Carlos Darwin Quintero). DT: Jaime de la Pava
CERRO PORTEÑO: Hilario Bernardo Navarro, Lorgio Álvarez, Fidel Amado Pérez, Nelson David Cabrera, Jorge Martín Núñez, Jorge Orlando Brítez (58 Osvaldo Hobecker), Édgar Daniel González, José Domingo Salcedo, Ernesto Rubén Cristaldo (67 Pablo Junior Giménez), César Augusto Ramírez (79 Eder Ricardo Godoy), Alejandro Damián Da Silva. DT: Gustavo Costas
Goal: Carlos Darwin Quintero (63).

CÚCUTA DEPORTIVO – CERRO PORTEÑO 1-1 (0-0)
General Santander, Cúcuta, 13.03.2007, Referee: Pablo Alejandro Lunati (ARG), Attendance: 16.789
CÚCUTA: Róbinson Zapata, Rubén Darío Bustos, Wálter José Moreno, Julián Hurtado, Joe Louis Raguá (78 Elvis Javier González), Nélson Alfonso Flores (60 David Camilo Córdoba), Dúmar Ricardo Rueda, Macnelly Torres, Roberto Carlos Bobadilla (56 Víctor Javier Cortés), Juan Manuel Martínez, Blas Antonio Miguel Pérez. DT: Jorge Luis Bernal
CERRO PORTEÑO: Hilario Bernardo Navarro, Lorgio Álvarez, Fidel Amado Pérez, Nelson David Cabrera, Jorge Martín Núñez, Édgar Daniel González, José Domingo Salcedo, Oscar Moisés Gamarra, Pablo Junior Giménez (24 Eder Ricardo Godoy), César Augusto Ramírez (68 Ernesto Rubén Cristaldo), Alejandro Damián Da Silva (87 Jorge Daniel Achucarro). DT: Gustavo Costas
Sent off: Núñez (65)
Goals: Blas Antonio Miguel Pérez (81) / César Augusto Ramírez (46).

DEPORTES TOLIMA – GRÊMIO FOOTBALL 1-0 (1-0)
Manuel Murillo Toro, Ibagué, 15.03.2007, Referee: Rafael Furchi (ARG)
DEPORTES TOLIMA: Agustín Julio, Gerardo Enrique Vallejo, Hilario Cuenú, Roller Cambindo, Jesús Brahman Sinisterra, Hernando Patiño, Yulián José Anchico, Juan Carlos Escobar, Jhon Jairo Charría (87 Franklin Emir González), Jorge Isaacs Perlaza (86 Gustavo Humberto Savoia), Carlos Darwin Quintero (76 Leiner Concepción Rolong). DT: Jaime de la Pava
GRÊMIO: Diego Sebastián Saja, PATRICIO Antônio Boques, Rolando Carlos Schiavi, WILLIAM Machado de Oliveira, LÚCIO Carlos Cajueiro Souza, Eduardo Martins NUNES, DIEGO de SOUZA Andrade (46 CARLOS EDUARDO Marques), LUCAS Pezzini Leiva, Ânderson Simas Luciano "TCHECO", RAMÓN Rodrigo de Freitas (83 ALOÍSIO dos Santos), EVERTON Santos. DT: Mano Menezes
Goal: Jorge Isaacs Perlaza (33).

CERRO PORTEÑO – CÚCUTA DEPORTIVO 2-1 (0-1)
Antonio Oddone Sarubbi, Ciudad del Este, 20.03.2007
Referee: Juan Pablo Pompei (ARG), Attendance: 10.000
CERRO PORTEÑO: Hilario Bernardo Navarro, Lorgio Álvarez, Fidel Amado Pérez, Nelson David Cabrera, Ernesto Rubén Cristaldo, Oscar Moisés Gamarra (46 Jorge Daniel Achucarro), Édgar Daniel González, José Domingo Salcedo, Eder Ricardo Godoy (62 Gustavo Eliseo Morínigo), César Augusto Ramírez, Alejandro Damián Da Silva (75 Jorge Orlando Brítez). DT: Gustavo Costas
CÚCUTA: Róbinson Zapata, Rubén Darío Bustos, Julián Hurtado, Wálter José Moreno, Joe Louis Raguá, Nélson Alfonso Flores, Dúmar Ricardo Rueda (72 Alexander Del Castillo), Macnelly Torres, Charles Castro (68 David Camilo Córdoba), Blas Antonio Miguel Pérez, Juan Manuel Martínez (74 Víctor Javier Cortés). DT: Jorge Luis Bernal
Goals: César Augusto Ramírez (52), Alejandro Damián Da Silva (65) /
Blas Antonio Miguel Pérez (35 penalty).

GRÊMIO FOOTBALL – DEPORTES TOLIMA 1-0 (1-0)
Olímpico Monumental, Porto Alegre, 27.03.2007, Referee: Martín Vázquez (URU)
GRÊMIO: Diego Sebastián Saja, PATRICIO Antônio Boques, Rolando Carlos Schiavi, WILLIAM Machado de Oliveira, LÚCIO Carlos Cajueiro Souza, EDMÍLSON Carlos Abel, LUCAS Pezzini Leiva, Ânderson Simas Luciano "TCHECO", RAMÓN Rodrigo de Freitas (77 DIEGO de SOUZA Andrade), CARLOS EDUARDO Marques (85 Wender Coelho da Silva "TECO"), Moacir Bastos "TUTA" (69 DOUGLAS de Oliveira). DT: Mano Menezes
DEPORTES TOLIMA: Agustín Julio, Gerardo Enrique Vallejo, Hilario Cuenú, Roller Cambindo, Jesús Brahman Sinisterra, Franklin Emir González (64 Leiner Concepción Rolong), Hernando Patiño, Juan Carlos Escobar, Jhon Jairo Charría, Yulián José Anchico (82 Carlos Darwin Quintero), Jorge Isaacs Perlaza. DT: Jaime de la Pava
Goal: Moacir Bastos "TUTA" (21).

CERRO PORTEÑO – DEPORTES TOLIMA 1-0 (0-0)
Defensores del Chaco, Asunción, 10.04.2007
Referee: Roberto Carlos Silvera (URU), Attendance: 5.000
CERRO PORTEÑO: Hilario Bernardo Navarro, Alfredo David Rojas, Fidel Amado Pérez, Nelson David Cabrera, Lorgio Álvarez (69 Eder Ricardo Godoy), Gustavo Eliseo Morínigo, Jorge Orlando Brítez (53 Jorge Daniel Achucarro), Édgar Daniel González, José Domingo Salcedo, César Augusto Ramírez (88 Jorge Martín Núñez), Alejandro Damián Da Silva. DT: Gustavo Costas
DEPORTES TOLIMA: Agustín Julio, Gerardo Enrique Vallejo, Hilario Cuenú, Roller Cambindo, Jesús Brahman Sinisterra, Yulián José Anchico, Hernando Patiño, Juan Carlos Escobar, Jhon Jairo Charría, Gustavo Humberto Savoia (46 Carlos Darwin Quintero), Jorge Isaacs Perlaza (76 Leiner Concepción Rolong). DT: Jaime de la Pava
Sent off: Ancico (58)
Goal: Gustavo Eliseo Morínigo (81).

CÚCUTA DEPORTIVO – GRÊMIO FOOTBALL 3-1 (1-0)
General Santander, Cúcuta, 11.04.2007, Referee: René Marcelo Ortubé (BOL), Attendance: 30.000
CÚCUTA: Róbinson Zapata, Rubén Darío Bustos, Pedro Paulo Portocarrero, Wálter José Moreno, Joe Louis Raguá, Nélson Alfonso Flores (59 Víctor Javier Cortés), Dúmar Ricardo Rueda, Charles Castro (59 Alexander Del Castillo), Macnelly Torres, Juan Manuel Martínez (78 Braynner Yesid García), Blas Antonio Miguel Pérez. DT: Jorge Luis Bernal
GRÊMIO: Diego Sebastián Saja, PATRICIO Antônio Boques, WILLIAM Machado de Oliveira, Rolando Carlos Schiavi, LÚCIO Carlos Cajueiro Souza, LUCAS Pezzini Leiva, RAMÓN Rodrigo de Freitas, DIEGO de SOUZA Andrade (76 CARLOS EDUARDO Marques), WILLIAM Henrique ANTUNES, Ânderson Simas Luciano "TCHECO" (83 EVERTON Santos), Moacir Bastos "TUTA".
DT: Mano Menezes
Goals: Rubén Darío Bustos (43), Blas Antonio Miguel Pérez (73), Alexander Del Castillo (87) /
Wálter José Moreno (51 own goal).

DEPORTES TOLIMA – CÚCUTA DEPORTIVO 3-4 (1-2)
Manuel Murillo Toro, Ibagué, 24.04.2007, Referee: Óscar Julián Ruiz (COL)
DEPORTES TOLIMA: Agustín Julio, Roller Cambindo, Gerardo Enrique Vallejo, Hilario Cuenú, Franklin Emir González (46 César Augusto Rivas), Jesús Brahman Sinisterra, Hernando Patiño, Juan Carlos Escobar, Jhon Jairo Charría, Carlos Darwin Quintero (83 Leiner Concepción Rolong), Jorge Isaacs Perlaza (74 Gustavo Adolfo Bolívar). DT: Hernán Torres
CÚCUTA: Róbinson Zapata, Rubén Darío Bustos, Julián Hurtado (46 Pedro Paulo Portocarrero), Wálter José Moreno, Dúmar Ricardo Rueda, Charles Castro (55 Víctor Javier Cortés), Joe Louis Raguá, Alexander Del Castillo (69 David Camilo Córdoba), Macnelly Torres, Juan Manuel Martínez, Blas Antonio Miguel Pérez. DT: Jorge Luis Bernal
Goals: Jhon Jairo Charría (38, 63 penalty), Carlos Darwin Quintero (49) /
Alexander Del Castillo (19), Juan Manuel Martínez (41), Blas Antonio Miguel Pérez (71, 86).

GRÊMIO FOOTBALL – CERRO PORTEÑO 1-0 (0-0)
Olímpico Monumental, Porto Alegre, 24.04.2007
Referee: Sergio Fabián Pezzotta (ARG), Attendance: 40.620
GRÊMIO: Diego Sebastián Saja, PATRICIO Antônio Boques, WILLIAM Machado de Oliveira, LÚCIO Carlos Cajueiro Souza, Wender Coelho da Silva "TECO", DIEGO de SOUZA Andrade, CARLOS EDUARDO Marques (74 EDMÍLSON Carlos Abel), SANDRO "GOIANO" Gomes Luz, Eduardo Martins NUNES (64 EVERTON Santos), Ânderson Simas Luciano "TCHECO" (84 WILLIAM Henrique ANTUNES), Moacir Bastos "TUTA". DT: Mano Menezes
CERRO PORTEÑO: Hilario Bernardo Navarro, Alfredo David Rojas, Fidel Amado Pérez, Nelson David Cabrera, Lorgio Álvarez, Gustavo Eliseo Morínigo (72 Alejandro Damián Da Silva), Jorge Orlando Brítez (81 Ernesto Rubén Cristaldo), Édgar Daniel González, Jorge Daniel Achucarro (76 Eder Ricardo Godoy), José Domingo Salcedo, César Augusto Ramírez. DT: Gustavo Costas
Goal: EVERTON Santos (69).

1	GRÊMIO FOOTBALL	6	3	1	2	4	4	10
2	CÚCUTA DEPORTIVO	6	2	3	1	9	7	9
3	Deportes Tolima	6	2	1	3	5	6	7
4	Cerro Porteño	6	2	1	3	4	5	7

GROUP 4

EMELEC – VÉLEZ SARSFIELD 0-1 (0-1)
George Capwell, Guayaquil, 13.02.2007, Referee: Antonio Javier Arias (PAR), Attendance: 22.000
EMELEC: Marcelo Ramón Elizaga, Carlos Andrés Quiñónez, Marco Antonio Quiñónez, Facundo Jesús Corozo, Silvano de los Santos Estacio, José Luis Quiñónez, Michael Antonio Arroyo, Luis Guillermo Rivera (78 Jaime Ramiro Caicedo), Sebastián Hernández (61 Óscar Maximiliano Asís), Israel Rodrigo Rodríguez, Jerónimo Morales Neumann (61 Jorge Washington Ladines). DT: Carlos Torres Garcés
VÉLEZ SARSFIELD: Gastón Alejandro Sessa, Hernán Darío Pellerano, Maximiliano Pellegrino, Marcelo Hernán Bustamante, Mario Méndez, Maximiliano Andrés Bustos, Emiliano Ramiro Papa, Damián Ariel Escudero (66 Ariel Esteban Broggi), Iván Diego Moreno y Fabianesi, Lucas Martín Castromán (81 Ramón Dario Ocampo), Mauro Matías Zárate (71 Gustavo Alberto Balvorín). DT: Ricardo La Volpe
Goal: Marcelo Hernán Bustamante (13).

NACIONAL MONTEVIDEO – INTERNACIONAL 3-1 (0-1)
Parque Central, Montevideo, 21.02.2007, Referee: Sergio Fabián Pezzotta (ARG), Attendance: 9.582
NACIONAL: Washington Alexis Viera, Pablo Álvarez, Alejandro Rodríguez, Diego Roberto Godín, Agustín Viana, Marcelo Carlo Broli (41 Jorge Andrés Martínez), Marco Eduardo Vanzini (65 Gonzalo Castro), Javier Omar Delgado, Marcos Marcelo Tejera (65 Marcelo Fabian Sosa), Andrés Leonardo Márquez, Diego Vera. DT: Daniel Carreño

INTERNACIONAL: CLEMER Melo da Silva, ELDER da Silva GRANJA, EDIGLÉ Quaresma Farías, RAFAEL Alves SANTOS, Martín Emilio Hidalgo, Edimo Ferreira Campos "EDINHO", WELLINGTON de Oliveira MONTEIRO, ALEX Raphael Meschini (74 Cleiton Eduardo Vicente "PERDIGÃO"), Carlos ADRIANO de Souza Vieira (82 MICHEL Neves Dias), Pedro IARLEY Lima Dantas, LUIZ ADRIANO Souza da Silva (64 Fernando Lúcio da Costa "FERNANDÃO"). DT: Abel Braga
Sent off: Rodríguez (61) / Monteiro (74)
Goals: Diego Vera (72), Javier Omar Delgado (75), Jorge Andrés Martínez (90+2) / Martín Emilio Hidalgo (37).

VÉLEZ SARSFIELD – NACIONAL MONTEVIDEO 1-1 (1-0)
José Amalfitani, Buenos Aires, 28.02.2007
Referee: Sálvio Spínola Fagundes (BRA), Attendance: 8.661
VÉLEZ SARSFIELD: Gastón Alejandro Sessa, Hernán Darío Pellerano, Maximiliano Pellegrino, Sergio Román Sena (60 Ariel Esteban Broggi), Mario Méndez, Maximiliano Andrés Bustos, Iván Diego Moreno y Fabianesi (60 Javier Sebastián Robles), Emiliano Ramiro Papa (78 Marcelo Hernán Bustamante), Damián Ariel Escudero, Gustavo Alberto Balvorín, Mauro Matías Zárate. DT: Ricardo La Volpe
NACIONAL: Washington Alexis Viera, Pablo Álvarez, Diego Jaume, Diego Roberto Godín, Agustín Viana, Mathías Cardaccio (62 Hugo Diego Arismendi), Marcelo Carlo Broli (84 Marco Eduardo Vanzini), Marcelo Fabian Sosa, Hector Ignacio La Luz (46 Gonzalo Castro), Jorge Andrés Martínez, Diego Vera. DT: Daniel Carreño
Goals: Damián Ariel Escudero (45) / Diego Vera (46).

INTERNACIONAL – EMELEC 3-0 (1-0)
José Pinheiro Borda, Porto Alegre, 28.02.2007
Referee: Rubén Marcos Selman (CHI), Attendance: 34.327
INTERNACIONAL: CLEMER Melo da Silva, Marcos Venâncio de Albuquerque "CEARÁ", Marcos Antonio de Lima "ÍNDIO" (76 WILSON Roberto dos Santos), RAFAEL Alves SANTOS, Martín Emilio Hidalgo, Edimo Ferreira Campos "EDINHO", Cleiton Eduardo Vicente "PERDIGÃO", ALEX Raphael Meschini (68 MAYCON Vieira da Silva), Fernando Lúcio da Costa "FERNANDÃO", Pedro IARLEY Lima Dantas, ALEXANDRE "PATO" Rodrigues da Silva (80 Carlos ADRIANO de Souza Vieira). DT: Abel Braga
EMELEC: Marcelo Ramón Elizaga, Facundo Jesús Corozo, Carlos Andrés Quiñónez, Banner Geovanny Caicedo (56 Israel Rodrigo Rodríguez), Marco Antonio Quiñónez, Silvano de los Santos Estacio, Jaime Ramiro Caicedo, José Luis Quiñónez, Luis Guillermo Rivera, Sebastián Hernández (70 Michael Antonio Arroyo), Jerónimo Morales Neumann (77 Jorge Washington Ladines). DT: Carlos Torres Garcés
Goals: Cleiton Eduardo Vicente "PERDIGÃO" (26), Marcos Antonio de Lima "ÍNDIO" (55), ALEXANDRE "PATO" Rodrigues da Silva (66).

VÉLEZ SARSFIELD – INTERNACIONAL 3-0 (2-0)
José Amalfitani, Buenos Aires, 14.03.2007, Referee: Carlos Amarilla (PAR), Attendance: 14.000
VÉLEZ SARSFIELD: Gastón Alejandro Sessa, Hernán Darío Pellerano, Mariano Esteban Uglessich, Marcelo Hernán Bustamante, Mario Méndez, Maximiliano Pellegrino, Iván Diego Moreno y Fabianesi, Emiliano Ramiro Papa (75 Gastón Eduardo Montero), Damián Ariel Escudero, Mauro Matías Zárate (85 Gustavo Alberto Balvorín), Lucas Martín Castromán (66 Ramón Dario Ocampo). DT: Ricardo La Volpe
INTERNACIONAL: CLEMER Melo da Silva, Marcos Venâncio de Albuquerque "CEARÁ", Marcos Antonio de Lima "ÍNDIO", WILSON Roberto dos Santos, Martín Emilio Hidalgo, Edimo Ferreira Campos "EDINHO", MAYCON Vieira da Silva, MICHEL Neves Dias (75 Emilio Fabián Andrés Vargas), Fernando Lúcio da Costa "FERNANDÃO", Carlos ADRIANO de Souza Vieira (46 ALEXANDRE "PATO" Rodrigues da Silva), Pedro IARLEY Lima Dantas (46 CHRISTIAN Correa Dionísio). DT: Abel Braga
Goals: Lucas Martín Castromán (16), Damián Ariel Escudero (21, 81).

EMELEC – NACIONAL MONTEVIDEO 1-0 (0-0)
George Capwell, Guayaquil, 22.03.2007, Referee: Rubén Marcos Selman (CHI), Attendance: 8.000
EMELEC: Marcelo Ramón Elizaga, Carlos Andrés Quiñónez, Banner Geovanny Caicedo, Luis Alberto Zambrano, Marco Antonio Quiñónez, José Luis Quiñónez, Tilson Oswaldo Minda (63 Michael Antonio Arroyo), Luis Guillermo Rivera, Sebastián Hernández (73 Silvano de los Santos Estacio), Lucas Ezequiel Viatri, Jerónimo Morales Neumann (66 Jorge Washington Ladines). DT: Carlos Torres Garcés
NACIONAL: Washington Alexis Viera, Pablo Álvarez, Diego Jaume, Diego Roberto Godín, Agustín Viana, Mathías Cardaccio (77 Javier Omar Delgado), Marcelo Carlo Broli, Marcelo Fabian Sosa, Hector Ignacio La Luz (71 Alejandro Rodríguez), Jorge Andrés Martínez, Diego Vera (79 Gonzalo Castro). DT: Daniel Carreño
Sent off: Quiñónez (67), Caicedo (90) / Jaume (67)
Goal: Carlos Andrés Quiñónez (89).

INTERNACIONAL – VÉLEZ SARSFIELD 0-0
José Pinheiro Borda, Porto Alegre, 28.03.2007
Referee: Jorge Luis Larrionda (URU), Attendance: 35.258
INTERNACIONAL: CLEMER Melo da Silva, Marcos Venâncio de Albuquerque "CEARÁ", Marcos Antonio de Lima "ÍNDIO", Martín Emilio Hidalgo, RUBENS Vanderlei Tavares CARDOSO, Edimo Ferreira Campos "EDINHO", MAYCON Vieira da Silva, Fernando Lúcio da Costa "FERNANDÃO" (77 Carlos ADRIANO de Souza Vieira), ALEX Raphael Meschini (74 Cleiton Eduardo Vicente "PERDIGÃO"), CHRISTIAN Correa Dionísio, Pedro IARLEY Lima Dantas (46 ALEXANDRE "PATO" Rodrigues da Silva). DT: Abel Braga   Sent off: Dionísio (27)
VÉLEZ SARSFIELD: Gastón Alejandro Sessa, Mariano Esteban Uglessich, Maximiliano Pellegrino, Hernán Darío Pellerano, Marcelo Hernán Bustamante (27 Ariel Esteban Broggi), Mario Méndez, Iván Diego Moreno y Fabianesi (81 Sergio Román Sena), Maximiliano Andrés Bustos, Damián Ariel Escudero, Emiliano Ramiro Papa, Mauro Matías Zárate (71 Gustavo Alberto Balvorín). DT: La Volpe

NACIONAL MONTEVIDEO – EMELEC 3-1 (3-0)
Parque Central, Montevideo, 3.04.2007, Referee: Carlos Amarilla (PAR), Attendance: 10.246
NACIONAL: Néstor Fernando Muslera, Pablo Álvarez, Diego Roberto Godín, Jorge Da Rosa, Agustín Viana, Marcelo Fabian Sosa, Marco Eduardo Vanzini (72 Mathías Cardaccio), Javier Omar Delgado, Jorge Andrés Martínez, Carlos Alberto Juárez (72 Andrés Leonardo Márquez), Gonzalo Castro (82 Marcos Marcelo Tejera). DT: Daniel Carreño
EMELEC: Marcelo Ramón Elizaga, Carlos Andrés Quiñónez, Facundo Jesús Corozo, José Luis Quiñónez, Silvano de los Santos Estacio, Jaime Ramiro Caicedo, Luis Guillermo Rivera (59 Jaime Javier Ayoví), Tilson Oswaldo Minda, Michael Antonio Arroyo, Sebastián Hernández (46 Lorenzo Javier Mercado), Lucas Ezequiel Viatri (74 Jerónimo Morales Neumann). DT: Carlos Torres Garcés
Goals: Agustín Viana (19), Javier Omar Delgado (30), Carlos Alberto Juárez (45+1) /
Jerónimo Morales Neumann (90+2).

EMELEC – INTERNACIONAL 1-2 (1-1)
George Capwell, Guayaquil, 10.04.2007, Referee: Víctor Hugo Rivera (PER), Attendance: 5.000
EMELEC: Robert Andrés Angulo, Lorenzo Javier Mercado (76 Facundo Jesús Corozo), Banner Geovanny Caicedo, José Luis Quiñónez, Silvano de los Santos Estacio, Jaime Ramiro Caicedo, Luis Guillermo Rivera, Sebastián Hernández, Michael Antonio Arroyo, Lucas Ezequiel Viatri (61 Jaime Javier Ayoví), Jerónimo Morales Neumann (70 Jorge Washington Ladines). DT: Carlos Torres Garcés
INTERNACIONAL: CLEMER Melo da Silva, Marcos Venâncio de Albuquerque "CEARÁ", Marcos Antonio de Lima "ÍNDIO" (70 EDIGLÉ Quaresma Farías), RUBENS Vanderlei Tavares CARDOSO, WELLINGTON de Oliveira MONTEIRO, Martín Emilio Hidalgo, Emilio Fabián Andrés Vargas, Edimo Ferreira Campos "EDINHO", Fernando Lúcio da Costa "FERNANDÃO", Pedro IARLEY Lima Dantas (83 MICHEL Neves Dias), ALEXANDRE "PATO" Rodrigues da Silva (90 MAYCON Vieira da Silva). DT: Abel Braga
Sent off: Arroyo (87)
Goals: Michael Antonio Arroyo (45) /
Pedro IARLEY Lima Dantas (36), ALEXANDRE "PATO" Rodrigues da Silva (52).

NACIONAL MONTEVIDEO – VÉLEZ SARSFIELD 2-0 (1-0)
Parque Central, Montevideo, 12.04.2007, Referee: Carlos Luis Chandía (CHI), Attendance: 15.000
NACIONAL: Néstor Fernando Muslera, Pablo Álvarez, Diego Jaume, Diego Roberto Godín, Agustín Viana, Marcelo Fabian Sosa, Marco Eduardo Vanzini (50 Mathías Cardaccio), Javier Omar Delgado, Jorge Andrés Martínez, Diego Vera, Gonzalo Castro (78 Marcelo Carlo Broli). DT: Daniel Carreño
VÉLEZ SARSFIELD: Gastón Alejandro Sessa, Mariano Esteban Uglessich, Maximiliano Pellegrino, Hernán Darío Pellerano (46 Emiliano Ramiro Papa), Marco Natanel Torsiglieri, Mario Méndez (78 Sebastián Adolfo Ereros), Iván Diego Moreno y Fabianesi, Maximiliano Andrés Bustos, Damián Ariel Escudero, Ramón Dario Ocampo, Gustavo Alberto Balvorín (46 Sergio Román Sena). DT: Ricardo La Volpe
Goals: Diego Roberto Godín (33), Gonzalo Castro (75).

INTERNACIONAL – NACIONAL MONTEVIDEO 1-0 (0-0)
José Pinheiro Borda, Porto Alegre, 19.04.2007
Referee: Rubén Marcos Selman (CHI), Attendance: 38.853
INTERNACIONAL: CLEMER Melo da Silva, Marcos Venâncio de Albuquerque "CEARÁ", Marcos Antonio de Lima "ÍNDIO", Martín Emilio Hidalgo, RUBENS Vanderlei Tavares CARDOSO (63 Cleiton Eduardo Vicente "PERDIGÃO"), WELLINGTON de Oliveira MONTEIRO, Emilio Fabián Andrés Vargas (70 MICHEL Neves Dias), Edimo Ferreira Campos "EDINHO", Fernando Lúcio da Costa "FERNANDÃO", Pedro IARLEY Lima Dantas, ALEXANDRE "PATO" Rodrigues da Silva. DT: Abel Braga
NACIONAL: Néstor Fernando Muslera, Adrián Marcelo Romero, Diego Jaume, Diego Roberto Godín, Agustín Viana, Pablo Álvarez, Marco Eduardo Vanzini (81 Hugo Diego Arismendi), Marcelo Fabian Sosa, Javier Omar Delgado (46 Mathías Cardaccio), Jorge Andrés Martínez, Gonzalo Castro (56 Diego Vera). DT: Daniel Carreño
Sent off: Índio (65)
Goal: Fernando Lúcio da Costa "FERNANDÃO" (80).

VÉLEZ SARSFIELD – EMELEC 1-0 (0-0)
José Amalfitani, Buenos Aires, 19.04.2007, Referee: Ricardo Grance (PAR), Attendance: 13.000
VÉLEZ SARSFIELD: Gastón Alejandro Sessa, Mariano Esteban Uglessich (46 Ramón Dario Ocampo), Maximiliano Pellegrino, Hernán Darío Pellerano, Marcelo Hernán Bustamante, Mario Méndez, Iván Diego Moreno y Fabianesi (80 Sergio Román Sena), Maximiliano Andrés Bustos, Damián Ariel Escudero, Mauro Matías Zárate, Lucas Martín Castromán (76 Emiliano Ramiro Papa). DT: Ricardo La Volpe
EMELEC: Robert Andrés Angulo, Lorenzo Javier Mercado, Facundo Jesús Corozo, Banner Geovanny Caicedo, Marco Antonio Quiñónez, Silvano de los Santos Estacio, José Luis Quiñónez, Luis Guillermo Rivera (80 Jaime Javier Ayoví), Sebastián Hernández (69 Jerónimo Morales Neumann), Jaime Ramiro Caicedo, Lucas Ezequiel Viatri. DT: Carlos Torres Garcés
Goal: Damián Ariel Escudero (64).

1	VÉLEZ SARSFIELD	6	3	2	1	6	3	11
2	NACIONAL M	6	3	1	2	9	5	10
3	Internacional	6	3	1	2	7	7	10
4	Emelec	6	1	0	5	3	10	3

GROUP 5

BAMIN REAL POTOSÍ – FLAMENGO 2-2 (2-0)
Mario Mercado Vaca Guzmán, Potosí, 14.02.2007
Referee: Víctor Hugo Rivera (PER), Attendance: 15.000
BAMIN REAL: José Pablo Burtovoy, Nicolás Suárez, Edemir Rodríguez, Santos Amador, Gerson Luis García (86 Percy Colque), Luis Gatty Ribeiro, Marco David Paz, Franz Álvaro Calustro (75 Fernando Ariel Brandán), Darwin Peña, Carlos Eduardo "EDÚ" Monteiro, Rubén Darío Aguilera (61 Líder Paz). DT: Félix Berdeja
FLAMENGO: BRUNO Das Dores de Souza, Leonardo da Silva "LEO" MOURA, THIAGO Pimentel Gosling (61 Oswaldo Giroldo Júnior "JUNINHO PAULISTA"), MOISÉS Moura Pinheiro, RONALDO Simões ANGELIM, JUAN Maldonado Jaimez Júnior (46 Roniéliton Pereira Santos "RONI"), Paulo Benedito Maximiano "PAULINHO", CLAITON Alberto dos Santos, Carlos RENATO de Abreu, RENATO Soares de Oliveira AUGUSTO, Manuel de Brito Filho "OBINA" (72 Rodrigo de SOUZA Cardoso). DT: Ney Franco
Goals: Carlos Eduardo "EDÚ" Monteiro (13), Rubén Darío Aguilera (43) /
Roniéliton Pereira Santos "RONI" (48), Manuel de Brito Filho "OBINA" (66).

UNIÓN ATLÉTICO MARACAIBO – PARANÁ CLUBE 2-4 (1-1)
José 'Pachencho' Romero, Maracaibo, 15.02.2007, Referee: Samuel Haro (ECU), Attendance: 12.000
UA MARACAIBO: Gilberto Angelucci, Luis José Vallenilla, Lucas Alfredo Bovaglio, Juan José Fuenmayor, Elvis Alfonso Martínez, Pedro Alfonso Fernández, Miguel Ángel Mea Vitali, Darío Damián Figueroa (58 Emilio Rentería), Gabriel José Urdaneta (75 Wilton Almeida), Cristian Alfonso Cásseres, Daniel Enrique Arismendi (69 Orlando Enrique Ballesteros). DT: Jorge Pellicer
PARANÁ: FLÁVIO Emidio dos Santos Vieira, DANIEL MARQUES da Silva, Anderson da Silva de Jesús "NEGUETE", ANDRÉ LUIZ de Oliveira Regatieri, Clennyson Silva do Nascimento "XAVES", Valberto Amorim Santos "BETO", José GERSON Ramos, DINELSON dos Santos Lima (85 Alexsandro Ferreira "ALEX"), EGÍDIO de Araújo Pereira Júnior, HENRIQUE Dias Carvalho (72 JOELSON dos Santos Silva), JOSIEL da Rocha (79 Rodrigo LIMA dos Santos). DT: Armelino Donizetti Quagliato 'Zetti'
Goals: Daniel Enrique Arismendi (44), Cristian Alfonso Cásseres (66) / JOSIEL da Rocha (38), DINELSON dos Santos Lima (55), HENRIQUE Dias Carvalho (56), José GERSON Ramos (68).

PARANÁ CLUBE – BAMIN REAL POTOSÍ 2-0 (0-0)
Durival Brito e Silva, Curitiba, 21.02.2007, Referee: Saúl Laverni (ARG)
PARANÁ: FLÁVIO Emidio dos Santos Vieira, ANDRÉ LUIZ de Oliveira Regatieri, DANIEL MARQUES da Silva, JOÃO PAULO Pereira Mendes Bersch, EGÍDIO de Araújo Pereira Júnior, Valberto Amorim Santos "BETO", Emerson Bueno dos Santos "GOIANO" (67 VINICIUS Pacheco dos Santos), José GERSON Ramos, DINELSON dos Santos Lima (85 JOELSON dos Santos Silva), JOSIEL da Rocha, HENRIQUE Dias Carvalho (80 Clennyson Silva do Nascimento "XAVES"). DT: Armelino Donizetti Quagliato 'Zetti'
BAMIN REAL: José Pablo Burtovoy, Percy Colque, Nicolás Suárez, Edemir Rodríguez, Santos Amador, Luis Gatty Ribeiro, Marco David Paz, Franz Álvaro Calustro, Darwin Peña, Carlos Eduardo "EDÚ" Monteiro, Líder Paz (67 Fernando Ariel Brandán). DT: Félix Berdeja
Sent off: Paz (60)
Goals: DINELSON dos Santos Lima (62), DANIEL MARQUES da Silva (73).

FLAMENGO – UNIÓN ATLÉTICO MARACAIBO 3-1 (3-0)
Mario Filho 'Maracanã', Río de Janeiro, 21.02.2007, Referee: Enrique Ossés (CHI), Attendance: 31.240
FLAMENGO: BRUNO Das Dores de Souza, Leonardo da Silva "LEO" MOURA, MOISÉS Moura Pinheiro, IRINEU Calixto Couto, JUAN Maldonado Jaimez Júnior, Paulo Benedito Maximiano "PAULINHO" (77 Oswaldo Giroldo Júnior "JUNINHO PAULISTA"), CLAITON Alberto dos Santos, Carlos RENATO de Abreu, RENATO Soares de Oliveira AUGUSTO (76 Leandro SALINO Carmo), Rodrigo de SOUZA Cardoso, Manuel de Brito Filho "OBINA" (67 Roniéliton Pereira Santos "RONI"). DT: Ney Franco

UA MARACAIBO: Gilberto Angelucci, Pedro Alfonso Fernández, Rafael Loreto Mea Vitali, Juan José Fuenmayor, Elvis Alfonso Martínez, Miguel Ángel Mea Vitali, Gabriel José Urdaneta, Vicente Antonio Suanno (46 Darío Damián Figueroa), Andrée Aníbal González, Emilio Rentería (67 Daniel Enrique Arismendi), Cristian Alfonso Cásseres (58 Julio César Laffatigue). DT: Jorge Pellicer
Goals: Carlos RENATO de Abreu (16), Rodrigo de SOUZA Cardoso (36), Manuel de Brito Filho "OBINA" (45) / Daniel Enrique Arismendi (89).

UNIÓN ATLÉTICO MARACAIBO – BAMIN REAL POTOSÍ 1-1 (0-0)
José 'Pachencho' Romero, Maracaibo, 13.03.2007
Referee: Jorge Hernán Hoyos (COL), Attendance: 8.000
UA MARACAIBO: Gilberto Angelucci, Pedro Alfonso Fernández, Rafael Loreto Mea Vitali, Juan José Fuenmayor, Elvis Alfonso Martínez, Andrée Aníbal González (46 Luis José Vallenilla), Miguel Ángel Mea Vitali, Darío Damián Figueroa, Rubén Gastón Galván (70 Julio César Laffatigue), Cristian Alfonso Cásseres, Daniel Enrique Arismendi (32 Orlando Enrique Ballesteros). DT: Jorge Pellicer
BAMIN REAL: José Pablo Burtovoy, Gerson Luis García, Luis Gatty Ribeiro, Edemir Rodríguez, Eduardo Fabiano Ortiz (80 Gerardo César Yecerotte), Nicolás Suárez, Franz Álvaro Calustro, Darwin Peña, Fernando Ariel Brandán (75 Adrián Cuéllar), Rubén Darío Aguilera (73 Carlos Eduardo "EDÚ" Monteiro), Líder Paz. DT: Félix Berdeja
Goals: Pedro Alfonso Fernández (72) / Darwin Peña (64).

PARANÁ CLUBE – FLAMENGO 0-1 (0-1)
Durival Brito e Silva, Curitiba, 14.03.2007
Referee: Leonardo GACIBA da Silva (BRA), Attendance: 15.614
PARANÁ: FLÁVIO Emidio dos Santos Vieira, Anderson da Silva de Jesús "NEGUETE", JOÃO VITOR da Silva (67 JOELSON dos Santos Silva), DANIEL MARQUES da Silva, ANDRÉ LUIZ de Oliveira Regatieri, Clennyson Silva do Nascimento "XAVES" (60 VINICIUS Pacheco dos Santos), Valberto Amorim Santos "BETO", José GERSON Ramos, EGÍDIO de Araújo Pereira Júnior, HENRIQUE Dias Carvalho (66 Rodrigo LIMA dos Santos), JOSIEL da Rocha. DT: Armelino Donizetti Quagliato 'Zetti'
FLAMENGO: BRUNO Das Dores de Souza, Leonardo da Silva "LEO" MOURA, IRINEU Calixto Couto, RONALDO Simões ANGELIM, JUAN Maldonado Jaimez Júnior, Paulo Benedito Maximiano "PAULINHO", Carlos RENATO de Abreu, RENATO Soares de Oliveira AUGUSTO, Oswaldo Giroldo Júnior "JUNINHO PAULISTA" (58 Leandro SALINO Carmo), Roniéliton Pereira Santos "RONI" (87 Leandro Ferreira "LEO" MEDEIROS), Rodrigo de SOUZA Cardoso (77 LEONARDO Gonçalves Silva). DT: Ney Franco
Sent off: Neguete (88)
Goal: Carlos RENATO de Abreu (24).

BAMIN REAL POTOSÍ – UNIÓN ATLÉTICO MARACAIBO 2-2 (2-1)
Mario Mercado Vaca Guzmán, Potosí, 20.03.2007
Referee: José Patricio Carpio (ECU), Attendance: 12.000
BAMIN REAL: José Pablo Burtovoy, Luis Gatty Ribeiro, Edemir Rodríguez, Gerson Luis García, Santos Amador, Franz Álvaro Calustro (58 Líder Paz), Marco David Paz, Nicolás Suárez, Darwin Peña, Carlos Eduardo "EDÚ" Monteiro, Rubén Darío Aguilera (67 Fernando Ariel Brandán). DT: Félix Berdeja
UA MARACAIBO: Manuel Sanhouse, Luis José Vallenilla, Juan José Fuenmayor, Rafael Loreto Mea Vitali, Elvis Alfonso Martínez, Pedro Alfonso Fernández, Miguel Ángel Mea Vitali, Julio César Machado, Rubén Gastón Galván (55 Darío Damián Figueroa), Cristian Alfonso Cásseres (90+1 Julio César Laffatigue), Orlando Enrique Ballesteros (75 Emilio Rentería). DT: Jorge Pellicer
Goals: Carlos Eduardo "EDÚ" Monteiro (12 penalty, 40) / Cristian Alfonso Cásseres (36), Orlando Enrique Ballesteros (55).

FLAMENGO – PARANÁ CLUBE 1-0 (0-0)
Mario Filho 'Maracanã', Río de Janeiro, 21.03.2007, Referee: Carlos Eugênio Simón (BRA)
FLAMENGO: BRUNO Das Dores de Souza, Leonardo da Silva "LEO" MOURA, IRINEU Calixto Couto, RONALDO Simões ANGELIM, JUAN Maldonado Jaimez Júnior, Paulo Benedito Maximiano "PAULINHO", Carlos RENATO de Abreu, RENATO Soares de Oliveira AUGUSTO, Oswaldo Giroldo Júnior "JUNINHO PAULISTA" (89 JAILTON da Cruz Alves), Roniéliton Pereira Santos "RONI" (70 LEONARDO Gonçalves Silva), Rodrigo de SOUZA Cardoso (90 Leandro Ferreira "LEO" MEDEIROS). DT: Ney Franco
PARANÁ: FLÁVIO Emidio dos Santos Vieira, ANDRÉ LUIZ de Oliveira Regatieri, JOÃO PAULO Pereira Mendes Bersch, DANIEL MARQUES da Silva, EGÍDIO de Araújo Pereira Júnior, Clennyson Silva do Nascimento "XAVES", Valberto Amorim Santos "BETO", José GERSON Ramos (69 VINICIUS Pacheco dos Santos), DINELSON dos Santos Lima (79 Rodrigo LIMA dos Santos), HENRIQUE Dias Carvalho (74 Alexsandro Ferreira "ALEX"), JOSIEL da Rocha. DT: Armelino Donizetti Quagliato 'Zetti'
Goal: Rodrigo de SOUZA Cardoso (87).

UNIÓN ATLÉTICO MARACAIBO – FLAMENGO 1-2 (0-1)
José 'Pachencho' Romero, Maracaibo, 4.04.2007
Referee: Víctor Hugo Carrillo (PER), Attendance: 12.000
UA MARACAIBO: Manuel Sanhouse, Elvis Alfonso Martínez (62 Renier Alexander Rodríguez), Juan José Fuenmayor, Rafael Loreto Mea Vitali, Julio César Machado, Miguel Ángel Mea Vitali, Pedro Alfonso Fernández, Luis José Vallenilla (62 Dickson Díaz), Darío Damián Figueroa (69 Guillermo Fabián Beraza), Cristian Alfonso Cásseres, Orlando Enrique Ballesteros. DT: Jorge Pellicer
FLAMENGO: BRUNO Das Dores de Souza, Paulo Benedito Maximiano "PAULINHO", IRINEU Calixto Couto, RONALDO Simões ANGELIM, JUAN Maldonado Jaimez Júnior, Leonardo da Silva "LEO" MOURA, CLAITON Alberto dos Santos (85 MOISÉS Moura Pinheiro), Carlos RENATO de Abreu, RENATO Soares de Oliveira AUGUSTO (90 JAILTON da Cruz Alves), Oswaldo Giroldo Júnior "JUNINHO PAULISTA" (90+2 GERSON Alencar de Lima Júnior), Rodrigo de SOUZA Cardoso. DT: Ney Franco
Sent off: Mea Vitali (90+3)
Goals: Paulo Benedito Maximiano "PAULINHO" (77 own goal) /
Carlos RENATO de Abreu (12), RENATO Soares de Oliveira AUGUSTO (81).

BAMIN REAL POTOSÍ – PARANÁ CLUBE 3-1 (1-1)
Mario Mercado Vaca Guzmán, Potosí, 10.04.2007, Referee: Ricardo Grance (PAR), Attendance: 8.000
BAMIN REAL: José Pablo Burtovoy, Ronald Eguino, Luis Gatty Ribeiro (89 Rubén Darío Aguilera), Edemir Rodríguez (68 Líder Paz), Marco David Paz, Percy Colque, Franz Álvaro Calustro, Nicolás Suárez, Fernando Ariel Brandán, Darwin Peña (79 Gerardo César Yecerotte), Carlos Eduardo "EDÚ" Monteiro. DT: Mauricio Soria
PARANÁ: FLÁVIO Emidio dos Santos Vieira, Antônio Bezerra Brandão "TONINHO", DANIEL MARQUES da Silva, JOÃO PAULO Pereira Mendes Bersch, Emerson Bueno dos Santos "GOIANO" (76 VINICIUS Pacheco dos Santos), Clennyson Silva do Nascimento "XAVES", Valberto Amorim Santos "BETO", José GERSON Ramos (66 Alexsandro Ferreira "ALEX"), EGÍDIO de Araújo Pereira Júnior, DINELSON dos Santos Lima (85 JOELSON dos Santos Silva), HENRIQUE Dias Carvalho. DT: Armelino Donizetti Quagliato 'Zetti'
Goals: Edemir Rodríguez (23), Fernando Ariel Brandán (70), Carlos Eduardo "EDÚ" Monteiro (75) / José GERSON Ramos (29).

FLAMENGO – BAMIN REAL POTOSÍ 1-0 (1-0)
Mario Filho 'Maracanã', Río de Janeiro, 18.04.2007
Referee: Líber Tabare Prudente (URU), Attendance: 14.964
FLAMENGO: BRUNO Das Dores de Souza, Leonardo da Silva "LEO" MOURA, RONALDO Simões ANGELIM, IRINEU Calixto Couto, JUAN Maldonado Jaimez Júnior, Paulo Benedito Maximiano "PAULINHO", CLAITON Alberto dos Santos (77 Leandro SALINO Carmo), Carlos RENATO de

Abreu, RENATO Soares de Oliveira AUGUSTO, Rodrigo de SOUZA Cardoso (46 Leandro Ferreira "LEO" MEDEIROS), Roniéliton Pereira Santos "RONI". DT: Ney Franco
BAMIN REAL: José Pablo Burtovoy, Ronald Eguino, Luis Gatty Ribeiro, Edemir Rodríguez, Marco David Paz (70 Santos Amador), Percy Colque (86 Líder Paz), Franz Álvaro Calustro, Nicolás Suárez, Fernando Ariel Brandán (76 Rubén Darío Aguilera), Darwin Peña, Carlos Eduardo "EDÚ" Monteiro. DT: Mauricio Soria
Goal: Rodrigo de SOUZA Cardoso (12).

PARANÁ CLUBE – UNIÓN ATLÉTICO MARACAIBO 2-1 (2-0)
Durival Brito e Silva, Curitiba, 18.04.2007, Referee: Juan Pablo Pompei (ARG), Attendance: 6.551
PARANÁ: FLÁVIO Emidio dos Santos Vieira, Alexsandro Ferreira "ALEX", DANIEL MARQUES da Silva, JOÃO VITOR da Silva, EGÍDIO de Araújo Pereira Júnior, Clennyson Silva do Nascimento "XAVES", Valberto Amorim Santos "BETO", José GERSON Ramos, DINELSON dos Santos Lima (63 Emerson Bueno dos Santos "GOIANO"), JOSIEL da Rocha (69 Rodrigo LIMA dos Santos), VINICIUS Pacheco dos Santos (87 JOELSON dos Santos Silva). DT: Armelino Donizetti Quagliato 'Zetti'
UA MARACAIBO: Manuel Sanhouse, Renier Alexander Rodríguez, Lucas Alfredo Bovaglio (46 Luis José Vallenilla), Rafael Loreto Mea Vitali, Julio César Machado, Dickson Díaz, Pedro Alfonso Fernández, Gabriel José Urdaneta, Guillermo Fabián Beraza, Emilio Rentería (66 Orlando Enrique Ballesteros), Daniel Enrique Arismendi (66 Cristian Alfonso Cásseres). DT: Jorge Pellicer
Goals: EGÍDIO de Araújo Pereira Júnior (7), Valberto Amorim Santos "BETO" (14) /
Julio César Machado (70).

1	FLAMENGO	6	5	1	0	10	4	16
2	PARANÁ EC	6	3	0	3	9	8	9
3	Bamin Real Potosí	6	1	3	2	8	9	6
4	UA Maracaibo	6	0	2	4	8	14	2

GROUP 6

CARACAS FC – LIGA DEP. UNIVERSITARIA 1-0 (0-0)
Brígido Iriarte, Caracas, 22.02.2007, Referee: Víctor Hugo Carrillo (PER), Attendance: 3.000
CARACAS: Javier Eduardo Toyo, Leonel Vielma, José Manuel Rey, Oswaldo Augusto Vizcarrondo, Edder Alfonso Pérez, Luis Enrique Vera, Jorge Alberto Rojas, César Eduardo González (63 Weymar Franck Olivares), Alejandro Abraham Guerra (88 Enrique Andrés Rouga), Iván Jose Velásquez (61 Rafael Ernesto Castellín), Wilson Alberto Carpintero. DT: Noel Sanvicente
LDU: Cristian Rafael Mora, Jairo Rolando Campos, Norberto Carlos Araujo, Arlín Segundo Ayoví, Enrique Daniel Vera, Patricio Javier Urrutia, Alfonso Andrés Obregón (81 Luis Alberto Bolaños), Paul Vicente Ambrossi, Cristian Rolando Lara, Joffre David Guerrón (70 Franklin Agustín Salas), Luis Miguel Escalada. DT: Edgardo Bauza
Goal: Alejandro Abraham Guerra (75).

COLO COLO SANTIAGO – RIVER PLATE 1-2 (0-1)
Monumental, Santiago, 22.02.2007, Referee: Carlos Manuel Torres (PAR), Attendance: 48.000
COLO COLO: Christian Sebastian Cejas, Miguel Augusto Riffo, Arturo Erasmo Vidal, David Andrés Henríquez, Boris Igor González (57 Luis Arturo Mena), Rodrigo David Meléndez, Héctor Arturo Sanhueza, José Luis Jerez (57 Mario Édison Giménez), Giovanni Hernández, Alexis Alejandro Sánchez (78 Juan Gonzalo Lorca), Humberto Andrés Suazo. DT: Claudio Borghi
RIVER PLATE: Juan Pablo Carrizo, Paulo Andrés Ferrari, Danilo Telmo Gerlo, Nelson Enrique Rivas, Eduardo Nicolás Tuzzio, Diego Alberto Galván (76 Óscar Adrián Ahumada), Leonardo Daniel Ponzio, Fernando Daniel Belluschi, Rubens Oscar Sambueza (66 Víctor Eduardo Zapata), Radamel Falcao García, Ernesto Antonio Fariás. DT: Daniel Passarella
Sent off: Mena (89) / García (63)
Goals: Humberto Andrés Suazo (61) / Leonardo Daniel Ponzio (45+1), Ernesto Antonio Fariás (54).

LIGA DEP. UNIVERSITARIA – COLO COLO SANTIAGO 3-1 (0-1)
La Casa Blanca, Quito, 7.03.2007, Referee: Albert Duarte (COL), Attendance: 15.000
LDU: Cristian Rafael Mora, Enrique Daniel Vera, Arlín Segundo Ayoví, Norberto Carlos Araujo, Paul Vicente Ambrossi, Alfonso Andrés Obregón (63 Luis Alberto Bolaños), Diego Armando Calderón, Pedro Sebastián Larrea (74 Joffre David Guerrón), Cristian Rolando Lara, Franklin Agustín Salas (84 Luis Alberto Ortiz), Luis Miguel Escalada. DT: Edgardo Bauza
COLO COLO: Christian Sebastian Cejas, Miguel Augusto Riffo, Arturo Erasmo Vidal, David Andrés Henríquez, Gonzalo Antonio Fierro, Rodrigo David Meléndez, Héctor Arturo Sanhueza, José Luis Jerez (58 Boris Igor González), Giovanni Hernández (81 Juan Gonzalo Lorca), Alexis Alejandro Sánchez (72 Mario Édison Giménez), Humberto Andrés Suazo. DT: Claudio Borghi
Sent off: Lara (80) / Henríquez (74)
Goals: Alfonso Andrés Obregón (46), Franklin Agustín Salas (74 penalty), Joffre David Guerrón (85) / Humberto Andrés Suazo (32).

RIVER PLATE – CARACAS FC 0-1 (0-1)
Antonio V. Liberti 'Monumental', Buenos Aires, 8.03.2007, Referee: Pablo Antonio Pozo (CHI)
RIVER PLATE: Juan Pablo Carrizo, Paulo Andrés Ferrari (84 Andrés Lorenzo Ríos), Danilo Telmo Gerlo, Nelson Enrique Rivas, Eduardo Nicolás Tuzzio, Diego Alberto Galván (46 Augusto Matías Fernández), Óscar Adrián Ahumada, Fernando Daniel Belluschi, Víctor Eduardo Zapata (75 Rubens Oscar Sambueza), Ernesto Antonio Fariás, Marco Gastón Rubén. DT: Daniel Passarella
CARACAS: Javier Eduardo Toyo, Leonel Vielma, José Manuel Rey, Oswaldo Augusto Vizcarrondo, Edder Alfonso Pérez (66 Enrique Andrés Rouga), Luis Enrique Vera, Jorge Alberto Rojas, Alejandro Abraham Guerra, César Eduardo González (86 Jaime Andrés Bustamante), Iván Jose Velásquez (71 Franklin José Lucena), Wilson Alberto Carpintero. DT: Noel Sanvicente
Goal: Iván Jose Velásquez (9).

LIGA DEP. UNIVERSITARIA – RIVER PLATE 1-1 (1-0)
La Casa Blanca, Quito, 15.03.2007, Referee: Carlos Luis Chandía (CHI), Attendance: 24.135
LDU: Cristian Rafael Mora, Enrique Daniel Vera, Arlín Segundo Ayoví, Norberto Carlos Araujo, Paul Vicente Ambrossi, Diego Armando Calderón, Alfonso Andrés Obregón (56 Joffre David Guerrón), Pedro Sebastián Larrea (81 Ángel Enrique Pután), Luis Alberto Bolaños (66 José Nicolás Vizcarra), Franklin Agustín Salas, Luis Miguel Escalada. DT: Edgardo Bauza
RIVER PLATE: Juan Pablo Carrizo, Paulo Andrés Ferrari, Danilo Telmo Gerlo, Federico Guillermo Lussenhoff, Cristián Carlos Villagra, Fernando Daniel Belluschi, Leonardo Daniel Ponzio (89 Víctor Eduardo Zapata), Óscar Adrián Ahumada, Rubens Oscar Sambueza, Ernesto Antonio Fariás, Marco Gastón Rubén (73 René Martín Lima). DT: Daniel Passarella
Sent off: Escalada (49) / Sambueza (40)
Goals: Enrique Daniel Vera (15) / Ernesto Antonio Fariás (54).

CARACAS FC – COLO COLO SANTIAGO 0-4 (0-2)
General Santander, Cúcuta (COL), 20.03.2007
Referee: José Hernando Buitrago (COL), Attendance: 8.000
CARACAS: Javier Eduardo Toyo, Leonel Vielma, José Manuel Rey, Oswaldo Augusto Vizcarrondo (46 Franklin José Lucena), Edder Alfonso Pérez, Luis Enrique Vera, Jorge Alberto Rojas, César Eduardo González (67 Rafael Ernesto Castellín), Alejandro Abraham Guerra, Iván Jose Velásquez (63 Habinson Escobar), Wilson Alberto Carpintero. DT: Noel Sanvicente
COLO COLO: Christian Sebastian Cejas, Luis Arturo Mena, Miguel Augusto Riffo, Arturo Erasmo Vidal, Moisés Fermin Villarroel, Rodrigo David Meléndez, José Luis Jerez (87 Gerson Elías Acevedo), Gonzalo Antonio Fierro, Giovanni Hernández (82 Rodrigo Javier Millar), Alexis Alejandro Sánchez, Mario Édison Giménez (53 Gonzalo Alejandro Jara). DT: Claudio Borghi
Goals: Alexis Alejandro Sánchez (21, 60, 88), Mario Édison Giménez (27).

RIVER PLATE – LIGA DEP. UNIVERSITARIA 0-0
Antonio V. Liberti 'Monumental', Buenos Aires, 29.03.2007
Referee: Carlos Eugênio Simón (BRA), Attendance: 15.707
RIVER PLATE: Juan Pablo Carrizo, Paulo Andrés Ferrari, Danilo Telmo Gerlo, Nelson Enrique Rivas, Cristián Carlos Villagra, Fernando Daniel Belluschi, Augusto Matías Fernández, Leonardo Daniel Ponzio, Víctor Eduardo Zapata, Ernesto Antonio Fariás (71 Marco Gastón Rubén), Mauro Damián Rosales (82 Ariel Arnaldo Ortega). DT: Daniel Passarella
LDU: Cristian Rafael Mora, Arlín Segundo Ayoví, Norberto Carlos Araujo, Jairo Rolando Campos, Luis Alberto Bolaños (62 Joffre David Guerrón), Pedro Sebastián Larrea (79 Alfonso Andrés Obregón), Enrique Daniel Vera, Diego Armando Calderón, Paul Vicente Ambrossi, Franklin Agustín Salas (86 José Nicolás Vizcarra), Cristian Rolando Lara. DT: Edgardo Bauza

COLO COLO SANTIAGO – CARACAS FC 2-1 (1-0)
Monumental, Santiago, 30.03.2007, Referee: Manuel Alejandro Garay (PER), Attendance: 11.310
COLO COLO: Christian Sebastian Cejas, Miguel Augusto Riffo, Luis Arturo Mena, Arturo Erasmo Vidal, Gonzalo Antonio Fierro, Rodrigo David Meléndez, Moisés Fermin Villarroel (75 Rodrigo Javier Millar), José Luis Jerez (55 Héctor Arturo Sanhueza), Giovanni Hernández, Alexis Alejandro Sánchez, Mario Édison Giménez (55 Humberto Andrés Suazo). DT: Claudio Borghi
CARACAS: Javier Eduardo Toyo, Leonel Vielma, José Manuel Rey, Enrique Andrés Rouga, Edder Alfonso Pérez , Luis Enrique Vera, Jorge Alberto Rojas, Alejandro Abraham Guerra (84 Franklin José Lucena), César Eduardo González (68 Weymar Franck Olivares), Wilson Alberto Carpintero, Iván Jose Velásquez (46 Habinson Escobar). DT: Noel Sanvicente
Goals: Gonzalo Antonio Fierro (43), Humberto Andrés Suazo (90+2 penalty) /
César Eduardo González (67).

COLO COLO SANTIAGO – LIGA DEP. UNIVERSITARIA 4-0 (0-0)
Monumental, Santiago, 3.04.2007, Referee: Roberto Carlos Silvera (URU)
COLO COLO: Christian Sebastian Cejas, Miguel Augusto Riffo, Luis Arturo Mena, Arturo Erasmo Vidal (80 Gonzalo Alejandro Jara), Gonzalo Antonio Fierro, Héctor Arturo Sanhueza, Rodrigo David Meléndez, José Luis Jerez, Giovanni Hernández (87 Moisés Fermin Villarroel), Humberto Andrés Suazo, Alexis Alejandro Sánchez (77 Rodrigo Javier Millar). DT: Claudio Borghi
LDU: Cristian Rafael Mora, Jairo Rolando Campos, Norberto Carlos Araujo, Arlín Segundo Ayoví, Enrique Daniel Vera (34 Luis Alberto Bolaños), Paul Vicente Ambrossi, Pedro Sebastián Larrea, Diego Armando Calderón (57 Joffre David Guerrón), Cristian Rolando Lara (77 Luis Alberto Ortiz), Luis Miguel Escalada, Franklin Agustín Salas. DT: Edgardo Bauza
Goals: Gonzalo Antonio Fierro (50 penalty, 72), Humberto Andrés Suazo (65),
Rodrigo Javier Millar (78).

CARACAS FC – RIVER PLATE 3-1 (3-1)
General Santander, Cúcuta (COL), 5.04.2007
Referee: Jorge Luis Larrionda (URU), Attendance: 20.000
CARACAS: Javier Eduardo Toyo, Leonel Vielma, José Manuel Rey, Oswaldo Augusto Vizcarrondo, Enrique Andrés Rouga, Franklin José Lucena, Weymar Franck Olivares, Alejandro Abraham Guerra (87 José Caraballo), César Eduardo González (46 Bremer Alfredo Piñango), Wilson Alberto Carpintero, Habinson Escobar (67 Jaime Andrés Bustamante). DT: Noel Sanvicente
RIVER PLATE: Juan Pablo Carrizo, Paulo Andrés Ferrari, Danilo Telmo Gerlo, Nelson Enrique Rivas, Cristián Carlos Villagra, Fernando Daniel Belluschi, Augusto Matías Fernández, Leonardo Daniel Ponzio (82 René Martín Lima), Víctor Eduardo Zapata, Ernesto Antonio Fariás (73 Diego Alberto Galván), Mauro Damián Rosales (46 Marco Gastón Rubén). DT: Daniel Passarella
Sent off: Lucena (42) / Zapata (42)
Goals: José Manuel Rey (15), Habinson Escobar (32, 36) / Ernesto Antonio Fariás (28).

LIGA DEP. UNIVERSITARIA – CARACAS FC 3-1 (2-0)
La Casa Blanca, Quito, 25.04.2007, Referee: Georges Buckley (PER), Attendance: 2.000
LDU: Cristian Rafael Mora, Jairo Rolando Campos, Renán Calle (69 Norberto Carlos Araujo), Diego Armando Calderón, Enrique Daniel Vera, Patricio Javier Urrutia, Pedro Sebastián Larrea, Luis Alberto Bolaños (77 Alfonso Andrés Obregón), Paul Vicente Ambrossi, Joffre David Guerrón (73 Ángel Enrique Pután), Orlando Ayovi. DT: Edgardo Bauza
CARACAS: Javier Eduardo Toyo, Leonel Vielma, Enrique Andrés Rouga, Jaime Andrés Bustamante, Jobanny De Jesús Rivero (46 Oswaldo Augusto Vizcarrondo), Bremer Alfredo Piñango (46 César Eduardo González), Weymar Franck Olivares, José Caraballo (69 Luis Enrique Vera), Jorge Alberto Rojas, Habinson Escobar, Wilson Alberto Carpintero. DT: Noel Sanvicente
Goals: Orlando Ayovi (23), Jairo Rolando Campos (40), Joffre David Guerrón (55) / César Eduardo González (63).

RIVER PLATE – COLO COLO SANTIAGO 1-0 (0-0)
Antonio V. Liberti 'Monumental', Buenos Aires, 25.04.2007, Referee: Paulo César De Oliveira (BRA)
RIVER PLATE: Juan Marcelo Ojeda, Danilo Telmo Gerlo, Nelson Enrique Rivas, Federico Guillermo Lussenhoff, Cristián Carlos Villagra (68 Paulo Andrés Ferrari), Óscar Adrián Ahumada (46 Fernando Daniel Belluschi), Diego Alberto Galván, Rubens Oscar Sambueza, Ariel Arnaldo Ortega, Marco Antonio Rubén (46 René Martín Lima), Andrés Lorenzo Ríos. DT: Daniel Passarella
COLO COLO: Christian Sebastian Cejas, Rodrigo David Meléndez, Arturo Erasmo Vidal, Gonzalo Alejandro Jara (70 Juan Pablo Areñas), Moisés Fermin Villarroel, Héctor Arturo Sanhueza, Gonzalo Antonio Fierro, José Luis Jerez (64 Gerson Elías Acevedo), Rodrigo Javier Millar, Mario Édison Giménez (64 Juan Gonzalo Lorca), Humberto Andrés Suazo. DT: Claudio Borghi
Goal: Diego Alberto Galván (62).

1	COLO COLO	6	3	0	3	12	7	9
2	CARACAS FC	6	3	0	3	7	10	9
3	LDU de Quito	6	2	2	2	7	8	8
4	River Plate	6	2	2	2	5	6	8

GROUP 7

BOLÍVAR LA PAZ – BOCA JUNIORS 0-0
Hernando Siles, La Paz, 16.02.2007, Referee: Ricardo Grance (PAR), Attendance: 3.413
BOLÍVAR: Joel Fernando Zayas, Zackary Flores, Juan Doyle Vaca, Carlos Hugo Tordoya, Ignacio Awad García, Leonel Alfredo Reyes, Gabriel Alejandro Viglianti, THIAGO Leitão Polieri, Julio César Baldivieso, Carlos Saucedo (70 Justo Rolando Meza), Luis Hernán Sillero. DT: Víctor Hugo Antelo
BOCA JUNIORS: Mauricio Ariel Caranta, Hugo Benjamín Ibarra, Claudio Marcelo Morel, Sebastián Alejandro Battaglia, Jonathan Ramón Maidana, Daniel Alberto Díaz, Sergio Daniel Orteman, Neri Raúl Cardozo (84 Guillermo Barros Schelotto), Ever Maximiliano David Banega (69 Pablo Martín Ledesma), Martín Palermo, Rodrigo Sebastián Palacio (62 Bruno Marioni). DT: Miguel Ángel Russo

CIENCIANO – CD TOLUCA 1-2 (1-0)
Inca Gracilaso de la Vega, Cusco, 21.02.2007, Referee: Mauricio Javier Reinoso (ECU)
CIENCIANO: Juan Ángel Flores, Paolo Giancarlo De La Haza, Nicolás Osvaldo Pisano, Juan Francisco Hernández, Carlos Oswaldo Fernández, Juan Carlos Bazalar, Juan Carlos Mariño, Julio Edson Uribe (62 Guillermo Alejandro Guizasola), Julio César García (46 Miguel Ángel Mostto), Miguel Ángel Torres, Rodrigo Alonso Saraz (46 Jaime Alfonso Ruiz). DT: Julio César Uribe
CD TOLUCA: César Amado Lozano, Jonathan Arias, Manuel Alejandro De la Torre, Carlos Esquivel, José Manuel Cruzalta (46 Juan Carlos Núñez), Erik Osvaldo Espinosa, Miguel Ángel Almazán, Josué Castillejos (62 Moisés Adrián Velasco), José García, Diego Javier De La Torre, Ismael Valadez (82 Emilio Hassan Viades). DT: Pablo Marino
Goals: Juan Francisco Hernández (37) / Diego Javier De La Torre (71), Moisés Adrián Velasco (87).

CD TOLUCA – BOLÍVAR LA PAZ 1-2 (1-0)
Nemesio Díaz, Toluca, 27.02.2007, Referee: Manuel Candelario Andarcia (VEN)
CD TOLUCA: Rolando Hernán Cristante, Paulo César Da Silva, Miguel Ángel Almazán, Manuel Alejandro De la Torre, Sergio Amaury Ponce (61 Ismael Valadez), Ariel Javier Rosada, Vicente Martín Sánchez, Antonio Naelson Matías "ZINHA", Diego Javier De La Torre, Carlos Esquivel, Érwin Lorenzo Ávalos (46 Moisés Adrián Velasco). DT: Américo Gallego
BOLÍVAR: Joel Fernando Zayas, Diego Esteban Salvatierra, Carlos Hugo Tordoya, Ariel Juárez, Ignacio Awad García, Rubén Melgar (88 Carlos Oswaldo Camacho), Gabriel Alejandro Viglianti, Leonel Alfredo Reyes, Adalberto Cuéllar (67 Justo Rolando Meza), Luis Hernán Sillero (90+1 Ovidio Guatía), THIAGO Leitão Polieri. DT: Víctor Hugo Antelo
Goals: Paulo César Da Silva (2) / Gabriel Alejandro Viglianti (55), Luis Hernán Sillero (58).

BOCA JUNIORS – CIENCIANO 1-0 (0-0)
Pedro Bidegain, Buenos Aires, 1.03.2007, Referee: Héber Roberto Lopes (BRA), Attendance: 11.800
BOCA JUNIORS: Mauricio Ariel Caranta, Hugo Benjamín Ibarra, Jonathan Ramón Maidana, Daniel Alberto Díaz, Claudio Marcelo Morel (85 Clemente Juan Rodríguez), Sergio Daniel Orteman (68 Guillermo Andrés Marino), Ever Maximiliano David Banega, Neri Raúl Cardozo (90 Pablo Martín Ledesma), Juan Román Riquelme, Bruno Marioni, Martín Palermo. DT: Miguel Ángel Russo
CIENCIANO: Juan Ángel Flores, Paolo Giancarlo De La Haza, Nicolás Osvaldo Pisano, Juan Francisco Hernández, Carlos Oswaldo Fernández (46 Édgar Harry Villamarín), Miguel Ángel Torres (46 Miguel Ángel Mostto), Juan Carlos Bazalar, Julio César García, Julio Edson Uribe (67 Miguel Ángel Huertas), Juan Carlos Mariño, Rodrigo Alonso Saraz. DT: Julio César Uribe
Sent off: Mariano (81)
Goal: Hugo Benjamín Ibarra (81).

CIENCIANO – BOLÍVAR LA PAZ 5-1 (0-1)
Inca Gracilaso de la Vega, Cusco, 8.03.2007, Referee: Samuel Haro (ECU)
CIENCIANO: Juan Ángel Flores, Édgar Harry Villamarín, Juan Francisco Hernández, Nicolás Osvaldo Pisano, Paolo Giancarlo De La Haza, Juan Carlos Bazalar, Julio César García (64 William Medardo Chiroque), Julio Edson Uribe, Juan Carlos Mariño, Miguel Ángel Torres (36 Miguel Ángel Mostto), Rodrigo Alonso Saraz (46 Jaime Alfonso Ruiz). DT: Julio César Uribe
BOLÍVAR: Joel Fernando Zayas, Ariel Juárez (80 Carlos Saucedo), Diego Esteban Salvatierra (75 Faustino Abraham García), Carlos Hugo Tordoya, Ignacio Awad García, THIAGO Leitão Polieri, Gabriel Alejandro Viglianti, Leonel Alfredo Reyes, Rubén Melgar, Luis Hernán Sillero, Adalberto Cuéllar (66 Julio César Baldivieso). DT: Víctor Hugo Antelo
Sent off: Melgar (68)
Goals: Miguel Ángel Mostto (63, 79), Juan Carlos Mariño (69 penalty, 82), Jaime Alfonso Ruiz (88) / Adalberto Cuéllar (16).

CD TOLUCA – BOCA JUNIORS 2-0 (1-0)
Nemesio Díaz, Toluca, 14.03.2007, Referee: Jorge Luis Larrionda (URU)
CD TOLUCA: Rolando Hernán Cristante, Paulo César Da Silva, José Manuel Cruzalta, Emilio Hassan Viades (57 Jonathan Arias), Ariel Javier Rosada, Sergio Amaury Ponce (64 Carlos Esquivel), Carlos Adrián Morales, Erik Osvaldo Espinosa, Diego Javier De La Torre, Antonio Naelson Matías "ZINHA" (76 Érwin Lorenzo Ávalos), Vicente Martín Sánchez. DT: Américo Gallego
BOCA JUNIORS: Mauricio Ariel Caranta, Hugo Benjamín Ibarra, Jonathan Ramón Maidana, Daniel Alberto Díaz, Pablo Martín Ledesma, Claudio Marcelo Morel (72 Clemente Juan Rodríguez), Sebastián Alejandro Battaglia (84 Sergio Daniel Orteman), Ever Maximiliano David Banega, Neri Raúl Cardozo, Mauro Boselli (24 Matías Agustín Silvestre), Bruno Marioni. DT: Miguel Ángel Russo
Sent off: Cata Díaz (22)
Goals: Sergio Amaury Ponce (7), Vicente Martín Sánchez (57).

BOCA JUNIORS – CD TOLUCA 3-0 (2-0)
José Amalfitani, Buenos Aires, 22.03.2007, Referee: Carlos Amarilla (PAR), Attendance: 25.000
BOCA JUNIORS: Mauricio Ariel Caranta, Hugo Benjamín Ibarra, Jonathan Ramón Maidana, Claudio Marcelo Morel, Clemente Juan Rodríguez, Pablo Martín Ledesma, Ever Maximiliano David Banega, Neri Raúl Cardozo (84 Jesús Alberto Dátolo), Juan Román Riquelme, Marcos Gustavo Mondaini (75 Bruno Marioni), Martín Palermo (82 Mauro Boselli). DT: Miguel Ángel Russo
CD TOLUCA: Rolando Hernán Cristante, Sergio Amaury Ponce, José Manuel Cruzalta, Paulo César Da Silva, Jonathan Arias (46 Miguel Ángel Almazán), Erik Osvaldo Espinosa, Carlos Adrián Morales (59 Carlos Esquivel), Ariel Javier Rosada, Antonio Naelson Matías "ZINHA", Diego Javier De La Torre (66 Érwin Lorenzo Ávalos), Vicente Martín Sánchez. DT: Américo Gallego
Sent off: Cruzalta (40)
Goals: Jonathan Ramón Maidana (15), Juan Román Riquelme (23), Mauro Boselli (82).

BOLÍVAR LA PAZ – CIENCIANO 2-3 (1-1)
Hernando Siles, La Paz, 28.03.2007, Referee: Saúl Laverni (ARG), Attendance: 10.000
BOLÍVAR: Joel Fernando Zayas, Ariel Juárez (88 Rudy David Montaño), Carlos Hugo Tordoya, Juan Doyle Vaca, Carlos Oswaldo Camacho, Leonel Alfredo Reyes, Diego Esteban Salvatierra (46 Zackary Flores), Gabriel Alejandro Viglianti, THIAGO Leitão Polieri, Faustino Abraham García (53 Adalberto Cuéllar), Carlos Saucedo. DT: Víctor Hugo Antelo
CIENCIANO: Juan Ángel Flores, Cristian Guevara (56 Carlos Oswaldo Fernández), Guillermo Alejandro Guizasola, Nicolás Osvaldo Pisano, Javier Salazar, Juan Carlos Bazalar, Paolo Giancarlo De La Haza, William Medardo Chiroque (67 Julio Edson Uribe), Juan Carlos Mariño, Juan Diego GONZÁLEZ VIGIL, Miguel Ángel Mostto (75 Jaime Alfonso Ruiz). DT: José Basualdo
Goals: THIAGO Leitão Polieri (12, 66) / Juan Carlos Mariño (33), Juan Diego González Vigil (63), Julio Edson Uribe (81 penalty).

CIENCIANO – BOCA JUNIORS 3-0 (0-0)
Inca Gracilaso de la Vega, Cusco, 4.04.2007, Referee: Óscar Julián Ruiz (COL), Attendance: 40.000
CIENCIANO: Juan Ángel Flores, Nicolás Osvaldo Pisano, Javier Salazar, Édgar Harry Villamarín, Cristian Guevara (59 Miguel Ángel Torres), Juan Carlos Bazalar, Paolo Giancarlo De La Haza, Juan Carlos Mariño (23 Carlos Oswaldo Fernández), Miguel Ángel Mostto, William Medardo Chiroque (68 Miguel Ángel Huertas), Juan Diego GONZÁLEZ VIGIL. DT: José Basualdo
BOCA JUNIORS: Mauricio Ariel Caranta, Daniel Alberto Díaz, Claudio Marcelo Morel, Jonathan Ramón Maidana (81 Matías Agustín Silvestre), Clemente Juan Rodríguez, Sebastián Alejandro Battaglia (72 Jesús Alberto Dátolo), Pablo Martín Ledesma, Neri Raúl Cardozo, Sergio Daniel Orteman (64 Ever Maximiliano David Banega), Bruno Marioni, Mauro Boselli. DT: Miguel Ángel Russo
Sent off: Mostto (83) / Cardozo (38)
Goals: Juan Diego González Vigil (48), Miguel Ángel Mostto (79), Miguel Ángel Torres (90+1).

BOLÍVAR LA PAZ – CD TOLUCA 0-2 (0-1)
Hernando Siles, La Paz, 12.04.2007, Referee: Antonio Javier Arias (PAR), Attendance: 45.000
BOLÍVAR: Joel Fernando Zayas, Ariel Juárez, Juan Doyle Vaca, Carlos Hugo Tordoya, Carlos Oswaldo Camacho, Leonel Alfredo Reyes, Diego Esteban Salvatierra (65 Justo Rolando Meza), Gabriel Alejandro Viglianti, THIAGO Leitão Polieri, Rubén Melgar (83 Adalberto Cuéllar), Carlos Saucedo. DT: Marco Antonio Sandy
CD TOLUCA: Rolando Hernán Cristante, Paulo César Da Silva, Jonathan Arias, Emilio Hassan Viades, Sergio Amaury Ponce, Erik Osvaldo Espinosa, Ariel Javier Rosada, Antonio Naelson Matías "ZINHA" (63 Josué Castillejos), Diego Javier De La Torre (68 Manuel Alejandro De la Torre), Carlos Esquivel (82 Érwin Lorenzo Ávalos), Vicente Martín Sánchez. DT: Américo Gallego
Goals: Sergio Amaury Ponce (14), Vicente Martín Sánchez (88).

CD TOLUCA – CIENCIANO 3-0 (1-0)
Nemesio Díaz, Toluca, 26.04.2007, Referee: Carlos Luis Chandía (CHI)
CD TOLUCA: Rolando Hernán Cristante, José Manuel Cruzalta, Paulo César Da Silva, Emilio Hassan Viades, Ariel Javier Rosada, Sergio Amaury Ponce, Antonio Naelson Matías "ZINHA", Carlos Adrián

Morales (80 Erik Osvaldo Espinosa), Carlos Esquivel (78 Manuel Alejandro De la Torre), Diego Javier De La Torre (75 Érwin Lorenzo Ávalos), Vicente Martín Sánchez. DT: Américo Gallego
CIENCIANO: Juan Ángel Flores, Cristian Guevara (62 Guillermo Alejandro Guizasola), Nicolás Osvaldo Pisano, Édgar Harry Villamarín, Paolo Giancarlo De La Haza, Javier Salazar, Juan Carlos Bazalar, William Medardo Chiroque, Miguel Ángel Torres, Rodrigo Alonso Saraz (52 Jaime Alfonso Ruiz), Juan Diego GONZÁLEZ VIGIL. DT: José Basualdo
Goals: Carlos Adrián Morales (32 penalty, 48), Vicente Martín Sánchez (70).

BOCA JUNIORS – BOLÍVAR LA PAZ 7-0 (3-0)
José Amalfitani, Buenos Aires, 26.04.2007, Referee: Ricardo Grance (PAR), Attendance: 38.000
BOCA JUNIORS: Mauricio Ariel Caranta, Hugo Benjamín Ibarra, Daniel Alberto Díaz, Claudio Marcelo Morel, Clemente Juan Rodríguez, Pablo Martín Ledesma, Ever Maximiliano David Banega, Jesús Alberto Dátolo, Juan Román Riquelme (75 Guillermo Andrés Marino), Rodrigo Sebastián Palacio (63 Bruno Marioni), Martín Palermo (63 Mauro Boselli). DT: Miguel Ángel Russo
BOLÍVAR: Joel Fernando Zayas, Carlos Hugo Tordoya, Juan Doyle Vaca, Diego Esteban Salvatierra, Ariel Juárez, Carlos Oswaldo Camacho, Leonel Alfredo Reyes, Rubén Melgar, Juan Enrique Bustillos, THIAGO Leitão Polieri (46 Gabriel Alejandro Viglianti), Carlos Saucedo (70 Luis Hernán Sillero). DT: Marco Antonio Sandy
Goals: Rodrigo Sebastián Palacio (32, 45), Martín Palermo (37 penalty),
Carlos Hugo Tordoya (51 own goal), Jesús Alberto Dátolo (57), Bruno Marioni (64, 85).

1	CD TOLUCA	6	4	0	2	10	6	12
2	BOCA JUNIORS	6	3	1	2	11	5	10
3	Cienciano	6	3	0	3	12	9	9
4	Bolívar	6	1	1	4	5	18	4

GROUP 8

DEFENSOR SPORTING–GIMNASIA y ESGRIMA LA PLATA 3-0 (1-0)
Centenario, Montevideo, 13.02.2007, Referee: Pablo Antonio Pozo (CHI), Attendance: 7.385
DEFENSOR SPORTING: Martín Silva, Gonzalo Matías Maulella, Williams Guillermo Martínez, José Martín Cáceres, Álvaro Rafael González, Victorio Maximiliano Pereira (74 Carlos Díaz), Fernando Fadeuille (68 Miguel Ángel Amado), Sergio Sebastián Ariosa, Diego Alejandro De Souza, Mauro Adrián Vila, Carlos María Morales (76 Sebastián Bruno Fernández). DT: Jorge Da Silva
GIMNASIA Y ESGRIMA: Carlos José Kletnicki, Germán Rodrigo Basualdo, Diego Armando Herner, Jorge Héctor San Esteban, Lucas León Landa, Álvaro Andrés Ormeño (46 Antonio Piergüidi), Ignacio Piatti, Matías Leonardo Escobar, Héctor Daniel Romero (46 Jonathan Daniel Chávez), Antonio Pacheco (51 Luciano Félix Leguizamón), Santiago Martín Silva. DT: Pedro Troglio
Goals: Sergio Sebastián Ariosa (36), Carlos María Morales (63), Victorio Maximiliano Pereira (72).

DEPORTIVO PASTO – SANTOS FC 0-1 (0-0)
Libertad, Pasto, 21.02.2007, Referee: Manuel Candelario Andarcia (VEN), Attendance: 12.000
DEPORTIVO PASTO: Carlos Alberto Barahona, Jamell Orlando Ramos, José Hermes Mera, Wilmer Díaz, Fernando Monroy, Jhon Alexander Jaramillo, Harold Antonio Rodríguez (66 Rolan De La Cruz), Jorge Hernando Vidal, Ferley Raúl Villamil (70 Luis Omar Valencia), Juan Enrique García (65 Oscar Darío Martínez), Carlos Andrés Rodas. DT: Álvaro de Jesús Gómez
SANTOS: FÁBIO COSTA, PEDRO Alves da Silva, ADAÍLTON José dos Santos Filho, ANTÔNIO CARLOS Zago, Cristiano Espíndola de ÁVALOS, KLÉBER de Carvalho Corrêa, Claudio Andrés del Transito Maldonado, CLÉBER SANTANA Loureiro, José "ZÉ" ROBERTO da Silva Júnior (78 Pedro Paulo de Oliveira "PEDRINHO"), MARCOS AURÉLIO de Oliveira Lima (65 JONAS Gonçalves Oliveira), RODRIGO "TIUÍ" Bonifácio da Rocha (85 RODRIGO Barbosa TABATA). DT: Vanderlei Luxemburgo
Goal: Claudio Andrés del Transito Maldonado (61).

SANTOS FC – DEFENSOR SPORTING 1-0 (0-0)
Urbano Caldeira, Santos, 1.03.2007, Referee: Héctor Walter Baldassi (ARG), Attendance: 9.409
SANTOS: FÁBIO COSTA, DÊNIS Oliveira de Souza, ADAÍLTON José dos Santos Filho, ANTÔNIO CARLOS Zago, KLÉBER de Carvalho Corrêa, RODRIGO Ribeiro SOUTO, Claudio Andrés del Transito Maldonado, José "ZÉ" ROBERTO da Silva Júnior, CLÉBER SANTANA Loureiro (71 Cristiano Espíndola de ÁVALOS), MARCOS AURÉLIO de Oliveira Lima (87 JONAS Gonçalves Oliveira), RODRIGO "TIUÍ" Bonifácio da Rocha (72 Pedro Paulo de Oliveira "PEDRINHO").
DEFENSOR SPORTING: Martín Silva, Ignacio Ithurralde, Williams Guillermo Martínez, José Martín Cáceres, Carlos Díaz (77 Carlos María Morales), Victorio Maximiliano Pereira (65 Diego Alejandro De Souza), Fernando Fadeuille, Álvaro Rafael González, Paulo César Pezzolano (65 Sergio Sebastián Ariosa), Sebastián Bruno Fernández, Danilo Javier Peinado. DT: Jorge Da Silva
Goal: José "ZÉ" ROBERTO da Silva Júnior (48).

GIMNASIA Y ESGRIMA LA PLATA – DEPORTIVO PASTO 3-2 (1-1)
Ciudad de La Plata, La Plata, 6.03.2007, Referee: Rubén Marcos Selman (CHI), Attendance: 22.000
GIMNASIA Y ESGRIMA: Carlos José Kletnicki, Germán Rodrigo Basualdo, Gustavo Adrián Semino, Lucas León Landa, Héctor Daniel Romero (73 Álvaro Andrés Ormeño), Ignacio Piatti, Reinaldo Andrés Alderete, Oscar Roberto Cornejo, Antonio Pacheco (88 Jorge Héctor San Esteban), Antonio Piergüidi, Sergio William Leal (73 Santiago Martín Silva). DT: Pedro Troglio
DEPORTIVO PASTO: Carlos Alberto Barahona, Jamell Orlando Ramos, José Hermes Mera, Wilmer Díaz, Fernando Monroy, Jhon Alexander Jaramillo, Harold Antonio Rodríguez, Jorge Hernando Vidal, Ferley Raúl Villamil (64 Luis Omar Valencia), Carlos Andrés Rodas, Juan Enrique García (69 Oscar Darío Martínez). DT: Álvaro de Jesús Gómez
Goals: Sergio William Leal (28), Antonio Pacheco (49), Antonio Piergüidi (86) /
Carlos Andrés Rodas (19), Luis Omar Valencia (70).

SANTOS FC – GIMNASIA Y ESGRIMA LA PLATA 3-0 (1-0)
Urbano Caldeira, Santos, 14.03.2007, Referee: Ricardo Grance (PAR), Attendance: 6.855
SANTOS: FÁBIO COSTA, DÊNIS Oliveira de Souza, ADAÍLTON José dos Santos Filho, ANTÔNIO CARLOS Zago, KLÉBER de Carvalho Corrêa, RODRIGO Ribeiro SOUTO, Claudio Andrés del Transito Maldonado, CLÉBER SANTANA Loureiro (77 Pedro Paulo de Oliveira "PEDRINHO"), José "ZÉ" ROBERTO da Silva Júnior, MARCOS AURÉLIO de Oliveira Lima (70 RODRIGO Barbosa TABATA), RODRIGO "TIUÍ" Bonifácio da Rocha (59 Cristiano Espíndola de ÁVALOS). DT: Vanderlei Luxemburgo
GIMNASIA Y ESGRIMA: Carlos José Kletnicki, Gustavo Adrián Semino, Jorge Héctor San Esteban, Santiago Juan Gentiletti, Germán Rodrigo Basualdo, Álvaro Andrés Ormeño, Matías Leonardo Escobar (72 Héctor Daniel Romero), Oscar Roberto Cornejo (57 Sebastián Dubarbier), Antonio Pacheco, Sergio William Leal (57 Santiago Martín Silva), Antonio Piergüidi. DT: Pedro Troglio
Carlos José Kletnicki saved a penalty taken by RODRIGO Barbosa TABATA after 90+2 minutes.
Goals: Germán Rodrigo Basualdo (6 own goal), CLÉBER SANTANA Loureiro (52),
José "ZÉ" ROBERTO da Silva Júnior (69).

DEPORTIVO PASTO – DEFENSOR SPORTING 1-2 (1-0)
Libertad, Pasto, 15.03.2007, Referee: Víctor Hugo Rivera (PER)
DEPORTIVO PASTO: Carlos Alberto Barahona, Jamell Orlando Ramos, José Hermes Mera, Walden Alexis Vargas, Fernando Monroy (84 Oscar Darío Martínez), Jhon Alexander Jaramillo, Ferley Raúl Villamil, Jorge Hernando Vidal, Luis Omar Valencia (51 Jhonatan René Rosero), Carlos Daniel Hidalgo, Carlos Andrés Rodas (70 Einer Viveros). DT: Álvaro de Jesús Gómez
DEFENSOR SPORTING: Martín Silva, Williams Guillermo Martínez, Ignacio Ithurralde (69 Mauro Adrián Vila), José Martín Cáceres, Álvaro Rafael González, Sergio Sebastián Ariosa (64 Diego Alejandro De Souza), Carlos Díaz (59 Danilo Javier Peinado), Fernando Fadeuille, Victorio Maximiliano Pereira, Carlos María Morales, Sebastián Bruno Fernández. DT: Jorge Da Silva
Sent off: Jaramillo (46), Ramos (65) / Fernández (56), Vila (71)
Goals: Carlos Andrés Rodas (26) /
Williams Guillermo Martínez (80), Diego Alejandro De Souza (90+1).

GIMNASIA Y ESGRIMA LA PLATA – SANTOS FC 1-2 (0-1)
Ciudad de La Plata, La Plata, 22.03.2007, Referee: Roberto Carlos Silvera (URU), Attendance: 11.799
GIMNASIA YE.LP: Carlos José Kletnicki, Germán Rodrigo Basualdo, Gustavo Adrián Semino, Lucas León Landa, Héctor Daniel Romero (77 Sergio William Leal), Ignacio Piatti, Reinaldo Andrés Alderete, Antonio Pacheco (67 Luciano Félix Leguizamón), Sebastián Dubarbier, Antonio Piergüidi, Santiago Martín Silva. DT: Pedro Troglio
SANTOS: FÁBIO COSTA, ADAÍLTON José dos Santos Filho, ANTÔNIO CARLOS Zago, LEONARDO José Aparecido Moura (63 MARCELO Antonio Guedes Filho), DÊNIS Oliveira de Souza (74 PEDRO Alves da Silva), RODRIGO Ribeiro SOUTO, KLÉBER de Carvalho Corrêa, José "ZÉ" ROBERTO da Silva Júnior, CLÉBER SANTANA Loureiro, RODRIGO "TIUÍ" Bonifácio da Rocha, MARCOS AURÉLIO de Oliveira Lima (63 Pedro Paulo de Oliveira "PEDRINHO"). DT: Vanderlei Luxemburgo
Goals: Sergio William Leal (88) / MARCOS AURÉLIO de Oliveira Lima (3), José "ZÉ" ROBERTO da Silva Júnior (90).

DEFENSOR SPORTING – DEPORTIVO PASTO 3-0 (2-0)
Centenario, Montevideo, 28.03.2007, Referee: Leonardo Gaciba (BRA), Attendance: 8.500
DEFENSOR SPORTING: Martín Silva, Ignacio Ithurralde, Williams Guillermo Martínez, José Martín Cáceres, Álvaro Rafael González (62 Carlos Díaz), Victorio Maximiliano Pereira, Fernando Fadeuille, Sergio Sebastián Ariosa, Diego Alejandro De Souza (74 Paulo César Pezzolano), Carlos María Morales (62 Tabaré Uruguay Viudez), Danilo Javier Peinado. DT: Jorge Da Silva
DEPORTIVO PASTO: Carlos Alberto Barahona, Einer Viveros (85 Jhonatan René Rosero), José Hermes Mera, Walden Alexis Vargas, Fernando Monroy, Carlos Eduardo Salazar (88 Carlos Daniel Hidalgo), Rolan De La Cruz, Jorge Hernando Vidal, Ferley Raúl Villamil, Juan Enrique García (54 Oscar Darío Martínez), Carlos Andrés Rodas. DT: Álvaro de Jesús Gómez
Goals: Ignacio Ithurralde (16), Carlos María Morales (26 penalty), Danilo Javier Peinado (90+3).

DEFENSOR SPORTING – SANTOS FC 0-2 (0-0)
Centenario, Montevideo, 5.04.2007, Referee: Antonio Javier Arias (PAR), Attendance: 33.848
DEFENSOR SPORTING: Martín Silva, Ignacio Ithurralde, Williams Guillermo Martínez (73 Tabaré Uruguay Viudez), José Martín Cáceres, Álvaro Rafael González, Fernando Fadeuille (73 Danilo Javier Peinado), Carlos Díaz, Sergio Sebastián Ariosa (64 Victorio Maximiliano Pereira), Diego Alejandro De Souza, Carlos María Morales, Mauro Adrián Vila. DT: Jorge Da Silva
SANTOS: FÁBIO COSTA, DÊNIS Oliveira de Souza (46 PEDRO Alves da Silva), ADAÍLTON José dos Santos Filho, MARCELO Antonio Guedes Filho, KLÉBER de Carvalho Corrêa, Claudio Andrés del Transito Maldonado, RODRIGO Ribeiro SOUTO, CLÉBER SANTANA Loureiro (67 Pedro Paulo de Oliveira "PEDRINHO"), José "ZÉ" ROBERTO da Silva Júnior, MARCOS AURÉLIO de Oliveira Lima, JONAS Gonçalves Oliveira (67 RODRIGO Barbosa TABATA). DT: Vanderlei Luxemburgo
Goals: MARCOS AURÉLIO de Oliveira Lima (68), RODRIGO Barbosa TABATA (84).

DEPORTIVO PASTO – GIMNASIA Y ESGRIMA LA PLATA 0-2 (0-1)
Libertad, Pasto, 5.04.2007, Referee: Alfredo Stalin Intriago (ECU)
DEPORTIVO PASTO: Nelson Fernando Ramos, Einer Viveros (56 Jamell Orlando Ramos), Luis Eduardo Lora, Carlos Alfredo Saa, Walden Alexis Vargas, Jhonatan René Rosero, Harold Antonio Rodríguez (56 Ferley Raúl Villamil), Oscar Darío Martínez, Luis Omar Valencia, Carlos Eduardo Salazar (75 Amir Buelvas), Carlos Daniel Hidalgo. DT: Álvaro de Jesús Gómez
GIMNASIA Y ESGRIMA: Pablo Martín Bangardino, Gustavo Adrián Semino, Jorge Héctor San Esteban, Fernando Javier Crosa, Ariel Horacio Franco, Germán Rodrigo Basualdo, Reinaldo Andrés Alderete, Héctor Daniel Romero, Antonio Pacheco (85 Oscar Roberto Cornejo), Luciano Félix Leguizamón (52 Sergio William Leal), Antonio Piergüidi (65 Jonathan Daniel Chávez). DT: Víctor Bernay
Sent off: Ramos (58)
Goals: Antonio Pacheco (15), Sergio William Leal (75).

GIMNASIA y ESGRIMA LA PLATA–DEFENSOR SPORTING 3-0 (2-0)
Ciudad de La Plata, La Plata, 19.04.2007
Referee: Sálvio Spínola Fagundes (BRA), Attendance: 17.000
GIMNASIA Y ESGRIMA: Juan Carlos Olave, Ariel Horacio Franco, Gustavo Adrián Semino, Fernando Javier Crosa, Héctor Daniel Romero, Oscar Roberto Cornejo (58 Santiago Martín Silva), Reinaldo Andrés Alderete, Jonathan Daniel Chávez (66 Sebastián Dubarbier), Antonio Pacheco, Sergio William Leal (58 Germán Rodrigo Basualdo), Luciano Félix Leguizamón. DT: Ricardo Kuzemka
DEFENSOR SPORTING: Martín Silva, José Martín Cáceres, Ignacio Ithurralde, Williams Guillermo Martínez, Álvaro Rafael González, Carlos Díaz (74 Victorio Maximiliano Pereira), Fernando Fadeuille, Sergio Sebastián Ariosa, Diego Alejandro De Souza (79 Paulo César Pezzolano), Carlos María Morales (59 Mauro Adrián Vila), Danilo Javier Peinado. DT: Jorge Da Silva
Goals: Luciano Félix Leguizamón (24, 72), Ignacio Ithurralde (44 own goal).

SANTOS FC – DEPORTIVO PASTO 3-0 (2-0)
Urbano Caldeira, Santos, 19.04.2007, Referee: Óscar Maldonado (BOL), Attendance: 3.253
SANTOS: FÁBIO COSTA, DÊNIS Oliveira de Souza, ADAÍLTON José dos Santos Filho, MARCELO Antonio Guedes Filho, Carlos Andrade Souza "CARLINHOS", Claudio Andrés del Transito Maldonado (46 RODRIGO Ribeiro SOUTO), CLÉBER SANTANA Loureiro (46 José "ZÉ" ROBERTO da Silva Júnior), Pedro Paulo de Oliveira "PEDRINHO", RODRIGO Barbosa TABATA, MARCOS AURÉLIO de Oliveira Lima (61 RODRIGO "TIUÍ" Bonifácio da Rocha), JONAS Gonçalves Oliveira. DT: Vanderlei Luxemburgo
DEPORTIVO PASTO: Carlos Alberto Barahona (82 Nelson Fernando Ramos), Einer Viveros, Carlos Alfredo Saa, Walden Alexis Vargas, Luis Eduardo Lora, Rolan De La Cruz, Jhonatan René Rosero (56 Ferley Raúl Villamil), Luis Omar Valencia, Juan Fernando Rebolledo, Carlos Andrés Rodas (56 Oscar Darío Martínez), Juan Enrique García. DT: Álvaro de Jesús Gómez
Goals: Carlos Andrade Souza "CARLINHOS" (7), Pedro Paulo de Oliveira "PEDRINHO" (45), RODRIGO "TIUÍ" Bonifácio da Rocha (84).

1	SANTOS FC	6	6	0	0	12	1	18
2	DEFENSOR SPORTING	6	3	0	3	8	7	9
3	Gimnasia y Esgrima	6	3	0	3	9	10	9
4	Deportivo Pasto	6	0	0	6	3	14	0

ROUND OF 16

CARACAS FC – SANTOS FC 2-2 (0-1)
Olímpico Universitario, Caracas, 2.05.2007
Referee: Mauricio Javier Reinoso (ECU), Attendance: 16.087
CARACAS: Javier Eduardo Toyo, Leonel Vielma, José Manuel Rey, Enrique Andrés Rouga, Edder Alfonso Pérez, Luis Enrique Vera, Jorge Alberto Rojas (71 José Caraballo), César Eduardo González, Weymar Franck Olivares, Iván Jose Velásquez, Habinson Escobar (68 Wilson Alberto Carpintero). DT: Noel Sanvicente
SANTOS: FÁBIO COSTA, DÊNIS Oliveira de Souza (5 DIONISIO de Oliveira Alves), ANTÔNIO CARLOS Zago (42 Cristiano Espíndola de ÁVALOS), ADAÍLTON José dos Santos Filho, MARCELO Antonio Guedes Filho, KLÉBER de Carvalho Corrêa, RODRIGO Ribeiro SOUTO, Claudio Andrés del Transito Maldonado, CLÉBER SANTANA Loureiro, José "ZÉ" ROBERTO da Silva Júnior, MARCOS AURÉLIO de Oliveira Lima (75 RODRIGO Barbosa TABATA). DT: Vanderlei Luxemburgo
Sent off: Dionisio (53)
Goals: Iván Jose Velásquez (55), Leonel Vielma (87) /
José "ZÉ" ROBERTO da Silva Júnior (16), KLÉBER de Carvalho Corrêa (64).

SANTOS FC – CARACAS FC 3-2 (2-2)
Urbano Caldeira, Santos, 10.05.2007, Referee: Carlos Amarilla (PAR), Attendance: 10.826
SANTOS: FÁBIO COSTA, Claudio Andrés del Transito Maldonado, ADAÍLTON José dos Santos Filho, Cristiano Espíndola de ÁVALOS, KLÉBER de Carvalho Corrêa, RODRIGO Ribeiro SOUTO, CLÉBER SANTANA Loureiro, Pedro Paulo de Oliveira "PEDRINHO" (63 RODRIGO Barbosa TABATA), José "ZÉ" ROBERTO da Silva Júnior, MARCOS AURÉLIO de Oliveira Lima (71 MARCELO Antonio Guedes Filho), JONAS Gonçalves Oliveira (63 Renato Carlos Martins Júnior "RENATINHO"). DT: Vanderlei Luxemburgo
CARACAS: Javier Eduardo Toyo, Enrique Andrés Rouga, Oswaldo Augusto Vizcarrondo, José Manuel Rey, Edder Alfonso Pérez, Luis Enrique Vera (71 Alejandro Abraham Guerra), Weymar Franck Olivares (83 Edgar Hernán Jiménez), Jorge Alberto Rojas, César Eduardo González, Iván Jose Velásquez (78 Rafael Ernesto Castellín), Wilson Alberto Carpintero. DT: Noel Sanvicente
Sent off: Adaílton (90+2)
Goals: ADAÍLTON José dos Santos Filho (34), José "ZÉ" ROBERTO da Silva Júnior (40, 66) / José Manuel Rey (23), Wilson Alberto Carpintero (30).

CF AMÉRICA – COLO COLO SANTIAGO 3-0 (2-0)
Azteca, México City, 2.05.2007, Referee: Antonio Javier Arias (PAR), Attendance: 47.307
CF AMÉRICA: Francisco Guillermo Ochoa, José Antonio Castro, Ismael de Jesús Rodríguez, Duilio César Davino, Ricardo Francisco Rojas, Alejandro Argüello, Raúl Alvin Mendoza, Germán Villa, Cuauhtémoc Bravo Blanco, Salvador Cabañas (87 Daniel Rubén Bilos), Santiago Fernández (81 Felipe Abdiel Baloy). DT: Luis Fernando Tena
COLO COLO: Christian Sebastian Cejas, Luis Arturo Mena, Miguel Augusto Riffo, Gonzalo Alejandro Jara (46 José Luis Jerez), Gonzalo Antonio Fierro, Héctor Arturo Sanhueza, Rodrigo David Meléndez, Arturo Erasmo Vidal, Giovanni Hernández (63 Boris Igor González), Alexis Alejandro Sánchez (56 Mario Édison Giménez), Humberto Andrés Suazo. DT: Claudio Borghi
Sent off: Davino (80)
Goals: Salvador Cabañas (26), Santiago Fernández (29), Ricardo Francisco Rojas (53).

COLO COLO SANTIAGO – CF AMÉRICA 2-1 (0-0)
Monumental, Santiago, 8.05.2007, Referee: Jorge Luis Larrionda (URU), Attendance: 12.569
COLO COLO: Christian Sebastian Cejas, Miguel Augusto Riffo, Luis Arturo Mena (75 Mario Édison Giménez), Arturo Erasmo Vidal, Gonzalo Antonio Fierro, Rodrigo David Meléndez, Héctor Arturo Sanhueza, Moisés Fermin Villarroel (57 Juan Gonzalo Lorca), Giovanni Hernández, Alexis Alejandro Sánchez (84 Juan Pablo Areñas), Humberto Andrés Suazo. DT: Claudio Borghi
CF AMÉRICA: Francisco Guillermo Ochoa, Felipe Abdiel Baloy, Rodrigo Iñigo, Ricardo Francisco Rojas, José Antonio Castro, Raúl Alvin Mendoza (77 Carlos Jesús Infante), Alejandro Argüello, Ignacio Torres, Luis Ernesto Pérez (71 Daniel Rubén Bilos), Salvador Cabañas, Santiago Fernández (73 Nelson Rafael Cuevas). DT: Luis Fernando Tena
Sent off: Meléndez (90+2)
Goals: José Antonio Castro (70 own goal), Humberto Andrés Suazo (88) / Carlos Jesús Infante (86).

DEFENSOR SPORTING – FLAMENGO 3-0 (1-0)
Centenario, Montevideo, 2.05.2007, Referee: Carlos Luis Chandía (CHI), Attendance: 26.921
DEFENSOR SPORTING: Martín Silva, Gonzalo Sorondo, Williams Guillermo Martínez, José Martín Cáceres, Álvaro Rafael González, Victorio Maximiliano Pereira, Fernando Fadeuille, Diego Alejandro De Souza (87 Miguel Ángel Amado), Danilo Javier Peinado (82 Carlos María Morales), Álvaro Damián Navarro, Paulo César Pezzolano (74 Sebastián Bruno Fernández). DT: Jorge Da Silva
FLAMENGO: BRUNO Das Dores de Souza, Leonardo da Silva "LEO" MOURA, IRINEU Calixto Couto, MOISÉS Moura Pinheiro, JUAN Maldonado Jaimez Júnior, Leandro SALINO Carmo (56 Leonardo "LÉO" LIMA da Silva), Carlos RENATO de Abreu, Paulo Benedito Maximiano "PAULINHO" (84 JAILTON da Cruz Alves), Oswaldo Giroldo Júnior "JUNINHO PAULISTA" (46 Roniéliton Pereira Santos "RONI"), RENATO Soares de Oliveira AUGUSTO, Rodrigo de SOUZA Cardoso. DT: Ney Franco
Goals: Álvaro Damián Navarro (5 penalty, 75), Álvaro Rafael González (49).

FLAMENGO – DEFENSOR SPORTING 2-0 (1-0)
Mario Filho 'Maracanã', Río de Janeiro, 9.05.2007
Referee: Héctor Walter Baldassi (ARG), Attendance: 57.767
FLAMENGO: BRUNO Das Dores de Souza, Leonardo da Silva "LEO" MOURA, IRINEU Calixto Couto, JUAN Maldonado Jaimez Júnior, RONALDO Simões ANGELIM, Carlos RENATO de Abreu, Paulo Benedito Maximiano "PAULINHO" (77 Leonardo "LÉO" LIMA da Silva), CLAITON Alberto dos Santos (69 PAULO SERGIO Luiz de Souza), RENATO Soares de Oliveira AUGUSTO, Rodrigo de SOUZA Cardoso, Roniéliton Pereira Santos "RONI". DT: Ney Franco
DEFENSOR SPORTING: Martín Silva, Gonzalo Sorondo, Williams Guillermo Martínez, José Martín Cáceres, Álvaro Rafael González, Sergio Sebastián Ariosa, Miguel Ángel Amado, Fernando Fadeuille, Diego Alejandro De Souza, Danilo Javier Peinado (65 Carlos María Morales), Paulo César Pezzolano (46 Sebastián Bruno Fernández). DT: Jorge Da Silva
Goals: Carlos RENATO de Abreu (35, 47).

SÃO PAULO FC – GRÊMIO FOOTBALL 1-0 (0-0)
Cícero Pompeu de Toledo 'Morumbí', São Paulo, 2.05.2007
Referee: Wagner Tardelli Azevedo (BRA), Attendance: 33.387
SÃO PAULO: ROGÉRIO CENI, Ilson Pereira Dias Júnior "ILSINHO" (86 ANDRÉ Gonçalves DIAS), ALEX Sandro da SILVA, João MIRANDA de Souza Filho, José JADÍLSON dos Santos Silva, JOSUÉ de Oliviera, RICHARLYSON Barbosa Felisbino, HUGO Assis do Nascimento, Williamis de SOUZA Silva, ALOÍSIO José da Silva (86 MARCEL Augusto Ortolan), LEANDRO Lessa Azevedo (46 DAGOBERTO Pelentier). DT: Muricy Ramalho
GRÊMIO: Diego Sebastián Saja, PATRICIO Antônio Boques, WILLIAM Machado de Oliveira, LÚCIO Carlos Cajueiro Souza, Wender Coelho da Silva "TECO", EDMÍLSON Carlos Abel, SANDRO "GOIANO" Gomes Luz (57 Diego Antonio Gavilán), Ânderson Simas Luciano "TCHECO", DIEGO de SOUZA Andrade, Moacir Bastos "TUTA" (85 EVERTON Santos), CARLOS EDUARDO Marques (66 Márcio AMOROSO dos Santos). DT: Mano Menezes
Goal: João MIRANDA de Souza Filho (56).

GRÊMIO FOOTBALL – SÃO PAULO FC 2-0 (1-0)
Olímpico Monumental, Porto Alegre, 9.05.2007
Referee: Carlos Luis Chandía (CHI), Attendance: 42.669
GRÊMIO: Diego Sebastián Saja, PATRICIO Antônio Boques, WILLIAM Machado de Oliveira, Wender Coelho da Silva "TECO", LÚCIO Carlos Cajueiro Souza, EDMÍLSON Carlos Abel, SANDRO "GOIANO" Gomes Luz (66 Márcio AMOROSO dos Santos), Ânderson Simas Luciano "TCHECO" (42 Diego Antonio Gavilán), DIEGO de SOUZA Andrade, Moacir Bastos "TUTA", CARLOS EDUARDO Marques (87 Rolando Carlos Schiavi). DT: Mano Menezes
SÃO PAULO: ROGÉRIO CENI, Ilson Pereira Dias Júnior "ILSINHO", ALEX Sandro da SILVA, João MIRANDA de Souza Filho, José JADÍLSON dos Santos Silva (46 JORGE WAGNER Góes Conceição), JOSUÉ de Oliviera, RICHARLYSON Barbosa Felisbino, Williamis de SOUZA Silva, HUGO Assis do Nascimento (46 DAGOBERTO Pelentier), LEANDRO Lessa Azevedo (87 MARCEL Augusto Ortolan), ALOÍSIO José da Silva. DT: Muricy Ramalho
Goals: Ânderson Simas Luciano "TCHECO" (17), DIEGO de SOUZA Andrade (75).

BOCA JUNIORS – VÉLEZ SARSFIELD 3-0 (1-0)
Alberto J. Armando 'La Bombonera', Buenos Aires, 2.05.2007
Referee: Héctor Walter Baldassi (ARG), Attendance: 28.657
BOCA JUNIORS: Mauricio Ariel Caranta, Hugo Benjamín Ibarra, Matías Agustín Silvestre, Claudio Marcelo Morel, Clemente Juan Rodríguez, Pablo Martín Ledesma, Ever Maximiliano David Banega (87 Nicolás Santiago Bertolo), Neri Raúl Cardozo, Juan Román Riquelme, Rodrigo Sebastián Palacio, Martín Palermo (86 Mauro Boselli). DT: Miguel Ángel Russo

VÉLEZ SARSFIELD: Gastón Alejandro Sessa, Hernán Darío Pellerano, Maximiliano Pellegrino, Marcelo Hernán Bustamante, Mario Méndez, Maximiliano Andrés Bustos, Mariano Esteban Uglessich, Damián Ariel Escudero (72 Alejandro Ariel Cabral), Lucas Martín Castromán, Mauro Matías Zárate (25 Sebastián Darío Peratta), Iván Diego Moreno y Fabianesi (72 Emiliano Ramiro Papa). DT: Ricardo La Volpe
Sent off: Sessa (25)
Goals: Juan Román Riquelme (9), Martín Palermo (60), Clemente Juan Rodríguez (89).

VÉLEZ SARSFIELD – BOCA JUNIORS 3-1 (2-1)
José Amalfitani, Buenos Aires, 9.05.2007, Referee: Saúl Laverni (ARG), Attendance: 10.232
VÉLEZ SARSFIELD: Sebastián Darío Peratta, Hernán Darío Pellerano, Maximiliano Pellegrino, Marcelo Hernán Bustamante (60 Gustavo Alberto Balvorín), Mario Méndez, Maximiliano Andrés Bustos, Alejandro Ariel Cabral (60 Ariel Esteban Broggi), Ramón Dario Ocampo, Damián Ariel Escudero, Lucas Martín Castromán (63 Iván Diego Moreno y Fabianesi), Mauro Matías Zárate. DT: Ricardo La Volpe
BOCA JUNIORS: Mauricio Ariel Caranta, Hugo Benjamín Ibarra, Matías Agustín Silvestre, Claudio Marcelo Morel, Clemente Juan Rodríguez, Pablo Martín Ledesma, Ever Maximiliano David Banega, Neri Raúl Cardozo (46 Nicolás Santiago Bertolo), Juan Román Riquelme, Rodrigo Sebastián Palacio (82 Mauro Boselli), Martín Palermo (86 Sergio Daniel Orteman). DT: Miguel Ángel Russo
Sent off: Castromán (82 got the red card after he was substituted), Méndez (90+3) / Ledesma (34)
Goals: Mauro Matías Zárate (14, 36), Ramón Dario Ocampo (79) / Juan Román Riquelme (32).

PARANÁ CLUBE – LIBERTAD ASUNCIÓN 1-2 (0-0)
Durival Brito e Silva, Curitiba, 3.05.2007, Referee: Roberto Carlos Silvera (URU), Attendance: 8.393
PARANÁ: FLÁVIO Emidio dos Santos Vieira, Leonardo "LÉO" de MATOS Cruz, Anderson da Silva de Jesús "NEGUETE", DANIEL MARQUES da Silva, EGÍDIO de Araújo Pereira Júnior, Valberto Amorim Santos "BETO", Clennyson Silva do Nascimento "XAVES", José GERSON Ramos (71 ADRIANO Ferreira Silvestre), DINELSON dos Santos Lima, Rodrigo LIMA dos Santos (79 JOÃO PAULO Pereira Mendes Bersch), JOSIEL da Rocha. DT: Armelino Donizetti Quagliato 'Zetti'
LIBERTAD: Horacio Javier González, Carlos Bonet, Ricardo Julián Martínez, Deivis Barone, Édgar Gabriel Balbuena (24 Raúl Hernán Damiani), Sergio Daniel Aquino, Víctor Javier Cáceres, Pablo Horacio Guiñazú, Osvaldo David Martínez (68 Vladimir Marín), Roberto Carlos Gamarra (68 Freddy José Bareiro), Hernán Rodrigo López. DT: Sergio Markarian
Sent off: Neguete (77)
Goals: JOSIEL da Rocha (51) / Vladimir Marín (71), Deivis Barone (89).

LIBERTAD ASUNCIÓN – PARANÁ CLUBE 1-1 (1-0)
Defensores del Chaco, Asunción, 10.05.2007
Referee: Rubén Marcos Selman (CHI), Attendance: 1.554
LIBERTAD: Jorge Rodrigo Bava, Carlos Bonet, Ricardo Julián Martínez, Pedro Alcides Sarabia, Édgar Gabriel Balbuena, Sergio Daniel Aquino (75 Vladimir Marín), Víctor Javier Cáceres, Cristian Miguel Riveros, Pablo Horacio Guiñazú (88 Freddy José Bareiro), Roberto Carlos Gamarra (55 Osvaldo David Martínez), Hernán Rodrigo López. DT: Sergio Markarian
PARANÁ: FLÁVIO Emidio dos Santos Vieira, Leonardo "LÉO" de MATOS Cruz (90 José GERSON Ramos), DANIEL MARQUES da Silva, EGÍDIO de Araújo Pereira Júnior (32 JOÃO PAULO Pereira Mendes Bersch), Antônio Bezerra Brandão "TONINHO", Valberto Amorim Santos "BETO", Clennyson Silva do Nascimento "XAVES", JOELSON dos Santos Silva, DINELSON dos Santos Lima, VINICIUS Pacheco dos Santos, JOSIEL da Rocha. DT: Armelino Donizetti Quagliato 'Zetti'
Sent off: Vinicius (86)
Goals: Roberto Carlos Gamarra (12) / JOELSON dos Santos Silva (84).

NACIONAL MONTEVIDEO – NECAXA 3-2 (2-1)
Parque Central, Montevideo, 3.05.2007, Referee: Sálvio Spínola Fagundes (BRA), Attendance: 13.204
NACIONAL: Néstor Fernando Muslera, Pablo Álvarez, Diego Roberto Godín, Diego Jaume, Agustín Viana, Mathías Cardaccio (89 Adrián Marcelo Romero), Marcelo Fabian Sosa, Marco Eduardo Vanzini (79 Pablo Caballero), Javier Omar Delgado (73 Gonzalo Castro), Jorge Andrés Martínez, Diego Vera. DT: Daniel Carreño
NECAXA: Federico Vilar, Pablo Javier Quattrocchi, Joaquín Beltrán, Horacio Javier Cervantes, Jaime Ruiz, Gerardo Gabriel Galindo (60 Luis Omar Hernández), Óscar Emilio Rojas, EVERALDO Vergne de Assis BARBOSA, Alfredo David Moreno (64 Juan Manuel Salgueiro), Héctor Horacio Giménez (46 Leandro Gracián), KLÉBER João BOAS Pereira. DT: José Luis Trejo
Sent off: Vera (82) / Barbosa (82)
Goals: Diego Vera (7), Diego Roberto Godín (23), Jorge Andrés Martínez (55) / KLÉBER João BOAS Pereira (10), Diego Roberto Godín (53 own goal).

NECAXA – NACIONAL MONTEVIDEO 0-1 (0-0)
Azteca, México City, 10.05.2007, Referee: Sergio Fabián Pezzotta (ARG), Attendance: 21.314
NECAXA: Federico Vilar, Pablo Javier Quattrocchi, Joaquín Beltrán, Horacio Javier Cervantes, Luis Omar Hernández (46 Emmanuel Sánchez), Óscar Emilio Rojas (53 Alfredo David Moreno), Juan Manuel Salgueiro (55 Leandro Gracián), Jaime Ruiz, Gerardo Gabriel Galindo, KLÉBER João BOAS Pereira, Héctor Horacio Giménez. DT: José Luis Trejo
NACIONAL: Néstor Fernando Muslera, Pablo Álvarez, Diego Roberto Godín, Diego Jaume, Agustín Viana, Mathías Cardaccio, Adrián Marcelo Romero, Javier Omar Delgado (66 Pablo Caballero), Marcelo Fabian Sosa, Gonzalo Castro (59 Andrés Leonardo Márquez), Jorge Andrés Martínez. DT: Daniel Carreño
Goal: Jorge Andrés Martínez (88).

CÚCUTA DEPORTIVO – CD TOLUCA 5-1 (4-1)
General Santander, Cúcuta, 3.05.2007, Referee: Saúl Laverni (ARG), Attendance: 26.304
CÚCUTA: Róbinson Zapata, Rubén Darío Bustos, Elvis Javier González, Wálter José Moreno, Julián Hurtado, Dúmar Ricardo Rueda (75 Nélson Alfonso Flores), Alexander Del Castillo, Charles Castro, Macnelly Torres, Juan Manuel Martínez (80 Lionard Fernando Pajoy), Blas Antonio Miguel Pérez. DT: Jorge Luis Bernal
CD TOLUCA: Rolando Hernán Cristante, Paulo César Da Silva, José Manuel Cruzalta (46 Carlos Esquivel), Édgar Esteban Dueñas (68 Ignacio Martín Scocco), Emilio Hassan Viades, Sergio Amaury Ponce, Ariel Javier Rosada, Carlos Adrián Morales, Antonio Naelson Matías "ZINHA", Juan Francisco Palencia (46 Diego Javier De La Torre), Vicente Martín Sánchez. DT: Américo Gallego
Sent off: Morales (26)
Goals: Juan Manuel Martínez (33, 42, 45), Charles Castro (34), Alexander Del Castillo (89) / Vicente Martín Sánchez (1).

CD TOLUCA – CÚCUTA DEPORTIVO 2-0 (1-0)
Nemesio Diez, Toluca, 8.05.2007
Referee: Manuel Candelario Andarcia (VEN), Attendance: 6.557
CD TOLUCA: Rolando Hernán Cristante, Jonathan Arias, Paulo César Da Silva, Sergio Amaury Ponce, Diego Javier De La Torre (64 Manuel Alejandro De la Torre), Carlos Esquivel (74 Josué Castillejos), Ariel Javier Rosada, Ignacio Martín Scocco, Antonio Naelson Matías "ZINHA", Juan Francisco Palencia (56 Érwin Lorenzo Ávalos), Vicente Martín Sánchez. DT: Américo Gallego
CÚCUTA: Róbinson Zapata, Rubén Darío Bustos, Elvis Javier González, Wálter José Moreno, Julián Hurtado, Dúmar Ricardo Rueda, Alexander Del Castillo, Charles Castro, Macnelly Torres (87 Lionard Fernando Pajoy), Juan Manuel Martínez (67 Nélson Alfonso Flores), Blas Antonio Miguel Pérez (80 Víctor Javier Cortés). DT: Jorge Luis Bernal
Goals: Antonio Naelson Matías "ZINHA" (21), Ignacio Martín Scocco (90).

QUARTER-FINALS

CÚCUTA DEPORTIVO – NACIONAL MONTEVIDEO 2-0 (0-0)
General Santander, Cúcuta, 15.05.2007, Referee: Carlos Eugênio Simón (BRA), Attendance: 32.400
CÚCUTA: Róbinson Zapata, Rubén Darío Bustos, Elvis Javier González, Wálter José Moreno, Julián Hurtado, Dúmar Ricardo Rueda (75 Nélson Alfonso Flores), Alexander Del Castillo, Charles Castro (46 David Camilo Córdoba), Macnelly Torres, Juan Manuel Martínez (78 Víctor Javier Cortés), Blas Antonio Miguel Pérez. DT: Jorge Luis Bernal
NACIONAL: Néstor Fernando Muslera, Pablo Álvarez, Diego Roberto Godín, José Ignacio Pallas, Agustín Viana, Mathías Cardaccio (56 Pablo Caballero), Adrián Marcelo Romero, Javier Omar Delgado (75 Marcelo Carlo Broli), Marcelo Fabian Sosa, Diego Vera (81 Andrés Leonardo Márquez), Jorge Andrés Martínez. DT: Daniel Carreño
Sent off: Pallas (30)
Goals: Macnelly Torres (65), Blas Antonio Miguel Pérez (89).

NACIONAL MONTEVIDEO – CÚCUTA DEPORTIVO 2-2 (1-1)
Parque Central, Montevideo, 22.05.2007, Referee: Sergio Fabián Pezzotta (ARG), Attendance: 13.842
NACIONAL: Néstor Fernando Muslera, Pablo Álvarez, Diego Roberto Godín, Diego Jaume, Agustín Viana, Mathías Cardaccio (46 Jorge Andrés Martínez), Javier Omar Delgado, Marcelo Fabian Sosa, Diego Vera, Andrés Leonardo Márquez (51 Pablo Caballero), Gonzalo Castro (63 Carlos Alberto Juárez). DT: Daniel Carreño
CÚCUTA: Róbinson Zapata, Rubén Darío Bustos, Elvis Javier González, Wálter José Moreno, Julián Hurtado, Dúmar Ricardo Rueda, Alexander Del Castillo, Charles Castro (87 Braynner Yesid García), Macnelly Torres (73 David Camilo Córdoba), Juan Manuel Martínez (69 Lionard Fernando Pajoy), Blas Antonio Miguel Pérez. DT: Jorge Luis Bernal
Goals: Gonzalo Castro (11), Diego Vera (84) / Rubén Darío Bustos (21), Lionard Fernando Pajoy (90).

DEFENSOR SPORTING – GRÊMIO FOOTBALL 2-0 (2-0)
Centenario, Montevideo, 16.05.2007, Referee: Rubén Marcos Selman (CHI), Attendance: 28.468
DEFENSOR SPORTING: Martín Silva, Gonzalo Sorondo, Williams Guillermo Martínez, José Martín Cáceres, Álvaro Rafael González, Victorio Maximiliano Pereira, Fernando Fadeuille, Danilo Javier Peinado, Diego Alejandro De Souza (77 Carlos Díaz), Mauro Adrián Vila (66 Sebastián Bruno Fernández), Carlos María Morales (43 Miguel Ángel Amado). DT: Jorge Da Silva
GRÊMIO: Diego Sebastián Saja, PATRICIO Antônio Boques, WILLIAM Machado de Oliveira, Wender Coelho da Silva "TECO", LÚCIO Carlos Cajueiro Souza, Eduardo Martins NUNES (46 Márcio AMOROSO dos Santos), Diego Antonio Gavilán, DIEGO de SOUZA Andrade, Ânderson Simas Luciano "TCHECO", CARLOS EDUARDO Marques (76 EVERTON Santos), Moacir Bastos "TUTA" (83 RAMÓN Rodrigo de Freitas). DT: Mano Menezes
Sent off: González (37)
Goals: Gonzalo Sorondo (1), Williams Guillermo Martínez (34).

GRÊMIO FOOTBALL – DEFENSOR SPORTING 2-0 (2-0), 4-2 penalties
Olímpico Monumental, Porto Alegre, 23.05.2007, Referee: Carlos Amarilla (PAR), Attendance: 42.387
GRÊMIO: Diego Sebastián Saja, PATRICIO Antônio Boques, WILLIAM Machado de Oliveira, Wender Coelho da Silva "TECO", LÚCIO Carlos Cajueiro Souza, Diego Antonio Gavilán (62 DOUGLAS de Oliveira), SANDRO "GOIANO" Gomes Luz, Ânderson Simas Luciano "TCHECO" (60 RAMÓN Rodrigo de Freitas), Márcio AMOROSO dos Santos, CARLOS EDUARDO Marques, Moacir Bastos "TUTA" (84 EVERTON Santos). DT: Mano Menezes
DEFENSOR SPORTING: Martín Silva, Gonzalo Sorondo (15 Andrés Lamas), Williams Guillermo Martínez, José Martín Cáceres (61 Mauro Adrián Vila), Miguel Ángel Amado (46 Carlos Díaz), Sergio Sebastián Ariosa, Victorio Maximiliano Pereira, Fernando Fadeuille, Danilo Javier Peinado, Diego Alejandro De Souza, Sebastián Bruno Fernández. DT: Jorge Da Silva
Sent off: Amoroso (90+1) / Díaz (80)
Goals: Ânderson Simas Luciano "TCHECO" (23), Wender Coelho da Silva "TECO" (45).

Penalties: * Fernando Fadeuille, 1-0 PATRICIO Antônio Boques, * Danilo Javier Peinado, 2-0 LÚCIO Carlos Cajueiro Souza, 2-1 Diego Alejandro De Souza, 3-1 DOUGLAS de Oliveira, 3-2 Victorio Maximiliano Pereira, 4-2 RAMÓN Rodrigo de Freitas

CF AMÉRICA – SANTOS FC 0-0
Azteca, México City, 16.05.2007, Referee: Roberto Carlos Silvera (URU), Attendance: 69.157
CF AMÉRICA: Francisco Guillermo Ochoa, Carlos Jesús Infante, Felipe Abdiel Baloy, Diego Alberto Cervantes, Óscar Adrián Rojas, Fabián Peña, Rodrigo Iñigo (58 Cuauhtémoc Bravo Blanco), Ignacio Torres, Juan Carlos Mosqueda (58 Salvador Cabañas), Luis Ernesto Pérez (67 Santiago Fernández), Nelson Rafael Cuevas. DT: Luis Fernando Tena
SANTOS: FÁBIO COSTA, ALESSANDRO Mori Nunes, KLÉBER de Carvalho Corrêa, Cristiano Espíndola de ÁVALOS, DOMINGOS Nascimento dos Santos Filho, MARCELO Antonio Guedes Filho, RODRIGO Ribeiro SOUTO (75 Pedro Paulo de Oliveira "PEDRINHO"), CLÉBER SANTANA Loureiro, Claudio Andrés del Transito Maldonado, José "ZÉ" ROBERTO da Silva Júnior, MARCOS AURÉLIO de Oliveira Lima (75 RODRIGO Barbosa TABATA). DT: Vanderlei Luxemburgo

SANTOS FC – CF AMÉRICA 2-1 (0-1)
Urbano Caldeira, Santos, 23.05.2007, Referee: Óscar Julián Ruiz (COL), Attendance: 11.925
SANTOS: FÁBIO COSTA, ADAÍLTON José dos Santos Filho, KLÉBER de Carvalho Corrêa, ALESSANDRO Mori Nunes (46 Pedro Paulo de Oliveira "PEDRINHO"), RODRIGO Ribeiro SOUTO, Cristiano Espíndola de ÁVALOS, JONAS Gonçalves Oliveira (79 DIONISIO de Oliveira Alves), Claudio Andrés del Transito Maldonado, MARCOS AURÉLIO de Oliveira Lima, José "ZÉ" ROBERTO da Silva Júnior, CLÉBER SANTANA Loureiro (75 MARCELO Antonio Guedes Filho). DT: Vanderlei Luxemburgo
CF AMÉRICA: Armando Navarrete, Carlos Jesús Infante, Felipe Abdiel Baloy, Diego Alberto Cervantes, Óscar Adrián Rojas, Fabián Peña, Rodrigo Iñigo (74 Daniel Omar Márquez), Ignacio Torres, Juan Carlos Mosqueda (70 Luis Ernesto Pérez), Daniel Rubén Bilos, Raúl Alvin Mendoza.
Goals: JONAS Gonçalves Oliveira (65), RODRIGO Ribeiro SOUTO (71) / Daniel Rubén Bilos (32).

BOCA JUNIORS – LIBERTAD ASUNCIÓN 1-1 (0-0)
Alberto J. Armando 'La Bombonera', Buenos Aires, 17.05.2007
Referee: Óscar Julián Ruiz (COL), Attendance: 31.397
BOCA JUNIORS: Mauricio Ariel Caranta, Hugo Benjamín Ibarra, Matías Agustín Silvestre, Claudio Marcelo Morel, Clemente Juan Rodríguez, Nicolás Santiago Bertolo (58 Jesús Alberto Dátolo), Ever Maximiliano David Banega, Neri Raúl Cardozo, Juan Román Riquelme, Martín Palermo, Rodrigo Sebastián Palacio. DT: Miguel Ángel Russo
LIBERTAD: Jorge Rodrigo Bava, Carlos Bonet, Pedro Alcides Sarabia, Ricardo Julián Martínez, Édgar Gabriel Balbuena, Sergio Daniel Aquino (73 Edgar Arnulfo Robles), Cristian Miguel Riveros, Víctor Javier Cáceres, Pablo Horacio Guiñazú, Vladimir Marín (64 Osvaldo David Martínez), Hernán Rodrigo López (90+1 Freddy José Bareiro). DT: Sergio Markarian
Goals: Martín Palermo (90) / Osvaldo David Martínez (82).

LIBERTAD ASUNCIÓN – BOCA JUNIORS 0-2 (0-0)
Defensores del Chaco, Asunción, 24.05.2007, Referee: Carlos Luis Chandía (CHI), Attendance: 27.137
LIBERTAD: Jorge Rodrigo Bava, Carlos Bonet, Pedro Alcides Sarabia, Édgar Gabriel Balbuena, Víctor Javier Cáceres, Cristian Miguel Riveros (74 Osvaldo David Martínez), Sergio Daniel Aquino (65 Vladimir Marín), Ricardo Julián Martínez, Pablo Horacio Guiñazú, Roberto Carlos Gamarra (74 Freddy José Bareiro), Hernán Rodrigo López. DT: Sergio Markarian
BOCA JUNIORS: Mauricio Ariel Caranta, Hugo Benjamín Ibarra, Daniel Alberto Díaz, Claudio Marcelo Morel (84 Matías Agustín Silvestre), Clemente Juan Rodríguez, Pablo Martín Ledesma, Ever Maximiliano David Banega (56 Jesús Alberto Dátolo), Neri Raúl Cardozo (75 Sergio Daniel Orteman), Juan Román Riquelme, Martín Palermo, Rodrigo Sebastián Palacio. DT: Miguel Ángel Russo
Goals: Juan Román Riquelme (61), Rodrigo Sebastián Palacio (71).

SEMI-FINALS

GRÊMIO FOOTBALL – SANTOS FC 2-0 (2-0)
Olímpico Monumental, Porto Alegre, 30.05.2007
Referee: Sergio Fabián Pezzotta (ARG), Attendance: 44.646
GRÊMIO: Diego Sebastián Saja, PATRICIO Antônio Boques, WILLIAM Machado de Oliveira, Wender Coelho da Silva "TECO", LÚCIO Carlos Cajueiro Souza, Diego Antonio Gavilán, SANDRO "GOIANO" Gomes Luz, DIEGO de SOUZA Andrade (80 EDMÍLSON Carlos Abel), Ânderson Simas Luciano "TCHECO" (46 RAMÓN Rodrigo de Freitas), CARLOS EDUARDO Marques, Moacir Bastos "TUTA". DT: Mano Menezes
SANTOS: FÁBIO COSTA, ADAÍLTON José dos Santos Filho, KLÉBER de Carvalho Corrêa, ALESSANDRO Mori Nunes (46 RODRIGO Barbosa TABATA), Cristiano Espíndola de ÁVALOS, RODRIGO Ribeiro SOUTO, JONAS Gonçalves Oliveira (46 Pedro Paulo de Oliveira "PEDRINHO"), Claudio Andrés del Transito Maldonado, CLÉBER SANTANA Loureiro (66 Aluísio Chaves Ribeiro MORAES Júnior), José "ZÉ" ROBERTO da Silva Júnior, MARCOS AURÉLIO de Oliveira Lima. DT: Vanderlei Luxemburgo
Goals: Ânderson Simas Luciano "TCHECO" (35 penalty), CARLOS EDUARDO Marques (37).

SANTOS FC – GRÊMIO FOOTBALL 3-1 (1-1)
Urbano Caldeira, Santos, 6.06.2007, Referee: Carlos Manuel Torres (PAR), Attendance: 19.788
SANTOS: FÁBIO COSTA, ADAÍLTON José dos Santos Filho, KLÉBER de Carvalho Corrêa, ALESSANDRO Mori Nunes (58 RODRIGO Barbosa TABATA), RODRIGO Ribeiro SOUTO, DOMINGOS Nascimento dos Santos Filho, Pedro Paulo de Oliveira "PEDRINHO" (50 Aluísio Chaves Ribeiro MORAES Júnior), Renato Carlos Martins Júnior "RENATINHO" (72 JONAS Gonçalves Oliveira), CLÉBER SANTANA Loureiro, José "ZÉ" ROBERTO da Silva Júnior, MARCOS AURÉLIO de Oliveira Lima. DT: Vanderlei Luxemburgo
GRÊMIO: Diego Sebastián Saja, PATRICIO Antônio Boques, WILLIAM Machado de Oliveira, Wender Coelho da Silva "TECO", LÚCIO Carlos Cajueiro Souza, Diego Antonio Gavilán, SANDRO "GOIANO" Gomes Luz, DIEGO de SOUZA Andrade, Ânderson Simas Luciano "TCHECO" (81 EDMÍLSON Carlos Abel), DOUGLAS de Oliveira (62 LUCAS Pezzini Leiva), CARLOS EDUARDO Marques (28 RAMÓN Rodrigo de Freitas). DT: Mano Menezes
Goals: Renato Carlos Martins Júnior "RENATINHO" (45+2, 61), José "ZÉ" ROBERTO da Silva (77) / DIEGO de SOUZA Andrade (24).

CÚCUTA DEPORTIVO – BOCA JUNIORS 3-1 (1-1)
General Santander, Cúcuta, 31.05.2007, Referee: Carlos Amarilla (PAR), Attendance: 42.000
CÚCUTA: Róbinson Zapata, Rubén Darío Bustos, Elvis Javier González, Wálter José Moreno, Julián Hurtado, Dúmar Ricardo Rueda (77 Lionard Fernando Pajoy), Charles Castro (32 David Camilo Córdoba, 72 Nélson Alfonso Flores), Alexander Del Castillo, Macnelly Torres, Juan Manuel Martínez, Blas Antonio Miguel Pérez. DT: Jorge Luis Bernal
BOCA JUNIORS: Mauricio Ariel Caranta (46 Aldo Antonio Bobadilla), Hugo Benjamín Ibarra, Daniel Alberto Díaz, Claudio Marcelo Morel, Clemente Juan Rodríguez (77 Matías Agustín Silvestre), Pablo Martín Ledesma, Ever Maximiliano David Banega, Neri Raúl Cardozo (66 Jesús Alberto Dátolo), Juan Román Riquelme, Martín Palermo, Rodrigo Sebastián Palacio. DT: Miguel Ángel Russo
Goals: Blas Antonio Miguel Pérez (39, 65), Rubén Darío Bustos (83) / Pablo Martín Ledesma (27).

BOCA JUNIORS – CÚCUTA DEPORTIVO 3-0 (1-0)
Alberto J. Armando 'La Bombonera', Buenos Aires, 7.06.2007
Referee: Roberto Carlos Silvera (URU), Attendance: 37.488
BOCA JUNIORS: Aldo Antonio Bobadilla, Hugo Benjamín Ibarra, Daniel Alberto Díaz, Claudio Marcelo Morel (84 Matías Agustín Silvestre), Clemente Juan Rodríguez, Pablo Martín Ledesma, Ever Maximiliano David Banega, Neri Raúl Cardozo (85 Sebastián Alejandro Battaglia), Juan Román Riquelme, Martín Palermo, Rodrigo Sebastián Palacio. DT: Miguel Ángel Russo
CÚCUTA: Róbinson Zapata, Rubén Darío Bustos, Elvis Javier González, Wálter José Moreno, Julián Hurtado, Dúmar Ricardo Rueda (90+1 Braynner Yesid García), Nélson Alfonso Flores (67 David Camilo Córdoba), Macnelly Torres, Lionard Fernando Pajoy, Alexander Del Castillo (79 Víctor Javier Cortés), Juan Manuel Martínez. DT: Jorge Luis Bernal
Goals: Juan Román Riquelme (44), Martín Palermo (61), Sebastián Alejandro Battaglia (90).

FINALS

BOCA JUNIORS – GRÊMIO FOOTBALL 3-0 (1-0)
Alberto J. Armando 'La Bombonera', Buenos Aires, 13.06.2007
Referee: Jorge Luis Larrionda (URU), Attendance: 39.993
BOCA JUNIORS: Mauricio Ariel Caranta, Hugo Benjamín Ibarra, Daniel Alberto Díaz, Claudio Marcelo Morel, Clemente Juan Rodríguez, Pablo Martín Ledesma, Ever Maximiliano David Banega (81 Sebastián Alejandro Battaglia), Neri Raúl Cardozo (67 Jesús Alberto Dátolo), Juan Román Riquelme, Martín Palermo, Rodrigo Sebastián Palacio. DT: Miguel Ángel Russo
GRÊMIO: Diego Sebastián Saja, PATRICIO Antônio Boques, WILLIAM Machado de Oliveira, Wender Coelho da Silva "TECO", LÚCIO Carlos Cajueiro Souza, SANDRO "GOIANO" Gomes Luz, Diego Antonio Gavilán, Ânderson Simas Luciano "TCHECO" (80 DOUGLAS de Oliveira), DIEGO de SOUZA Andrade, CARLOS EDUARDO Marques, Moacir Bastos "TUTA" (72 LUCAS Pezzini Leiva). DT: Mano Menezes
Sent off: Sandro Goiano (58)
Goals: Rodrigo Sebastián Palacio (18), Juan Román Riquelme (73), PATRICIO Antônio Boques (89 own goal).

GRÊMIO FOOTBALL – BOCA JUNIORS 0-2 (0-0)
Olímpico Monumental, Porto Alegre, 20.06.2007
Referee: Óscar Julián Ruiz (COL), Attendance: 43.952
GRÊMIO: Diego Sebastián Saja, PATRICIO Antônio Boques, WILLIAM Machado de Oliveira, Wender Coelho da Silva "TECO" (35 Rolando Carlos Schiavi), LÚCIO Carlos Cajueiro Souza, LUCAS Pezzini Leiva, Diego Antonio Gavilán, Ânderson Simas Luciano "TCHECO" (46 Márcio AMOROSO dos Santos), DIEGO de SOUZA Andrade, CARLOS EDUARDO Marques, Moacir Bastos "TUTA" (70 EVERTON Santos). DT: Mano Menezes
BOCA JUNIORS: Mauricio Ariel Caranta, Hugo Benjamín Ibarra, Daniel Alberto Díaz, Claudio Marcelo Morel, Clemente Juan Rodríguez, Pablo Martín Ledesma, Ever Maximiliano David Banega (82 Sergio Daniel Orteman), Neri Raúl Cardozo (59 Sebastián Alejandro Battaglia), Juan Román Riquelme, Martín Palermo, Rodrigo Sebastián Palacio (87 Mauro Boselli). DT: Miguel Ángel Russo
Martín Palermo missed a penalty in the 83rd minute
Goals: Juan Román Riquelme (69, 81).

2008

FIRST ROUND

ARSENAL - MINEROS DE GUAYANA 2-0 (1-0)
Julio Humberto Grondona, Sarandí - Buenos Aires, 29.01.2008, Referee: Enrique Ossés (CHI)
ARSENAL: Mario Eduardo Cuenca, Javier Marcelo Gandolfi, Jossimar Mosquera, Aníbal Samuel Matellán, Cristian Leonel Díaz, Sebastián Carrera (63 Diego Nicolás Villar), Carlos Damián Casteglione, Andrés San Martín (78 Cristian Alberto Pellerano), Martín Ezequiel Andrizzi, Alejandro Darío Gómez (63 Luciano Félix Leguizamón), José Luis Calderón. DT: Gustavo Alfaro
MINEROS: Euro Iván Guzmán, Wilson Cuero, Atahualpa Gabriel González, Jailson Dos Santos, Flavio De Jesús, Gregory Luzardo (73 Juan Carlos Lira), José Javier Caraballo (85 Giancarlos Sensi), Jarrín García, Ederlei Aparecido Pereira, Nicolás Massia (86 Cristian Jeandet), Jhonny Carneiro. DT: Stalin Rivas
Goals: José Luis Calderón (41), Luciano Félix Leguizamón (78)

MINEROS DE GUAYANA – ARSENAL 2-1 (1-0)
CTE Cachamay, Puerto Ordaz, 5.02.2008, Referee: Leonardo Gaciba (BRA)
MINEROS: Euro Iván Guzmán, Wilson Cuero, Atahualpa Gabriel González, Jailson Dos Santos, Flavio De Jesús (69 José Javier Caraballo), Gregory Luzardo, Jarrín García, Ederlei Aparecido Pereira (76 Elías Leal), Nicolás Massia, Jhonny Carneiro, Cristian Jeandet (65 Alexis Acuña). DT: Stalin Rivas
ARSENAL: Catrinel Iván Orcellet, Javier Marcelo Gandolfi, Jossimar Mosquera, Aníbal Samuel Matellán, Cristian Leonel Díaz, Sebastián Carrera (60 Pablo Sebastián Garnier), Carlos Damián Casteglione, Andrés San Martín, Martín Ezequiel Andrizzi (66 Javier Orlando Yacuzzi), Alejandro Darío Gómez (76 Leonardo Ángel Biagini), José Luis Calderón. DT: Gustavo Alfaro
Sent off: García (90)
Goals: Ederlei Aparecido Pereira (45 penalty), Jailson Dos Santos (58) / José Luis Calderón (46)

CRUZEIRO - CERRO PORTEÑO 3-1 (1-0)
Magalhães Pinto 'Mineirão', Belo Horizonte, 30.01.2008, Referee: Jorge Larrionda (URU)
CRUZEIRO: FÁBIO Deivson Lopes Maciel, Antonio Marcos Silva Filho 'MARQUINHO PARANÁ', THIAGO MARTINELLI Silva, THIAGO HELENO Henrique Ferreira, José JADÍLSON dos Santos Silva, FABRICIO De Souza, CHARLES Fernando Basílio Silva, RAMIRES Santos Nascimento, WAGNER Ferreira Dos Santos (69 Fernando Alves Santa Clara 'FERNANDINHO'), GUILHERME Mihomem Gusmão (60 KERLON Moura Souza, 76 Marcio Rocha Da Silva 'MARCINHO'), Marcelo Martins Moreno. DT: Adilson Batista
CERRO PORTEÑO: Diego Daniel Barreto, Fidel Amado Pérez, Nelson David Cabrera, Jorge Orlando Brítez, César Augusto Ramírez (67 Víctor Ramón Ferreira), Pablo Junior Giménez, Jorge Martín Núñez, Walter Milciades Fretes (53 Luis Enrique Cáceres), Osvaldo Hobecker (46 Lorgio Álvarez), Marcelo Alejandro Estigarribia, Rodrigo Ramón Burgos. DT: Javier Torrente
Goals: RAMIRES Santos Nascimento (40, 89), Marcelo Martins Moreno (55) /
Nelson Cabrera (74 penalty)

CERRO PORTEÑO – CRUZEIRO 2-3 (1-1)
Defensores del Chaco, Asunción, 6.02.2008, Referee: Carlos Chandía (CHI)
CERRO PORTEÑO: Diego Daniel Barreto, Alfredo David Rojas (64 Walter Milciades Fretes), Fidel Amado Pérez, Nelson David Cabrera, Jorge Orlando Brítez, César Augusto Ramírez, Luis Enrique Cáceres, Ernesto Rubén Cristaldo (46 Víctor Ramón Ferreira), Lorgio Álvarez, Jorge Martín Núñez, Marcelo Alejandro Estigarribia. DT: Javier Torrente

CRUZEIRO: FÁBIO Deivson Lopes Maciel, Antonio Marcos Silva Filho 'MARQUINHO PARANÁ', THIAGO HELENO Henrique Ferreira, José JADÍLSON dos Santos Silva, FABRICIO De Souza, CHARLES Fernando Basílio Silva (67 LUIS ALBERTO Santos Dos Santos), RAMIRES Santos Nascimento, WAGNER Ferreira Dos Santos, THIAGO MARTINELLI Silva, Marcelo Martins Moreno, LEANDRO DOMINGUES Barbosa (46 Fernando Alves Santa Clara 'FERNANDINHO'). DT: Adilson Batista
Goals: Lorgio Álvarez (42, 63) / THIAGO HELENO Henrique Ferreira (5), Marcelo Martins Moreno (53 penalty), RAMIRES Santos Nascimento (57)
The match was abandoned due to crowd trouble in the 70th minute but the result was allowed to stand.

ATLAS GUADALAJARA - LA PAZ FC 2-0 (1-0)
Jalisco, Guadalajara, 30.01.2008, Referee: Georges Buckley (PER)
ATLAS: Jorge Rodrigo Bava, Omar Alejandro Flores, Diego Daniel Colotto, Juan Carlos Medina (58 Luis Enrique Robles), Emanuel Adrian Centurión (63 Óscar Salvador Vera), Jorge Hernández, Hugo Ayala, Christian de Jesús Valdez, Ulises Mendivil (84 Flavio Jesús Santos), Bruno Marioni, Eduardo Rergis. DT: Miguel Ángel Brindisi
LA PAZ: Mauro Machado, Miguel Ángel Hurtado, Juan Carlos Paz García, Rómulo Alaca, Édgar Clavijo, Diómedes Peña (66 Julio César Cortez), Edgar Rolando Olivares (85 Kyle Zenoni), Helmut Enrique Gutiérrez, Augusto Andaverís, Didí Torrico, Regis Adair Quaresma. DT: Sergio Apaza
Goals: Ulises Mendivil (6), Eduardo Rergis (72)

LA PAZ FC – ATLAS GUADALAJARA 1-0 (0-0)
Hernando Siles, La Paz, 6.02.2008, Referee: Antonio Arias (PAR)
LA PAZ: Mauro Machado, Miguel Ángel Hurtado (76 Juan Eduardo Fierro), Juan Carlos Paz García, Rómulo Alaca, Édgar Clavijo, Diómedes Peña, Julio César Cortez, Helmut Enrique Gutiérrez (89 Kyle Zenoni), Augusto Andaverís, Didí Torrico, Regis Adair Quaresma. DT: Sergio Apaza
ATLAS: Jorge Rodrigo Bava, Luis Enrique Robles, Jorge Emmanuel Torres, Bruno Marioni, Néstor Vicente Vidrio, Jorge Hernández, Gerardo Flores, Hugo Ayala, Christian de Jesús Valdez, Ulises Mendivil (67 Jorge Daniel Achucarro), Eduardo Rergis. DT: Miguel Ángel Brindisi
Goal: Edgar Clavijo (51)

OLMEDO RIOBAMBA – LANÚS 1-0 (0-0)
Olímpico, Riobamba, 31.01.2008, Referee: Víctor Hugo Rivera (Peru)
OLMEDO: Edwin Alberto Villafuerte, Omar Eduardo Ledesma, Carlos Javier Caicedo (46 Freddy Samaniego), José Luis Perlaza, Juan Keli Guerrón, Elvis Élber Bone, Andrés Alejandro Vinueza, Sebastian Vezzani (65 Gonzalo Javier Chila), Lucas Godoy (46 Estuardo Cristian Quiñónez), John Jairo Tenorio, Maximiliano Antonelli. DT: Armando Osma
LANÚS: Carlos Gustavo Bossio, Rodolfo Graieb, Carlos Gustavo Quintana, Emir Saúl Faccioli, Maximiliano Velázquez, Sebastián Blanco (80 Adrián Peralta), Agustín Pelletieri, Matías Fritzler, Diego Valeri, Lautaro Acosta (74 Diego Lagos), José Gustavo Sand. DT: Ramón Cabrero
Goal: Estuardo Cristian Quiñónez (71)

LANÚS – OLMEDO RIOBAMBA 3-0 (0-0)
Néstor Díaz Pérez, Ciudad de Lanús, Referee: Heber Lopes (BRA)
LANÚS: Carlos Gustavo Bossio, Rodolfo Graieb, Carlos Gustavo Quintana, Emir Saúl Faccioli, Maximiliano Velázquez, Sebastián Blanco (84 Sebastián Salomón), Agustín Pelletieri, Matías Fritzler, Diego Valeri (86 Adrián Peralta), Lautaro Acosta (56 Santiago Biglieri), José Gustavo Sand. DT: Ramón Cabrero
OLMEDO: Edwin Alberto Villafuerte (27 Francisco Manuel Caicedo), Omar Eduardo Ledesma, Freddy Samaniego, José Luis Perlaza, Juan Keli Guerrón, Elvis Élber Bone, Gustavo Nazareno (60 Andrés Alejandro Vinueza), Sebastian Vezzani, John Jairo Tenorio, Maximiliano Antonelli, Cristian Badaracco (60 Estuardo Cristian Quiñónez). DT: Armando Osma
Sent off: J.J. Tenorio (90)
Goals: Matías Fritzler (58), Santiago Biglieri (77), Maximiliano Velázquez (83)

CIENCIANO - MONTEVIDEO WANDERERS 1-0 (1-0)
Inca Gracilaso de la Vega, Cusco, 31.01.2008, Referee: Carlos Vera (ECU)
CIENCIANO: Juan Ángel Flores, Luis Manuel Marengo, Carlos Solís, Julio Romaña (76 Daniel Peláez), Roberto Carlos Guizasola, César Camilo Ccahuantico, Juan Carlos Bazalar (70 Aldo Ítalo Olcese), William Medardo Chiroque, Julio César García (70 Julio Edson Uribe), Gustavo Enrique Vassallo, Masakatsu Sawa. DT: Franco Navarro
MONTEVIDEO WANDERERS: Sergio Antonio Martínez, Emiliano Mathias Tellechea, Edgar Leonardo Martínez, Miguel Ángel Britos, Juan Daniel Álvez, Álvaro Fernández, Víctor Adrián Fagúndez, Fernando Fadeuille, Simon Vanderhoeght (66 Matías Quagliotti), Facundo Martín Martínez (76 Diego Gonzalo Chavez), Danilo Javier Peinado (86 Jonathan Charquero). DT: Jorge Gonçalvez
Goal: Masakatsu Sawa (13)

MONTEVIDEO WANDERERS – CIENCIANO 0-0
Centenario, Montevideo, 7.02.2008, Referee: Federico Beligoy (ARG)
MONTEVIDEO WANDERERS: Sergio Antonio Martínez, Emiliano Mathias Tellechea (75 Christian Abraham Yeladian), Edgar Leonardo Martínez, Miguel Ángel Britos, Juan Daniel Álvez, Álvaro Fernández, Víctor Adrián Fagúndez, Fernando Fadeuille (57 Jonathan Alexis Pérez), Facundo Martín Martínez, Manuel Abreu (74 Jonathan Charquero), Danilo Javier Peinado. DT: Jorge Gonçalvez
CIENCIANO: Juan Ángel Flores, Roberto Carlos Guizasola, Luis Manuel Marengo, Carlos Solís, Julio Romaña, César Camilo Ccahuantico, Juan Carlos Bazalar (90 César Andres Ortiz), Julio César García (80 Aldo Ítalo Olcese), William Medardo Chiroque, Gustavo Enrique Vassallo (72 Víctor Hugo Manique), Masakatsu Sawa. DT: Franco Navarro

BOYACÁ CHICÓ FC - AUDAX ITALIANO 4-3 (2-1)
Nemesio Camacho, Bogota, 7.02.2008
Referee: Juan Soto (VEN)
BOYACÁ CHICÓ: Walter Henry Noriega, Ever Antonio Palacios, Leoncio Alejandro Alegría (71 Edwin Dayan Móvil), Jules Eric Ntarnak (46 Juan Gabriel Galicia), Óscar Díaz, Víctor Danilo Pacheco, Miguel Eduardo Caneo, Pedro Macario Pino, Juna Alejandro Mahecha (46 Leonardo Fábio López), Rodrigo Alonso Saraz, Néstor Fabían Salazar. DT: Alberto Gamero
AUDAX: Mario Eduardo Villasanti, Boris Alexis Rieloff, Carlos Alberto Garrido, Sebastián Rocco, Patricio Javier Gutiérrez, Marcelo Carlo Broli, Braulio Antonio Leal, Miguel Ángel Romero (89 Nicolás Ignacio Corvetto), Carlos Andrés Villanueva, Renato Andrés Ramos (74 Renzo Alberto Yáñez), Fabian Ariel Orellana. DT: Raúl Toro
Sent off: Saraz (78)
Goals: Néstor Salazar (8, 90), Víctor Pacheco (37), Miguel Caneo (76 penalty) /
Jules Ntarnak (1 own goal), Carlos Villanueva (21), Fabián Orellana (61)

AUDAX ITALIANO - BOYACÁ CHICÓ FC 1-0 (0-0)
Monumental, Santiago, 12.02.2008, Referee: Óscar Maldonado (BOL)
AUDAX: Mario Eduardo Villasanti, Boris Alexis Rieloff (72 Manuel Francisco Ibarra), Carlos Alberto Garrido, Sebastián Rocco, Patricio Javier Gutiérrez, Marcelo Carlo Broli, Braulio Antonio Leal, Miguel Ángel Romero, Carlos Andrés Villanueva, Renato Andrés Ramos (72 Renzo Alberto Yáñez), Fabian Ariel Orellana. DT: Raúl Toro
BOYACÁ CHICÓ: Edigson Velásquez, Mario Humberto García (62 Jesús Brahaman Sinisterra), Ever Antonio Palacios, Pedro Macario Pino, Juan Gabriel Galicia, Rubén Darío Velásquez (83 Wilmer Jesús Beltre), Óscar Díaz, Miguel Eduardo Caneo (74 Ferley Raúl Villamil), Edwin Dayan Móvil, Víctor Danilo Pacheco, Néstor Fabían Salazar. DT: Alberto Gamero
Goal: Marcelo Carlo Broli (80)

SECOND PHASE

GROUP 1

CARACAS FC - SAN LORENZO 2-0 (1-0)
Olímpico, Caracas, 12.02.2008, Referee: Alberto Duarte (COL)
CARACAS: Vicente Rosales, Franklin José Lucena, José Hermes Mera, Jaime Andrés Bustamante, Juan Valencia, Luis Enrique Vera, Edgar Hernán Jiménez (86 John Ocoro), Ronald Alejandro Vargas, Juan Cominges (77 Bremer Alfredo Piñango), Rafael Castellín, Pablo Emanuel Bastianini (80 Emilio Rentería). DT: Noel Sanvicente
SAN LORENZO: Agustín Ignacio Orión, Christian Alberto Tula, Sebastián Ariel Méndez, Jonathan Pablo Bottinelli, Diego Rodolfo Placente, Diego Alejandro Rivero (46 Hernán Adrián González), Jorge Alberto Ortiz (86 Santiago Hirsig), Juan Manuel Torres, Román Aureliano Torres (73 Bernardo Daniel Romeo), Andrés Nicolás D'Alessandro, Néstor Andrés Silvera. DT: Ramón Díaz
Sent off: Tula (42), J.M. Torres (89)
Goals: Ronald Alejandro Vargas (40), Rafael Castellín (70)

CRUZEIRO - REAL POTOSÍ 3-0 (0-0)
Governador Magalhães Pinto 'Mineirão', Belo Horizonte, 13.02.2008, Referee: Roberto Silva (BRA)
CRUZEIRO: FÁBIO Deivson Lopes Maciel, Antonio Marcos Silva Filho 'MARQUINHO PARANÁ' (78 Luis Dialisson De Souza Alves 'APODI'), THIAGO HELENO Henrique Ferreira, Giovanny Patricio Espinoza, José JADÍLSON dos Santos Silva (46 Fernando Alves Santa Clara 'FERNANDINHO'), FABRICIO De Souza, CHARLES Fernando Basílio Silva, RAMIRES Santos Nascimento, WAGNER Ferreira Dos Santos (65 Marcio Rocha Da Silva 'MARCINHO'), GUILHERME Mihomem Gusmão, Marcelo Martins Moreno. DT: Adilson Batista
REAL POTOSÍ: Hugo Suárez, Luis Gatty Ribeiro, Edemir Rodríguez, Nicolás Sartori, Marco David Paz, Nicolás Suárez, Eduardo Fabiano Ortiz, Miguel Oswaldo Loayza (59 Adrián Cuéllar), Gonzalo Germán Galindo (55 Percy Colque), Álvaro Gabriel Pintos, Isidro Candia (75 Ronald Eguino). DT: Mauricio Soria.
Goals: Marcelo Martins Moreno (46), RAMIRES Santos Nascimento (52), GUILHERME Mihomem Gusmão (66)

SAN LORENZO - CRUZEIRO 0-0
Pedro Bidegain, Buenos Aires, 21.02.2008, Referee: Carlos Amarilla (PAR)
SAN LORENZO: Agustín Ignacio Orión, Hernán Adrián González, Gastón Damián Aguirre, Diego Rodolfo Placente, Wálter Aníbal Acevedo, Jonathan Pablo Bottinelli, Néstor Andrés Silvera, Santiago Hirsig (71 Román Aureliano Torres), Daniel Rubén Bilos (64 Jorge Alberto Ortiz), Andrés Nicolás D'Alessandro, Gonzalo Rubén Bergessio (66 Bernardo Daniel Romeo). DT: Ramón Díaz
CRUZEIRO: FÁBIO Deivson Lopes Maciel, Antonio Marcos Silva Filho 'MARQUINHO PARANÁ', THIAGO MARTINELLI Silva, Giovanny Patricio Espinoza, José JADÍLSON dos Santos Silva, FABRICIO De Souza, CHARLES Fernando Basílio Silva, RAMIRES Santos Nascimento, WAGNER Ferreira Dos Santos (46 Fernando Alves Santa Clara 'FERNANDINHO'), Marcelo Martins Moreno (84 MARCEL Augusto Ortolan), GUILHERME Mihomem Gusmão (60 Marcio Rocha Da Silva 'MARCINHO'). DT: Adilson Batista

CARACAS FC - REAL POTOSÍ 2-1 (2-0)
Olímpico, Caracas, 26.02.2008, Referee: José Buitrago (COL)
CARACAS: Vicente Rosales, José Hermes Mera, Jaime Andrés Bustamante, Juan Valencia, Luis Enrique Vera, Emilio Rentería (89 Giovanny Romero), Edgar Hernán Jiménez, Ronald Alejandro Vargas, Juan Cominges (77 John Ocoro), Pablo Emanuel Bastianini (13 Jorge Francisco Casanova), Franklin José Lucena. DT: Noel Sanvicente Sent off: Vargas (44)
BAMIN REAL POTOSÍ: Hugo Suárez, Luis Gatty Ribeiro, Ronald Eguino, Santos Amador (65 Marco David Paz), Nicolás Sartori, Nicolás Suárez, Eduardo Fabiano Ortiz, Percy Colque (57 Adrián Cuéllar), Gonzalo Germán Galindo, Álvaro Gabriel Pintos, Isidro Candia. DT: Mauricio Soria.
Goals: Emilio Rentería (3), Ronald Alejandro Vargas (38) / Gonzalo Germán Galindo (74)

CRUZEIRO - CARACAS FC 3-0 (2-0)
Governador Magalhães Pinto 'Mineirão', Belo Horizonte, 4.03.2008, Referee: Saúl Laverni (ARG)
CRUZEIRO: FÁBIO Deivson Lopes Maciel, JONATHAN Cícero Moreira, THIAGO HELENO Henrique Ferreira, Giovanny Patricio Espinoza, José JADÍLSON dos Santos Silva, Antonio Marcos Silva Filho 'MARQUINHO PARANÁ', CHARLES Fernando Basílio Silva, RAMIRES Santos Nascimento, WAGNER Ferreira Dos Santos (61 Marcio Rocha Da Silva 'MARCINHO'), Marcelo Martins Moreno (82 MARCEL Augusto Ortolan), GUILHERME Mihomem Gusmão (71 LEANDRO DOMINGUES Barbosa). DT: Adilson Batista
CARACAS: Vicente Rosales, Franklin José Lucena, José Hermes Mera, Jaime Andrés Bustamante, Juan Valencia, Luis Enrique Vera, Emilio Rentería (69 Ever Espinoza), Edgar Hernán Jiménez, Juan Cominges (84 Miguel Ángel Romero), Pablo Emanuel Bastianini, John Ocoro (46 Jorge Francisco Casanova). DT: Noel Sanvicente
Goals: GUILHERME Mihomem Gusmão (9), RAMIRES Santos Nascimento (28),
Marcelo Martins Moreno (64)

BAMIN REAL POTOSÍ - SAN LORENZO 2-3 (2-0)
Víctor Agustín Ugarte, Potosí, 11.03.2008, Referee: Jorge Larrionda (URU)
BAMIN REAL POTOSÍ: Hugo Suárez, Nicolás Sartori, Edemir Rodríguez, Santos Amador, Luis Gatty Ribeiro, Nicolás Suárez, Miguel Oswaldo Loayza, Isidro Candia (67 Marco David Paz), Gonzalo Germán Galindo, Álvaro Gabriel Pintos, Luis Hernán Sillero. DT: Mauricio Soria.
SAN LORENZO: Agustín Ignacio Orión, Hernán Adrián González (70 Cristian Gabriel Chávez), Gastón Damián Aguirre, Nicolás Bianchi Arce, Diego Rodolfo Placente, Juan Manuel Torres (75 Pablo Andrés Alvarado), Santiago Hirsig (46 Daniel Rubén Bilos), Diego Alejandro Rivero, Bernardo Daniel Romeo, Gonzalo Rubén Bergessio, Román Aureliano Torres. DT: Ramón Díaz
Sent off: Gonzalo Germán Galindo (50)
Goals: Miguel Oswaldo Loayza (17), Álvaro Gabriel Pintos (32) /
Bernardo Daniel Romeo (71), Cristian Gabriel Chávez (78), Román Aureliano Torres (88 penalty)

CARACAS FC - CRUZEIRO 1-1 (1-0)
Olímpico, Caracas, 18.03.2008, Referee: Óscar Julián Ruiz (COL)
CARACAS: Vicente Rosales, Franklin José Lucena, José Hermes Mera, Oswaldo Augusto Vizcarrondo, Juan Valencia, Luis Enrique Vera, Edgar Hernán Jiménez (81 Jorge Francisco Casanova), Ronald Alejandro Vargas, Juan Cominges (75 Gualberto Campos), Rafael Castellín, Pablo Emanuel Bastianini (65 Emilio Rentería). DT: Noel Sanvicente
CRUZEIRO: FÁBIO Deivson Lopes Maciel, JONATHAN Cícero Moreira, THIAGO MARTINELLI Silva, Giovanny Patricio Espinoza, Antonio Marcos Silva Filho 'MARQUINHO PARANÁ', RAMIRES Santos Nascimento, WAGNER Ferreira Dos Santos, Leonardo 'LEO' FORTUNATO Dos Santos, Marcio Rocha Da Silva 'MARCINHO', Marcelo Martins Moreno, Luis Dialisson De Souza Alves 'APODI'. DT: Adilson Batista
Sent off: Vizcarrondo (87)
Goals: Juan Valencia (30) / Marcelo Martins Moreno (55 penalty)

SAN LORENZO – BAMIN REAL POTOSÍ 1-0 (1-0)
Pedro Bidegain, Buenos Aires, 25.03.2008, Referee: Heber Lopes (BRA)
SAN LORENZO: Agustín Ignacio Orión, Hernán Adrián González, Diego Rodolfo Placente, Gastón Damián Aguirre, Juan Manuel Torres, Sebastián Ariel Méndez, Daniel Rubén Bilos (66 Román Aureliano Torres), Diego Alejandro Rivero, Bernardo Daniel Romeo, Andrés Nicolás D'Alessandro (81 Juan Carlos Menseguez), Gonzalo Rubén Bergessio (59 Néstor Andrés Silvera). DT: Ramón Díaz
BAMIN REAL POTOSÍ: Hugo Suárez, Nicolás Sartori, Edemir Rodríguez, Santos Amador, Luis Gatty Ribeiro, Miguel Oswaldo Loayza, Isidro Candia, Marco David Paz, Jesús Ronald Gallegos (51 Luis Hernán Sillero), Percy Colque (89 Adrián Cuéllar), Álvaro Gabriel Pintos. DT:Tito Montaño
Goal: Hernán Adrián González (29 penalty)

BAMIN REAL POTOSÍ - CARACAS FC 3-1 (2-1)
Víctor Agustín Ugarte, Potosí, 1.04.2008, Referee: Georges Buckley (PER)
BAMIN REAL POTOSÍ: Hugo Suárez, Nicolás Sartori, Edemir Rodríguez, Luis Gatty Ribeiro, Miguel Oswaldo Loayza, Isidro Candia (60 Gonzalo Germán Galindo), Santos Amador, Marco David Paz, Jesús Ronald Gallegos (83 Eduardo Fabiano Ortiz), Luis Hernán Sillero (71 Nicolás Suárez), Álvaro Gabriel Pintos. DT: Tito Montaño
CARACAS: Vicente Rosales, Franklin José Lucena, José Hermes Mera, Jaime Andrés Bustamante, Juan Valencia, Luis Enrique Vera, Rafael Castellín, Ronald Alejandro Vargas, Giovanny Romero (71 Edgar Hernán Jiménez), Pablo Emanuel Bastianini (62 Emilio Rentería), Juan Cominges (62 Jorge Francisco Casanova). DT: Noel Sanvicente
Goals: Isidro Candia (3), Hugo Suárez (25), Álvaro Gabriel Pintos (80) / Rafael Castellín (6)

CRUZEIRO - SAN LORENZO 3-1 (1-0)
Epaminondas Mendes Brito, Ipatinga, 3.04.2008, Referee: Carlos Chandía (CHI)
CRUZEIRO: FÁBIO Deivson Lopes Maciel, Leonardo 'LEO' FORTUNATO Dos Santos, HENRIQUE Pacheco de Lima (80 Marcio Rocha Da Silva 'MARCINHO'), Giovanny Patricio Espinoza, Luis Dialisson De Souza Alves 'APODI', Antonio Marcos Silva Filho 'MARQUINHO PARANÁ', RAMIRES Santos Nascimento, José JADÍLSON dos Santos Silva, WAGNER Ferreira dos Santos, GUILHERME Mihomem Gusmão (66 THIAGO HELENO Henrique Ferreira), Marcelo Martins Moreno. DT: Adilson Batista
SAN LORENZO: Agustín Ignacio Orión, Gastón Damián Aguirre, Sebastián Ariel Méndez, Jonathan Pablo Bottinelli, Hernán Adrián González (51 Daniel Rubén Bilos), Diego Alejandro Rivero, Pablo Andrés Alvarado, Diego Rodolfo Placente, Andrés Nicolás D'Alessandro (74 Wálter Aníbal Acevedo), Gonzalo Rubén Bergessio, Bernardo Daniel Romeo (60 Néstor Andrés Silvera). DT: Ramón Díaz
Goals: Marcelo Moreno (10, 70), WAGNER Ferreira Dos Santos (81) / Néstor Andrés Silvera (87)

BAMIN REAL POTOSÍ - CRUZEIRO 5-1 (2-1)
Víctor Agustín Ugarte, Potosí, 16.04.2008, Referee: Alfredo Intriago (ECU)
BAMIN REAL POTOSÍ: Hugo Suárez, Luis Gatty Ribeiro, Marco David Paz (79 Eduardo Fabiano Ortiz), Edemir Rodríguez, Ronald Eguino, Jesús Ronald Gallegos (76 Gonzalo Germán Galindo), Miguel Oswaldo Loayza (81 Gerardo César Yecerotte), Isidro Candia, Nicolás Suárez, Luis Hernán Sillero, Álvaro Gabriel Pintos. DT:Tito Montaño
CRUZEIRO: FÁBIO Deivson Lopes Maciel, Antonio Marcos Silva Filho 'MARQUINHO PARANÁ', Giovanny Patricio Espinoza, Leonardo 'LEO' FORTUNATO Dos Santos, RAMIRES Santos Nascimento, WAGNER Ferreira Dos Santos, THIAGO MARTINELLI Silva, HENRIQUE Pacheco De Lima, JONATHAN Cícero Moreira, Marcelo Martins Moreno, CHARLES Fernando Basílio Silva.
Goals: Miguel Oswaldo Loayza (3), Álvaro Gabriel Pintos (12, 51), Isidro Candia (66), Luis Gatty Ribeiro (86) / Marcelo Martins Moreno (29 penalty)

SAN LORENZO - CARACAS FC 3-0 (1-0)
Pedro Bidegain, Buenos Aires, 16.04.2008, Referee: Wilmar Roldán (COL)
SAN LORENZO: Agustín Ignacio Orión, Hernán Adrián González (66 Pablo Andrés Alvarado), Gastón Damián Aguirre, Sebastián Ariel Méndez, Diego Rodolfo Placente, Diego Alejandro Rivero (46 Jonathan Pablo Bottinelli), Juan Manuel Torres, Wálter Aníbal Acevedo, Andrés Nicolás D'Alessandro (83 Román Aureliano Torres), Néstor Andrés Silvera, Gonzalo Rubén Bergessio. DT: Ramón Díaz
CARACAS: Vicente Rosales, Franklin José Lucena, José Hermes Mera, Oswaldo Augusto Vizcarrondo, Juan Valencia, Luis Enrique Vera, Edgar Hernán Jiménez (46 Pablo Emanuel Bastianini), Rafael Castellín, Ronald Alejandro Vargas (67 Emilio Rentería), Juan Cominges, Alejandro Abraham Guerra (46 John Ocoro). DT: Noel Sanvicente
Goals: Gonzalo Rubén Bergessio (16), Vicente Rosales (35 own goal), Néstor Andrés Silvera (78)

1	CRUZEIRO	6	3	2	1	11	7	11
2	SAN LORENZO	6	3	1	2	8	7	10
3	Caracas FC	6	2	1	3	6	11	7
4	Bamin Real Potosí	6	2	0	4	11	11	6

GROUP 2

DEPORTIVO CUENCA - ESTUDIANTES LA PLATA 1-0 (1-0)
Alejandro Serrano Aguilar, Cuenca, 12.02.2008, Referee: Rubén Selman (CHI)
CUENCA: Javier Hernán Klimowicz, Marlon Patricio Moreno, Julio Marcelo Fleitas, Arlín Segundo Ayoví, Marcelo Cristian Bohórquez, Jimmy Alfredo Bran, Leonardo Javier Soledispa, Germán Castillo (89 Mariano Mina), Federico Barrionuevo (73 Jhon García), Javier Fabián Toledo (83 Gustavo Omar Figueroa), Mauricio Javier Ferradás. DT: Gabriel Perrone
ESTUDIANTES: Mariano Gonzalo Andújar, Marcos Alberto Angeleri, Agustín Alayes, Leandro Desabato, Juan Manuel Díaz (67 Enzo Nicolás Pérez), Juan Sebastián Verón, Rodrigo Braña, Leandro Damián Benítez, Juan Manuel Salgueiro (81 Pablo Ariel Lugüerico), Ezequiel Carlos Maggiolo (62 Leandro Hernán Lazzaro), Pablo Daniel Piatti. DT: Roberto Sensini
Goal: Mauricio Javier Ferradás (45)

LANÚS - DANUBIO 3-1 (1-1)
Néstor Díaz Pérez, Lanús, 14.02.2008, Referee: Carlos Galeano (PAR)
LANÚS: Carlos Gustavo Bossio, Rodolfo Graieb, Carlos Gustavo Quintana, Emir Saúl Faccioli, Nelson Benítez, Sebastián Blanco, Agustín Pelletieri, Sebastián Salomón (53 Diego Hernán González), Diego Valeri (81 Eduardo Ledesma), José Gustavo Sand, Lautaro Acosta (89 Germán Ezequiel Cano). DT: Ramón Cabrero
DANUBIO: Néstor Esteban Conde, Damián Alejandro Malrechauffe, Daniel Alejandro Lembo, Sergio Gonzalo Rodríguez, Leonardo Abelenda, Ribair Rodríguez, Pedro Richar Irala, Gabriel Aníbal Alcoba (56 Jorge Adrián García), Matías Cresseri (65 Mateo Figoli), Cristian Pedro Bardaro (75 Deley Yesid Mena), Carlos María Morales. DT: Gustavo Dalto
Goals: Agustín Pelletieri (8), Lautaro Acosta (58), José Gustavo Sand (87) / Leonardo Abelenda (37)

DEPORTIVO CUENCA - DANUBIO 0-0
Alejandro Serrano Aguilar, Cuenca, 21.02.2008, Referee: Georges Buckley (PER)
CUENCA: Javier Hernán Klimowicz, Marlon Patricio Moreno, Julio Marcelo Fleitas, Arlín Segundo Ayoví, Marcelo Cristian Bohórquez, Jimmy Alfredo Bran, Leonardo Javier Soledispa, Germán Castillo, Federico Barrionuevo (70 Édison Preciado), Javier Fabián Toledo (79 Cristian Valencia), Mauricio Javier Ferradás. DT: Gabriel Perrone
DANUBIO: Néstor Esteban Conde, Damián Alejandro Malrechauffe, Daniel Alejandro Lembo, Sergio Gonzalo Rodríguez, Matías Omar Pérez, Leonardo Abelenda, Ribair Rodríguez, Pedro Richar Irala, Carlos María Morales (75 Derlis Florentín), Mateo Figoli (65 Deley Yesid Mena), Cristian Pedro Bardaro (68 Raúl Freddy Ferro). DT: Gustavo Dalto

ESTUDIANTES LA PLATA - LANÚS 0-0
Ciudad de La Plata, La Plata, 26.02.2008, Referee: Gabriel Favale (ARG)
ESTUDIANTES: Mariano Gonzalo Andújar, Marcos Alberto Angeleri, Agustín Alayes, Leandro Desabato, Juan Sebastián Verón, Rodrigo Braña, Leandro Damián Benítez, Juan Manuel Salgueiro (35 Pablo Ariel Lugüerico), Iván Diego Moreno y Fabianesi (84 Enzo Nicolás Pérez), Ezequiel Carlos Maggiolo (65 Leandro Hernán Lazzaro), Pablo Daniel Piatti. DT: Roberto Sensini
LANÚS: Carlos Gustavo Bossio, Rodolfo Graieb, Carlos Gustavo Quintana (88 Leonardo Germán Sigali), Emir Saúl Faccioli, Nelson Benítez, Sebastián Blanco (78 Sebastián Salomón), Agustín Pelletieri, Diego Hernán González, Diego Valeri, José Gustavo Sand, Lautaro Acosta. DT: Ramón Cabrero

DANUBIO - ESTUDIANTES LA PLATA 1-2 (1-0)
Centenario, Montevideo, 5.03.2008, Referee: Enrique Osses (CHI)
DANUBIO: Néstor Esteban Conde, Damián Alejandro Malrechauffe, Daniel Alejandro Lembo, Sergio Gonzalo Rodríguez, Matías Omar Pérez, Ribair Rodríguez, Pedro Richar Irala, Gabriel Aníbal Alcoba (65 Mateo Figoli), Carlos María Morales (42 Álvaro Daniel Noble), Deley Yesid Mena, Cristian Pedro Bardaro (77 Enzo Scorza). DT: Gustavo Dalto

ESTUDIANTES: Mariano Gonzalo Andújar, Marcos Alberto Angeleri, Agustín Alayes, Leandro Desabato, Juan Sebastián Verón, Rodrigo Braña, Leandro Damián Benítez, Pablo Ariel Lugüerico (68 Enzo Nicolás Pérez), Iván Diego Moreno y Fabianesi (46 José María Basanta), Leandro Hernán Lazzaro, Pablo Daniel Piatti (46 Cristian Venancio Bogado). DT: Roberto Sensini
Sent off: Alayes (25)
Goals: Pedro Richar Irala (9) / Juan Sebastián Verón (61 penalty), Enzo Nicolás Pérez (87)

LANÚS - DEPORTIVO CUENCA 0-0
Néstor Díaz Pérez, Lanús, 13.03.2008, Referee: Enrique Osses (CHI)
LANÚS: Carlos Gustavo Bossio, Rodolfo Graieb, Carlos Gustavo Quintana, Emir Saúl Faccioli, Maximiliano Velázquez, Sebastián Blanco, Sebastián Salomón (74 Diego Hernán González), Agustín Pelletieri, Diego Valeri (53 Adrián Peralta), Santiago Biglieri (77 Nicolás Francisco Ramírez), Germán Ezequiel Cano. DT: Ramón Cabrero
CUENCA: Javier Hernán Klimowicz, Marlon Patricio Moreno, Julio Marcelo Fleitas, Arlín Segundo Ayoví, Marcelo Cristian Bohórquez, Polo Wila, Jimmy Alfredo Bran, Leonardo Javier Soledispa (81 Jhon García), Germán Castillo (88 Mariano Mina), Javier Fabián Toledo (71 Federico Barrionuevo), Mauricio Javier Ferradás. DT: Gabriel Perrone

ESTUDIANTES LA PLATA - DANUBIO 2-0 (1-0)
Ciudad de la Plata, La Plata, 18.03.2008, Referee: Leonardo Gaciba (BRA)
ESTUDIANTES: Mariano Gonzalo Andújar, Marcos Alberto Angeleri, Leandro Desabato, José María Basanta, Juan Manuel Salgueiro, Juan Sebastián Verón (80 Diego Alberto Galván), Rodrigo Braña, Leandro Damián Benítez, Iván Diego Moreno y Fabianesi (65 Enzo Nicolás Pérez), Ezequiel Carlos Maggiolo (65 Leandro Hernán Lazzaro), Pablo Daniel Piatti. DT: Roberto Sensini
DANUBIO: Néstor Esteban Conde, Damián Alejandro Malrechauffe, Daniel Alejandro Lembo, Sergio Gonzalo Rodríguez, Matías Omar Pérez, Raúl Freddy Ferro (80 Matías Cresseri), Ribair Rodríguez, Pedro Richar Irala, Mateo Figoli, Deley Yesid Mena (70 Cristiano Gomes Machado), Cristian Pedro Bardaro (70 Derlis Florentín). DT: Gustavo Dalto
Gals: Juan Sebastián Verón (44 penalty), Leandro Desabato (75)

DEPORTIVO CUENCA - LANÚS 1-1 (0-1)
Alejandro Serrano Aguilar, Cuenca, 20.03.2008, Referee: Salvio Fagundes (BRA)
CUENCA: Javier Hernán Klimowicz, Marlon Patricio Moreno, Julio Marcelo Fleitas, Arlín Segundo Ayoví, Marcelo Cristian Bohórquez, Federico Barrionuevo (60 Jhon García), Jimmy Alfredo Bran (60 Hólger Eduardo Matamoros), Leonardo Javier Soledispa, Germán Castillo, Javier Fabián Toledo, Mauricio Javier Ferradás. DT: Gabriel Perrone
LANÚS: Carlos Gustavo Bossio, Rodolfo Graieb, Carlos Gustavo Quintana, Santiago Abel Hoyos, Maximiliano Velázquez, Sebastián Blanco (64 Adrián Peralta), Sebastián Salomón, Diego Hernán González, Agustín Pelletieri, Santiago Biglieri (28 Nicolás Francisco Ramírez), Germán Ezequiel Cano (80 Eduardo Ledesma). DT: Ramón Cabrero
Goals: Jhon García (70) / Sebastián Salomón (7)

DANUBIO - DEPORTIVO CUENCA 2-0 (2-0)
Parque Central, Montevideo, 27.03.2008, Referee: Evandro Roman (BRA)
DANUBIO: Néstor Esteban Conde, Daniel Alejandro Lembo, Matías Omar Pérez, Raúl Freddy Ferro, Sergio Gonzalo Rodríguez, Pedro Richar Irala, Mateo Figoli (63 Carlos María Morales), Ribair Rodríguez, Cristian Pedro Bardaro (70 Jorge Adrián García), Damián Alejandro Malrechauffe, Deley Yesid Mena (84 Enzo Scorza). DT: Gustavo Dalto
CUENCA: Javier Hernán Klimowicz, Marlon Patricio Moreno, Julio Marcelo Fleitas, Arlín Segundo Ayoví, Marcelo Cristian Bohórquez, Jimmy Alfredo Bran, Leonardo Javier Soledispa (46 Jhon García), Polo Wila, Germán Castillo (46 Hólger Eduardo Matamoros), Javier Fabián Toledo, Mauricio Javier Ferradás (61 Federico Barrionuevo). DT: Gabriel Perrone
Goals: Damián Alejandro Malrechauffe (3), Daniel Alejandro Lembo (20)

LANÚS – ESTUDIANTES LA PLATA 3-3 (2-2)
Néstor Díaz Pérez, Lanús, 2.04.2008, Referee: Pablo Lunatti (ARG)
LANÚS: Carlos Gustavo Bossio, Carlos David Arce (72 Nicolás Francisco Ramírez), Carlos Gustavo Quintana, Santiago Abel Hoyos, Maximiliano Velázquez, Sebastián Blanco (86 Emir Saúl Faccioli), Agustín Pelletieri, Matías Fritzler, Diego Valeri, Lautaro Acosta, José Gustavo Sand. DT: R. Cabrero
ESTUDIANTES: Mariano Gonzalo Andújar, Marcos Alberto Angeleri (65 Juan Manuel Díaz), Leandro Desabato, Agustín Alayes, José María Basanta, Iván Diego Moreno y Fabianesi, Rodrigo Braña, Leandro Damián Benítez, Juan Manuel Salgueiro, Leandro Hernán Lazzaro (55 Ezequiel Carlos Maggiolo), Pablo Daniel Piatti (35 Diego Alberto Galván). DT: Roberto Sensini
Sent off: Alayes (45) / Hoyos (85)
Goals: José Gustavo Sand (10), Diego Valeri (15), Lautaro Acosta (77) /
Leandro Desábato (21), Leandro Damián Benítez (24), Iván Diego Moreno y Fabianesi (60)

DANUBIO - LANÚS 1-2 (0-0)
Parque Central, Montevideo, 15.04.2008, Referee: Heber Lopes (BRA)
DANUBIO: Néstor Esteban Conde, Damián Alejandro Malrechauffe, Daniel Alejandro Lembo, Sergio Gonzalo Rodríguez, Raúl Freddy Ferro, Cristiano Gomes Machado (54 Mateo Figoli), Pedro Richar Irala, Carlos María Morales, Deley Yesid Mena (61 Enzo Scorza), Cristian Pedro Bardaro, Jorge Adrián García (65 Matías Omar Pérez). DT: Gustavo Dalto
LANÚS: Carlos Gustavo Bossio, Rodolfo Graieb, Carlos Gustavo Quintana, Emir Saúl Faccioli, Maximiliano Velázquez (79 Carlos David Arce), Sebastián Blanco (74 Diego Hernán González), Agustín Pelletieri, Matías Fritzler, Diego Valeri, Lautaro Acosta (78 Nicolás Francisco Ramírez), José Gustavo Sand. DT: Ramón Cabrero
Goals: Cristian Pedro Bardaro (87) / Sebastián Blanco (53), José Gustavo Sand (63)

ESTUDIANTES LA PLATA - DEPORTIVO CUENCA 2-0 (1-0)
Ciudad de la Plata, La Plata, 15.04.2008, Referee: Carlos Amarilla (PAR)
ESTUDIANTES: Mariano Gonzalo Andújar, Leonardo Agustín Sánchez, Leandro Desabato (85 Juan Manuel Díaz), José María Basanta, Iván Diego Moreno y Fabianesi, Juan Sebastián Verón, Rodrigo Braña, Leandro Damián Benítez, Juan Manuel Salgueiro (65 Diego Alberto Galván), Leandro Hernán Lazzaro (71 Ezequiel Carlos Maggiolo), Pablo Daniel Piatti. DT: Roberto Sensini
CUENCA: Javier Hernán Klimowicz, Marlon Patricio Moreno (77 Hólger Eduardo Matamoros), Julio Marcelo Fleitas, Mariano Mina, Marcelo Cristian Bohórquez, Polo Wila, Jhon García, Jimmy Alfredo Bran, Germán Castillo, Mauricio Javier Ferradás, Federico Barrionuevo (46 Édison Preciado). DT: Gabriel Perrone
Goals: Leandro Hernán Lazzaro (11), Polo Wila (87 own goal)

1	ESTUDIANTES	6	3	2	1	9	5	11
2	LANÚS	6	2	4	0	9	6	10
3	Deportivo Cuenca	6	1	3	2	2	5	6
4	Danubio	6	1	1	4	5	9	4

GROUP 3

UA MARACAIBO - BOCA JUNIORS 1-1 (0-0)
José Encarnación Romero, Maracaibo, 20.02.2008, Referee: Carlos Torres (PAR)
UA MARACAIBO: Juan Carlos Henao, Pedro Fernández, Claudio Muñoz, Gregory Evans Lancken, Juan José Fuenmayor, Miguel Ángel Mea Vitali, Gabriel José Urdaneta, Darío Damián Figueroa, Jorge Alberto Rojas (67 Guillermo Fabián Beraza), Nicolás Saucedo (89 Heiber Díaz), Armando Rafael Maita (78 Víctor Guaza). DT: Jorge Pellicer
BOCA JUNIORS: Mauricio Ariel Caranta, Jonathan Ramón Maidana, Julio César Cáceres, Gabriel Alejandro Paletta, Claudio Marcelo Morel, Álvaro Rafael González (70 Fabián Andrés Vargas), Sebastián Alejandro Battaglia, Neri Raúl Cardozo (70 Jesús Alberto Dátolo), Juan Román Riquelme, Martín Palermo, Rodrigo Sebastián Palacio. DT: Carlos Ischia
Goals: Miguel Ángel Mea Vitali (80), Sebastián Alejandro Battaglia (83)

ATLAS GUADALAJARA - COLO COLO SANTIAGO 3-0 (2-0)
Jalisco, Guadalajara, 21.02.2008, Referee: Federico Beligoy (ARG)
ATLAS: Jorge Rodrigo Bava, Diego Daniel Colotto, Ricardo Adán Jiménez, Néstor Vicente Vidrio, Juan Carlos Medina, Christian de Jesús Valdez, Eduardo Rergis (78 Óscar Salvador Vera), Emanuel Adrian Centurión (82 Édgar Iván Pacheco), Gerardo Flores, Jorge Daniel Achucarro (65 Ulises Mendivil), Bruno Marioni. DT: Miguel Ángel Brindisi
COLO COLO: Cristian Fernando Muñoz, Miguel Augusto Riffo, Luis Arturo Mena, Ricardo Francisco Rojas, Gonzalo Antonio Fierro, Moisés Fermin Villarroel, Héctor Arturo Sanhueza, José Domingo Salcedo, Carlos Eduardo Salazar (53 Eduardo Javier Rubio), Gustavo Biscayzacú (67 Jhon Jairo Castillo), Lucas Barrios (53 Cristóbal Jorquera). DT: Claudio Borghi
Goals: Bruno Marioni (7), Diego Daniel Colotto (41), Juan Carlos Medina (67)

UA MARACAIBO - COLO COLO 1-3 (0-0)
José Encarnación Romero, Maracaibo, 28.02.2008, Referee: Samuel Haro (ECU)
UA MARACAIBO: Juan Carlos Henao, Pedro Fernández, Claudio Muñoz, Gregory Evans Lancken, Juan José Fuenmayor, Miguel Ángel Mea Vitali, Gabriel José Urdaneta, Darío Damián Figueroa, Guillermo Fabián Beraza (68 Jorge Alberto Rojas), Nicolás Saucedo (55 Víctor Guaza), Armando Rafael Maita (75 Heiber Díaz). DT: Jorge Pellicer
COLO COLO: Cristian Fernando Muñoz, Miguel Augusto Riffo, Luis Arturo Mena, Ricardo Francisco Rojas, Gonzalo Antonio Fierro, Moisés Fermin Villarroel, Héctor Arturo Sanhueza, José Domingo Salcedo (60 Gonzalo Alejandro Jara), Cristóbal Jorquera, Eduardo Javier Rubio (65 Gustavo Biscayzacú), Lucas Barrios (70 Carlos Eduardo Salazar). DT: Claudio Borghi
Goals: Heiber Díaz (90+2) / Gonzalo Antonio Fierro (48), Gustavo Biscayzacú (68), Gregory Evans Lancken (86 own goal)

BOCA JUNIORS - ATLAS GUADALAJARA 3-0 (1-0)
Alberto J. Armando 'La Bombonera', Buenos Aires, 6.03.2008, Referee: Roberto Silvera (URU)
BOCA JUNIORS: Mauricio Ariel Caranta, Jonathan Ramón Maidana, Julio César Cáceres, Gabriel Alejandro Paletta, Claudio Marcelo Morel, Sebastián Alejandro Battaglia, Fabián Andrés Vargas (77 Jesús Alberto Dátolo), Pablo Martín Ledesma, Juan Román Riquelme (82 Leandro Gracián), Martín Palermo, Rodrigo Sebastián Palacio (84 Lucas Castromán). DT: Carlos Ischia
ATLAS: Jorge Rodrigo Bava, Diego Daniel Colotto, Luis Enrique Robles, Néstor Vicente Vidrio, Gerardo Flores, Eduardo Rergis, Christian de Jesús Valdez, Juan Carlos Medina (69 Édgar Iván Pacheco)), Emanuel Adrian Centurión (60 Óscar Salvador Vera), Jorge Daniel Achucarro, Bruno Marioni (69 Ulises Mendivil). DT: Miguel Ángel Brindisi
Sent off: Vidrio (89)
Goals: Rodrigo Sebastián Palacio (32, 81), Martín Palermo (83)

ATLAS GUADALAJARA - UA MARACAIBO 3-0 (1-0)
Jalisco, Guadalajara, 12.03.2008, Referee: Carlos Vera (ECU)
ATLAS: Jorge Rodrigo Bava, Diego Daniel Colotto, Luis Enrique Robles, Ricardo Adán Jiménez, Juan Carlos Medina, Gerardo Flores (70 Óscar Salvador Vera), Eduardo Rergis, Emanuel Adrian Centurión (81 Édgar Iván Pacheco), Christian de Jesús Valdez, Jorge Daniel Achucarro, Ulises Mendivil (26 Bruno Marioni). DT: Miguel Ángel Brindisi
UA MARACAIBO: Juan Carlos Henao, Jorge Alberto Rojas, Pedro Fernández, Claudio Muñoz, Gregory Evans Lancken, Miguel Ángel Mea Vitali, Víctor Villarreal (61 Armando Rafael Maita), Gabriel José Urdaneta, Darío Damián Figueroa (83 Nicolás Saucedo), Guillermo Fabián Beraza, Heiber Díaz (67 Víctor Guaza). DT: Jorge Pellicer
Goals: Gerardo Flores (41), Jorge Daniel Achucarro (62), Bruno Marioni (67)

COLO COLO - BOCA JUNIORS 2-0 (2-0)
Monumental, Santiago, 20.03.2008, Referee: Martín Vázquez (URU)
COLO COLO: Cristian Fernando Muñoz, Luis Arturo Mena, Jorge Antonio Carrasco, Ricardo Francisco Rojas, Gonzalo Antonio Fierro, Moisés Fermin Villarroel (86 Gonzalo Alejandro Jara), Héctor Arturo Sanhueza, José Domingo Salcedo, Cristóbal Jorquera (69 Carlos Eduardo Salazar), Gustavo Biscayzacú (78 Rodolfo Antonio Moya), Lucas Barrios. DT: Claudio Borghi
BOCA JUNIORS: Mauricio Ariel Caranta, Jonathan Ramón Maidana, Julio César Cáceres, Gabriel Alejandro Paletta, Claudio Marcelo Morel, Sebastián Alejandro Battaglia, Fabián Andrés Vargas (46 Jesús Alberto Dátolo), Pablo Martín Ledesma (64 Leandro Gracián), Juan Román Riquelme (75 Mauro Boselli), Martín Palermo, Rodrigo Sebastián Palacio. DT: Carlos Ischia
Goals: Cristóbal Jorquera (2), Gustavo Biscayzacú (34)

UA MARACAIBO - ATLAS GUADALAJARA 1-1 (0-0)
José Encarnación Romero, Maracaibo, 25.03.2008, Referee: Wilmar Roldán (COL)
UA MARACAIBO: Juan Carlos Henao, Jorge Alberto Rojas, Pedro Fernández, Claudio Muñoz, Gregory Evans Lancken, Miguel Ángel Mea Vitali (74 Víctor Villarreal), Gabriel José Urdaneta, Darío Damián Figueroa, Guillermo Fabián Beraza (69 Armando Rafael Maita), Heiber Díaz (81 Nicolás Saucedo), Yhonatan Del Valle. DT: Jorge Pellicer
ATLAS: Jorge Rodrigo Bava, Diego Daniel Colotto, Hugo Ayala (69 Néstor Vicente Vidrio), Omar Alejandro Flores, Gerardo Flores, Eduardo Rergis, Luis Enrique Robles, Emanuel Adrian Centurión (69 Édgar Iván Pacheco), Christian de Jesús Valdez, Juan Carlos Medina (83 Flavio Jesús Santos), Bruno Marioni. DT: Miguel Ángel Brindisi
Sent off: Colotto (85)
Goals: Darío Damián Figueroa (80 penalty) / Bruno Marioni (56 penalty)

BOCA JUNIORS - COLO COLO SANTIAGO 4-3 (1-2)
Alberto J. Armando 'La Bombonera', Buenos Aires, 27.03.2008, Referee: Carlos Amarilla (PAR)
BOCA JUNIORS: Mauricio Ariel Caranta, Hugo Benjamín Ibarra, Jonathan Ramón Maidana, Julio César Cáceres, Luciano Fabián Monzón, Fabián Andrés Vargas (64 Neri Raúl Cardozo), Sebastián Alejandro Battaglia, Jesús Alberto Dátolo (82 Álvaro Rafael González), Leandro Gracián (68 Facundo Roncaglia), Rodrigo Sebastián Palacio, Martín Palermo. DT: Carlos Ischia
COLO COLO: Cristian Fernando Muñoz, Luis Arturo Mena, Jorge Antonio Carrasco, Ricardo Francisco Rojas, Gonzalo Antonio Fierro, Moisés Fermin Villarroel, Héctor Arturo Sanhueza, José Domingo Salcedo (70 Carlos Eduardo Salazar), Cristóbal Jorquera (56 Rodolfo Antonio Moya), Jhon Jairo Castillo (46 José Luis Cabión), Gustavo Biscayzacú. DT: Claudio Borghi
Sent off: Monzón (22)
Goals: Martín Palermo (29), Leandro Gracián (49), Rodrigo Sebastián Palacio (66), Nery Raúl Cardozo (88) / Gustavo Bizcayzacú (24, 42), Rodolfo Antonio Moya (90+1)

ATLAS GUADALAJARA - BOCA JUNIORS 3-1 (1-1)
Jalisco, Guadalajara, 8.04.2008, Referee: Óscar Julián Ruiz (COL)
ATLAS: Jorge Rodrigo Bava, Omar Alejandro Flores, Ricardo Adán Jiménez, Néstor Vicente Vidrio, Gerardo Flores, Eduardo Rergis, Juan Carlos Medina, Luis Enrique Robles, Emanuel Adrian Centurión (46 Jorge Hernández), Jorge Daniel Achucarro (27 Ulises Mendivil, 56 Christian de Jesús Valdez), Bruno Marioni. DT: Miguel Ángel Brindisi
BOCA JUNIORS: Mauricio Ariel Caranta, Álvaro Rafael González, Jonathan Ramón Maidana, Julio César Cáceres, Claudio Marcelo Morel, Sebastián Alejandro Battaglia, Fabián Andrés Vargas, Jesús Alberto Dátolo (73 Neri Raúl Cardozo), Leandro Gracián (73 Cristian Manuel Chávez), Rodrigo Sebastián Palacio, Martín Palermo. DT: Carlos Ischia
Goals: Gerardo Flores (21), Bruno Marioni (58, 76) / Sebastián Alejandro Battaglia (31)

COLO COLO SANTIAGO - UA MARACAIBO 2-0 (0-0)
Monumental, Santiago, 10.04.2008, Referee: René Ortubé (BOL)
COLO COLO: Cristian Fernando Muñoz, Luis Arturo Mena, Jorge Antonio Carrasco, Ricardo Francisco Rojas, Gonzalo Antonio Fierro, Moisés Fermin Villarroel, Héctor Arturo Sanhueza, José Domingo Salcedo, Daniel González (77 Carlos Eduardo Salazar), Gustavo Biscayzacú, Lucas Barrios (82 Rodolfo Antonio Moya). DT: Fernando Astengo
UA MARACAIBO: Juan Carlos Henao (54 Tulio Hernández), Jorge Alberto Rojas, Pedro Fernández, Claudio Muñoz, Rafael Loreto Mea Vitali, Juan José Fuenmayor (64 Víctor Villarreal), Miguel Ángel Mea Vitali, Gabriel José Urdaneta, Darío Damián Figueroa (54 Nicolás Saucedo), Guillermo Fabián Beraza, Armando Rafael Maita. DT: Jorge Pellicer
Goals: Gustavo Bizcayzacú (47), Lucas Barrios (50)

COLO COLO SANTIAGO - ATLAS GUADALAJARA 1-1 (1-0)
Monumental, Santiago, 22.04.2008, Referee: Jorge Larrionda (URU)
COLO COLO: Cristian Fernando Muñoz, Luis Arturo Mena, Jorge Antonio Carrasco, Ricardo Francisco Rojas, Gonzalo Antonio Fierro, Héctor Arturo Sanhueza, José Domingo Salcedo (75 Eduardo Javier Rubio), Gonzalo Alejandro Jara, Boris Sagredo, Gustavo Biscayzacú (81 Rodolfo Antonio Moya), Lucas Barrios. DT: Fernando Astengo
ATLAS: Jorge Rodrigo Bava, Omar Alejandro Flores, Jorge Emmanuel Torres, Néstor Vicente Vidrio, Diego Daniel Colotto, Eduardo Rergis, Juan Carlos Medina (81 Christian de Jesús Valdez), Luis Enrique Robles, Jorge Hernández (46 Gerardo Flores), Ulises Mendivil, Bruno Marioni (84 Emanuel Adrian Centurión). DT: Miguel Ángel Brindisi
Goals: Ricardo Francisco Rojas (5) / Diego Daniel Colotto (65)

BOCA JUNIORS - UA MARACAIBO 3-0 (2-0)
Alberto J. Armando 'La Bombonera', Buenos Aires, 22.04.2008, Referee: Víctor Hugo Rivera (PER)
BOCA JUNIORS: Mauricio Ariel Caranta, Álvaro Rafael González, Julio César Cáceres, Gabriel Alejandro Paletta (14 Jonathan Ramón Maidana), Luciano Fabián Monzón, Sebastián Alejandro Battaglia, Fabián Andrés Vargas (52 Leandro Gracián), Jesús Alberto Dátolo (71 Neri Raúl Cardozo), Juan Román Riquelme, Rodrigo Sebastián Palacio, Martín Palermo. DT: Carlos Ischia
UA MARACAIBO: Juan Carlos Henao, Gregory Evans Lancken, Claudio Muñoz, Julio César Machado, Juan José Fuenmayor, Miguel Ángel Mea Vitali, Pedro Fernández, Gabriel José Urdaneta, Guillermo Fabián Beraza (46 Darío Damián Figueroa), Jorge Alberto Rojas (83 Nicolás Saucedo), Armando Rafael Maita. DT: Jorge Pellicer
Goals: Gabriel Alejandro Paletta (9), Jesús Alberto Dátolo (20), Juan Román Riquelme (73)

1	ATLAS	6	3	2	1	11	6	11
2	BOCA JUNIORS	6	3	1	2	12	9	10
3	Colo Colo	6	3	1	2	11	9	10
4	UA Maracaibo	6	0	2	4	3	13	2

GROUP 4

CORONEL BOLOGNESI - FLAMENGO 0-0
Jorge Basadre, Tacna, 13.02.2008, Referee: Mauricio Reinoso (ECU)
CORONEL: Diego Penny, Jaime Linares, Adán Adolfo Balbín, Juan Diego Gonzales Vigil (83 Miguel Ángel Mostto), Renzo Revoredo, Jorge Johann Vásquez, Miguel Ostersen, Jesús Martín Álvarez, Luis Alberto Ramírez (89 Enio Joao Novoa), Douglas Junior Ross (71 Jesús Chávez), Eduardo Alberto Uribe. DT: Juan Reynoso
FLAMENGO: BRUNO Fernandes Souza, Leonardo 'LÉO' Da Silva MOURA, FABIO LUCIANO, RONALDO Simões ANGELIM, JONATAS Domingos, JUAN Maldonado Jaimez, IBSON Barreto Da Silva, Rafael TORÓ Ferreira Francisco (41 José KLÉBERSON Pereira), Rodrigo de SOUZA Cardoso (85 Márcio José de Oliveira 'MARCINHO'), DIEGO TARDELLI Martins (77 Manuel De Brito Filho 'OBINA'), JAILTON Da Cruz Alves. DT: Joel Santana

CIENCIANO - NACIONAL MONTEVIDEO 2-1 (0-0)
Inca Gracilaso de la Vega, Cusco, 14.02.2008, Referee: Enrique Osses (CHI)
CIENCIANO: Juan Ángel Flores, Luis Manuel Marengo, Carlos Solís, Julio Romaña, César Camilo Ccahuantico, Juan Carlos Bazalar, Julio César García (75 Víctor Hugo Manique), Gustavo Enrique Vassallo (75 Aldo Ítalo Olcese), Masakatsu Sawa (90 José Alberto Corcuera), Roberto Carlos Guizasola, William Medardo Chiroque. DT: Franco Navarro
NACIONAL: Washington Alexis Viera, Pablo Rodrigo Melo, Mauricio Bernardo Victorino, Hugo Diego Arismendi, Bruno Fornaroli (70 Juan Pereyra), Martín Ricardo Ligüera (88 Nicolás Lodeiro), Adrián Marcelo Romero, Pablo Caballero, Gastón Filgueira (30 Deivis Barone), Óscar Javier Morales, Richard Javier Morales. DT: Gerardo Pelusso
Sent off: Romero (43)
Goals: Gustavo Vasallo (54, 67) / Mauricio Bernardo Victorino (89)

CORONEL BOLOGNESI - NACIONAL MONTEVIDEO 0-1 (0-1)
Jorge Basadre, Tacna, 19.02.2008, Referee: Jorge Gasso (MEX)
CORONEL: Diego Penny, Adrián Cortez, Jaime Linares (29 Enio Joao Novoa), Adán Adolfo Balbín, Juan Diego Gonzales Vigil (77 Juan José Barros), Jorge Johann Vásquez, Miguel Ostersen, Jesús Martín Álvarez, Luis Alberto Ramírez, Douglas Junior Ross, Eduardo Alberto Uribe (46 Miguel Ángel Mostto). DT: Juan Reynoso
NACIONAL: Washington Alexis Viera, Deivis Barone, Mauricio Bernardo Victorino, Hugo Diego Arismendi, Bruno Fornaroli (68 Nicolás Bertolo), Martín Ricardo Ligüera (83 Juan Pereyra), Mathías Cardaccio, Pablo Caballero, Gastón Filgueira, Óscar Javier Morales, Richard Javier Morales. DT: Gerardo Pelusso
Goal: Bruno Fornaroli (9)

FLAMENGO - CIENCIANO 2-1 (1-1)
Mario Filho 'Maracanã', Rio de Janeiro, 27.02.2008, Referee: Ricardo Grance (PAR)
FLAMENGO: BRUNO Fernandes Souza, Leonardo 'LÉO' Da Silva MOURA, FABIO LUCIANO, RONALDO Simões ANGELIM, JUAN Maldonado Jaimez, IBSON Barreto Da Silva, CRISTIAN Mark Baroni, Rafael TORÓ Ferreira Francisco (66 Manuel De Brito Filho 'OBINA'), José KLÉBERSON Pereira (84 JONATAS Domingos), Rodrigo de SOUZA Cardoso, DIEGO TARDELLI Martins (66 Márcio José de Oliveira 'MARCINHO'). DT: Joel Santana
CIENCIANO: Juan Ángel Flores, Luis Manuel Marengo, Carlos Solís, Julio Romaña, Roberto Carlos Guizasola, Juan Carlos Bazalar, Julio César García, César Andres Ortiz, Masakatsu Sawa (77 José Alberto Corcuera), William Medardo Chiroque, Gustavo Enrique Vassallo. DT: Franco Navarro
Goals: Rodrigo de SOUZA Cardoso (37), Márcio José de Oliveira 'MARCINHO' (88) / Gustavo Enrique Vassallo (45)

NACIONAL MONTEVIDEO - FLAMENGO 3-0 (1-0)
Parque Central, Montevideo, 6.03.2008, Referee: Pablo Pozo (CHI)
NACIONAL: Washington Alexis Viera, Gerardo Acosta, Deivis Barone, Mauricio Bernardo Victorino, Adrián Marcelo Romero, Mathías Cardaccio, Óscar Javier Morales, Hugo Diego Arismendi (71 Martín Ricardo Ligüera), Nicolás Bertolo, Bruno Fornaroli (84 Diego Perrone), Richard Javier Morales (75 Juan Pereyra). DT: Gerardo Pelusso
FLAMENGO: BRUNO Fernandes Souza, Leonardo 'LÉO' Da Silva MOURA, FABIO LUCIANO, RONALDO Simões ANGELIM, JUAN Maldonado Jaimez, IBSON Barreto Da Silva, CRISTIAN Mark Baroni, José KLÉBERSON Pereira (52 JAILTON Da Cruz Alves), Rodrigo de SOUZA Cardoso (69 JONATAS Domingos), DIEGO TARDELLI Martins (46 Márcio José de Oliveira 'MARCINHO'), Rafael TORÓ Ferreira Francisco. DT: Joel Santana
Goals: Richard Javier Morales (41, 66), Bruno Fornaroli (69)

CIENCIANO - CORONEL BOLOGNESI 1-0 (0-0)
Inca Gracilaso de la Vega, Cusco, 11.03.2008, Referee: Víctor Hugo Carrillo (PER)
CIENCIANO: Juan Ángel Flores, Luis Manuel Marengo, Carlos Solís, Julio Romaña, Roberto Carlos Guizasola, Juan Carlos Bazalar (81 César Camilo Ccahuantico), Julio César García (88 Cristian Guevara), César Andres Ortiz, Masakatsu Sawa (86 Natalio Portillo), William Medardo Chiroque, Gustavo Enrique Vassallo. DT: Franco Navarro
CORONEL: Diego Penny, Adrián Cortez, Jaime Linares (86 Jesús Chávez), Adán Adolfo Balbín, Enio Joao Novoa, Miguel Ángel Mostto, Renzo Revoredo, Jorge Johann Vásquez, Miguel Ostersen, Luis Alberto Ramírez, Eduardo Alberto Uribe (80 Douglas Junior Ross). DT: Juan Reynoso
Goal: Carlos Solís (75)

FLAMENGO - NACIONAL MONTEVIDEO 2-0 (1-0)
Mario Filho 'Maracanã', Rio de Janeiro, 19.03.2008, Referee: Carlos Amarilla (PAR)
FLAMENGO: BRUNO Fernandes Souza, Luiz Antônio De Oliveira 'LUIZINHO', FABIO LUCIANO, RONALDO Simões ANGELIM, JUAN Maldonado Jaimez, IBSON Barreto Da Silva, CRISTIAN Mark Baroni, José KLÉBERSON Pereira, RENATO Soares AUGUSTO, Márcio José de Oliveira 'MARCINHO' (85 Maximiliano Biancucchi), Rodrigo de SOUZA Cardoso (77 Manuel De Brito Filho 'OBINA'). DT: Joel Santana
NACIONAL: Washington Alexis Viera, Gerardo Acosta, Deivis Barone, Mauricio Bernardo Victorino, Adrián Marcelo Romero, Mathías Cardaccio, Óscar Javier Morales, Hugo Diego Arismendi, Nicolás Bertolo (65 Martín Ricardo Ligüera), Bruno Fornaroli (82 Diego Vera), Richard Javier Morales. DT: Gerardo Pelusso
Goals: Márcio José de Oliveira 'MARCINHO' (25, 65)

CORONEL BOLOGNESI - CIENCIANO 0-0
Jorge Basadre, Tacna, 25.03.2008, Referee: Héctor Pacheco (PER)
CORONEL: Diego Penny, Rafael Farfán (77 Jorge Johann Vásquez), Jaime Linares, Adán Adolfo Balbín, Miguel Ángel Mostto, Jesús Chávez (59 Juan Diego Gonzales Vigil), Renzo Revoredo, Miguel Ostersen, Luis Alberto Ramírez, Eduardo Alberto Uribe, Douglas Junior Ross. DT: Juan Reynoso
CIENCIANO: Juan Ángel Flores, Luis Manuel Marengo, Carlos Solís, Julio Romaña, Gustavo Enrique Vassallo, Roberto Carlos Guizasola, Juan Carlos Bazalar, César Andres Ortiz, Masakatsu Sawa, William Medardo Chiroque (59 José Alberto Corcuera), Julio Edson Uribe (60 Aldo Ítalo Olcese). DT: Franco Navarro

NACIONAL MONTEVIDEO - CORONEL BOLOGNESI 1-0 (1-0)
Parque Central, Montevideo, 3.04.2008, Referee: Paulo César Oliveira (BRA)
NACIONAL: Washington Alexis Viera, Pablo Caballero, Deivis Barone, Mauricio Bernardo Victorino, Adrián Marcelo Romero, Hugo Diego Arismendi, Óscar Javier Morales, Nicolás Bertolo (60 Mathías Cardaccio), Martín Ricardo Ligüera (89 Nicolás Lodeiro), Bruno Fornaroli (77 Diego Vera), Richard Javier Morales. DT: Gerardo Pelusso
CORONEL: Alexandro Álvarez, Rafael Farfán, Adrián Cortez, Jaime Linares, Adán Adolfo Balbín, Juan Diego Gonzales Vigil, Enio Joao Novoa (63 Luis Alberto Ramírez), Miguel Ángel Mostto, Mario Jorge Soto, Eduardo Alberto Uribe (80 Juan José Barros), Jesús Martín Álvarez. DT: Juan Reynoso
Sent off: Ramírez (90)
Goal: Deivis Barone (30)

CIENCIANO - FLAMENGO 0-3 (0-0)
Inca Gracilaso de la Vega, Cusco, 9.04.2008, Referee: Sergio Pezzotta (ARG)
CIENCIANO: Juan Ángel Flores, Luis Manuel Marengo, Carlos Solís, Julio Romaña, Gustavo Enrique Vassallo, Roberto Carlos Guizasola, Juan Carlos Bazalar, César Andres Ortiz, Julio Edson Uribe (60 Cristian Guevara), Masakatsu Sawa, Natalio Portillo (71 Jimmy Corrales). DT: Franco Navarro

FLAMENGO: BRUNO Fernandes Souza, Leonardo 'LÉO' Da Silva MOURA, FABIO LUCIANO, RONALDO Simões ANGELIM, JUAN Maldonado Jaimez, IBSON Barreto Da Silva (90+2 JAILTON Da Cruz Alves), CRISTIAN Mark Baroni, José KLÉBERSON Pereira, RENATO Soares AUGUSTO (87 Manuel De Brito Filho 'OBINA'), Rafael TORÓ Ferreira Francisco, Rodrigo de SOUZA Cardoso (87 Márcio José de Oliveira 'MARCINHO'). DT: Joel Santana
Sent off: Bazalar (63)
Goals: RENATO Soares AUGUSTO (58), Rafael TORÓ Ferreira Francisco (77), JUAN Maldonado Jaimez (90+2)

FLAMENGO - CORONEL BOLOGNESI 2-0 (0-0)
Mario Filho 'Maracanã', Rio de Janeiro, 23.04.2008, Referee: Iván Gamboa (BOL)
FLAMENGO: BRUNO Fernandes Souza, Leonardo 'LÉO' Da Silva MOURA, FABIO LUCIANO, RONALDO Simões ANGELIM, JUAN Maldonado Jaimez, JAILTON Da Cruz Alves, CRISTIAN Mark Baroni (46 DIEGO TARDELLI Martins), José KLÉBERSON Pereira, Rafael TORÓ Ferreira Francisco (68 Manuel De Brito Filho 'OBINA'), Rodrigo de SOUZA Cardoso (83 Diego Antonio GAVILÁN), Márcio José de Oliveira 'MARCINHO'. DT: Joel Santana
CORONEL: Diego Penny, Renzo Revoredo (85 Rafael Farfán), Adán Adolfo Balbín, Miguel Ostersen, Adrián Cortez, Eduardo Alberto Uribe, Jorge Johann Vásquez, Jaime Linares (62 Enio Joao Novoa), Jesús Martín Álvarez, Juan Diego Gonzales Vigil (59 Miguel Ángel Mostto), Douglas Junior Ross. DT: Juan Reynoso
Goals: BRUNO Fernandes Souza (82), Manuel De Brito Filho 'OBINA' (88)

NACIONAL MONTEVIDEO – CIENCIANO 3-1 (1-0)
Parque Central, Montevideo, 23.04.2008, Referee: Carlos Chandía (CHI)
NACIONAL: Washington Alexis Viera, Mauricio Bernardo Victorino, Deivis Barone, Pablo Caballero, Adrián Marcelo Romero, Mathías Cardaccio, Óscar Javier Morales, Nicolás Bertolo, Martín Ricardo Ligüera (80 Hugo Diego Arismendi), Bruno Fornaroli (73 Juan Pereyra), Richard Javier Morales (65 Diego Vera). DT: Gerardo Pelusso
CIENCIANO: Juan Ángel Flores, Luis Manuel Marengo, Carlos Solís, César Camilo Ccahuantico (7 Cristian Guevara), Julio Romaña, Gustavo Enrique Vassallo, Roberto Carlos Guizasola, César Andres Ortiz, José Alberto Corcuera, Masakatsu Sawa (65 Natalio Portillo), Aldo Ítalo Olcese (69 Julio César García). DT: Franco Navarro
Sent off: Romaña (84)
Goals: Martín Ricardo Ligüera (38), Mathías Cardaccio (54), Diego Vera (90+2) / Cristian Guevara (82)

1	FLAMENGO	6	4	1	1	9	4	13
2	NACIONAL	6	4	0	2	9	5	12
3	Cienciano	6	2	1	3	5	9	7
4	Coronel Bolognesi	6	0	2	4	0	5	2

GROUP 5

UNIVERSIDAD SAN MARTÍN - RIVER PLATE 2-0 (1-0)
Monumental, Lima, 13.02.2008, Referee: Leonardo Gaciba (BRA)
USM: Leao Butrón, Jorge Raúl Huamán, Orlando Contreras, Jorge Enrique Reyes (46 Bruno Félix Bianchi), Guillermo Sandro Salas, Mario Evaristo Leguizamón (67 José Luis Díaz), John Christopher Hinostroza, Edwin Pérez, Fernando Daniel Del Solar, Pedro Alejandro García (69 Alexander Gustavo Sánchez), Roberto Ovelar. DT: Víctor Rivera
RIVER PLATE: Juan Pablo Carrizo, Paulo Andrés Ferrari, Gustavo Daniel Cabral, Eduardo Nicolás Tuzzio, Cristian Carlos Villagra, Leonardo Daniel Ponzio, Nicolás Mario Domingo (46 Radamel Falcao García), Augusto Matías Fernández (77 Matías Enrique Abelairas), Ariel Arnaldo Ortega, Alexis Alejandro Sánchez (69 Mauro Damián Rosales), Washington Sebastián Abreu. DT: Diego Simeone
Goals: Roberto Ovelar (14), Jose Luis Díaz (90)

CF AMÉRICA - UNIVERSIDAD CATÓLICA 2-1 (1-0)
Azteca, México DF, 20.02.2008, Referee: Saúl Laverni (ARG)
AMÉRICA: Armando Navarrete, Diego Alberto Cervantes, Óscar Adrián Rojas, Ismael Rodríguez, Carlos Jesús Infante (6 Jesús Armando Sánchez), José Antonio Castro, Alejandro Argüello, Germán Villa, Richard Núñez (62 Federico Higuaín), Salvador Cabañas, Hernán Rodrigo López (76 Juan Carlos Mosqueda). DT: Rubén Omar Romano
UNIVERSIDAD CATÓLICA: José María Buljubasich, Marcos Andrés González, Facundo Jorge Imboden, Jorge Andrés Ormeño, Eros Roque Pérez, Gary Medel, Rodrigo Ignacio Valenzuela, Iván Vásquez, Darío Botinelli (82 Rodrigo Toloza), José Ailton Da Silva (56 Luis Núñez), Héctor Santiago Tapia (90 Francisco Silva). DT: Fernando Carvallo
Goals: Salvador Cabañas (39), Federico Higuaín (90+2) / Darío Botinelli (70)

UNIVERSIDAD SAN MARTÍN - UNIVERSIDAD CATÓLICA 0-1 (0-1)
Monumental, Lima, 26.02.2008, Referee: René Ortubé (BOL)
USM: Leao Butrón, Jair Edson Céspedes, Orlando Contreras, Bruno Félix Bianchi, Guillermo Sandro Salas, Mario Evaristo Leguizamón (60 José Luis Díaz), John Christopher Hinostroza, Edwin Pérez, Fernando Daniel Del Solar (71 Roberto Enrique Silva), Pedro Alejandro García (62 Alexander Gustavo Sánchez), Roberto Ovelar. DT: Víctor Rivera
UNIVERSIDAD CATÓLICA: José María Buljubasich, Marcos Andrés González, Facundo Jorge Imboden, Jorge Andrés Ormeño, Eros Roque Pérez, Gary Medel, Rodrigo Ignacio Valenzuela (84 Boris Igor González), Iván Vásquez, Darío Botinelli, José Ailton Da Silva (74 Roberto Gutiérrez), Luis Núñez. DT: Fernando Carvallo
Goals: Darío Bottinelli (30)

RIVER PLATE – CF AMÉRICA 2-1 (1-1)
Antonio V. Liberti, Buenos Aires, 27.02.2008, Referee: Rubén Selman (CHI)
RIVER PLATE: Juan Pablo Carrizo, Paulo Andrés Ferrari (46 Alexis Alejandro Sánchez), Gustavo Daniel Cabral, Eduardo Nicolás Tuzzio, Cristian Carlos Villagra, Oscar Adrián Ahumada, Augusto Matías Fernández, Matías Enrique Abelairas (62 Diego Mario Buonanotte), Ariel Arnaldo Ortega, Radamel Falcao García, Washington Sebastián Abreu. DT: Diego Simeone
AMÉRICA: Armando Navarrete, Diego Alberto Cervantes, Óscar Adrián Rojas, Ismael Rodríguez, José Antonio Castro, Alejandro Argüello, Germán Villa, Juan Carlos Mosqueda (67 Richard Núñez), Sebastián Domínguez (35 Jesús Armando Sánchez), Salvador Cabañas, Hernán Rodrigo López (46 Federico Higuaín). DT: Rubén Omar Romano
Sent off: García (90) / Castro (90)
Goals: Radamel Falcao García (37), Ariel Arnaldo Ortega (90+3) / Salvador Cabañas (18)

UNIVERSIDAD CATÓLICA - RIVER PLATE 1-2 (0-1)
San Carlos de Apoquindo, Santiago, 12.03.2008, Referee: Salvio Fagundes (BRA)
UNIVERSIDAD CATÓLICA: José María Buljubasich, Marcos Andrés González, Facundo Jorge Imboden, Jorge Andrés Ormeño, Eros Roque Pérez, Gary Medel, Rodrigo Ignacio Valenzuela, Iván Vásquez, Darío Botinelli, José Ailton Da Silva (75 Luis Núñez), Roberto Gutiérrez. DT: Fernando Carvallo
RIVER PLATE: Juan Pablo Carrizo, Paulo Andrés Ferrari, Gustavo Daniel Cabral, Eduardo Nicolás Tuzzio, Cristian Carlos Villagra, Leonardo Daniel Ponzio, Augusto Matías Fernández, Matías Enrique Abelairas (66 Diego Mario Buonanotte), Ariel Arnaldo Ortega (90 Oscar Adrián Ahumada), Alexis Alejandro Sánchez (66 Mauro Damián Rosales), Washington Sebastián Abreu. DT: Diego Simeone
Goals: Roberto Gutiérrez (47) / Washington Sebastián Abreu (43), Mauro Damián Rosales (87)

CF AMÉRICA - UNIVERSIDAD SAN MARTÍN 3-1 (1-1)
Azteca, México DF, 13.03.2008, Referee: Carlos Amarilla (PAR)
AMÉRICA: Armando Navarrete, Diego Alberto Cervantes, Óscar Adrián Rojas, Richard Núñez (55 Carlos Alberto Sánchez), Jesús Armando Sánchez, Alejandro Argüello, Rodrigo Iñigo (67 Salvador Cabañas), José de Jesús Mosqueda (55 Juan Carlos Mosqueda), Luis Hermilo Villegas, Daniel Omar Márquez, Hernán Rodrigo López. DT: Norberto Scoponi

USM: Leao Butrón, Jorge Raúl Huamán, Orlando Contreras, Bruno Félix Bianchi, Guillermo Sandro Salas, Mario Evaristo Leguizamón (63 Pedro Alejandro García), Víctor Wílmer Carrillo, Edwin Pérez, Roberto Enrique Silva, Alexander Gustavo Sánchez (59 José Luis Díaz), Roberto Ovelar (68 Fernando Daniel Del Solar). DT: Víctor Rivera
Goals: Daniel O. Márquez (40), Rodrigo Iñigo (47), Salvador Cabañas (71) / Roberto Enrique Silva (7)

RIVER PLATE - UNIVERSIDAD CATÓLICA 2-0 (1-0)
Antonio V. Liberti, Buenos Aires, 26.03.2008, Referee: Carlos Torres (PAR)
RIVER PLATE: Juan Pablo Carrizo, Paulo Andrés Ferrari, Gustavo Daniel Cabral, Eduardo Nicolás Tuzzio (51 Danilo Telmo Gerlo), Cristian Carlos Villagra, Oscar Adrián Ahumada (43 Leonardo Daniel Ponzio), Matías Enrique Abelairas, Diego Mario Buonanotte, Radamel Falcao García (56 Nicolás Mario Domingo), Mauro Damián Rosales, Washington Sebastián Abreu. DT: Diego Simeone
UNIVERSIDAD CATÓLICA: José María Buljubasich, Rodrigo Ignacio Valenzuela, Marcos Andrés González, Facundo Jorge Imboden, Eros Roque Pérez, Gary Medel, Jorge Andrés Ormeño, Rodrigo Toloza (66 Luis Núñez), Darío Botinelli, José Ailton Da Silva, Héctor Santiago Tapia (63 Roberto Gutiérrez). DT: Fernando Carvallo Sent off: Núñez (69)
Goals: Radamel Falcao García (1), Washington Sebastián Abreu (72)

UNIVERSIDAD SAN MARTÍN – CF AMÉRICA 1-0 (1-0)
Monumental, Lima, 26.03.2008
Referee: Juan Soto (VEN)
USM: Leao Butrón, Jorge Raúl Huamán, Orlando Contreras, Bruno Félix Bianchi, Guillermo Sandro Salas, John Christopher Hinostroza, Edwin Pérez, Mario Evaristo Leguizamón (79 Pedro Alejandro García), Alexander Gustavo Sánchez (85 Jair Edson Céspedes), Roberto Enrique Silva, José Luis Díaz (90+3 Ryan Zonath Salazar). DT: Víctor Rivera
AMÉRICA: Francisco Guillermo Ochoa, Sebastián Domínguez, Diego Alberto Cervantes, José Antonio Castro, Ismael Rodríguez, Óscar Adrián Rojas, Juan Carlos Mosqueda (84 Daniel Omar Márquez), Jesús Armando Sánchez (57 Enrique Esqueda), Alejandro Argüello, Federico Higuaín (66 Richard Núñez), Salvador Cabañas. DT: Norberto Scoponi
Goal: Mario Evaristo Leguizamón (36)

UNIVERSIDAD CATÓLICA - UNIVERSIDAD SAN MARTÍN 1-0 (0-0)
San Carlos de Apoquindo, Santiago, 1.04.2008, Referee: Antonio Arias (PAR)
UNIVERSIDAD CATÓLICA: José María Buljubasich, Marcos Andrés González, Facundo Jorge Imboden, Jorge Andrés Ormeño (28 Iván Vásquez), Eros Roque Pérez, Gary Medel, Rodrigo Ignacio Valenzuela, Rodrigo Toloza, Darío Botinelli, José Ailton Da Silva, Héctor Santiago Tapia (68 Julio Gutiérrez). DT: Fernando Carvallo
USM: Leao Butrón, Guillermo Sandro Salas, Jorge Raúl Huamán, Orlando Contreras, Bruno Félix Bianchi, John Christopher Hinostroza, Edwin Pérez, Mario Evaristo Leguizamón (75 Jair Edson Céspedes), José Luis Díaz, Alexander Gustavo Sánchez (82 Josepmir Aarón Ballón), Roberto Enrique Silva. DT: Víctor Rivera Sent off: J.L. Díaz (36)
Goal: Julio Gutiérrez (88)

CF AMÉRICA - RIVER PLATE 4-3 (0-1)
Azteca, México DF, 2.04.2008, Referee: Roberto Silveira (URU)
AMÉRICA: Francisco Guillermo Ochoa, Rodrigo Iñigo, Diego Alberto Cervantes, Ismael Rodríguez, Óscar Adrián Rojas, Germán Villa, Alejandro Argüello, José Antonio Castro, Juan Carlos Mosqueda (70 Richard Núñez), Federico Higuaín (52 Salvador Cabañas), Enrique Esqueda (83 José de Jesús Mosqueda). DT: Norberto Scoponi
RIVER PLATE: Juan Pablo Carrizo, Paulo Andrés Ferrari (86 Andrés Lorenzo Ríos), Nicolás Gabriel Sánchez, Cristian Javier Nasuti, Cristian Carlos Villagra, Rodrigo Javier Archubi (75 Nicolás Mario Domingo), Leonardo Daniel Ponzio, Matías Enrique Abelairas, Radamel Falcao García, Alexis Alejandro Sánchez, Washington Sebastián Abreu. DT: Diego Simeone
Goals: Rodrigo Iñigo (52), Enrique Esqueda (53), Diego Alberto Cervantes (62), Salvador Cabañas (70) / Rodrigo Javier Archubi (7), Diego A. Cervantes (55 own goal), Washington Sebastián Abreu (63)

UNIVERSIDAD CATÓLICA - CF AMÉRICA 2-0 (0-0)
San Carlos de Apoquindo, Santiago, 17.04.2008, Referee: Leonardo Gaciba (BRA)
UNIVERSIDAD CATÓLICA: José María Buljubasich, Rodrigo Ignacio Valenzuela, Marcos Andrés González, Facundo Jorge Imboden, Eros Roque Pérez, Gary Medel (83 Nicolás Núñez), Iván Vásquez, Luis Núñez, Darío Botinelli, Roberto Gutiérrez, José Ailton Da Silva. DT: Fernando Carvallo
AMÉRICA: Francisco Guillermo Ochoa, José Antonio Castro, Rodrigo Iñigo, Diego Alberto Cervantes, Ismael Rodríguez, Óscar Adrián Rojas, Juan Carlos Mosqueda (89 Daniel Omar Márquez), Jesús Armando Sánchez, Juan Carlos Silva, Enrique Esqueda (76 Federico Higuaín), Salvador Cabañas. DT: Norberto Scoponi
Goals: Gary Medel (52), Dario Botinelli (90)

RIVER PLATE - UNIVERSIDAD SAN MARTÍN 5-0 (2-0)
Antonio V. Liberti, Buenos Aires, 17.04.2008, Referee: Óscar Luiz (COL)
RIVER PLATE: Juan Pablo Carrizo, Paulo Andrés Ferrari, Gustavo Daniel Cabral, Nicolás Gabriel Sánchez, Cristian Carlos Villagra, Rodrigo Javier Archubi, Leonardo Daniel Ponzio (46 Oscar Adrián Ahumada), Matías Enrique Abelairas (54 Diego Mario Buonanotte), Radamel Falcao García (61 Andrés Lorenzo Ríos), Alexis Alejandro Sánchez, Washington Sebastián Abreu. DT: Diego Simeone
USM: Leao Butrón, Jorge Raúl Huamán, Orlando Contreras, Bruno Félix Bianchi, Guillermo Sandro Salas, Alexander Gustavo Sánchez, John Christopher Hinostroza, Edwin Pérez, Fernando Daniel Del Solar (46 Ronald Quinteros), Pedro Alejandro García (68 Jair Edson Céspedes), Roberto Ovelar (53 Roberto Enrique Silva). DT: Víctor Rivera
Goals: Washington Sebastián Abreu (14, 51, 90+1), Radamel Falcao García (27), Andrés Ríos (82)

1	RIVER PLATE	6	4	0	2	14	8	12
2	CF AMÉRICA	6	3	0	3	10	10	9
3	Universidad Católica	6	3	0	3	6	6	9
4	Universidad San Martín	6	2	0	4	4	10	6

GROUP 6

CÚCUTA DEPORTIVO - SANTOS FC 0-0
General Santander, Cúcuta, 13.02.2008, Referee: Víctor Rivera (PER)
CÚCUTA: Andrés Leandro Castellanos, Elvis Antonio Rivas, Pedro Paulo Portocarrero, Flavio Armando Córdoba, Elvis Javier González, Charles Castro, Nelson Alfonso Florez, James Enrique Castro (66 Édison Fonseca), Macnelly Torres, Lin Carlos Henry (55 Eudalio Eulises Arriaga), Diego Aroldo Cabrera. DT: Pedro Sarmiento
SANTOS: FÁBIO COSTA, ADRIANO Santos, Ebert Amancio 'BETÃO', ADAÍLTON José dos Santos Filho, DOMINGOS Nascimento dos Santos Filho, Thiago CARLETO, Márcio Glad 'MARCINHO GUERREIRO', RODRIGO Ribeiro SOUTO, Mauricio Alejandro Molina, KLÉBER BOAS PEREIRA, Michael Jackson Quiñónez (46 WESLEY Beltrame). DT: Emerson Leão

CD GUADALAJARA - SAN JOSÉ 2-0 (1-0)
Jalisco, Guadalajara, 19.02.2008, Referee: Alfredo Intriago (ECU)
GUADALAJARA: Luis Ernesto Michel, José Jonny Magallón, Francisco Javier Rodríguez, Juan Antonio Ocampo (60 Marco Jhonfai Fabián), Gonzalo Pineda, Édgar Iván Solís (77 Jesús Andrés Padilla), Xavier Iván Báez, Alberto Medina, Ramón Morales, Sergio Alejandro Santana (73 Javier Hernández), Omar Antonio Bravo. DT: Efraín Flores
SAN JOSÉ: Daniel Vaca, Enrique Parada, Luis Mario Palacios, Carlos De Castro, Carlos Alvarenga, Gerson Luis García, Sandro Coelho Leite, Rolando Ribera, Darwin Peña, Alex da Rosa (89 Martín Adrián Palavicini), Luis David Cerutti. DT: Marcos Ferrufino
Goals: Edgar Iván Solís (28), Sergio Alejandro Santana (53 penalty)

CÚCUTA DEPORTIVO - SAN JOSÉ 0-0
General Santander, Cúcuta, 28.02.2008
Referee: Juan Soto (VEN)
CÚCUTA: Andrés Leandro Castellanos, Braynner Yezid García, Pedro Paulo Portocarrero, Flavio Armando Córdoba, Fredy Arizala (46 Matías Héctor Urbano), Charles Castro, Nelson Alfonso Florez (8 James Enrique Castro), Macnelly Torres, José Alberto Amarilla, Eudalio Eulises Arriaga (63 Leandro Abel Vargas), Diego Aroldo Cabrera. DT: Pedro Sarmiento
SAN JOSÉ: Daniel Vaca, Enrique Parada, Luis Mario Palacios, Carlos De Castro, Carlos Alvarenga, Gerson Luis García, Rolando Ribera, Sandro Coelho Leite (53 Limbert Percy Pizarro), Darwin Peña, Alex da Rosa (56 Mauricio Saucedo), Luis David Cerutti (71 Martín Adrián Palavicini). DT: Marcos Ferrufino
Sent off: Castro (86), Amarilla (88)

SANTOS FC – CD GUADALAJARA 1-0 (1-0)
Urbano Caldeira, Santos, 4.03.2008, Referee: Carlos Amarilla (PAR)
SANTOS: FÁBIO COSTA, ADRIANO Santos, Ebert Amancio 'BETÃO', DOMINGOS Nascimento dos Santos Filho, Thiago CARLETO, Márcio Glad 'MARCINHO GUERREIRO', RODRIGO Ribeiro SOUTO, WESLEY Beltrame (61 Michael Jackson Quiñónez), Mauricio Alejandro Molina (80 ANDERSON SALLES), KLÉBER BOAS PEREIRA, Mariano Tripodi (59 TIAGO Martins 'LUIS'). DT: Emerson Leão
GUADALAJARA: Luis Ernesto Michel, José Jonny Magallón, Héctor Reynoso, Francisco Javier Rodríguez, Xavier Iván Báez, Gonzalo Pineda (60 Julio César Nava), Édgar Iván Solís (71 Javier Hernández), Alberto Medina, Ramón Morales (81 Marco Jhonfai Fabián), Sergio Alejandro Santana, Omar Antonio Bravo. DT: Efraín Flores
Goal: Mauricio Alejandro Molina (22)

CD GUADALAJARA - CÚCUTA DEPORTIVO 0-1 (0-1)
Jalisco, Guadalajara, 11.03.2008, Referee: Alfredo Intriago (ECU)
GUADALAJARA: Luis Ernesto Michel, José Jonny Magallón, Héctor Reynoso, Francisco Javier Rodríguez, Xavier Iván Báez (46 Alberto Medina), Gonzalo Pineda (60 Omar Alejandro Esparza), Édgar Iván Solís (54 Javier Hernández), Ramón Morales, Marco Jhonfai Fabián, Sergio Alejandro Santana, Omar Antonio Bravo. DT: Efraín Flores
CÚCUTA: Andrés Leandro Castellanos, Braynner Yezid García, Flavio Armando Córdoba, Pedro Paulo Portocarrero, Fredy Arizala, James Enrique Castro, William Román Zapata, Lin Carlos Henry (35 Danovis Banguero), Elvis Antonio Rivas, Macnelly Torres, Matías Héctor Urbano (79 Leandro Abel Vargas). DT: Pedro Sarmiento
Sent off: Fabián (90)
Goal: Matías Héctor Urbano (44)

SAN JOSÉ - SANTOS FC 2-1 (1-1)
Jesús Bermúdez, Oruro, 19.03.2008, Referee: Samuel Haro (ECU)
SAN JOSÉ: Daniel Vaca, Enrique Parada, Luis Mario Palacios, Carlos De Castro, Carlos Alvarenga, Gerson Luis García (86 Límberg Ronald Morejón), Rolando Ribera, Sandro Coelho Leite, Darwin Peña (73 Mauricio Saucedo), Alex da Rosa (88 Richard José Rojas), Luis David Cerutti. DT: Marcos Ferrufino
SANTOS: FÁBIO COSTA, ADRIANO Santos, Ebert Amancio 'BETÃO', DOMINGOS Nascimento dos Santos Filho, KLÉBER de Carvalho Corrêa, Márcio Glad 'MARCINHO GUERREIRO' (57 ANDERSON SALLES, 72 Mariano Tripodi), RODRIGO Ribeiro SOUTO, WESLEY Beltrame, Mauricio Alejandro Molina, KLÉBER BOAS PEREIRA, Sebastián Pinto (46 EVALDO Santos). DT: Emerson Leão
Goals: Luis David Cerutti (11), Gerson Luis García (61) / Kléber Boas Pereira (7)

CÚCUTA DEPORTIVO – CD GUADALAJARA 1-0 (0-0)
General Santander, Cúcuta, 27.03.2008, Referee: Óscar Maldonado (BOL)
CÚCUTA: Andrés Leandro Castellanos, Braynner Yezid García, Flavio Armando Córdoba, Pedro Paulo Portocarrero, Elvis Javier González, Charles Castro, William Román Zapata, James Enrique Castro, José Alberto Amarilla (79 Lin Carlos Henry), Macnelly Torres, Matías Héctor Urbano (79 Diego Aroldo Cabrera). DT: Pedro Sarmiento
GUADALAJARA: Luis Ernesto Michel, José Jonny Magallón, Héctor Reynoso, Francisco Javier Rodríguez, Gonzalo Pineda, Sergio Gabriel Ávila (62 Omar Arellano), Édgar Iván Solís (55 Sergio Alejandro Santana), Xavier Iván Báez, Ramón Morales, Alberto Medina (67 Julio César Nava), Omar Antonio Bravo. DT: Efraín Flores
Goal: Matías Héctor Urbano (62)

SANTOS FC - SAN JOSÉ 7-0 (3-0)
Urbano Caldeira, Santos, 1.04.2008, Referee: Liber Prudente (URU)
SANTOS: FÁBIO COSTA, DÊNIS Oliveira de Souza (68 José Fabio Azevedo 'FABÃO'), DOMINGOS Nascimento dos Santos Filho, Ebert Amancio 'BETÃO', KLÉBER de Carvalho Corrêa, Márcio Glad 'MARCINHO GUERREIRO', RODRIGO Ribeiro SOUTO, Mauricio Alejandro Molina, Rodrigo TABATA (73 Michael Jackson Quiñónez), WESLEY Beltrame (64 TIAGO Martins 'LUIS'), KLÉBER BOAS PEREIRA. DT: Emerson Leão
SAN JOSÉ: Daniel Vaca, Enrique Parada, Luis Mario Palacios, Carlos De Castro, Carlos Alvarenga, Gerson Luis García, Rolando Ribera, Sandro Coelho Leite, Darwin Peña (59 Mauricio Saucedo), Alex da Rosa (61 Martín Adrián Palavicini), Luis David Cerutti (83 Límberg Ronald Morejón). DT: Marcos Ferrufino
Goals: DOMINGOS Nascimento dos Santos Filho (17), Mauricio Alejandro Molina (22, 32, 63, 87), Kléber Boas Pereira (79), Michael Quiñónez (81)

SAN JOSÉ - CÚCUTA DEPORTIVO 2-4 (0-2)
Jesús Bermúdez, Oruro, 8.04.2008, Referee: Ricardo Grance (PAR)
SAN JOSÉ: Daniel Vaca, Enrique Parada, René Oliva (44 Fernando Batistte), Carlos De Castro, Carlos Alvarenga, Gerson Luis García (37 Darwin Peña), Rolando Ribera, Sandro Coelho Leite, Alex da Rosa, Martín Adrián Palavicini (67 Mauricio Saucedo), Luis David Cerutti. DT: Marcos Ferrufino
CÚCUTA: Andrés Leandro Castellanos, Braynner Yezid García, Flavio Armando Córdoba, Pedro Paulo Portocarrero, Elvis Javier González, Charles Castro, William Román Zapata, James Enrique Castro (75 Lin Carlos Henry), José Alberto Amarilla (87 Roberto Antonio Peñaloza), Macnelly Torres, Matías Héctor Urbano (85 Leandro Abel Vargas). DT: Pedro Sarmiento
Goals: Luis David Cerutti (46), Enrique Parada (77) / Matías Héctor Urbano (35, 38, 78), Macnelly Torres (53)

CD GUADALAJARA - SANTOS FC 3-2 (2-1)
Jalisco, Guadalajara, 9.04.2008, Referee: José Buitrago (COL)
GUADALAJARA: Luis Ernesto Michel, Édgar Iván Solís, José Jonny Magallón, Héctor Reynoso, Francisco Javier Rodríguez, Gonzalo Pineda, Ramón Morales (70 Patricio Gabriel Araujo), Sergio Gabriel Ávila, Alberto Medina, Omar Arellano (63 Omar Antonio Bravo), Sergio Alejandro Santana (69 Omar Alejandro Esparza). DT: Efraín Flores
SANTOS: FÁBIO COSTA, Ebert Amancio 'BETÃO', José Fabio Azevedo 'FABÃO', DOMINGOS Nascimento dos Santos Filho (39 EVALDO Santos), DÊNIS Oliveira de Souza (62 Michael Jackson Quiñónez), Márcio Glad 'MARCINHO GUERREIRO', RODRIGO Ribeiro SOUTO, Mauricio Alejandro Molina (73 TIAGO Martins 'LUIS'), KLÉBER de Carvalho Corrêa, WESLEY Beltrame, KLÉBER BOAS PEREIRA. DT: Emerson Leão
Goals: Omar Arellano (13), Francisco Javier Rodríguez (34), Sergio Alejandro Santana (47) / Kléber Boas Pereira (39), KLÉBER de Carvalho Corrêa (55)

SAN JOSÉ – CD GUADALAJARA 0-3 (0-2)
Jesús Bermúdez, Oruro, 16.04.2008, Referee: Pablo Pozo (CHI)
SAN JOSÉ: Daniel Vaca, Enrique Parada, Franklin Juan Herrera (46 Gerson Luis García), Luis Mario Palacios, Carlos Alvarenga, Límberg Ronald Morejón, Rolando Ribera, Sandro Coelho Leite, Martín Adrián Palavicini (67 Mauricio Saucedo), Darwin Peña (46 Luis David Cerutti), Alex da Rosa. DT: Marcos Ferrufino
GUADALAJARA: Luis Ernesto Michel, José Jonny Magallón (66 Arturo Javier Ledezma), Héctor Reynoso, Francisco Javier Rodríguez, Xavier Iván Báez, Gonzalo Pineda, Sergio Gabriel Ávila (75 Jesús Andrés Padilla), Alberto Medina, Marco Jhonfai Fabián (69 Julio César Nava), Omar Arellano, Omar Antonio Bravo. DT: Efraín Flores
Sent off: Coelho Leite (55)
Goals: Sergio Gabriel Ávila (29, 43), Gonzalo Pineda (55)

SANTOS FC - CÚCUTA DEPORTIVO 2-1 (0-1)
Urbano Caldeira, Santos, 16.04.2008, Referee: Jorge Larrionda (URU)
SANTOS: FÁBIO COSTA, Ebert Amancio 'BETÃO', José Fabio Azevedo 'FABÃO', DOMINGOS Nascimento dos Santos Filho, KLÉBER de Carvalho Corrêa, Márcio Glad 'MARCINHO GUERREIRO', RODRIGO Ribeiro SOUTO, Mauricio Alejandro Molina, Rodrigo TABATA (46 Mariano Tripodi), WESLEY Beltrame, KLÉBER BOAS PEREIRA. DT: Emerson Leão
CÚCUTA: Andrés Leandro Castellanos, Braynner Yezid García, Flavio Armando Córdoba, Pedro Paulo Portocarrero, Elvis Javier González, Charles Castro (90+5 Eudalio Eulises Arriaga), Elvis Antonio Rivas (58 Matías Héctor Urbano), William Román Zapata, Lin Carlos Henry, Macnelly Torres, Leandro Abel Vargas (58 James Enrique Castro). DT: Pedro Sarmiento
Goals: Kléber Boas Pereira (68), Mariano Tripodi (88) / Lin Carlos Henry (22)

1	CÚCUTA DEPORTIVO	6	3	2	1	7	4	11
2	SANTOS FC	6	3	1	2	13	6	10
3	CD Guadalajara	6	3	0	3	8	5	9
4	San José Oruro	6	1	1	4	4	17	4

GROUP 7

AUDAX ITALIANO - SPORTIVO LUQUEÑO 1-2 (1-1)
David Arellano, Santiago, 19.02.2008, Referee: Heber Lopes (BRA)
AUDAX: Mario Eduardo Villasanti, Boris Alexis Rieloff (79 Matías Leonardo Vidangossy), Carlos Alberto Garrido, Sebastián Rocco, Patricio Javier Gutiérrez, Marcelo Carlo Broli, Braulio Antonio Leal, Miguel Ángel Romero, Carlos Andrés Villanueva, Fabian Ariel Orellana, Renzo Alberto Yáñez (71 Renato Andrés Ramos). DT: Raúl Toro
SPORTIVO LUQUEÑO: Enrique García, Ignacio Ramón Paniagua, Rober Antonio Servín, Diego Martínez, Reinaldo Román, Carlos Antonio Mereles, Víctor Quintana (39 Luis Alejandro Núñez), Derlis Fabián Ortiz (80 Juan Gabriel Abente), Charles da Silva, Marcos Antonio Lazaga (65 Claudio David Vargas), Rubén Darío Gigena. DT: Daniel Lanata
Sent off: Núñez (90)
Goals: Miguel Ángel Romero (11) / Rober Antonio Servín (9), Luis Alejandro Núñez (72)

ATLÉTICO NACIONAL - SÃO PAULO FC 1-1 (1-1)
Atanasio Girardot, Medellín, 27.02.2008, Referee: Víctor Rivera (PER)
ATLÉTICO NACIONAL: David Ospina, Humberto Antonio Mendoza, Wálter José Moreno, Juan Camilo Zúñiga, Juan Estiven Vélez, Diego Mauricio Toro, Luis Felipe Chará, Elkin Antonio Murillo, David Camilo Córdoba (75 Marlon Piedrahita), Sergio Alejandro Galván Rey, Carmelo Valencia. DT: Oscar Quintabani
SÃO PAULO: ROGÉRIO CENI, ANDRÉ Gonçalves DIAS, João MIRANDA de Souza Filho, JORGE WAGNER Goes Conceição, ÉDER LUIS De Oliveira, ADRIANO Leite Ribeiro, JOILSON Rodrigues Macedo (73 EDER Schiola Santana), Anderson HERNANES Andrade Lima, Humberlito BORGES Teixeira (90 CARLOS ALBERTO Gomes de Jesus), RICHARLYSON Barbosa Felisbino, José 'ZÉ' LUIS Santos Da Visitação. DT: Muricy Ramalho
Goals: David Camilo Córdoba (8) / João MIRANDA De Souza Filho (32)

SÃO PAULO FC - AUDAX ITALIANO 2-1 (0-0)
Cícero Pompeu de Toledo 'Morumbí', 5.03.2008, Referee: Sergio Pezzotta (ARG)
SÃO PAULO: ROGÉRIO CENI, ANDRÉ Gonçalves DIAS, João MIRANDA De Souza Filho, JORGE WAGNER Goes Conceição, ÉDER LUIS De Oliveira (87 JOILSON Rodrigues Macedo), ADRIANO Leite Ribeiro, FÁBIO dos SANTOS Barbosa (70 ALOÍSIO José da Silva), Anderson HERNANES Andrade Lima, Humberlito BORGES Teixeira, RICHARLYSON Barbosa Felisbino (61 Jenilson Angelo De Souza 'JÚNIOR'), José 'ZÉ' LUIS Santos Da Visitação. DT: Muricy Ramalho
AUDAX: Mario Eduardo Villasanti, Boris Alexis Rieloff, Carlos Alberto Garrido, Sebastián Rocco, Patricio Javier Gutiérrez, Marcelo Carlo Broli, Braulio Antonio Leal, Miguel Ángel Romero, Carlos Andrés Villanueva (73 Cristián Eduardo Reynero), Fabian Ariel Orellana, Renzo Alberto Yáñez (46 Renato Andrés Ramos). DT: Raúl Toro
Sent off: Rocco (74)
Goals: ADRIANO Leite Ribeiro (73, 85) / Carlos Andrés Villanueva (62)

ATLÉTICO NACIONAL - SPORTIVO LUQUEÑO 3-0 (2-0)
Atanasio Girardot, Medellín, 6.03.2008, Referee: Jorge Larrionda (URU)
ATLÉTICO NACIONAL: David Ospina, Humberto Antonio Mendoza, Juan Camilo Zúñiga (83 Marlon Piedrahita), Juan Camilo Pérez, Juan Estiven Vélez, Diego Mauricio Toro, José Antonio Amaya, Elkin Antonio Murillo (74 David Camilo Córdoba), Sergio Alejandro Galván Rey, Carlos Wilson Villagra, León Darío Muñoz (48 Carmelo Valencia). DT: Oscar Quintabani
SPORTIVO LUQUEÑO: Enrique García, Celso Esquivel, Rober Antonio Servín, Diego Martínez, Reinaldo Román, Víctor Quintana, Sinecio León (75 Juan Ángel Hermosilla), Derlis Fabián Ortiz, Charles da Silva, Marcos Antonio Lazaga (48 Adriano Javier Duarte), Rubén Darío Gigena (53 Claudio David Vargas). DT: Daniel Lanata
Goals: Sergio Alejandro Galván Rey (21), Carlos Wilson Villagra (43), Carmelo Valencia (81)

AUDAX ITALIANO - ATLÉTICO NACIONAL 1-0 (0-0)
David Arellano, Santiago, 18.03.2008, Referee: Fernando Cabrera (URU)
AUDAX: Mario Eduardo Villasanti, Boris Alexis Rieloff, Carlos Alberto Garrido, César Elías Santis, Patricio Javier Gutiérrez, Cristián Eduardo Reynero, Braulio Antonio Leal, Miguel Ángel Romero, Carlos Andrés Villanueva, Fabian Ariel Orellana, Renzo Alberto Yáñez (78 Oliver Adrián Toledo). DT: Raúl Toro
ATLÉTICO NACIONAL: David Ospina, Luis Felipe Chará, Juan Camilo Pérez, Humberto Antonio Mendoza, Juan Estiven Vélez, Juan Camilo Zúñiga, José Antonio Amaya, Diego Mauricio Toro (58 Carlos Wilson Villagra), Elkin Antonio Murillo (73 Marlon Piedrahita), Sergio Alejandro Galván Rey, Carmelo Valencia (78 Francisco Arrué). DT: Oscar Quintabani
Goal: Fabián Ariel Orellana (48)

SPORTIVO LUQUEÑO - SÃO PAULO FC 1-1 (0-0)
Feliciano Cáceres, Luque, 20.03.2008, Referee: Sergio Pezzotta (ARG)
SPORTIVO LUQUEÑO: Enrique García, Ignacio Ramón Paniagua, Rober Antonio Servín, Diego Martínez, Reinaldo Román, Víctor Quintana (71 Juan Rodolfo Romero), Luis Alejandro Núñez, Celso Esquivel (80 Juan Ángel Hermosilla), Juan Gabriel Abente (66 Adriano Javier Duarte), Charles da Silva, Marcos Antonio Lazaga. DT: Daniel Lanata
SÃO PAULO: ROGÉRIO CENI, ANDRÉ Gonçalves DIAS, João MIRANDA De Souza Filho (41 Anselmo Vendrechovski Júnior 'JUNINHO'), JORGE WAGNER Goes Conceição, ÉDER LUIS De Oliveira (85 CARLOS ALBERTO Gomes de Jesus), ADRIANO Leite Ribeiro, Anderson HERNANES Andrade Lima, Humberlito BORGES Teixeira (56 ALOÍSIO José da Silva), RICHARLYSON Barbosa Felisbino, EDER Schiola Santana, José 'ZÉ' LUIS Santos Da Visitação. DT: Muricy Ramalho
Goals: Adriano Javier Duarte (90+3) / ALOÍSIO José Da Silva (59)

SÃO PAULO FC - SPORTIVO LUQUEÑO 1-0 (0-0)
Cícero Pompeu de Toledo 'Morumbí', 2.04.2008, Referee: Martín Vázquez (URU)
SÃO PAULO: ROGÉRIO CENI, José 'ZÉ' LUIS Santos Da Visitação, ANDRÉ Gonçalves DIAS, João MIRANDA De Souza Filho, RICHARLYSON Barbosa Felisbino, Anderson HERNANES Andrade Lima, FÁBIO dos SANTOS Barbosa (66 DAGOBERTO Pelentier), ÉDER LUIS De Oliveira (72 CARLOS ALBERTO Gomes de Jesus), JORGE WAGNER Goes Conceição, Humberlito BORGES Teixeira, ADRIANO Leite Ribeiro. DT: Muricy Ramalho
SPORTIVO LUQUEÑO: Enrique García, Ignacio Ramón Paniagua, Rober Antonio Servín, Diego Martínez, Reinaldo Román, Víctor Quintana (54 Luis Alejandro Núñez), Celso Esquivel, Carlos Antonio Mereles, Claudio David Vargas (76 Bladimiro Duarte), Charles da Silva (62 Juan Gabriel Abente), Marcos Antonio Lazaga. DT: Daniel Lanata
Goal: ADRIANO Leite Ribeiro (90+3)

ATLÉTICO NACIONAL - AUDAX ITALIANO 1-1 (0-0)
Atanasio Girardot, Medellín, 3.04.2008, Referee: Carlos Vera (ECU)
ATLÉTICO NACIONAL: David Ospina, Juan Camilo Zúñiga, Humberto Antonio Mendoza, Wálter José Moreno, Juan Estiven Vélez, Diego Mauricio Toro, José Antonio Amaya, Francisco Arrué (74 David Camilo Córdoba), Fernando Patricio Martel (66 Marlon Piedrahita), Sergio Alejandro Galván Rey, Carlos Wilson Villagra. DT: Oscar Quintabani
AUDAX: Mario Eduardo Villasanti, Boris Alexis Rieloff (62 Oliver Adrián Toledo), Carlos Alberto Garrido, Sebastián Rocco, Patricio Javier Gutiérrez, Cristián Eduardo Reynero, Braulio Antonio Leal, Marcelo Carlo Broli, Miguel Ángel Romero, Fabian Ariel Orellana, Renzo Alberto Yáñez (28 Nicolás Ignacio Corvetto, 76 Matías Leonardo Vidangossy). DT: Raúl Toro
Goals: Carlos Wilson Villagra (59) / Fabián Ariel Orellana (78)

AUDAX ITALIANO - SÃO PAULO FC 1-0 (0-0)
Nacional, Santiago, 10.04.2008, Referee: Héctor Baldassi (ARG)
AUDAX: Mario Eduardo Villasanti, Boris Alexis Rieloff, Carlos Alberto Garrido, Sebastián Rocco, Patricio Javier Gutiérrez, Cristián Eduardo Reynero, Braulio Antonio Leal, Miguel Ángel Romero (78 Nicolás Ignacio Corvetto), Marco Antonio Medel (46 Renato Andrés Ramos), Oliver Adrián Toledo (90 César Elías Santis), Fabian Ariel Orellana. DT: Raúl Toro
SÃO PAULO: ROGÉRIO CENI, ANDRÉ Gonçalves DIAS, João MIRANDA De Souza Filho, JORGE WAGNER Goes Conceição, ÉDER LUIS De Oliveira (63 Jenilson Angelo De Souza 'JÚNIOR'), ADRIANO Leite Ribeiro, JOILSON Rodrigues Macedo, Anderson HERNANES Andrade Lima, Humberlito BORGES Teixeira (70 DAGOBERTO Pelentier), RICHARLYSON Barbosa Felisbino, EDER Schiola Santana (82 HUGO Henrique Assis Do Nascimento). DT: Muricy Ramalho
Goal: Renato Andrés Ramos (77)

SPORTIVO LUQUEÑO - ATLÉTICO NACIONAL 1-3 (0-1)
Feliciano Cáceres, Luque, 10.04.2008, Referee: Saúl Laverni (ARG)
SPORTIVO LUQUEÑO: Bryan López, Ignacio Ramón Paniagua, Rober Antonio Servín, Diego Martínez, Reinaldo Román, Víctor Quintana (46 Marcos Antonio Lazaga), Celso Esquivel, Carlos Antonio Mereles, Claudio David Vargas (46 Luis Alejandro Núñez), Charles da Silva (61 Juan Ángel Hermosilla), Rubén Darío Gigena. DT: Daniel Lanata
ATLÉTICO NACIONAL: David Ospina, Juan Camilo Zúñiga, Humberto Antonio Mendoza, Wálter José Moreno, Harold Martínez, Francisco Arrué (85 David Camilo Córdoba), José Antonio Amaya, Diego Mauricio Toro (82 Luis Felipe Chará), Fernando Patricio Martel (73 Carlos Alberto Díaz), Sergio Alejandro Galván Rey, Carlos Wilson Villagra. DT: Oscar Quintabani
Sent off: Paniagua (88), Mendoza (88)
Goals: Mauro Antonio Lazaga (71) /
Carlos Wilson Villagra (38), Sergio Alejandro Galván Rey (50 penalty), David Camilo Córdoba (90+2)

SPORTIVO LUQUEÑO - AUDAX ITALIANO 4-1 (4-0)
Feliciano Cáceres, Luque, 23.04.2008, Referee: Roberto Silvera (URU)
SPORTIVO LUQUEÑO: Enrique García, Rober Antonio Servín, Celso Esquivel, Diego Martínez, Reinaldo Román, Luis Alejandro Núñez, Carlos Antonio Mereles, Juan Gabriel Abente, Juan Ángel Hermosilla (65 Claudio David Vargas), Charles da Silva (59 Víctor Quintana), Rubén Darío Gigena (60 Marcos Antonio Lazaga). DT: Daniel Lanata
AUDAX: Mario Eduardo Villasanti, Boris Alexis Rieloff, Carlos Alberto Garrido, Sebastián Rocco, Patricio Javier Gutiérrez (46 César Elías Santis), Cristián Eduardo Reynero, Braulio Antonio Leal, Carlos Andrés Villanueva, Nicolás Ignacio Corvetto (69 Renzo Alberto Yáñez), Fabian Ariel Orellana, Renato Andrés Ramos (46 Matías Leonardo Vidangossy). DT: Raúl Toro
Goals: Juan Abente (1, 28), Rubén Gigena (7), Celso Esquivel (43) / Carlos Villanueva (55)

SÃO PAULO FC - ATLÉTICO NACIONAL 1-0 (1-0)
Cícero Pompeu de Toledo 'Morumbí', 23.04.2008, Referee: Carlos Torres (PAR)
SÃO PAULO: ROGÉRIO CENI, João MIRANDA De Souza Filho, ALEX Sandro da SILVA, ANDRÉ Gonçalves DIAS (60 EDER Schiola Santana), José 'ZÉ' LUIS Santos Da Visitação, RICHARLYSON Barbosa Felisbino, Anderson HERNANES Andrade Lima, ÉDER LUIS De Oliveira (83 FÁBIO dos SANTOS Barbosa), JORGE WAGNER Goes Conceição, Humberlito BORGES Teixeira (64 DAGOBERTO Pelentier), ADRIANO Leite Ribeiro. DT: Muricy Ramalho
ATLÉTICO NACIONAL: David Ospina, Juan Camilo Zúñiga, Carlos Alberto Díaz, Wálter José Moreno, Harold Martínez, José Antonio Amaya, Luis Felipe Chará, Juan Carlos Ramírez (71 Juan Estiven Vélez), David Camilo Córdoba (62 Elkin Antonio Murillo), Sergio Alejandro Galván Rey, Carlos Wilson Villagra (74 Carmelo Valencia. DT: Oscar Quintabani
Goal: ALEX Sandro da SILVA (38)

1	SÃO PAULO FC	6	3	2	1	6	4	11
2	ATLÉTICO NACIONAL	6	2	2	2	8	5	8
3	Sportivo Luqueño	6	2	1	3	8	10	7
4	Audax Italiano	6	2	1	3	6	9	7

GROUP 8

ARSENAL - LIBERTAD 1-0 (0-0)
Julio Humberto Grondona, Sarandí, 20.02.2008, Referee: Salvio Fagundes (BRA)
ARSENAL: Mario Eduardo Cuenca, Cristian Alberto Pellerano (67 Diego Nicolás Villar), José Luis Calderón, Luciano Félix Leguizamón, Carlos Damián Casteglione, Javier Marcelo Gandolfi (39 Darío Espínola), Aníbal Samuel Matellán, Cristian Leonel Díaz, Jossimar Mosquera, Sebastián Carrera (26 Alejandro Darío Gómez), Javier Orlando Yacuzzi. DT: Gustavo Alfaro
LIBERTAD: Horacio Javier González, Pedro Juan Benítez, Derlis Cardozo, Édgar Gabriel Balbuena, Omar Heber Pouso, Edgar Arnulfo Robles, Vladimir Marín (76 Hugo Américo Luzardi), Roberto Carlos Gamarra (76 Nelson Rafael Cuevas), Dante López (56 Nelson David Romero), Pedro Alcides Sarabia, Sergio Daniel Aquino. DT: Rubén Israel
Goal: Luciano Félix Leguizamón (78)

LDU QUITO - FLUMINENSE 0-0
La Casa Blanca, Quito, 20.02.2008, Referee: Albert Duarte (COL)
LDU: José Francisco Cevallos, Jairo Rolando Campos, Norberto Carlos Araujo, Renán Calle, Paul Vicente Ambrossi (46 Jaime Iván Kaviedes), Enrique Daniel Vera, Patricio Javier Urrutia, Luis Alberto Bolaños, Damián Alejandro Manso, Joffre David Guerrón (74 Christian Andrés Suárez), Claudio Daniel Bieler (68 Agustín Javier Delgado). DT: Edgardo Bauza
FLUMINENSE: FERNANDO HENRIQUE Dos Anjos, GABRIEL Rodrigues Dos Santos, THIAGO Emiliano Da SILVA, LUIZ ALBERTO Da Silva Oliveira, YGOR Maciel Santiago, JUNIOR CESAR Eduardo Machado, LEANDRO Camara do AMARAL (74 Darío Leonardo Conca), Marcos AROUCA da Silva, WASHINGTON Stecanela Cerqueira, THIAGO NEVES Augusto (81 ROGER Machado Marques), MAURÍCIO José Da Silveira Junior (46 CÍCERO Santos). DT: Renato Portaluppi

LDU QUITO - LIBERTAD 2-0 (0-0)
La Casa Blanca, Quito, 4.03.2008, Referee: Óscar Ruiz (COL)
LDU: José Francisco Cevallos, Jairo Rolando Campos, Norberto Carlos Araujo, Diego Armando Calderón, Paul Vicente Ambrossi (60 Luis Alberto Bolaños), Joffre David Guerrón, Enrique Daniel Vera, Patricio Javier Urrutia, Damián Alejandro Manso (73 William Francisco Araujo), Agustín Javier Delgado (60 Franklin Agustín Salas), Claudio Daniel Bieler. DT: Edgardo Bauza
LIBERTAD: Horacio Javier González, Celso Pablo González, Pedro Alcides Sarabia, Pedro Juan Benítez, Derlis Cardozo, Sergio Daniel Aquino (79 Dante López), Víctor Javier Cáceres, Edgar Arnulfo Robles, Vladimir Marín (72 Roberto Carlos Gamarra), Osvaldo David Martínez (72 Omar Heber Pouso), Juan Eduardo Samudio. DT: Rubén Israel
Goals: Patricio Javier Urrutia (71), Joffre David Guerrón (82)

FLUMINENSE - ARSENAL 6-0 (3-0)
Mario Filho 'Maracanã', Rio de Janeiro, 5.03.2008, Referee: Carlos Torres (PAR)
FLUMINENSE: FERNANDO HENRIQUE Dos Anjos, GABRIEL Rodrigues Dos Santos, THIAGO Emiliano Da SILVA, LUIZ ALBERTO Da Silva Oliveira, YGOR Maciel Santiago, JUNIOR CESAR Eduardo Machado (74 ROGER Machado Marques), Marcos AROUCA da Silva (74 Fábio De Jesus 'FABINHO'), WASHINGTON Stecanela Cerqueira, THIAGO NEVES Augusto (68 CÍCERO Santos), Ricardo Lucas 'DODÔ', Darío Leonardo Conca. DT: Renato Portaluppi
ARSENAL: Mario Eduardo Cuenca, Darío Espínola, Andrés San Martín (18 Cristian Alberto Pellerano), José Luis Calderón, Leonardo Ángel Biagini (62 Luciano Félix Leguizamón), Carlos Damián Casteglione, Aníbal Samuel Matellán, Cristian Leonel Díaz, Jossimar Mosquera, Sebastián Carrera (62 Alejandro Darío Gómez), Javier Orlando Yacuzzi. DT: Gustavo Alfaro
Goals: THIAGO NEVES Augusto (13), Ricardo Lucas 'DODÔ' (24, 50), GABRIEL Rodrigues Dos Santos (44), WASHINGTON Stecanela Cerqueira (71), CÍCERO Santos (85)

ARSENAL - LDU QUITO 0-1 (0-0)
Julio Humberto Grondona, Sarandí, 12.03.2008, Referee: Carlos Chandía (CHI)
ARSENAL: Mario Eduardo Cuenca, Carlos Alberto Báez (46 Cristian Leonel Díaz), Darío Espínola, Cristian Alberto Pellerano, José Luis Calderón, Luciano Félix Leguizamón (62 Leonardo Ángel Biagini), Alejandro Darío Gómez, Carlos Damián Casteglione, Aníbal Samuel Matellán, Jossimar Mosquera, Javier Orlando Yacuzzi (67 Sebastián Carrera). DT: Gustavo Alfaro
LDU: José Francisco Cevallos, Jairo Rolando Campos, Norberto Carlos Araujo, Diego Armando Calderón, Paul Vicente Ambrossi, Joffre David Guerrón, William Francisco Araujo (87 Andrés Arrunategui), Patricio Javier Urrutia, Luis Alberto Bolaños (73 Pedro Sebastián Larrea), Damián Alejandro Manso (82 Franklin Agustín Salas), Claudio Daniel Bieler. DT: Edgardo Bauza
Goal: Patricio Urrutia (79 penalty)

LIBERTAD - FLUMINENSE 1-2 (1-1)
Defensores del Chaco, Asunción, 19.03.2008, Referee: Héctor Baldassi (ARG)
LIBERTAD: Horacio Javier González, Pedro Juan Benítez, Derlis Cardozo, Édgar Gabriel Balbuena (53 Vladimir Marín), Omar Heber Pouso, Edgar Arnulfo Robles, Osvaldo David Martínez, Pedro Alcides Sarabia, Sergio Daniel Aquino, Juan Eduardo Samudio (67 Roberto Carlos Gamarra), Juan Manuel Olivera (61 Nelson Rafael Cuevas). DT: Rubén Israel
FLUMINENSE: FERNANDO HENRIQUE Dos Anjos, GABRIEL Rodrigues Dos Santos, THIAGO Emiliano Da SILVA, LUIZ ALBERTO Da Silva Oliveira, YGOR Maciel Santiago, JUNIOR CESAR Eduardo Machado (80 ROGER Machado Marques), Marcos AROUCA da Silva (67 MAURÍCIO José Da Silveira Junior), WASHINGTON Stecanela Cerqueira, THIAGO NEVES Augusto (74 Vinicius Silva Soares 'TARTÁ'), CÍCERO Santos, Darío Leonardo Conca. DT: Renato Portaluppi
Goals: Juan Eduardo Samudio (30) / WASHINGTON Stecanela Cerqueira (40, 50)

LDU QUITO - ARSENAL 6-1 (4-1)
La Casa Blanca, Quito, 26.03.2008, Referee: Armando Archundia (MEX)
LDU: José Francisco Cevallos, Jairo Rolando Campos, Norberto Carlos Araujo, Diego Armando Calderón, Paul Vicente Ambrossi, Enrique Daniel Vera, Patricio Javier Urrutia, Joffre David Guerrón (78 Alfonso Andrés Obregón), Luis Alberto Bolaños, Damián Alejandro Manso (74 Edder Javier Vaca), Claudio Daniel Bieler (66 Agustín Javier Delgado). DT: Edgardo Bauza
ARSENAL: Mario Eduardo Cuenca, Darío Espínola, Carlos Alberto Báez, Aníbal Samuel Matellán, Cristian Leonel Díaz (61 Martín Ezequiel Andrizzi), Pablo Sebastián Garnier, Cristian Alberto Pellerano, Carlos Damián Casteglione, Javier Orlando Yacuzzi, Luciano Félix Leguizamón (75 Sebastián Carrera), Leonardo Ángel Biagini (22 José Luis Calderón). DT: Gustavo Alfaro
Sent off: Casteglione (72)
Goals: Patricio Javier Urrutia (15), Damián Alejandro Manso (19), Luis Alberto Bolaños (28, 42), Claudio Daniel Bieler (64), Alfonso Andrés Obregón (89) / Luciano Félix Leguizamón (4)

FLUMINENSE - LIBERTAD 2-0 (1-0)
Mario Filho 'Maracanã', Rio de Janeiro, 2.04.2008, Referee: Rubén Selman (CHI)
FLUMINENSE: FERNANDO HENRIQUE Dos Anjos, GABRIEL Rodrigues Dos Santos (68 RAFAEL Pereira Da Silva), THIAGO Emiliano Da SILVA, LUIZ ALBERTO Da Silva Oliveira, YGOR Maciel Santiago, JUNIOR CESAR Eduardo Machado, Marcos AROUCA da Silva, WASHINGTON Stecanela Cerqueira, THIAGO NEVES Augusto (82 Vinicius Silva Soares 'TARTÁ'), CÍCERO Santos (90 ROGER Machado Marques), Darío Leonardo Conca. DT: Renato Portaluppi
LIBERTAD: Horacio Javier González, Pedro Juan Benítez, Arnaldo Andrés Vera, Édgar Gabriel Balbuena, Vladimir Marín (66 Wilson Osmar Pittoni), Roberto Carlos Gamarra (70 Omar Heber Pouso), Osvaldo David Martínez, Pedro Alcides Sarabia, Sergio Daniel Aquino, Víctor Javier Cáceres, Nelson Rafael Cuevas (57 Dante López). DT: Rubén Israel
Goals: CÍCERO Santos (30), THIAGO Emiliano Da SILVA (51)

LIBERTAD - LDU QUITO 3-1 (2-0)
Defensores del Chaco, Asunción, 8.04.2008, Referee: Jorge Larrionda (URU)
LIBERTAD: Víctor Hugo Centurión, Celso Pablo González, Pedro Juan Benítez, Adalberto Román, Arnaldo Andrés Vera, Wilson Osmar Pittoni, Sergio Daniel Aquino (46 Víctor Javier Cáceres), Edgar Arnulfo Robles, Hugo Américo Luzardi (66 Vladimir Marín), Dante López, Juan Manuel Olivera (46 Nelson Rafael Cuevas). DT: Rubén Israel
LDU: Daniel Jimmy Viteri, Andrés Arrunategui, Renán Calle, Byron Camacho, Paul Vicente Ambrossi, Pedro Sebastián Larrea (57 Christian Andrés Suárez), William Francisco Araujo, Alfonso Andrés Obregón, Edder Javier Vaca, Claudio Daniel Bieler (57 Enrique Daniel Vera), Franklin Agustín Salas (68 Luis Alberto Bolaños). DT: Edgardo Bauza
Goals: Dante López (10), Juan Manuel Olivera (14), Nelson Rafael Cuevas (63) /
Alfonso Andrés Obregón (65)

ARSENAL - FLUMINENSE 2-0 (0-0)
Julio Humberto Grondona, Sarandí, 9.04.2008, Referee: Víctor Rivera (PER)
ARSENAL: Catrinel Iván Orcellet, Darío Espínola, Carlos Alberto Báez, Cristian Alberto Pellerano, Leonardo Ángel Biagini (87 Alejandro Darío Gómez), Alexander Leonel Corro, Pablo Sebastián Garnier, Jossimar Mosquera, Gustavo Toranzo, Javier Orlando Yacuzzi (81 José Luis Calderón), Juan Eduardo Bottaro (74 Luciano Félix Leguizamón). DT: Gustavo Alfaro
FLUMINENSE: FERNANDO HENRIQUE Dos Anjos, GABRIEL Rodrigues Dos Santos, THIAGO Emiliano Da SILVA, LUIZ ALBERTO Da Silva Oliveira, JUNIOR CESAR Eduardo Machado, YGOR Maciel Santiago (73 DAVID Oliveira e Silva), Marcos AROUCA da Silva (62 Vinicius Silva Soares 'TARTÁ'), MAURÍCIO José Da Silveira Junior, Darío Leonardo Conca, CÍCERO Santos (81 ROMEU Pereira Dos Santos), THIAGO NEVES Augusto. DT: Renato Portaluppi
Sent off: Thiago Neves (73)
Goals: Leonardo Ángel Biagini (59), Juan Eduardo Bottaro (65)

LIBERTAD - ARSENAL 1-2 (1-1)
Defensores del Chaco, Asunción, 16.04.2008, Referee: Óscar Maldonado (BOL)
LIBERTAD: Víctor Hugo Centurión, Celso Pablo González, Adalberto Román, Arnaldo Andrés Vera, Derlis Cardozo, Omar Heber Pouso, Edgar Arnulfo Robles, Wilson Osmar Pittoni (63 Osvaldo David Martínez), Hugo Américo Luzardi (63 Dante López), Juan Manuel Olivera, Nelson Rafael Cuevas (73 Nelson David Romero). DT: Rubén Israel
ARSENAL: Mario Eduardo Cuenca, Darío Espínola (32 Aníbal Samuel Matellán), Carlos Alberto Báez, Jossimar Mosquera, Gustavo Toranzo, Pablo Sebastián Garnier (46 Javier Orlando Yacuzzi), Carlos Damián Casteglione, Sebastián Carrera, Martín Ezequiel Andrizzi (61 Alejandro Darío Gómez), Juan Eduardo Bottaro, Leonardo Ángel Biagini. DT: Gustavo Alfaro
Sent off: Pouso (76)
Goals: Nelson Cuevas (23) / Juan Bottaro (10), Javier Yacuzzi (68)

FLUMINENSE - LDU QUITO 1-0 (1-0)
Mario Filho 'Maracanã', Rio de Janeiro, 17.04.2008, Referee: Roberto Silveira (URU)
FLUMINENSE: FERNANDO HENRIQUE Dos Anjos, GABRIEL Rodrigues Dos Santos, THIAGO Emiliano Da SILVA, LUIZ ALBERTO Da Silva Oliveira, JUNIOR CESAR Eduardo Machado, YGOR Maciel Santiago, Marcos AROUCA da Silva, DAVID Oliveira e Silva (66 MAURÍCIO José Da Silveira Junior), Vinicius Silva Soares 'TARTÁ' (77 ROMEU Pereira Dos Santos), Darío Leonardo Conca (90+2 ROGER Machado Marques), CÍCERO Santos. DT: Renato Portaluppi
LDU: Daniel Jimmy Viteri, Byron Camacho, Renán Calle, Diego Armando Calderón, Alfonso Andrés Obregón, Paul Vicente Ambrossi, Pedro Sebastián Larrea (71 Jairo Rolando Campos), William Francisco Araujo, Edder Javier Vaca (73 Franklin Agustín Salas), Christian Andrés Suárez (64 Joffre David Guerrón), Agustín Javier Delgado. DT: Edgardo Bauza
Goal: CÍCERO Santos (30)

1	FLUMINENSE	6	4	1	1	11	3	13
2	LDU QUITO	6	3	1	2	10	5	10
3	Arsenal Buenos Aires	6	3	0	3	6	14	9
4	Libertad	6	1	0	5	5	10	3

ROUND OF 16

LANÚS - ATLAS GUADALAJARA 0-1 (0-1)
Néstor Díaz Pérez, Lanús, 29.04.2008, Referee: Víctor Hugo Rivera (PER)
LANÚS: Carlos Gustavo Bossio, Rodolfo Graieb, Emir Saúl Faccioli, Carlos Gustavo Quintana, Maximiliano Velázquez (48 Nelson Benítez), Sebastián Blanco (71 Santiago Biglieri), Agustín Pelletieri, Matías Fritzler, Diego Valeri, Nicolás Francisco Ramírez (59 Germán Ezequiel Cano), José Gustavo Sand. DT: Ramón Cabrero
ATLAS: Jorge Rodrigo Bava, Néstor Vicente Vidrio, Diego Daniel Colotto, Jorge Emmanuel Torres, Omar Alejandro Flores, Juan Carlos Medina (72 Emanuel Adrian Centurión), Luis Enrique Robles, Gerardo Flores (59 Jorge Hernández), Eduardo Rergis, Ulises Mendivil (53 Danilo Gomes), Bruno Marioni. DT: Miguel Ángel Brindisi
Goal: Bruno Marioni (37)

ATLAS GUADALAJARA – LANÚS 2-2 (1-0)
Jalisco, Guadalajara, 6.05.2008, Referee: Carlos Torres (PAR)
ATLAS: Jorge Rodrigo Bava, Néstor Vicente Vidrio, Diego Daniel Colotto, Jorge Emmanuel Torres, Omar Alejandro Flores, Juan Carlos Medina (80 Ricardo Adán Jiménez), Luis Enrique Robles, Gerardo Flores (55 Jorge Hernández), Eduardo Rergis, Ulises Mendivil (79 Danilo Gomes), Bruno Marioni. DT: Miguel Ángel Brindisi
LANÚS: Carlos Gustavo Bossio, Rodolfo Graieb, Carlos Gustavo Quintana, Santiago Abel Hoyos, Maximiliano Velázquez (74 Adrián Peralta), Sebastián Blanco (70 Santiago Biglieri), Agustín Pelletieri, Matías Fritzler, Diego Valeri, Lautaro Acosta, José Gustavo Sand. DT: Ramón Cabrero
Goals: Bruno Marioni (29), Ulises Mendívil (78) / José Gustavo Sand (64), Lautaro Acosta (90+1)

LDU QUITO- ESTUDIANTES LA PLATA 2-0 (0-0)
Casa Blanca, Quito, 29.04.2008, Referee: Leonardo Gaciba (BRA)
LDU: José Francisco Cevallos, Jairo Rolando Campos, Norberto Carlos Araujo, Diego Armando Calderón, Joffre David Guerrón, Enrique Daniel Vera (90 William Francisco Araujo), Patricio Javier Urrutia, Paul Vicente Ambrossi, Luis Alberto Bolaños, Damián Alejandro Manso, Claudio Daniel Bieler (68 Agustín Javier Delgado). DT: Edgardo Bauza
ESTUDIANTES: Mariano Gonzalo Andújar, Marcos Alberto Angeleri, Leandro Desabato, José María Basanta, Juan Manuel Díaz, Diego Alberto Galván (73 Iván Diego Moreno y Fabianesi), Juan Sebastián Verón, Édgar Daniel González, Leandro Damián Benítez, Leandro Hernán Lazzaro (83 Ezequiel Carlos Maggiolo), Pablo Ariel Lugüerico (65 Pablo Daniel Piatti). DT: Roberto Sensini
Sent off: Díaz (89)
Goals: Joffre David Guerrón (63), Damián Alejandro Manso (77)

ESTUDIANTES LA PLATA – LDU QUITO 2-1 (1-1)
Ciudad de La Plata, La Plata, 6.05.2008, Referee: Óscar Julián Ruiz (COL)
ESTUDIANTES: Mariano Gonzalo Andújar, Marcos Alberto Angeleri, Agustín Alayes, Leandro Desabato, José María Basanta (46 Enzo Nicolás Pérez), Diego Alberto Galván (62 Ezequiel Carlos Maggiolo), Juan Sebastián Verón, Leandro Damián Benítez, Juan Manuel Salgueiro, Leandro Hernán Lazzaro, Pablo Daniel Piatti (77 Pablo Ariel Lugüerico). DT: Roberto Sensini

LDU: José Francisco Cevallos, Jairo Rolando Campos, Norberto Carlos Araujo, Diego Armando Calderón (16 Renán Calle), Paul Vicente Ambrossi, Joffre David Guerrón, Enrique Daniel Vera, Patricio Javier Urrutia, Luis Alberto Bolaños (69 William Francisco Araujo), Damián Alejandro Manso (77 Byron Camacho), Víctor Estupiñán. DT: Edgardo Bauza
Sent off: Pérez (90)
Goals: Agustín Alayes (45), Ezequiel Carlos Maggiolo (66) / Luis Alberto Bolaños (25)

ATLÉTICO NACIONAL - FLUMINENSE 1-2 (0-1)
Atanasio Girardot, Medellín, 30.04.2008, Referee: Martín Vázquez (URU)
ATLÉTICO NACIONAL: David Ospina, Juan Camilo Zúñiga, Humberto Antonio Mendoza, Wálter José Moreno, Juan Estiven Vélez, David Camilo Córdoba (20 Carlos Alberto Barahona), José Antonio Amaya, Harold Martínez, Francisco Arrué, León Darío Muñoz (46 Sergio Alejandro Galván Rey), Carlos Wilson Villagra (66 Fernando Patricio Martel). DT: Oscar Quintabani
FLUMINENSE: FERNANDO HENRIQUE Dos Anjos, GABRIEL Rodrigues Dos Santos, THIAGO Emiliano Da SILVA (55 ROGER Machado Marques), LUIZ ALBERTO Da Silva Oliveira, YGOR Maciel Santiago, JUNIOR CESAR Eduardo Machado, Marcos AROUCA da Silva, WASHINGTON Stecanela Cerqueira, THIAGO NEVES Augusto (62 MAURÍCIO José Da Silveira Junior), CÍCERO Santos, Darío Leonardo Conca (77 Ricardo Lucas 'DODÔ'). DT: Renato Portaluppi
Sent off: Ospina (18)
Goals: Francisco Arrué (53) / THIAGO NEVES Augusto (22 penalty), Darío Leonardo Conca (72)

FLUMINENSE - ATLÉTICO NACIONAL 1-0 (0-0)
Mario Filho 'Maracanã', Rio de Janeiro, 6.05.2008, Referee: Víctor Hugo Rivera (PER)
FLUMINENSE: FERNANDO HENRIQUE Dos Anjos, GABRIEL Rodrigues Dos Santos (82 Carlos Henrique Carneiro Marinho 'CARLINHOS'), ROGER Machado Marques, LUIZ ALBERTO Da Silva Oliveira, YGOR Maciel Santiago, JUNIOR CESAR Eduardo Machado, WASHINGTON Stecanela Cerqueira (72 Vinicius Silva Soares 'TARTÁ'), THIAGO NEVES Augusto (66 MAURÍCIO José Da Silveira Junior), CÍCERO Santos, Ricardo Lucas 'DODÔ', Darío Leonardo Conca. DT: Renato Portaluppi
ATLÉTICO NACIONAL: Carlos Alberto Barahona, Juan Camilo Zúñiga (78 David Camilo Córdoba), Humberto Antonio Mendoza, Wálter José Moreno, Juan Estiven Vélez, Francisco Arrué, José Antonio Amaya, Harold Martínez (79 Diego Mauricio Toro), Fernando Patricio Martel (62 Elkin Antonio Murillo), León Darío Muñoz, Sergio Alejandro Galván Rey. DT: Oscar Quintabani
Goal: ROGER Machado Marques (52)

BOCA JUNIORS - CRUZEIRO 2-1 (1-0)
Alberto J. Armando 'La Bombonera', Buenos Aires, 30.04.2008, Referee: Jorge Larrionda (URU)
BOCA JUNIORS: Mauricio Ariel Caranta, Álvaro Rafael González, Jonathan Ramón Maidana, Julio César Cáceres, Luciano Fabián Monzón, Fabián Andrés Vargas (82 Pablo Martín Ledesma), Sebastián Alejandro Battaglia, Jesús Alberto Dátolo (82 Cristian Manuel Chávez), Juan Román Riquelme, Rodrigo Sebastián Palacio, Martín Palermo. DT: Carlos Ischia
CRUZEIRO: FÁBIO Deivson Lopes Maciel, CHARLES Fernando Basílio Silva, THIAGO HELENO Henrique Ferreira, Giovanny Patricio Espinoza, Antonio Marcos Silva Filho 'MARQUINHO PARANÁ', HENRIQUE Pacheco de Lima, FABRICIO De Souza, RAMIRES Santos Nascimento, WAGNER Ferreira Dos Santos (74 Marcio Rocha Da Silva 'MARCINHO'), GUILHERME Mihomem Gusmão (60 JONATHAN Cícero Moreira), Marcelo Martins Moreno. DT: Adilson Batista
Goals: Juan Román Riquelme (6), Jesús Dátolo (65) / FABRICIO De Souza (78)
The match was suspended after 90+1 minutes of play but the result was allowed to stand.

CRUZEIRO – BOCA JUNIORS 1-2 (0-2)
Governador Magalhães Pinto 'Mineirão', Belo Horizonte, 7.05.2008, Referee: Carlos Chandía (CHI)
CRUZEIRO: FÁBIO Deivson Lopes Maciel, JONATHAN Cícero Moreira (60 Luis Dialisson De Souza Alves 'APODI'), THIAGO HELENO Henrique Ferreira, Giovanny Patricio Espinoza, Antonio Marcos Silva Filho 'MARQUINHO PARANÁ', FABRICIO De Souza, CHARLES Fernando Basílio Silva (71 HENRIQUE Pacheco de Lima), RAMIRES Santos Nascimento, WAGNER Ferreira Dos Santos, Marcelo Martins Moreno, GUILHERME Mihomem Gusmão (46 Marcio Rocha Da Silva 'MARCINHO'). DT: Adilson Batista
BOCA JUNIORS: Mauricio Ariel Caranta, Jonathan Ramón Maidana, Julio César Cáceres, Claudio Marcelo Morel, Luciano Fabián Monzón, Fabián Andrés Vargas (71 Pablo Martín Ledesma), Sebastián Alejandro Battaglia, Jesús Alberto Dátolo (87 Álvaro Rafael González), Juan Román Riquelme, Rodrigo Sebastián Palacio, Martín Palermo (82 Mauro Boselli). DT: Carlos Ischia
Sent off: Ramires (82)
Goals: WAGNER Ferreira Dos Santos (56) / Rodrigo Sebastián Palacio (36), Martín Palermo (43)

CF AMÉRICA - FLAMENGO 2-4 (1-1)
Azteca, México, 30.04.2008, Referee: Carlos Chandía (CHI)
AMÉRICA: Francisco Guillermo Ochoa, Ismael Rodríguez, José Antonio Castro, Óscar Adrián Rojas, Diego Alberto Cervantes, Sebastián Domínguez, Salvador Cabañas, Juan Carlos Mosqueda (46 Federico Higuaín), Germán Villa, Enrique Esqueda, Juan Carlos Silva (81 Richard Núñez). DT: Rubén Romano
FLAMENGO: BRUNO Fernandes Souza, Luiz Antônio De Oliveira 'LUIZINHO', FABIO LUCIANO, RONALDO Simões ANGELIM, JAILTON Da Cruz Alves, JUAN Maldonado Jaimez (46 Leonardo 'LÉO' Da Silva MOURA), IBSON Barreto Da Silva, CRISTIAN Mark Baroni (80 DIEGO TARDELLI Martins), José KLÉBERSON Pereira, Rodrigo de SOUZA Cardoso (46 Manuel De Brito Filho 'OBINA'), Márcio José de Oliveira 'MARCINHO'. DT: Joel Santana
Goals: Diego Alberto Cervantes (45), Enrique Esqueda (72) / Márcio José de Oliveira 'MARCINHO' (44, 70), DIEGO TARDELLI Martins (89), Leonardo 'LÉO' Da Silva MOURA (90)

FLAMENGO - CF AMÉRICA 0-3 (0-2)
Mario Filho 'Maracanã', Rio de Janeiro, 7.05.2008, Referee: Alfredo Intriago (ECU)
FLAMENGO: BRUNO Fernandes Souza, Leonardo 'LÉO' Da Silva MOURA, LEONARDO Devanir de Paula, RONALDO Simões ANGELIM, JAILTON Da Cruz Alves (79 RENATO Soares AUGUSTO), JUAN Maldonado Jaimez, IBSON Barreto Da Silva, José KLÉBERSON Pereira (46 Manuel De Brito Filho 'OBINA'), Rafael TORÓ Ferreira Francisco, Rodrigo de SOUZA Cardoso (55 DIEGO TARDELLI Martins), Márcio José de Oliveira 'MARCINHO'. DT: Joel Santana
AMÉRICA: Francisco Guillermo Ochoa, Sebastián Domínguez, José Antonio Castro, Óscar Adrián Rojas, Ismael Rodríguez, Alejandro Argüello (76 Juan Carlos Mosqueda), Carlos Alberto Sánchez, Salvador Cabañas (90 Federico Higuaín), Germán Villa, Enrique Esqueda (79 Rodrigo Iñigo), Juan Carlos Silva. DT: Rubén Romano
Sent off: Juan (84)
Goals: Salvador Cabañas (20, 77), Enrique Esqueda (38)

NACIONAL MONTEVIDEO - SÃO PAULO FC 0-0
Parque Central, Montevideo, 30.04.2008, Referee: Rubén Selman (CH)
NACIONAL: Washington Alexis Viera, Pablo Caballero, Mauricio Bernardo Victorino, Deivis Barone, Adrián Marcelo Romero, Mathías Cardaccio, Óscar Javier Morales (66 Nicolás Bertolo), Hugo Diego Arismendi, Martín Ricardo Ligüera (73 Diego Vera), Bruno Fornaroli, Richard Javier Morales. DT: Gerardo Pelusso
SÃO PAULO: ROGÉRIO CENI, ALEX Sandro da SILVA, João MIRANDA de Souza Filho, JORGE WAGNER Goes Conceição (66 HUGO Henrique Assis Do Nascimento), ÉDER LUIS De Oliveira, ADRIANO Leite Ribeiro, Anderson HERNANES Andrade Lima, Humberlito BORGES Teixeira, RICHARLYSON Barbosa Felisbino, EDER Schiola Santana, José 'ZÉ' LUIS Santos Da Visitação (46 FÁBIO dos SANTOS Barbosa). DT: Muricy Ramalho

SÃO PAULO FC – NACIONAL MONTEVIDEO 2-0 (1-0)
Cícero Pompeu de Toledo 'Morumbí', São Paulo, 7.05.2008, Referee: Héctor Baldassi (ARG)
SÃO PAULO: ROGÉRIO CENI, EDER Schiola Santana, ALEX Sandro da SILVA, João MIRANDA de Souza Filho, RICHARLYSON Barbosa Felisbino, José 'ZÉ' LUIS Santos Da Visitação, Anderson HERNANES Andrade Lima, HUGO Henrique Assis Do Nascimento (90 Jenilson Angelo De Souza 'JÚNIOR'), ÉDER LUIS De Oliveira (61 DAGOBERTO Pelentier), ADRIANO Leite Ribeiro, Humberlito BORGES Teixeira (80 FÁBIO dos SANTOS Barbosa). DT: Muricy Ramalho
NACIONAL: Washington Alexis Viera, Pablo Caballero, Mauricio Bernardo Victorino, Deivis Barone, Adrián Marcelo Romero, Mathías Cardaccio (70 Martín Ricardo Ligüera), Óscar Javier Morales, Nicolás Bertolo, Hugo Diego Arismendi, Bruno Fornaroli, Richard Javier Morales (70 Diego Vera). DT: Gerardo Pelusso
Sent off: Caballero (46)
Goals: ADRIANO Leite Ribeiro (37), DAGOBERTO Pelentier (88)

SAN LORENZO - RIVER PLATE 2-1 (1-1)
Pedro Bidegain, Buenos Aires, 30.04.2008, Referee: Héctor Baldassi (ARG)
SAN LORENZO: Agustín Ignacio Orión, Hernán Adrián González, Diego Rodolfo Placente, Gastón Damián Aguirre, Sebastián Ariel Méndez, Diego Alejandro Rivero (90 Christian Alberto Tula), Wálter Aníbal Acevedo (70 Santiago Hirsig), Juan Manuel Torres, Andrés Nicolás D'Alessandro, Gonzalo Rubén Bergessio, Néstor Andrés Silvera (46 Bernardo Daniel Romeo). DT: Ramón Díaz
RIVER PLATE: Juan Pablo Carrizo, Oscar Adrián Ahumada, Cristian Carlos Villagra, Radamel Falcao García, Matías Enrique Abelairas, Paulo Andrés Ferrari, Gustavo Daniel Cabral, Eduardo Nicolás Tuzzio, Washington Sebastián Abreu (81 Ariel Arnaldo Ortega), Rodrigo Javier Archubi (62 Diego Mario Buonanotte), Augusto Matías Fernández (75 Alexis Alejandro Sánchez). DT: Diego Simeone
Goals: Néstor Andrés Silvera (27), Hernán Adrián González (87 penalty) / Radamel Falcao García (30)

RIVER PLATE - SAN LORENZO 2-2 (1-0)
Antonio V. Liberti 'Monumental', Buenos Aires, 8.05.2008, Referee: Sergio Pezzotta (ARG)
RIVER PLATE: Juan Pablo Carrizo, Paulo Andrés Ferrari, Gustavo Daniel Cabral, Eduardo Nicolás Tuzzio, Cristian Carlos Villagra, Augusto Matías Fernández (64 Mauro Damián Rosales), Oscar Adrián Ahumada, Matías Enrique Abelairas, Diego Mario Buonanotte (73 Alexis Alejandro Sánchez), Radamel Falcao García, Washington Sebastián Abreu. DT: Diego Simeone
SAN LORENZO: Agustín Ignacio Orión, Hernán Adrián González, Diego Rodolfo Placente, Sebastián Ariel Méndez (46 Gastón Damián Aguirre), Jonathan Pablo Bottinelli, Diego Alejandro Rivero, Wálter Aníbal Acevedo (64 Pablo Andrés Alvarado), Román Aureliano Torres, Andrés Nicolás D'Alessandro, Gonzalo Rubén Bergessio, Néstor Andrés Silvera (78 Santiago Hirsig). DT: Ramón Díaz
Sent off: Rivero (42), Bottinelli (58), Tuzzio (90)
Goals: Matías Enrique Abelairas (11), Washington Sebastián Abreu (61 penalty) /
Gonzalo Rubén Bergessio (69, 72)

SANTOS FC - CÚCUTA DEPORTIVO 2-0 (1-0)
Urbano Caldeira, Santos, 1.05.2008, Referee: Marco Rodríguez (MEX)
SANTOS: FÁBIO COSTA, MARCELO Antônio Guedes Filho, KLÉBER de Carvalho Corrêa, Ebert Amancio 'BETÃO', RODRIGO Ribeiro SOUTO, José Fabio Azevedo 'FABÃO', Márcio Glad 'MARCINHO GUERREIRO' (64 ADRIANO Santos), Rodrigo LIMA Santos (88 Mariano Tripodi), Mauricio Alejandro Molina (78 Rodrigo TABATA), KLÉBER BOAS PEREIRA, WESLEY Beltrame. DT: Emerson Leão
CÚCUTA: Andrés Leandro Castellanos, Braynner Yezid García (77 Diego Aroldo Cabrera), Flavio Armando Córdoba, Pedro Paulo Portocarrero, Elvis Javier González, James Enrique Castro (65 Lionard Fernando Pajoy), José Alberto Amarilla (89 Mauricio Romero), William Román Zapata, Charles Castro, Macnelly Torres, Matías Héctor Urbano. DT: Pedro Sarmiento
Sent off: Wesley (73)
Goals: Rodrigo LIMA Santos (18), Mauricio Alejandro Molina (71)

CÚCUTA DEPORTIVO – SANTOS FC 0-2 (0-1)
General Santander, Cúcuta, 8.05.2008, Referee: Carlos Amarilla (PAR)
CÚCUTA: Andrés Leandro Castellanos, Elvis Antonio Rivas (68 Eudalio Eulises Arriaga), Flavio Armando Córdoba, Pedro Paulo Portocarrero, Elvis Javier González, Charles Castro, José Alberto Amarilla, James Enrique Castro (74 Lin Carlos Henry), Macnelly Torres, Matías Héctor Urbano, Diego Aroldo Cabrera. DT: Pedro Sarmiento
SANTOS: FÁBIO COSTA, MARCELO Antônio Guedes Filho, KLÉBER de Carvalho Corrêa, Ebert Amancio 'BETÃO', ADRIANO Santos, RODRIGO Ribeiro SOUTO (80 ANDERSON SALLES), José Fabio Azevedo 'FABÃO', Márcio Glad 'MARCINHO GUERREIRO', Rodrigo LIMA Santos (74 Mariano Tripodi), Mauricio Alejandro Molina (68 Michael Jackson Quiñónez), KLÉBER BOAS PEREIRA. DT: Emerson Leão
Goals: Kléber Boas Pereira (40), Rodrigo LIMA Santos (53)

QUARTER-FINALS

SÃO PAULO FC – FLUMINENSE 1-0 (1-0)
Cícero Pompeu de Toledo 'Morumbí', São Paulo, 14.05.2008, Referee: Julián Ruiz (COL)
SÃO PAULO: ROGÉRIO CENI, JANCARLOS De Oliveira Barros, ALEX Sandro da SILVA, João MIRANDA de Souza Filho, RICHARLYSON Barbosa Felisbino, José 'ZÉ' LUIS Santos Da Visitação, FÁBIO dos SANTOS Barbosa, Anderson HERNANES Andrade Lima, HUGO Henrique Assis do Nascimento, DAGOBERTO Pelentier (77 ALOÍSIO José da Silva), ADRIANO Leite Ribeiro. DT: Muricy Ramalho
FLUMINENSE: FERNANDO HENRIQUE Dos Anjos, GABRIEL Rodrigues Dos Santos, LUIZ ALBERTO Da Silva Oliveira, ROGER Machado Marques, JUNIOR CESAR Eduardo Machado, YGOR Maciel Santiago, Marcos AROUCA da Silva, CÍCERO Santos, THIAGO NEVES Augusto (60 Darío Leonardo Conca), Ricardo Lucas 'DODÔ', WASHINGTON Stecanela Cerqueira. DT: Renato Portaluppi
Goal: ADRIANO Leite Ribeiro (19)

FLUMINENSE – SÃO PAULO FC 3-1 (1-0)
Mario Filho 'Maracanã', Rio de Janeiro, 21.05.2008, Referee: Carlos Amarilla (PAR)
FLUMINENSE: FERNANDO HENRIQUE Dos Anjos, GABRIEL Rodrigues Dos Santos (88 ALAN Douglas Borges De Carvalho), LUIZ ALBERTO Da Silva Oliveira, THIAGO Emiliano Da SILVA, JUNIOR CESAR Eduardo Machado, YGOR Maciel Santiago (81 MAURÍCIO José Da Silveira Junior), Marcos AROUCA da Silva (54 Ricardo Lucas 'DODÔ'), CÍCERO Santos, Darío Leonardo Conca, THIAGO NEVES Augusto, WASHINGTON Stecanela Cerqueira. DT: Renato Portaluppi
SÃO PAULO: ROGÉRIO CENI, JANCARLOS De Oliveira Barros (46 JOILSON Rodrigues Macedo), ALEX Sandro da SILVA, João MIRANDA de Souza Filho, RICHARLYSON Barbosa Felisbino, José 'ZÉ' LUIS Santos Da Visitação, FÁBIO dos SANTOS Barbosa, Anderson HERNANES Andrade Lima, HUGO Henrique Assis do Nascimento (78 JORGE WAGNER Goes Conceição), DAGOBERTO Pelentier (57 ALOÍSIO José da Silva), ADRIANO Leite Ribeiro. DT: Muricy Ramalho
Sent off: Joilson (84)
Goals: WASHINGTON Stecanela Cerqueira (11, 90+1), Ricardo Lucas 'DODÔ' (71) / ADRIANO Leite Ribeiro (70)

BOCA JUNIORS – ATLAS GUADALAJARA 2-2 (1-1)
José Amalfitani, Buenos Aires, 14.05.2008, Referee: Wilmar Roldán (COL)
BOCA JUNIORS: Mauricio Ariel Caranta, Jonathan Ramón Maidana (60 Álvaro Rafael González), Julio César Cáceres, Luciano Fabián Monzón, Claudio Marcelo Morel, Fabián Andrés Vargas (60 Cristian Manuel Chávez), Sebastián Alejandro Battaglia, Jesús Alberto Dátolo, Juan Román Riquelme, Martín Palermo, Rodrigo Sebastián Palacio. DT: Carlos Ischia

ATLAS: Jorge Rodrigo Bava, Jorge Emmanuel Torres, Hugo Ayala, Diego Daniel Colotto, Omar Alejandro Flores, Eduardo Rergis (74 Ricardo Adán Jiménez), Luis Enrique Robles (50 Gerardo Flores), Juan Carlos Medina, Christian de Jesús Valdez, Bruno Marioni (90 Jorge Hernández), Ulises Mendivil. DT: Miguel Ángel Brindisi
Goals: Hugo Ayala (36 own goal), Julio Cáceres (75) /
Omar Alejandro Flores (5), Jorge Emmanuel Torres (88)

ATLAS GUADALAJARA – BOCA JUNIORS 0-3 (0-3)
Jalisco, Guadalajara, 21.05.2008, Referee: Rubén Selman (Chile)
ATLAS: Jorge Rodrigo Bava, Omar Alejandro Flores, Diego Daniel Colotto, Jorge Emmanuel Torres, Gerardo Flores (46 Emanuel Adrian Centurión), Luis Enrique Robles (34 Danilo Gomes), Juan Carlos Medina, Christian de Jesús Valdez, Eduardo Rergis (50 Pedro Hernández), Bruno Marioni, Ulises Mendivil. DT: Miguel Ángel Brindisi
BOCA JUNIORS: Pablo Alejandro Migliore, Jonathan Ramón Maidana, Julio César Cáceres, Gabriel Alejandro Paletta (59 Luciano Fabián Monzón), Claudio Marcelo Morel, Cristian Manuel Chávez (62 Fabián Andrés Vargas), Sebastián Alejandro Battaglia, Jesús Alberto Dátolo (71 Pablo Martín Ledesma), Juan Román Riquelme, Martín Palermo, Rodrigo Sebastián Palacio. DT: Carlos Ischia
Sent off: Bava (50)
Goals: Martín Palermo (20, 34, 38)

CF AMÉRICA – SANTOS FC 2-0 (1-0)
Azteca, Ciudad de México, 15.05.2008, Referee: Héctor Baldassi (ARG)
AMÉRICA: Francisco Guillermo Ochoa, Ismael Rodríguez, José Antonio Castro, Carlos Alberto Sánchez (68 Rodrigo Iñigo), Sebastián Domínguez, Óscar Adrián Rojas, Alejandro Argüello (90 Jesús Armando Sánchez), Juan Carlos Silva, Germán Villa, Enrique Esqueda (86 Juan Carlos Mosqueda), Salvador Cabañas. DT: Juan Antonio Luna
SANTOS: FÁBIO COSTA, Ebert Amancio 'BETÃO', MARCELO Antônio Guedes Filho, José Fabio Azevedo 'FABÃO', KLÉBER de Carvalho Corrêa, Márcio Glad 'MARCINHO GUERREIRO' (80 ADRIANO Santos), RODRIGO Ribeiro SOUTO, WESLEY Beltrame (65 MARIANO TRÍPODI), Mauricio Alejandro Molina (46 Rodrigo TABATA), Rodrigo Santos LIMA, KLÉBER BOAS PEREIRA. DT: Emerson Leão
Goals: Salvador Cabañas (24, 62)

SANTOS FC – CF AMÉRICA 1-0 (0-0)
Urbano Caldeira, Santos, 22.05.2008, Referee: Jorge Larrionda (URU)
SANTOS: FÁBIO COSTA, MARCELO Antônio Guedes Filho, José Fabio Azevedo 'FABÃO', Ebert Amancio 'BETÃO' (61 Michael Jackson Quiñónez), KLÉBER de Carvalho Corrêa, Márcio Glad 'MARCINHO GUERREIRO', RODRIGO Ribeiro SOUTO, WESLEY Beltrame (46 MARIANO TRÍPODI), Mauricio Alejandro Molina, Rodrigo Santos LIMA, KLÉBER BOAS PEREIRA. DT: Emerson Leão
AMÉRICA: Francisco Guillermo Ochoa, Ismael Rodríguez (84 Rodrigo Iñigo), José Antonio Castro, Carlos Alberto Sánchez, Sebastián Domínguez, Óscar Adrián Rojas, Alejandro Argüello (72 Jesús Armando Sánchez), Juan Carlos Silva, Germán Villa, Enrique Esqueda (80 Juan Carlos Mosqueda), Salvador Cabañas. DT: Juan Antonio Luna.
Goal: Kléber Boas Pereira (62)

SAN LORENZO – LIGA DEP. UNIVERSITARIA 1-1 (1-1)
Pedro Bidegain, Buenos Aires, 15.05.2008, Referee: Carlos Simón (Brasil)
SAN LORENZO: Agustín Ignacio Orión, Hernán Adrián González, Christian Alberto Tula, Gastón Damián Aguirre, Diego Rodolfo Placente (64 Pablo Andrés Alvarado), Juan Manuel Torres, Santiago Hirsig (38 Germán Voboril), Wálter Aníbal Acevedo (64 Juan Carlos Menseguez), Andrés Nicolás D'Alessandro, Gonzalo Rubén Bergessio, Néstor Andrés Silvera. DT: Ramón Díaz.

LDU: José Francisco Cevallos, Jairo Rolando Campos, Norberto Carlos Araujo, Renán Calle, Paul Vicente Ambrossi, Joffre David Guerrón (90 Alfonso Andrés Obregón), Patricio Javier Urrutia, Enrique Daniel Vera, Damián Alejandro Manso (86 Christian Andrés Suárez), Luis Alberto Bolaños (79 William Francisco Araujo), Claudio Daniel Bieler. DT: Edgardo Bauza.
Goals: Hernán Adrián González (38) / Claudio Daniel Bieler (35)

LIGA DEP. UNIVERSITARIA - SAN LORENZO 1-1 (1-0), 5-3 penalties
La Casa Blanca, Quito, 22.05.2008, Referee: Marco Rodríguez (MEX), Attendance: 40.000
LDU: José Francisco Cevallos, Jairo Rolando Campos, Norberto Carlos Araujo, Renán Calle, Paul Vicente Ambrossi, Joffre David Guerrón, Patricio Javier Urrutia, Enrique Daniel Vera, Damián Alejandro Manso (92 Edder Javier Vaca), Luis Alberto Bolaños (73 Agustín Javier Delgado), Claudio Daniel Bieler. DT: Edgardo Bauza.
SAN LORENZO: Agustín Ignacio Orión, Hernán Adrián González, Christian Alberto Tula, Gastón Damián Aguirre, Diego Rodolfo Placente, Juan Manuel Torres, Diego Alejandro Rivero (70 Pablo Andrés Alvarado), Santiago Hirsig (82 Nicolás Bianchi Arce), Andrés Nicolás D'Alessandro, Gonzalo Rubén Bergessio, Bernardo Daniel Romeo (51 Román Aureliano Torres). DT: Ramón Díaz.
Sent off: Torres (30)
Goals: Damián Manso (26) / Gonzalo Bergessio (47)
Penalties: Patricio Urrutia, Jairo Campos, Edder Vaca, Joffre Guerrón, Claudio Bieler / Adrián González, Andrés D'Alessandro, Pablo Alvarado. Missed: Román Torres.

SEMI-FINALS

CF AMÉRICA - LIGA DEP. UNIVERSITARIA 1-1 (0-0)
Azteca, Ciudad de México, 28.05.2008, Referee: Martín Vázquez (URU)
AMÉRICA: Francisco Guillermo Ochoa, Rodrigo Iñigo (67 Hernán Rodrigo López), José Antonio Castro, Carlos Alberto Sánchez, Sebastián Domínguez, Óscar Adrián Rojas, Alejandro Argüello (46 Federico Higuaín), Juan Carlos Silva, Germán Villa, Enrique Esqueda (85 Richard Núñez), Salvador Cabañas. DT: Juan Antonio Luna
LDU: José Francisco Cevallos, Renán Calle, Norberto Carlos Araujo, Jairo Rolando Campos, Enrique Daniel Vera, Patricio Javier Urrutia, Paul Vicente Ambrossi, Damián Alejandro Manso (85 William Francisco Araujo), Luis Alberto Bolaños, Joffre David Guerrón (90 Byron Camacho), Claudio Daniel Bieler (53 Agustín Javier Delgado). DT: Edgardo Bauza.
Sent off: Domínguez (74) / Bolaños (74)
Goals: Enrique Esqueda (72) / Luis Bolaños (62)

LIGA DEP. UNIVERSITARIA – CF AMÉRICA 0-0
La Casa Blanca, Quito, 3.06.2008, Referee: Pablo Pozo (CHI)
LDU: José Francisco Cevallos, Renán Calle, Norberto Carlos Araujo, Jairo Rolando Campos, Enrique Daniel Vera, Patricio Javier Urrutia, Paul Vicente Ambrossi, Franklin Agustín Salas (74 Edder Javier Vaca), Damián Alejandro Manso (80 William Francisco Araujo), Joffre David Guerrón, Claudio Daniel Bieler (78 Agustín Javier Delgado). DT: Edgardo Bauza.
AMÉRICA: Francisco Guillermo Ochoa, Ismael Rodríguez, José Antonio Castro, Carlos Alberto Sánchez, Óscar Adrián Rojas, Juan Carlos Silva (74 Juan Carlos Mosqueda), Jesús Armando Sánchez, Germán Villa, Hernán Rodrigo López (65 Alejandro Argüello), Enrique Esqueda (71 Federico Higuaín), Salvador Cabañas. DT: Juan Antonio Luna
Sent off: Sánchez (60), Argüello (90)

BOCA JUNIORS - FLUMINENSE 2-2 (1-1)
Juan Domingo Perón, Buenos Aires, 28.05.2008, Referee: Roberto Silvera (URU)
BOCA JUNIORS: Pablo Alejandro Migliore, Jonathan Ramón Maidana (61 Hugo Benjamín Ibarra), Julio César Cáceres, Gabriel Alejandro Paletta, Claudio Marcelo Morel, Cristian Manuel Chávez (66 Neri Raúl Cardozo), Sebastián Alejandro Battaglia (76 Fabián Andrés Vargas), Jesús Alberto Dátolo, Juan Román Riquelme, Martín Palermo, Rodrigo Sebastián Palacio. DT: Carlos Ischia

FLUMINENSE: FERNANDO HENRIQUE Dos Anjos, GABRIEL Rodrigues Dos Santos, LUIZ ALBERTO Da Silva Oliveira, THIAGO Emiliano Da SILVA, JUNIOR CESAR Eduardo Machado, MAURÍCIO José Da Silveira Junior (63 ROMEU Pereira Dos Santos), Marcos AROUCA da Silva, CÍCERO Santos, Darío Leonardo Conca, THIAGO NEVES Augusto (88 ROGER Machado Marques), WASHINGTON Stecanela Cerqueira (79 Ricardo Lucas 'DODÔ'). DT: Renato Portaluppi
Goals: Juan Román Riquelme (12, 65) /
THIAGO Emiliano Da SILVA (16), THIAGO NEVES Augusto (77)

FLUMINENSE - BOCA JUNIORS 3-1 (0-0)
Mario Filho 'Maracanã', Rio de Janeiro, 4.06.2008, Referee: Carlos Torres (PAR)
FLUMINENSE: FERNANDO HENRIQUE Dos Anjos, GABRIEL Rodrigues Dos Santos, LUIZ ALBERTO Da Silva Oliveira, THIAGO Emiliano Da SILVA, JUNIOR CESAR Eduardo Machado, YGOR Maciel Santiago (61 Ricardo Lucas 'DODÔ'), Marcos AROUCA da Silva, CÍCERO Santos, Darío Leonardo Conca, THIAGO NEVES Augusto (79 MAURÍCIO José Da Silveira Junior), WASHINGTON Stecanela Cerqueira (90+2 ROGER Machado Marques). DT: Renato Portaluppi
BOCA JUNIORS: Pablo Alejandro Migliore, Hugo Benjamín Ibarra, Julio César Cáceres, Gabriel Alejandro Paletta, Claudio Marcelo Morel (79 Mauro Boselli), Sebastián Alejandro Battaglia, Fabián Andrés Vargas (46 Pablo Martín Ledesma)), Jesús Alberto Dátolo (85 Cristian Manuel Chávez), Juan Román Riquelme, Martín Palermo, Rodrigo Sebastián Palacio. DT: Carlos Ischia
Goals: WASHINGTON Stecanela Cerqueira (63), Darío Leonardo Conca (70),
Ricardo Lucas 'DODÔ' (90+3) / Martín Palermo (58)

FINALS

LIGA DEP. UNIVERSITARIA – FLUMINENSE 4-2 (4-1)
La Casa Blanca, Quito, 25.06.2008, Carlos Chandía (CHI), Attendance: 45.000
LDU: José Francisco Cevallos, Renán Calle, Norberto Carlos Araujo, Jairo Rolando Campos, Joffre David Guerrón, Enrique Daniel Vera, Patricio Javier Urrutia, Paul Vicente Ambrossi, Luis Alberto Bolaños, Damián Alejandro Manso (74 William Francisco Araujo), Claudio Daniel Bieler (82 Agustín Javier Delgado). DT: Edgardo Bauzá
FLUMINENSE: FERNANDO HENRIQUE Dos Anjos, GABRIEL Rodrigues Dos Santos, LUIZ ALBERTO Da Silva Oliveira, THIAGO Emiliano Da SILVA, JUNIOR CESAR Eduardo Machado, YGOR Maciel Santiago, Marcos AROUCA da Silva (67 MAURÍCIO José Da Silveira Junior), Darío Leonardo Conca, CÍCERO Santos, THIAGO NEVES Augusto (90 ROGER Machado Marques), WASHINGTON Stecanela Cerqueira (72 Ricardo Lucas 'DODÔ'). DT: Renato Portaluppi
Goals: Claudio Bieler (2), Joffre Guerrón (29), Jairo Campos (34), Patricio Urrutia (45) /
Darío Leonardo Conca (12), THIAGO NEVES Augusto (52)

FLUMINENSE - LIGA DEP. UNIVERSITARIA 3-1 (2-1); 1-3 penalties
Mario Filho 'Maracanã', Rio de Janeiro, 2.07.2008
Referee: Héctor Baldassi (ARG), Attendance: 86.027
FLUMINENSE: FERNANDO HENRIQUE Dos Anjos, GABRIEL Rodrigues Dos Santos (105 MAURÍCIO José Da Silveira Junior), THIAGO Emiliano Da SILVA, LUIZ ALBERTO Da Silva Oliveira, JUNIOR CESAR Eduardo Machado, YGOR Maciel Santiago (46 Ricardo Lucas 'DODÔ'), Marcos AROUCA da Silva (110 ROGER Machado Marques), THIAGO NEVES Augusto, Darío Leonardo Conca, CÍCERO Santos, WASHINGTON Stecanela Cerqueira. DT: Renato Portaluppi.
LDU: José Francisco Cevallos, Jairo Rolando Campos, Norberto Carlos Araujo, Renán Calle, Paul Vicente Ambrossi, Patricio Javier Urrutia, Enrique Daniel Vera, Joffre David Guerrón, Luis Alberto Bolaños (105 Franklin Agustín Salas), Damián Alejandro Manso (88 William Francisco Araujo), Claudio Daniel Bieler. DT: Edgardo Bauza.
Sent off: Luiz Alberto (120)
Goals: Thiago Neves (12, 28, 58) / Luis Bolaños (6)
Penalties: 0-1 Patricio Urrutia, Conca (miss), Jairo Campos (miss), Thiago Neves (miss), 0-2 Franklin Salas, 1-2 Cícero, 1-3 Joffre Guerrón, Washington (miss)

2009

FIRST STAGE

CD EL NACIONAL – CLUB NACIONAL ASUNCIÓN 0-5 (0-0)
Estadio Olímpico Atahualpa, Quito, 27.01.2009
Referee: José Hernando BUITRAGO Arango (COL), Attendance: 6.757
CD EL NACIONAL: Rafael Cristhian MORA Medrano, Erik Rolando DE JESÚS Delgado, Johan Roberto GÓMEZ Marcos (61 Fricson Vinicio GEORGE Tenorio), Pavel Cipriano CAICEDO Renteria, Bolívar Efrén GÓMEZ Valencia, Juan Carlos GODOY Cuero (54 Jorge Washington LADINES Garces), Michael Jackson QUIÑONEZ Cabeza, Wellington Eduardo SÁNCHEZ Luzuriaga, Marwin Jonathan PITA Mora (54 Moisés Antonio CANDELARIO Diaz), Orlindo AYOVÍ Caicedo, Edmundo Salomon ZURA de Jesus. DT: Jorge CÉLICO
CLUB NACIONAL ASUNCIÓN: Ignacio Oscar DON, Arnaldo Andrés ESPÍNOLA Benítez, Diego Raúl ARÉVALOS, Raúl Eduardo PIRIS, Ricardo MAZACOTTE, Ignacio Ramón CÁCERES Cabañas, Glaucineis Martins da Silva "INCA", Carlos Luis RUIZ Peralta (81 Gustavo Eliseo MORÍNIGO Vázquez), Jorge Daniel NÚÑEZ Espínola, Héber Alberto ARRIOLA (72 Fabio ESCOBAR Benítez), Raúl Basilio ROMÁN Garay (87 Marcos Antonio MELGAREJO). DT: Daniel Eduardo RASCHLE Matucheski.
Goals: Raúl Basilio ROMÁN Garay (51), Jorge Daniel NÚÑEZ Espínola (56, 85), Ignacio Ramón CÁCERES Cabañas (70), Marcos Antonio MELGAREJO (87).

CLUB NACIONAL ASUNCIÓN – CD EL NACIONAL 3-3 (3-3)
General Pablo Rojas, Asunción, 5.02.2009
Referee: Sergio Fabián PEZZOTTA (ARG), Attendance: 2.801
CLUB NACIONAL ASUNCIÓN: Ignacio Oscar DON, Arnaldo Andrés ESPÍNOLA Benítez, Diego Raúl ARÉVALOS, Raúl Eduardo PIRIS, Ricardo MAZACOTTE, Ignacio Ramón CÁCERES Cabañas, Glaucineis Martins da Silva "INCA", Carlos Luis RUIZ Peralta (56 Gustavo Eliseo MORÍNIGO Vázquez), Jorge Daniel NÚÑEZ Espínola, Héber Alberto ARRIOLA (69 Fabio ESCOBAR Benítez), Raúl Basilio ROMÁN Garay (78 Guillermo Alexis BELTRÁN). DT: Daniel E. RASCHLE Matucheski
CD EL NACIONAL: Rafael Cristhian MORA Medrano, Jorge Daniel GUAGUA Tamayo (87 Bolívar Efrén GÓMEZ Valencia), Fricson Vinicio GEORGE Tenorio (32 Erik Rolando DE JESÚS Delgado), William Angelis CUERO Quiñónez, Pavel Cipriano CAICEDO Renteria, Juan Carlos GODOY Cuero, Michael Jackson QUIÑONEZ Cabeza, Wellington Eduardo SÁNCHEZ Luzuriaga, Marwin Jonathan PITA Mora, Edmundo Salomon ZURA de Jesus (85 Orlindo AYOVÍ Caicedo), Jorge Washington LADINES Garces. DT: Juan Carlos BURBANO de Lara Torres
Goals: Jorge Daniel NÚÑEZ Espínola (9, 14), Héber Alberto ARRIOLA (28) / Marwin Jonathan PITA Mora (32), Jorge Washington LADINES Garces (35), Edmundo Salomon ZURA de Jesus (43).

CF UNIVERSIDAD DE CHILE – CF PACHUCA 1-0 (1-0)
Estadio Santa Laura, Santiago, 28.01.2009
Referee: Héber Roberto LOPES (BRA), Attendance: 16.000
CF UNIVERSIDAD DE CHILE: Miguel Ángel PINTO Jérez, Rafael Andrés OLARRA Guerrero, José Manuel ROJAS Bahamondes, Juan Claudio GONZÁLEZ Calderón, Marcelo Alfonso DÍAZ Rojas, Mauricio Antonio ARIAS González, Manuel Rolando ITURRA Urrutia, Marco Andrés ESTRADA Quinteros, Felipe Ignacio SEYMOUR Dobud (75 Sebastián Eduardo PARDO Campos), Emilio Exequiel HERNÁNDEZ Hernández (75 Hugo César NOTARIO), Juan Manuel OLIVERA López (85 Manuel Arturo VILLALOBOS Salvo). DT: Sergio Apraham MARKARIÁN Abrahamian
CF PACHUCA: Miguel Ángel CALERO Rodríguez, Marco Iván PÉREZ Riego, Paul Nicolás AGUILAR Rojas, Javier David MUÑOZ Mustafá, Carlos Gerardo RODRÍGUEZ Serrano, Jaime CORREA Córdoba, Damián Ariel ÁLVAREZ, José Francisco TORRES Mezzell (70 Luis Arturo MONTES Jiménez), Blas Antonio Miguel PÉREZ Ortega (80 Ulises MENDIVIL Armenta), José María CÁRDENAS López, Edgar Milciades BENÍTEZ Santander (65 Juan Carlos ROJAS Guerra).
Goal: Marcelo Alfonso DÍAZ Rojas (4).

CF PACHUCA – CF UNIVERSIDAD DE CHILE 2-1 (1-0)
Estadio Hidalgo, Pachuca, 4.02.2009
Referee: Alfredo Stalin INTRIAGO Ortega (ECU), Attendance: 13.140
CF PACHUCA: Miguel Ángel CALERO Rodríguez, Marco Iván PÉREZ Riego, Paul Nicolás AGUILAR Rojas, Javier David MUÑOZ Mustafá, Carlos Gerardo RODRÍGUEZ Serrano, Jaime CORREA Córdoba (63 Juan Carlos ROJAS Guerra), Damián Ariel ÁLVAREZ, José Francisco TORRES Mezzell, Blas Antonio Miguel PÉREZ Ortega, José María CÁRDENAS López (68 Luis Arturo MONTES Jiménez), Edgar Milciades BENÍTEZ Santander (57 Christian GIMÉNEZ). DT: Enrique Everardo MEZA Enríquez
CF UNIVERSIDAD DE CHILE: Miguel Ángel PINTO Jérez, Rafael Andrés OLARRA Guerrero, José Manuel ROJAS Bahamondes, Juan Claudio GONZÁLEZ Calderón, Marcelo Alfonso DÍAZ Rojas (85 José Raúl CONTRERAS Arrau), Mauricio Antonio ARIAS González, Manuel Rolando ITURRA Urrutia, Marco Andrés ESTRADA Quinteros, Felipe Ignacio SEYMOUR Dobud (46 Osvaldo Alexis GONZÁLEZ Sepúlveda), Emilio Exequiel HERNÁNDEZ Hernández (68 Sebastián Eduardo PARDO Campos), Juan Manuel OLIVERA López. DT: Sergio Apraham MARKARIÁN Abrahamian.
Sent off: Álvarez (90+2), Muñoz (90+3) / Arias (11)
Goals: Carlos Gerardo RODRÍGUEZ Serrano (24 penalty), Damián Ariel ÁLVAREZ (86) / Marco Andrés ESTRADA Quinteros (58).

CD INDEPENDIENTE MEDELLÍN – CA PEÑAROL MONTEVIDEO 4-0 (3-0)
Estadio Atanasio Girardot, Medellín, 28.02.2009
Referee: Víctor Hugo RIVERA Chavez (PER), Attendance: 15.750
CD INDEPENDIENTE MEDELLÍN: Aldo Antonio BOBADILLA Ávalos, Samuel Antonio VANEGAS Luna, Andrés Felipe ORTIZ Agudelo, Juan David MURIEL Cruz, John Javier RESTREPO Pérez, Juan Esteban ORTIZ Blandón, Jair BENÍTEZ Sinisterra, Isidro Ramón CANDIÁ Morales (78 Luis Carlos ARIAS Cardona), Diego Aroldo CABRERA Flores (69 William Francisco ARBOLEDA Perea), Jackson Arley MARTÍNEZ Valencia (87 Carlos Daniel HIDALGO Cadena), Iván Arturo CORREDOR Hurtado. DT: Santiago ESCOBAR Saldarriaga
CA PEÑAROL MONTEVIDEO: Pablo Oscar CAVALLERO, Darío Octavio RODRÍGUEZ Peña, Gerardo ALCOBA Rebollo, Jonathan Alberto PÍRIZ Palacio, Danilo ASCONEGUY Ruiz, Richard Dario NÚÑEZ Pereyra, Maximiliano BAJTER Ugollini (75 Maximiliano LOMBARDI Rodríguez), Julio Fabián MOZZO Valdéz (46 Nicolás Ezequiel ROTUNDO Ferrero), Omar Mario PÉREZ Aguado (66 José María FRANCO Ramallo), Antonio PACHECO D'Agosti, Carlos Héber BUENO Suárez. DT: Julio César RIBAS
Goals: Jackson Arley MARTÍNEZ Valencia (15, 18, 46), Iván Arturo CORREDOR Hurtado (34)

CA PEÑAROL MONTEVIDEO – CD INDEPENDIENTE MEDELLÍN 0-0
Estadio Centenario, Montevideo, 3.02.2009
Referee: Carlos Manuel TORRES Nuñez (PAR), Attendance: 19.590
CA PEÑAROL MONTEVIDEO: Pablo Oscar CAVALLERO, Darío Octavio RODRÍGUEZ Peña, Gerardo ALCOBA Rebollo, Jonathan Alberto PÍRIZ Palacio, Danilo ASCONEGUY Ruiz, Richard Dario NÚÑEZ Pereyra, Maximiliano BAJTER Ugollini (63 Fernando Edgardo CORREA Ayala), Julio Fabián MOZZO Valdéz, Antonio PACHECO D'Agosti, Carlos Héber BUENO Suárez, José María FRANCO Ramallo. DT: Julio César RIBAS
CD INDEPENDIENTE MEDELLÍN: Aldo Antonio BOBADILLA Ávalos, Samuel Antonio VANEGAS Luna, Andrés Felipe ORTIZ Agudelo, Juan David MURIEL Cruz, John Javier RESTREPO Pérez, Juan Esteban ORTIZ Blandón, Jair BENÍTEZ Sinisterra, Isidro Ramón CANDIÁ Morales (84 William Francisco ARBOLEDA Perea), Diego Aroldo CABRERA Flores (74 Luis Carlos ARIAS Cardona), Jackson Arley MARTÍNEZ Valencia, Iván Arturo CORREDOR Hurtado (87 Carlos Daniel HIDALGO Cadena). DT: Santiago ESCOBAR Saldarriaga

SE PALMEIRAS – CLUB BAMIN REAL POTOSÍ 5-1 (3-1)
Estádio Palestra Itália (Parque Antárctica), São Paulo, 29.01.2009
Referee: Roberto Carlos SILVERA Calcerrada (URU), Attendance: 23.694
SE PALMEIRAS: MARCOS Roberto Silveira Reis, EDMÍLSON José Gomes de Moraes, DANILO Laranjeira, Pablo Estifer ARMERO, MAURÍCIO Donizete RAMOS Júnior, Antônio Fábio Francez Cavalcante "FABINHO CAPIXABA", CLEITON Ribeiro XAVIER, DIEGO de SOUZA Andrade (74 EVANDRO Goebel), Lucas PIERRE Santos Oliveira (62 JUMAR José da Costa Júnior), WILLIANS dos Santos Santana (66 LENNY Fernandes Coelho Felisbino), KEIRRISON de Souza Carneiro. DT: Vanderlei LUXEMBURGO da Silva
CLUB BAMIN REAL POTOSÍ: MAURO MACHADO da Silva, Juan Carlos PAZ García, Nicolás SUÁREZ Vaca, Edhemir RODRÍGUEZ Mercado, César Gerardo YECEROTTE Soruco, Gonzalo Germán GALINDO Sánchez, Roberto Carlos CORREA Arias (75 Marco David PAZ Alvarez), Luis Gatty RIBEIRO Roca, Ronald EGUINO Segovia, Eduardo ORTIZ Cuéllar, José Horacio CHIORAZZO (46 Darwin PEÑA Arce). DT: Vladimir SORIA Camacho
Goals: KEIRRISON de Souza Carneiro (3, 20 penalty), DIEGO de SOUZA Andrade (39), CLEITON Ribeiro XAVIER (58), EDMÍLSON José Gomes de Moraes (90+1) /
Edhemir RODRÍGUEZ Mercado (22).

CLUB BAMIN REAL POTOSÍ – SE PALMEIRAS 0-2 (0-1)
Estadio Víctor Agustín Ugarte, Potosí, 4.02.2009
Referee: Carlos GALEANO Rios (PAR), Attendance: 3.055
CLUB BAMIN REAL POTOSÍ: MAURO MACHADO da Silva, Nicolás SUÁREZ Vaca, Edhemir RODRÍGUEZ Mercado, César Gerardo YECEROTTE Soruco, Gonzalo Germán GALINDO Sánchez, Roberto Carlos CORREA Arias (46 Marco David PAZ Alvarez), Luis Gatty RIBEIRO Roca, Ronald EGUINO Segovia, Eduardo ORTIZ Cuéllar (46 Gerson Luis GARCÍA Galvez), José Horacio CHIORAZZO (55 Cristian Maciel RUIZ), Horacio Ramón FERNÁNDEZ. DT: Vladimir SORIA Camacho
SE PALMEIRAS: BRUNO Cortez Cardoso, EDMÍLSON José Gomes de Moraes, DANILO Laranjeira (77 Jecimauro José Borge dos Santos "JECI"), Pablo Estifer ARMERO, MAURÍCIO Donizete RAMOS Júnior, Antônio Fábio Francez Cavalcante "FABINHO CAPIXABA", CLEITON Ribeiro XAVIER, DIEGO de SOUZA Andrade (61 LENNY Fernandes Coelho Felisbino), Lucas PIERRE Santos Oliveira, WILLIANS dos Santos Santana (55 JUMAR José da Costa Júnior), KEIRRISON de Souza Carneiro. DT: Vanderlei LUXEMBURGO da Silva
Goals: CLEITON Ribeiro XAVIER (29), KEIRRISON de Souza Carneiro (74).

CLUB SPORTING CRISTAL LIMA – CA ESTUDIANTES DE LA PLATA 2-1 (1-1)
Estadio San Martín de Porres, Lima, 29.01.2009
Referee: Carlos Luis CHANDÍA Alarcón (CHI), Attendance: 16.302
CLUB SPORTING CRISTAL LIMA: Manuel Alexander HEREDIA Rojas, Miguel Ángel VILLALTA Hurtado, Jeickson Gustavo REYES Aparcana, Wenceslao Ernesto FERNÁNDEZ Donayre, Alejandro Damián GONZÁLEZ Hernandez, Edwin Alberto PÉREZ León, Carlos Augusto LOBATÓN Espejo, Roberto Carlos PALACIOS Mestas (90 Daniel Alonso SÁNCHEZ Albujar), Antonio Yosimar LIZARBE Merino, Héctor Hugo HURTADO Salazar (86 Juan Luis QUIÑONEZ López), Franco Junior ALIBERTI Barreto (75 Renzo Santiago SHEPUT Rodríguez). DT: Juan Carlos OBLITAS Saba
CA ESTUDIANTES DE LA PLATA: Mariano Gonzalo ANDÚJAR, Marcos Alberto ANGELERI, Leandro DESÁBATO, Cristian Ariel CELLAY, Juan Manuel DÍAZ Martínez, Juan Sebastián VERÓN, Diego Alberto GALVÁN (59 Iván Diego MORENO Y FABIANESI), Enzo Nicolás PÉREZ, Matías Ariel SÁNCHEZ, Gastón Nicolás FERNÁNDEZ (81 Juan Manuel SALGUEIRO Silva), Ramón LENTINI (72 José Luis CALDERÓN). DT: Leonardo Rubén ASTRADA
Goals: Roberto Carlos PALACIOS Mestas (42), Héctor Hugo HURTADO Salazar (55) /
Enzo Nicolás PÉREZ (29).

CD ESTUDIANTES DE LA PLATA – CLUB SPORTING CRISTAL LIMA 1-0 (0-0)
Estadio Ciudad de La Plata, La Plata, 4.02.2009
Referee: LEONARDO GACIBA da Silva (BRA), Attendance: 20.426
CA ESTUDIANTES DE LA PLATA: Mariano Gonzalo ANDÚJAR, Agustín ALAYES, Marcos Alberto ANGELERI, Leandro DESÁBATO, Cristian Ariel CELLAY, Juan Sebastián VERÓN, Enzo Nicolás PÉREZ (62 Diego Alberto GALVÁN), Matías Ariel SÁNCHEZ, Mauro BOSELLI, Juan Manuel SALGUEIRO Silva (70 Ramón LENTINI), Gastón Nicolás FERNÁNDEZ (60 José Luis CALDERÓN). DT: Leonardo Rubén ASTRADA
CLUB SPORTING CRISTAL LIMA: Manuel Alexander HEREDIA Rojas, Miguel Ángel VILLALTA Hurtado, Jeickson Gustavo REYES Aparcana, Wenceslao Ernesto FERNÁNDEZ Donayre, Alejandro Damián GONZÁLEZ Hernandez, Edwin Alberto PÉREZ León, Carlos Augusto LOBATÓN Espejo, Roberto Carlos PALACIOS Mestas, Antonio Yosimar LIZARBE Merino (78 Flavio Francisco MAESTRI Andrade), Héctor Hugo HURTADO Salazar, Franco Junior ALIBERTI Barreto (75 Renzo Santiago SHEPUT Rodríguez). DT: Juan Carlos OBLITAS Saba
Sent off : Pérez (90+3)
Goal: Ramón LENTINI (76).

DEPORTIVO ANZOATEGUI SC – CLUB DEPORTIVO CUENCA 2-0 (1-0)
Estadio José Antonio Anzoátegui, Puerto La Cruz, 29.01.2009
Referee: Víctor Hugo CARRILLO Casanova (PER), Attendance: 10.000
DEPORTIVO ANZOATEGUI SC: José Leonardo MORALES Larez, Pedro Luis BOADA Noya, Giacomo DI GIORGI, Grendy Andrián PEROZO, José YEGÜÉZ, Rubén YORI, Nicolás MASSÍA Arias (85 José David MORENO), José Ricardo DUNO, Édgard Fabián ESPÍNDOLA (70 Alexander RONDÓN Heredia), Jhonny José GONZÁLEZ Barreto, Emerson Mariano PANIGUTTI (80 Luis Miguel LOBO). DT: Félix José HERNÁNDEZ
CLUB DEPORTIVO CUENCA: Carlos Antonio MORÁN Jalón, Marco Antonio QUIÑÓNEZ Angulo, Marlon Patricio MORENO Vargas, Marcelo Cristian BOHÓRQUEZ Valencia, Norberto Javier ORREGO, José Eduardo GRANDA Vicuña (65 Juan Carlos PAREDES Reasco), Giancarlo Pablo RAMOS Barrios, Jhon Antonio GARCÍA Figueroa, Hólger Eduardo MATAMOROS Chunga (70 Christian Santiago CORDERO Rodríguez), RODRIGO TEIXEIRA Pereira (58 Édison Andrés PRECIADO Bravo), Ismael Oscar VILLALBA. DT: Guillermo DURÓ
Sent off : Quiñónez (87)
Goals: Édgard Fabián ESPÍNDOLA (11), Jhonny José GONZÁLEZ Barreto (51).

CLUB DEPORTIVO CUENCA – DEPORTIVO ANZOATEGUI SC 3-0 (1-0)
Estadio Alejandro Serrano Aguilar, Cuenca, 3.02.2009
Referee: Óscar MALDONADO Urey (BOL), Attendance: 7.275
CLUB DEPORTIVO CUENCA: Carlos Antonio MORÁN Jalón, Juan Kely GUERRÓN Vásquez, Jaime Javier CHILA Cortéz, Norberto Javier ORREGO, José Eduardo GRANDA Vicuña, Giancarlo Pablo RAMOS Barrios, Hólger Eduardo MATAMOROS Chunga (87 Jhon Antonio GARCÍA Figueroa), William Osvaldo ESPAÑA España, RODRIGO TEIXEIRA Pereira, Ismael Oscar VILLALBA (78 Mauricio Bladimir HURTADO Alvarado), Juan Carlos PAREDES Reasco (71 Édison Andrés PRECIADO Bravo). DT: Guillermo DURÓ
DEPORTIVO ANZOATEGUI SC: José Leonardo MORALES Larez, Pedro Luis BOADA Noya, Giacomo DI GIORGI, Grendy Andrián PEROZO, José YEGÜÉZ (46 Edixon Vladimir CUEVAS), Rubén YORI, Nicolás MASSÍA Arias, José Ricardo DUNO, Édgard Fabián ESPÍNDOLA (72 Alexander RONDÓN Heredia), Jhonny José GONZÁLEZ Barreto, Emerson Mariano PANIGUTTI (59 Luis Miguel LOBO). DT: Félix José HERNÁNDEZ
Sent off : Cuevas (67), Lobo (89)
Goals: RODRIGO TEIXEIRA Pereira (27, 68), Ismael Oscar VILLALBA (74).

SECOND PHASE – GROUP 1

LIGA DEPORTIVA UNIVERSITARIA DE QUITO – SE PALMEIRAS 3-2 (2-1)
Estadio de LDU (La Casa Blanca), Quito, 17.02.2009
Referee: Wilmar Alexander ROLDÁN Pérez (COL), Attendance: 8.000
LDU: José Francisco CEVALLOS Villavicencio, Vicente Paúl AMBROSI Zambrano (61 Diego Armando CALDERÓN Espinoza), Néicer REASCO Yano, Renán CALLE Camacho, Norberto Carlos ARAUJO, Jairo Rolando CAMPOS León, Patricio Javier URRUTIA Espinoza (86 Pedro Sebastián LARREA Arellano), William Francisco ARAUJO Ogonaga, Damián Alejandro MANSO, Claudio Daniel BIELER, Walter Richard CALDERÓN Carcelén (64 Alfonso Andrés OBREGÓN Cancino).
DT: Jorge Daniel FOSSATI Lurachi
SE PALMEIRAS: MARCOS Roberto Silveira Reis, EDMÍLSON José Gomes de Moraes, DANILO Laranjeira, Pablo Estifer ARMERO, MAURÍCIO Donizete RAMOS Júnior (46 Marcos Antônio da Silva Gonçalves "MARQUINHOS"), Antônio Fábio Francez Cavalcante "FABINHO CAPIXABA" (72 EVANDRO Goebel), CLEITON Ribeiro XAVIER, DIEGO de SOUZA Andrade, Lucas PIERRE Santos Oliveira, WILLIANS dos Santos Santana (69 LENNY Fernandes Coelho Felisbino), KEIRRISON de Souza Carneiro. DT: Vanderlei LUXEMBURGO da Silva Sent off: Armero (90)
Goals: Walter Richard CALDERÓN Carcelén (23, 34), Damián Alejandro MANSO (58) / WILLIANS dos Santos Santana (28), EDMÍLSON José Gomes de Moraes (46).

CSD COLO COLO SANTIAGO – SPORT CLUB DO RECIFE 1-2 (0-2)
Estadio Monumental David Arellano, Santiago, 18.02.2009
Referee: Saúl Esteban LAVERNI (ARG), Attendance: 23.427
CSD COLO COLO SANTIAGO: Cristian Fernando MUÑOZ, Rodrigo Javier MILLAR Carvajal, Gonzalo Alejandro JARA Reyes (68 Yerson Flavio OPAZO Riquelme), Rodrigo Fabian RIQUELME Cabrera, Luis Arturo MENA Irarrázabal, Macnelly TORRES Berrio (70 Gerardo Elías CORTÉS Hermosilla), Héctor Arturo SANHUEZA Medel, José Domingo SALCEDO González, Rodrigo David MELÉNDEZ Araya (46 César Alberto CARRANZA), Lucas Ramón BARRIOS, Rodolfo Antonio MOYA Spuler. DT: Marcelo Pablo BARTICCIOTTO
SPORT CLUB DO RECIFE: Alessandro Beti Rosa "MAGRÃO", IGOR Nascimento Soares, PAULO César BAIER (72 José Fernando FUMAGALLI), Severino dos Ramos DURVAL da Silva, Antonio Monteiro DUTRA, CÉSAR Ricardo de LUCENA, João Henrique de ANDRADE Amaral, MOACIR Costa da Silva, HAMILTON Henio Ferreira Calheiros, WILSON Rodrigues Fonseca (81 SANDRO "GOIANO" Gomes Luz), CIRO Henrique Alves Ferreira e Silva (65 WELDON Santos de Andrade).
DT: NELSINHO BAPTISTA Júnior
Goals: Lucas R. BARRIOS (70) / CIRO Henrique Alves Ferreira e Silva (7), WILSON R. Fonseca (44).

SE PALMEIRAS – CSD COLO COLO SANTIAGO 1-3 (0-1)
Estádio Palestra Itália (Parque Antárctica), São Paulo, 3.03.2009
Referee: Sergio Fabián PEZZOTTA (ARG), Attendance: 23.285
SE PALMEIRAS: BRUNO Cortez Cardoso, EDMÍLSON José Gomes de Moraes, Marcos Alberto Skavinski "MARCÃO" (46 JUMAR José da Costa Júnior), DANILO Laranjeira, MAURÍCIO Donizete RAMOS Júnior (46 JEFFERSON Nascimento), Antônio Fábio Francez Cavalcante "FABINHO CAPIXABA" (63 LENNY Fernandes Coelho Felisbino), CLEITON Ribeiro XAVIER, DIEGO de SOUZA Andrade, Lucas PIERRE Santos Oliveira, WILLIANS dos Santos Santana, KEIRRISON de Souza Carneiro. DT: Vanderlei LUXEMBURGO da Silva
CSD COLO COLO SANTIAGO: Cristian Fernando MUÑOZ, Rodrigo Javier MILLAR Carvajal, Miguel Augusto RIFFO Garay, Luis Arturo MENA Irarrázabal, Macnelly TORRES Berrio (86 Yerson Flavio OPAZO Riquelme), Héctor Arturo SANHUEZA Medel, Luis Pedro FIGUEROA Sepúlveda, José Domingo SALCEDO González, Rodrigo David MELÉNDEZ Araya, César Alberto CARRANZA (52 Rafael Antonio CAROCA Cordero), Lucas Ramón BARRIOS (78 Sebastián Ignacio GONZÁLEZ Valdés). DT: Marcelo Pablo BARTICCIOTTO
Sent off: Meléndez (49)
Goals: KEIRRISON de Souza Carneiro (70) / Lucas Ramón BARRIOS (44), Macnelly TORRES Berrio (54), Sebastián Ignacio GONZÁLEZ Valdés (79).

SPORT CLUB DO RECIFE – LIGA DEPORTIVA UNIVERSITARIA DE QUITO 2-0 (1-0)
Estádio Adelmar da Costa Carvalho (Ilha do Retiro), Recife, 4.03.2009
Referee: Jorge Luis LARRIONDA Pietrafesa (URU), Attendance: 20.184
SPORT CLUB DO RECIFE: Alessandro Beti Rosa "MAGRÃO", IGOR Nascimento Soares, PAULO César BAIER (75 José Fernando FUMAGALLI), Severino dos Ramos DURVAL da Silva, Antonio Monteiro DUTRA, CÉSAR Ricardo de LUCENA, DANIEL "PAULISTA" Pollo Barion (82 SANDRO "GOIANO" Gomes Luz), MOACIR Costa da Silva, HAMILTON Henio Ferreira Calheiros, WILSON Rodrigues Fonseca, CIRO Henrique Alves Ferreira e Silva (52 Augusto Pacheco Fraga "GUTO"). DT: NELSINHO BAPTISTA Júnior
LDU: José Francisco CEVALLOS Villavicencio, Diego Armando CALDERÓN Espinoza, Néicer REASCO Yano (71 Daniel Jimmy VITERI Vinces), Renán CALLE Camacho, Norberto Carlos ARAUJO, Jairo Rolando CAMPOS León, Patricio Javier URRUTIA Espinoza, William Francisco ARAUJO Ogonaga, Damián Alejandro MANSO, Claudio Daniel BIELER (85 Pedro Sebastián LARREA Arellano), Walter Richard CALDERÓN Carcelén (53 Richard Javier MORALES Aguirre). DT: Jorge Daniel FOSSATI Lurachi
Sent off: Cevallos (69)
Goals: DANIEL "PAULISTA" Pollo Barion (13), PAULO César BAIER (72 penalty).

CSD COLO COLO SANTIAGO – LIGA DEPORTIVA UNIVERSITARIA DE QUITO 3-0 (0-0)
Estadio Monumental David Arellano, Santiago, 12.03.2009
Referee: Carlos Arecio AMARILLA Demarqui (PAR), Attendance: 30.000
CSD COLO COLO SANTIAGO: Cristian Fernando MUÑOZ, Luis Arturo MENA Irarrázabal, Roberto Andrés CERECEDA Guajardo, Miguel Augusto RIFFO Garay, Luis Pedro FIGUEROA Sepúlveda, Macnelly TORRES Berrio (87 Rodolfo Antonio MOYA Spuler), César Alberto CARRANZA (72 Sebastián Ignacio GONZÁLEZ Valdés), Rodrigo Javier MILLAR Carvajal (70 Rafael Antonio CAROCA Cordero), Héctor Arturo SANHUEZA Medel, José Domingo SALCEDO González, Lucas Ramón BARRIOS. DT: Marcelo Pablo BARTICCIOTTO
LDU: Alexander DOMÍNGUEZ Carabalí, Renán CALLE Camacho, Vicente Paúl AMBROSI Zambrano (63 Miler Alejandro BOLAÑOS Reasco), Néicer REASCO Yano, William Francisco ARAUJO Ogonaga (70 Carlos Alberto ESPÍNOLA Oviedo), Jairo Rolando CAMPOS León, Patricio Javier URRUTIA Espinoza, Diego Armando CALDERÓN Espinoza, Damián Alejandro MANSO (84 Danny Alejandro VERA Carpio), Richard Javier MORALES Aguirre, Claudio Daniel BIELER. DT: Jorge Daniel FOSSATI Lurachi
Goals: César Alberto CARRANZA (56), Roberto Andrés CERECEDA Guajardo (61), Lucas Ramón BARRIOS (65).

SPORT CLUB DO RECIFE – SE PALMEIRAS 0-2 (0-1)
Estádio Adelmar da Costa Carvalho (Ilha do Retiro), Recife, 8.04.2009
Referee: Carlos Manuel TORRES (PAR), Attendance: 19.386
SPORT CLUB DO RECIFE: Alessandro Beti Rosa "MAGRÃO", PAULO César BAIER, CÉSAR Ricardo de LUCENA, IGOR Nascimento Soares, Severino dos Ramos DURVAL da Silva, Antonio Monteiro DUTRA, João Henrique de ANDRADE Amaral, DANIEL "PAULISTA" Pollo Barion (46 SANDRO "GOIANO" Gomes Luz), CIRO Henrique Alves Ferreira e Silva, Vanderson da Silva Souza "VANDINHO" (70 WELDON Santos de Andrade), MOACIR Costa da Silva (46 LUCIANO HENRIQUE de Gouveia). DT: NELSINHO BAPTISTA Júnior
SE PALMEIRAS: MARCOS Roberto Silveira Reis, EDMÍLSON José Gomes de Moraes, MAURÍCIO Donizete RAMOS Júnior (80 Marcos Alberto Skavinski "MARCÃO"), DANILO Laranjeira, Lucas PIERRE Santos Oliveira, Pablo Estifer ARMERO, DIEGO de SOUZA Andrade, WILLIANS dos Santos Santana (53 José María ORTIGOZA Ortíz), CLEITON Ribeiro XAVIER, Antônio Fábio Francez Cavalcante "FABINHO CAPIXABA", KEIRRISON de Souza Carneiro (77 SANDRO Laurindo da SILVA). DT: Vanderlei LUXEMBURGO da Silva
Goals: KEIRRISON de Souza Carneiro (23), DIEGO de SOUZA Andrade (73).

LIGA DEPORTIVA UNIVERSITARIA DE QUITO – CSD COLO COLO SANTIAGO 1-1 (0-0)
Estadio de LDU (La Casa Blanca), Quito, 9.04.2009
Referee: Benito Armando ARCHUNDIA Tellez (MEX), Attendance: 18.000
LDU: José Francisco CEVALLOS Villavicencio, Norberto Carlos ARAUJO, Renán CALLE Camacho, Vicente Paúl AMBROSI Zambrano (86 Diego Armando CALDERÓN Espinoza), Néicer REASCO Yano, William Francisco ARAUJO Ogonaga (63 Pedro Sebastián LARREA Arellano), Jairo Rolando CAMPOS León, Patricio Javier URRUTIA Espinoza, Damián Alejandro MANSO, Walter Richard CALDERÓN Carcelén (74 Edder Javier VACA Quinde), Claudio Daniel BIELER. DT: Jorge Daniel FOSSATI Lurachi
CSD COLO COLO SANTIAGO: Cristian Fernando MUÑOZ, Rodrigo Fabian RIQUELME Cabrera, Luis Arturo MENA Irarrázabal, Roberto Andrés CERECEDA Guajardo (80 Rafael Antonio CAROCA Cordero), Luis Pedro FIGUEROA Sepúlveda, Macnelly TORRES Berrio, César Alberto CARRANZA (67 Sebastián Ignacio GONZÁLEZ Valdés), Rodrigo Javier MILLAR Carvajal (82 Daud Jared GAZALE Álvarez), Héctor Arturo SANHUEZA Medel, José Domingo SALCEDO González, Lucas Ramón BARRIOS. DT: Marcelo Pablo BARTICCIOTTO
Goals: Jairo Rolando CAMPOS León (48) / Claudio Daniel BIELER (90+2 own goal).

SE PALMEIRAS – SPORT CLUB DO RECIFE 1-1 (1-1)
Estádio Palestra Itália (Parque Antárctica), São Paulo, 15.04.2009:
Referee: Roberto Carlos SILVERA Calcerrada (URU), Attendance: 22.372
SE PALMEIRAS: MARCOS Roberto Silveira Reis, EDMÍLSON José Gomes de Moraes (52 EVANDRO Goebel), MAURÍCIO Donizete RAMOS Júnior, DANILO Laranjeira, Lucas PIERRE Santos Oliveira, Pablo Estifer ARMERO, DIEGO de SOUZA Andrade, CLEITON Ribeiro XAVIER, Antônio Fábio Francez Cavalcante "FABINHO CAPIXABA" (69 Marcos Antônio da Silva Gonçalves "MARQUINHOS"), KEIRRISON de Souza Carneiro, LENNY Fernandes Coelho Felisbino (69 José María ORTIGOZA Ortíz). DT: Vanderlei LUXEMBURGO da Silva
SPORT CLUB DO RECIFE: Alessandro Beti Rosa "MAGRÃO", PAULO César BAIER (67 José Fernando FUMAGALLI), CÉSAR Ricardo de LUCENA, IGOR Nascimento Soares, Severino dos Ramos DURVAL da Silva, Antonio Monteiro DUTRA, João Henrique de ANDRADE Amaral (87 SANDRO "GOIANO" Gomes Luz), DANIEL "PAULISTA" Pollo Barion, WILSON Rodrigues Fonseca, Vanderson da Silva Souza "VANDINHO" (81 Augusto Pacheco Fraga "GUTO"), MOACIR Costa da Silva. DT: NELSINHO BAPTISTA Júnior
Sent off: Wilson (45)
Goals: KEIRRISON de Souza Carneiro (14 penalty) / WILSON Rodrigues Fonseca (45).

SE PALMEIRAS – LIGA DEPORTIVA UNIVERSITARIA DE QUITO 2-0 (0-0)
Estádio Palestra Itália (Parque Antárctica), São Paulo, 21.04.2009
Referee: Jorge Luis LARRIONDA Pietrafesa (URU), Attendance: 19.205
SE PALMEIRAS: MARCOS Roberto Silveira Reis, Marcos Alberto Skavinski "MARCÃO", MAURÍCIO Donizete RAMOS Júnior, DANILO Laranjeira, Lucas PIERRE Santos Oliveira, Pablo Estifer ARMERO, DIEGO de SOUZA Andrade, CLEITON Ribeiro XAVIER, Antônio Fábio Francez Cavalcante "FABINHO CAPIXABA" (46 Marcos Antônio da Silva Gonçalves "MARQUINHOS"), KEIRRISON de Souza Carneiro, LENNY Fernandes Coelho Felisbino (73 SANDRO Laurindo da SILVA, 80 WENDEL Santana Pereira Santos). DT: Vanderlei LUXEMBURGO da Silva
LDU: José Francisco CEVALLOS Villavicencio (53 Alexander DOMÍNGUEZ Carabalí), Norberto Carlos ARAUJO, Renán CALLE Camacho (70 Danny Alejandro VERA Carpio), Néicer REASCO Yano, William Francisco ARAUJO Ogonaga, Jairo Rolando CAMPOS León, Carlos Alberto ESPÍNOLA Oviedo, Diego Armando CALDERÓN Espinoza, Edder Javier VACA Quinde (81 Gonzalo Javier CHILA Palma), Miler Alejandro BOLAÑOS Reasco, Walter Richard CALDERÓN Carcelén. DT: Jorge Daniel FOSSATI Lurachi
Sent off : Maequinhos (71) / Bolaños (71)
Goals: Marcos Alberto Skavinski "MARCÃO" (48), DIEGO de SOUZA Andrade (83).

SPORT CLUB DO RECIFE – CSD COLO COLO SANTIAGO 2-1 (0-0)
Estádio Adelmar da Costa Carvalho (Ilha do Retiro), Recife, 22.04.2009
Referee: Héctor Wálter BALDASSI (ARG), Attendance: 20.050
SPORT CLUB DO RECIFE: Alessandro Beti Rosa "MAGRÃO", PAULO César BAIER (73 Augusto Pacheco Fraga "GUTO"), CÉSAR Ricardo de LUCENA, IGOR Nascimento Soares, Severino dos Ramos DURVAL da Silva, Antonio Monteiro DUTRA, HAMILTON Henio Ferreira Calheiros (61 LUCIANO HENRIQUE de Gouveia), DANIEL "PAULISTA" Pollo Barion, CIRO Henrique Alves Ferreira e Silva (46 José Fernando FUMAGALLI), Vanderson da Silva Souza "VANDINHO", MOACIR Costa da Silva. DT: NELSINHO BAPTISTA Júnior
CSD COLO COLO SANTIAGO: Cristian Fernando MUÑOZ, Luis Arturo MENA Irarrázabal, Roberto Andrés CERECEDA Guajardo (60 Rafael Antonio CAROCA Cordero), Nelson David CABRERA Báez (88 César Alberto CARRANZA), Gonzalo Alejandro JARA Reyes, Luis Pedro FIGUEROA Sepúlveda, Macnelly TORRES Berrio, Rodrigo Javier MILLAR Carvajal, Rodrigo David MELÉNDEZ Araya (76 Sebastián Ignacio GONZÁLEZ Valdés), José Domingo SALCEDO González, Lucas Ramón BARRIOS. DT: Marcelo Pablo BARTICCIOTTO
Goals: MOACIR Costa da Silva (60), Vanderson da Silva Souza "VANDINHO" (75) /
Rodrigo Javier MILLAR Carvajal (50).

LIGA DEPORTIVA UNIVERSITARIA DE QUITO – SPORT CLUB DO RECIFE 2-3 (2-1)
Estadio de LDU (La Casa Blanca), Quito, 29.04.2009
Referee: Juan Ernesto SOTO (VEN), Attendance: 1.500
LDU: Daniel Jimmy VITERI Vinces, Renán CALLE Camacho, Carlos Alberto ESPÍNOLA Oviedo, Alfonso Andrés OBREGÓN Cancino (62 Vicente Paúl AMBROSI Zambrano), Alejandro Gabriel ESPINOSA Borja, Diego Armando CALDERÓN Espinoza, Gonzalo Javier CHILA Palma (62 Jairo Rolando CAMPOS León), Pedro Sebastián LARREA Arellano (75 Néicer REASCO Yano), Edder Javier VACA Quinde, Franklin Agustín SALAS Nárvaez, Danny Alejandro VERA Carpio. DT: Jorge Daniel FOSSATI Lurachi
SPORT CLUB DO RECIFE: Alessandro Beti Rosa "MAGRÃO", CÉSAR Ricardo de LUCENA, IGOR Nascimento Soares, Severino dos Ramos DURVAL da Silva, Antonio Monteiro DUTRA, José Fernando FUMAGALLI (81 BRUNO Martins TELES), João Henrique de ANDRADE Amaral, DANIEL "PAULISTA" Pollo Barion (76 SANDRO "GOIANO" Gomes Luz), WILSON Rodrigues Fonseca, Vanderson da Silva Souza "VANDINHO", MOACIR Costa da Silva (46 LUCIANO HENRIQUE de Gouveia). DT: NELSINHO BAPTISTA Júnior
Sent off : Salas (33), Calderón (90)
Goals: Carlos Alberto ESPÍNOLA Oviedo (2), Danny Alejandro VERA Carpio (41) / João Henrique de ANDRADE Amaral (23), IGOR Nascimento Soares (58), João Henrique de ANDRADE Amaral (77).

CSD COLO COLO SANTIAGO – SE PALMEIRAS 0-1 (0-0)
Estadio Monumental David Arellano, Santiago, 29.04.2009
Referee: Carlos Manuel TORRES (PAR), Attendance: 31.038
CSD COLO COLO: Cristian Fernando MUÑOZ, Luis Arturo MENA Irarrázabal, Miguel Augusto RIFFO Garay, Luis Pedro FIGUEROA Sepúlveda, Macnelly TORRES Berrio (17 Rafael Antonio CAROCA Cordero), César Alberto CARRANZA (85 Sebastián Ignacio GONZÁLEZ Valdés), Rodrigo Javier MILLAR Carvajal, Héctor Arturo SANHUEZA Medel, Rodrigo David MELÉNDEZ Araya (64 Gonzalo Alejandro JARA Reyes), José Domingo SALCEDO González, Lucas Ramón BARRIOS. DT: Gualberto JARA
SE PALMEIRAS: MARCOS Roberto Silveira Reis, Marcos Alberto Skavinski "MARCÃO", MAURÍCIO Donizete RAMOS Júnior, DANILO Laranjeira, Lucas PIERRE Santos Oliveira (60 EVANDRO Goebel), Pablo Estifer ARMERO, DIEGO de SOUZA Andrade, CLEITON Ribeiro XAVIER, WENDEL Santana Pereira Santos (46 WILLIANS dos Santos Santana), Elierce Barbosa de SOUZA (87 José María ORTIGOZA Ortíz), KEIRRISON de Souza Carneiro. DT: Vanderlei LUXEMBURGO da Silva
Sent off: Marcão (63)
Goal: CLEITON Ribeiro XAVIER (87).

1	SPORT RECIFE	6	4	1	1	10	7	13
2	PALMEIRAS	6	3	1	2	9	7	10
3	Colo Colo	6	2	1	3	9	7	7
4	Liga de Quito	6	1	1	4	6	13	4

GROUP 2

CLUB GUARANI ASUNCION – DEPORTIVO TACHIRA FC 1-2 (1-1)
Estadio General Pablo Rojas (La Olla), Asunción, 10.02.2009
Referee: Diego ABAL (ARG), Attendance: 3.000
CLUB GUARANI ASUNCION: Joel Alberto SILVA Estigarribia, Elvis Israel MARECOS, Eduardo FILIPPINI, Reinaldo ROMÁN Fernández, Héctor Federico CARBALLO, Luis Alejandro NÚÑEZ López (46 Jonathan FABBRO), Miguel Ángel PANIAGUA Rivarola, Cristian Gustavo SOSA, Julián Alfonso BENÍTEZ Franco, Pedro Julián CHÁVEZ Ruiz (66 Osvaldo Javier DÍAZ Giménez), José Edicarlos Lima NEGREIROS (80 Carlos Ariel NEUMANN Torres). DT: Félix Darío LEÓN
DEPORTIVO TACHIRA FC: Manuel Alejandro SANHOUSE Contreras, José Javier VILLAFRAZ Quintero, Emilio Martín HIDALGO Conde, Julio César MACHADO Cesareo, Lucas Alfredo BOVAGLIO Ibarra, Diego Alejandro GUERRERO Corredor, Jorge Francisco CASANOVA Canchila, Mario Evaristo LEGUIZAMÓN Martínez, Gerzon Armando CHACÓN Varela (75 José Francisco GONZÁLEZ Quijada), Nahuel Darío FIORETTO (63 Edgar Fernando PÉREZ Greco), Daniel Enrique ARISMENDI Marchan (66 Anderson ARIAS Zambrano). DT: Carlos Fabián MALDONADO Bineiro
Goals: Pedro Julián CHÁVEZ Ruiz (37) / Gerzon Armando CHACÓN Varela (40), Edgar Fernando PÉREZ Greco (79).

CA BOCA JUNIORS BUENOS AIRES – CLUB DEPORTIVO CUENCA 1-0 (1-0)
Estadio Alberto J.Armando (La Bombonera), Buenos Aires, 17.02.2009
Referee: Paulo César DE OLIVEIRA (BRA), Attendance: 50.328
CA BOCA JUNIORS: Roberto Carlos ABBONDANZIERI, Julio César CÁCERES López, Claudio Marcelo MOREL Rodríguez (81 Juan Ángel KRUPOVIESA), Hugo Benjamín IBARRA, Facundo Sebastián RONCAGLIA, Sebastián Alejandro BATTAGLIA, Juan Román RIQUELME, Fabián Andrés VARGAS Rivera, Pablo Nicolás MOUCHE (56 Osvaldo Nicolás Fabián GAITÁN), Rodrigo Sebastián PALACIO, Lucas Ezequiel VIATRI (63 Martín PALERMO). DT: Carlos Luis ISCHIA
CLUB DEPORTIVO CUENCA: Carlos Antonio MORÁN Jalón, Norberto Javier ORREGO, Juan Kely GUERRÓN Vásquez, William Osvaldo ESPAÑA España, Bernardo Javier CHILA Ayovi, Mauricio Bladimir HURTADO Alvarado (75 Jhon Antonio GARCÍA Figueroa), Giancarlo Pablo RAMOS Barrios, José Eduardo GRANDA Vicuña (60 Hólger Eduardo MATAMOROS Chunga), RODRIGO TEIXEIRA Pereira (75 Édison Andrés PRECIADO Bravo), Ismael Oscar VILLALBA, Juan Carlos PAREDES Reasco. DT: Guillermo DURÓ
Goal: Rodrigo Sebastián PALACIO (12).

CLUB DEPORTIVO CUENCA – CLUB GUARANÍ ASUNCIÓN 4-0 (1-0)
Estadio Alejandro Serrano Aguilar, Cuenca, 24.02.2009
Referee: Juan Ernesto SOTO (VEN), Attendance: 10.000
CLUB DEPORTIVO CUENCA: Carlos Antonio MORÁN Jalón, Norberto Javier ORREGO, Juan Kely GUERRÓN Vásquez, William Osvaldo ESPAÑA España, Bernardo Javier CHILA Ayovi, Hólger Eduardo MATAMOROS Chunga, Giancarlo Pablo RAMOS Barrios (81 Christian Santiago CORDERO Rodríguez), José Eduardo GRANDA Vicuña (62 Jhon Antonio GARCÍA Figueroa), RODRIGO TEIXEIRA Pereira (75 Édison Andrés PRECIADO Bravo), Ismael Oscar VILLALBA, Juan Carlos PAREDES Reasco. DT: Guillermo DURÓ
CLUB GUARANÍ ASUNCIÓN: Joel Alberto SILVA Estigarribia, Elvis Israel MARECOS, Eduardo FILIPPINI, Héctor Federico CARBALLO, Ariel Eleuterio ALVARENGA Sosa, Luis Alejandro NÚÑEZ López (81 Hermes Manuel VALDEZ Fernández), Miguel Ángel PANIAGUA Rivarola, WILLIAN SCHUSTER Dornelles da Silva (55 Cristian Gustavo SOSA), Julián Alfonso BENÍTEZ Franco (73 Carlos Ariel NEUMANN Torres), José Edicarlos Lima NEGREIROS, Jonathan FABBRO. DT: Félix Darío LEÓN
Goals: RODRIGO TEIXEIRA Pereira (45), José Eduardo GRANDA Vicuña (61), Ismael Oscar VILLALBA (74), Christian Santiago CORDERO Rodríguez (82).

DEPORTIVO TÁCHIRA FC – CA BOCA JUNIORS BUENOS AIRES 0-1 (0-0)
Estadio Pueblo Nuevo, San Cristóbal, 4.03.2009
Referee: Víctor Hugo RIVERA Chavez (PER), Attendance: 40.000
DEPORTIVO TÁCHIRA FC: Manuel Alejandro SANHOUSE Contreras, José Javier VILLAFRAZ Quintero, Emilio Martín HIDALGO Conde, Julio César MACHADO Cesareo, Lucas Alfredo BOVAGLIO Ibarra, Diego Alejandro GUERRERO Corredor, Jorge Francisco CASANOVA Canchila (76 Mario Evaristo LEGUIZAMÓN Martínez), Gerzon Armando CHACÓN Varela, Nahuel Darío FIORETTO, Alejandro Darío DELORTE (60 Edgar Fernando PÉREZ Greco), Daniel Enrique ARISMENDI Marchan (86 Anderson ARIAS Zambrano). DT: Carlos Fabián MALDONADO Bineiro
CA BOCA JUNIORS: Roberto Carlos ABBONDANZIERI, Julio César CÁCERES López, Juan Daniel FORLÍN, Facundo Sebastián RONCAGLIA, Juan Ángel KRUPOVIESA, Sebastián Alejandro BATTAGLIA, Juan Román RIQUELME, Fabián Andrés VARGAS Rivera, Osvaldo Nicolás Fabián GAITÁN (82 Leandro GRACIÁN), Ricardo Daniel NOIR (61 Pablo Nicolás MOUCHE), Lucas Ezequiel VIATRI (70 Luciano Gabriel "Lucho" FIGUEROA Herrera). DT: Carlos Luis ISCHIA
Goal: Luciano Gabriel "Lucho" FIGUEROA Herrera (87).

DEPORTIVO TÁCHIRA FC – CLUB DEPORTIVO CUENCA 1-0 (0-0)
Estadio Pueblo Nuevo, San Cristóbal, 11.03.2009
Referee: Albert DUARTE (COL), Attendance: 16.000
DEPORTIVO TÁCHIRA FC: Manuel Alejandro SANHOUSE Contreras, José Javier VILLAFRAZ Quintero, José Luis GRANADOS Asprilla, Julio César MACHADO Cesareo, Lucas Alfredo BOVAGLIO Ibarra, Gerzon Armando CHACÓN Varela (82 Diego Alejandro GUERRERO Corredor), Nahuel Darío FIORETTO, Edgar Fernando PÉREZ Greco, José Mauricio PARRA Perdomo (43 José Francisco GONZÁLEZ Quijada), Daniel Enrique ARISMENDI Marchan, Anderson ARIAS Zambrano (76 Jorge Francisco CASANOVA Canchila). DT: Carlos Fabián MALDONADO Bineiro
CLUB DEPORTIVO CUENCA: Carlos Antonio MORÁN Jalón, Norberto Javier ORREGO, Juan Kely GUERRÓN Vásquez, William Osvaldo ESPAÑA España, Bernardo Javier CHILA Ayovi, Hólger Eduardo MATAMOROS Chunga (66 Marlon Patricio MORENO Vargas), Giancarlo Pablo RAMOS Barrios, José Eduardo GRANDA Vicuña, RODRIGO TEIXEIRA Pereira, Ismael Oscar VILLALBA, Juan Carlos PAREDES Reasco (75 Édison Andrés PRECIADO Bravo). DT: Guillermo DURÓ
Sent off: Machado (39) / Guerrón (61)
Goal: José Javier VILLAFRAZ Quintero (66).

CLUB DEPORTIVO CUENCA – DEPORTIVO TÁCHIRA FC 3-1 (2-0)
Estadio Alejandro Serrano Aguilar, Cuenca, 17.03.2009
Referee: Raúl OROZCO (BOL), Attendance: 13.530
CLUB DEPORTIVO CUENCA: Carlos Antonio MORÁN Jalón, Norberto Javier ORREGO, Marcelo Cristian BOHÓRQUEZ Valencia, William Osvaldo ESPAÑA España, Bernardo Javier CHILA Ayovi, Hólger Eduardo MATAMOROS Chunga, Giancarlo Pablo RAMOS Barrios, José Eduardo GRANDA Vicuña (78 Mauricio Bladimir HURTADO Alvarado), RODRIGO TEIXEIRA Pereira, Ismael Oscar VILLALBA, Juan Carlos PAREDES Reasco (68 Édison Andrés PRECIADO Bravo). DT: Guillermo DURÓ
DEPORTIVO TÁCHIRA FC: Manuel Alejandro SANHOUSE Contreras, José Francisco GONZÁLEZ Quijada, José Javier VILLAFRAZ Quintero, José Luis GRANADOS Asprilla, Lucas Alfredo BOVAGLIO Ibarra, Diego Alejandro GUERRERO Corredor (55 José Mauricio PARRA Perdomo), Jorge Francisco CASANOVA Canchila, Gerzon Armando CHACÓN Varela, Nahuel Darío FIORETTO (42 Anderson ARIAS Zambrano, 69 Alejandro Darío DELORTE), Edgar Fernando PÉREZ Greco, Daniel Enrique ARISMENDI Marchan. DT: Carlos Fabián MALDONADO Bineiro
Sent off: Bovaglio
Goals: José Eduardo GRANDA Vicuña (18), RODRIGO TEIXEIRA Pereira (39, 67) / José Javier VILLAFRAZ Quintero (76).

CLUB GUARANÍ ASUNCIÓN – CA BOCA JUNIORS BUENOS AIRES 1-3 (1-0)
Estadio Manuel Ferreira, Asunción, 18.03.2009
Referee: Enrique Roberto OSSÉS Zencovich (CHI), Attendance: 5.927
CLUB GUARANÍ ASUNCIÓN: Pablo Fernando AURRECOCHEA Medina, Elvis Israel MARECOS, Eduardo FILIPPINI, Héctor Federico CARBALLO, Francisco Joel BENÍTEZ, Hermes Manuel VALDEZ Fernández, Miguel Ángel PANIAGUA Rivarola, Cristian Gustavo SOSA (81 Osvaldo Javier DÍAZ Giménez), Julián Alfonso BENÍTEZ Franco (79 WILLIAN SCHUSTER Dornelles da Silva), José Edicarlos Lima NEGREIROS (64 Federico Javier SANTANDER Mereles), Jonathan FABBRO. DT: Félix Darío LEÓN
CA BOCA JUNIORS: Roberto Carlos ABBONDANZIERI, Julio César CÁCERES López, Hugo Benjamín IBARRA, Juan Daniel FORLÍN, Facundo Sebastián RONCAGLIA, Juan Ángel KRUPOVIESA, Sebastián Alejandro BATTAGLIA, Juan Román RIQUELME, Fabián Andrés VARGAS Rivera, Pablo Nicolás MOUCHE (69 Martín PALERMO), Luciano Gabriel "Lucho" FIGUEROA Herrera (69 Rodrigo Sebastián PALACIO). DT: Carlos Luis ISCHIA
Goals: José Edicarlos Lima NEGREIROS (36) / Juan Román RIQUELME (65 penalty), Martín PALERMO (76), Rodrigo Sebastián PALACIO (85).

CA BOCA JUNIORS BUENOS AIRES – CLUB GUARANÍ ASUNCIÓN 3-1 (2-1)
Estadio Alberto J.Armando (La Bombonera), Buenos Aires, 9.04.2009
Referee: Víctor Hugo RIVERA Chavez (PER), Attendance: 22.651
CA BOCA JUNIORS: Roberto Carlos ABBONDANZIERI, Hugo Benjamín IBARRA, Juan Daniel FORLÍN, Facundo Sebastián RONCAGLIA, Juan Ángel KRUPOVIESA, Sebastián Alejandro BATTAGLIA, Juan Román RIQUELME, Fabián Andrés VARGAS Rivera, Osvaldo Nicolás Fabián GAITÁN (80 Leandro GRACIÁN), Martín PALERMO (80 Luciano Gabriel "Lucho" FIGUEROA Herrera), Rodrigo Sebastián PALACIO (77 Pablo Nicolás MOUCHE). DT: Carlos Luis ISCHIA
CLUB GUARANÍ ASUNCIÓN: Joel Alberto SILVA Estigarribia, Elvis Israel MARECOS, Eduardo FILIPPINI, Héctor Federico CARBALLO, Francisco Joel BENÍTEZ, Hermes Manuel VALDEZ Fernández, Miguel Ángel PANIAGUA Rivarola, Juan Carlos Manuel AGUILAR (83 Julián Alfonso BENÍTEZ Franco), Cristian Gustavo SOSA (68 Pedro Julián CHÁVEZ Ruiz), Jonathan FABBRO, Carlos Ariel NEUMANN Torres (59 José Edicarlos Lima NEGREIROS). DT: Félix Darío LEÓN
Goals: Martín PALERMO (33), Rodrigo Sebastián PALACIO (36), Juan Román RIQUELME (85 penalty) / Miguel Ángel PANIAGUA Rivarola (44).

DEPORTIVO TÁCHIRA FC – CLUB GUARANÍ ASUNCIÓN 2-1 (0-1)
Estadio Pueblo Nuevo, San Cristóbal, 16.04.2009
Referee: Manuel Alejandro GARAY Evia (PER), Attendance: 12.000
DEPORTIVO TÁCHIRA FC: Manuel Alejandro SANHOUSE Contreras, José Francisco GONZÁLEZ Quijada, José Javier VILLAFRAZ Quintero (12 Diego Alejandro GUERRERO Corredor), José Luis GRANADOS Asprilla, Julio César MACHADO Cesareo, Jorge Francisco CASANOVA Canchila, Gerzon Armando CHACÓN Varela, Edgar Fernando PÉREZ Greco, José Mauricio PARRA Perdomo (53 Marlon Antonio FERNÁNDEZ Jiménez), Daniel Enrique ARISMENDI Marchan (61 Yhonatan Alexander DEL VALLE Rodríguez), Anderson ARIAS Zambrano. DT: Carlos Fabián MALDONADO Bineiro
CLUB GUARANÍ ASUNCIÓN: Joel Alberto SILVA Estigarribia, Elvis Israel MARECOS, Eduardo FILIPPINI, Héctor Federico CARBALLO, Francisco Joel BENÍTEZ, Hermes Manuel VALDEZ Fernández (76 Osvaldo Javier DÍAZ Giménez), Miguel Ángel PANIAGUA Rivarola, WILLIAN SCHUSTER Dornelles da Silva (60 Juan Carlos Manuel AGUILAR), Cristian Gustavo SOSA (66 Luis Alejandro NÚÑEZ López), Julián Alfonso BENÍTEZ Franco, Carlos Ariel NEUMANN Torres. DT: Félix Darío LEÓN
Goals: Yhonatan Alexander DEL VALLE Rodríguez (68), Marlon A. FERNÁNDEZ Jiménez (75) / Carlos Ariel NEUMANN Torres (18).

CLUB DEPORTIVO CUENCA – CA BOCA JUNIORS BUENOS AIRES 1-0 (0-0)
Estadio Alejandro Serrano Aguilar, Cuenca, 23.04.2009
Referee: José Hernando BUITRAGO Arango (COL), Attendance: 20.000
CLUB DEPORTIVO CUENCA: Israel Cristopher ÁLVAREZ Vargas, Norberto Javier ORREGO, Juan Kely GUERRÓN Vásquez, William Osvaldo ESPAÑA España, Bernardo Javier CHILA Ayovi, Hólger Eduardo MATAMOROS Chunga (80 Mauricio Bladimir HURTADO Alvarado), Giancarlo Pablo RAMOS Barrios (75 Jhon Antonio GARCÍA Figueroa), José Eduardo GRANDA Vicuña, RODRIGO TEIXEIRA Pereira, Ismael Oscar VILLALBA, Juan Carlos PAREDES Reasco (67 Édison Andrés PRECIADO Bravo). DT: Guillermo DURÓ
CA BOCA JUNIORS: Roberto Carlos ABBONDANZIERI, Claudio Marcelo MOREL Rodríguez, Hugo Benjamín IBARRA, Facundo Sebastián RONCAGLIA, Ezequiel MUÑOZ, Juan Ángel KRUPOVIESA, Sebastián Alejandro BATTAGLIA, Fabián Andrés VARGAS Rivera (80 Ricardo Daniel NOIR), Osvaldo Nicolás Fabián GAITÁN (73 Damián Rodrigo DÍAZ), Pablo Nicolás MOUCHE (68 Rodrigo Sebastián PALACIO), Martín PALERMO. DT: Carlos Luis ISCHIA
Goal: Édison Andrés PRECIADO Bravo (77).

CLUB GUARANÍ ASUNCIÓN – CLUB DEPORTIVO CUENCA 1-1 (0-1)
Estadio Manuel Ferreira, Asunción, 30.04.2009
Referee: RICARDO MARQUES Ribeiro (BRA), Attendance: 1.000
CLUB GUARANÍ ASUNCIÓN: Pablo Fernando AURRECOCHEA Medina, Nelson Avelino AMARILLA Bogado, Eduardo FILIPPINI, Reinaldo ROMÁN Fernández, Héctor Federico CARBALLO, Hermes Manuel VALDEZ Fernández, Osvaldo Javier DÍAZ Giménez, WILLIAN SCHUSTER Dornelles da Silva (65 Carlos Ariel NEUMANN Torres), Juan Carlos Manuel AGUILAR (46 Juan Esteban ROMERO Patiño), Pedro Julián CHÁVEZ Ruiz, José Edicarlos Lima NEGREIROS (83 Miguel Ángel PANIAGUA Rivarola). DT: Pedro SANDOVAL
CLUB DEPORTIVO CUENCA: Israel Cristopher ÁLVAREZ Vargas, Norberto Javier ORREGO, Juan Kely GUERRÓN Vásquez, William Osvaldo ESPAÑA España, Bernardo Javier CHILA Ayovi, Jhon Antonio GARCÍA Figueroa, Hólger Eduardo MATAMOROS Chunga (85 Christian Santiago CORDERO Rodríguez), José Eduardo GRANDA Vicuña, RODRIGO TEIXEIRA Pereira (77 Mauricio Bladimir HURTADO Alvarado), Ismael Oscar VILLALBA, Juan Carlos PAREDES Reasco (69 Édison Andrés PRECIADO Bravo). DT: Guillermo DURÓ
Goals: Osvaldo Javier DÍAZ Giménez (55) / RODRIGO TEIXEIRA Pereira (2).

CA BOCA JUNIORS BUENOS AIRES – DEPORTIVO TACHIRA FC 3-0 (1-0)
Estadio Alberto J.Armando (La Bombonera), Buenos Aires, 30.04.2009
Referee: WILSON Luiz SENEME (BRA), Attendance: 38.000
CA BOCA JUNIORS: Roberto Carlos ABBONDANZIERI, Claudio Marcelo MOREL Rodríguez, Hugo Benjamín IBARRA, Juan Daniel FORLÍN, Facundo Sebastián RONCAGLIA, Sebastián Alejandro BATTAGLIA (81 Exequiel Emanuel BENAVÍDEZ), Leandro GRACIÁN, Fabián Andrés VARGAS Rivera, Osvaldo Nicolás Fabián GAITÁN (85 Damián Rodrigo DÍAZ), Martín PALERMO (72 Lucas Ezequiel VIATRI), Rodrigo Sebastián PALACIO. DT: Carlos Luis ISCHIA
DEPORTIVO TACHIRA FC: Manuel Alejandro SANHOUSE Contreras, José Javier VILLAFRAZ Quintero, José Luis GRANADOS Asprilla, Julio César MACHADO Cesareo, Lucas Alfredo BOVAGLIO Ibarra, Diego Alejandro GUERRERO Corredor, Jorge Francisco CASANOVA Canchila (80 Alejandro Darío DELORTE), Gerzon Armando CHACÓN Varela, Edgar Fernando PÉREZ Greco, Daniel Enrique ARISMENDI Marchan (66 Anderson ARIAS Zambrano), Yhonatan Alexander DEL VALLE Rodríguez (53 Marlon Antonio FERNÁNDEZ Jiménez). DT: Carlos Fabián MALDONADO Bineiro
Goals: Martín PALERMO (13, 63), Rodrigo Sebastián PALACIO (80).

1	BOCA JUNIORS	6	5	0	1	11	3	15
2	DEPORTIVO CUENCA	6	3	1	2	9	4	10
3	Deportivo Táchira	6	3	0	3	6	9	9
4	Guaraní	6	0	1	5	5	15	1

GROUP 3

CLUB NACIONAL MONTEVIDEO – CD UNIVERSIDAD SAN MARTÍN 2-1 (1-1)
Estadio Gran Parque Central, Montevideo, 12.02.2009
Referee: Carlos Luis CHANDÍA Alarcón (CHI), Attendance: 11.518
CLUB NACIONAL MONTEVIDEO: Rodrigo Martín MUÑOZ Salomón, Matiás Nicolás RODRÍGUEZ, Víctor Martín GALAIN Pécora, Federico Hernán DOMÍNGUEZ, Diego Sebastián RODRÍGUEZ Cano (70 Santiago Damián GARCÍA Correa), Hugo Diego ARISMENDI, Adrián Marcelo ROMERO González, Roberto Sebastián BRUM Gutiérrez, Álvaro FERNÁNDEZ Gay (80 Sergio Rubén BLANCO Soto), Alexander Jesús MEDINA Reobasco (70 Marcelo Nicolás LODEIRO Benítez, Marcos Gustavo MONDAINI. DT: Gerardo Cono PELUSSO Boyrie
CD UNIVERSIDAD SAN MARTÍN: Leao BUTRÓN Gotuzzo, Jorge Raúl HUAMÁN Salinas, Christian Guillermo Martín RAMOS Garagay, Guillermo Alejandro GIUZASOLA La Rosa, Atilio MUENTE Gionti, José Luis DÍAZ Sulca, Carlos Osvaldo FERNÁNDEZ Maldonado, John Cristopher HINOSTROZA Guzmán, Ronald QUINTEROS Sánchez (78 Josepmir Aarón BALLÓN Villacorta), Martín Enrique ARZUAGA Coronel (65 Pedro Alexandro GARCÍA De La Cruz), Gonzalo Emanuel LUDUEÑA (65 Orlando ALLENDE Huby). DT: Víctor Hugo RIVERA Coronado
Goals: Federico Hernán DOMÍNGUEZ (30), Marcelo Nicolás LODEIRO Benítez (90) /
Martín Enrique ARZUAGA Coronel (39).

CA RIVER PLATE BUENOS AIRES – CLUB NACIONAL ASUNCION 1-0 (0-0)
Estadio Antonio V.Liberti (El Monumental), Buenos Aires, 12.02.2009
Referee: Héber Roberto LOPES (BRA), Attendance: 17.673
CA RIVER PLATE: Juan Marcelo OJEDA, Nicolás Gabriel SÁNCHEZ, Cristian Carlos VILLAGRA, Paulo Andrés FERRARI, Gustavo Daniel CABRAL, Oscar Adrián AHUMADA, Matías Enrique ABELAIRAS (46 Robert Mario FLORES Bitolfi), Augusto Matías FERNÁNDEZ, Diego Mario BUONANOTTE Rende (90+2 Nicolás Mario DOMINGO), Mauro Damián ROSALES, Gustavo Martín FERNÁNDEZ (60 Cristian Gastón FABBIANI). DT: Néstor Raúl GOROSITO
CLUB NACIONAL ASUNCIÓN: Ignacio Oscar DON, Diego Raúl ARÉVALOS, Arnaldo Andrés ESPÍNOLA Benítez, Raúl Eduardo PIRIS, Ricardo MAZACOTTE, Glaucineis Martins da Silva "INCA", Jorge Daniel NÚÑEZ Espínola, Carlos Luis RUIZ Peralta, Ignacio Ramón CÁCERES Cabañas (90+2 Júlio César ORTELLADO Melgarejo), Héber Alberto ARRIOLA, Raúl Basilio ROMÁN Garay (72 Fabio ESCOBAR Benítez). DT: Daniel Eduardo RASCHLE Matucheski.
Sent off: Flores (90+2), Nuñéz (90+3)
Goal: CA River PLATE: 1-0 Diego Mario BUONANOTTE Rende (90).

CLUB NACIONAL ASUNCIÓN – CLUB NACIONAL MONTEVIDEO 0-3 (0-2)
Estadio General Pablo Rojas (La Olla), Asunción, 18.02.2009
Referee: LEONARDO GACIBA da Silva (BRA), Attendance: 1.307
CLUB NACIONAL ASUNCIÓN: Ignacio Oscar DON, Diego Raúl ARÉVALOS (86 Guillermo Alexis BELTRÁN), Arnaldo Andrés ESPÍNOLA Benítez (66 Herminio Antonio MIRANDA Ovelar), Raúl Eduardo PIRIS, Ricardo MAZACOTTE, Glaucineis Martins da Silva "INCA", Marcos Antonio MELGAREJO, Carlos Luis RUIZ Peralta, Ignacio Ramón CÁCERES Cabañas (41 Júlio César ORTELLADO Melgarejo), Héber Alberto ARRIOLA, Raúl Basilio ROMÁN Garay. DT: Daniel Eduardo RASCHLE Matucheski
CLUB NACIONAL MONTEVIDEO: Leonardo Fabián BURIÁN Castro, Cristian Martín RODRÍGUEZ Telis, Federico Hernán DOMÍNGUEZ (78 Víctor Martín GALAIN Pécora), Marcelo Nicolás LODEIRO Benítez, Adrián Marcelo ROMERO González, Roberto Sebastián BRUM Gutiérrez (60 Hugo Diego ARISMENDI), Pablo CABALLERO González, Óscar Javier MORALES Albornoz, Álvaro FERNÁNDEZ Gay (81 Mauricio Ernesto PEREYRA Antonini), Alexander Jesús MEDINA Reobasco, Marcos Gustavo MONDAINI. DT: Gerardo Cono PELUSSO Boyrie
Goals: Álvaro FERNÁNDEZ Gay (9), Marcelo Nicolás LODEIRO Benítez (38),
Marcos Gustavo MONDAINI (64).

CD UNIVERSIDAD SAN MARTÍN – CA RIVER PLATE BUENOS AIRES 2-1 (1-0)
Estadio Monumental, Lima, 5.03.2009
Referee: José Hernando BUITRAGO Arango (COL), Attendance: 20.000
CD UNIVERSIDAD SAN MARTÍN: Leao BUTRÓN Gotuzzo, Jorge Raúl HUAMÁN Salinas, Christian Guillermo Martín RAMOS Garagay, Adán Adolfo BALBÍN Silva (7 Josepmir Aarón BALLÓN Villacorta), Guillermo Alejandro GIUZASOLA La Rosa, José Luis DÍAZ Sulca, Pedro Alexandro GARCÍA De La Cruz (63 Ronald QUINTEROS Sánchez), Carlos Osvaldo FERNÁNDEZ Maldonado, John Cristopher HINOSTROZA Guzmán (86 Victor Wilmer CARRILLO Gonzáles), Martín Enrique ARZUAGA Coronel, Gonzalo Emanuel LUDUEÑA. DT: Víctor Hugo RIVERA Coronado
CA RIVER PLATE: Mariano Damián BARBOSA, Nicolás Gabriel SÁNCHEZ, Danilo Telmo GERLO (68 Gustavo Leonardo BOU), Gustavo Daniel CABRAL, Oscar Adrián AHUMADA, Rodrigo Javier ARCHUBI, Rubens Oscar SAMBUEZA (90+1 Diego Armando BARRADO), Nicolás Mario DOMINGO (61 Marcelo Daniel GALLARDO), Martín Sebastián GALMARINI, Mauro Damián ROSALES, Radamel Falcao GARCÍA Zárete. DT: Jorge Horacio BORELLI
Goals: José Luis DÍAZ Sulca (37 penalty), Gonzalo Emanuel LUDUEÑA (55) /
Radamel Falcao GARCÍA Zárete (68).

CD UNIVERSIDAD SAN MARTÍN – CLUB NACIONAL ASUNCIÓN 2-1 (0-0)
Estadio Alejandro Villanueva, Lima, 12.03.2009
Referee: Enrique Roberto OSSÉS Zencovich (CHI), Attendance: 5.000
CD UNIVERSIDAD SAN MARTÍN: Leao BUTRÓN Gotuzzo, Jorge Raúl HUAMÁN Salinas (75 Guillermo Sandro SALAS Suarez), Christian Guillermo Martín RAMOS Garagay, Jorge Enrique REYES Condori, Guillermo Alejandro GIUZASOLA La Rosa, José Luis DÍAZ Sulca, Pedro Alexandro GARCÍA De La Cruz (73 Ronald QUINTEROS Sánchez), John Cristopher HINOSTROZA Guzmán, Josepmir Aarón BALLÓN Villacorta, Martín Enrique ARZUAGA Coronel (81 Carlos Alberto PÉREZ Alcazar), Gonzalo Emanuel LUDUEÑA. DT: Víctor Hugo RIVERA Coronado
CLUB NACIONAL ASUNCIÓN: Ignacio Oscar DON, Arnaldo Andrés ESPÍNOLA Benítez, Herminio Antonio MIRANDA Ovelar, Raúl Eduardo PIRIS, Glaucineis Martins da Silva "INCA", Marcos Antonio MELGAREJO, Jorge Daniel NÚÑEZ Espínola, Ignacio Ramón CÁCERES Cabañas, Héber Alberto ARRIOLA, Éder Ricardo GODOY Rojas (58 Fabio ESCOBAR Benítez), Júlio César ORTELLADO Melgarejo (65 Guillermo Alexis BELTRÁN). DT: Daniel Eduardo RASCHLE Matucheski
Goals: Pedro Alexandro GARCÍA De La Cruz (53, 58) / Héber Alberto ARRIOLA (74).

CLUB NACIONAL MONTEVIDEO – CA RIVER PLATE BUENOS AIRES 3-0 (1-0)
Estadio Centenario, Montevideo, 19.03.2009
Referee: Carlos Luis CHANDÍA Alarcón (CHI), Attendance: 47.571
CLUB NACIONAL MONTEVIDEO: Rodrigo Martín MUÑOZ Salomón, Federico Hernán DOMÍNGUEZ, Mauricio Bernardo VICTORINO Dansilio, Matiás Nicolás RODRÍGUEZ, Hugo Diego ARISMENDI, Marcelo Nicolás LODEIRO Benítez, Adrián Marcelo ROMERO González, Óscar Javier MORALES Albornoz, Álvaro FERNÁNDEZ Gay (86 Roberto Sebastián BRUM Gutiérrez), Alexander Jesús MEDINA Reobasco (75 Santiago Damián GARCÍA Correa), Marcos Gustavo MONDAINI (66 Sergio Rubén BLANCO Soto). DT: Gerardo Cono PELUSSO Boyrie
CA RIVER PLATE: Mariano Damián BARBOSA, Nicolás Gabriel SÁNCHEZ, Cristian Carlos VILLAGRA, Paulo Andrés FERRARI, Facundo Hernan QUIROGA, Oscar Adrián AHUMADA, Marcelo Daniel GALLARDO (67 Diego Mario BUONANOTTE Rende), Rubens Oscar SAMBUEZA (84 Matías Enrique ABELAIRAS), Augusto Matías FERNÁNDEZ (84 Mauro Damián ROSALES), Radamel Falcao GARCÍA Zárete, Cristian Gastón FABBIANI. DT: Néstor Raúl GOROSITO
Sent off: García (90+3)
Goals: Álvaro FERNÁNDEZ Gay (40), Marcelo Nicolás LODEIRO Benítez (73), Mauricio VICTORINO (90+5).

CLUB NACIONAL ASUNCIÓN – CD UNIVERSIDAD SAN MARTÍN 1-1 (0-1)
Estadio General Pablo Rojas (La Olla), Asunción, 7.04.2009
Referee: Paulo César DE OLIVEIRA (BRA), Attendance: 193
CLUB NACIONAL ASUNCIÓN: Ignacio Oscar DON, Arnaldo Andrés ESPÍNOLA Benítez, Raúl Eduardo PIRIS, Glaucineis Martins da Silva "INCA", Marcos Antonio MELGAREJO, Jorge Daniel NÚÑEZ Espínola (78 Herminio Antonio MIRANDA Ovelar), Carlos Luis RUIZ Peralta (66 Gustavo David NOGUERA Domínguez), Ignacio Ramón CÁCERES Cabañas, Fabio ESCOBAR Benítez, Guillermo Alexis BELTRÁN, Éder Ricardo GODOY Rojas (55 Júlio César ORTELLADO Melgarejo). DT: Daniel Eduardo RASCHLE Matucheski
CD UNIVERSIDAD SAN MARTÍN: Leao BUTRÓN Gotuzzo, Christian Guillermo Martín RAMOS Garagay, Jorge Enrique REYES Condori, Guillermo Alejandro GIUZASOLA La Rosa, Guillermo Sandro SALAS Suarez, José Luis DÍAZ Sulca, Pedro Alexandro GARCÍA De La Cruz (69 Ronald QUINTEROS Sánchez), John Cristopher HINOSTROZA Guzmán (81 Orlando ALLENDE Huby), Josepmir Aarón BALLÓN Villacorta, Martín Enrique ARZUAGA Coronel (75 Carlos Alberto PÉREZ Alcazar), Gonzalo Emanuel LUDUEÑA. DT: Víctor Hugo RIVERA Coronado
Sent off: Melgarejo (90+3) / Ramos (89)
Goals: Fabio ESCOBAR Benítez (67) / Martín Enrique ARZUAGA Coronel (41).

CA RIVER PLATE BUENOS AIRES – CLUB NACIONAL MONTEVIDEO 0-0
Estadio Antonio V.Liberti (El Monumental), Buenos Aires, 7.04.2009
Referee: Sálvio Spínola FAGUNDES Filho (BRA), Attendance: 32.000
CA RIVER PLATE: Mariano Damián BARBOSA, Nicolás Gabriel SÁNCHEZ, Cristian Carlos VILLAGRA (63 Mauro Damián ROSALES), Paulo Andrés FERRARI, Gustavo Daniel CABRAL, Oscar Adrián AHUMADA, Marcelo Daniel GALLARDO, Rubens Oscar SAMBUEZA, Diego Armando BARRADO (76 Gustavo Martín FERNÁNDEZ), Radamel Falcao GARCÍA Zárete, Cristian Gastón FABBIANI. DT: Néstor Raúl GOROSITO
CLUB NACIONAL MONTEVIDEO: Rodrigo Martín MUÑOZ Salomón, Federico Hernán DOMÍNGUEZ, Mauricio Bernardo VICTORINO Dansilio, Matiás Nicolás RODRÍGUEZ, Hugo Diego ARISMENDI, Ángel Alejandro MORALES Santos (71 Marcos Gustavo MONDAINI), Marcelo Nicolás LODEIRO Benítez, Adrián Marcelo ROMERO González, Óscar Javier MORALES Albornoz, Álvaro FERNÁNDEZ Gay (41 Mauricio Ernesto PEREYRA Antonini), Alexander Jesús MEDINAReobasco (90 Sergio Rubén BLANCO Soto). DT: Gerardo Cono PELUSSO Boyrie

CD UNIVERSIDAD SAN MARTÍN – CLUB NACIONAL MONTEVIDEO 1-1 (0-0)
Estadio Alejandro Villanueva, Lima, 21.04.2009
Referee: Carlos Eugênio SIMÓN (BRA), Attendance: 5.000
CD UNIVERSIDAD SAN MARTÍN: Leao BUTRÓN Gotuzzo, Jorge Enrique REYES Condori, Guillermo Alejandro GIUZASOLA La Rosa, Guillermo Sandro SALAS Suarez, Pedro Alexandro GARCÍA De La Cruz, John Cristopher HINOSTROZA Guzmán (60 Carlos Alberto PÉREZ Alcazar), Ronald QUINTEROS Sánchez (38 Fernando Daniel DEL SOLAR Álvarez-Calderón, 72 Luis Gabriel GARCÍA), Victor Wilmer CARRILLO Gonzáles, Josepmir Aarón BALLÓN Villacorta, Martín Enrique ARZUAGA Coronel, Gonzalo Emanuel LUDUEÑA. DT: Víctor Hugo RIVERA Coronado
CLUB NACIONAL MONTEVIDEO: Rodrigo Martín MUÑOZ Salomón, Federico Hernán DOMÍNGUEZ, Mauricio Bernardo VICTORINO Dansilio, Matiás Nicolás RODRÍGUEZ, Hugo Diego ARISMENDI, Marcelo Nicolás LODEIRO Benítez, Adrián Marcelo ROMERO González, Óscar Javier MORALES Albornoz, Álvaro FERNÁNDEZ Gay (62 Mauricio Ernesto PEREYRA Antonini), Santiago Damián GARCÍA Correa (70 Ángel Alejandro MORALES Santos), Marcos Gustavo MONDAINI (81 Sergio Rubén BLANCO Soto). DT: Gerardo Cono PELUSSO Boyrie
Goals: Gonzalo Emanuel LUDUEÑA (88) / Marcos Gustavo MONDAINI (74).

CLUB NACIONAL ASUNCIÓN – CA RIVER PLATE BUENOS AIRES 4-2 (0-1)
Estadio Defensores del Chaco, Asunción, 23.04.2009
Referee: LEONARDO GACIBA da Silva (BRA), Attendance: 3.000
CLUB NACIONAL ASUNCIÓN: Ignacio Oscar DON, Gustavo David NOGUERA Domínguez, Herminio Antonio MIRANDA Ovelar, Raúl Eduardo PIRIS, Ricardo MAZACOTTE, Marcos Hernán RIVEROS, Glaucineis Martins da Silva "INCA", Ignacio Ramón CÁCERES Cabañas, Fabio ESCOBAR Benítez (65 Jorge Daniel NÚÑEZ Espínola), Héber Alberto ARRIOLA (69 Carlos Luis RUIZ Peralta), Guillermo Alexis BELTRÁN (82 Júlio César ORTELLADO Melgarejo). DT: Daniel Eduardo RASCHLE Matucheski
CA RIVER PLATE: Mario Daniel VEGA, Nicolás Gabriel SÁNCHEZ, Paulo Andrés FERRARI, Danilo Telmo GERLO, Gustavo Daniel CABRAL (70 Marcelo Daniel GALLARDO), Oscar Adrián AHUMADA, Rubens Oscar SAMBUEZA (70 Mauro Damián ROSALES), Nicolás Mario DOMINGO (46 Matías Enrique ABELAIRAS), Diego Mario BUONANOTTE Rende, Radamel Falcao GARCÍA Zárete, Cristian Gastón FABBIANI. DT: Néstor Raúl GOROSITO
Sent off: Buonanotte (59)
Goals: Fabio ESCOBAR Benítez (48 penalty), Jorge Daniel NÚÑEZ Espínola (66, 79), Carlos Luis RUIZ Peralta (74) / Radamel Falcao GARCÍA Zárete (44 penalty), Marcelo Daniel GALLARDO (82).

CLUB NACIONAL MONTEVIDEO – CLUB NACIONAL ASUNCIÓN 3-1 (1-1)
Estadio Centenario, Montevideo, 30.04.2009
Referee: René Marcelo ORTUBÉ Betancourt (BOL)
CLUB NACIONAL MONTEVIDEO: Rodrigo Martín MUÑOZ Salomón, Federico Hernán DOMÍNGUEZ (22 Pablo CABALLERO González), Mauricio Bernardo VICTORINO Dansilio, Sebastián COATES Nion, Hugo Diego ARISMENDI (67 Ángel Alejandro MORALES Santos), Marcelo Nicolás LODEIRO Benítez, Adrián Marcelo ROMERO González, Óscar Javier MORALES Albornoz, Álvaro FERNÁNDEZ Gay (78 Sergio Rubén BLANCO Soto), Santiago Damián GARCÍA Correa, Marcos Gustavo MONDAINI. DT: Gerardo Cono PELUSSO Boyrie
CLUB NACIONAL ASUNCIÓN: Derlis Venancio GÓMEZ López, Diego Raúl ARÉVALOS, Arnaldo Andrés ESPÍNOLA Benítez, Gustavo David NOGUERA Domínguez, Herminio Antonio MIRANDA Ovelar, Marcos Hernán RIVEROS, Marcos Antonio MELGAREJO, Jorge Daniel NÚÑEZ Espínola, Carlos Luis RUIZ Peralta, Gustavo Eliseo MORÍNIGO Vázquez (66 Raúl Eduardo PIRIS), Héber Alberto ARRIOLA. DT: Daniel Eduardo RASCHLE Matucheski
Sent off: Miranda (62)
Goals: Hugo Diego ARISMENDI (29), Sebastián COATES Nion (80), Marcelo Nicolás LODEIRO Benítez (90+1) / Jorge Daniel NÚÑEZ Espínola (9).

CA RIVER PLATE BUENOS AIRES – CD UNIVERSIDAD SAN MARTIN 3-0 (2-0)
Estadio Antonio V.Liberti (El Monumental), Buenos Aires, 30.04.2009
Referee: Carlos Arecio AMARILLA Demarqui (PAR), Attendance: 5.000
CA RIVER PLATE: Juan Marcelo OJEDA, Nicolás Gabriel SÁNCHEZ, Cristian Carlos VILLAGRA, Danilo Telmo GERLO, Rodrigo Javier ARCHUBI, Rubens Oscar SAMBUEZA, Robert Mario FLORES Bitolfi, Nicolás Mario DOMINGO, Diego Armando BARRADO, Gustavo Leonardo BOU, Gustavo Martín FERNÁNDEZ (78 Cristian Gastón FABBIANI). DT: Néstor Raúl GOROSITO
CD UNIVERSIDAD SAN MARTÍN: Leao BUTRÓN Gotuzzo, Christian Guillermo Martín RAMOS Garagay, Jorge Enrique REYES Condori, Guillermo Alejandro GIUZASOLA La Rosa, Guillermo Sandro SALAS Suarez, Pedro Alexandro GARCÍA De La Cruz (67 Carlos Alberto PÉREZ Alcazar), Carlos Osvaldo FERNÁNDEZ Maldonado, John Cristopher HINOSTROZA Guzmán (68 Josepmir Aarón BALLÓN Villacorta), Victor Wilmer CARRILLO Gonzáles, Martín Enrique ARZUAGA Coronel, Gonzalo Emanuel LUDUEÑA (71 Fernando Daniel DEL SOLAR Álvarez-Calderón). DT: Víctor Hugo RIVERA Coronado
Goals: Gustavo Leonardo BOU (17), Rubens Oscar SAMBUEZA (41), Diego A. BARRADO (60).

1	NACIONAL MONTEVIDEO	6	4	2	0	12	3	14
2	UNIVER. SAN MARTÍN	6	2	2	2	7	9	8
3	River Plate	6	2	1	3	7	9	7
4	Nacional Asunción	6	1	1	4	7	12	4

GROUP 4

DEFENSOR SPORTING CLUB – CD AMÉRICA DE CALI 1-0 (1-0)
Estadio Centenario, Montevideo, 10.02.2009
Referee: Enrique Roberto OSSÉS Zencovich (CHI), Attendance: 12.734
DEFENSOR SPORTING CLUB: Martín Andrés SILVA Leites, Jorge Wiston CURBELO-Gari, Mario Pablo RISSO, Pablo Daniel GAGLIANONE De León, Sergio Sebastián ARIOSA, Diego Alejandro DE SOUZA Carballo (73 Marcos Antonio García Nascimento "NASA"), Miguel Angel AMADO Alanís, Julio Javier MARCHANT (82 Carlos Richard DÍAZ), Pablo César PINTOS Cabral, Diego Daniel VERA Méndez, Mauro Adrián VILA Wilkins (73 Diego FERREIRA). DT: Jorge Orosmán DA SILVA Etcheberrito
CD AMÉRICA DE CALI: Julián Andrés MESA Orrego, Pedro Pablo TAVIMA Alba, Juan Camilo ANGULO Villegas, Gustavo Andrés VICTORIA Rave, Diego Ferney CHARÁ Zamora, Jhon Jairo VALENCIA Ortiz, Paulo César ARANGO Ambuila, Alexander DEL CASTILLO Molina, Jong Harold VIAFARA Campo Ramos, Wilmer PARRA Cadena (74 Víctor Javier CORTÉS), Gustavo Adrián RAMOS Vásquez. DT: Diego Edison UMAÑA
Goal: Pablo Daniel GAGLIANONE De León (38).

SÃO PAULO FC – CD INDEPENDIENTE MEDELLÍN 1-1 (0-0)
Estádio Cícero Pompeu de Toledo (Morumbí), São Paulo, 18.02.2009
Referee: Sergio Fabián PEZZOTTA (ARG), Attendance: 30.375
SÃO PAULO FC: João BOSCO de Freitas Chaves, ANDRÉ Gonçalves DIAS, João MIRANDA de Souza Filho, RENATO Assis da SILVA (87 ANDRÉ Luiz Barretto Silva LIMA), JORGE WAGNER Goes Conceição, Anderson HERNANES de Carvalho Andrade, JEAN Raphael Vanderlei Moreira, HUGO Henrique Assis do Nascimento (63 DAGOBERTO Pelentier), José "ZÉ" LUIS Santos da Visitação (84 Marcos AROUCA da Silva), WASHINGTON Stécanelo Cerqueira, Humberlito BORGES Teixeira. DT: MURICY RAMALHO
CD INDEPENDIENTE MEDELLÍN: Aldo Antonio BOBADILLA Ávalos, Andrés Felipe ORTIZ Agudelo, Jair BENÍTEZ Sinisterra, Samuel Antonio VANEGAS Luna, Juan Esteban ORTIZ Blandón, Isidro Ramón CANDIÁ Morales (73 Rafael Arlex CASTILLO Galviz), Juan David MURIEL Crúz, Iván Arturo CORREDOR Hurtado (89 Ricardo CALLE Estrada), John Javier RESTREPO Pérez, Jackson Arley MARTÍNEZ Valencia, Diego Aroldo CABRERA Flores (75 Luis Carlos ARIAS Cardona). DT: Santiago ESCOBAR Saldarriaga
Goals: Humberlito BORGES Teixeira (90+2) / Luis Carlos ARIAS Cardona (79).

CD INDEPENDIENTE MEDELLÍN – DEFENSOR SPORTING CLUB 0-0
Estadio Atanasio Girardot, Medellín, 24.02.2009
Referee: Carlos Alfredo VERA Rodríguez (ECU), Attendance: 12.734
CD INDEPENDIENTE MEDELLÍN: Aldo Antonio BOBADILLA Ávalos, Andrés Felipe ORTIZ Agudelo (73 Rafael Arlex CASTILLO Galviz), Jair BENÍTEZ Sinisterra, Samuel Antonio VANEGAS Luna, Juan Esteban ORTIZ Blandón, Isidro Ramón CANDIÁ Morales (46 William Francisco ARBOLEDA Perea), Juan David MURIEL Crúz, Iván Arturo CORREDOR Hurtado, John Javier RESTREPO Pérez, Jackson Arley MARTÍNEZ Valencia, Diego Aroldo CABRERA Flores (56 Luis Carlos ARIAS Cardona). DT: Santiago ESCOBAR Saldarriaga
DEFENSOR SPORTING CLUB: Martín Andrés SILVA Leites, Jorge Wiston CURBELO-Gari, Mario Pablo RISSO, Pablo Daniel GAGLIANONE De León (76 Diego FERREIRA), Sergio Sebastián ARIOSA, Diego Alejandro DE SOUZA Carballo, Miguel Angel AMADO Alanís, Julio Javier MARCHANT (84 Leandro Daniel CABRERA Sasla), Pablo César PINTOS Cabral, Diego Daniel VERA Méndez, Mauro Adrián VILA Wilkins (63 Rodrigo Nicanor MORA). DT: Jorge Orosmán DA SILVA Etcheberrito

CD AMÉRICA DE CALI – SÃO PAULO FC 1-3 (0-2)
Estadio Pascual Guerrero, Cali, 5.03.2009
Referee: Héctor Wálter BALDASSI (ARG), Attendance: 15.116
CD AMÉRICA DE CALI: Julián Andrés MESA Orrego, Pedro Pablo TAVIMA Alba, Juan Camilo ANGULO Villegas, José Iván VÉLEZ Castillo, Diego Ferney CHARÁ Zamora, José Harrison OTÁLVARO Arce (70 Wilmer PARRA Cadena), Jhon Jairo VALENCIA Ortiz, Paulo César ARANGO Ambuila, Jong Harold VIAFARA Campo Ramos, Gustavo Adrián RAMOS Vásquez, Víctor Javier CORTÉS. DT: Diego Edison UMAÑA
SÃO PAULO FC: ROGÉRIO CENI, ANDRÉ Gonçalves DIAS, João MIRANDA de Souza Filho, JÚNIOR CÉSAR Eduardo Machado, RENATO Assis da SILVA, JORGE WAGNER Goes Conceição, Anderson HERNANES de Carvalho Andrade, JEAN Raphael Vanderlei Moreira, José "ZÉ" LUIS Santos da Visitação, WASHINGTON Stécanelo Cerqueira (88 DAGOBERTO Pelentier), Humberlito BORGES Teixeira. DT: MURICY RAMALHO
Goals: Víctor Javier CORTÉS (85) /
WASHINGTON Stécanelo Cerqueira (2, 27), Humberlito BORGES Teixeira (49).

CD AMÉRICA DE CALI – CD INDEPENDIENTE MEDELLÍN 1-1 (0-0)
Estadio Pascual Guerrero, Cali, 10.03.2009
Referee: Luis Francisco PEÑUELA (COL)
CD AMÉRICA DE CALI: Julián Andrés MESA Orrego, Pedro Pablo TAVIMA Alba, Juan Camilo ANGULO Villegas, José Iván VÉLEZ Castillo, Diego Ferney CHARÁ Zamora (73 José Harrison OTÁLVARO Arce), Jhon Jairo VALENCIA Ortiz, Paulo César ARANGO Ambuila, Jong Harold VIAFARA Campo Ramos, Wilmer PARRA Cadena (68 Gabriel Arturo TORRES Tejada), Gustavo Adrián RAMOS Vásquez, Víctor Javier CORTÉS (46 Carlos Enrique VALDÉS Parra). DT: Diego Edison UMAÑA
CD INDEPENDIENTE MEDELLÍN: Aldo Antonio BOBADILLA Ávalos, Andrés Felipe ORTIZ Agudelo, Ricardo CALLE Estrada, Jair BENÍTEZ Sinisterra, Samuel Antonio VANEGAS Luna, Roger CAÑAS Henao, Isidro Ramón CANDIÁ Morales (63 William Francisco ARBOLEDA Perea), Juan David MURIEL Crúz, Iván Arturo CORREDOR Hurtado (78 Diego Aroldo CABRERA Flores), John Javier RESTREPO Pérez, Jackson Arley MARTÍNEZ Valencia (89 Rafael Arlex CASTILLO Galviz). DT: Santiago ESCOBAR Saldarriaga
Goals: Samuel Antonio VANEGAS Luna (81 own goal) / Samuel Antonio VANEGAS Luna (53).

CD INDEPENDIENTE MEDELLÍN – CD AMÉRICA DE CALI 0-0
Estadio Atanasio Girardot, Medellín, 17.03.2009
Referee: Óscar Julián RUIZ Acosta (COL), Attendance: 12.465
CD INDEPENDIENTE MEDELLÍN: Aldo Antonio BOBADILLA Ávalos, Andrés Felipe ORTIZ Agudelo, Jair BENÍTEZ Sinisterra, Samuel Antonio VANEGAS Luna, Roger CAÑAS Henao, Isidro Ramón CANDIÁ Morales (46 Luis Carlos ARIAS Cardona), Rafael Arlex CASTILLO Galviz (65 William Francisco ARBOLEDA Perea), Juan David MURIEL Crúz, Iván Arturo CORREDOR Hurtado, John Javier RESTREPO Pérez, Diego Aroldo CABRERA Flores (61 Carlos Daniel HIDALGO Cadena). DT: Santiago ESCOBAR Saldarriaga
CD AMÉRICA DE CALI: Julián Andrés MESA Orrego, Carlos Enrique VALDÉS Parra, Pedro Pablo TAVIMA Alba, Juan Camilo ANGULO Villegas, José Iván VÉLEZ Castillo, José Harrison OTÁLVARO Arce (46 Paulo César ARANGO Ambuila), Jhon Jairo VALENCIA Ortiz, Jorge Eliécer BANGUERO Viáfara, Jong Harold VIAFARA Campo Ramos (46 Víctor Javier CORTÉS), Wilmer PARRA Cadena (78 Diego Ferney CHARÁ Zamora), Gustavo Adrián RAMOS Vásquez. DT: Diego Edison UMAÑA
Sent off: Angulo (78)

DEFENSOR SPORTING CLUB – SÃO PAULO FC 0-1 (0-1)
Estadio Centenario, Montevideo, 18.03.2009
Referee: Carlos Arecio AMARILLA Demarqui (PAR), Attendance: 19.339
DEFENSOR SPORTING CLUB: Martín Andrés SILVA Leites, Jorge Wiston CURBELO-Gari, Mario Pablo RISSO, Pablo Daniel GAGLIANONE De León (71 Diego FERREIRA), Sergio Sebastián ARIOSA, Diego Alejandro DE SOUZA Carballo (61 Álvaro Damián NAVARRO Bica), Miguel Angel AMADO Alanís, Julio Javier MARCHANT, Pablo César PINTOS Cabral, Diego Daniel VERA Méndez, Rodrigo Nicanor MORA (61 Mauro Adrián VILA Wilkins). DT: Jorge Orosmán DA SILVA Etcheberrito
SÃO PAULO FC: ROGÉRIO CENI, RODRIGO Baldasso Da Costa, João MIRANDA de Souza Filho, JÚNIOR CÉSAR Eduardo Machado (90+1 AISLAN Paulo Lotici Back), RENATO Assis da SILVA, JORGE WAGNER Goes Conceição, Anderson HERNANES de Carvalho Andrade, Marcos AROUCA da Silva (80 RICHARLYSON Barbosa Felisbino), JEAN Raphael Vanderlei Moreira, WASHINGTON Stécanelo Cerqueira, Humberlito BORGES Teixeira. DT: MURICY RAMALHO
Goal: Humberlito BORGES Teixeira (39).

SÃO PAULO FC – DEFENSOR SPORTING CLUB 2-1 (0-1)
Estádio Cícero Pompeu de Toledo (Morumbí), São Paulo, 9.04.2009
Referee: Carlos Luis CHANDÍA Alarcón (CHI), Attendance: 47.205
SÃO PAULO FC: ROGÉRIO CENI, ANDRÉ Gonçalves DIAS, João MIRANDA de Souza Filho, JÚNIOR CÉSAR Eduardo Machado, JORGE WAGNER Goes Conceição, Anderson HERNANES de Carvalho Andrade, Marcos AROUCA da Silva, JEAN Raphael Vanderlei Moreira, José "ZÉ" LUIS Santos da Visitação (54 DAGOBERTO Pelentier), WASHINGTON Stécanelo Cerqueira, Humberlito BORGES Teixeira (85 RENATO Assis da SILVA). DT: MURICY RAMALHO
DEFENSOR SPORTING CLUB: Martín Andrés SILVA Leites, Jorge Wiston CURBELO-Gari, Mario Pablo RISSO, Carlos Richard DÍAZ (76 Marcos Antonio García Nascimento "NASA"), Robert Fabián HERRERA, Leandro Daniel CABRERA Sasla, Diego Alejandro DE SOUZA Carballo, Miguel Angel AMADO Alanís, Diego FERREIRA (80 Jonathan TECHERA), Julio Javier MARCHANT, Rodrigo Nicanor MORA (62 Pablo Daniel GAGLIANONE De León). DT: Jorge Orosmán DA SILVA Etcheberrito
Sent off: De Souza (89)
Goals: Humberlito BORGES Teixeira (70, 74) / Diego Alejandro DE SOUZA Carballo (38).

CD INDEPENDIENTE MEDELLÍN – SÃO PAULO FC 2-1 (2-1)
Estadio Atanasio Girardot, Medellín, 15.04.2009
Referee: Carlos Alfredo VERA Rodríguez (ECU)
CD INDEPENDIENTE MEDELLÍN: Aldo Antonio BOBADILLA Ávalos, Andrés Felipe ORTIZ Agudelo, Jair BENÍTEZ Sinisterra, Samuel Antonio VANEGAS Luna, Juan Guillermo CUADRADO Bello (73 Ricardo CALLE Estrada), Roger CAÑAS Henao, Rafael Arlex CASTILLO Galviz, Iván Arturo CORREDOR Hurtado (82 Ayron DEL VALLE Rodriguez), John Javier RESTREPO Pérez, Luis Carlos ARIAS Cardona, Diego Aroldo CABRERA Flores (66 William Francisco ARBOLEDA Perea). DT: Santiago ESCOBAR Saldarriaga
SÃO PAULO FC: João BOSCO de Freitas Chaves, WÁGNER DINIZ Gomes de Araújo (46 WELLINGTON Aparecido Martins), RODRIGO Baldasso Da Costa, RENATO Assis da SILVA, AISLAN Paulo Lotici Back, EDUARDO Nascimento COSTA (80 OSCAR dos Santos Emboaba Junior), JEAN Raphael Vanderlei Moreira, HUGO Henrique Assis do Nascimento, RICHARLYSON Barbosa Felisbino, DAGOBERTO Pelentier, ANDRÉ Luiz Barreto Silva LIMA. DT: MURICY RAMALHO
Goals: Diego Aroldo CABRERA Flores (17), Rafael Arlex CASTILLO Galviz (27) /
ANDRÉ Luiz Barreto Silva LIMA (39).

CD AMÉRICA DE CALI – DEFENSOR SPORTING CLUB 0-0
Estadio Pascual Guerrero, Cali, 16.04.2009
Referee: Saúl Esteban LAVERNI (ARG)
CD AMÉRICA DE CALI: Julián Andrés MESA Orrego, Carlos Enrique VALDÉS Parra, Pedro Pablo TAVIMA Alba, José Iván VÉLEZ Castillo, Diego Ferney CHARÁ Zamora, José Harrison OTÁLVARO Arce, Jhon Jairo VALENCIA Ortiz, Paulo César ARANGO Ambuila, Jong Harold VIAFARA Campo Ramos, Wilson David MORELO López (65 Wilmer PARRA Cadena), Víctor Javier CORTÉS. DT: Diego Edison UMAÑA
DEFENSOR SPORTING CLUB: Martín Andrés SILVA Leites, Jorge Wiston CURBELO-Gari, Mario Pablo RISSO, Pablo Daniel GAGLIANONE De León, Carlos Richard DÍAZ (68 Mauro Adrián VILA Wilkins), Sergio Sebastián ARIOSA, Miguel Angel AMADO Alanís, Marcos Antonio García Nascimento "NASA" (74 Jonathan TECHERA), Julio Javier MARCHANT (85 Diego FERREIRA), Pablo César PINTOS Cabral, Rodrigo Nicanor MORA. DT: Jorge Orosmán DA SILVA Etcheberrito
Sent off: Mora (80)

DEFENSOR SPORTING CLUB – CD INDEPENDIENTE MEDELLÍN 4-3 (2-1)
Estadio Centenario, Montevideo, 22.04.2009
Referee: Federico José BELIGOY (ARG)
DEFENSOR SPORTING CLUB: Martín Andrés SILVA Leites, Jorge Wiston CURBELO-Gari, Mario Pablo RISSO, Pablo Daniel GAGLIANONE De León, Sergio Sebastián ARIOSA (78 Mauro Adrián VILA Wilkins), Diego Alejandro DE SOUZA Carballo, Miguel Angel AMADO Alanís, Julio Javier MARCHANT (70 Diego FERREIRA), Pablo César PINTOS Cabral, Diego Daniel VERA Méndez (74 Jonathan TECHERA), Álvaro Damián NAVARRO Bica. DT: Jorge Orosmán DA SILVA Etcheberrito
CD INDEPENDIENTE MEDELLÍN: Aldo Antonio BOBADILLA Ávalos, Andrés Felipe ORTIZ Agudelo, Jair BENÍTEZ Sinisterra, Samuel Antonio VANEGAS Luna (46 Juan David MURIEL Crúz), Juan Guillermo CUADRADO Bello, Juan Esteban ORTIZ Blandón (75 William Francisco ARBOLEDA Perea), Rafael Arlex CASTILLO Galviz (78 Roger CAÑAS Henao), Iván Arturo CORREDOR Hurtado, John Javier RESTREPO Pérez, Luis Carlos ARIAS Cardona, Diego Aroldo CABRERA Flores. DT: Santiago ESCOBAR Saldarriaga
Sent off: Benítez (85)
Goals: Álvaro Damián NAVARRO Bica (14, 90+4), Diego Daniel VERA Méndez (35), 3-2 Diego Alejandro DE SOUZA Carballo (82) / Luis Carlos ARIAS Cardona (19), Andrés Felipe ORTIZ Agudelo (77), Diego Aroldo CABRERA Flores (89).

SÃO PAULO FC – CD AMÉRICA DE CALI 2-1 (0-1)
Estádio Cícero Pompeu de Toledo (Morumbí), São Paulo, 22.04.2009
Referee: Carlos Manuel TORRES (PAR), Attendance: 23.221
SÃO PAULO FC: João BOSCO de Freitas Chaves, RODRIGO Baldasso Da Costa (88 AISLAN Paulo Lotici Back), João MIRANDA de Souza Filho, JÚNIOR CÉSAR Eduardo Machado, RENATO Assis da SILVA, JORGE WAGNER Goes Conceição, Anderson HERNANES de Carvalho Andrade, JEAN Raphael Vanderlei Moreira, WASHINGTON Stécanelo Cerqueira, DAGOBERTO Pelentier, Humberlito BORGES Teixeira (83 HUGO Henrique Assis do Nascimento). DT: MURICY RAMALHO
CD AMÉRICA DE CALI: Julián Andrés MESA Orrego, Carlos Enrique VALDÉS Parra, Pedro Pablo TAVIMA Alba, Juan Camilo ANGULO Villegas, Diego Ferney CHARÁ Zamora, Jorge Eliécer BANGUERO Viáfara, Paulo César ARANGO Ambuila (87 Andrés Felipe CASAÑAS Sanclemente), Alexander DEL CASTILLO Molina, Oscar Alejandro RESTREPO Ramírez (77 José Harrison OTÁLVARO Arce), Jong Harold VIAFARA Campo Ramos, Wilmer PARRA Cadena (82 Wilson David MORELO López). Assitant coach: Álexander ESCOBAR Ganan
Goals: DAGOBERTO Pelentier (57, 76) / Wilmer PARRA Cadena (8).

1	SÃO PAULO FC	6	4	1	1	10	6	13
2	DEFENSOR SPORTING	6	2	2	2	6	6	8
3	Independiente Medellín	6	1	4	1	7	7	7
4	América	6	0	3	3	3	7	3

GROUP 5

CD UNIVERSITARIO DE SUCRE – SOCIEDAD DEPORTIVO QUITO 1-1 (0-0)
Estadio Olímpico Patria, Sucre, 12.02.2009
Referee: Manuel Alejandro GARAY Evia (PER), Attendance: 15.000
CD UNIVERSITARIO DE SUCRE: Carlos Emilio LAMPE Porras, Pedro ZABALA Pereira, Ronald Tylor RIVERO Khun, Axel Daniel BEJARANO Nuñez, Mauricio SAUCEDO Guardia, José MARCELO GÓMEZ (81 DIMAS Roberto da Silva), Sacha Silvestre LIMA Castedo (74 Jesús Ronald GALLEGOS Vera), Ángel Martín AGUIRRE, Rolando RIBERA Menacho, Nicolás RAIMONDI Schiaffarino, Luis Hernán SILLERO. DT: Eduardo VILLEGAS
SOCIEDAD DEPORTIVO QUITO: Oswaldo Geovanny IBARRA Carabali (65 Bonard Patricio GARCÍA Zambrano), Bánner Geovanny CAICEDO Quiñónez, Isaac Bryan MINA Arboleda, Franklin Orlando COROZO Quiñónez, Luis Armando CHECA Villamar, Édwin Rolando TENORIO Montano, Tilson Oswaldo MINDA Suscal (46 José Luis CORTÉZ Arroyo), Luis Fernando SARITAMA Padilla, Daniel Nevil MINA Arísola (61 Mauricio Alejandro DONOSO Pérez), Martín Roberto MANDRA, Léider Calimenio PRECIADO Guerrero. DT: Rubén Darío INSÚA Carballo
Goals: José MARCELO GÓMEZ (51) / Mauricio Alejandro DONOSO Pérez (68).

CRUZEIRO EC – CA ESTUDIANTES DE LA PLATA 3-0 (0-0)
Estádio Governador Magalhães Pinto (Mineirão), Belo Horizonte, 19.02.2009
Referee: Carlos Arecio AMARILLA Demarqui (PAR), Attendance: 33.969
CRUZEIRO EC: FÁBIO Deivson Lopes Maciel, JONATHAN Cícero Moreira, THIAGO HELENO Henrique Ferreira, LEONARDO Fabiano da SILVA e Silva, FABRICIO de Sousa (81 ELICARLOS Souza Santos), Fernando Alves Santa Clara "FERNANDINHO", Antônio Marcos da Silva Filho "MARQUINHOS PARANÁ", WÁGNER Ferreira dos Santos, HENRIQUE Pacheco de Lima (63 JANCARLOS de Oliveira Barros), WELLINGTON "PAULISTA" Pereira do Nascimento, THIAGO RIBEIRO Cardoso (60 KLÉBER Giacomace de Souza Freitas). DT: ADILSON Dias BATISTA
CA ESTUDIANTES DE LA PLATA: Mariano Gonzalo ANDÚJAR, Leandro DESÁBATO, Cristian Ariel CELLAY, Marcos Alberto ANGELERI, Germán David RÉ (76 Cristian Nicolás SÁNCHEZ Prette), Enzo Nicolás PÉREZ (79 Gastón Nicolás FERNÁNDEZ), Juan Sebastián VERÓN, Rodrigo BRAÑA, Leandro Damián BENÍTEZ, Juan Manuel SALGUEIRO Silva, Mauro BOSELLI (71 José Luis CALDERÓN). DT: Leonardo Rubén ASTRADA
Sent off: Kléber (75)
Goals: Fernando Alves Santa Clara "FERNANDINHO" (63 penalty),
KLÉBER Giacomace de Souza Freitas (69, 72).

SOCIEDAD DEPORTIVO QUITO – CRUZEIRO EC 1-1 (0-1)
Estadio Olímpico Atahualpa, Quito, 25.02.2009
Referee: Georges BUCKLEY (PER), Attendance: 11.000
SOCIEDAD DEPORTIVO QUITO: Bonard Patricio GARCÍA Zambrano, Bánner Geovanny CAICEDO Quiñónez, Isaac Bryan MINA Arboleda, Franklin Orlando COROZO Quiñónez, Luis Armando CHECA Villamar, José Luis CORTÉZ Arroyo (46 Tilson Oswaldo MINDA Suscal), Édwin Rolando TENORIO Montano, Daniel Nevil MINA Arísola (46 Luis Fernando SARITAMA Padilla), Mauricio Alejandro DONOSO Pérez, Martín Roberto MANDRA, Nicolás Geovanny ASENCIO Espinoza (62 Léider Calimenio PRECIADO Guerrero). DT: Rubén Darío INSÚA Carballo
CRUZEIRO EC: FÁBIO Deivson Lopes Maciel, JONATHAN Cícero Moreira, Leonardo "LÉO" FORTUNATO dos Santos, LEONARDO Fabiano da SILVA e Silva, FABRICIO de Sousa, Fernando Alves Santa Clara "FERNANDINHO", Antônio Marcos da Silva Filho "MARQUINHOS PARANÁ", RAMIRES Santos do Nascimento (79 Hiziel Souza SOARES), WÁGNER Ferreira dos Santos (67 HENRIQUE Pacheco de Lima), WELLINGTON "PAULISTA" Pereira do Nascimento, THIAGO RIBEIRO Cardoso (73 ELICARLOS Souza Santos). DT: ADILSON Dias BATISTA
Sent off: Checa (52) / Wellington Paulista (42), Fabricio (65)
Goals: Bánner Geovanny CAICEDO Quiñónez (90+1) / RAMIRES Santos do Nascimento (38).

CA ESTUDIANTES DE LA PLATA – CD UNIVERSITARIO DE SUCRE 1-0 (1-0)
Estadio Ciudad de La Plata (Único), La Plata, 26.02.2009
Referee: Pablo Antonio POZO Quinteros (CHI)
CA ESTUDIANTES DE LA PLATA: Mariano Gonzalo ANDÚJAR, Leandro DESÁBATO, Cristian Ariel CELLAY, Agustín ALAYES, Marcos Alberto ANGELERI, Matías Ariel SÁNCHEZ, Leandro Damián BENÍTEZ (57 Enzo Nicolás PÉREZ), Cristian Nicolás SÁNCHEZ Prette, Juan Manuel SALGUEIRO Silva, Gastón Nicolás FERNÁNDEZ (78 Diego Alberto GALVÁN), Mauro BOSELLI (69 José Luis CALDERÓN). DT: Leonardo Rubén ASTRADA
CD UNIVERSITARIO DE SUCRE: Carlos Emilio LAMPE Porras, Ángel Martín AGUIRRE, VANDERLEI dos Santos do Carlos, Pedro ZABALA Pereira, Ronald Tylor RIVERO Khun, Marvin Orlando BEJARANO Jiménez, Rolando RIBERA Menacho, Mauricio SAUCEDO Guardia, José MARCELO GÓMEZ (81 DIMAS Roberto da Silva), Sacha Silvestre LIMA Castedo (59 Nicolás RAIMONDI Schiaffarino), Luis Hernán SILLERO. DT: Eduardo VILLEGAS
Sent off: Aguirre (78)
Goal: Juan Manuel SALGUEIRO Silva (16).

CD UNIVERSITARIO DE SUCRE – CRUZEIRO EC 0-1 (0-1)
Estadio Olímpico Patria, Sucre, 4.03.2009
Referee: Roberto Carlos SILVERA Calcerrada (URU), Attendance: 25.000
CD UNIVERSITARIO DE SUCRE: Carlos Emilio LAMPE Porras, VANDERLEI dos Santos do Carlos, Pedro ZABALA Pereira, Ronald Tylor RIVERO Khun, Marvin Orlando BEJARANO Jiménez, Rolando RIBERA Menacho, Mauricio SAUCEDO Guardia (61 DIMAS Roberto da Silva), José MARCELO GÓMEZ (73 Jesús Ronald GALLEGOS Vera), Sacha Silvestre LIMA Castedo (79 Erland Gastón MEALLA Anachuri), Nicolás RAIMONDI Schiaffarino, Luis Hernán SILLERO. DT: Eduardo VILLEGAS
CRUZEIRO EC: FÁBIO Deivson Lopes Maciel, JONATHAN Cícero Moreira, Leonardo "LÉO" FORTUNATO dos Santos, LEONARDO Fabiano da SILVA e Silva, Fernando Alves Santa Clara "FERNANDINHO", Antônio Marcos da Silva Filho "MARQUINHOS PARANÁ", RAMIRES Santos do Nascimento (76 ELICARLOS Souza Santos), WÁGNER Ferreira dos Santos (65 Hiziel Souza SOARES), HENRIQUE Pacheco de Lima, THIAGO RIBEIRO Cardoso (54 JANCARLOS de Oliveira Barros), KLÉBER Giacomace de Souza Freitas. DT: ADILSON Dias BATISTA
Sent off: Kléber (68)
Goal: THIAGO RIBEIRO Cardoso (38).

SOCIEDAD DEPORTIVO QUITO – CA ESTUDIANTES DE LA PLATA 1-0 (0-0)
Estadio Olímpico Atahualpa, Quito, 10.03.2009
Referee: Juan Ernesto SOTO (VEN), Attendance: 8.030
SOCIEDAD DEPORTIVO QUITO: Bonard Patricio GARCÍA Zambrano, Bánner Geovanny CAICEDO Quiñónez, Isaac Bryan MINA Arboleda (46 Luis Alexis TENORIO Rivas), Franklin Orlando COROZO Quiñónez, José Luis CORTÉZ Arroyo, Édwin Rolando TENORIO Montano, Luis Fernando SARITAMA Padilla (71 Ángel Gabriel ESCOBAR Arce), Daniel Nevil MINA Arísola, Mauricio Alejandro DONOSO Pérez, Léider Calimenio PRECIADO Guerrero, Nicolás Geovanny ASENCIO Espinoza (46 Martín Roberto MANDRA). DT: Rubén Darío INSÚA Carballo
CA ESTUDIANTES DE LA PLATA: Mariano Gonzalo ANDÚJAR, Leandro DESÁBATO, Cristian Ariel CELLAY, Juan Manuel DÍAZ Martínez, Germán David RÉ (46 Agustín ALAYES), Matías Ariel SÁNCHEZ, Enzo Nicolás PÉREZ (60 Diego Alberto GALVÁN), Juan Sebastián VERÓN, Leandro Damián BENÍTEZ, Gastón Nicolás FERNÁNDEZ (57 José Luis CALDERÓN), Mauro BOSELLI. DT: Leonardo Rubén ASTRADA
Goal: Léider Calimenio PRECIADO Guerrero (85).

CRUZEIRO EC – CD UNIVERSITARIO DE SUCRE 2-0 (0-0)
Estádio Governador Magalhães Pinto (Mineirão), Belo Horizonte, 18.03.2009
Referee: Federico José BELIGOY (ARG), Attendance: 14.439
CRUZEIRO EC: FÁBIO Deivson Lopes Maciel, JONATHAN Cícero Moreira (86 JANCARLOS de Oliveira Barros), THIAGO HELENO Henrique Ferreira, LEONARDO Fabiano da SILVA e Silva, Juan Pablo SORÍN, FABRICIO de Sousa, Antônio Marcos da Silva Filho "MARQUINHOS PARANÁ", RAMIRES Santos do Nascimento, WÁGNER Ferreira dos Santos (16 GÉRSON "MAGRÃO" Alencar de Lima Junior), WELLINGTON "PAULISTA" Pereira do Nascimento, THIAGO RIBEIRO Cardoso (73 WANDERLEY dos Santos Monteiro Junior). DT: ADILSON Dias BATISTA
CD UNIVERSITARIO DE SUCRE: Carlos Emilio LAMPE Porras, Ángel Martín AGUIRRE, Pedro ZABALA Pereira, Ronald Tylor RIVERO Khun, Axel Daniel BEJARANO Nuñez, Rolando RIBERA Menacho, Mauricio SAUCEDO Guardia, José MARCELO GÓMEZ (86 VANDERLEI dos Santos do Carlos), Sacha Silvestre LIMA Castedo, Nicolás RAIMONDI Schiaffarino, Luis Hernán SILLERO (74 DIMAS Roberto da Silva). DT: Eduardo VILLEGAS
Sent off: Aguirre (62)
Goals: WELLINGTON "PAULISTA" Pereira do Nascimento (57 penalty, 90).

CA ESTUDIANTES DE LA PLATA – SOCIEDAD DEPORTIVO QUITO 4-0 (3-0)
Estadio Ciudad de La Plata (Único), La Plata, 19.03.2009
Referee: Carlos Eugênio SIMÓN (BRA), Attendance: 22.000
CA ESTUDIANTES DE LA PLATA: Mariano Gonzalo ANDÚJAR, Leandro DESÁBATO, Cristian Ariel CELLAY, Agustín ALAYES (35 Juan Manuel DÍAZ Martínez), Marcos Alberto ANGELERI, Enzo Nicolás PÉREZ, Juan Sebastián VERÓN, Rodrigo BRAÑA (65 Matías Ariel SÁNCHEZ), Leandro Damián BENÍTEZ, Gastón Nicolás FERNÁNDEZ (74 José Luis CALDERÓN), Mauro BOSELLI. DT: Alejandro Javier SABELLA
SOCIEDAD DEPORTIVO QUITO: Bonard Patricio GARCÍA Zambrano, Bánner Geovanny CAICEDO Quiñónez, Franklin Orlando COROZO Quiñónez, Luis Armando CHECA Villamar, José Luis CORTÉZ Arroyo, Édwin Rolando TENORIO Montano, Tilson Oswaldo MINDA Suscal, Luis Fernando SARITAMA Padilla (65 Ángel Gabriel ESCOBAR Arce), Daniel Nevil MINA Arísola (65 Mauricio Alejandro DONOSO Pérez), Martín Roberto MANDRA, Léider Calimenio PRECIADO Guerrero. DT: Rubén Darío INSÚA Carballo
Goals: Mauro BOSELLI (4, 25, 69), Enzo Nicolás PÉREZ (44).

CA ESTUDIANTES DE LA PLATA – CRUZEIRO EC 4-0 (2-0)
Estadio Ciudad de La Plata (Único), La Plata, 8.04.2009
Referee: Roberto Carlos SILVERA Calcerrada (URU), Attendance: 18.505
CA ESTUDIANTES DE LA PLATA: Mariano Gonzalo ANDÚJAR, Leandro DESÁBATO, Cristian Ariel CELLAY, Raúl Alejandro IBERBIA, Marcos Alberto ANGELERI, Enzo Nicolás PÉREZ, Juan Sebastián VERÓN (88 Matías Ariel SÁNCHEZ), Rodrigo BRAÑA, Leandro Damián BENÍTEZ, Gastón Nicolás FERNÁNDEZ (64 José Luis CALDERÓN), Mauro BOSELLI (69 Cristian Nicolás SÁNCHEZ Prette). DT: Alejandro Javier SABELLA
CRUZEIRO EC: FÁBIO Deivson Lopes Maciel, JONATHAN Cícero Moreira (46 BERNARDO Vieira de Souza), THIAGO HELENO Henrique Ferreira, JANCARLOS de Oliveira Barros (81 ELICARLOS Souza Santos), LEONARDO Fabiano da SILVA e Silva, FABRICIO de Sousa, Antônio Marcos da Silva Filho "MARQUINHOS PARANÁ", RAMIRES Santos do Nascimento, HENRIQUE Pacheco de Lima, GÉRSON "MAGRÃO" Alencar de Lima Junior, WELLINGTON "PAULISTA" Pereira do Nascimento (84 Hiziel Souza SOARES). DT: ADILSON Dias BATISTA
Goals: Juan Sebastián VERÓN (6), Gastón Nicolás FERNÁNDEZ (32),
Cristian Nicolás SÁNCHEZ Prette (74, 78).

SOCIEDAD DEPORTIVO QUITO – CD UNIVERSITARIO DE SUCRE 3-1 (2-1)
Estadio Olímpico Atahualpa, Quito, 14.04.2009
Referee: Marco Antonio RODRÍGUEZ Moreno (MEX), Attendance: 2.065
SOCIEDAD DEPORTIVO QUITO: Oswaldo Geovanny IBARRA Carabali, Bánner Geovanny CAICEDO Quiñónez, Isaac Bryan MINA Arboleda, Franklin Orlando COROZO Quiñónez (72 Luis Alexis TENORIO Rivas), Luis Armando CHECA Villamar, Édwin Rolando TENORIO Montano, Tilson Oswaldo MINDA Suscal, Luis Fernando SARITAMA Padilla, Mauricio Alejandro DONOSO Pérez, Léider Calimenio PRECIADO Guerrero (49 Bonard Patricio GARCÍA Zambrano), Nicolás Geovanny ASENCIO Espinoza (46 Jhonny Alejandro BALDEÓN Parreño). DT: Rubén Darío INSÚA Carballo   Sent off: Ibarra (47)
CD UNIVERSITARIO DE SUCRE: Juan Carlos ROBLES Rodríguez, VANDERLEI dos Santos do Carlos, Ronald Tylor RIVERO Khun, Marvin Orlando BEJARANO Jiménez, Axel Daniel BEJARANO Nuñez, Rolando RIBERA Menacho, DIMAS Roberto da Silva (68 Luis Hernán SILLERO), Mauricio SAUCEDO Guardia (78 Nicolás Darío TUDOR Sánchez), Jesús Ronald GALLEGOS Vera, Sacha Silvestre LIMA Castedo (46 José MARCELO GÓMEZ), Nicolás RAIMONDI Schiaffarino. DT: Eduardo VILLEGAS
Goals: Luis Fernando SARITAMA Padilla (11, 60 penalty), Léider Calimenio PRECIADO Guerrero (42 penalty) / Nicolás RAIMONDI Schiaffarino (26).

CD UNIVERSITARIO DE SUCRE – CA ESTUDIANTES DE LA PLATA 0-0
Estadio Olímpico Patria, Sucre, 22.04.2009
Referee: Carlos Luis CHANDÍA Alarcón (CHI), Attendance: 17.000
CD UNIVERSITARIO DE SUCRE: Carlos Emilio LAMPE Porras, Ángel Martín AGUIRRE, Ronald Tylor RIVERO Khun, Marvin Orlando BEJARANO Jiménez, Axel Daniel BEJARANO Nuñez, Rolando RIBERA Menacho, DIMAS Roberto da Silva (85 Erland Gastón MEALLA Anachuri), Mauricio SAUCEDO Guardia, José MARCELO GÓMEZ (64 Sacha Silvestre LIMA Castedo), Jesús Ronald GALLEGOS Vera, Nicolás RAIMONDI Schiaffarino. DT: Eduardo VILLEGAS
CA ESTUDIANTES DE LA PLATA: Mariano Gonzalo ANDÚJAR, Leandro DESÁBATO, Cristian Ariel CELLAY, Marcos Alberto ANGELERI, Germán David RÉ, Enzo Nicolás PÉREZ, Juan Sebastián VERÓN, Rodrigo BRAÑA (85 Matías Ariel SÁNCHEZ), Leandro Damián BENÍTEZ, Gastón Nicolás FERNÁNDEZ (71 Diego Alberto GALVÁN), Mauro BOSELLI (68 José Luis CALDERÓN). DT: Alejandro Javier SABELLA

CRUZEIRO EC – SOCIEDAD DEPORTIVO QUITO 2-0 (2-0)
Estádio Governador Magalhães Pinto (Mineirão), Belo Horizonte, 22.04.2009
Referee: Carlos Arecio AMARILLA Demarqui (PAR), Attendance: 34.175
CRUZEIRO EC: FÁBIO Deivson Lopes Maciel, JONATHAN Cícero Moreira, Leonardo "LÉO" FORTUNATO dos Santos, LEONARDO Fabiano da SILVA e Silva, FABRICIO de Sousa, Antônio Marcos da Silva Filho "MARQUINHOS PARANÁ", RAMIRES Santos do Nascimento (80 HENRIQUE Pacheco de Lima), WÁGNER Ferreira dos Santos (64 THIAGO RIBEIRO Cardoso), GÉRSON "MAGRÃO" Alencar de Lima Junior, WELLINGTON "PAULISTA" Pereira do Nascimento (71 BERNARDO Vieira de Souza), KLÉBER Giacomace de Souza Freitas. DT: ADILSON BATISTA
SOCIEDAD DEPORTIVO QUITO: Bonard Patricio GARCÍA Zambrano, Bánner Geovanny CAICEDO Quiñónez, Isaac Bryan MINA Arboleda, Franklin Orlando COROZO Quiñónez, Luis Armando CHECA Villamar, Luis Alexis TENORIO Rivas, Édwin Rolando TENORIO Montano, Tilson Oswaldo MINDA Suscal, Mauricio Alejandro DONOSO Pérez, Léider Calimenio PRECIADO Guerrero (63 Ángel Gabriel ESCOBAR Arce), Nicolás Geovanny ASENCIO Espinoza (63 Jhonny Alejandro BALDEÓN Parreño). DT: Rubén Darío INSÚA Carballo
Sent off: Fabricio (48) / Donoso (48), Minda (58)
Goals: Leonardo "LÉO" FORTUNATO dos Santos (14), WÁGNER Ferreira dos Santos (26).

1	CRUZEIRO	6	4	1	1	9	5	13
2	ESTUDIANTES LA PLATA	6	3	1	2	9	4	10
3	Deportivo Quito	6	2	2	2	6	9	8
4	Universitario de Sucre	6	0	2	4	2	8	2

GROUP 6

CA LANÚS – CD "CHIVAS" GUADALAJARA SA 1-1 (0-1)
Estadio Ciudad de Lanús (La Fortaleza), Lanús, 11.02.2009
Referee: Roberto Carlos SILVERA Calcerrada (URU), Attendance: 4.885
CA LANÚS: Carlos Gustavo BOSSIO, Maximiliano Nicolás VELÁZQUEZ, Rodolfo Moisés GRAIEB (63 Eduardo Fabián LEDESMA), JADSON Viera Castro, Santiago Abel HOYOS, Matías Lionel FRITZLER, Diego Hernán VALERI, Sebastián Marcelo BLANCO, Sebastián SALOMÓN (74 Germán Ezequiel CANO), Diego Eduardo LAGOS (23 Nicolás Francisco RAMÍREZ), José Gustavo SAND. DT: Luis Francisco ZUBELDÍA
CD GUADALAJARA SA: Luis Ernesto MICHEL Vergara, Héctor REYNOSO López, Gonzalo PINEDA Reyes, José Jonny MAGALLÓN Oliva, Édgar Eduardo MEJÍA Virrete, Ramón Heriberto Cortez MORALES Higuera, Sergio Gabriel ÁVILA Valle (68 Francisco Juan MENDOZA Martínez), Sergio Amaury PONCE Villegas (59 Omar Alejandro ESPARZA Morales), Xavier Iván BÁEZ Gamiño, Marco Jhonfai FABIÁN de la Mora, Jared Francisco BORGETTI Echavarría (74 Javier HERNÁNDEZ Balcazar). DT: Efraín FLORES Mercado
Goals: José Gustavo SAND (90+3) / Sergio Gabriel ÁVILA Valle (33).

CD EVERTON DE VIÑA DEL MAR – CARACAS FC 1-0 (1-0)
Estadio Sausalito, Viña del Mar, 17.02.2009
Referee: Antonio Javier ARIAS Alvarenga (PAR), Attendance: 12.200
CD EVERTON DE VIÑA DEL MAR: Gustavo Tulio DALSASSO, Cristián Gonzalo OVIEDO Molina, Leandro Javier DELGADO Plenkovich, Adrián Alejandro ROJAS Contreras, Nicolás Andrés FREITAS Silva, Jaime Eduardo RIVEROS Valenzuela (82 Marcos Ignacio VELÁSQUEZ Ahumada), Cristián Roberto URIBE Lara (25 Benjamín Ignacio RUIZ Herrera), Rodrigo Andrés RAMÍREZ Miranda, Fernando Antonio SAAVEDRA Valencia, Ezequiel Nicolás MIRALLES, Roberto Carlos GUTIÉRREZ Gamboa (65 Sebastián Ariel PENCO). DT: Nelson Bonifacio ACOSTA López
CARACAS FC: Javier Eduardo TOYO Barcenas, Deivis BARONE Farías, José Manuel REY Cortegoso, Gabriel Alejandro CICHERO Konarek, Franklin José LUCENA Peña, Jesús Javier GÓMEZ Mercado (67 Zamir VALOYES Nabollán), Bremer Alfredo PIÑANGO Arevalo, Édgar Hernán JIMÉNEZ González (62 Rolando Emilio ESCOBAR Batista), Darío Damián FIGUEROA (77 Emilio RENTERÍA García), Rafael Ernesto CASTELLÍN García, Rodrigo PRIETO Aubert. DT: Noel SANVINCENTE Bethelmy
Goal: Roberto Carlos GUTIÉRREZ Gamboa (45).

CARACAS FC – CA LANÚS 3-1 (0-0)
Estadio Olímpico, Caracas, 25.02.2009
Referee: Wilmar Alexander ROLDÁN Pérez (COL), Attendance: 6.533
CARACAS FC: Renny Vicente VEGA Hernández, Deivis BARONE Farías, José Manuel REY Cortegoso, Gabriel Alejandro CICHERO Konarek, Giovanny Michael ROMERO Armenio, Franklin José LUCENA Peña (46 Édgar Hernán JIMÉNEZ González), Jesús Javier GÓMEZ Mercado (80 Rolando Emilio ESCOBAR Batista), Bremer Alfredo PIÑANGO Arevalo, Darío Damián FIGUEROA, Rafael Ernesto CASTELLÍN García, Rodrigo PRIETO Aubert (86 Jaime Andrés BUSTAMANTE Suárez). DT: Noel SANVINCENTE Bethelmy
CA LANÚS: Carlos Gustavo BOSSIO, Maximiliano Nicolás VELÁZQUEZ, Rodolfo Moisés GRAIEB, JADSON Viera Castro, Santiago Abel HOYOS, Matías Lionel FRITZLER, Sebastián Marcelo BLANCO, Sebastián SALOMÓN (73 Diego Hernán GONZÁLEZ), José Gustavo SAND, Eduardo Antonio SALVIO (73 Santiago BIGLIERI), Germán Ezequiel CANO (60 Diego Hernán VALERI). DT: Luis Francisco ZUBELDÍA
Goals: José Manuel REY Cortegoso (47), Darío Damián FIGUEROA (49), Rafael Ernesto CASTELLÍN García (71) / José Gustavo SAND (84).

CD "CHIVAS" GUADALAJARA SA – CD EVERTON DE VIÑA DEL MAR 6-2 (4-0)
Estadio Jalisco, Guadalajara, 25.02.2009
Referee: Saúl Esteban LAVERNI (ARG), Attendance: 10.000
CD GUADALAJARA: Luis Ernesto MICHEL Vergara, Aarón GALINDO Rubio, Héctor REYNOSO López, Gonzalo PINEDA Reyes, José Jonny MAGALLÓN Oliva, Alberto MEDINA Briseño, Ramón Heriberto Cortez MORALES Higuera (57 Francisco Juan MENDOZA Martínez), Sergio Amaury PONCE Villegas, Xavier Iván BÁEZ Gamiño, Marco Jhonfai FABIÁN de la Mora (77 Jared Francisco BORGETTI Echavarría), Carlos Augusto OCHOA Mendoza (67 Javier HERNÁNDEZ Balcazar). DT: Efraín FLORES Mercado
CD EVERTON DE VIÑA DEL MAR: Gustavo Tulio DALSASSO, Cristián Gonzalo OVIEDO Molina, Francisco Javier SÁNCHEZ Silva (69 Matías Leonardo VIDANGOSSY Rebolledo), Leandro Javier DELGADO Plenkovich, Adrián Alejandro ROJAS Contreras, Nicolás Andrés FREITAS Silva, Jaime Eduardo RIVEROS Valenzuela (46 Roberto Ezequiel FLORIS), Rodrigo Andrés RAMÍREZ Miranda, Roberto Oscar CORNEJO (46 Roberto Carlos GUTIÉRREZ Gamboa), Fernando Antonio SAAVEDRA Valencia, Ezequiel Nicolás MIRALLES. DT: Nelson Bonifacio ACOSTA López
Goals: Sergio Amaury PONCE Villegas (18), Ramón Heriberto Cortez MORALES Higuera (23 penalty), Alberto MEDINA Briseño (32), Marco Jhonfai FABIÁN de la Mora (37), Javier HERNÁNDEZ Balcazar (78, 87) /
Roberto Carlos GUTIÉRREZ Gamboa (50), Ezequiel Nicolás MIRALLES (53 penalty).

CARACAS FC – CD "CHIVAS" GUADALAJARA SA 2-0 (1-0)
Estadio Olímpico, Caracas, 3.03.2009
Referee: Carlos Alfredo VERA Rodríguez (ECU), Attendance: 17.000
CARACAS FC: Renny Vicente VEGA Hernández, Deivis BARONE Farías, José Manuel REY Cortegoso (40 Jaime Andrés BUSTAMANTE Suárez), Gabriel Alejandro CICHERO Konarek, Giovanny Michael ROMERO Armenio, Jesús Javier GÓMEZ Mercado (78 Emilio RENTERÍA García), Bremer Alfredo PIÑANGO Arevalo, Édgar Hernán JIMÉNEZ González, Darío Damián FIGUEROA, Rafael Ernesto CASTELLÍN García, Rodrigo PRIETO Aubert (64 Franklin José LUCENA Peña). DT: Noel SANVINCENTE Bethelmy
CD GUADALAJARA SA: Luis Ernesto MICHEL Vergara, Aarón GALINDO Rubio, Héctor REYNOSO López, Patricio Gabriel ARAUJO Vázquez (49 Jared Francisco BORGETTI Echavarría), Gonzalo PINEDA Reyes, José Jonny MAGALLÓN Oliva, Alberto MEDINA Briseño, Ramón Heriberto Cortez MORALES Higuera, Sergio Amaury PONCE Villegas, Javier HERNÁNDEZ Balcazar (52 Sergio Gabriel ÁVILA Valle), Carlos Augusto OCHOA Mendoza (60 Xavier Iván BÁEZ Gamiño). DT: Efraín FLORES Mercado
Goals: Jaime Andrés BUSTAMANTE Suárez (45+1), Darío Damián FIGUEROA (51).

CD EVERTON DE VIÑA DEL MAR – CA LANÚS 1-1 (0-1)
Estadio Sausalito, Viña del Mar, 11.03.2009
Referee: Jorge Luis LARRIONDA Pietrafesa (URU), Attendance: 8.000
CD EVERTON DE VIÑA DEL MAR: Nicolás Miroslav PERIC Villarreal, Cristián Gonzalo OVIEDO Molina, Leandro Javier DELGADO Plenkovich, Roberto Ezequiel FLORIS, Adrián Alejandro ROJAS Contreras, Nicolás Andrés FREITAS Silva, Fernando Alejandro MANRÍQUEZ Hernández (46 Roberto Oscar CORNEJO), Jaime Eduardo RIVEROS Valenzuela, Rodrigo Andrés RAMÍREZ Miranda (72 Benjamin Ignacio RUIZ Herrera), Ezequiel Nicolás MIRALLES, Roberto Carlos GUTIÉRREZ Gamboa (76 Sebastián Ariel PENCO). DT: Nelson Bonifacio ACOSTA López
CA LANÚS: Carlos Gustavo BOSSIO, Maximiliano Nicolás VELÁZQUEZ, Rodolfo Moisés GRAIEB, Santiago Abel HOYOS, Emir Saúl FACCIOLI, Matías Lionel FRITZLER, Sebastián Marcelo BLANCO (80 Diego Hernán VALERI), Diego Hernán GONZÁLEZ, Santiago BIGLIERI (65 Diego Eduardo LAGOS), José Gustavo SAND, Nicolás Francisco RAMÍREZ (65 Eduardo Fabián LEDESMA). DT: Luis Francisco ZUBELDÍA
Sent off: Cornejo (58) / Graieb (58)
Goals: Ezequiel Nicolás MIRALLES (55 penalty) / Diego Hernán GONZÁLEZ (45).

CD "CHIVAS" GUADALAJARA SA – CARACAS FC 1-0 (0-0)
Estadio Jalisco, Guadalajara, 11.03.2009
Referee: Víctor Hugo CARRILLO Casanova (PER), Attendance: 13.319
CD GUADALAJARA SA: Luis Ernesto MICHEL Vergara, Aarón GALINDO Rubio, Gonzalo PINEDA Reyes, José Jonny MAGALLÓN Oliva, Alberto MEDINA Briseño, Sergio Gabriel ÁVILA Valle (72 Omar Alejandro ESPARZA Morales), Sergio Amaury PONCE Villegas, Xavier Iván BÁEZ Gamiño, Francisco Juan MENDOZA Martínez, Jared Francisco BORGETTI Echavarría (62 Patricio Gabriel ARAUJO Vázquez), Carlos Augusto OCHOA Mendoza (51 Omar ARELLANO Riverón). DT: Efraín FLORES Mercado
CARACAS FC: Renny Vicente VEGA Hernández, Deivis BARONE Farías, Gabriel Alejandro CICHERO Konarek, Jaime Andrés BUSTAMANTE Suárez, Giovanny Michael ROMERO Armenio (75 Zamir VALOYES Nabollán), Luis Enrique VERA Martineau, Jesús Javier GÓMEZ Mercado, Édgar Hernán JIMÉNEZ González (81 Rolando Emilio ESCOBAR Batista), Darío Damián FIGUEROA, Rafael Ernesto CASTELLÍN García (32 Jámerson RENTERÍA Mena), Rodrigo PRIETO Aubert. DT: Noel SANVINCENTE Bethelmy
Sent off: Magallón (68)
Goal: Aarón GALINDO Rubio (79).

CA LANÚS – CD EVERTON DE VIÑA DEL MAR 1-2 (1-0)
Estadio Ciudad de Lanús (La Fortaleza), Lanús, 17.03.2009
Referee: Paulo César DE OLIVEIRA (BRA), Attendance: 13.000
CA LANÚS: Carlos Gustavo BOSSIO, Maximiliano Nicolás VELÁZQUEZ, JADSON Viera Castro, Santiago Abel HOYOS, Matías Lionel FRITZLER, Diego Hernán VALERI, Sebastián Marcelo BLANCO (64 Nicolás Francisco RAMÍREZ), Eduardo Fabián LEDESMA, Sebastián SALOMÓN (75 Diego Hernán GONZÁLEZ), Santiago BIGLIERI (69 Diego Eduardo LAGOS), José Gustavo SAND. DT: Luis Francisco ZUBELDÍA
CD EVERTON DE VIÑA DEL MAR: Gustavo Tulio DALSASSO, Cristián Gonzalo OVIEDO Molina, Leandro Javier DELGADO Plenkovich, Roberto Ezequiel FLORIS, Adrián Alejandro ROJAS Contreras, Nicolás Andrés FREITAS Silva, Jaime Eduardo RIVEROS Valenzuela (83 Diego Antonio FIGUEREDO Matiauda), Rodrigo Andrés RAMÍREZ Miranda, Ezequiel Nicolás MIRALLES, Roberto Carlos GUTIÉRREZ Gamboa (87 José Luis MUÑOZ Muñoz), Matías Leonardo VIDANGOSSY Rebolledo (80 Fernando Alejandro MANRÍQUEZ Hernández). DT: Nelson Bonifacio ACOSTA López
Goals: Santiago BIGLIERI (29) /
Roberto Carlos GUTIÉRREZ Gamboa (53), José Luis MUÑOZ Muñoz (90+3).

CARACAS FC – CD EVERTON DE VIÑA DEL MAR 1-0 (0-0)
Estadio Olímpico, Caracas, 14.04.2009
Referee: Albert DUARTE (COL), Attendance: 15.000
CARACAS FC: Renny Vicente VEGA Hernández, Deivis BARONE Farías, José Manuel REY Cortegoso, Gabriel Alejandro CICHERO Konarek, Giovanny Michael ROMERO Armenio, Luis Enrique VERA Martineau, Jesús Javier GÓMEZ Mercado (71 Franklin José LUCENA Peña), Édgar Hernán JIMÉNEZ González, Darío Damián FIGUEROA (90 Zamir VALOYES Nabollán), Rafael Ernesto CASTELLÍN García (56 Emilio RENTERÍA García), Rodrigo PRIETO Aubert. DT: Noel SANVINCENTE Bethelmy
CD EVERTON DE VIÑA DEL MAR: Gustavo Tulio DALSASSO, Cristián Gonzalo OVIEDO Molina, Leandro Javier DELGADO Plenkovich, Adrián Alejandro ROJAS Contreras, Nicolás Andrés FREITAS Silva, Jaime Eduardo RIVEROS Valenzuela (75 José Luis MUÑOZ Muñoz), Cristián Roberto URIBE Lara (72 Marcos Ignacio VELÁSQUEZ Ahumada), Rodrigo Andrés RAMÍREZ Miranda, Fernando Antonio SAAVEDRA Valencia, Ezequiel Nicolás MIRALLES, Roberto Carlos GUTIÉRREZ Gamboa (76 Sebastián Ariel PENCO). DT: Nelson Bonifacio ACOSTA López
Sent off: Ramírez (67)
Goal: Darío Damián FIGUEROA (62 penalty).

CD "CHIVAS" GUADALAJARA SA – CA LANÚS 0-0
Estadio Jalisco, Guadalajara, 14.04.2009
Referee: Carlos Manuel TORRES (PAR)
CD GUADALAJARA: Luis Ernesto MICHEL Vergara, Héctor REYNOSO López, Patricio Gabriel ARAUJO Vázquez, Gonzalo PINEDA Reyes, Édgar Eduardo MEJÍA Virrete, Édgar Iván SOLÍS Castillón (46 Ramón Heriberto Cortez MORALES Higuera), Sergio Amaury PONCE Villegas (62 Marco Jhonfai FABIÁN de la Mora), Xavier Iván BÁEZ Gamiño (58 Alberto MEDINA Briseño), Omar ARELLANO Riverón, Javier HERNÁNDEZ Balcazar, Jared Francisco BORGETTI Echavarría. DT: Omar ARELLANO Nuño
CA LANÚS: Carlos Gustavo BOSSIO, Maximiliano Nicolás VELÁZQUEZ, Rodolfo Moisés GRAIEB, Santiago Abel HOYOS, Emir Saúl FACCIOLI, Matías Lionel FRITZLER (73 Sebastián Marcelo BLANCO), Eduardo Fabián LEDESMA, Cristian Matías MENÉNDEZ, Diego Hernán GONZÁLEZ, Santiago BIGLIERI (58 Carlos Darío ARCE), Eduardo Antonio SALVIO (68 Nicolás Francisco RAMÍREZ). DT: Luis Francisco ZUBELDÍA
Sent off: Velázquez (54)

CD EVERTON DE VIÑA DEL MAR – CD "CHIVAS" GUADALAJARA SA 1-1 (0-1)
Estadio Sausalito, Viña del Mar, 29.04.2009
Referee: Héctor Wálter BALDASSI (ARG), Attendance: 15.000
CD EVERTON DE VIÑA DEL MAR: Gustavo Tulio DALSASSO, Cristián Gonzalo OVIEDO Molina, Leandro Javier DELGADO Plenkovich, Roberto Ezequiel FLORIS (75 José Luis MUÑOZ Muñoz), Adrián Alejandro ROJAS Contreras, Nicolás Andrés FREITAS Silva, Jaime Eduardo RIVEROS Valenzuela, Cristián Roberto URIBE Lara (56 Roberto Oscar CORNEJO), Fernando Antonio SAAVEDRA Valencia, Ezequiel Nicolás MIRALLES, Roberto Carlos GUTIÉRREZ Gamboa (75 Sebastián Ariel PENCO). DT: Nelson Bonifacio ACOSTA López
CD GUADALAJARA SA: Luis Ernesto MICHEL Vergara, Aarón GALINDO Rubio, Héctor REYNOSO López, Patricio Gabriel ARAUJO Vázquez, Gonzalo PINEDA Reyes, Édgar Eduardo MEJÍA Virrete, Alberto MEDINA Briseño, Édgar Iván SOLÍS Castillón, Sergio Amaury PONCE Villegas, Marco Jhonfai FABIÁN de la Mora (62 Jesús Andrés PADILLA Cisneros), Javier HERNÁNDEZ Balcazar (75 Jared Francisco BORGETTI Echavarría). DT: Francisco Javier RAMÍREZ Gamez
Sent off: Miralles (87) / Pineda (87)
Goals: Jaime Eduardo RIVEROS Valenzuela (47) / Javier HERNÁNDEZ Balcazar (8).

CA LANÚS – CARACAS FC 1-1 (1-1)
Estadio Ciudad de Lanús (La Fortaleza), Lanús, 29.04.2009
Referee: Carlos Alfredo VERA Rodríguez (ECU), Attendance: 793
CA LANÚS: Agustín Federico MARCHESÍN, Emir Saúl FACCIOLI, Carlos Darío ARCE, Iván Ricardo MACALIK, Eduardo Fabián LEDESMA, Cristian Matías MENÉNDEZ, Leandro Raúl BENÍTEZ, Diego Hernán GONZÁLEZ (84 Rodolfo Moisés GRAIEB), Santiago BIGLIERI, Nicolás Francisco RAMÍREZ (75 Sebastián SALOMÓN), Germán Ezequiel CANO (72 Diego Eduardo LAGOS). DT: Luis Francisco ZUBELDÍA
CARACAS FC: Renny Vicente VEGA Hernández, Deivis BARONE Farías, José Manuel REY Cortegoso, Gabriel Alejandro CICHERO Konarek, Giovanny Michael ROMERO Armenio, Luis Enrique VERA Martineau, Franklin José LUCENA Peña, Jesús Javier GÓMEZ Mercado (75 Zamir VALOYES Nabollán), Darío Damián FIGUEROA (81 Rolando Emilio ESCOBAR Batista), Rafael Ernesto CASTELLÍN García, Emilio RENTERÍA García (57 Rodrigo PRIETO Aubert). DT: Noel SANVINCENTE Bethelmy
Goal: Iván Ricardo MACALIK (39) / Darío Damián FIGUEROA (30).

1	CARACAS FC	6	3	1	2	7	4	10
2	CD GUADALAJARA	6	2	3	1	9	6	9
3	Everton	6	2	2	2	7	10	8
4	CA Lanús	6	0	4	2	5	8	4

GROUP 7

CLUB AURORA COCHABAMBA – BOYACÁ CHICÓ FC 0-3 (0-1)
Estadio Félix Capriles, Cochabamba, 10.02.2009
Referee: Víctor Hugo CARRILLO Casanova (PER), Attendance: 25.000
CLUB AURORA COCHABAMBA: Silvio Marcos DULCICH, Julio César HURTADO Sánchez, Germán Gabriel LEONFORTE (46 Nelson SOSSA Chávez), Ronald RODRÍGUEZ Cabrera (58 Cristian Alberto LÓPEZ Narvaez), Iván Enrique HUAYHUATA Romero, Edward Mauro ZENTENO Alvarez, Christian FERNÁNDEZ, Edson Marcelo ZENTENO Alvarez, Jaime CARDOZO Tahua, Oliver Christian FERNÁNDEZ Ocaña (46 Límbert MÉNDEZ Justiniano), Derlis Miguel PAREDES Ortiz. DT: Julio César BALDIVIESO Rico
BOYACÁ CHICÓ FC: Edigson de Jesús VELÁZQUEZ Cano, Pedro Macario PINO Romero, Juan Alejandro MAHECHA Molina, Ormedis MADERA Blanco, Mario Humberto GARCÍA Caboara, Juan Gabriel GALICIA Molina, Anthony David TAPIA Gil (88 Yedinson PALACIOS León), Juan Gilberto NUÑEZ Castillo (64 Jhonny Albeiro RAMÍREZ Lozano), Edwin Dayan MÓVIL Cabrera, Leonardo Favio LÓPEZ Méndez, Wiston Manuel GIRÓN Amaya (87 Raúl Alexander ASPRILLA Moreno). DT: Alberto Miguel GAMERO Morillo
Sent off: Huyahuata (82)
Goals: Anthony David TAPIA Gil (45, 79), Juan Alejandro MAHECHA Molina (90+1).

GRÊMIO FOOT-BALL PORTO ALEGRENSE – CF UNIVERSIDAD DE CHILE 0-0
Estádio Olímpico Monumental, Porto Alegre, 25.02.2009
Referee: Martín Emilio VÁZQUEZ Broquetas (URU), Attendance: 33.431
GRÊMIO FOOT-BALL PORTO ALEGRENSE: VICTOR Leandro Bagy, José JADÍLSON dos Santos Silva (79 REINALDO de Souza), RÉVER Humberto Alves Araújo, Leonardo "LÉO" Renan Simoes de Lacerda (77 DOUGLAS Costa de Souza), RUY Bueno Neto, RAFAEL MARQUES Pinto (84 FÁBIO SANTOS Romeu), Anderson Simas Luciano "TCHECO", ADÍLSON Warken, Williamis de SOUZA Silva, Alexander "ALEX MINEIRO" Pereira Cardoso, JONAS Gonçalves Oliveira. DT: CELSO Juarez ROTH
CF UNIVERSIDAD DE CHILE: Miguel Ángel PINTO Jérez, Rodrigo Osvaldo RIVERA Godoy, Osvaldo Alexis GONZÁLEZ Sepúlveda, José Manuel ROJAS Bahamondes, Rafael Andrés OLARRA Guerrero, Marcelo Alfonso DÍAZ Rojas, Manuel Rolando ITURRA Urrutia (55 José Raúl CONTRERAS Arrau), Felipe Ignacio SEYMOUR Dobud, Ángel Orlando ROJAS Ortega (55 Nelson Rafael CUEVAS Amarilla), Juan Manuel OLIVERA López, Emilio Exequiel HERNÁNDEZ Hernández (75 Juan Claudio GONZÁLEZ Calderón). DT: Sergio Apraham MARKARIÁN Abrahamian
Sent off: Díaz (71)

CF UNIVERSIDAD DE CHILE – CLUB AURORA COCHABAMBA 3-0 (1-0)
Estadio Francisco Sánchez Rumoroso, Coquimbo, 4.03.2009
Referee: Carlos GALEANO Rios (PAR), Attendance: 12.896
CF UNIVERSIDAD DE CHILE: Miguel Ángel PINTO Jérez, Osvaldo Alexis GONZÁLEZ Sepúlveda, José Manuel ROJAS Bahamondes, Rafael Andrés OLARRA Guerrero, José Raúl CONTRERAS Arrau (46 Marco Andrés ESTRADA Quinteros), Mauricio Antonio ARIAS González, Manuel Rolando ITURRA Urrutia, Felipe Ignacio SEYMOUR Dobud, Juan Manuel OLIVERA López, Emilio Exequiel HERNÁNDEZ Hernández (84 Ángel Orlando ROJAS Ortega), Nelson Rafael CUEVAS Amarilla (67 Manuel Arturo VILLALOBOS Salvos). DT: Sergio Apraham MARKARIÁN Abrahamian
CLUB AURORA COCHABAMBA: Silvio Marcos DULCICH, Límbert MÉNDEZ Justiniano, Julio César HURTADO Sánchez, Germán Gabriel LEONFORTE, Edward Mauro ZENTENO Alvarez, Christian FERNÁNDEZ (68 Diego Marcelo BLANCO Vallejo), Joe Emanuel ESCOBAR Aliaga, Edson Marcelo ZENTENO Alvarez (87 Darwin Jesús LORA Vidaurre), Jaime CARDOZO Tahua (46 Nelson SOSSA Chávez), Federico Alejandro BONGIOANNI, Derlis Miguel PAREDES Ortiz. DT: Julio César BALDIVIESO Rico
Goals: Manuel Rolando ITURRA Urrutia (23), Manuel Arturo VILLALOBOS Salvos (80), José Manuel ROJAS Bahamondes (88).

BOYACÁ CHICÓ FC – GRÊMIO FOOT-BALL PORTO ALEGRENSE 0-1 (0-1)
Estadio La Independencia, Tunja, 11.03.2009
Referee: Sergio Fabián PEZZOTTA (ARG), Attendance: 15.000
BOYACÁ CHICÓ FC: Edigson de Jesús VELÁZQUEZ Cano, Pedro Macario PINO Romero, Juan Alejandro MAHECHA Molina, Ormedis MADERA Blanco (60 Juan Gilberto NUÑEZ Castillo), Mario Humberto GARCÍA Caboara, Juan Gabriel GALICIA Molina, Anthony David TAPIA Gil, Jhonny Albeiro RAMÍREZ Lozano, Edwin Dayan MÓVIL Cabrera (76 Wiston Manuel GIRÓN Amaya), Marco Jhonnier PÉREZ Murillo (82 Éver Antonio PALACIOS Palacios), Miguel Eduardo CANEO. DT: Alberto Miguel GAMERO Morillo
GRÊMIO FOOT-BALL PORTO ALEGRENSE: VICTOR Leandro Bagy, RUY Bueno Neto, RÉVER Humberto Alves Araújo, RAFAEL MARQUES Pinto, Leonardo "LÉO" Renan Simoes de Lacerda, FÁBIO SANTOS Romeu, Anderson Simas Luciano "TCHECO" (56 Leandro dos Santos de Jesus "MAKELELE"), Williamis de SOUZA Silva, ADÍLSON Warken, JONAS Gonçalves Oliveira (82 REINALDO de Souza), Alexander "ALEX MINEIRO" Pereira Cardoso (56 Germán Gustavo HERRERA). DT: CELSO Juarez ROTH
Sent off: Mahecha (70)
Goal: Williamis de SOUZA Silva (31).

BOYACÁ CHICÓ FC – CF UNIVERSIDAD DE CHILE 3-0 (2-0)
Estadio La Independencia, Tunja, 18.03.2009
Referee: Carlos Alfredo VERA Rodríguez (ECU), Attendance: 10.000
BOYACÁ CHICÓ FC: Edigson de Jesús VELÁZQUEZ Cano, Ormedis MADERA Blanco, Mario Humberto GARCÍA Caboara, Pedro Macario PINO Romero, Éver Antonio PALACIOS Palacios, Juan Gilberto NUÑEZ Castillo (75 Anthony David TAPIA Gil), Edwin Dayan MÓVIL Cabrera, Jhonny Albeiro RAMÍREZ Lozano, Wiston Manuel GIRÓN Amaya (85 Gustavo LÓPEZ Bustamante), Miguel Eduardo CANEO, Marco Jhonnier PÉREZ Murillo (90+2 Raúl Alexander ASPRILLA Moreno). DT: Alberto Miguel GAMERO Morillo
CF UNIVERSIDAD DE CHILE: Miguel Ángel PINTO Jérez, Osvaldo Alexis GONZÁLEZ Sepúlveda, José Manuel ROJAS Bahamondes, Rafael Andrés OLARRA Guerrero, Marcelo Alfonso DÍAZ Rojas, Marco Andrés ESTRADA Quinteros, Mauricio Antonio ARIAS González (30 Wálter Damián MONTILLO), Manuel Rolando ITURRA Urrutia, Ángel Orlando ROJAS Ortega (30 Felipe Ignacio SEYMOUR Dobud), Juan Manuel OLIVERA López, Emilio Exequiel HERNÁNDEZ Hernández (75 Nelson Rafael CUEVAS Amarilla). DT: Sergio Apraham MARKARIÁN Abrahamian
Goals: Edwin Dayan MÓVIL Cabrera (4), Wiston Manuel GIRÓN Amaya (22), Juan Gilberto NUÑEZ Castillo (70).

CLUB AURORA COCHABAMBA – GRÊMIO FOOT-BALL PORTO ALEGRENSE 1-2 (0-1)
Estadio Félix Capriles, Cochabamba, 25.03.2009
Referee: Juan Ernesto SOTO (VEN), Attendance: 18.000
CLUB AURORA COCHABAMBA: Silvio Marcos DULCICH, Límbert MÉNDEZ Justiniano, Germán Gabriel LEONFORTE, Edward Mauro ZENTENO Alvarez, Christian FERNÁNDEZ, Joe Emanuel ESCOBAR Aliaga, Vladimir CASTELLÓN Colque (81 Ronald RODRÍGUEZ Cabrera), Edson Marcelo ZENTENO Alvarez (46 Cristian Alberto LÓPEZ Narvaez), Jaime CARDOZO Tahua (80 Nelson SOSSA Chávez), Federico Alejandro BONGIOANNI, Derlis Miguel PAREDES Ortiz. DT: Julio César BALDIVIESO Rico
GRÊMIO FOOT-BALL PORTO ALEGRENSE: VICTOR Leandro Bagy, Leonardo "LÉO" Renan Simoes de Lacerda, FÁBIO SANTOS Romeu, RUY Bueno Neto (85 Leandro dos Santos de Jesus "MAKELELE"), RÉVER Humberto Alves Araújo, RAFAEL MARQUES Pinto, ADÍLSON Warken (90 Willian THIEGO de Jesus), Anderson Simas Luciano "TCHECO", Williamis de SOUZA Silva, JONAS Gonçalves Oliveira, Alexander "ALEX MINEIRO" Pereira Cardoso (65 Germán Gustavo HERRERA). DT: CELSO Juarez ROTH
Sent off: Jonas (59)
Goals: Derlis Miguel PAREDES Ortiz (53) / JONAS Gonçalves Oliveira (41), Anderson Simas Luciano "TCHECO" (87).

GRÊMIO FOOT-BALL PORTO ALEGRENSE – CLUB AURORA COCHABAMBA 3-0 (1-0)
Estádio Olímpico Monumental, Porto Alegre, 7.04.2009
Referee: Antonio Javier ARIAS Alvarenga (PAR), Attendance: 27.638
GRÊMIO FOOT-BALL PORTO ALEGRENSE: VICTOR Leandro Bagy, FÁBIO SANTOS Romeu (80 José JADÍLSON dos Santos Silva), RÉVER Humberto Alves Araújo, RAFAEL MARQUES Pinto, Leonardo "LÉO" Renan Simoes de Lacerda, Anderson Simas Luciano "TCHECO", Williamis de SOUZA Silva, ADÍLSON Warken, Leandro dos Santos de Jesus "MAKELELE" (88 DIOGO Antunes de Oliveira), Maximiliano Gastón "MAXI" LÓPEZ, Germán Gustavo HERRERA (82 Sergio Daniel ORTEMAN Rodríguez). DT: Marcelo ROSPIDE
CLUB AURORA COCHABAMBA: Silvio Marcos DULCICH, Julio César HURTADO Sánchez, Germán Gabriel LEONFORTE, Iván Enrique HUAYHUATA Romero, Humberto VIVIANI Ribera, Edward Mauro ZENTENO Alvarez, Christian FERNÁNDEZ, Joe Emanuel ESCOBAR Aliaga (90 Vladimir CASTELLÓN Colque), Federico Alejandro BONGIOANNI (57 Jaime CARDOZO Tahua), Nelson SOSSA Chávez (88 Aldo Enry GUTIÉRREZ Torrico), Derlis Miguel PAREDES Ortiz. DT: Julio César BALDIVIESO Rico
Goals: RAFAEL MARQUES Pinto (32), Maximiliano Gastón "MAXI" LÓPEZ (64), RÉVER Humberto Alves Araújo (81).

CF UNIVERSIDAD DE CHILE – BOYACÁ CHICÓ FC 3-0 (1-0)
Estadio Nacional, Santiago, 8.04.2009
Referee: Gabriel Norberto FAVALE (ARG), Attendance: 34.651
CF UNIVERSIDAD DE CHILE: Miguel Ángel PINTO Jérez, Osvaldo Alexis GONZÁLEZ Sepúlveda, José Manuel ROJAS Bahamondes, Rafael Andrés OLARRA Guerrero, Marcelo Alfonso DÍAZ Rojas, José Raul CONTRERAS Arrau, Marco Andrés ESTRADA Quinteros, Wálter Damián MONTILLO (46 Nelson Rafael CUEVAS Amarilla), Manuel Rolando ITURRA Urrutia, Juan Manuel OLIVERA López (83 Manuel Arturo VILLALOBOS Salvos), Emilio Exequiel HERNÁNDEZ Hernández (70 Felipe Ignacio SEYMOUR Dobud). DT: Sergio Apraham MARKARIÁN Abrahamian
BOYACÁ CHICÓ FC: Edigson de Jesús VELÁZQUEZ Cano, Pedro Macario PINO Romero (65 Anthony David TAPIA Gil), Éver Antonio PALACIOS Palacios, Juan Alejandro MAHECHA Molina, Ormedis MADERA Blanco, Mario Humberto GARCÍA Caboara, Jhonny Albeiro RAMÍREZ Lozano, Juan Gilberto NUÑEZ Castillo, Leonardo Favio LÓPEZ Méndez (75 Gustavo LÓPEZ Bustamante), Marco Jhonnier PÉREZ Murillo, Miguel Eduardo CANEO. DT: Alberto Miguel GAMERO Morillo
Goals: Emilio Exequiel HERNÁNDEZ Hernández (22), Juan Manuel OLIVERA López (47), Nelson Rafael CUEVAS Amarilla (90).

CF UNIVERSIDAD DE CHILE – GRÊMIO FOOT-BALL PORTO ALEGRENSE 0-2 (0-1)
Estadio Nacional, Santiago, 15.04.2009
Referee: Carlos Arecio AMARILLA Demarqui (PAR), Attendance: 33.140
CF UNIVERSIDAD DE CHILE: Miguel Ángel PINTO Jérez, Osvaldo Alexis GONZÁLEZ Sepúlveda, José Manuel ROJAS Bahamondes, Rafael Andrés OLARRA Guerrero, Marcelo Alfonso DÍAZ Rojas, José Raul CONTRERAS Arrau, Marco Andrés ESTRADA Quinteros, Manuel Rolando ITURRA Urrutia, Juan Manuel OLIVERA López, Emilio Exequiel HERNÁNDEZ Hernández (73 Manuel Arturo VILLALOBOS Salvos), Nelson Rafael CUEVAS Amarilla (65 Mauricio Alejandro GÓMEZ Ríos). DT: Sergio Apraham MARKARIÁN Abrahamian
GRÊMIO FOOT-BALL PORTO ALEGRENSE: VICTOR Leandro Bagy, Leonardo "LÉO" Renan Simoes de Lacerda (65 Willian THIEGO de Jesus), FÁBIO SANTOS Romeu, RÉVER Humberto Alves Araújo, RAFAEL MARQUES Pinto, Leandro dos Santos de Jesus "MAKELELE", ADÍLSON Warken, Anderson Simas Luciano "TCHECO", Williamis de SOUZA Silva, Maximiliano Gastón "MAXI" LÓPEZ (88 Sergio Daniel ORTEMAN Rodríguez), JONAS Gonçalves Oliveira (70 Germán Gustavo HERRERA). DT: Marcelo ROSPIDE
Sent off: Olivera (71)
Goals: Leonardo "LÉO" Renan Simoes de Lacerda (32), Maximiliano Gastón "MAXI" LÓPEZ (66).

BOYACÁ CHICÓ FC – CLUB AURORA COCHABAMBA 2-1 (0-0)
Estadio La Independencia, Tunja, 16.04.2009
Referee: Samuel Rolando HARO Inca (ECU), Attendance: 2.500
BOYACÁ CHICÓ FC: Edigson de Jesús VELÁZQUEZ Cano, Éver Antonio PALACIOS Palacios, Juan Alejandro MAHECHA Molina, Ormedis MADERA Blanco, Mario Humberto GARCÍA Caboara, Anthony David TAPIA Gil (67 Pedro Macario PINO Romero), Jhonny Albeiro RAMÍREZ Lozano, Juan Gilberto NUÑEZ Castillo (87 Gustavo LÓPEZ Bustamante), Leonardo Favio LÓPEZ Méndez (74 Michael Andrés RADA Gutiérrez), Marco Jhonnier PÉREZ Murillo, Miguel Eduardo CANEO. DT: Alberto Miguel GAMERO Morillo Sent off: Mahecha (75)
CLUB AURORA COCHABAMBA: Silvio Marcos DULCICH, Julio César HURTADO Sánchez, Germán Gabriel LEONFORTE, Iván Enrique HUAYHUATA Romero, Humberto VIVIANI Ribera, Edward Mauro ZENTENO Alvarez, Christian FERNÁNDEZ, Joe Emanuel ESCOBAR Aliaga (66 Jaime CARDOZO Tahua), Federico Alejandro BONGIOANNI (56 Nelson SOSSA Chávez), Cristian Alberto LÓPEZ Narvaez, Derlis Miguel PAREDES Ortiz. DT: Julio César BALDIVIESO Rico
Goals: Miguel E. CANEO (49 penalty), Marco J. PÉREZ Murillo (69) / Christian FERNÁNDEZ (87).

CLUB AURORA COCHABAMBA – CF UNIVERSIDAD DE CHILE 1-2 (1-1)
Estadio Félix Capriles, Cochabamba, 28.04.2009
Referee: Víctor Hugo RIVERA Chavez (PER), Attendance: 7.000
CLUB AURORA COCHABAMBA: Silvio Marcos DULCICH, Límbert MÉNDEZ Justiniano (28 Jaime CARDOZO Tahua), Julio César HURTADO Sánchez, Germán Gabriel LEONFORTE, Iván Enrique HUAYHUATA Romero, Edward Mauro ZENTENO Alvarez, Christian FERNÁNDEZ (78 Oliver Christian FERNÁNDEZ Ocaña), Vladimir CASTELLÓN Colque, Edson Marcelo ZENTENO Alvarez, Nelson SOSSA Chávez (73 Cristian Alberto LÓPEZ Narvaez), Derlis Miguel PAREDES Ortiz. DT: Julio César BALDIVIESO Rico
CF UNIVERSIDAD DE CHILE: Miguel Ángel PINTO Jérez, Osvaldo Alexis GONZÁLEZ Sepúlveda, José Manuel ROJAS Bahamondes, Juan Claudio GONZÁLEZ Calderon, Marcelo Alfonso DÍAZ Rojas (61 Nelson Rafael CUEVAS Amarilla), José Raul CONTRERAS Arrau, Marco Andrés ESTRADA Quinteros, Wálter Damián MONTILLO (72 Sebastián Eduardo PARDO Campos), Manuel Rolando ITURRA Urrutia, Manuel Arturo VILLALOBOS Salvos (84 Felipe Ignacio SEYMOUR Dobud), Emilio Exequiel HERNÁNDEZ Hernández. DT: Sergio Apraham MARKARIÁN Abrahamian
Goals: Derlis Miguel PAREDES Ortiz (20) / Marco Andrés ESTRADA Quinteros (14), Juan Claudio GONZÁLEZ Calderon (73).

GRÊMIO FOOT-BALL PORTO ALEGRENSE – BOYACÁ CHICÓ FC 3-0 (3-0)
Estádio Olímpico Monumental, Porto Alegre, 28.04.2009
Referee: Jorge Luis LARRIONDA Pietrafesa (URU), Attendance: 34.974
GRÊMIO FOOT-BALL PORTO ALEGRENSE: VICTOR Leandro Bagy, Leonardo "LÉO" Renan Simoes de Lacerda, FÁBIO SANTOS Romeu (83 José JADÍLSON dos Santos Silva), RUY Bueno Neto, RÉVER Humberto Alves Araújo, RAFAEL MARQUES Pinto, ADÍLSON Warken, Anderson Simas Luciano "TCHECO" (72 Sergio Daniel ORTEMAN Rodríguez), Williamis de SOUZA Silva, Maximiliano Gastón "MAXI" LÓPEZ (68 Alexander "ALEX MINEIRO" Pereira Cardoso), JONAS Gonçalves Oliveira. DT: Marcelo ROSPIDE
BOYACÁ CHICÓ FC: Edigson de Jesús VELÁZQUEZ Cano, Éver Antonio PALACIOS Palacios, Ormedis MADERA Blanco, Mario Humberto GARCÍA Caboara, Pedro Macario PINO Romero, Juan Gilberto NUÑEZ Castillo, Juan Andrés TEJERA Arachichu (46 Wiston Manuel GIRÓN Amaya), Anthony David TAPIA Gil (68 Michael Andrés RADA Gutiérrez), Jhonny Albeiro RAMÍREZ Lozano, Miguel Eduardo CANEO, Marco Jhonnier PÉREZ Murillo (86 Luis Eduardo DURÁN Aguirre). DT: Alberto Miguel GAMERO Morillo
Goals: Williamis de SOUZA Silva (13, 17), Leonardo "LÉO" Renan Simoes de Lacerda (30).

1	GRÊMIO	6	5	1	0	11	1	16
2	UNIVERSIDAD DE CHILE	6	3	1	2	8	6	10
3	Boyacá Chicó	6	3	0	3	8	8	9
4	Aurora	6	0	0	6	3	15	0

GROUP 8

CA SAN LORENZO DE ALMAGRO – SAN LUIS FC 4-1 (3-0)
Estadio Pedro Bidegain (El Nuevo Gasómetro), Buenos Aires, 11.02.2009
Referee: LEONARDO GACIBA da Silva (BRA), Attendance: 30.000
CA SAN LORENZO DE ALMAGRO: Agustín Ignacio ORIÓN, Jonathan Pablo BOTTINELLI, Gastón Damián AGUIRRE, Hernán Adrián GONZÁLEZ, Juan Manuel TORRES, Santiago Hernán SOLARI, Pablo Cesar BARRIENTOS (67 Diego Alejandro RIVERO), Aureliano TORRES Román, Cristian Raúl LEDESMA (81 Jonathan SANTANA Ghere), Néstor Andrés SILVERA (57 Cristian Gabriel CHÁVEZ), Gonzalo Rubén BERGESSIO. DT: Miguel Ángel RUSSO
SAN LUIS FC: Adrián MARTÍNEZ Flores, Omar MONJARAZ Campos, Óscar Yaroslav MASCORRO Ábrego, José Alfredo GONZÁLEZ Tahuilán, Armando Leonel OLMEDO Pérez (84 Rodolfo SALINAS Ortiz), Egidio Raúl ARÉVALO Ríos, Jairo Leonard PATIÑO Rosero (63 Víctor Hugo LOJERO Alexanderson), Ignacio TORRES Olvera, Arturo ALVARADO Pérez, Diego Andrés ÁLVAREZ Sánchez (46 Noé MAYA Vilches), Néstor Fabián BAREIRO Leguizamón. DT: Luis Américo SCATOLARO
Goals: Néstor Andrés SILVERA (3, 16), Gonzalo Rubén BERGESSIO (31),
Pablo Cesar BARRIENTOS (48) / Víctor Hugo LOJERO Alexanderson (70).

CLUB LIBERTAD ASUNCIÓN – UNIVERSITARIO DE LIMA 2-1 (1-0)
Estadio Feliciano Cáceres, Luque, 11.02.2009
Referee: Federico José BELIGOY (ARG), Attendance: 1.000
CLUB LIBERTAD ASUNCIÓN: Víctor Hugo CENTURIÓN Miranda, Adalberto ROMÁN Benítez, Édgar Gabriel BALBUENA Adorno, Lorgio ÁLVAREZ Roca (74 Édgar Arnulfo ROBLES Coronel), Pedro Alcides SARABIA Achucarro, Miguel Ángel SAMUDIO, Sergio Daniel AQUINO, Luis Alberto RAMÍREZ Lucay (75 Juan Eduardo SAMUDIO Serna), Víctor Javier CÁCERES Centurión, Manuel José MACIEL Fernández, Miguel Alejandro XIMÉNEZ Acosta (75 Roberto Carlos GAMARRA Varela). DT: Javier TORRENTE
UNIVERSITARIO DE LIMA: Raúl FERNÁNDEZ Valverde, John Christian GALLIQUIO Castro, Carlos Alberto GALVÁN Méndez, Renzo REVOREDO Suazo, Antonio GONZÁLES Canchari (46 Nolberto SOLANO Todco), Rainer TORRES Salas, Nelinho Minzun QUINA Asín, Jorge Johan VÁSQUEZ Rosales, Rodolfo ESPINOZA Díaz (80 Enio Joao NOVOA Heredia), Juan Manuel PERILLO (65 RONAILLE CALHEIRA Seara), Piero Fernando ALVA Niezen. DT: Juan Máximo REYNOSO Guzmán
Goals: Manuel José MACIEL Fernández (42), Adalberto ROMÁN Benítez (83) /
Norberto Albino SOLANO Todco (63).

UNIVERSITARIO DE LIMA – CA SAN LORENZO DE ALMAGRO 1-0 (1-0)
Estadio Monumental, Lima, 19.02.2009
Referee: Sálvio Spínola FAGUNDES Filho (BRA), Attendance: 60.000
UNIVERSITARIO DE LIMA: Raúl FERNÁNDEZ Valverde, John Christian GALLIQUIO Castro, Carlos Alberto GALVÁN Méndez, Renzo REVOREDO Suazo, Rainer TORRES Salas, Miguel Ángel TORRES Quintana, Nelinho Minzun QUINA Asín, Rodolfo ESPINOZA Díaz (62 Juan Manuel PERILLO, 82 Enio Joao NOVOA Heredia), Nolberto SOLANO Todco, RONAILLE CALHEIRA Seara, Piero Fernando ALVA Niezen (83 Jorge Johan VÁSQUEZ Rosales). DT: Juan Máximo REYNOSO Guzmán
CA SAN LORENZO DE ALMAGRO: Agustín Ignacio ORIÓN, Jonathan Pablo BOTTINELLI, Gastón Damián AGUIRRE, Hernán Adrián GONZÁLEZ, Juan Manuel TORRES, Santiago Hernán SOLARI (83 Cristian Gabriel CHÁVEZ), Pablo Cesar BARRIENTOS, Aureliano TORRES Román, Cristian Raúl LEDESMA (72 Jonathan SANTANA Ghere), Néstor Andrés SILVERA (80 Alejandro Darío GÓMEZ), Gonzalo Rubén BERGESSIO. DT: Miguel Ángel RUSSO
Sent off: Bottinelli (20)
Goal: Nolberto SOLANO Todco (21 penalty).

SAN LUIS FC – CLUB LIBERTAD ASUNCIÓN 0-1 (0-1)
Estadio Alfonso Lastras Ramírez, San Luis Potosí, 26.02.2009
Referee: Héctor Wálter BALDASSI (ARG)
SAN LUIS FC: Adrián MARTÍNEZ Flores, Adrián Israel GARCÍA Arias (46 Diego Andrés ÁLVAREZ Sánchez), Michael OROZCO Fiscal, Armando Leonel OLMEDO Pérez (75 Jairo Leonard PATIÑO Rosero), Egidio Raúl ARÉVALO Ríos, José Israel MARTÍNEZ Salas, Braulio LUNA Guzmán, Jesús Alejandro PALACIOS Olague, Néstor Fabián BAREIRO Leguizamón (46 Noé MAYA Vilches), Malher Tressor MORENO Baldrich, Víctor Hugo LOJERO Alexanderson. DT: Luis Américo SCATOLARO
CLUB LIBERTAD ASUNCIÓN: Jorge Rodrigo BAVA, Édgar Gabriel BALBUENA Adorno, Vladimir MARÍN Rios (46 Manuel José MACIEL Fernández), Pedro Alcides SARABIA Achucarro, Julio César MANZUR, Miguel Ángel SAMUDIO, Sergio Daniel AQUINO, Luis Alberto RAMÍREZ Lucay (75 Arnaldo Andrés VERA Chamorro), Víctor Javier CÁCERES Centurión, Édgar Arnulfo ROBLES Coronel, Juan Eduardo SAMUDIO Serna (75 Omar Héber POUSO Osores). DT: Javier TORRENTE
Sent off: Cáceres (75)
Goal: Luis Alberto RAMÍREZ Lucay (15).

CLUB LIBERTAD ASUNCIÓN – CA SAN LORENZO DE ALMAGRO 2-0 (2-0)
Estadio Feliciano Cáceres, Luque, 5.03.2009
Referee: Carlos Luis CHANDÍA Alarcón (CHI), Attendance: 5.000
CLUB LIBERTAD ASUNCIÓN: Jorge Rodrigo BAVA, Édgar Gabriel BALBUENA Adorno, Vladimir MARÍN Rios (72 Manuel José MACIEL Fernández), Pedro Alcides SARABIA Achucarro, Julio César MANZUR, Omar Héber POUSO Osores, Miguel Ángel SAMUDIO, Sergio Daniel AQUINO (75 Lorgio ÁLVAREZ Roca), Luis Alberto RAMÍREZ Lucay, Édgar Arnulfo ROBLES Coronel, Miguel Alejandro XIMÉNEZ Acosta (61 Juan Eduardo SAMUDIO Serna). DT: Javier TORRENTE
CA SAN LORENZO DE ALMAGRO: Agustín Ignacio ORIÓN (9 Bruno Emiliano CENTENO), Nicolás Alexis BIANCHI Arce, Gastón Damián AGUIRRE, Hernán Adrián GONZÁLEZ, Juan Manuel TORRES, Aureliano TORRES Román, Jonathan SANTANA Ghere (59 Diego Alejandro RIVERO), Alejandro Darío GÓMEZ (76 Bruno FORNAROLI Mezza), Cristian Raúl LEDESMA, Néstor Andrés SILVERA, Gonzalo Rubén BERGESSIO. DT: Miguel Ángel RUSSO
Goals: Miguel Alejandro XIMÉNEZ Acosta (25), Sergio Daniel AQUINO (37).

UNIVERSITARIO DE LIMA – SAN LUIS FC 0-0
Estadio Monumental, Lima, 10.03.2009
Referee: Jorge Joaquín ANTEQUERA Castedo (BOL), Attendance: 32.567
UNIVERSITARIO DE LIMA: Raúl FERNÁNDEZ Valverde, John Christian GALLIQUIO Castro, Carlos Alberto GALVÁN Méndez, Renzo REVOREDO Suazo, Rainer TORRES Salas (78 Diego Enrique BUSTAMANTE Gutiérrez), Miguel Ángel TORRES Quintana, Nelinho Minzun QUINA Asín, Rodolfo ESPINOZA Díaz, Nolberto SOLANO Todco (69 Jorge Johan VÁSQUEZ Rosales), RONAILLE CALHEIRA Seara, Piero Fernando ALVA Niezen (69 Carlos Alberto OREJUELA Pita). DT: Juan Máximo REYNOSO Guzmán
SAN LUIS FC: Adrián MARTÍNEZ Flores, Omar MONJARAZ Campos, Adrián Israel GARCÍA Arias, Noé MAYA Vilches (81 Rodolfo SALINAS Ortiz), José Alfredo GONZÁLEZ Tahuilán, Armando Leonel OLMEDO Pérez, Jairo Leonard PATIÑO Rosero, Ignacio TORRES Olvera, Jesús Alejandro PALACIOS Olague (78 Egidio Raúl ARÉVALO Ríos), Malher Tressor MORENO Baldrich, Víctor Hugo LOJERO Alexanderson (46 Michael OROZCO Fiscal). DT: Luis Américo SCATOLARO
Sent off: Espinoza (29) . González (29)

CA SAN LORENZO DE ALMAGRO – CLUB LIBERTAD ASUNCIÓN 0-1 (0-0)
Estadio Pedro Bidegain (El Nuevo Gasómetro), Buenos Aires, 18.03.2009
Referee: Roberto Carlos SILVERA Calcerrada (URU), Attendance: 22.000
CA SAN LORENZO DE ALMAGRO: Hilario Bernardo NAVARRO, Jonathan Pablo BOTTINELLI, Gastón Damián AGUIRRE, Hernán Adrián GONZÁLEZ, Juan Manuel TORRES, Diego Alejandro RIVERO, Aureliano TORRES Román (46 Germán Ariel VOBORIL), Alejandro Darío GÓMEZ, Cristian Raúl LEDESMA (67 Hernán Gastón PEIRONE), Gonzalo Rubén BERGESSIO, Bruno FORNAROLI Mezza (55 Cristian Gabriel CHÁVEZ). DT: Miguel Ángel RUSSO
CLUB LIBERTAD ASUNCIÓN: Jorge Rodrigo BAVA, Édgar Gabriel BALBUENA Adorno, Vladimir MARÍN Rios (77 Manuel José MACIEL Fernández), Pedro Alcides SARABIA Achucarro, Julio César MANZUR, Omar Héber POUSO Osores, Miguel Ángel SAMUDIO, Sergio Daniel AQUINO, Luis Alberto RAMÍREZ Lucay (85 Lorgio ÁLVAREZ Roca), Édgar Arnulfo ROBLES Coronel, Juan Eduardo SAMUDIO Serna (63 Miguel Alejandro XIMÉNEZ Acosta). DT: Javier TORRENTE
Goal: Gastón Damián AGUIRRE (53 own goal).

SAN LUIS FC – UNIVERSITARIO DE LIMA 2-2 (1-1)
Estadio Alfonso Lastras Ramírez, San Luis Potosí, 18.03.2009
Referee: Alfredo Stalin INTRIAGO Ortega (ECU)
SAN LUIS FC: Adrián MARTÍNEZ Flores, Omar MONJARAZ Campos, Adrián Israel GARCÍA Arias, Noé MAYA Vilches (56 Víctor Hugo LOJERO Alexanderson), Michael OROZCO Fiscal, Armando Leonel OLMEDO Pérez, Egidio Raúl ARÉVALO Ríos, José Israel MARTÍNEZ Salas, Jairo Leonard PATIÑO Rosero (70 Rodolfo SALINAS Ortiz), José Rodolfo REYES Machado (78 Ignacio TORRES Olvera), Malher Tressor MORENO Baldrich. DT: Luis Américo SCATOLARO
UNIVERSITARIO DE LIMA: Raúl FERNÁNDEZ Valverde, John Christian GALLIQUIO Castro, Carlos Alberto GALVÁN Méndez, Renzo REVOREDO Suazo, Rainer TORRES Salas (86 Alberto Gianfranco LABARTHE Tome), Nelinho Minzun QUINA Asín, Jorge Johan VÁSQUEZ Rosales, Giancarlo CARMONA Maldonado, Nolberto SOLANO Todco (74 Enio Joao NOVOA Heredia), RONAILLE CALHEIRA Seara, Piero Fernando ALVA Niezen. DT: Juan Máximo REYNOSO Guzmán
Goals: José Rodolfo REYES Machado (25), Michael OROZCO Fiscal (77) /
Piero Fernando ALVA Niezen (34), Alberto Gianfranco LABARTHE Tome (90+1).

UNIVERSITARIO DE LIMA – CLUB LIBERTAD ASUNCIÓN 2-1 (1-1)
Estadio Monumental, Lima, 7.04.2009
Referee: Carlos Alfredo VERA Rodríguez (ECU), Attendance: 24.923
UNIVERSITARIO DE LIMA: Raúl FERNÁNDEZ Valverde, John Christian GALLIQUIO Castro, Manuel CALDERÓN Maraví, Renzo REVOREDO Suazo, Rainer TORRES Salas (84 Enio Joao NOVOA Heredia), Miguel Ángel TORRES Quintana (77 Alberto Gianfranco LABARTHE Tome), Nelinho Minzun QUINA Asín, Rodolfo ESPINOZA Díaz, Nolberto SOLANO Todco (68 Jorge Johan VÁSQUEZ Rosales), RONAILLE CALHEIRA Seara, Piero Fernando ALVA Niezen. DT: Juan Máximo REYNOSO Guzmán
CLUB LIBERTAD ASUNCIÓN: Jorge Rodrigo BAVA, Édgar Gabriel BALBUENA Adorno, Vladimir MARÍN Rios (76 Manuel José MACIEL Fernández), Lorgio ÁLVAREZ Roca, Pedro Alcides SARABIA Achucarro, Julio César MANZUR, Omar Héber POUSO Osores, Miguel Ángel SAMUDIO, Sergio Daniel AQUINO, Luis Alberto RAMÍREZ Lucay (64 Nelson David ROMERO Cárdenas), Miguel Alejandro XIMÉNEZ Acosta (64 Juan Eduardo SAMUDIO Serna). DT: Javier TORRENTE
Goals: RONAILLE CALHEIRA Seara (28), Piero Fernando ALVA Niezen (61) /
Miguel Alejandro XIMÉNEZ Acosta (21).

SAN LUIS FC – CA SAN LORENZO DE ALMAGRO 2-0 (1-0)
Estadio Alfonso Lastras Ramírez, San Luis Potosí, 8.04.2009
Referee: Jorge Luis LARRIONDA Pietrafesa (URU)
SAN LUIS FC: Adrián MARTÍNEZ Flores, Omar MONJARAZ Campos, Adrián Israel GARCÍA Arias (46 José Alfredo GONZÁLEZ Tahuilán), Óscar Yaroslav MASCORRO Ábrego, Noé MAYA Vilches, Egidio Raúl ARÉVALO Ríos, Jairo Leonard PATIÑO Rosero, Jesús Alejandro PALACIOS Olague, José Rodolfo REYES Machado, Néstor Fabián BAREIRO Leguizamón (46 Ignacio TORRES Olvera), Rodolfo SALINAS Ortiz (66 Braulio LUNA Guzmán). DT: Luis Américo SCATOLARO
CA SAN LORENZO DE ALMAGRO: Hilario Bernardo NAVARRO, Jonathan Pablo BOTTINELLI, Gastón Damián AGUIRRE, Hernán Adrián GONZÁLEZ, Juan Manuel TORRES, Santiago Hernán SOLARI (46 Alejandro Darío GÓMEZ), Diego Alejandro RIVERO (54 Cristian Gabriel CHÁVEZ), Aureliano TORRES Román, Cristian Raúl LEDESMA, Néstor Andrés SILVERA, Gonzalo Rubén BERGESSIO. DT: Miguel Ángel RUSSO
Sent off: Monjaraz (45) / Silvera (45)
Goals: Jesús Alejandro PALACIOS Olague (43), José Rodolfo REYES Machado (67).

CA SAN LORENZO DE ALMAGRO – UNIVERSITARIO DE LIMA 2-0 (2-0)
Estadio Pedro Bidegain (El Nuevo Gasómetro), Buenos Aires, 28.04.2009
Referee: Enrique Roberto OSSÉS Zencovich (CHI), Attendance: 2.856
CA SAN LORENZO DE ALMAGRO: Hilario Bernardo NAVARRO, Germán Ariel VOBORIL, Jonathan Pablo BOTTINELLI, Nicolás Alexis BIANCHI Arce, Hernán Adrián GONZÁLEZ, Juan Manuel TORRES (60 Cristian Raúl LEDESMA), Alejandro Darío GÓMEZ (46 Diego Alejandro RIVERO), Salvador Agustín REYNOSO, Bruno FORNAROLI Mezza (46 Gonzalo Rubén BERGESSIO), Cristian Gabriel CHÁVEZ, Hernán Gastón PEIRONE. DT: Diego Pablo SIMEONE
UNIVERSITARIO DE LIMA: Raúl FERNÁNDEZ Valverde, John Christian GALLIQUIO Castro, Carlos Alberto GALVÁN Méndez, Renzo REVOREDO Suazo, Rainer TORRES Salas (46 Nolberto SOLANO Todco, 70 Alberto Gianfranco LABARTHE Tome), Miguel Ángel TORRES Quintana, Nelinho Minzun QUINA Asín, Jorge Johan VÁSQUEZ Rosales, Rodolfo ESPINOZA Díaz, RONAILLE CALHEIRA Seara (41 Juan Manuel PERILLO), Piero Fernando ALVA Niezen. DT: Juan Máximo REYNOSO Guzmán
Goals: RONAILLE CALHEIRA Seara (21 own goal), Alejandro Darío GÓMEZ (24).

CLUB LIBERTAD ASUNCIÓN – SAN LUIS FC 0-2 (0-0)
Estadio Feliciano Cáceres, Luque, 28.04.2009
Referee: Paulo César DE OLIVEIRA (BRA), Attendance: 3.227
CLUB LIBERTAD ASUNCIÓN: Jorge Rodrigo BAVA, Édgar Gabriel BALBUENA Adorno, Vladimir MARÍN Rios, Lorgio ÁLVAREZ Roca, Pedro Alcides SARABIA Achucarro, Julio César MANZUR, Omar Héber POUSO Osores, Sergio Daniel AQUINO, Luis Alberto RAMÍREZ Lucay (65 Rodolfo Vicente GAMARRA Varela), Juan Eduardo SAMUDIO Serna (72 Miguel Alejandro XIMÉNEZ Acosta), Javier Mercedes GONZÁLEZ González (53 Manuel José MACIEL Fernández). DT: Javier TORRENTE
SAN LUIS FC: Adrián MARTÍNEZ Flores, Óscar Yaroslav MASCORRO Ábrego, Noé MAYA Vilches, José Alfredo GONZÁLEZ Tahuilán, Michael OROZCO Fiscal, Egidio Raúl ARÉVALO Ríos, Braulio LUNA Guzmán, Néstor Fabián BAREIRO Leguizamón (73 Ignacio TORRES Olvera), Malher Tressor MORENO Baldrich, Víctor Hugo LOJERO Alexanderson (46 Jairo Leonard PATIÑO Rosero), Rodolfo SALINAS Ortiz (46 José Rodolfo REYES Machado). DT: Luis Américo SCATOLARO
Goals: Jairo Leonard PATIÑO Rosero (58), José Rodolfo REYES Machado (90+1).

1	LIBERTAD	6	4	0	2	7	5	12
2	SAN LUÍS FC	6	2	2	2	7	7	8
3	Universitario	6	2	2	2	6	7	8
4	San Lorenzo	6	2	0	4	6	7	6

ROUND OF 16

CD Guadalajara SA and San Luis FC were forced to withdraw from the tournament due to a severe outbreak of influenza in Mexico.

Club Nacional Montevideo and São Paulo FC therefore automatically progressed to the quarter-finals.

SE PALMEIRAS – SPORT CLUB DO RECIFE 1-0 (0-0)
Estádio Palestra Itália (Parque Antarctica), São Paulo, 5.05.2009
Referee: Sergio Fabián PEZZOTTA (ARG), Attendance: 23.991
SE PALMEIRAS: MARCOS Roberto Silveira Reis, DANILO Laranjeira, MAURÍCIO Donizete RAMOS Júnior, Lucas PIERRE Santos Oliveira, Pablo Estifer ARMERO (80 JEFFERSON Nascimento), DIEGO de SOUZA Andrade, WILLIANS dos Santos Santana (65 Junior Santos Batista MOZART), CLEITON Ribeiro XAVIER, Marcos Antônio da Silva Gonçalves "MARQUINHOS" (65 José María ORTIGOZA Ortíz), WENDEL Santana Pereira Santos, KEIRRISON de Souza Carneiro. DT: Vanderlei LUXEMBURGO da Silva
SPORT CLUB DO RECIFE: Alessandro Beti Rosa "MAGRÃO", PAULO César BAIER, CÉSAR Ricardo de LUCENA, IGOR Nascimento Soares, Severino dos Ramos DURVAL da Silva, Antonio Monteiro DUTRA, HAMILTON Henio Ferreira Calheiros, DANIEL "PAULISTA" Pollo Barion (65 LUCIANO HENRIQUE de Gouveia), WILSON Rodrigues Fonseca (76 João Henrique de ANDRADE Amaral), Vanderson da Silva Souza "VANDINHO" (63 CIRO Henrique Alves Ferreira e Silva), MOACIR Costa da Silva. DT: NELSINHO BAPTISTA Júnior
Sent off: Hamilton (73)
Goal: José María ORTIGOZA Ortíz (74).

SPORT CLUB DO RECIFE – SE PALMEIRAS 1-0 (0-0); 1-3 penalties
Estádio Adelmar Costa Carvalho (Ilha do Retiro), Recife, 12.05.2009
Referee: Carlos Luis CHANDÍA Alarcón (CHI), Attendance: 28.487
SPORT CLUB DO RECIFE: Alessandro Beti Rosa "MAGRÃO", PAULO César BAIER (46 José Fernando FUMAGALLI), CÉSAR Ricardo de LUCENA, IGOR Nascimento Soares, Severino dos Ramos DURVAL da Silva, Antonio Monteiro DUTRA, João Henrique de ANDRADE Amaral (65 MOACIR Costa da Silva), LUCIANO HENRIQUE de Gouveia, DANIEL "PAULISTA" Pollo Barion (21 SANDRO "GOIANO" Gomes Luz), CIRO Henrique Alves Ferreira e Silva, WILSON Rodrigues Fonseca. DT: NELSINHO BAPTISTA Júnior
SE PALMEIRAS: MARCOS Roberto Silveira Reis, Marcos Alberto Skavinski "MARCÃO", DANILO Laranjeira, MAURÍCIO Donizete RAMOS Júnior, Lucas PIERRE Santos Oliveira, Pablo Estifer ARMERO, DIEGO de SOUZA Andrade (65 WILLIANS dos Santos Santana), CLEITON Ribeiro XAVIER, WENDEL Santana Pereira Santos, Elierce Barbosa de SOUZA (76 Junior Santos Batista MOZART), KEIRRISON de Souza Carneiro (65 José María ORTIGOZA Ortíz). DT: Vanderlei LUXEMBURGO da Silva
Sent off: Wendel (90)
Goal: WILSON Rodrigues Fonseca (83).
Penalties: * Junior Santos Batista MOZART, * LUCIANO HENRIQUE de Gouveia, 1-0 Marcos Alberto Skavinski "MARCÃO", 1-1 IGOR Nascimento Soares, 2-1 DANILO Laranjeira, * José Fernando FUMAGALLI, 3-1 Pablo Estifer ARMERO, * Antonio Monteiro DUTRA

CD UNIVERSIDAD SAN MARTÍN – GRÊMIO FOOT-BALL PORTO ALEGRENSE 1-3 (1-1)
Estadio Alejandro Villanueva, Lima, 6.05.2009
Referee: Carlos Alfredo VERA Rodríguez (ECU), Attendance: 7.000
CD UNIVERSIDAD SAN MARTÍN: Leao BUTRÓN Gotuzzo, Christian Guillermo Martín RAMOS Garagay, Guillermo Alejandro GIUZASOLA La Rosa (47 Jorge Raúl HUAMÁN Salinas), Guillermo Sandro SALAS Suarez, Mauro Emiliano CEJAS (62 Roberto Enrique SILVA Pro), José Luis DÍAZ Sulca (68 Victor Wilmer CARRILLO Gonzáles), Pedro Alexandro GARCÍA De La Cruz, Carlos Osvaldo FERNÁNDEZ Maldonado, John Cristopher HINOSTROZA Guzmán, Josepmir Aarón BALLÓN Villacorta, Martín Enrique ARZUAGA Coronel. DT: Víctor Hugo RIVERA Coronado
GRÊMIO FOOT-BALL PORTO ALEGRENSE: VICTOR Leandro Bagy, Leonardo "LÉO" Renan Simoes de Lacerda, FÁBIO SANTOS Romeu, RUY Bueno Neto, RÉVER Humberto Alves Araújo, RAFAEL MARQUES Pinto, ADÍLSON Warken, Anderson Simas Luciano "TCHECO" (90+1 DOUGLAS Costa de Souza), Williamis de SOUZA Silva, Maximiliano Gastón "MAXI" LÓPEZ (72 Germán Gustavo HERRERA), JONAS Gonçalves Oliveira (76 TÚLIO Lustosa Seixas Pinheiros). DT: Marcelo ROSPIDE
Goals: Martín Enrique ARZUAGA Coronel (34) /
Williamis de SOUZA Silva (9), Maximiliano Gastón "MAXI" LÓPEZ (46, 61).

GRÊMIO FOOT-BALL PORTO ALEGRENSE – CD UNIVERSIDAD SAN MARTÍN 2-0 (1-0)
Estádio Olímpico Monumental, Porto Alegre, 13.05.2009
Referee: Antonio Javier ARIAS Alvarenga (PAR), Attendance: 23.839
GRÊMIO FOOT-BALL PORTO ALEGRENSE: VICTOR Leandro Bagy, RAFAEL MARQUES Pinto, FÁBIO SANTOS Romeu (46 José JADÍLSON dos Santos Silva), Willian THIEGO de Jesus (84 TÚLIO Lustosa Seixas Pinheiros), RUY Bueno Neto, RÉVER Humberto Alves Araújo, ADÍLSON Warken, Anderson Simas Luciano "TCHECO", Williamis de SOUZA Silva, Maximiliano Gastón "MAXI" LÓPEZ, JONAS Gonçalves Oliveira (63 Germán Gustavo HERRERA). DT: Marcelo ROSPIDE
CD UNIVERSIDAD SAN MARTÍN: Leao BUTRÓN Gotuzzo, Jorge Raúl HUAMÁN Salinas, Christian Guillermo Martín RAMOS Garagay, Jorge Enrique REYES Condori, Guillermo Sandro SALAS Suarez, José Luis DÍAZ Sulca, Pedro Alexandro GARCÍA De La Cruz (77 Orlando ALLENDE Huby), John Cristopher HINOSTROZA Guzmán, Victor Wilmer CARRILLO Gonzáles, Josepmir Aarón BALLÓN Villacorta, Martín Enrique ARZUAGA Coronel (70 Carlos Alberto PÉREZ Alcaraz). DT: Víctor Hugo RIVERA Coronado
Goals: JONAS Gonçalves Oliveira (17), Germán Gustavo HERRERA (74).

CLUB DEPORTIVO CUENCA – CARACAS FC 2-1 (0-1)
Estadio Alejandro Serrano Aguilar, Cuenca, 7.05.2009
Referee: Víctor Hugo RIVERA Chavez (PER), Attendance: 20.000
CLUB DEPORTIVO CUENCA: Israel Cristopher ÁLVAREZ Vargas, Norberto Javier ORREGO, Juan Kely GUERRÓN Vásquez (85 Jhon Antonio GARCÍA Figueroa), William Osvaldo ESPAÑA España (37 Édison Andrés PRECIADO Bravo), Bernardo Javier CHILA Ayovi, Hólger Eduardo MATAMOROS Chunga, Giancarlo Pablo RAMOS Barrios, José Eduardo GRANDA Vicuña, RODRIGO TEIXEIRA Pereira, Ismael Oscar VILLALBA, Juan Carlos PAREDES Reasco. DT: Guillermo DURÓ
CARACAS FC: Renny Vicente VEGA Hernández, Deivis BARONE Farías, José Manuel REY Cortegoso, Gabriel Alejandro CICHERO Konarek, Gerardo Joaquín TORRES Herrera, Luis Enrique VERA Martineau (34 Jaime Andrés BUSTAMANTE Suárez), Franklin José LUCENA Peña, Jesús Javier GÓMEZ Mercado (35 Jámerson RENTERÍA Mena, 63 Zamir VALOYES Nabollán), Darío Damián FIGUEROA, Rafael Ernesto CASTELLÍN García, Rodrigo PRIETO Aubert. DT: Noel SANVINCENTE Bethelmy
Sent off: Castellín (20)
Goals: RODRIGO TEIXEIRA Pereira (58), Ismael Oscar VILLALBA (69) /
Gabriel Alejandro CICHERO Konarek (3).

CARACAS FC – CLUB DEPORTIVO CUENCA 4-0 (2-0)
Estadio Olímpico UCV, Caracas, 12.05.2009
Referee: Pablo Alejandro LUNATI (ARG), Attendance: 20.000
CARACAS FC: Renny Vicente VEGA Hernández, Deivis BARONE Farías, José Manuel REY Cortegoso, Gabriel Alejandro CICHERO Konarek, Gerardo Joaquín TORRES Herrera (50 Bremer Alfredo PIÑANGO Arevalo), Luis Enrique VERA Martineau (71 Giovanny Michael ROMERO Armenio), Franklin José LUCENA Peña, Jesús Javier GÓMEZ Mercado, Darío Damián FIGUEROA, Emilio RENTERÍA García (76 Zamir VALOYES Nabollán), Rodrigo PRIETO Aubert. DT: Noel SANVINCENTE Bethelmy
CLUB DEPORTIVO CUENCA: Israel Cristopher ÁLVAREZ Vargas, Norberto Javier ORREGO, Juan Kely GUERRÓN Vásquez, William Osvaldo ESPAÑA España, Bernardo Javier CHILA Ayovi, Hólger Eduardo MATAMOROS Chunga (81 Christian Santiago CORDERO Rodríguez), Giancarlo Pablo RAMOS Barrios (62 Jhon Antonio GARCÍA Figueroa), José Eduardo GRANDA Vicuña, RODRIGO TEIXEIRA Pereira, Ismael Oscar VILLALBA, Juan Carlos PAREDES Reasco (46 Édison Andrés PRECIADO Bravo). DT: Guillermo DURÓ
Goals: Darío Damián FIGUEROA (24 penalty), Rodrigo PRIETO Aubert (42), Emilio RENTERÍA García (52), José Manuel REY Cortegoso (73).

CA ESTUDIANTES DE LA PLATA – CLUB LIBERTAD ASUNCION 3-0 (1-0)
Estadio Ciudad de la Plata (Único), La Plata, 7.05.2009
Referee: Carlos Eugênio SIMÓN (BRA), Attendance: 20.912
CA ESTUDIANTES DE LA PLATA: Mariano Gonzalo ANDÚJAR, Leandro DESÁBATO, Cristian Ariel CELLAY, Marcos Alberto ANGELERI, Germán David RÉ, Enzo Nicolás PÉREZ (79 Juan Augusto HUERTA), Juan Sebastián VERÓN, Rodrigo BRAÑA, Leandro Damián BENÍTEZ (87 Raúl Alejandro IBERBIA), Gastón Nicolás FERNÁNDEZ (46 Maximiliano Exequiel NÚÑEZ), Mauro BOSELLI. DT: Alejandro Javier SABELLA
CLUB LIBERTAD ASUNCIÓN: Jorge Rodrigo BAVA, Édgar Gabriel BALBUENA Adorno, Vladimir MARÍN Rios, Lorgio ÁLVAREZ Roca, Pedro Alcides SARABIA Achucarro (82 Adalberto ROMÁN Benítez), Julio César MANZUR, Omar Héber POUSO Osores, Miguel Ángel SAMUDIO, Sergio Daniel AQUINO (78 Miguel Alejandro XIMÉNEZ Acosta), Luis Alberto RAMÍREZ Lucay, Juan Eduardo SAMUDIO Serna (65 Manuel José MACIEL Fernández). DT: Javier TORRENTE
Sent off: Samudio (62)
Goals: Gastón Nicolás FERNÁNDEZ (1), Mauro BOSELLI (64 penalty, 70).

CLUB LIBERTAD ASUNCIÓN – CA ESTUDIANTES DE LA PLATA 0-0
Estadio Feliciano Cáceres, Asunción, 14.05.2009
Referee: Roberto Carlos SILVERA Calcerrada (URU), Attendance: 1.987
CLUB LIBERTAD ASUNCIÓN: Jorge Rodrigo BAVA, Arnaldo Andrés VERA Chamorro, Édgar Gabriel BALBUENA Adorno (61 Nestor Abraham CAMACHO Ledesma), Lorgio ÁLVAREZ Roca, Pedro Alcides SARABIA Achucarro, Julio César MANZUR, Omar Héber POUSO Osores, Víctor Javier CÁCERES Centurión, Manuel José MACIEL Fernández, Miguel Alejandro XIMÉNEZ Acosta (64 Juan Eduardo SAMUDIO Serna), Javier Mercedes GONZÁLEZ González (55 Rodolfo Vicente GAMARRA Varela). DT: Javier TORRENTE
CA ESTUDIANTES DE LA PLATA: Mariano Gonzalo ANDÚJAR, Leandro DESÁBATO, Cristian Ariel CELLAY, Marcos Alberto ANGELERI, Germán David RÉ, Enzo Nicolás PÉREZ (76 Diego Alberto GALVÁN), Juan Sebastián VERÓN, Rodrigo BRAÑA, Leandro Damián BENÍTEZ (65 Raúl Alejandro IBERBIA), Gastón Nicolás FERNÁNDEZ (15 José Luis CALDERÓN), Mauro BOSELLI. DT: Alejandro Javier SABELLA
Sent off: Pouso (67)

CF UNIVERSIDAD DE CHILE – CRUZEIRO EC 1-2 (0-1)
Estadio Nacinal, Santiago, 7.05.2009
Referee: Jorge Luis LARRIONDA Pietrafesa (URU), Attendance: 35.000
CF UNIVERSIDAD DE CHILE: Miguel Ángel PINTO Jérez, Osvaldo Alexis GONZÁLEZ Sepúlveda, José Manuel ROJAS Bahamondes, Rafael Andrés OLARRA Guerrero, Marcelo Alfonso DÍAZ Rojas (61 Sebastián Eduardo PARDO Campos), José Raul CONTRERAS Arrau, Wálter Damián MONTILLO (54 Nelson Rafael CUEVAS Amarilla), Manuel Rolando ITURRA Urrutia, Felipe Ignacio SEYMOUR Dobud, Juan Manuel OLIVERA López (72 Manuel Arturo VILLALOBOS Salvos), Emilio Exequiel HERNÁNDEZ Hernández. DT: Sergio Apraham MARKARIÁN Abrahamian
CRUZEIRO EC: FÁBIO Deivson Lopes Maciel, JONATHAN Cícero Moreira (83 JANCARLOS de Oliveira Barros), Leonardo "LÉO" FORTUNATO dos Santos, LEONARDO Fabiano da SILVA e Silva, Antônio Marcos da Silva Filho "MARQUINHOS PARANÁ", RAMIRES Santos do Nascimento, WÁGNER Ferreira dos Santos (69 ATHIRSON Mazzoli de Oliveira), HENRIQUE Pacheco de Lima, GÉRSON "MAGRÃO" Alencar de Lima Junior, Hiziel de Souza SOARES (43 THIAGO RIBEIRO Cardoso), KLÉBER Giacomace de Souza Freitas. DT: ADILSON Dias BATISTA
Sent off: Olarra (87)
Goals: Manuel Arturo VILLALOBOS Salvos (85) / Hiziel de Souza SOARES (8), Antônio Marcos da Silva Filho "MARQUINHOS PARANÁ" (52).

CRUZEIRO EC – CF UNIVERSIDAD DE CHILE 1-0 (0-0)
Estádio Governador Magalhães Pinto (Mineirão), Belo Horizonte, 14.05.2009
Referee: Héctor Wálter BALDASSI (ARG), Attendance: 36.898
CRUZEIRO EC: FÁBIO Deivson Lopes Maciel, JONATHAN Cícero Moreira (77 JANCARLOS de Oliveira Barros), Leonardo "LÉO" FORTUNATO dos Santos, LEONARDO Fabiano da SILVA e Silva, Antônio Marcos da Silva Filho "MARQUINHOS PARANÁ", RAMIRES Santos do Nascimento, WÁGNER Ferreira dos Santos (44 ATHIRSON Mazzoli de Oliveira), HENRIQUE Pacheco de Lima, GÉRSON "MAGRÃO" Alencar de Lima Junior (58 ELICARLOS Souza Santos), THIAGO RIBEIRO Cardoso, KLÉBER Giacomace de Souza Freitas. DT: ADILSON Dias BATISTA
CF UNIVERSIDAD DE CHILE: Miguel Ángel PINTO Jérez, Osvaldo Alexis GONZÁLEZ Sepúlveda, José Manuel ROJAS Bahamondes, Juan Claudio GONZÁLEZ Calderon, Marcelo Alfonso DÍAZ Rojas (46 Nelson Rafael CUEVAS Amarilla), José Raul CONTRERAS Arrau, Marco Andrés ESTRADA Quinteros, Sebastián Eduardo PARDO Campos (46 Felipe Ignacio SEYMOUR Dobud), Manuel Rolando ITURRA Urrutia, Juan Manuel OLIVERA López (67 Manuel Arturo VILLALOBOS Salvos), Emilio Exequiel HERNÁNDEZ Hernández. DT: Sergio Apraham MARKARIÁN Abrahamian
Goal: KLÉBER Giacomace de Souza Freitas (74).

DEFENSOR SPORTING CLUB – CA BOCA JUNIORS BUENOS AIRES 2-2 (1-1)
Estadio Centenario, Montevideo, 14.05.2009
Referee: Carlos Manuel TORRES Nuñez (PAR), Attendance: 30.000
DEFENSOR SPORTING CLUB: Martín Andrés SILVA Leites, Jorge Wiston CURBELO-Gari, Walter Fernando IBÁÑEZ Costa, Pablo Daniel GAGLIANONE De León, Sergio Sebastián ARIOSA (69 Rodrigo Nicanor MORA), Diego Alejandro DE SOUZA Carballo, Miguel Angel AMADO Alanís, Julio Javier MARCHANT (82 Marcos Antonio García Nascimento "NASA"), Pablo César PINTOS Cabral, Diego Daniel VERA Méndez, Mauro Adrián VILA Wilkins (46 Álvaro Damián NAVARRO Bica). DT: Jorge Orosmán DA SILVA Etcheberrito
CA BOCA JUNIORS: Roberto Carlos ABBONDANZIERI, Julio César CÁCERES López, Claudio Marcelo MOREL Rodríguez, Hugo Benjamín IBARRA (85 Facundo Sebastián RONCAGLIA), Juan Daniel FORLÍN, Sebastián Alejandro BATTAGLIA, Cristian Manuel CHÁVEZ, Fabián Andrés VARGAS Rivera, Osvaldo Nicolás Fabián GAITÁN (78 Juan Ángel KRUPOVIESA), Martín PALERMO, Rodrigo Sebastián PALACIO (78 Lucas Ezequiel VIATRI). DT: Carlos Luis ISCHIA
Goals: Pablo Daniel GAGLIANONE De León (45), Rodrigo Nicanor MORA (84) /
Martín PALERMO (3), Rodrigo Sebastián PALACIO (56).

CA BOCA JUNIORS BUENOS AIRES – DEFENSOR SPORTING CLUB 0-1 (0-1)
Estadio Alberto J.Armando (La Bombonera), Buenos Aires, 21.05.2009
Referee: Sálvio Spínola FAGUNDES Filho (BRA), Attendance: 44.000
CA BOCA JUNIORS: Roberto Carlos ABBONDANZIERI, Julio César CÁCERES López, Claudio Marcelo MOREL Rodríguez (63 Osvaldo Nicolás Fabián GAITÁN), Juan Daniel FORLÍN, Facundo Sebastián RONCAGLIA, Sebastián Alejandro BATTAGLIA (69 Leandro GRACIÁN), Juan Román RIQUELME, Cristian Manuel CHÁVEZ (63 Luciano Gabriel "Lucho" FIGUEROA Herrera), Fabián Andrés VARGAS Rivera, Martín PALERMO, Rodrigo Sebastián PALACIO. DT: Carlos Luis ISCHIA
DEFENSOR SPORTING CLUB: Martín Andrés SILVA Leites, Jorge Wiston CURBELO-Gari, Mario Pablo RISSO, Pablo Daniel GAGLIANONE De León, Leandro Daniel CABRERA Sasla, Diego Alejandro DE SOUZA Carballo (83 Mauro Adrián VILA Wilkins), Miguel Angel AMADO Alanís, Diego FERREIRA (69 Rodrigo Nicanor MORA), Julio Javier MARCHANT, Pablo César PINTOS Cabral, Diego Daniel VERA Méndez (75 Álvaro Damián NAVARRO Bica). DT: Jorge Orosmán DA SILVA Etcheberrito
Goal: Diego Alejandro DE SOUZA Carballo (27).

QUARTER-FINALS

CRUZEIRO EC – SÃO PAULO FC 2-1 (1-0)
Estádio Governador Magalhães Pinto (Mineirão), Belo Horizonte, 27.05.2009
Referee: Carlos Luis CHANDÍA Alarcón (CHI), Attendance: 52.906
CRUZEIRO EC: FÁBIO Deivson Lopes Maciel, JONATHAN Cícero Moreira, THIAGO HELENO Henrique Ferreira, LEONARDO Fabiano da SILVA e Silva, FABRICIO de Sousa, Antônio Marcos da Silva Filho "MARQUINHOS PARANÁ", RAMIRES Santos do Nascimento, HENRIQUE Pacheco de Lima, GÉRSON "MAGRÃO" Alencar de Lima Junior (62 José "ZÉ" CARLOS Ferreira Filho), THIAGO RIBEIRO Cardoso (46 ATHIRSON Mazzoli de Oliveira), KLÉBER Giacomace de Souza Freitas. DT: ADILSON Dias BATISTA
SÃO PAULO FC: DÊNIS César de Matos, ANDRÉ Gonçalves DIAS, João MIRANDA de Souza Filho, JORGE WAGNER Goes Conceição, EDUARDO Nascimento COSTA, Anderson HERNANES de Carvalho Andrade, JEAN Raphael Vanderlei Moreira, RICHARLYSON Barbosa Felisbino, José "ZÉ" LUIS Santos da Visitação, WASHINGTON Stécanelo Cerqueira (75 ANDRÉ Luiz Barretto Silva LIMA), DAGOBERTO Pelentier (71 Humberlito BORGES Teixeira). DT: MURICY RAMALHO
Goals: LEONARDO Fabiano da SILVA e Silva (45), José "ZÉ" CARLOS Ferreira Filho (66) / WASHINGTON Stécanelo Cerqueira (57).

SÃO PAULO FC – CRUZEIRO EC 0-2 (0-0)
Estádio Cícero Pompeu de Toledo (Morumbí), São Paulo, 18.06.2009
Referee: Sergio Fabián PEZZOTTA (ARG), Attendance: 52.809
SÃO PAULO FC: DÊNIS César de Matos, ANDRÉ Gonçalves DIAS, JÚNIOR CÉSAR Eduardo Machado (46 Anderson HERNANES de Carvalho Andrade), RENATO Assis da SILVA, EDUARDO Nascimento COSTA, JEAN Raphael Vanderlei Moreira, MARLOS Romero Bonfim, RICHARLYSON Barbosa Felisbino, José "ZÉ" LUIS Santos da Visitação (76 ANDRÉ Luiz Barretto Silva LIMA), WASHINGTON Stécanelo Cerqueira (46 DAGOBERTO Pelentier), Humberlito BORGES Teixeira. DT: MURICY RAMALHO
CRUZEIRO EC: FÁBIO Deivson Lopes Maciel, JONATHAN Cícero Moreira (71 THIAGO HELENO Henrique Ferreira), Leonardo "LÉO" FORTUNATO dos Santos, LEONARDO Fabiano da SILVA e Silva, Antônio Marcos da Silva Filho "MARQUINHOS PARANÁ", WÁGNER Fereira dos Santos (66 JANCARLOS de Oliveira Barros), HENRIQUE Pacheco de Lima, ELICARLOS Souza Santos (75 BERNARDO Vieira de Souza), GÉRSON "MAGRÃO" Alencar de Lima Junior, WELLINGTON "PAULISTA" Pereira do Nascimento, KLÉBER Giacomace de Souza Freitas. DT: ADILSON Dias BATISTA
Sent off: Eduardo Costa (43), André Dias (80)
Goals: HENRIQUE Pacheco de Lima (65), KLÉBER Giacomace de Souza Freitas (81 penalty).

CARACAS FC – GRÊMIO FOOT-BALL PORTO ALEGRENSE 1-1 (1-0)
Estadio Olímpico, Caracas, 27.05.2009
Referee: Roberto Carlos SILVERA Calcerrada (URU), Attendance: 20.000
CARACAS FC: Renny Vicente VEGA Hernández, Deivis BARONE Farías, José Manuel REY Cortegoso, Gabriel Alejandro CICHERO Konarek, Giovanny Michael ROMERO Armenio, Luis Enrique VERA Martineau, Jesús Javier GÓMEZ Mercado (79 Rolando Emilio ESCOBAR Batista), Bremer Alfredo PIÑANGO Arevalo, Darío Damián FIGUEROA (65 Alejandro Abraham GUERRA Morales), Emilio RENTERÍA García (16 Rodrigo PRIETO Aubert), Rafael Ernesto CASTELLÍN García. DT: Noel SANVINCENTE Bethelmy
GRÊMIO FOOT-BALL PORTO ALEGRENSE: VICTOR Leandro Bagy, RAFAEL MARQUES Pinto, Leonardo "LÉO" Renan Simoes de Lacerda, FÁBIO SANTOS Romeu, RUY Bueno Neto, RÉVER Humberto Alves Araújo, ADÍLSON Warken, Anderson Simas Luciano "TCHECO", Williamis de SOUZA Silva (89 TÚLIO Lustosa Seixas Pinheiros), Maximiliano Gastón "MAXI" LÓPEZ, JONAS Gonçalves Oliveira (51 Alexander "ALEX MINEIRO" Pereira Cardoso). DT: PAULO AUTUORI de Mello).
Goals: Gabriel Alejandro CICHERO Konarek (2) / FÁBIO SANTOS Romeu (75).

GRÊMIO FOOT-BALL PORTO ALEGRENSE – CARACAS FC 0-0
Estádio Olímpico Monumental, Porto Alegre, 17.06.2009
Referee: Carlos Manuel TORRES Nuñez (PAR), Attendance: 36.725
GRÊMIO FOOT-BALL PORTO ALEGRENSE: MARCELO GROHE, RUY Bueno Neto, RÉVER Humberto Alves Araújo, Leonardo "LÉO" Renan Simoes de Lacerda, FÁBIO SANTOS Romeu, TÚLIO Lustosa Seixas Pinheiros, Anderson Simas Luciano "TCHECO", Williamis de SOUZA Silva, ADÍLSON Warken, Maximiliano Gastón "MAXI" LÓPEZ, Alexander "ALEX MINEIRO" Pereira Cardoso (58 Germán Gustavo HERRERA). DT: PAULO AUTUORI de Mello
CARACAS FC: Renny Vicente VEGA Hernández, Deivis BARONE Farías, José Manuel REY Cortegoso, Gabriel Alejandro CICHERO Konarek, Giovanny Michael ROMERO Armenio, Luis Enrique VERA Martineau, Franklin José LUCENA Peña, Jesús Javier GÓMEZ Mercado (70 Rodrigo PRIETO Aubert), Darío Damián FIGUEROA (66 Alejandro Abraham GUERRA Morales), Jámerson RENTERÍA Mena (56 Zamir VALOYES Nabollán), Rafael Ernesto CASTELLÍN García. DT: Noel SANVINCENTE Bethelmy

DEFENSOR SPORTING CLUB – CA ESTUDIANTES DE LA PLATA 0-1 (0-1)
Estadio Centenario, Montevideo, 28.05.2009
Referee: Juan Ernesto SOTO (VEN), Attendance: 15.000
DEFENSOR SPORTING CLUB: Martín Andrés SILVA Leites, Jorge Wiston CURBELO-Gari, Mario Pablo RISSO, Pablo Daniel GAGLIANONE De León, Sergio Sebastián ARIOSA (82 Marcos Antonio García Nascimento "NASA"), Diego Alejandro DE SOUZA Carballo, Miguel Angel AMADO Alanís, Julio Javier MARCHANT (56 Rodrigo Nicanor MORA), Pablo César PINTOS Cabral, Diego Daniel VERA Méndez, Álvaro Damián NAVARRO Bica (65 Mauro Adrián VILA Wilkins). DT: Jorge Orosmán DA SILVA Etcheberrito
CA ESTUDIANTES DE LA PLATA: Mariano Gonzalo ANDÚJAR, Leandro DESÁBATO, Cristian Ariel CELLAY, Marcos Alberto ANGELERI, Germán David RÉ, Enzo Nicolás PÉREZ, Juan Sebastián VERÓN, Rodrigo BRAÑA, Leandro Damián BENÍTEZ (81 Federico FERNÁNDEZ), Juan Manuel SALGUEIRO Silva (69 Diego Alberto GALVÁN), Mauro BOSELLI (88 José Luis CALDERÓN). DT: Alejandro Javier SABELLA
Sent off: Curbelo (26) / Angeleri (26)
Goal: Leandro DESÁBATO (12).

CA ESTUDIANTES DE LA PLATA – DEFENSOR SPORTING CLUB 1-0 (1-0)
Estadio Ciudad de la Plata (Único), La Plata, 18.06.2009
Referee: Óscar Julián RUIZ Acosta (COL), Attendance: 27.855
CA ESTUDIANTES DE LA PLATA: Mariano Gonzalo ANDÚJAR, Leandro DESÁBATO, Cristian Ariel CELLAY (46 Federico FERNÁNDEZ), Juan Manuel DÍAZ Martínez, Germán David RÉ, Enzo Nicolás PÉREZ, Juan Sebastián VERÓN, Rodrigo BRAÑA, Leandro Damián BENÍTEZ (89 Faustino Marcos Alberto ROJO), Juan Manuel SALGUEIRO Silva (55 Gastón Nicolás FERNÁNDEZ), Mauro BOSELLI. DT: Alejandro Javier SABELLA
DEFENSOR SPORTING CLUB: Martín Andrés SILVA Leites, Wálter Fernando IBÁÑEZ Costa, Mario Pablo RISSO (59 Alejandro Pablo TRAVERSA Machado), Carlos Richard DÍAZ, Leandro Daniel CABRERA Sasla, Miguel Angel AMADO Alanís, Marcos Antonio García Nascimento "NASA", Julio Javier MARCHANT (68 Mauro Adrián VILA Wilkins), Pablo César PINTOS Cabral, Diego Daniel VERA Méndez, Rodrigo Nicanor MORA (46 Diego Alejandro DE SOUZA Carballo). DT: Jorge Orosmán DA SILVA Etcheberrito
Sent off: Carlos Díaz (82)
Goal: Leandro Damián BENÍTEZ (13).

SE PALMEIRAS – CLUB NACIONAL MONTEVIDEO 1-1 (0-0)
Estádio Palestra Itália (Parque Antárctica), São Paulo, 28.05.2009
Referee: Carlos Manuel TORRES Nuñez (PAR), Attendance: 24.737
SE PALMEIRAS: MARCOS Roberto Silveira Reis, Marcos Alberto Skavinski "MARCÃO", MAURÍCIO Donizete RAMOS Júnior, DANILO Laranjeira, Lucas PIERRE Santos Oliveira, Pablo Estifer ARMERO, DIEGO de SOUZA Andrade, CLEITON Ribeiro XAVIER, Antônio Fábio Francez Cavalcante "FABINHO CAPIXABA" (28 Marcos Antônio da Silva Gonçalves "MARQUINHOS"), Elierce Barbosa de SOUZA (28 Manoel de Brito Filho "OBINA"), KEIRRISON de Souza Carneiro (74 JUMAR José da Costa Júnior). DT: Vanderlei LUXEMBURGO da Silva
CLUB NACIONAL MONTEVIDEO: Rodrigo Martín MUÑOZ Salomón, Mauricio Bernardo VICTORINO Dansilio, Matías Nicolás RODRÍGUEZ, Sebastián COATES Nion, Hugo Diego ARISMENDI, Marcelo Nicolás LODEIRO Benítez (90 Roberto Sebastián BRUM Gutiérrez), Adrián Marcelo ROMERO González, Óscar Javier MORALES Albornoz, Álvaro FERNÁNDEZ Gay, Alexander Jesús MEDINA Reobasco (74 Santiago Damián GARCÍA Correa), Gustavo Javier BISCAYZACÚ Perea (68 Ángel Alejandro MORALES Santos). DT: Gerardo Cono PELUSSO Boyrie
Sent off: Brum (90+3)
Goals: DIEGO de SOUZA Andrade (55) / Santiago Damián GARCÍA Correa (80).

CLUB NACIONAL MONTEVIDEO – SE PALMEIRAS 0-0
Estadio Centenario, Montevideo, 17.06.2009
Referee: Carlos Alfredo VERA Rodríguez (ECU), Attendance: 46.269
CLUB NACIONAL MONTEVIDEO: Rodrigo Martín MUÑOZ Salomón, Federico Hernán DOMÍNGUEZ, Mauricio Bernardo VICTORINO Dansilio, Matías Nicolás RODRÍGUEZ, Sebastián COATES Nion, Hugo Diego ARISMENDI, Marcelo Nicolás LODEIRO Benítez (90 Mauricio Ernesto PEREYRA Antonini), Adrián Marcelo ROMERO González, Óscar Javier MORALES Albornoz, Alexander Jesús MEDINA Reobasco (87 Ángel Alejandro MORALES Santos), Gustavo Javier BISCAYZACÚ Perea (58 Santiago Damián GARCÍA Correa). DT: Gerardo Cono PELUSSO Boyrie
SE PALMEIRAS: MARCOS Roberto Silveira Reis, Marcos Alberto Skavinski "MARCÃO" (64 Manoel de Brito Filho "OBINA"), MAURÍCIO Donizete RAMOS Júnior, DANILO Laranjeira, Lucas PIERRE Santos Oliveira, Pablo Estifer ARMERO, DIEGO de SOUZA Andrade, WILLIANS dos Santos Santana (55 José María ORTIGOZA Ortíz), CLEITON Ribeiro XAVIER, WENDEL Santana Pereira Santos (68 Elierce Barbosa de SOUZA), KEIRRISON de Souza Carneiro. DT: Vanderlei LUXEMBURGO da Silva

SEMI-FINALS

CRUZEIRO EC – GRÊMIO FOOT-BALL PORTO ALEGRENSE 3-1 (1-0)
Estádio Governador Magalhães Pinto (Mineirão), Belo Horizonte, 24.06.2009
Referee: Enrique Roberto OSSÉS Zencovich (CHI), Attendance: 51.696
CRUZEIRO EC: FÁBIO Deivson Lopes Maciel, JONATHAN Cícero Moreira, THIAGO HELENO Henrique Ferreira, LEONARDO Fabiano da SILVA e Silva, Antônio Marcos da Silva Filho "MARQUINHOS PARANÁ", WÁGNER Fereira dos Santos (86 BERNARDO Vieira de Souza), HENRIQUE Pacheco de Lima, ELICARLOS Souza Santos (85 JANCARLOS de Oliveira Barros), Fábio Alves Félix "FABINHO", WELLINGTON "PAULISTA" Pereira do Nascimento, KLÉBER Giacomace de Souza Freitas. DT: ADILSON Dias BATISTA
GRÊMIO FOOT-BALL PORTO ALEGRENSE: MARCELO GROHE, Willian THIEGO de Jesus, RÉVER Humberto Alves Araújo, Leonardo "LÉO" Renan Simoes de Lacerda, FÁBIO SANTOS Romeu, TÚLIO Lustosa Seixas Pinheiros, Anderson Simas Luciano "TCHECO", Williamis de SOUZA Silva, ADÍLSON Warken, Maximiliano Gastón "MAXI" LÓPEZ, Alexander "ALEX MINEIRO" Pereira Cardoso (69 Germán Gustavo HERRERA). DT: PAULO AUTUORI de Mello
Goals: WELLINGTON "PAULISTA" Pereira do Nascimento (38), WÁGNER Fereira dos Santos (47), Fábio Alves Félix "FABINHO" (67) / Williamis de SOUZA Silva (78).

GRÊMIO FOOT-BALL PORTO ALEGRENSE – CRUZEIRO EC 2-2 (0-2)
Estádio Olímpico Monumental, Porto Alegre, 2.07.2009
Referee: Óscar Julián RUIZ Acosta (COL), Attendance: 40.452
GRÊMIO FOOT-BALL PORTO ALEGRENSE: VICTOR Leandro Bagy, RÉVER Humberto Alves Araújo, Leonardo "LÉO" Renan Simoes de Lacerda, FÁBIO SANTOS Romeu, Willian THIEGO de Jesus, Williamis de SOUZA Silva, ADÍLSON Warken, TÚLIO Lustosa Seixas Pinheiros, Anderson Simas Luciano "TCHECO", Maximiliano Gastón "MAXI" LÓPEZ, Germán Gustavo HERRERA (78 Edixon PEREA Valencia). DT: PAULO AUTUORI de Mello
CRUZEIRO EC: FÁBIO Deivson Lopes Maciel, JONATHAN Cícero Moreira, THIAGO HELENO Henrique Ferreira, LEONARDO Fabiano da SILVA e Silva (51 ANDERSON Cléber Beraldo), Antônio Marcos da Silva Filho "MARQUINHOS PARANÁ", RAMIRES Santos do Nascimento, WÁGNER Fereira dos Santos, GÉRSON "MAGRÃO" Alencar de Lima Junior (60 ELICARLOS Souza Santos), Fábio Alves Félix "FABINHO", WELLINGTON "PAULISTA" Pereira do Nascimento (71 THIAGO RIBEIRO Cardoso), KLÉBER Giacomace de Souza Freitas. DT: ADILSON Dias BATISTA
Sent off: Adílson (60)
Goals: RÉVER Humberto Alves Araújo (54), Williamis de SOUZA Silva (74) / WELLINGTON "PAULISTA" Pereira do Nascimento (34, 36).

CA ESTUDIANTES DE LA PLATA – CLUB NACIONAL MONTEVIDEO 1-0 (1-0)
Estadio Ciudad de la Plata (Único), La Plata, 25.06.2009
Referee: René Marcelo ORTUBÉ Betancourt (BOL)
CA ESTUDIANTES DE LA PLATA: Mariano Gonzalo ANDÚJAR, Leandro DESÁBATO, Cristian Ariel CELLAY (80 Juan Manuel DÍAZ Martínez), Rolando Carlos SCHIAVI, Germán David RÉ, Juan Sebastián VERÓN (46 Matías Ariel SÁNCHEZ), Diego Alberto GALVÁN (58 Maximiliano Ezequiel NÚÑEZ), Rodrigo BRAÑA, Leandro Damián BENÍTEZ, Gastón Nicolás FERNÁNDEZ, Mauro BOSELLI. DT: Alejandro Javier SABELLA
CLUB NACIONAL MONTEVIDEO: Rodrigo Martín MUÑOZ Salomón, Mauricio Bernardo VICTORINO Dansilio, Matías Nicolás RODRÍGUEZ, Sebastián COATES Nion, Hugo Diego ARISMENDI, Marcelo Nicolás LODEIRO Benítez, Adrián Marcelo ROMERO González, Óscar Javier MORALES Albornoz, Álvaro FERNÁNDEZ Gay (73 Federico Hernán DOMÍNGUEZ), Alexander Jesús MEDINA Reobasco (46 Santiago Damián GARCÍA Correa), Gustavo Javier BISCAYZACÚ Perea (65 Ángel Alejandro MORALES Santos). DT: Gerardo Cono PELUSSO Boyrie
Goal: Diego Alberto GALVÁN (14).

CLUB NACIONAL MONTEVIDEO – CA ESTUDIANTES DE LA PLATA 1-2 (0-0)
Estadio Centenario, Montevideo, 1.07.2009
Referee: Carlos Manuel TORRES Nuñez (PAR), Attendance: 46.983
CLUB NACIONAL MONTEVIDEO: Rodrigo Martín MUÑOZ Salomón, Federico Hernán DOMÍNGUEZ (59 Santiago Damián GARCÍA Correa), Mauricio Bernardo VICTORINO Dansilio, Matías Nicolás RODRÍGUEZ (68 Álvaro FERNÁNDEZ Gay), Sebastián COATES Nion, Hugo Diego ARISMENDI, Adrián Marcelo ROMERO González, Ángel Alejandro MORALES Santos (46 Marcelo Nicolás LODEIRO Benítez), Óscar Javier MORALES Albornoz, Alexander Jesús MEDINA Reobasco, Marcos Gustavo MONDAINI. DT: Gerardo Cono PELUSSO Boyrie
CA ESTUDIANTES DE LA PLATA: Mariano Gonzalo ANDÚJAR, Leandro DESÁBATO, Juan Manuel DÍAZ Martínez, Rolando Carlos SCHIAVI, Germán David RÉ, Matías Ariel SÁNCHEZ, Enzo Nicolás PÉREZ (71 Diego Alberto GALVÁN), Rodrigo BRAÑA, Leandro Damián BENÍTEZ, Gastón Nicolás FERNÁNDEZ (68 Juan Manuel SALGUEIRO Silva), Mauro BOSELLI (90+2 José Luis CALDERÓN). DT: Alejandro Javier SABELLA
Goals: Alexander Jesús MEDINA Reobasco (75) / Mauro BOSELLI (52, 90+1).

FINALS

CA ESTUDIANTES DE LA PLATA – CRUZEIRO EC 0-0
Estadio Ciudad de la Plata (Único), La Plata, 8.07.2009
Referee: Jorge Luis LARRIONDA Pietrafesa (URU)
CA ESTUDIANTES DE LA PLATA: Mariano Gonzalo ANDÚJAR, Leandro DESÁBATO, Cristian Ariel CELLAY, Rolando Carlos SCHIAVI, Germán David RÉ, Enzo Nicolás PÉREZ, Juan Sebastián VERÓN, Rodrigo BRAÑA, Leandro Damián BENÍTEZ (74 Maximiliano Ezequiel NÚÑEZ), Gastón Nicolás FERNÁNDEZ (81 Juan Manuel SALGUEIRO Silva), Mauro BOSELLI. DT: Alejandro Javier SABELLA
CRUZEIRO EC: FÁBIO Deivson Lopes Maciel, JONATHAN Cícero Moreira, ANDERSON Cléber Beraldo, LEONARDO Fabiano da SILVA e Silva, Antônio Marcos da Silva Filho "MARQUINHOS PARANÁ", RAMIRES Santos do Nascimento, WÁGNER Fereira dos Santos, HENRIQUE Pacheco de Lima, GÉRSON "MAGRÃO" Alencar de Lima Junior (85 Fábio Alves Félix "FABINHO"), WELLINGTON "PAULISTA" Pereira do Nascimento, KLÉBER Giacomace de Souza Freitas. DT: ADILSON Dias BATISTA

CRUZEIRO EC – CA ESTUDIANTES DE LA PLATA 1-2 (0-0)
Estádio Governador Magalhães Pinto (Mineirão), Belo Horizonte, 15.07.2009
Referee: Carlos Luis CHANDÍA Alarcón (CHI), Attendance: 60.000
CRUZEIRO EC: FÁBIO Deivson Lopes Maciel, JONATHAN Cícero Moreira, THIAGO HELENO Henrique Ferreira, LEONARDO Fabiano da SILVA e Silva, Antônio Marcos da Silva Filho "MARQUINHOS PARANÁ", RAMIRES Santos do Nascimento, WÁGNER Fereira dos Santos (71 ATHIRSON Mazzoli de Oliveira), HENRIQUE Pacheco de Lima, GÉRSON "MAGRÃO" Alencar de Lima Junior, WELLINGTON "PAULISTA" Pereira do Nascimento (75 THIAGO RIBEIRO Cardoso), KLÉBER Giacomace de Souza Freitas. DT: ADILSON Dias BATISTA
CA ESTUDIANTES DE LA PLATA: Mariano Gonzalo ANDÚJAR, Leandro DESÁBATO, Cristian Ariel CELLAY, Rolando Carlos SCHIAVI, Germán David RÉ, Enzo Nicolás PÉREZ, Juan Sebastián VERÓN, Rodrigo BRAÑA (87 Matías Ariel SÁNCHEZ), Leandro Damián BENÍTEZ (80 Juan Manuel DÍAZ Martínez), Gastón Nicolás FERNÁNDEZ (90 José Luis CALDERÓN), Mauro BOSELLI. DT: Alejandro Javier SABELLA
Goals: HENRIQUE Pacheco de Lima (52) / Gastón Nicolás FERNÁNDEZ (57), Mauro BOSELLI (72).

2010

FIRST STAGE

CA COLON DE SANTA FE – CD UNIVERSIDAD CATOLICA 3-2 (1-1)
Estadio Brigadier General Estanislao López, Santa Fé, 26.01.2010
Referee: Jorge Luis LARRIONDA Pietrafesa (URU), Attendance: 14.902
CA COLON DE SANTA FE: Diego Raúl POZO, Marcelo Jesús GOUX, Salustiano Antonio CANDÍA Gaieano, Germán Ezequiel RIVAROLA, Ariel Hernán GARCÉ, Alejandro Rubén CAPURRO, Iván Diego MORENO Y FABIANESI (54 Eduardo Germán COUDET), Ricardo Ernesto GÓMEZ (46 Juan Manuel LUCERO Campos), Facundo BERTOGLIO, Federico NIETO, Esteban Oscar FUERTES (76 Cristian Alberto PELLERANO). DT: Antonio Ricardo MOHAMED Matijevich
CD UNIVERSIDAD CATÓLICA: Paulo Andrés GARCÉS Contreras, Ismael Ignacio FUENTES Castro, Hans MARTÍNEZ Cabrera, David Andrés HENRÍQUEZ Espinoza, Damián Rodrigo DÍAZ, Rodrigo Alejandro TOLOZA Vilches (77 Pablo Andrés VRANJICAN), Jorge ORMEÑO Guerra, Rodrigo Ignatio VALENZUELA Avilés, Francisco Andrés SILVA Gajardo (42 Ángel Rodrigo CARREÑO Ballesteros), Milovan Petar MIROSEVIC Albornoz (67 Fernando Andrés MENESES Cornejo), Juan José MORALES. DT: Marco Antonio FIGUEROA Montero
Sent off: Ormeño (90+2)
Goals: Federico NIETO (5), Esteban Oscar FUERTES (66), Facundo BERTOGLIO (69) /
Juan José MORALES (35, 81).

CD UNIVERSIDAD CATÓLICA – CA COLÓN DE SANTA FÉ 3-2 (1-0); 5-3 penalties
Estadio San Carlos de Apoquindo, Santiago, 9.02.2010
Referee: Carlos Manuel TORRES Nuñez (PAR), Attendance: 12.272
CD UNIVERSIDAD CATÓLICA: Paulo Andrés GARCÉS Contreras, Ismael Ignacio FUENTES Castro, Leonel Jonathan MENA Gutiérrez, Hans MARTÍNEZ Cabrera, David Andrés HENRÍQUEZ Espinoza, Damián Rodrigo DÍAZ, Rodrigo Alejandro TOLOZA Vilches, Rodrigo Ignatio VALENZUELA Avilés (76 Rodrigo Martín MANNARA), Ángel Rodrigo CARREÑO Ballesteros (57 Pablo Andrés VRANJICAN), Milovan Petar MIROSEVIC Albornoz, Juan José MORALES. DT: Marco Antonio FIGUEROA Montero
CA COLÓN DE SANTA FÉ: Diego Raúl POZO, Marcelo Jesús GOUX, Salustiano Antonio CANDÍA Gaieano, Germán Ezequiel RIVAROLA, Ariel Hernán GARCÉ (44 Eduardo Germán COUDET), Alejandro Rubén CAPURRO, Iván Diego MORENO Y FABIANESI, Nicolás Emanuel TORRES, Facundo BERTOGLIO (72 Josimar MOSQUERA Angulo), Federico NIETO, Esteban Oscar FUERTES (59 Cristian Alberto PELLERANO). DT: Antonio Ricardo MOHAMED Matijevich
Sent off: Candía (69)
Goals: David Andrés HENRÍQUEZ Espinoza (40), Rodrigo Alejandro TOLOZA Vilches (75),
Juan José MORALES (83) /
Iván Diego MORENO Y FABIANESI (53), Esteban Oscar FUERTES (56 penalty).
Penalties: 1-0 Rodrigo Alejandro TOLOZA Vilches, 1-1 Eduardo Germán COUDET, 2-1 Milovan Petar MIROSEVIC Albornoz, * Iván Diego MORENO Y FABIANESI, 3-1 Pablo Andrés VRANJICAN, 3-2 Cristian Alberto PELLERANO, 4-2 Damián Rodrigo DÍAZ, 4-3 Germán Ezequiel RIVAROLA, 5-3 Rodrigo Martín MANNARA

DEPORTIVO TÁCHIRA FC – CLUB LIBERTAD ASUNCIÓN 1-0 (1-0)
Estadio Polideportivo de Pueblo Nuevo, San Cristóbal, 26.01.2010
Referee: José Hernando BUITRAGO Arango (COL), Attendance: 16.382
DEPORTIVO TÁCHIRA FC: Manuel Alejandro SANHOUSE Contreras, Daniel Eduardo BENÍTEZ Pernía, Gerzon Armando CHACÓN Varela, José Luis GRANADOS Asprilla, Jong Harold VIÁFARA Ramos, Pedro Alfonzo FERNÁNDEZ Camacho, Nicolás Ignacioa DIEZ Parajón (63 Jorge Alberto ROJAS Méndez), Édgar Fernando PÉREZ Greco (76 Yeison David YBARROLA Silva), José Javier VILLAFRAZ Quintero, Daniel Enrique ARISMENDI Marchán (72 José Mauricio PARRA Perdomo), Armando Rafael MAITA Urbáez. DT: Carlos Fabián MALDONADO Piñeiro
CLUB LIBERTAD ASUNCIÓN: Bernardo David MEDINA, Pedro Alcides SARABIA Achucarro, Ismael BENEGAS, Édgar Arnulfo ROBLES Coronel (56 José Ariel NÚÑEZ Portelli), Víctor Javier CÁCERES Centurión, Miguel Ángel Ramón SAMUDIO, Víctor Hugo AYALA Núñez, Jorge Luis CABALLERO Alonzo, Rodrigo ALBORNO Ortega (66 Rodolfo Vicente GAMARRA Varela), Roberto Carlos GAMARRA Acosta (67 Javier Mercedes GONZÁLEZ González), Pablo César VELÁZQUEZ Centurión. DT: Javier TORRENTE
Sent off: Fernández (69)
Goal: Armando Rafael MAITA (27).

CLUB LIBERTAD ASUNCIÓN – DEPORTIVO TÁCHIRA FC 3-1 (1-1)
Estadio Defensores del Chaca, Asunción, 2.02.2010
Referee: Héctor Wálter BALDASSI (ARG), Attendance: 1.252
CLUB LIBERTAD ASUNCIÓN: Bernardo David MEDINA, Pedro Alcides SARABIA Achucarro, Ismael BENEGAS (72 Jorge Luis CABALLERO Alonzo), Sergio Daniel AQUINO, Víctor Javier CÁCERES Centurión, Miguel Ángel Ramón SAMUDIO, Gustavo Alberto CRISTALDO Brítez (46 Javier Mercedes GONZÁLEZ González), Jorge Luis MOREIRA Ferreira (55 Wilson Omar PITTONI Rodríguez), Víctor Hugo AYALA Núñez, Pablo César VELÁZQUEZ Centurión, Rodolfo Vicente GAMARRA Varela. DT: Javier TORRENTE
DEPORTIVO TÁCHIRA FC: Manuel Alejandro SANHOUSE Contreras, Pedro Luis BOADA Noya, Daniel Eduardo BENÍTEZ Pernía, Gerzon Armando CHACÓN Varela (82 David Eduardo SOLARI), José Luis GRANADOS Asprilla, Jong Harold VIÁFARA Ramos, Jorge Alberto ROJAS Méndez, Nicolás Ignacioa DIEZ Parajón, José Javier VILLAFRAZ Quintero, Armando Rafael MAITA Urbáez (78 Daniel Enrique ARISMENDI Marchán), Yeison David YBARROLA Silva (68 Édgar Fernando PÉREZ Greco). DT: Carlos Fabián MALDONADO Piñeiro
Goals: Rodolfo Vicente GAMARRA Varela (40), Pablo César VELÁZQUEZ Centurión (67), Pablo César VELÁZQUEZ Centurión (81) / Pedro Luis BOADA Noya (29).

CA NEWELL'S OLD BOYS – CS EMELEC 0-0
Estadio Marcelo Alberto Bielsa, Rosario, 27.01.2010
Referee: Roberto Carlos SILVERA Calcerrada (URU), Attendance: 15.292
CA NEWELL'S OLD BOYS: Sebastián Darío PERATTA, Agustín ALAYES, Rolando Carlos SCHIAVI, Juan Manuel INSAURRALDE, Lucas Ademar BERNARDI (71 Cristian Nicolás SÁNCHEZ PRETTE), Leonel Jesús VANGIONI, Diego MATEO Alustiza, Carlos ROSELLI (46 Diego Alberto TORRES), Mauro Abel FÓRMICA, Jorge Daniel ACHUCARRO (82 Juan Leandro QUIROGA), Antonio Joaquín BOGHOSSIAN. DT: Roberto Néstor SENSINI
CS EMELEC: Marcelo Ramón ELIZAGA Ferrero, Gabriel Eduardo ACHILIER Zurita, Julio Marcelo FLEITAS Silveira, Mariano Florencio MINA Orobio, Carlos Andrés QUIÑÓNEZ Valencia (75 Silvano de los Santos ESTACIO Montaño), Miguel David QUIROZ Villón, Pablo Javier PÉREZ (90+3 Hernán Gastón PEIRONE), Pedro Ángel QUIÑÓNEZ Rodríguez, Santiago BIGLIERI, Joao Robin ROJAS Menzoza, Enner Remberto VALENCIA Lastra (57 José Luis QUIÑÓNEZ Quiñónez). DT: Jorge Luis SAMPAOLI

CS EMELEC – CA NEWELL'S OLD BOYS 2-1 (0-0)
Estadio George Capwell, Guayaquil, 10.02.2010
Referee: Óscar Julián RUÍZ Acosta (COL), Attendance: 14.634
CS EMELEC: Marcelo Ramón ELIZAGA Ferrero, Gabriel Eduardo ACHILIER Zurita, Julio Marcelo FLEITAS Silveira, Mariano Florencio MINA Orobio, Miguel David QUIROZ Villón (79 Carlos Andrés QUIÑÓNEZ Valencia), Pablo Javier PÉREZ, Fernando Augusto GIMÉNEZ Solis (26 José Luis QUIÑÓNEZ Quiñónez), Pedro Ángel QUIÑÓNEZ Rodríguez, Santiago BIGLIERI (90+2 Eduardo Javier MORANTE Rosas), Joao Robin ROJAS Menzoza, Jaime Javier AYOVÍ Corozo. DT: Jorge Luis SAMPAOLI
CA NEWELL'S OLD BOYS: Sebastián Darío PERATTA, Agustín ALAYES, Rolando Carlos SCHIAVI, Juan Manuel INSAURRALDE, Lucas Ademar BERNARDI (79 Mauricio Ezequiel SPERDUTTI), Hugo Alberto BARRIENTOS, Leonel Jesús VANGIONI (70 Marcelo Alejandro ESTIGARRIBIA Balmori), Pablo Franco DOLCI, Mauro Abel FÓRMICA, Jorge Daniel ACHUCARRO (86 Cristian Manuel NÚÑEZ), Antonio Joaquín BOGHOSSIAN. DT: Roberto Néstor SENSINI
Sent off: Schiavi (85)
Goals: Joao Robin ROJAS Menzoza (46), José Luis QUIÑÓNEZ Quiñónez (66) /
Hugo Alberto BARRIENTOS (53).

CLUB BAMIN REAL POTOSÍ – CRUZEIRO EC 1-1 (0-1)
Estadio Víctor Agustín Ugarte, Potosí, 27.01.2010
Referee: Víctor Hugo RIVERA Chavez (PER), Attendance: 7.064
CLUB BAMIN REAL POTOSÍ: MAURO MACHADO da Silva, Édgar CLAVIJO Peralta (46 Augusto ANDAVERIS Iriondo), Edhemar RODRÍGUEZ Mercado, Álvaro RICALDI Alcócer, Gonzalo Germán GALINDO Sánchez, Ronald EGUINO Segovia, Eduardo ORTIZ Cuéllar (27 Roberto Carlos CORREA Arias), Miguel Oswaldo LOAYZA Tardío, Fernando ARGARAÑAZ, César Gerardo YECEROTTI Soruco, Cristian Maciel RUIZ (73 Jorge Daniel FLORENTÍN Cáceres). DT: Sergio APAZA
CRUZEIRO EC: Deivison Lopes Maciel "FÁBIO", LEANDRO Fabiano da SILVA e Silva, DIEGO RENÁN de Lima Ferreira, Carlos Gilberto Nascimento da Silva e Silva "GIL", GILBERTO da Silva Melo, Antônio Marcos da Silva Filho "MARQUINHOS PARANÁ", HENRIQUE Pacheco de Lima, ELICARLOS Souza Santos, PEDRO KEN Morimoto Moreira (74 Fábio Alves Félix "FABINHO"), WELLINGTON "PAULISTA" Pereira do Nascimento (51 JONATHAN Cícero Moreira), KLÉBER Giacomace de Souza Freitas (68 THIAGO RIBEIRO Cardoso). DT: ADÍLSON Dias BATISTA
Sent off: Gilberto (22)
Goals: Roberto Carlos CORREA Arias (88) /
WELLINGTON "PAULISTA" Pereira do Nascimento (7).

CRUZEIRO EC – CLUB BAMIN REAL POTOSÍ 7-0 (4-0)
Estaádio Governador Magalhães Pinto, Belo Horizonte, 3.02.2010
Referee: Diego Hernán ABAL (ARG), Attendance: 36.574
CRUZEIRO EC: Deivison Lopes Maciel "FÁBIO", JONATHAN Cícero Moreira, LEANDRO Fabiano da SILVA e Silva, DIEGO RENÁN de Lima Ferreira, Carlos Gilberto Nascimento da Silva e Silva "GIL", Antônio Marcos da Silva Filho "MARQUINHOS PARANÁ", HENRIQUE Pacheco de Lima, ELICARLOS Souza Santos (48 Joffre David GUERRÓN Méndez), WELLINGTON "PAULISTA" Pereira do Nascimento (66 BERNARDO Vieira de Souza), KLÉBER Giacomace de Souza Freitas (73 ELIANDRO dos Santos Gonzaga), THIAGO RIBEIRO Cardoso. DT: ADÍLSON Dias BATISTA
CLUB BAMIN REAL POTOSÍ: MAURO MACHADO da Silva, Édgar CLAVIJO Peralta, Edhemar RODRÍGUEZ Mercado, Helmut Enrique GUTIÉRREZ Zapata, Álvaro RICALDI Alcócer, Gonzalo Germán GALINDO Sánchez, Ronald EGUINO Segovia, Eduardo ORTIZ Cuéllar, Fernando ARGARAÑAZ (64 Miguel Oswaldo LOAYZA Tardío), Augusto ANDAVERIS Iriondo (87 Pastor Buenaventura TORRES Quiroz), César Gerardo YECEROTTI Soruco. DT: Sergio APAZA
Sent off: Yecerotti (46), Galindo (74)
Goals: Antônio Marcos da Silva Filho "MARQUINHOS PARANÁ" (28), THIAGO RIBEIRO Cardoso (30), KLÉBER Giacomace de Souza Freitas (39), JONATHAN Cícero Moreira (45), ELIANDRO dos Santos Gonzaga (87), BERNARDO Vieira de Souza (88), Joffre David GUERRÓN Méndez (90+1).

CLUB JUAN AURICH – CF ESTUDIANTES TECOS 2-0 (1-0)
Estadio Elías Aguirre, Chiclayo, 27.01.2010
Referee: Pablo Antonio POZO Quinteros (CHI), Attendance: 10.312
CLUB JUAN AURICH: Diego Hernán MORALES, Roberto Carlos GUIZASOLA La Rosa, Jesús Martín ÁLVAREZ Hurtado, Jorge Martín ARAUJO Paredes, Willy Alexander RIVAS Asin, Juan Carlos LA ROSA Llontop, Renato Gianfranco ESPEJO Reyes, Luis Carlos TEJADA Hansel (81 Manuel Francisco BARRETO Sayón), Herlyn Ysrael ZÚÑIGA Yáñez (57 Ricardo Manuel CICILIANO Bustillo), Pedro Luis ASCOY Cortez (90+1 Franco Giovanni MENDOZA Breña), Reimond MANCO Albarracin. DT: Luis Fernando SUÁREZ
CF ESTUDIANTES TECOS: Mario RODRÍGUEZ Cervantes, Juan Carlos LEAÑO Del Castillo, Diego Octavio JIMÉNEZ Villa, Marcelo Guadalupe ALATORRE Maldonado (86 Jorge Damián ZAMOGILNY), Joel SÁNCHEZ Ramos (61 Fredy José BAREIRO Gamarra), Oswaldo ALANÍS Pantoja (86 Jorge Damián ZAMOGILNY), Rafael MEDINA Rodríguez, Elgabry Ricardo RANGEL Especiano, Mauro Emiliano CEJAS, Alberto RAMÍREZ Torres (56 Rubens Oscar SAMBUEZA), Rodrigo Patricio RUIZ De Barbieri. DT: Miguel Ernesto HERRERA Aguirre
Goals: Luis Carlos TEJADA Hansel (11, 60).

CF ESTUDIANTES TECOS – CLUB JUAN AURICH 1-2 (0-1)
Estadio Tres de Marzo, Zapopan, 3.02.2010
Referee: Juan Ernesto SOTO Arevalo (VEN), Attendance: 3.000
CF ESTUDIANTES TECOS: Mario RODRÍGUEZ Cervantes, Juan Carlos LEAÑO Del Castillo, Diego Octavio JIMÉNEZ Villa, Marcelo Guadalupe ALATORRE Maldonado (20 Samuel (Sammy) OCHOA Oregel), Daniel ALCÁNTAR García (46 Roberto Carlos GUTIÉRREZ Gamboa), Rafael MEDINA Rodríguez (46 Mauro Emiliano CEJAS), Elgabry Ricardo RANGEL Especiano, Jorge Damián ZAMOGILNY, Rubens Oscar SAMBUEZA, Rodrigo Patricio RUIZ De Barbieri, Fredy José BAREIRO Gamarra. DT: Miguel Ernesto HERRERA Aguirre
CLUB JUAN AURICH: Diego Hernán MORALES, Roberto Carlos GUIZASOLA La Rosa, Jesús Martín ÁLVAREZ Hurtado, Jorge Martín ARAUJO Paredes, Willy Alexander RIVAS Asin, Ricardo Manuel CICILIANO Bustillo, Juan Carlos LA ROSA Llontop, Renato Gianfranco ESPEJO Reyes, Luis Carlos TEJADA Hansel (81 Herlyn Ysrael ZÚÑIGA Yáñez), Pedro Luis ASCOY Cortez (61 José Luis GUEVARA Tnoco), Reimond MANCO Albarracin (77 César Alberto SÁNCHEZ Aurich). DT: Luis Fernando SUÁREZ
Sent off: Rivas (66)
Goals: Fredy José BAREIRO Gamarra (76) /
Luis Carlos TEJADA Hansel (43), Ricardo Manuel CICILIANO Bustillo (74).

CPD ATLÉTICO JUNIOR – RACING CLUB DE MONTEVIDEO 2-2 (1-1)
Estadio Metropolitano Roberto Meléndez, Barranquilla, 28.01.2010
Referee: Carlos Alfredo VERA Rodríguez (ECU), Attendance: 18.026
CPD ATLÉTICO JUNIOR: Adrián BERBIA Pose, Román Aureliano TORRES Morcillo, César Augusto FAWCETT Lebolo (79 John Alexander VALENCIA Hinestroza), Hayder Guillermo PALACIO Álvarez, Roller CAMBINDO Ibarra, Giovanni HERNÁNDEZ Soto, Paulo César ARANGO Ambuila, Jhon Alexander JARAMILLO Gómez, Jorge Daniel CASANOVA Curbelo (62 Martín Enrique ARZUAGA Coronel), Emerson de Jesús ACUÑA Juviano (81 Víctor Javier CORTEZ), Carlos Arturo BACCA Ahumada. DT: Diego Edison UMAÑA
RACING CLUB DE MONTEVIDEO: Jorge Wálter CONTRERAS Rodríguez, José Ignacio PALLÁS Martínez, Héctor Roberto HERNÁNDEZ, Rodrigo Nicolás BRASESCO Pérez, Danny TEJERA, Diego Martín SCOTTI Ponce de León, Darío Antonio FLORES Bitolfi (78 Alejandro Cléber REYES Sosa), Santiago Humberto OSTOLAZA Chimelir, Claudio Matías MIRABAJE Correa (66 Jean Pierre Augustín BARRIENTOS Díaz), Líber Daniel QUIÑÓNEZ Prieto (62 Néstor Fabián SILVA Fros), Martín CAUTERRUCCIO. DT: Juan José VERZERI Casas
Sent off: Cambindo (74) / Cauterruccio (45)
Goals: Emerson de Jesús ACUÑA Juviano (13), Martín Enrique ARZUAGA Coronel (90+2) /
Claudio Matías MIRABAJE Correa (29), José Ignacio PALLÁS Martínez (68).

RACING CLUB DE MONTEVIDEO – CPD ATLÉTICO JUNIOR 2-0 (1-0)
Estadio Gran Parque Central, Montevideo, 4.02.2010
Referee: Paulo César DE OLIVEIRA (BRA), Attendance: 4.768
RACING CLUB DE MONTEVIDEO: Jorge Wálter CONTRERAS Rodríguez, José Ignacio PALLÁS Martínez, Héctor Roberto HERNÁNDEZ, Rodrigo Nicolás BRASESCO Pérez, Danny TEJERA, Darío Antonio FLORES Bitolfi (79 Gastón MACHADO), Santiago Humberto OSTOLAZA Chimelir, Claudio Matías MIRABAJE Correa (68 Jean Pierre Augustín BARRIENTOS Díaz), Héctor Federico VEGA Ataídes, Néstor Fabián SILVA Fros (71 Román Marcelo CUELLO Arizmendi), Líber Daniel QUIÑÓNEZ Prieto. DT: Juan José VERZERI Casas
CPD ATLÉTICO JUNIOR: Adrián BERBIA Pose, Román Aureliano TORRES Morcillo, César Augusto FAWCETT Lebolo, Hayder Guillermo PALACIO Álvarez, Pedro Pablo TAVIMA Parra, Giovanni HERNÁNDEZ Soto, Paulo César ARANGO Ambuila, Jhon Alexander JARAMILLO Gómez (51 Víctor Javier CORTEZ), Jorge Daniel CASANOVA Curbelo, Emerson de Jesús ACUÑA Juviano (77 Frank Enrique PACHECO Cardona), Carlos Arturo BACCA Ahumada (46 Martín Enrique ARZUAGA Coronel). DT: Diego Edison UMAÑA
Sent off: Cortez (90+3)
Goals: Líber Daniel QUIÑÓNEZ Prieto (13 penalty, 88).

SECOND PHASE – GROUP 1

CLUB CERRO PORTEÑO – CD INDEPENDIENTE MEDELLÍN 1-1 (0-1)
Estadio Defensores del Chaco, Asunción, 11.02.2010
Referee: Saúl Esteban LAVERNI (ARG), Attendance: 15.219
CLUB CERRO PORTEÑO: Diego Daniel BARRETO Cáceres, Diego Armando HERNER, Miguel Ángel TORRÉN, David Bernardo MENDOZA Ayala (46 Julio Daniel DOS SANTOS Rodríguez), Iván Rodrigo PIRIS Leguizamón, Iván Emmanuel GONZÁLEZ Ferreira (46 Carlos Ariel RECALDE), Javier Alejandro VILLARREAL, César Augusto RAMÍREZ Caje, Luis Enrique CÁCERES Centurión, Alberto MARTÍNEZ Jara (70 Rodrigo Ramón BURGOS Oviedo), Pablo Daniel ZEBALLOS Ocampos. DT: Pedro Antonio TROGLIO
CD INDEPENDIENTE MEDELLÍN: Aldo Antonio BOBADILLA Ávalos, Ricardo CALLE Estrada, Juan David VALENCIA, Anselmo de Almeida MACHADO, Leiton JIMÉNEZ Romero, Malher Tressor MORENO Baldrich (66 Nelson Alberto BARAHONA Collins), Juan Esteban ORTÍZ Blandón, Juan Esteban LÓPEZ Mosquera, Édgar Felipe PARDO Castro (87 César Augusto RIVAS Tejada), Mario Edison GIMÉNEZ (46 César Augusto VALOYES Córdoba), Luis Carlos ARIAS Cardona. DT: Leonel de Jesús ÁLVAREZ Zuleta
Goals: César Augusto RAMÍREZ Caje (56) / Édgar Felipe PARDO Castro (17).

SC CORINTHIANS PAULISTA – RACING CLUB DE MONTEVIDEO 2-1 (1-1)
Estádio Municipal Paulo Machado de Carvalho, São Paulo, 24.02.2010
Referee: Raúl OROZCO Delgadillo (BOL), Attendance: 31.035
SC CORINTHIANS PAULISTA: Luiz FELIPE Ventura dos Santos, ROBERTO CARLOS da Silva, Anderson Sebastião Cardoso "CHICÃO", WILLIAM Machado de Oliveira, ALESSANDRO Mori Nunes (71 JUCILEI da Silva), Anderson Simas Luciano "TCHECO", Matías Adrián DEFEDERICO (46 Rodrigo de SOUZA Cardoso), ELÍAS Mendes Trinidade, RALF de Souza Teles, RONALDO Luis Nazário de Lima, JORGE HENRIQUE de Souza (84 Bruno Ferreira Bonfim "DENTINHO"). DT: Luiz Antonio "MANO" Venker MENEZES
RACING CLUB DE MONTEVIDEO: Jorge Wálter CONTRERAS Rodríguez, José Ignacio PALLÁS Martínez, Héctor Roberto HERNÁNDEZ, Rodrigo Nicolás BRASESCO Pérez, Danny TEJERA, Darío Antonio FLORES Bitolfi, Santiago Humberto OSTOLAZA Chimelir, Claudio Matías MIRABAJE Correa (65 Carlos KEOSSEIÁN), Héctor Federico VEGA Ataídes, Líber Daniel QUIÑÓNEZ Prieto (71 Jean Pierre Augustín BARRIENTOS Díaz), Martín CAUTERUCCIO (83 Nicolás LÓPEZ Araja). DT: Juan José VERZERI Casas
Sent off: Flores (57)
Goals: ELÍAS Mendes Trinidade (11, 71) / Martín CAUTERUCCIO (1).

RACING CLUB DE MONTEVIDEO – CLUB CERRO PORTEÑO 2-1 (1-0)
Estadio Gran Parque Central, Montevideo, 9.03.2010
Referee: Federico José BELIGOY (ARG), Attendance: 1.435
RACING CLUB DE MONTEVIDEO: Jorge Wálter CONTRERAS Rodríguez, José Ignacio PALLÁS Martínez, Héctor Roberto HERNÁNDEZ, Rodrigo Nicolás BRASESCO Pérez, Danny TEJERA, Santiago Humberto OSTOLAZA Chimelir, Claudio Matías MIRABAJE Correa (86 Néstor Fabián SILVA Fros), Héctor Federico VEGA Ataídes, Líber Daniel QUIÑÓNEZ Prieto (59 Jorge Luis CAZULO), Jean Pierre Augustín BARRIENTOS Díaz (74 Gonzalo AGUILAR Camacho), Martín CAUTERUCCIO. DT: Juan José VERZERI Casas
CLUB CERRO PORTEÑO: Diego Daniel BARRETO Cáceres, Diego Armando HERNER, Miguel Ángel TORRÉN, Luis Carlos CARDOZO Espillage (46 Julio Daniel DOS SANTOS Rodríguez), Julio César IRRAZÁBAL León, Iván Rodrigo PIRIS Leguizamón, Javier Alejandro VILLARREAL, César Augusto RAMÍREZ Caje (74 Sebastián Adolfo EREROS), Luis Enrique CÁCERES Centurión, Carlos Ariel RECALDE (59 Ramón Idalecio CARDOZO), Pablo Daniel ZEBALLOS Ocampos. DT: Pedro Antonio TROGLIO
Sent off: Villarreal (78)
Goals: Claudio Matías MIRABAJE Correa (19), Martín CAUTERUCCIO (69) /
Luis Enrique CÁCERES Centurión (84).

CD INDEPENDIENTE MEDELLÍN – SC CORINTHIANS PAULISTA 1-1 (0-0)
Estadio Nemesio Camacho "El Campín", Bogotá, 10.03.2010
Referee: Sergio Fabián PEZZOTTA (ARG), Attendance: 23.886
CD INDEPENDIENTE MEDELLÍN: Aldo Antonio BOBADILLA Ávalos, Ricardo CALLE Estrada, Juan David VALENCIA, Anselmo de Almeida MACHADO, Leiton JIMÉNEZ Romero, Jhon Javier RESTREPO Pérez, Juan Esteban ORTÍZ Blandón, Nelson Alberto BARAHONA Collins (69 César Augusto VALOYES Córdoba), Édgar Felipe PARDO Castro (86 César Augusto RIVAS Tejada), Mario Edison GIMÉNEZ (56 Malher Tressor MORENO Baldrich), Luis Carlos ARIAS Cardona. DT: Leonel de Jesús ÁLVAREZ Zuleta
SC CORINTHIANS PAULISTA: Luiz FELIPE Ventura dos Santos, ROBERTO CARLOS da Silva, Anderson Sebastião Cardoso "CHICÃO", WILLIAM Machado de Oliveira, DANILO Gabriel de Andrade (58 Bruno Ferreira Bonfim "DENTINHO"), MARCELO Mendonça de MATTOS Terra (82 Manoel de MORIAS Amorim), ELÍAS Mendes Trinidade, RALF de Souza Teles, JUCILEI da Silva, RONALDO Luis Nazário de Lima (73 Rodrigo de SOUZA Cardoso), JORGE HENRIQUE de Souza. DT: Luiz Antonio "MANO" Venker MENEZES
Goals: César Augusto VALOYES Córdoba (76) / Bruno Ferreira Bonfim "DENTINHO" (84).

CLUB CERRO PORTEÑO – SC CORINTHIANS PAULISTA 0-1 (0-1)
Estadio Defensores del Chaco, Asunción, 17.03.2010
Referee: Pablo Antonio POZO Quinteros (CHI), Attendance: 17.321
CLUB CERRO PORTEÑO: Diego Daniel BARRETO Cáceres, Diego Armando HERNER (77 Luis Carlos CARDOZO Espillage), Miguel Ángel TORRÉN, Julio César IRRAZÁBAL León, Iván Rodrigo PIRIS Leguizamón, Julio Daniel DOS SANTOS Rodríguez, César Augusto RAMÍREZ Caje (64 Sebastián Adolfo EREROS), Jorge Orlando BRÍTEZ Larramendi, Luis Enrique CÁCERES Centurión (71 Carlos Ariel RECALDE), Jorge Daniel NÚÑEZ Espínola, Pablo Daniel ZEBALLOS Ocampos. DT: Pedro Antonio TROGLIO
SC CORINTHIANS PAULISTA: Luiz FELIPE Ventura dos Santos, ROBERTO CARLOS da Silva, Anderson Sebastião Cardoso "CHICÃO", WILLIAM Machado de Oliveira, DANILO Gabriel de Andrade (77 Anderson Simas Luciano "TCHECO"), ELÍAS Mendes Trinidade, MOACIR Costa da Silva, RALF de Souza Teles, JUCILEI da Silva, RONALDO Luis Nazário de Lima (83 Rodrigo de SOUZA Cardoso), Bruno Ferreira Bonfim "DENTINHO" (71 JORGE HENRIQUE de Souza).DT: Luiz Antonio "MANO" Venker MENEZES
Sent off: Brítez (83)
Goal: RONALDO Luis Nazário de Lima (41).

CD INDEPENDIENTE MEDELLÍN – RACING CLUB DE MONTEVIDEO 0-0
Estadio Palogrande, Manizales, 18.03.2010
Referee: Juan Ernesto SOTO Arevalo (VEN), Attendance: 4.651
CD INDEPENDIENTE MEDELLÍN: Aldo Antonio BOBADILLA Ávalos, Ricardo CALLE Estrada (72 Lewis Alexander OCHOA Cassiani), Juan David VALENCIA, Anselmo de Almeida MACHADO, Leiton JIMÉNEZ Romero, Jhon Javier RESTREPO Pérez, Juan Esteban ORTÍZ Blandón (61 Malher Tressor MORENO Baldrich), Nelson Alberto BARAHONA Collins (80 Mario Edison GIMÉNEZ), César Augusto VALOYES Córdoba, Édgar Felipe PARDO Castro, Luis Carlos ARIAS Cardona. DT: Leonel de Jesús ÁLVAREZ Zuleta
RACING CLUB DE MONTEVIDEO: Jorge Wálter CONTRERAS Rodríguez, José Ignacio PALLÁS Martínez, Héctor Roberto HERNÁNDEZ, Rodrigo Nicolás BRASESCO Pérez, Danny TEJERA, Santiago Humberto OSTOLAZA Chimelir, Claudio Matías MIRABAJE Correa (84 Alejandro Cléber REYES Sosa), Héctor Federico VEGA Ataídes, Jorge Luis CAZULO (46 Jean Pierre Augustín BARRIENTOS Díaz), Líber Daniel QUIÑÓNEZ Prieto (69 Néstor Fabián SILVA Fros), Martín CAUTERUCCIO. DT: Juan José VERZERI Casas
Sent off: Valoyes (66), Ochoa (89)

RACING CLUB DE MONTEVIDEO – CD INDEPENDIENTE MEDELLÍN 1-0 (0-0)
Estadio Gran Parque Central. Montevideo, 25.03.2010
Referee: Diego Hernán ABAL (ARG), Attendance: 2.492
RACING CLUB DE MONTEVIDEO: Jorge Wálter CONTRERAS Rodríguez, José Ignacio PALLÁS Martínez, Héctor Roberto HERNÁNDEZ, Rodrigo Nicolás BRASESCO Pérez, Danny TEJERA, Santiago Humberto OSTOLAZA Chimelir, Claudio Matías MIRABAJE Correa (83 Mathías Nicolás ABERO Villan), Héctor Federico VEGA Ataídes, Jorge Luis CAZULO (62 Jean Pierre Augustín BARRIENTOS Díaz), Néstor Fabián SILVA Fros (73 Líber Daniel QUIÑÓNEZ Prieto), Martín CAUTERUCCIO. DT: Juan José VERZERI Casas
CD INDEPENDIENTE MEDELLÍN: Aldo Antonio BOBADILLA Ávalos, Ricardo CALLE Estrada, Juan David VALENCIA, Anselmo de Almeida MACHADO, Leiton JIMÉNEZ Romero, Jhon Javier RESTREPO Pérez, Juan Esteban ORTÍZ Blandón, Héctor Alejandro VASCO Osorio (77 Nelson Alberto BARAHONA Collins), Édgar Felipe PARDO Castro (84 César Augusto RIVAS Tejada), Mario Edison GIMÉNEZ, Luis Carlos ARIAS Cardona. DT: Leonel de Jesús ÁLVAREZ Zuleta
Sent off: Giménez (84)
Goal: Santiago Humberto OSTOLAZA Chimelir (74).

SC CORINTHIANS PAULISTA – CLUB CERRO PORTEÑO 2-1 (1-0)
Estádio Municipal Paulo Machado de Carvalho, São Paulo, 1.04.2010
Referee: Víctor Hugo CARRILLO Casanova (PER), Attendance: 30.321
SC CORINTHIANS PAULISTA: RAFAEL de Carvalho SANTOS, ROBERTO CARLOS da Silva, Anderson Sebastião Cardoso "CHICÃO", WILLIAM Machado de Oliveira, DANILO Gabriel de Andrade (90+1 Anderson Simas Luciano "TCHECO"), ELÍAS Mendes Trinidade, MOACIR Costa da Silva, RALF de Souza Teles, JUCILEI da Silva, RONALDO Luis Nazário de Lima (87 Pedro IARLEY Lima Dantas), Bruno Ferreira Bonfim "DENTINHO" (83 JORGE HENRIQUE de Souza). DT: Luiz Antonio "MANO" Venker MENEZES
CLUB CERRO PORTEÑO: Diego Daniel BARRETO Cáceres, Diego Armando HERNER, Luis Carlos CARDOZO Espillage, Ernesto Rubén CRISTALDO Santacruz, Iván Rodrigo PIRIS Leguizamón, Julio Daniel DOS SANTOS Rodríguez, Javier Alejandro VILLARREAL, Rodrigo Ramón BURGOS Oviedo (74 Luis Enrique CÁCERES Centurión), Jorge Daniel NÚÑEZ Espínola (60 Julio César IRRAZÁBAL León), Pablo Daniel ZEBALLOS Ocampos, Roberto Antonio NANNI (71 Sebastián Adolfo EREROS). DT: Pedro Antonio TROGLIO
Goals: RONALDO Luis Nazário de Lima (36), Anderson Sebastião Cardoso "CHICÃO" (63) / Julio Daniel DOS SANTOS Rodríguez (79).

CD INDEPENDIENTE MEDELLÍN – CLUB CERRO PORTEÑO 1-0 (0-0)
Estadio Atanasio Girardot, Medellín, 8.04.2010
Referee: Georges BUCKLEY de Meritens (PER), Attendance: 8.066
CD INDEPENDIENTE MEDELLÍN: Aldo Antonio BOBADILLA Ávalos, Ricardo CALLE Estrada, Juan David VALENCIA, Anselmo de Almeida MACHADO, Leiton JIMÉNEZ Romero, Malher Tressor MORENO Baldrich (46 Nelson Alberto BARAHONA Collins), Jhon Javier RESTREPO Pérez, Juan Esteban ORTÍZ Blandón, César Augusto VALOYES Córdoba (90 César Augusto RIVAS Tejada), Édgar Felipe PARDO Castro (84 Héctor Alejandro VASCO Osorio), Luis Carlos ARIAS Cardona. DT: Leonel de Jesús ÁLVAREZ Zuleta
CLUB CERRO PORTEÑO: Ezequiel Luis MEDRÁN, Fidel Amado PÉREZ, Luis Carlos CARDOZO Espillage, Ernesto Rubén CRISTALDO Santacruz, Iván Rodrigo PIRIS Leguizamón, Rodrigo Ramón BURGOS Oviedo, Jorge Daniel NÚÑEZ Espínola, Carlos Ariel RECALDE (78 Sebastián Adolfo EREROS), Alberto MARTÍNEZ Jara (59 Luis Enrique CÁCERES Centurión), Ramón Idalecio CARDOZO, Roberto Antonio NANNI (78 Julio Daniel DOS SANTOS Rodríguez). DT: Pedro Antonio TROGLIO
Sent off: Burgos (68)
Goal: Luis Carlos ARIAS Cardona (56).

RACING CLUB DE MONTEVIDEO – SC CORINTHIANS PAULISTA 0-2 (0-1)
Estadio Gran Parque Central, Montevideo, 14.04.2010
Referee: Héctor Wálter BALDASSI (ARG), Attendance: 2.669
RACING CLUB DE MONTEVIDEO: Jorge Wálter CONTRERAS Rodríguez, José Ignacio PALLÁS Martínez, Héctor Roberto HERNÁNDEZ (83 Alejandro Cléber REYES Sosa), Rodrigo Nicolás BRASESCO Pérez, Danny TEJERA, Santiago Humberto OSTOLAZA Chimelir, Claudio Matías MIRABAJE Correa, Héctor Federico VEGA Ataídes (81 Nicolás LÓPEZ Arajo), Jorge Luis CAZULO (64 Jean Pierre Augustín BARRIENTOS Díaz), Líber Daniel QUIÑÓNEZ Prieto, Martín CAUTERUCCIO. DT: Juan José VERZERI Casas
SC CORINTHIANS PAULISTA: JÚLIO CÉSAR de Souza Santos, ROBERTO CARLOS da Silva, Anderson Sebastião Cardoso "CHICÃO", WILLIAM Machado de Oliveira, DANILO Gabriel de Andrade (83 PAULO ANDRÉ Cren Benini), ELÍAS Mendes Trinidade, MOACIR Costa da Silva, RALF de Souza Teles, JUCILEI da Silva, RONALDO Luis Nazário de Lima (70 JORGE HENRIQUE de Souza), Bruno Ferreira Bonfim "DENTINHO" (73 Pedro IARLEY Lima Dantas). DT: Luiz Antonio "MANO" Venker MENEZES
Goals: Bruno Ferreira Bonfim "DENTINHO" (18), ELÍAS Mendes Trinidade (87).

CLUB CERRO PORTEÑO – RACING CLUB DE MONTEVIDEO 0-0
Estadio Defensores del Chaco, Asunción, 22.04.2010
Referee: Víctor Hugo RIVERA Chavez (PER), Attendance: 2.728
CLUB CERRO PORTEÑO: Ezequiel Luis MEDRÁN, Miguel Ángel TORRÉN, Fidel Amado PÉREZ, Julio César IRRAZÁBAL León, Iván Rodrigo PIRIS Leguizamón, Iván Emmanuel GONZÁLEZ Ferreira (63 Ernesto Rubén CRISTALDO Santacruz), Javier Alejandro VILLARREAL, Carlos Ariel RECALDE, Alberto MARTÍNEZ Jara, Sebastián Adolfo EREROS (67 César Augusto RAMÍREZ Caje), Roberto Antonio NANNI (81 Ramón Idalecio CARDOZO). DT: Pedro Antonio TROGLIO
RACING CLUB DE MONTEVIDEO: Jorge Wálter CONTRERAS Rodríguez, José Ignacio PALLÁS Martínez, Héctor Roberto HERNÁNDEZ (55 Jean Pierre Augustín BARRIENTOS Díaz), Rodrigo Nicolás BRASESCO Pérez, Danny TEJERA, Santiago Humberto OSTOLAZA Chimelir, Claudio Matías MIRABAJE Correa, Héctor Federico VEGA Ataídes (79 Alejandro Cléber REYES Sosa), Jorge Luis CAZULO, Líber Daniel QUIÑÓNEZ Prieto (70 Néstor Fabián SILVA Fros), Martín CAUTERUCCIO. DT: Juan José VERZERI Casas

SC CORINTHIANS PAULISTA – CD INDEPENDIENTE MEDELLÍN 1-0 (1-0)
Estádio Municipal Paulo Machado de Carvalho, São Paulo, 22.04.2010
Referee: Federico José BELIGOY (ARG), Attendance: 29.541
SC CORINTHIANS PAULISTA: JÚLIO CÉSAR de Souza Santos, ROBERTO CARLOS da Silva, Anderson Sebastião Cardoso "CHICÃO", WILLIAM Machado de Oliveira, DANILO Gabriel de Andrade (88 Eduardo César Daude "EDU" GASPAR), ELÍAS Mendes Trinidade, MOACIR Costa da Silva, RALF de Souza Teles, JUCILEI da Silva, Pedro IARLEY Lima Dantas (78 Rodrigo de SOUZA Cardoso), Bruno Ferreira Bonfim "DENTINHO" (65 JORGE HENRIQUE de Souza).
CD INDEPENDIENTE MEDELLÍN: Aldo Antonio BOBADILLA Ávalos, Ricardo CALLE Estrada, Juan David VALENCIA, Anselmo de Almeida MACHADO, Leiton JIMÉNEZ Romero, Jhon Javier RESTREPO Pérez, Juan Esteban ORTÍZ Blandón, Héctor Alejandro VASCO Osorio (46 Malher Tressor MORENO Baldrich), Nelson Alberto BARAHONA Collins (78 Hernán Enrique PERTÚZ Ortega), Édgar Felipe PARDO Castro, Mario Edison GIMÉNEZ (58 César Augusto VALOYES Córdoba). DT: Leonel de Jesús ÁLVAREZ Zuleta
Goal: Juan David VALENCIA (23 own goal).

1	CORINTHIANS	6	5	1	0	9	3	16
2	RACING	6	2	2	2	4	5	8
3	Independiente Medellín	6	1	3	2	3	4	6
4	Cerro Porteño	6	0	2	4	3	7	2

GROUP 2

CLUB NACIONAL ASUNCIÓN – CD ONCE CALDAS 0-2 (0-1)
Estadio Defensores del Chaco, Asunción, 9.02.2010
Referee: Federico José BELIGOY (ARG), Attendance: 966
CLUB NACIONAL ASUNCIÓN: Germán Martín CAFFA, Raúl Eduardo PIRIS (70 Celso Pablo GONZÁLEZ Ferreira), Ricardo MAZACOTTE, Arturo David AQUINO Ríos, Marcos MIERS, Fabio Ramón RAMOS Mereles, Marcos Benjamín MELGAREJO (46 Ignacio Ramón CÁCERES Canañas), Aldo Andrés PANIAGUA Benítez (46 Fabián Orlando CABALLERO), Marcos Antonio RIVEROS, Guillermo Alexis BELTRÁN, Víctor Marelino AQUINO Romero. DT: Ever Hugo ALMEIDA
CD ONCE CALDAS: Héctor Fabio LANDÁZURI, Oswaldo Augusto VIZCARRONDO Araujo, Alexis Héctor HENRÍQUEZ Charales, Luis Alberto NUÑEZ Charales, José Iván VÉLEZ Castillo, Diego Armando AMAYA Solano, Jaime Alberto CASTRILLÓN Vásquez, Diego Alejandro ARIAS Hincapié, Fernando Antonio CÁRDENAS Arredondo (74 Juan Guillermo BAENA), Danny Manuel SANTOYA Otero (67 John Jairo VALENCIA Ortiz), Fernando URIBE Himcapie (80 Sebastián Lucas TAGLIABÚE). DT: Juan Carlos OSORIO Arbelaez
Goals: Jaime Alberto CASTRILLÓN Vásquez (23), Danny Manuel SANTOYA Otero (65).

SÃO PAULO FC – CF MONTERREY AC 2-0 (1-0)
Estádio Cícero Pompeu de Toledo, São Paulo, 10.02.2010
Referee: Sergio Fabián PEZZOTTA (ARG), Attendance: 34.501
SÃO PAULO FC: ROGÉRIO Rodrigo CENI, João MIRANDA de Souza Filho, RENATO Assís da SILVA, Alexandre Luiz Reame "XANDÃO", JORGE WÁGNER Goes Conceição, Marcelo dos Santos "MARCELINHO" (83 MARLOS Romero Bonfim), RICHARLYSON Barbosa Felisbino (75 Cícero João de Cezare "CICINHO"), Anderson HERNANES de Carvalho Andrade Lima, CLÉBER SANTANA Loureiro, JEAN Raphael Vanderlei de Moreira (90+1 Leonardo "LÉO" LIMA da Silva), WASHINGTON Stecanela Cerqueira. DT: Raymundo RICARDO GOMES
CF MONTERREY AC: Omar ORTÍZ Uribe, Eduardo GUEVARA Martínez, Juan Carlos MEDINA Alonso, Sérgio PÉREZ Moya, Diego Alberto CERVANTES Chávez, Gerardo Gabriel GALINDO Martínez (72 Luis Alfonso RODRÍGUEZ Alanís), Héctor Miguel MORALES Llanas, José de Jesús ARELLANO Alcocer (61 Sergio Alejandro SANTANA Piedra), Jesús Eduardo ZAVALA Castañeda, Osvaldo Félix Souza "VAL BAIANO" (61 Osvaldo David MARTÍNEZ Arce), Abraham Darío CARREÑO Rohan. DT: Víctor Manuel VUCETICH Rojas
Goals: WASHINGTON Stecanela Cerqueira (13, 76).

CF MONTERREY AC – CLUB NACIONAL ASUNCIÓN 2-1 (0-0)
Estadio Tecnológico, Monterrey, 24.02.2010
Referee: Víctor Hugo RIVERA Chavez (PER), Attendance: 20.366
CF MONTERREY AC: Omar ORTÍZ Uribe, José María BASANTA, Juan Carlos MEDINA Alonso (62 Osvaldo Félix Souza "VAL BAIANO"), Sérgio PÉREZ Moya, Diego Alberto CERVANTES Chávez (62 Neri Raúl CARDOZO), Luis Ernesto PÉREZ Gómez, Wálter Orlando AYOVÍ Corozo, Osvaldo David MARTÍNEZ Arce, Héctor Miguel MORALES Llanas, José de Jesús ARELLANO Alcocer (72 Gerardo Gabriel GALINDO Martínez), Sergio Alejandro SANTANA Piedra. DT: Víctor Manuel VUCETICH Rojas
CLUB NACIONAL ASUNCIÓN: Germán Martín CAFFA, Herminio MIRANDA Ovelar, Alfredo David ROJAS, Ricardo MAZACOTTE, Arturo David AQUINO Ríos, Ignacio Ramón CÁCERES Canañas (69 Marcos Benjamín MELGAREJO), Carlos Gabriel RUIZ Peralta, Marcos Antonio RIVEROS, Orlando Rubén BORDÓN Achucarro, Fabián Orlando CABALLERO, Ariel Gregorio BOGADO Llanos (46 Guillermo Alexis BELTRÁN). DT: Ever Hugo ALMEIDA
Goals: Sergio Alejandro SANTANA Piedra (61), Osvaldo David MARTÍNEZ Arce (68) / Herminio MIRANDA Ovelar (67 penalty).

CD ONCE CALDAS – SÃO PAULO FC 2-1 (0-1)
Estadio Palogrande, Manizales, 25.02.2010
Referee: Pablo Antonio POZO Quinteros (CHI), Attendance: 21.766
CD ONCE CALDAS: Luis Enrique MARTÍNEZ Rodríguez, Oswaldo Augusto VIZCARRONDO Araujo, Alexis Héctor HENRÍQUEZ Charales, Luis Alberto NUÑEZ Charales, José Iván VÉLEZ Castillo, Dayro Mauricio MORENO Galindo, John Jairo VALENCIA Ortiz, Jaime Alberto CASTRILLÓN Vásquez (46 Fernando Antonio CÁRDENAS Arredondo), Diego Alejandro ARIAS Hincapié, Danny Manuel SANTOYA Otero (71 Juan Guillermo BAENA), Fernando URIBE Himcapie (81 Diego Armando AMAYA Solano). DT: Juan Carlos OSORIO Arbelaez
SÃO PAULO FC: ROGÉRIO Rodrigo CENI, Cícero João de Cezare "CICINHO", João MIRANDA de Souza Filho, Alexandre Luiz Reame "XANDÃO", JORGE WÁGNER Goes Conceição, Marcelo dos Santos "MARCELINHO" (75 RODRIGO Ribeiro SOUTO), RICHARLYSON Barbosa Felisbino, Anderson HERNANES de Carvalho Andrade Lima, CLÉBER SANTANA Loureiro, JEAN Raphael Vanderlei de Moreira, WASHINGTON Stecanela Cerqueira. DT: Raymundo RICARDO GOMES
Goals: Fernando URIBE Himcapie (49), Dayro Mauricio MORENO Galindo (71) / ROGÉRIO Rodrigo CENI (33).

CD ONCE CALDAS – CF MONTERREY AC 1-1 (0-1)
Estadio Palogrande, Manizales, 10.03.2010
Referee: Jorge Joaquín ANTEQUERA Castedo (BOL), Attendance: 20.127
CD ONCE CALDAS: Luis Enrique MARTÍNEZ Rodríguez, Oswaldo Augusto VIZCARRONDO Araujo, Alexis Héctor HENRÍQUEZ Charales, Luis Alberto NUÑEZ Charales, José Iván VÉLEZ Castillo, Dayro Mauricio MORENO Galindo, John Jairo VALENCIA Ortiz, Jaime Alberto CASTRILLÓN Vásquez (46 Diego Armando AMAYA Solano), Diego Alejandro ARIAS Hincapié, Fernando Antonio CÁRDENAS Arredondo (56 Danny Manuel SANTOYA Otero), Fernando URIBE Himcapie (77 Juan Guillermo BAENA). DT: Juan Carlos OSORIO Arbelaez
CF MONTERREY AC: Jonathan Emmanuel OROZCO Domínguez, José María BASANTA, Wiliam Alberto PAREDES Barbudo (72 Gerardo Gabriel GALINDO Martínez), Sérgio PÉREZ Moya, Duilio César Jen-Pierre DAVINO Rodríguez, Neri Raúl CARDOZO, Wálter Orlando AYOVÍ Corozo, Osvaldo David MARTÍNEZ Arce (77 Severo Efraín MEZA Mayorga), Héctor Miguel MORALES Llanas, Sergio Alejandro SANTANA Piedra (63 Osvaldo Félix Souza "VAL BAIANO"), Jesús Eduardo ZAVALA Castañeda. DT: Víctor Manuel VUCETICH Rojas
Sent off: Zavala (57), Galindo (83)
Goals: John Jairo VALENCIA Ortiz (58) / Héctor Miguel MORALES Llanas (32).

CLUB NACIONAL ASUNCIÓN – SÃO PAULO FC 0-2 (0-0)
Estadio Defensores del Chaco, Asunción, 11.03.2010
Referee: Enrique Roberto OSSÉS Zencovich (CHI), Attendance: 700
CLUB NACIONAL ASUNCIÓN: Germán Martín CAFFA, Herminio MIRANDA Ovelar, Raúl Eduardo PIRIS, Ricardo MAZACOTTE, Marcos MIERS, Fabio Ramón RAMOS Mereles, Marcos Benjamín MELGAREJO (59 Guillermo Alexis BELTRÁN), Carlos Gabriel RUIZ Peralta (24 Arturo David AQUINO Ríos), Marcos Antonio RIVEROS, Orlando Rubén BORDÓN Achucarro, Víctor Marelino AQUINO Romero (72 Ariel Gregorio BOGADO Llanos). DT: Ever Hugo ALMEIDA
SÃO PAULO FC: ROGÉRIO Rodrigo CENI, Cícero João de Cezare "CICINHO" (69 RODRIGO Ribeiro SOUTO), João MIRANDA de Souza Filho, JÚNIOR CÉSAR Eduardo Machado, ALEX Sandro da SILVA, Marcelo dos Santos "MARCELINHO" (46 CLÉBER SANTANA Loureiro), RICHARLYSON Barbosa Felisbino, Anderson HERNANES de Carvalho Andrade Lima, JEAN Raphael Vanderlei de Moreira, WASHINGTON Stecanela Cerqueira, DAGOBERTO Pelentier (83 Luiz Fernando Pereira da Silva "FERNANDINHO"). DT: Raymundo RICARDO GOMES
Goals: WASHINGTON Stecanela Cerqueira (58, 89).

CF MONTERREY AC – CD ONCE CALDAS 2-2 (1-1)
Estadio Tecnológico, Monterrey, 17.03.2010
Referee: Georges BUCKLEY de Meritens (PER), Attendance: 26.725
CF MONTERREY AC: Jonathan Emmanuel OROZCO Domínguez, José María BASANTA, Severo Efraín MEZA Mayorga (62 Diego Alberto CERVANTES Chávez), Wiliam Alberto PAREDES Barbudo, Duilio César Jen-Pierre DAVINO Rodríguez (67 Aldo Jesús DE NIGRIS Guajardo), Neri Raúl CARDOZO, Wálter Orlando AYOVÍ Corozo, Osvaldo David MARTÍNEZ Arce, Héctor Miguel MORALES Llanas, Sergio Alejandro SANTANA Piedra (62 Sérgio PÉREZ Moya), Abraham Darío CARREÑO Rohan. DT: Víctor Manuel VUCETICH Rojas
CD ONCE CALDAS: Luis Enrique MARTÍNEZ Rodríguez, Oswaldo Augusto VIZCARRONDO Araujo, Alexis Héctor HENRÍQUEZ Charales, Luis Alberto NUÑEZ Charales, José Iván VÉLEZ Castillo, Diego Armando AMAYA Solano (56 Dayron Alexander PÉREZ Calle), Dayro Mauricio MORENO Galindo, John Jairo VALENCIA Ortiz, Diego Alejandro ARIAS Hincapié, Danny Manuel SANTOYA Otero (46 Jaime Alberto CASTRILLÓN Vásquez), Fernando URIBE Himcapie (46 Fernando Antonio CÁRDENAS Arredondo). DT: Juan Carlos OSORIO Arbelaez
Goals: Osvaldo David MARTÍNEZ Arce (18 penalty), Neri Raúl CARDOZO (46) /
Dayro Mauricio MORENO Galindo (1), Jaime Alberto CASTRILLÓN Vásquez (66).

SÃO PAULO FC – CLUB NACIONAL ASUNCIÓN 3-0 (2-0)
Estádio Cícero Pompeu de Toledo, São Paulo, 18.03.2010
Referee: Darío Agustín UBRIACO Mederos (URU), Attendance: 31.411
SÃO PAULO FC: ROGÉRIO Rodrigo CENI, João MIRANDA de Souza Filho, JÚNIOR CÉSAR Eduardo Machado, ALEX Sandro da SILVA, Leonardo "LÉO" LIMA da Silva, RICHARLYSON Barbosa Felisbino (79 RODRIGO Ribeiro SOUTO), Anderson HERNANES de Carvalho Andrade Lima, CLÉBER SANTANA Loureiro, JEAN Raphael Vanderlei de Moreira (75 Cícero João de Cezare "CICINHO"), WASHINGTON Stecanela Cerqueira (72 Luiz Fernando Pereira da Silva "FERNANDINHO"), DAGOBERTO Pelentier. DT: Raymundo RICARDO GOMES
CLUB NACIONAL ASUNCIÓN: Germán Martín CAFFA, Herminio MIRANDA Ovelar, Alfredo David ROJAS (46 Víctor Marelino AQUINO Romero), Raúl Eduardo PIRIS, Ricardo MAZACOTTE (46 Arturo David AQUINO Ríos), Marcos MIERS, Ignacio Ramón CÁCERES Cabañas, Aldo Andrés PANIAGUA Benítez, Blas Bernardo IRALA, Marcos Antonio RIVEROS, Guillermo Alexis BELTRÁN (64 Orlando Rubén BORDÓN Achucarro). DT: Ever Hugo ALMEIDA
Goals: DAGOBERTO Pelentier (30), Leonardo "LÉO" LIMA da Silva (33), WASHINGTON Stecanela Cerqueira (54).

CF MONTERREY AC – SÃO PAULO FC 0-0
Estadio Tecnológico, Monterrey, 31.03.2010
Referee: Saúl Esteban LAVERNI (ARG), Attendance: 28.472
CF MONTERREY AC: Jonathan Emmanuel OROZCO Domínguez, José María BASANTA, Wiliam Alberto PAREDES Barbudo, Sérgio PÉREZ Moya (83 Juan Carlos MEDINA Alonso), Neri Raúl CARDOZO, Wálter Orlando AYOVÍ Corozo, Osvaldo David MARTÍNEZ Arce, Héctor Miguel MORALES Llanas, Sergio Alejandro SANTANA Piedra (59 Abraham Darío CARREÑO Rohan), Jesús Eduardo ZAVALA Castañeda, Osvaldo Félix Souza "VAL BAIANO" (59 José de Jesús ARELLANO Alcocer). DT: Víctor Manuel VUCETICH Rojas
SÃO PAULO FC: ROGÉRIO Rodrigo CENI, Cícero João de Cezare "CICINHO" (72 JEAN Raphael Vanderlei de Moreira), João MIRANDA de Souza Filho, JÚNIOR CÉSAR Eduardo Machado, ALEX Sandro da SILVA, JORGE WÁGNER Goes Conceição, RODRIGO Ribeiro SOUTO, Anderson HERNANES de Carvalho Andrade Lima (82 Alexandre Luiz Reame "XANDÃO"), CLÉBER SANTANA Loureiro, WASHINGTON Stecanela Cerqueira, DAGOBERTO Pelentier (57 Luiz Fernando Pereira da Silva "FERNANDINHO"). DT: Raymundo RICARDO GOMES

CD ONCE CALDAS – CLUB NACIONAL ASUNCIÓN 1-0 (1-0)
Estadio Palogrande, Manizales, 1.04.2010
Referee: Mayker Alain GÓMEZ (VEN), Attendance: 17.086
CD ONCE CALDAS: Héctor Fabio LANDÁZURI, Oswaldo Augusto VIZCARRONDO Araujo, Alexis Héctor HENRÍQUEZ Charales, Luis Alberto NUÑEZ Charales, José Iván VÉLEZ Castillo, Dayro Mauricio MORENO Galindo, John Jairo VALENCIA Ortiz, Jaime Alberto CASTRILLÓN Vásquez (75 Diego Armando AMAYA Solano), Diego Alejandro ARIAS Hincapié, Danny Manuel SANTOYA Otero (56 Fernando Antonio CÁRDENAS Arredondo), Fernando URIBE Himcapie (70 Sebastián HERNÁNDEZ Mejía). DT: Juan Carlos OSORIO Arbelaez
CLUB NACIONAL ASUNCIÓN: Germán Martín CAFFA, Herminio MIRANDA Ovelar, Raúl Eduardo PIRIS, Ricardo MAZACOTTE, Marcos MIERS, Ignacio Ramón CÁCERES Cabañas (88 Sergio GÓMEZ), Fabio Ramón RAMOS Mereles, Marcos Benjamín MELGAREJO (62 Arturo David AQUINO Ríos), Blas Bernardo IRALA, Orlando Rubén BORDÓN Achucarro, Fabián Orlando CABALLERO (69 Víctor Marelino AQUINO Romero). DT: Ever Hugo ALMEIDA
Goal: John Jairo VALENCIA Ortiz (14).

CLUB NACIONAL ASUNCIÓN – CF MONTERREY AC 2-0 (1-0)
Estadio Defensores del Chaco, Asunción, 21.04.2010
Referee: Raúl OSORCO Delgadillo (BOL), Attendance: 341
CLUB NACIONAL ASUNCIÓN: Germán Martín CAFFA, Herminio MIRANDA Ovelar, Alfredo David ROJAS, Raúl Eduardo PIRIS (46 Gilberto Ariel VELÁZQUEZ Gómez), Marcos MIERS, Ignacio Ramón CÁCERES Cabañas, Aldo Andrés PANIAGUA Benítez, Blas Bernardo IRALA, Orlando Rubén BORDÓN Achucarro, Fabián Orlando CABALLERO (73 Fabio Ramón RAMOS Mereles), Víctor Marelino AQUINO Romero (61 Guillermo Alexis BELTRÁN). DT: Ever Hugo ALMEIDA
CF MONTERREY AC: Jonathan Emmanuel OROZCO Domínguez, Eduardo GUEVARA Martínez (71 Wiliam Alberto PAREDES Barbudo), Juan Carlos MEDINA Alonso, Sérgio PÉREZ Moya, Diego Alberto CERVANTES Chávez, José Óscar RECIO Arreola (72 Abraham Darío CARREÑO Rohan), Luis Alfonso RODRÍGUEZ Alanís, José de Jesús ARELLANO Alcocer (78 Osvaldo David MARTÍNEZ Arce), Jesús Eduardo ZAVALA Castañeda, Osvaldo Félix Souza "VAL BAIANO", Brayan Adan MARTÍNEZ Arizpe. DT: Víctor Manuel VUCETICH Rojas
Goals: Aldo Andrés PANIAGUA Benítez (4), Guillermo Alexis BELTRÁN (67).

SÃO PAULO FC – CD ONCE CALDAS 1-0 (1-0)
Estádio Cícero Pompeu de Toledo, São Paulo, 21.04.2010
Referee: Diego Hernán ABAL (ARG), Attendance: 50.461
SÃO PAULO FC: ROGÉRIO Rodrigo CENI, Cícero João de Cezare "CICINHO", João MIRANDA de Souza Filho, ALEX Sandro da SILVA, JORGE WÁGNER Goes Conceição (69 WASHINGTON Stecanela Cerqueira), RODRIGO Ribeiro SOUTO, RICHARLYSON Barbosa Felisbino, Anderson HERNANES de Carvalho Andrade Lima (87 CLÉBER SANTANA Loureiro), MARLOS Romero Bonfim, DAGOBERTO Pelentier, Luiz Fernando Pereira da Silva "FERNANDINHO" (61 JEAN Raphael Vanderlei de Moreira). DT: Raymundo RICARDO GOMES
CD ONCE CALDAS: Luis Enrique MARTÍNEZ Rodríguez, Oswaldo Augusto VIZCARRONDO Araujo, Alexis Héctor HENRÍQUEZ Charales, Luis Alberto NUÑEZ Charales, José Iván VÉLEZ Castillo, Dayro Mauricio MORENO Galindo, Dayron Alexander PÉREZ Calle (46 Fernando Antonio CÁRDENAS Arredondo), John Jairo VALENCIA Ortiz, Jaime Alberto CASTRILLÓN Vásquez (71 Diego Armando AMAYA Solano), Diego Alejandro ARIAS Hincapié, Danny Manuel SANTOYA Otero (71 Fernando URIBE Himcapie). DT: Juan Carlos OSORIO Arbelaez
Goal: Luiz Fernando Pereira da Silva "FERNANDINHO" (41).

1	SÃO PAULO FC	6	4	1	1	9	2	13
2	ONCE CALDAS	6	3	2	1	8	5	11
3	Monterrey	6	1	3	2	5	8	6
4	Nacional Asunción	6	1	0	5	3	10	3

GROUP 3

BOLÍVAR IU LA PAZ – CLUB ALIANZA LIMA 1-3 (0-0)
Estadio Hernando Siles, La Paz, 10.02.2010
Referee: Samuel Rolando HARO Inca (ECU), Attendance: 16.852
BOLÍVAR IU LA PAZ: Carlos Edwin ARIAS Eguez, Límbert MÉNDEZ Rocha, Ignacio ITHURRALDE Sáez (46 Werther Thiers CHARLES da Silva Mota), Ronald Tylor RIVERO Khun, Leonel Alfredo REYES Saravia (67 Enrique PARADA Salvatierra), Didí TORRICO Camacho, ALEX Rodrigo DA ROSA Dorneles, Wálter Alberto FLORES Condarco, Abdón REYES Cardozo, ANDERSON Gonzaga Martins (57 José Gabriel RÍOS Benegas), William FERREIRA Martínez. DT: Santiago ESCOBAR Saldarriaga
CLUB ALIANZA LIMA: Salomón Alexis LIBMAN Pastor, Carlos Javier SOLÍS Alvarado, Amilton Jair PRADO Barron, Héctor Vidal SOSA Gaona, Édgar VILLAMARÍN Arguedas, Édgar Daniel GONZÁLEZ Brítez, Henry Edson QUINTEROS Sánchez (62 Juan José JAYO Legario), Jean Carlos TRAGODARA Gálvez, Joel Melchor SÁNCHEZ Alegría (66 Alexander Gustavo SÁNCHEZ Reyes), José Carlos FERNÁNDEZ Piedra (80 Johnnier Esteiner MONTAÑO Bolaño), Wilmer Alexander AGUIRRE Vasquez. DT: Gustavo Adolfo COSTAS
Goals: William FERREIRA Martínez (89 penalty) / José Carlos FERNÁNDEZ Piedra (72, 74), Johnnier Esteiner MONTAÑO Bolaño (90+2).

CA ESTUDIANTES DE LA PLATA – CLUB JUAN AURICH 5-1 (2-1)
Estadio Centenario Dr. José Luis Meiszner, Quilmes, 11.02.2010
Referee: Sálvio Spínosa FAGUNDES Filho (BRA), Attendance: 10.704
CA ESTUDIANTES DE LA PLATA: Agustín Ignacio ORIÓN, Leandro DESÁBATO, Christian Ariel CELLAY, Germán David RÉ (64 Faustino Marcos Alberto ROJO), Clemente Juan RODRÍGUEZ, Juan Sebastián VERÓN, Rodrigo BRAÑA, Leandro Damián BENÍTEZ, Enzo Nicolás PÉREZ (76 Maximiliano Ezequiel NÚÑEZ), José Ernesto SOSA (82 Leandro GONZÁLEZ), Mauro BOSELLI. DT: Alejandro Javier SABELLA
CLUB JUAN AURICH: Diego Hernán MORALES, Roberto Carlos GUIZASOLA La Rosa, Jesús Martín ÁLVAREZ Hurtado, Jorge Martín ARAUJO Paredes, Jersson VÁSQUEZ Shapiama, Ricardo Manuel CICILIANO Bustillo, Juan Carlos LA ROSA Llontop (68 Herlyn Ysrael ZÚÑIGA Yáñez), Renato Gianfranco ESPEJO Reyes, Luis Carlos TEJADA Hansel, Pedro Luis ASCOY Cortez (46 César Alberto SÁNCHEZ Aurich), Reimond MANCO Albarracin (57 José Luis GUEVARA Tinoco). DT: Luis Fernando SUÁREZ
Sent off: Guizasola (44)
Goals: Mauro BOSELLI (7 penalty, 59, 72), Germán David RÉ (43), Leandro GONZÁLEZ (89) / Luis Carlos TEJADA Hansel (34).

CLUB ALIANZA LIMA – CA ESTUDIANTES DE LA PLATA 4-1 (2-1)
Estadio Alejandro Villanueva, Lima, 18.02.2010
Referee: Marlon Giovanny ESCALANTE Alvarez (VEN), Attendance: 16.310
CLUB ALIANZA LIMA: Salomón Alexis LIBMAN Pastor, Carlos Javier SOLÍS Alvarado, Amilton Jair PRADO Barron, Héctor Vidal SOSA Gaona, Édgar VILLAMARÍN Arguedas, Édgar Daniel GONZÁLEZ Brítez, Henry Edson QUINTEROS Sánchez (76 Juan José JAYO Legario), Jean Carlos TRAGODARA Gálvez (86 Wálter Ricardo VÍLCHEZ Soto), Joel Melchor SÁNCHEZ Alegría (70 Alexander Gustavo SÁNCHEZ Reyes), José Carlos FERNÁNDEZ Piedra, Wilmer Alexander AGUIRRE Vasquez. DT: Gustavo Adolfo COSTAS
CA ESTUDIANTES DE LA PLATA: Agustín Ignacio ORIÓN, Leandro DESÁBATO, Christian Ariel CELLAY, Germán David RÉ, Clemente Juan RODRÍGUEZ, Juan Sebastián VERÓN, Rodrigo BRAÑA, Leandro Damián BENÍTEZ (63 Jerónimo MORALES NEUMANN), Enzo Nicolás PÉREZ (47 Maximiliano Ezequiel NÚÑEZ), José Ernesto SOSA (90+3 Faustino Marcos Alberto ROJO), Mauro BOSELLI. DT: Alejandro Javier SABELLA
Goals: Wilmer Alexander AGUIRRE Vasquez (17, 33, 74), José Carlos FERNÁNDEZ Piedra (83) / José Ernesto SOSA (1).

CLUB JUAN AURICH – BOLÍVAR IU LA PAZ 2-0 (2-0)
Estadio Elías Aguirre, Chiclayo, 24.02.2010
Referee: Patricio Antonio POLIC Orellana (CHI), Attendance: 10.759
CLUB JUAN AURICH: Diego Hernán MORALES, Jesús Martín ÁLVAREZ Hurtado, Jorge Martín ARAUJO Paredes, Willy Alexander RIVAS Asin, Ricardo Manuel CICILIANO Bustillo (46 William CHIROQUE Tavara), Juan Carlos LA ROSA Llontop, Renato Gianfranco ESPEJO Reyes, José Luis GUEVARA Tinoco, Luis Carlos TEJADA Hansel (83 Herlyn Ysrael ZÚÑIGA Yáñez), Pedro Luis ASCOY Cortez, Reimond MANCO Albarracin (69 Franco Giovanni MENDOZA Breña),. DT: Luis Fernando SUÁREZ
BOLÍVAR IU LA PAZ: Carlos Edwin ARIAS Eguez, Límbert MÉNDEZ Rocha (78 Enrique PARADA Salvatierra), Ignacio ITHURRALDE Sáez, Ronald Tylor RIVERO Khun, Leonel Alfredo REYES Saravia, ALEX Rodrigo DA ROSA Dorneles, Luis Aníbal TORRICO Valverde (62 ANDRÉ MARTINS Saraiva), Wálter Alberto FLORES Condarco, Abdón REYES Cardozo (46 Werther Thiers CHARLES da Silva Mota), ANDERSON Gonzaga Martins (62 Didí TORRICO Camacho), William FERREIRA Martínez. DT: Santiago ESCOBAR Saldarriaga
Sent off: Ascoy (39)
Goals: Ricardo Manuel CICILIANO Bustillo (11), Luis Carlos TEJADA Hansel (37).

BOLÍVAR IU LA PAZ – CA ESTUDIANTES DE LA PLATA 0-0
Estadio Hernando Siles, La Paz, 9.03.2010
Referee: Carlos Horacio GALEANO Rios (PAR), Attendance: 7.887
BOLÍVAR IU LA PAZ: Carlos Edwin ARIAS Eguez, Ignacio ITHURRALDE Sáez, Ronald Tylor RIVERO Khun, Leonel Alfredo REYES Saravia, Didí TORRICO Camacho (59 José Gabriel RÍOS Benegas), ALEX Rodrigo DA ROSA Dorneles (72 ANDERSON Gonzaga Martins), Enrique PARADA Salvatierra, Wálter Alberto FLORES Condarco, Werther Thiers CHARLES da Silva Mota, Abdón REYES Cardozo, William FERREIRA Martínez. DT: Santiago ESCOBAR Saldarriaga
CA ESTUDIANTES DE LA PLATA: Agustín Ignacio ORIÓN, Marcos Alberto ANGELERI, Leandro DESÁBATO, Christian Ariel CELLAY, Germán David RÉ, Clemente Juan RODRÍGUEZ, Juan Sebastián VERÓN, Rodrigo BRAÑA, Enzo Nicolás PÉREZ (58 Matías Ariel SÁNCHEZ), José Ernesto SOSA (74 Maximiliano Ezequiel NÚÑEZ), Mauro BOSELLI (90 Leandro GONZÁLEZ). DT: Alejandro Javier SABELLA

CLUB ALIANZA LIMA – CLUB JUAN AURICH 2-0 (1-0)
Estadio Alejandro Villanueva, Lima, 10.03.2010
Referee: Percy Jesús ROJAS Nuñez (PER), Attendance: 24.742
CLUB ALIANZA LIMA: Salomón Alexis LIBMAN Pastor, Carlos Javier SOLÍS Alvarado, Amilton Jair PRADO Barron, Héctor Vidal SOSA Gaona, Édgar VILLAMARÍN Arguedas, Édgar Daniel GONZÁLEZ Brítez, Henry Edson QUINTEROS Sánchez (75 Wálter Ricardo VÍLCHEZ Soto), Jean Carlos TRAGODARA Gálvez (74 Alexander Gustavo SÁNCHEZ Reyes), Joel Melchor SÁNCHEZ Alegría, José Carlos FERNÁNDEZ Piedra (84 Johnnier Esteiner MONTAÑO Bolaño), Wilmer Alexander AGUIRRE Vasquez. DT: Gustavo Adolfo COSTAS
CLUB JUAN AURICH: Diego Hernán MORALES, Roberto Carlos GUIZASOLA La Rosa, Jesús Martín ÁLVAREZ Hurtado, Jorge Martín ARAUJO Paredes, Willy Alexander RIVAS Asin, Ricardo Manuel CICILIANO Bustillo, Juan Carlos LA ROSA Llontop, Renato Gianfranco ESPEJO Reyes (46 Reimond MANCO Albarracin), Miguel Ángel CEVASCO Abad (58 Franco Giovanni MENDOZA Breña), Luis Carlos TEJADA Hansel, William CHIROQUE Tavara (66 Herlyn Ysrael ZÚÑIGA Yáñez),. DT: Luis Fernando SUÁREZ
Goals: José Carlos FERNÁNDEZ Piedra (41), Jean Carlos TRAGODARA Gálvez (59).

CLUB JUAN AURICH – CLUB ALIANZA LIMA 4-2 (2-1)
Estadio Elías Aguirre, Chiclayo, 16.03.2010
Referee: Carlos Eugênio SIMÓN, Attendance: 13.253
CLUB JUAN AURICH: Diego Hernán MORALES, Roberto Carlos GUIZASOLA La Rosa, Jesús Martín ÁLVAREZ Hurtado, Jorge Martín ARAUJO Paredes, Willy Alexander RIVAS Asin (51 Jersson VÁSQUEZ Shapiama), Ricardo Manuel CICILIANO Bustillo (73 Herlyn Ysrael ZÚÑIGA Yáñez), Juan Carlos LA ROSA Llontop, Renato Gianfranco ESPEJO Reyes, Luis Carlos TEJADA Hansel, Pedro Luis ASCOY Cortez, Reimond MANCO Albarracin (86 William CHIROQUE Tavara). DT: Luis Fernando SUÁREZ
CLUB ALIANZA LIMA: Salomón Alexis LIBMAN Pastor, Carlos Javier SOLÍS Alvarado, Amilton Jair PRADO Barron, Héctor Vidal SOSA Gaona, Édgar VILLAMARÍN Arguedas, Édgar Daniel GONZÁLEZ Brítez, Henry Edson QUINTEROS Sánchez (69 Johnnier Esteiner MONTAÑO Bolaño), Jean Carlos TRAGODARA Gálvez (82 Óscar Cristopher VÍLCHEZ Soto), Joel Melchor SÁNCHEZ Alegría, José Carlos FERNÁNDEZ Piedra (63 Roberto OVELAR Maldonado), Wilmer Alexander AGUIRRE Vasquez. DT: Gustavo Adolfo COSTAS
Goals: Roberto Carlos GUIZASOLA La Rosa (24), Luis Carlos TEJADA Hansel (43),
Reimond MANCO Albarracin (59), Pedro Luis ASCOY Cortez (86) /
Joel Melchor SÁNCHEZ Alegría (3), Roberto OVELAR Maldonado (71).

CA ESTUDIANTES DE LA PLATA – BOLÍVAR IU LA PAZ 2-0 (0-0)
Estadio Centenario Dr. José Luis Meiszner, Quilmes, 23.03.2010
Referee: Henrique MARCELO de Lima (BRA), Attendance: 8.907
CA ESTUDIANTES DE LA PLATA: Agustín Ignacio ORIÓN, Marcos Alberto ANGELERI, Leandro DESÁBATO, Christian Ariel CELLAY, Germán David RÉ, Juan Sebastián VERÓN, Rodrigo BRAÑA, Enzo Nicolás PÉREZ (46 Marcelo Adriám CARRUSCA), José Ernesto SOSA (86 Jerónimo MORALES NEUMANN), Mauro BOSELLI, Gastón Nicolás FERNÁNDEZ (64 Maximiliano Ezequiel NÚÑEZ). DT: Alejandro Javier SABELLA
BOLÍVAR IU LA PAZ: Carlos Edwin ARIAS Eguez, Ignacio ITHURRALDE Sáez, Ronald Tylor RIVERO Khun, Leonel Alfredo REYES Saravia, ALEX Rodrigo DA ROSA Dorneles (61 ANDERSON Gonzaga Martins), Mario Alberto OVANDO Padilla (84 Rudy Alejandro CARDOZO Fernández), Luis Aníbal TORRICO Valverde, Wálter Alberto FLORES Condarco, Werther Thiers CHARLES da Silva Mota, Abdón REYES Cardozo (61 Enrique PARADA Salvatierra), William FERREIRA Martínez. DT: Santiago ESCOBAR Saldarriaga
Goals: José Ernesto SOSA (51), Mauro BOSELLI (79).

CLUB JUAN AURICH – CA ESTUDIANTES DE LA PLATA 0-2 (0-0)
Estadio Eliás Aguirre, Chiclayo, 30.03.2010
Referee: Carlos Arecio AMARILLA Demarqui (PAR), Attendance: 19.904
CLUB JUAN AURICH: Diego Hernán MORALES, Roberto Carlos GUIZASOLA La Rosa, Jesús Martín ÁLVAREZ Hurtado, Jorge Martín ARAUJO Paredes, Jersson VÁSQUEZ Shapiama, Ricardo Manuel CICILIANO Bustillo, Juan Carlos LA ROSA Llontop (61 William CHIROQUE Tavara), Renato Gianfranco ESPEJO Reyes, Luis Carlos TEJADA Hansel, Pedro Luis ASCOY Cortez (84 Herlyn Ysrael ZÚÑIGA Yáñez), Reimond MANCO Albarracin (88 Víctor Julio BALTA Mori). DT: Luis Fernando SUÁREZ
CA ESTUDIANTES DE LA PLATA: Agustín Ignacio ORIÓN, Marcos Alberto ANGELERI, Leandro DESÁBATO, Christian Ariel CELLAY, Germán David RÉ, Clemente Juan RODRÍGUEZ (83 Faustino Marcos Alberto ROJO), Juan Sebastián VERÓN, Rodrigo BRAÑA, José Ernesto SOSA (89 Matías Ariel SÁNCHEZ), Mauro BOSELLI, Gastón Nicolás FERNÁNDEZ (64 Enzo Nicolás PÉREZ). DT: Alejandro Javier "Alex" SABELLA
Sent off: Álvarez (86), Tejada (90+1)
Goals: Gastón Nicolás FERNÁNDEZ (52), Rodrigo BRAÑA (68).

CLUB ALIANZA LIMA – BOLÍVAR IU LA PAZ 1-0 (1-0)
Estadio Alejandro Villanueva, Lima, 8.04.2010
Referee: Juan Ernesto SOTO Arevalo (VEN), Attendance: 11.285
CLUB ALIANZA LIMA: Salomón Alexis LIBMAN Pastor, Wálter Ricardo VÍLCHEZ Soto, Amilton Jair PRADO Barron, Héctor Vidal SOSA Gaona, Édgar VILLAMARÍN Arguedas, Édgar Daniel GONZÁLEZ Brítez, Henry Edson QUINTEROS Sánchez, Jean Carlos TRAGODARA Gálvez (83 Eduardo Alberto URIBE Oshiro), Joel Melchor SÁNCHEZ Alegría (64 Roberto OVELAR Maldonado), José Carlos FERNÁNDEZ Piedra (64 Alexander Gustavo SÁNCHEZ Reyes), Wilmer Alexander AGUIRRE Vasquez. DT: Gustavo Adolfo COSTAS
BOLÍVAR IU LA PAZ: Carlos Edwin ARIAS Eguez, Ignacio ITHURRALDE Sáez, Ariel JUÁREZ Montaño, Ronald Tylor RIVERO Khun, Leonel Alfredo REYES Saravia (77 ALEX Rodrigo DA ROSA Dorneles), Wálter Alberto FLORES Condarco, Rudy Alejandro CARDOZO Fernández, Werther Thiers CHARLES da Silva Mota, Abdón REYES Cardozo (87 José Gabriel RÍOS Benegas), ANDERSON Gonzaga Martins (77 Didí TORRICO Camacho), William FERREIRA Martínez. DT: Santiago ESCOBAR Saldarriaga
Sent off: Villamarín (87)
Goal: José Carlos FERNÁNDEZ Piedra (6).

BOLIVAR IU LA PAZ – CLUB JUAN AURICH 2-0 (0-0)
Estadio Hernando Siles, La Paz, 20.04.2010
Referee: Jorge Luis OSORIO Reyes (CHI), Attendance: 2.484
BOLÍVAR IU LA PAZ: Carlos Edwin ARIAS Eguez, Ignacio ITHURRALDE Sáez, Ariel JUÁREZ Montaño (87 Enrique PARADA Salvatierra), Ronald Tylor RIVERO Khun, Leonel Alfredo REYES Saravia, Wálter Alberto FLORES Condarco, Rudy Alejandro CARDOZO Fernández (58 José Gabriel RÍOS Benegas), Werther Thiers CHARLES da Silva Mota, Abdón REYES Cardozo, ANDERSON Gonzaga Martins (68 ALEX Rodrigo DA ROSA Dorneles), William FERREIRA Martínez. DT: Santiago ESCOBAR Saldarriaga
CLUB JUAN AURICH: Diego Hernán MORALES, Jorge Martín ARAUJO Paredes, Jersson VÁSQUEZ Shapiama, Johnny Javier LALOPÚ Mera, César Alberto SÁNCHEZ Aurich, Juan Carlos LA ROSA Llontop, Renato Gianfranco ESPEJO Reyes (75 Miguel Ángel CEVASCO Abad), Franco Giovanni MENDOZA Breña, Herlyn Ysrael ZÚÑIGA Yáñez, William CHIROQUE Tavara (80 Fernando Rafael GARCÍA López), Manuel Francisco BARRETO Sayón (64 Gary Jeamsen CORREA Gogin). DT: Luis Fernando SUÁREZ
Goals: Wálter Alberto FLORES Condarco (71), ALEX Rodrigo DA ROSA Dorneles (86 penalty).

CA ESTUDIANTES DE LA PLATA – CLUB ALIANZA LIMA 1-0 (0-0)
Estadio Centenario Dr. José Luis Meiszner, Quilmes, 20.04.2010
Referee: Roberto Carlos SILVERA Calcerrada (URU), Attendance: 14.982
CA ESTUDIANTES DE LA PLATA: Agustín Ignacio ORIÓN, Marcos Alberto ANGELERI, Leandro DESÁBATO, Christian Ariel CELLAY, Clemente Juan RODRÍGUEZ (88 Germán David RÉ), Juan Sebastián VERÓN, Rodrigo BRAÑA, Enzo Nicolás PÉREZ, José Ernesto SOSA, Maximiliano Ezequiel NÚÑEZ (82 Leandro GONZÁLEZ), Mauro BOSELLI. DT: Alejandro Javier "Alex" SABELLA
CLUB ALIANZA LIMA: George Patrick FORSYTH Somer, Wálter Ricardo VÍLCHEZ Soto, Carlos Javier SOLÍS Alvarado, Amilton Jair PRADO Barron, Héctor Vidal SOSA Gaona, Édgar Daniel GONZÁLEZ Brítez, Henry Edson QUINTEROS Sánchez (81 Óscar Cristopher VÍLCHEZ Soto), Jean Carlos TRAGODARA Gálvez (86 Eduardo Alberto URIBE Oshiro), Joel Melchor SÁNCHEZ Alegría, José Carlos FERNÁNDEZ Piedra (73 Johnnier Esteiner MONTAÑO Bolaño), Wilmer Alexander AGUIRRE Vasquez. DT: Gustavo Adolfo COSTAS Sent off: Vílchez (90+3)
Goal: Juan Sebastián VERÓN (90+5).

1	ESTUDIANTES LA PLATA	6	4	1	1	11	5	13
2	ALIANZA LIMA	6	4	0	2	12	7	12
3	Juan Aurich	6	2	0	4	7	13	6
4	Bolívar	6	1	1	4	3	8	4

GROUP 4

CA LANÚS – CLUB LIBERTAD ASUNCIÓN 0-2 (0-0)
Estadio Ciudad de Lanús – Néstor Díaz Pérez, Lanús, 9.02.2010
Referee: Wilson Luiz SENEME, Attendance: 4.220
CA LANÚS: Agustín Federico MARCHESÍN, Maximiliano Nicolás VELÁZQUEZ, Santiago Abel HOYOS, JADSON Viera Castro, Hernán Gustavo GRANA (79 Cristian MENÉNDEZ), Agustín Daniel PELLETIERI, Matías Lionel FRITZLER, Marcos Sebastián AGUIRRE (67 Santiago Gabriel SALCEDO González), Sebastián Marcelo BLANCO, Diego Eduardo LAGOS (67 Eduardo Fabián LEDESMA Trinidad), Gonzalo Rubén CASTILLEJOS. DT: Luis Francisco ZUBELDÍA
CLUB LIBERTAD ASUNCIÓN: Bernardo David MEDINA, Pedro Alcides SARABIA Achucarro, Ismael BENEGAS, Sergio Daniel AQUINO, Víctor Javier CÁCERES Centurión, Miguel Ángel Ramón SAMUDIO, Jorge Luis MOREIRA Ferreira (46 Wilson Omar PITTONI Rodríguez), Víctor Hugo AYALA Núñez, Javier Mercedes GONZÁLEZ González (77 Gustavo Ramón MENCIA Avalos), Pablo César VELÁZQUEZ Centurión, Rodolfo Vicente GAMARRA Varela (68 Omar Héber POUSO Osores). DT: Javier TORRENTE
Goals: Rodolfo Vicente GAMARRA Varela (67), Pablo César VELÁZQUEZ Centurión (73).

CSCD BLOOMING – UNIVERSITARIO DE DEPORTES 1-2 (0-0)
Estadio Ramón "Tahuichi" Aguilera Costas, Santa Cruz, 11.02.2010
Referee: Julio Cesar QUINTANA Rodriguez (PAR), Attendance: 10.600
CSCD BLOOMING: Andrés Martín JEMIO Amenabar, Lorgio ÁLVAREZ Roca, Andrés Roberto IMPERIALE, Juan Carlos SÁNCHEZ Ampuero (61 David Raúl VILLALBA Candía), Wilder ZABALA Perrogón, FABRICIO BRANDÃO Santos, Jesús Alejandro GÓMEZ Lanza, José Luis CHÁVEZ Sánchez, LUIZ CARLOS Vieira Junior (58 Róger SUÁREZ Sandoval), José Alfredo CASTILLO Parada (57 Julio César HURTADO Sánchez), Damián Emilio AKERMAN. DT: Víctor Hugo ANDRADA Canalis
UNIVERSITARIO DE DEPORTES: Raúl FERNÁNDEZ Valverde, John Cristian GALLIQUIO Castro, Carlos Alberto GALVÁN, Rodolfo ESPINOZA Díaz, Renzo REVOREDO Zuazo, Rainer TORRES Salas (80 Luis Alberto RAMÍREZ Lucay), Jesús RABANAL Dávila, Antonio Emiliano GONZÁLEZ Canchari (70 Luis Alberto HERNÁNDEZ Díaz), Jorge Johan VÁZQUEZ Rosales, Piero Fernando ALVA Niezen, Carlos Alberto OREJUELA Pita (65 Alberto Gianfranco LABARTHE Tome). DT: Juan Máximo REYNOSO Guzmán
Goals: Jesús Alejandro GÓMEZ Lanza (89) /
Carlos Alberto OREJUELA Pita (52), Rodolfo ESPINOZA Díaz (76).

CLUB LIBERTAD ASUNCIÓN – CSCD BLOOMING 4-0 (1-0)
Estadio Defensores del Chaco, Asunción, 16.02.2010
Referee: Roberto Carlos SILVERA Calcerrada (URU), Attendance: 457
CLUB LIBERTAD ASUNCIÓN: Bernardo David MEDINA, Pedro Alcides SARABIA Achucarro, Ismael BENEGAS, Sergio Daniel AQUINO (69 Omar Héber POUSO Osores), Víctor Javier CÁCERES Centurión, Miguel Ángel Ramón SAMUDIO, Jorge Luis MOREIRA Ferreira (38 Wilson Omar PITTONI Rodríguez), Víctor Hugo AYALA Núñez, Javier Mercedes GONZÁLEZ González (66 Rodrigo ALBORNO Ortega), Pablo César VELÁZQUEZ Centurión, Rodolfo Vicente GAMARRA Varela. DT: Javier TORRENTE
CSCD BLOOMING: Andrés Martín JEMIO Amenabar, Lorgio ÁLVAREZ Roca, Andrés Roberto IMPERIALE, Juan Carlos SÁNCHEZ Ampuero, Wilder ZABALA Perrogón, FABRICIO BRANDÃO Santos, Jesús Alejandro GÓMEZ Lanza, Jorge Marco ANDIA Pizarro (69 Raúl René GONZÁLEZ Guzmán), José Luis CHÁVEZ Sánchez, LUIZ CARLOS Vieira Junior (53 Omar Jesús MORALES Paz), Damián Emilio AKERMAN (67 Julio César HURTADO Sánchez). DT: Víctor Hugo ANDRADA Canalis
Sent off: Fabricio Brandão (49), Imperiale (52)
Goals: Víctor Javier CÁCERES Centurión (45), Rodolfo Vicente GAMARRA Varela (68, 90+1), Víctor Hugo AYALA Núñez (90).

UNIVERSITARIO DE DEPORTES – CA LANÚS 2-0 (1-0)
Estadio Monumental, Lima, 17.02.2010
Referee: Juan Ernesto SOTO Arevalo (VEN), Attendance: 12.507
UNIVERSITARIO DE DEPORTES: Raúl FERNÁNDEZ Valverde, John Cristian GALLIQUIO Castro, Carlos Alberto GALVÁN, Rodolfo ESPINOZA Díaz, Renzo REVOREDO Zuazo, Rainer TORRES Salas, Jesús RABANAL Dávila, Antonio Emiliano GONZÁLEZ Canchari (59 Alberto Gianfranco LABARTHE Tome), Jorge Johan VÁZQUEZ Rosales (86 Giancarlo CARMONA Maldonado), Piero Fernando ALVA Niezen, Carlos Alberto OREJUELA Pita (69 Luis Alberto RAMÍREZ Lucay). DT: Juan Máximo REYNOSO Guzmán
CA LANÚS: Agustín Federico MARCHESÍN, Maximiliano Nicolás VELÁZQUEZ, JADSON Viera Castro, Eduardo Fabián LEDESMA Trinidad, Hernán Gustavo GRANA (84 Cristian MENÉNDEZ), Matías Lionel FRITZLER, Sebastián Marcelo BLANCO (64 Diego Eduardo LAGOS), Rodrigo ERRAMUSPE, Guido PIZARRO (73 Marcos Sebastián AGUIRRE), Santiago Gabriel SALCEDO González, Gonzalo Rubén CASTILLEJOS. DT: Luis Francisco ZUBELDÍA
Goals: Piero Fernando ALVA Niezen (18), Alberto Gianfranco LABARTHE Tome (88).

CSCD BLOOMING – CA LANÚS 1-4 (1-2)
Estadio Ramón "Tahuichi" Aguilera Costas, Santa Cruz, 25.02.2010
Referee: Evandro Rogério ROMÁN (BRA), Attendance: 3.709
CSCD BLOOMING: Andrés Martín JEMIO Amenabar, Lorgio ÁLVAREZ Roca, Juan Carlos SÁNCHEZ Ampuero, Wilder ZABALA Perrogón, David Raúl VILLALBA Candía (46 Jorge Marco ANDIA Pizarro), Jesús Alejandro GÓMEZ Lanza, Omar Jesús MORALES Paz, José Luis CHÁVEZ Sánchez, LUIZ CARLOS Vieira Junior (61 Julio César HURTADO Sánchez), Luis Hernán SILLERO (57 Róger SUÁREZ Sandoval), Damián Emilio AKERMAN. DT: Víctor Hugo ANDRADA Canalis
CA LANÚS: Agustín Federico MARCHESÍN, Maximiliano Nicolás VELÁZQUEZ (46 Carlos Darío ARCE), Santiago Abel HOYOS, JADSON Viera Castro, Hernán Gustavo GRANA, Agustín Daniel PELLETIERI, Matías Lionel FRITZLER, Sebastián Marcelo BLANCO (83 Nelson Javier CARRASCO), Rodrigo ERRAMUSPE, Santiago Gabriel SALCEDO González, Gonzalo Rubén CASTILLEJOS (57 Diego Eduardo LAGOS). DT: Luis Francisco ZUBELDÍA
Goals: LUIZ CARLOS Vieira Junior (9) / Sebastián Marcelo BLANCO (24), Santiago Gabriel SALCEDO González (39), Diego Eduardo LAGOS (60, 76).

UNIVERSITARIO DE DEPORTES – CLUB LIBERTAD ASUNCIÓN 0-0
Estadio Monumental, Lima, 25.02.2010
Referee: Omar Andres PONCE Manzo (ECU), Attendance: 16.530
UNIVERSITARIO DE DEPORTES: Raúl FERNÁNDEZ Valverde, John Cristian GALLIQUIO Castro, Carlos Alberto GALVÁN, Rodolfo ESPINOZA Díaz, Luis Alberto RAMÍREZ Lucay, Renzo REVOREDO Zuazo, Rainer TORRES Salas, Jesús RABANAL Dávila, Antonio Emiliano GONZÁLEZ Canchari (61 Alberto Gianfranco LABARTHE Tome), Víctor Enrique PÍRIZ Álvez, Piero Fernando ALVA Niezen. DT: Juan Máximo REYNOSO Guzmán
CLUB LIBERTAD ASUNCIÓN: Bernardo David MEDINA, Pedro Alcides SARABIA Achucarro, Adalberto ROMÁN Benítez, Ismael BENEGAS, Sergio Daniel AQUINO (78 Omar Héber POUSO Osores),Víctor Javier CÁCERES Centurión, Miguel Ángel Ramón SAMUDIO, Víctor Hugo AYALA Núñez, Javier Mercedes GONZÁLEZ González (74 Jorge Luis MOREIRA Ferreira), Pablo César VELÁZQUEZ Centurión, Rodolfo Vicente GAMARRA Varela (63 Rodrigo ALBORNO Ortega). DT: Javier TORRENTE

CLUB LIBERTAD ASUNCIÓN – UNIVERSITARIO DE DEPORTES 1-1 (0-0)
Estadio Defensores del Chaco, Asunción, 23.03.2010
Referee: Sálvio Spínosa FAGUNDES Filho (BRA), Attendance: 270
CLUB LIBERTAD ASUNCIÓN: Bernardo David MEDINA, Pedro Alcides SARABIA Achucarro, Adalberto ROMÁN Benítez, Sergio Daniel AQUINO, Édgar Arnulfo ROBLES Coronel (80 Jorge Luis MOREIRA Ferreira), Víctor Javier CÁCERES Centurión, Miguel Ángel Ramón SAMUDIO, Víctor Hugo AYALA Núñez, Javier Mercedes GONZÁLEZ González (46 Wilson Omar PITTONI Rodríguez), Pablo César VELÁZQUEZ Centurión, Rodolfo Vicente GAMARRA Varela. DT: Javier TORRENTE
UNIVERSITARIO DE DEPORTES: Raúl FERNÁNDEZ Valverde, John Cristian GALLIQUIO Castro, Carlos Alberto GALVÁN, Rodolfo ESPINOZA Díaz, Luis Alberto RAMÍREZ Lucay, Giancarlo CARMONA Maldonado, Rainer TORRES Salas, Jesús RABANAL Dávila, Antonio Emiliano GONZÁLEZ Canchari (73 Jorge Johan VÁZQUEZ Rosales), Piero Fernando ALVA Niezen (84 Carlos Alberto OREJUELA Pita), Alberto Gianfranco LABARTHE Tome (66 Víctor Enrique PÍRIZ Álvez). DT: Juan Máximo REYNOSO Guzmán
Goals: Víctor Hugo AYALA Núñez (56) / Luis Alberto RAMÍREZ Lucay (87).

CA LANÚS – CSCD BLOOMING 1-0 (1-0)
Estadio Ciudad de Lanús – Néstor Díaz Pérez, Lanús, 24.03.2010
Referee: Patricio Antonio POLIC Orellana (CHI), Attendance: 4.271
CA LANÚS: Agustín Federico MARCHESÍN, Maximiliano Nicolás VELÁZQUEZ, Santiago Abel HOYOS, JADSON Viera Castro, Eduardo Fabián LEDESMA Trinidad (70 Guido PIZARRO), Hernán Gustavo GRANA (78 Marcos Sebastián AGUIRRE), Agustín Daniel PELLETIERI, Sebastián Marcelo BLANCO, Rodrigo ERRAMUSPE, Santiago Gabriel SALCEDO González, Gonzalo Rubén CASTILLEJOS (60 Diego Eduardo LAGOS). DT: Luis Francisco ZUBELDÍA
CSCD BLOOMING: Andrés Martín JEMIO Amenabar, Lorgio ÁLVAREZ Roca, Andrés Roberto IMPERIALE, FABRICIO BRANDÃO Santos, Raúl René GONZÁLEZ Guzmán, David Raúl VILLALBA Candía (57 Wilder ZABALA Perrogón), Jesús Alejandro GÓMEZ Lanza, Jorge Marco ANDIA Pizarro, José Luis CHÁVEZ Sánchez (82 Julio César HURTADO Sánchez), LUIZ CARLOS Vieira Junior, José Alfredo CASTILLO Parada. DT: Carlos ARAGONÉS Espinoza
Goal: Santiago Gabriel SALCEDO González (71penalty).

CLUB LIBERTAD ASUNCIÓN – CA LANÚS 1-1 (1-0)
Estadio Defensores del Chaco, Asunción, 30.03.2010
Referee: Paulo César DE OLIVEIRA (BRA), Attendance: 902
CLUB LIBERTAD ASUNCIÓN: Bernardo David MEDINA, Pedro Alcides SARABIA Achucarro, Adalberto ROMÁN Benítez, Sergio Daniel AQUINO, Édgar Arnulfo ROBLES Coronel, Víctor Javier CÁCERES Centurión, Miguel Ángel Ramón SAMUDIO (66 Gustavo Ramón MENCIA Avalos), Wilson Omar PITTONI Rodríguez (70 Rodrigo ALBORNO Ortega), Víctor Hugo AYALA Núñez, Roberto Carlos GAMARRA Acosta, Pablo César VELÁZQUEZ Centurión (77 Javier Mercedes GONZÁLEZ González). DT: Javier TORRENTE
CA LANÚS: Agustín Federico MARCHESÍN, Maximiliano Nicolás VELÁZQUEZ, Santiago Abel HOYOS (60 Marcos Sebastián AGUIRRE), JADSON Viera Castro, Eduardo Fabián LEDESMA Trinidad, Hernán Gustavo GRANA, Agustín Daniel PELLETIERI (60 Matías Lionel FRITZLER), Sebastián Marcelo BLANCO, Diego Eduardo LAGOS (60 Leandro Nicolás DÍAZ), Rodrigo ERRAMUSPE, Santiago Gabriel SALCEDO González. DT: Luis Francisco ZUBELDÍA
Sent off: Salcedo (41)
Goals: Adalberto ROMÁN Benítez (3) / Maximiliano Nicolás VELÁZQUEZ (83).

UNIVERSITARIO DE DEPORTES – CSCD BLOOMING 0-0
Estadio Monumental, Lima, 6.04.2010
Referee: Héber Roberto LOPES (BRA), Attendance: 18.884
UNIVERSITARIO DE DEPORTES: Raúl FERNÁNDEZ Valverde, John Cristian GALLIQUIO Castro, Carlos Alberto GALVÁN, Rodolfo ESPINOZA Díaz, Luis Alberto RAMÍREZ Lucay, Renzo REVOREDO Zuazo, Rainer TORRES Salas, Jesús RABANAL Dávila, Antonio Emiliano GONZÁLEZ Canchari (46 Giancarlo CARMONA Maldonado), Piero Fernando ALVA Niezen, Alberto Gianfranco LABARTHE Tome (68 Carlos Alberto OREJUELA Pita). DT: Juan Máximo REYNOSO Guzmán
CSCD BLOOMING: Andrés Martín JEMIO Amenabar, Lorgio ÁLVAREZ Roca, Andrés Roberto IMPERIALE, Wilder ZABALA Perrogón, FABRICIO BRANDÃO Santos, David Raúl VILLALBA Candía (82 Jorge Marco ANDIA Pizarro), Jesús Alejandro GÓMEZ Lanza, Omar Jesús MORALES Paz, José Luis CHÁVEZ Sánchez, LUIZ CARLOS Vieira Junior (90+1 Julio César HURTADO Sánchez), José Alfredo CASTILLO Parada (80 Luis Hernán SILLERO). DT: Carlos ARAGONÉS Espinoza

CSCD BLOOMING – CLUB LIBERTAD ASUNCIÓN 1-2 (1-1)
Estadio Ramón "Tahuichi" Aguilera Costas, Santa Cruz, 15.04.2010
Referee: Jorge Luis LARRIONDA Pietrafesa (URU), Attendance: 804
CSCD BLOOMING: Andrés Martín JEMIO Amenabar, Andrés Roberto IMPERIALE, Wilder ZABALA Perrogón, Dustin MALDONADO Antelo, David Raúl VILLALBA Candía, Julio César HURTADO Sánchez, Omar Jesús MORALES Paz, Jorge Marco ANDIA Pizarro, Jorge GONZÁLEZ Suárez (46 Damián Emilio AKERMAN), Luis Hernán SILLERO (46 Lorgio ÁLVAREZ Roca), José Alfredo CASTILLO Parada (62 LUIZ CARLOS Vieira Junior). DT: Carlos ARAGONÉS Espinoza
CLUB LIBERTAD ASUNCIÓN: Bernardo David MEDINA, Pedro Alcides SARABIA Achucarro, Adalberto ROMÁN Benítez, Ismael BENEGAS, Sergio Daniel AQUINO, Víctor Javier CÁCERES Centurión, Miguel Ángel Ramón SAMUDIO, Víctor Hugo AYALA Núñez, Javier Mercedes GONZÁLEZ González (46 Gustavo Alberto CRISTALDO Brítez), Pablo César VELÁZQUEZ Centurión (77 Roberto Carlos GAMARRA Acosta), Rodolfo Vicente GAMARRA Varela (82 Édgar Arnulfo ROBLES Coronel). DT: Gregorio Elso PÉREZ Perdigón
Goals: Julio César HURTADO Sánchez (27) /
Adalberto ROMÁN Benítez (38), Rodolfo Vicente GAMARRA Varela (53).

CA LANÚS – UNIVERSITARIO DE DEPORTES 0-0
Estadio Ciudad de Lanús – Néstor Díaz Pérez, Lanús, 15.04.2010
Referee: Carlos Eugênio SIMÓN (BRA), Attendance: 4.198
CA LANÚS: Agustín Federico MARCHESÍN, Maximiliano Nicolás VELÁZQUEZ, Santiago Abel HOYOS, JADSON Viera Castro, Agustín Daniel PELLETIERI, Marcos Sebastián AGUIRRE (75 Nelson Javier CARRASCO), Sebastián Marcelo BLANCO, Rodrigo ERRAMUSPE (46 Hernán Gustavo GRANA), Guido PIZARRO, Gonzalo Rubén CASTILLEJOS (75 Cristian MENÉNDEZ), Leandro Nicolás DÍAZ. DT: Luis Francisco ZUBELDÍA
UNIVERSITARIO DE DEPORTES: Raúl FERNÁNDEZ Valverde, John Cristian GALLIQUIO Castro, Carlos Alberto GALVÁN, Rodolfo ESPINOZA Díaz, Renzo REVOREDO Zuazo, Giancarlo CARMONA Maldonado, Rainer TORRES Salas (90 Jorge Johan VÁZQUEZ Rosales), Jesús RABANAL Dávila, Antonio Emiliano GONZÁLEZ Canchari (60 Raúl RUIDÍAZ), Piero Fernando ALVA Niezen, Alberto Gianfranco LABARTHE Tome (69 Víctor Enrique PÍRIZ Álvez).
Sent off: Pelletieri (90+5), Díaz (90+5) / Fernández (90+5), Galliquio (90+5)

1	LIBERTAD	6	3	3	0	10	3	12
2	UNIVERSITARIO	6	2	4	0	5	2	10
3	CA Lanús	6	2	2	2	6	6	8
4	Blooming	6	0	1	5	3	13	1

GROUP 5

CA CERRO MONTEVIDEO – SOCIEDAD DEPORTIVO QUITO 2-0 (1-0)
Estadio Centenario, Montevideo, 9.02.2010
Referee: Jorge Luis OSORIO Reyes (CHI), Attendance: 6.021
CA CERRO MONTEVIDEO: Damián FRASCARELLI, Pablo Rodrigo MELO, Wálter Fernando IBÁÑEZ Costa, Daniel LEITES, Danilo ASCONEGUY Ruiz, Claudio Martín DADÓMO Minervini (90 Jorge Fabián TRUJILLO Caceres), Richard Javier PELLEJERO Ferreira, Sebastián Marcelo SUÁREZ López, Pablo Eduardo CABALLERO Sebastiani, Álvaro Alejandro MELLO Silvera, Rodrigo Nicanor MORA Núñez (86 Raúl César MOLINA). DT: Pablo REPETTO
SOCIEDAD DEPORTIVO QUITO: Oswaldo Giovanny IBARRA Carabalí, Iván Jacinto HURTADO Angulo, Pedro Luis ESTERILLA Delgado (74 José Jacobo VISCAÍNO Rosales), Roberto Michael CASTRO Cadena (65 Juan Carlos PAREDES Reasco), Luis Armando CHECA Villamar, Banner Geovanny CAICEDO Quiñónez, Luis Fernando SARITAMA Padilla, Ángel Gabriel ESCOBAR Arce, Michael Antonio ARROYO Mina, Marcos Emiliano PIRCHIO, Iván Emilio BORGHELLO (40 Franco NIELL). DT: Rubén Darío INSÚA
Goals: Claudio Martín DADÓMO Minervini (20), Rodrigo Nicanor MORA Núñez (62).

SC INTERNACIONAL – CS EMELEC 2-1 (0-0)
Estádio José Pinheiro Borda (Beira-Rio), Porto Alegre, 23.02.2010
Referee: Diego Hernán ABAL (ARG), Attendance: 39.304
SC INTERNACIONAL: Roberto Carlos ABBONDANZIERI, Gonzalo SORONDO Amaro, Fabián Guedes "BOLÍVAR", Claudinei Cardoso Félix da Silva "NEI" (64 TAISON Barcellos Freda), KLÉBER de Carvalho Correa, DANILO da Silva, Pablo Horacio GUIÑAZÚ, GIULIANO Victor de Paula (81 André Luiz Tavares "ANDREZINHO"), SANDRO Guimaraes Cordeiro Ranieri, Luis Eduardo Schmidt "EDÚ" (76 WALTER Henrique da Silva), ALECSANDRO Barbosa Felisbino. DT: Jorge Daniel FOSATTI Lurachi
CS EMELEC: Marcelo Ramón ELIZAGA Ferrero, Gabriel Eduardo ACHILIER Zurita, Julio Marcelo FLEITAS Silveira, Mariano Florencio MINA Orobio, Miguel David QUIROZ Villón, Pablo Javier PÉREZ, Pedro Ángel QUIÑÓNEZ Rodríguez, Eduardo Javier MORANTE Rosas (74 José Luis QUIÑÓNEZ Quiñónez), Joao Robin ROJAS Mendoza, Jaime Javier AYOVÍ Corozo (90+4 Hernán Gastón PEIRONE), Enner Remberto VALENCIA Lastra (46 Santiago BIGLIERI). DT: Jorge Luis SAMPAOLI
Goals: Claudinei Cardoso Félix da Silva "NEI" (53), ALECSANDRO Barbosa Felisbino (87) / Miguel David QUIROZ Villón (49).

CS EMELEC – CA CERRO MONTEVIDEO 1-2 (0-0)
Estadio George Capwell, Guayaquil, 11.03.2010
Referee: Víctor Hugo CARRILLO Casanova (PER), Attendance: 9.793
CS EMELEC: Marcelo Ramón ELIZAGA Ferrero, Gabriel Eduardo ACHILIER Zurita, Julio Marcelo FLEITAS Silveira, Mariano Florencio MINA Orobio (82 Ángel Israel MENA Delgado), Miguel David QUIROZ Villón, Pablo Javier PÉREZ, Pedro Ángel QUIÑÓNEZ Rodríguez, Santiago BIGLIERI, Joao Robin ROJAS Mendoza, Jaime Javier AYOVÍ Corozo, Enner Remberto VALENCIA Lastra (54 Hernán Gastón PEIRONE). DT: Jorge Luis SAMPAOLI
CA CERRO MONTEVIDEO: Mathías ROLERO, Pablo Rodrigo MELO, Wálter Fernando IBÁÑEZ Costa, Daniel LEITES, Danilo ASCONEGUY Ruiz, Claudio Martín DADÓMO Minervini, Richard Javier PELLEJERO Ferreira, Sebastián Marcelo SUÁREZ López, Pablo Eduardo CABALLERO Sebastiani (82 Marcelo Adrián MANSILLA Iriarte), Álvaro Alejandro MELLO Silvera (79 Jorge Fabián TRUJILLO Caceres), Rodrigo Nicanor MORA Núñez (89 Raúl César MOLINA). DT: Pablo REPETTO
Goals: Pablo Javier PÉREZ (70) / Pablo Eduardo CABALLERO Sebastiani (51), Claudio Martín DADÓMO Minervini (67).

SOCIEDAD DEPORTIVO QUITO – SC INTERNACIONAL 1-1 (1-1)
Estadio Olímpico Atahualpa, Quito, 11.03.2010
Referee: José Hernando BUITRAGO Arango (COL), Attendance: 4.088
SOCIEDAD DEPORTIVO QUITO: Oswaldo Giovanny IBARRA Carabalí, Iván Jacinto HURTADO Angulo, Roberto Michael CASTRO Cadena, Luis Armando CHECA Villamar, Isaac Bryan MINA Arboleda, José Ramón AGUIRRE Icaza, Luis Fernando SARITAMA Padilla, Tilson Oswaldo MINDA Suscal, Michael Antonio ARROYO Mina (62 Iván Emilio BORGHELLO), Franco NIELL, Marcos Emiliano PIRCHIO (62 Mauricio Alejandro DONOSO Pérez). DT: Rubén Darío INSÚA
SC INTERNACIONAL: Roberto Carlos ABBONDANZIERI, BRUNO Ramón SILVA Barone, Gonzalo SORONDO Amaro, KLÉBER de Carvalho Correa, Marcos Antônio de Lima "ÍNDIO", JUAN Guilherme Nunes Jesus, Pablo Horacio GUIÑAZÚ, GIULIANO Victor de Paula (80 WILSON TIAGO Mathías), SANDRO Guimaraes Cordeiro Ranieri, Luis Eduardo Schmidt "EDÚ" (70 Andrés Nicolás D'ALESSANDRO), ALECSANDRO Barbosa Felisbino (85 TAISON Barcellos Freda). DT: Jorge Daniel FOSATTI Lurachi
Goals: Tilson Oswaldo MINDA Suscal (33) / GIULIANO Victor de Paula (40).

CA CERRO MONTEVIDEO – SC INTERNACIONAL 0-0
Estadio Atilio Paiva Olivera, Rivera, 18.03.2010
Referee: Saúl Esteban LAVERNI (ARG), Attendance: 25.510
CA CERRO MONTEVIDEO: Mathías ROLERO, Pablo Rodrigo MELO, Wálter Fernando IBÁÑEZ Costa, Daniel LEITES, Danilo ASCONEGUY Ruiz, Claudio Martín DADÓMO Minervini, Richard Javier PELLEJERO Ferreira, Sebastián Marcelo SUÁREZ López, Pablo Eduardo CABALLERO Sebastiani, Álvaro Alejandro MELLO Silvera (87 Raúl César MOLINA), Rodrigo Nicanor MORA Núñez (79 Maximiliano LOMBARDI Rodríguez). DT: Pablo REPETTO
SC INTERNACIONAL: Roberto Carlos ABBONDANZIERI, BRUNO Ramón SILVA Barone (58 Claudinei Cardoso Félix da Silva "NEI"), Gonzalo SORONDO Amaro, KLÉBER de Carvalho Correa, Marcos Antônio de Lima "ÍNDIO", Andrés Nicolás D'ALESSANDRO (72 André Luiz Tavares "ANDREZINHO"), Pablo Horacio GUIÑAZÚ, GIULIANO Victor de Paula (80 TAISON Barcellos Freda), SANDRO Guimaraes Cordeiro Ranieri, Luis Eduardo Schmidt "EDÚ", ALECSANDRO Barbosa Felisbino. DT: Jorge Daniel FOSATTI Lurachi

SOCIEDAD DEPORTIVO QUITO – CS EMELEC 1-0 (0-0)
Estadio Olímpico Atahualpa, Quito, 25.03.2010
Referee: José Luis ESPINEL Mena (ECU), Attendance: 5.719
SOCIEDAD DEPORTIVO QUITO: Oswaldo Giovanny IBARRA Carabalí, Pedro Luis ESTERILLA Delgado, Luis Armando CHECA Villamar, Luis Alexis TENORIO Rivas, Banner Geovanny CAICEDO Quiñónez, Luis Fernando SARITAMA Padilla, Ángel Gabriel ESCOBAR Arce, Tilson Oswaldo MINDA Suscal, Michael Antonio ARROYO Mina (88 José Jacobo VISCAÍNO Rosales), Franco NIELL (84 Marcos Emiliano PIRCHIO), Iván Emilio BORGHELLO (85 Roberto Michael CASTRO Cadena). DT: Rubén Darío INSÚA
CS EMELEC: Marcelo Ramón ELIZAGA Ferrero, Gabriel Eduardo ACHILIER Zurita, Mariano Florencio MINA Orobio, Luis Alberto ZAMBRANO Santacruz, Miguel David QUIROZ Villón, Pedro Ángel QUIÑÓNEZ Rodríguez, José Luis QUIÑÓNEZ Quiñónez, Eduardo Javier MORANTE Rosas, Hernán Gastón PEIRONE (63 Jaime Javier AYOVÍ Corozo), Joao Robin ROJAS Mendoza (70 Silvano de los Santos ESTACIO Montaño), Enner Remberto VALENCIA Lastra (46 Santiago BIGLIERI). DT: Jorge Luis SAMPAOLI
Goal: Michael Antonio ARROYO Mina (64).

SC INTERNACIONAL – CA CERRO MONTEVIDEO 2-0 (0-0)
Estádio José Pinheiro Borda (Beira-Rio), Porto Alegre, 31.03.2010
Referee: Carlos Manuel TORRES Nuñez (PAR), Attendance: 36.897
SC INTERNACIONAL: Roberto Carlos ABBONDANZIERI, Fabián Guedes "BOLÍVAR", Claudinei Cardoso Félix da Silva "NEI", KLÉBER de Carvalho Correa, Marcos Antônio de Lima "ÍNDIO", Andrés Nicolás D'ALESSANDRO (76 André Luiz Tavares "ANDREZINHO"), Pablo Horacio GUIÑAZÚ, GIULIANO Victor de Paula (89 WILSON TIAGO Mathías), SANDRO Guimaraes Cordeiro Ranieri, ALECSANDRO Barbosa Felisbino, WALTER Henrique da Silva (83 TAISON Barcellos Freda). DT: Jorge Daniel FOSATTI Lurachi
CA CERRO MONTEVIDEO: Damián FRASCARELLI, Pablo Rodrigo MELO, Claudio Martín DADÓMO Minervini (81 Maximiliano LOMBARDI Rodríguez), Wálter Fernando IBÁÑEZ Costa, Daniel LEITES, Danilo ASCONEGUY Ruiz, Richard Javier PELLEJERO Ferreira, Sebastián Marcelo SUÁREZ López (83 Jorge Fabián TRUJILLO Caceres), Pablo Eduardo CABALLERO Sebastiani, Álvaro Alejandro MELLO Silvera, Rodrigo Nicanor MORA Núñez (64 Sergio SUFFO). DT: Pablo REPETTO
Goals: Wálter Fernando IBÁÑEZ Costa (58 own goal), ALECSANDRO Barbosa Felisbino (72).

CS EMELEC – SOCIEDAD DEPORTIVO QUITO 0-1 (0-0)
Estadio George Capwell, Guayaquil, 1.04.2010
Referee: Samuel Rolando HARO Inca (ECU), Attendance: 4.217
CS EMELEC: Marcelo Ramón ELIZAGA Ferrero, Gabriel Eduardo ACHILIER Zurita, Julio Marcelo FLEITAS Silveira, Mariano Florencio MINA Orobio, Luis Alberto ZAMBRANO Santacruz, Miguel David QUIROZ Villón, José Luis QUIÑÓNEZ Quiñónez, Santiago BIGLIERI, Hernán Gastón PEIRONE (46 Silvano de los Santos ESTACIO Montaño), Joao Robin ROJAS Mendoza (68 Enner Remberto VALENCIA Lastra), Jaime Javier AYOVÍ Corozo. DT: Jorge Luis SAMPAOLI
SOCIEDAD DEPORTIVO QUITO: Oswaldo Giovanny IBARRA Carabalí, Iván Jacinto HURTADO Angulo, Pedro Luis ESTERILLA Delgado (60 Mauricio Alejandro DONOSO Pérez), Luis Armando CHECA Villamar, Isaac Bryan MINA Arboleda, Luis Fernando SARITAMA Padilla, Ángel Gabriel ESCOBAR Arce, Tilson Oswaldo MINDA Suscal, Michael Antonio ARROYO Mina (74 Juan Carlos PAREDES Reasco), Franco NIELL, Iván Emilio BORGHELLO (46 Marcos Emiliano PIRCHIO). DT: Rubén Darío INSÚA
Sent off: Achilier (79)
Goal: Iván Jacinto HURTADO Angulo (90+3 penalty).

SOCIEDAD DEPORTIVO QUITO – CA CERRO MONTEVIDEO 2-1 (1-1)
Estadio Olímpico Atahualpa, Quito, 13.04.2010
Referee: Óscar Julián RUÍZ Acosta (COL), Attendance: 8.836
SOCIEDAD DEPORTIVO QUITO: Oswaldo Giovanny IBARRA Carabalí, Iván Jacinto HURTADO Angulo, Luis Armando CHECA Villamar, Isaac Bryan MINA Arboleda, Luis Fernando SARITAMA Padilla, Ángel Gabriel ESCOBAR Arce (46 Mauricio Alejandro DONOSO Pérez), Tilson Oswaldo MINDA Suscal, Michael Antonio ARROYO Mina, Juan Carlos PAREDES Reasco (68 Roberto Michael CASTRO Cadena), Franco NIELL, Marcos Emiliano PIRCHIO (78 Daniel Alejandro SOLANO Valarezco). DT: Rubén Darío INSÚA
CA CERRO MONTEVIDEO: Damián FRASCARELLI, Pablo Rodrigo MELO, Claudio Martín DADÓMO Minervini (88 Jonathan SOTO), Wálter Fernando IBÁÑEZ Costa, Daniel LEITES, Danilo ASCONEGUY Ruiz, Richard Javier PELLEJERO Ferreira, Sebastián Marcelo SUÁREZ López, Pablo Eduardo CABALLERO Sebastiani (82 Marcelo Adrián MANSILLA Iriarte), Álvaro Alejandro MELLO Silvera (74 Jorge Fabián TRUJILLO Caceres), Rodrigo Nicanor MORA Núñez. DT: Pablo REPETTO
Goals: Isaac Bryan MINA Arboleda (20), Luis Armando CHECA Villamar (86) /
Claudio Martín DADÓMO Minervini (27 penalty).

CS EMELEC – SC INTERNACIONAL 0-0
Estadio George Capwell, Guayaquil, 4.04.2010
Referee: Marlon Giovanny ESCALANTE Alvarez (VEN), Attendance: 3.774
CS EMELEC: Javier Hernán KLIMOWICZ Laganá, Julio Marcelo FLEITAS Silveira, Mariano Florencio MINA Orobio, Luis Alberto ZAMBRANO Santacruz, Fernando Augusto GIMÉNEZ Solis (72 Fernando Vicente GAIBOR Orellana), Pedro Ángel QUIÑÓNEZ Rodríguez (68 Polo Raúl WILA Cangá), José Luis QUIÑÓNEZ Quiñónez, Santiago BIGLIERI, Hernán Gastón PEIRONE, Silvano de los Santos ESTACIO Montaño, Enner Remberto VALENCIA Lastra (78 Ángel Israel MENA Delgado). DT: Jorge Luis SAMPAOLI
SC INTERNACIONAL: Roberto Carlos ABBONDANZIERI, Gonzalo SORONDO Amaro, Fabián Guedes "BOLÍVAR", Claudinei Cardoso Félix da Silva "NEI", KLÉBER de Carvalho Correa, Andrés Nicolás D'ALESSANDRO (86 Luis Eduardo Schmidt "EDÚ"), Pablo Horacio GUIÑAZÚ, GIULIANO Victor de Paula (71 André Luiz Tavares "ANDREZINHO"), SANDRO Guimaraes Cordeiro Ranieri, ALECSANDRO Barbosa Felisbino, WALTER Henrique da Silva (66 TAISON Barcellos Freda). DT: Jorge Daniel FOSATTI Lurachi

SC INTERNACIONAL – SOCIEDAD DEPORTIVO QUITO 3-0 (1-0)
Estádio José Pinheiro Borda (Beira-Rio), Porto Alegre, 22.04.2010
Referee: Carlos Alberto AMARILLA Demarqui (PAR), Attendance: 31.360
SC INTERNACIONAL: Roberto Carlos ABBONDANZIERI, Gonzalo SORONDO Amaro, Fabián Guedes "BOLÍVAR", Claudinei Cardoso Félix da Silva "NEI", KLÉBER de Carvalho Correa (80 FABIANO ELLER dos Santos), Andrés Nicolás D'ALESSANDRO, Pablo Horacio GUIÑAZÚ, André Luiz Tavares "ANDREZINHO" (86 GIULIANO Victor de Paula), SANDRO Guimaraes Cordeiro Ranieri, ALECSANDRO Barbosa Felisbino, WALTER Henrique da Silva (68 Luis Eduardo Schmidt "EDÚ"). DT: Jorge Daniel FOSATTI Lurachi
SOCIEDAD DEPORTIVO QUITO: Oswaldo Giovanny IBARRA Carabalí, Iván Jacinto HURTADO Angulo, Pedro Luis ESTERILLA Delgado (46 Roberto Michael CASTRO Cadena), Luis Armando CHECA Villamar, Isaac Bryan MINA Arboleda, Banner Geovanny CAICEDO Quiñónez, Luis Fernando SARITAMA Padilla (76 Franco NIELL), Tilson Oswaldo MINDA Suscal, Michael Antonio ARROYO Mina, Marcos Emiliano PIRCHIO (46 Mauricio Alejandro DONOSO Pérez), Iván Emilio BORGHELLO. DT: Rubén Darío INSÚA
Sent off: Edú (89)
Goals: André Luiz Tavares "ANDREZINHO" (4), Fabián Guedes "BOLÍVAR" (61), GIULIANO Victor de Paula (90+3).

CA CERRO MONTEVIDEO – CS EMELEC 0-0
Estadio Luis Tróccoli, Montevideo, 22.04.2010
Referee: Iván Igor GAMBOA Zizold (BOL), Attendance: 2.669
CA CERRO MONTEVIDEO: Damián FRASCARELLI, Ignacio Enrique AMARILLA Carames (46 Fernando Daniel ÁLVES Olivera), Claudio Martín DADÓMO Minervini, Wálter Fernando IBÁÑEZ Costa, Daniel LEITES (64 Jonathan SOTO), Danilo ASCONEGUY Ruiz, Richard Javier PELLEJERO Ferreira, Sebastián Marcelo SUÁREZ López, Pablo Eduardo CABALLERO Sebastiani, Álvaro Alejandro MELLO Silvera (74 Ricardo QUEIRO), Rodrigo Nicanor MORA Núñez. DT: Pablo REPETTO
CS EMELEC: Marcelo Ramón ELIZAGA Ferrero, Gabriel Eduardo ACHILIER Zurita, Julio Marcelo FLEITAS Silveira, Miguel David QUIROZ Villón, Fernando Augusto GIMÉNEZ Solis, Pedro Ángel QUIÑÓNEZ Rodríguez, Eduardo Javier MORANTE Rosas, Santiago BIGLIERI (58 Enner Remberto VALENCIA Lastra), Joao Robin ROJAS Mendoza (90+3 José Luis QUIÑÓNEZ Quiñónez), Jaime Javier AYOVÍ Corozo (62 Hernán Gastón PEIRONE), Silvano de los Santos ESTACIO Montaño. DT: Jorge Luis SAMPAOLI
Sent off: Suárez (56) / Quiroz (80)

1	INTERNACIONAL	6	3	3	0	8	2	12
2	DEPORTIVO QUITO	6	3	1	2	5	7	10
3	CA Cerro	6	2	2	2	5	5	8
4	Emelec	6	0	2	4	2	6	2

GROUP 6

CA BANFIELD – CA MONARCAS MORELIA 2-1 (0-0)
Estadio Florencio Solá, Banfield, 10.02.2010
Referee: Antonio Javier ARIAS Alvarenga (PAR), Attendance: 5.804
CA BANFIELD: Cristian David LUCCHETTI, Jonathan Ramón MAIDANA, Víctor Rubén LÓPEZ, Walter Marcelo BUSTAMANTE, Roberto Miguel BATTIÓN, Julio Eduardo BARRAZA, Wálter Daniel ERVITI (81 Ariel Emmanuel PÍO), Marcelo Nildo QUINTEROS (89 Julio Javier MARCHANT), James David RODRÍGUEZ Rubio, Rubén Darío RAMÍREZ, Sebastián Bruno FERNÁNDEZ Miglierina. DT: Julio César FALCIONI
CA MONARCAS MORELIA: Moisés Alberto MUÑOZ Rodríguez, Fernando SALAZAR Lomelí, Marvin Gabriel CABRERA Ibarra, Martín Mauricio ROMERO, Hugo Patricio DROGUETT Diocares, Adrián Alexei ALDRETE Rodríguez, Gabriel Ernesto PEREYRA Vázquez (69 Elías Hernán HERNÁNDEZ Jacuinde), Jorge HERNÁNDEZ González, Aldo Leão RAMÍREZ Sierra, Jared Francisco BORGETTI Echavarría (58 Jaime DURÁN Gómez), Miguel SABAH Rodríguez (81 Luis Gabriel REY Villamizar). DT: Tomás Juan BOY Espinoza
Sent off: Aldrete (52)
Goals: James David RODRÍGUEZ Rubio (55), Roberto Miguel BATTIÓN (79) /
Luis Gabriel REY Villamizar (90+1).

CLUB NACIONAL MONTEVIDEO – CLUB DEPORTIVO CUENCA 3-2 (0-1)
Estadio Gran Parque Central, Montevideo, 11.02.2010
Referee: Enrique Roberto OSSÉS Zencovich (CHI), Attendance: 11.299
CLUB NACIONAL MONTEVIDEO: Rodrigo Martín MUÑOZ Salomón, Alejandro Daniel LEMBO Betancor, Christian Washington NÚÑEZ Medina, Sebastián COATES Nion, Gustavo Antonio VARELA Rodríguez, Álvaro Rafael GONZÁLEZ Luengo (70 Sergio Rubén BLANCO Soto), Ángel Alejandro MORALES Santos, Óscar Javier MORALES Albornoz, Mauricio Ernesto PEREYRA Antonini, Mario Ignacio REGUEIRO Pintos (79 Sebastián Andrés BALSAS Bruno), Santiago Damián GARCÍA Correa (60 Diego Daniel VERA Méndez). DT: Eduardo Mario ACEVEDO Cardozo
CLUB DEPORTIVO CUENCA: Esteban Javier DREER, Diego Adrián IANIERO, Juan Kely GUERRÓN Vásquez, Jaime Javier CHILA Cortez, Arlin Secundo AYOVÍ Ayoví, Gabriel Antonio MÉNDEZ, José Eduardo GRANDA Vicuña (76 Christian Santiago CORDERO Rodríguez), Giancarlo Pablo RAMOS Barrios, Jhon Antonio GARCÍA Figueroa, Mauricio Bladimir HURTADO Alvarado (67 William Osvaldo ESPAÑA España), Luis Miguel ESCALADA (81 Darwín Deivis CAICEDO Wila).
DT: Paúl VÉLEZ
Goals: Mario Ignacio REGUEIRO Pintos (46, 65), Óscar Javier MORALES Albornoz (85 penalty) /
José Eduardo GRANDA Vicuña (25), Luis Miguel ESCALADA (68).

CLUB DEPORTIVO CUENCA – CA BANFIELD 1-4 (0-2)
Estadio Alejandro Serrano Aguilar, Cuenca, 17.02.2010
Referee: Wilmar Alexander ROLDÁN Pérez (COL), Attendance: 11.345
CLUB DEPORTIVO CUENCA: Esteban Javier DREER, Diego Adrián IANIERO (74 Christian Santiago CORDERO Rodríguez), Juan Kely GUERRÓN Vásquez, Jaime Javier CHILA Cortez, Arlin Secundo AYOVÍ Ayoví, Gabriel Antonio MÉNDEZ, José Eduardo GRANDA Vicuña, Giancarlo Pablo RAMOS Barrios, Jhon Antonio GARCÍA Figueroa (46 Jorge Washington LADINES Garcés), Mauricio Bladimir HURTADO Alvarado (46 William Osvaldo ESPAÑA España), Luis Miguel ESCALADA.
DT: Paúl VÉLEZ
CA BANFIELD: Cristian David LUCCHETTI, Jonathan Ramón MAIDANA, Víctor Rubén LÓPEZ, Walter Marcelo BUSTAMANTE, Roberto Miguel BATTIÓN, Julio Eduardo BARRAZA, Wálter Daniel ERVITI (74 Ariel Emmanuel PÍO), Marcelo Nildo QUINTEROS, James David RODRÍGUEZ Rubio, Rubén Darío RAMÍREZ (86 José Alberto SHAFFER), Sebastián Bruno FERNÁNDEZ Miglierina (80 Cristian Andrés GARCÍA). DT: Julio César FALCIONI
Sent off: Bustamante (85)
Goals: Gabriel Antonio MÉNDEZ (86 penalty) / Wálter Daniel ERVITI (35), Sebastián Bruno FERNÁNDEZ Miglierina (38, 60), James David RODRÍGUEZ Rubio (71).

CA MONARCAS MORELIA – CLUB NACIONAL MONTEVIDEO 0-0
Estadio Generalísimo José María Morelos y Pavón, Morelia, 23.02.2010
Referee: Luis Francisco PEÑUELA Fajardo (COL), Attendance: 21.493
CA MONARCAS MORELIA: Moisés Alberto MUÑOZ Rodríguez, Fernando SALAZAR Lomelí, Jaime DURÁN Gómez, Martín Mauricio ROMERO, Hugo Patricio DROGUETT Diocares, Jorge HERNÁNDEZ González (61 Miguel SABAH Rodríguez), Aldo Leão RAMÍREZ Sierra (74 Luis Fernando SILVA Ochoa), Enrique PÉREZ Herrera, Jared Francisco BORGETTI Echavarría, Luis Gabriel REY Villamizar, Elías Hernán HERNÁNDEZ Jacuinde (54 Gabriel Ernesto PEREYRA Vázquez). DT: Tomás Juan BOY Espinoza
CLUB NACIONAL MONTEVIDEO: Rodrigo Martín MUÑOZ Salomón, Alejandro Daniel LEMBO Betancor, Christian Washington NÚÑEZ Medina, Ernesto GOÑI Ameijenda, Sebastián COATES Nion, Gustavo Antonio VARELA Rodríguez, Álvaro Rafael GONZÁLEZ Luengo (61 Sebastián Andrés BALSAS Bruno), Óscar Javier MORALES Albornoz, Raúl Freddy FERRO Olivera (78 Sergio Rubén BLANCO Soto), Mauricio Ernesto PEREYRA Antonini (69 Maximiliano Matías CALZADA Fuentes), Mario Ignacio REGUEIRO Pintos. DT: Eduardo Mario ACEVEDO Cardozo
Sent off: Sabah (84)

CLUB DEPORTIVO CUENCA – CA MONARCAS MORELIA 2-0 (0-0)
Estadio Alejandro Serrano Aguilar, Cuenca, 9.03.2010
Referee: Giovanni PERLUZZO Diaz (VEN), Attendance: 7.700
CLUB DEPORTIVO CUENCA: Esteban Javier DREER, Diego Adrián IANIERO, Juan Kely GUERRÓN Vásquez, Marco Antonio QUIÑÓNEZ Angulo, Jaime Javier CHILA Cortez, John William NARVÁEZ Arroyo, Gabriel Antonio MÉNDEZ (88 Fernando Rafael FAJARDO Avila), José Eduardo GRANDA Vicuña (46 William Osvaldo ESPAÑA España), Giancarlo Pablo RAMOS Barrios, Jhon Antonio GARCÍA Figueroa, Luis Miguel ESCALADA (84 Jorge Washington LADINES Garcés). DT: Paúl VÉLEZ
CA MONARCAS MORELIA: Moisés Alberto MUÑOZ Rodríguez, Fernando SALAZAR Lomelí, Marvin Gabriel CABRERA Ibarra, Jaime DURÁN Gómez, Martín Mauricio ROMERO, Hugo Patricio DROGUETT Diocares, Jorge HERNÁNDEZ González (68 Pedro Luis BELTRÁN García), Ismael PINEDA Jácome, Jared Francisco BORGETTI Echavarría, Luis Gabriel REY Villamizar (78 Miguel Ángel SANSORES Sánchez), Elías Hernán HERNÁNDEZ Jacuinde (79 Mario Antonio MORENO González). DT: Tomás Juan BOY Espinoza
Sent off: Ramos (87) / Moreno (86)
Goals: Gabriel Antonio MÉNDEZ (59), Luis Miguel ESCALADA (82).

CLUB NACIONAL MONTEVIDEO – CA BANFIELD 2-2 (2-2)
Estadio Centenario, Montevideo, 10.03.2010
Referee: Héber Roberto LOPES (BRA), Attendance: 34.468
CLUB NACIONAL MONTEVIDEO: Rodrigo Martín MUÑOZ Salomón, Alejandro Daniel LEMBO Betancor, Christian Washington NÚÑEZ Medina (59 Maximiliano Matías CALZADA Fuentes), Ernesto GOÑI Ameijenda (84 Sergio Rubén BLANCO Soto), Sebastián COATES Nion, Gustavo Antonio VARELA Rodríguez, Álvaro Rafael GONZÁLEZ Luengo, Ángel Alejandro MORALES Santos, Óscar Javier MORALES Albornoz, Raúl Freddy FERRO Olivera (70 Santiago Damián GARCÍA Correa), Mario Ignacio REGUEIRO Pintos. DT: Eduardo Mario ACEVEDO Cardozo
CA BANFIELD: Cristian David LUCCHETTI, Jonathan Ramón MAIDANA, Víctor Rubén LÓPEZ, José Alberto SHAFFER, Roberto Miguel BATTIÓN, Julio Eduardo BARRAZA, Wálter Daniel ERVITI (79 Ariel Emmanuel PÍO), Marcelo Nildo QUINTEROS (85 Santiago Andrés LADINO), James David RODRÍGUEZ Rubio (89 Mathias Adolfo CARDACCIO Alaguich), Rubén Darío RAMÍREZ, Sebastián Bruno FERNÁNDEZ Miglierina. DT: Julio César FALCIONI
Goals: Gustavo Antonio VARELA Rodríguez (5), Mario Ignacio REGUEIRO Pintos (40) / James David RODRÍGUEZ Rubio (18, 36 penalty).

CA BANFIELD – CLUB NACIONAL MONTEVIDEO 0-2 (0-2)
Estadio Florencio Solá, Banfield, 16.03.2010
Referee: Wilson Luiz SENEME (BRA), Attendance: 9.507
CA BANFIELD: Cristian David LUCCHETTI, Jonathan Ramón MAIDANA, Víctor Rubén LÓPEZ, Walter Marcelo BUSTAMANTE (70 Cristian Andrés GARCÍA), Roberto Miguel BATTIÓN (66 Mathias Adolfo CARDACCIO Alaguich), Julio Eduardo BARRAZA (83 Ariel Emmanuel PÍO), Wálter Daniel ERVITI, Marcelo Nildo QUINTEROS, James David RODRÍGUEZ Rubio, Rubén Darío RAMÍREZ, Sebastián Bruno FERNÁNDEZ Miglierina. DT: Julio César FALCIONI
CLUB NACIONAL MONTEVIDEO: Rodrigo Martín MUÑOZ Salomón, Alejandro Daniel LEMBO Betancor (22 Gonzalo GODOY), Ernesto GOÑI Ameijenda, Sebastián COATES Nion, Gustavo Antonio VARELA Rodríguez, Álvaro Rafael GONZÁLEZ Luengo, Ángel Alejandro MORALES Santos (72 Mauricio Ernesto PEREYRA Antonini), Óscar Javier MORALES Albornoz, Raúl Freddy FERRO Olivera (59 Sebastián Andrés BALSAS Bruno), Maximiliano Matías CALZADA Fuentes, Mario Ignacio REGUEIRO Pintos. DT: Eduardo Mario ACEVEDO Cardozo
Goals: Sebastián COATES Nion (34), Gonzalo GODOY (42).

CA MONARCAS MORELIA – CLUB DEPORTIVO CUENCA 2-1 (2-0)
Estadio Generalísimo José María Morelos y Pavón, Morelia, 16.03.2010
Referee: Víctor Hugo RIVERA Chavez (PER), Attendance: 14.066
CA MONARCAS MORELIA: Moisés Alberto MUÑOZ Rodríguez, Fernando SALAZAR Lomelí, Marvin Gabriel CABRERA Ibarra (62 Enrique PÉREZ Herrera), Christian Emmanuel SÁNCHEZ Narváez, Jaime DURÁN Gómez, Martín Mauricio ROMERO, Hugo Patricio DROGUETT Diocares, Pedro Luis BELTRÁN García (68 Jorge Kanú GASTELUM Ocampo), Jared Francisco BORGETTI Echavarría, Luis Gabriel REY Villamizar (66 Oscar Emilio ROJAS Ruíz), Elías Hernán HERNÁNDEZ Jacuinde. DT: Tomás Juan BOY Espinoza
CLUB DEPORTIVO CUENCA: Esteban Javier DREER, Diego Adrián IANIERO, Juan Kely GUERRÓN Vásquez, Marco Antonio QUIÑÓNEZ Angulo, Jaime Javier CHILA Cortez (59 Christian Santiago CORDERO Rodríguez), John William NARVÁEZ Arroyo, Gabriel Antonio MÉNDEZ, José Eduardo GRANDA Vicuña (85 Jefferson Alexander NÁJERA Recalde), Jhon Antonio GARCÍA Figueroa, William Osvaldo ESPAÑA España, Luis Miguel ESCALADA (73 Jorge Washington LADINES Garcés). DT: Paúl VÉLEZ
Goals: Jared Francisco BORGETTI Echavarría (19, 27) / Jorge Washington LADINES Garcés (76).

CA MONARCAS MORELIA – CA BANFIELD 1-1 (0-0)
Estadio Generalísimo José María Morelos y Pavón, Morelia, 31.03.2010
Referee: Óscar Julián RUÍZ Acosta (COL), Attendance: 16.516
CA MONARCAS MORELIA: Moisés Alberto MUÑOZ Rodríguez, Fernando SALAZAR Lomelí (46 Jared Francisco BORGETTI Echavarría), Christian Emmanuel SÁNCHEZ Narváez, Jaime DURÁN Gómez, Martín Mauricio ROMERO, Adrián Alexei ALDRETE Rodríguez (46 Hugo Patricio DROGUETT Diocares), Gabriel Ernesto PEREYRA Vázquez (80 Jorge HERNÁNDEZ González), Enrique PÉREZ Herrera, Jorge Kanú GASTELUM Ocampo, Miguel SABAH Rodríguez, Elías Hernán HERNÁNDEZ Jacuinde. DT: Tomás Juan BOY Espinoza
CA BANFIELD: Cristian David LUCCHETTI, Jonathan Ramón MAIDANA, Santiago Andrés LADINO, Víctor Rubén LÓPEZ, Mauro Javier DOS SANTOS, Roberto Miguel BATTIÓN, Wálter Daniel ERVITI, Cristian Andrés GARCÍA (62 Luis Ángel SALMERÓN), Marcelo Nildo QUINTEROS (88 Maximiliano LASO), James David RODRÍGUEZ Rubio, Sebastián Bruno FERNÁNDEZ Miglierina (68 Ariel Emmanuel PÍO). DT: Julio César FALCIONI
Sent off: Gastelum (74) / Battión (66)
Goals: Jared Francisco BORGETTI Echavarría (78) / Maximiliano LASO (90+2).

CLUB DEPORTIVO CUENCA – CLUB NACIONAL MONTEVIDEO 0-0
Estadio Alejandro Serrano Aguilar, Cuenca, 7.04.2010
Referee: Pablo Antonio POZO Quinteros (CHI), Attendance: 4.683
CLUB DEPORTIVO CUENCA: Esteban Javier DREER, Diego Adrián IANIERO, Juan Kely GUERRÓN Vásquez, Arlin Secundo AYOVÍ Ayoví, John William NARVÁEZ Arroyo, Gabriel Antonio MÉNDEZ, Giancarlo Pablo RAMOS Barrios (86 José Eduardo GRANDA Vicuña), Jhon Antonio GARCÍA Figueroa, Mauricio Bladimir HURTADO Alvarado (55 William Osvaldo ESPAÑA España), Jorge Washington LADINES Garcés (76 Jefferson Alexander NÁJERA Recalde), Luis Miguel ESCALADA. DT: Paúl VÉLEZ
CLUB NACIONAL MONTEVIDEO: Rodrigo Martín MUÑOZ Salomón, Gonzalo GODOY, Ernesto GOÑI Ameijenda, Sebastián COATES Nion, Gustavo Antonio VARELA Rodríguez (90+4 Christian Washington NÚÑEZ Medina), Álvaro Rafael GONZÁLEZ Luengo, Óscar Javier MORALES Albornoz, Raúl Freddy FERRO Olivera, Maximiliano Matías CALZADA Fuentes (78 Gianni Bismark GUIGOU Martínez), Mario Ignacio REGUEIRO Pintos, Sergio Rubén BLANCO Soto (61 Mauricio Ernesto PEREYRA Antonini). DT: Eduardo Mario ACEVEDO Cardozo
Sent off: Morales (90+1)

CLUB NACIONAL MONTEVIDEO – CA MONARCAS MORELIA 2-0 (1-0)
Estadio Gran Parque Central, Montevideo, 21.04.2010
Referee: Paulo César DE OLIVEIRA (BRA), Attendance: 12.780
CLUB NACIONAL MONTEVIDEO: Rodrigo Martín MUÑOZ Salomón, Alejandro Daniel LEMBO Betancor, Ernesto GOÑI Ameijenda, Sebastián COATES Nion, Gustavo Antonio VARELA Rodríguez, Álvaro Rafael GONZÁLEZ Luengo (58 Christian Washington NÚÑEZ Medina), Ángel Alejandro MORALES Santos (74 Mauricio Ernesto PEREYRA Antonini), Raúl Freddy FERRO Olivera, Matías Julio CABRERA Acevedo (87 Sergio Rubén BLANCO Soto), Maximiliano Matías CALZADA Fuentes, Mario Ignacio REGUEIRO Pintos. DT: Eduardo Mario ACEVEDO Cardozo
CA MONARCAS MORELIA: Miguel Ángel FRAGA Licona, Marvin Gabriel CABRERA Ibarra, Jaime DURÁN Gómez, Luis Fernando SILVA Ochoa, Oscar Emilio ROJAS Ruíz, Pedro Luis BELTRÁN García, Jorge HERNÁNDEZ González, Enrique PÉREZ Herrera, Mario Antonio MORENO González (63 Miguel Ángel SANSORES Sánchez), Ismael PINEDA Jácome (71 Elías Hernán HERNÁNDEZ Jacuinde), Jared Francisco BORGETTI Echavarría. DT: Tomás Juan BOY Espinoza
Goals: Mario Ignacio REGUEIRO Pintos (3), Mauricio Ernesto PEREYRA Antonini (78).

CA BANFIELD – CLUB DEPORTIVO CUENCA 4-1 (0-0)
Estadio Florencio Solá, Banfield, 21.04.2010
Referee: Carlos Horacio GALEANO Rios (PAR), Attendance: 5.486
CA BANFIELD: Cristian David LUCCHETTI, Jonathan Ramón MAIDANA, Santiago Andrés LADINO, Víctor Rubén LÓPEZ, Julio Eduardo BARRAZA (46 Mathias Adolfo CARDACCIO Alaguich), Federico Javier SARDELLA, Wálter Daniel ERVITI, Cristian Andrés GARCÍA (53 Sebastián Bruno FERNÁNDEZ Miglierina), Marcelo Nildo QUINTEROS, James David RODRÍGUEZ Rubio (79 Mauro Javier DOS SANTOS), Rubén Darío RAMÍREZ. DT: Julio César FALCIONI
CLUB DEPORTIVO CUENCA: Esteban Javier DREER, Diego Adrián IANIERO, Juan Kely GUERRÓN Vásquez, Arlin Secundo AYOVÍ Ayoví, John William NARVÁEZ Arroyo, Gabriel Antonio MÉNDEZ, José Eduardo GRANDA Vicuña (80 Pablo Xavier ARÉVALO Jiménez), Michael Leonardo ENDARA Leones, Christian Santiago CORDERO Rodríguez (82 José Alberto VALDIVIEZO Ordóñez), Fernando Rafael FAJARDO Avila, Luis Miguel ESCALADA (76 Jefferson Alexander NÁJERA Recalde). DT: Paúl VÉLEZ
Goals: Rubén Darío RAMÍREZ (48, 68), Wálter Daniel ERVITI (87), Cristian David LUCCHETTI (90 penalty) / Gabriel Antonio MÉNDEZ (72).

1	NACIONAL	6	3	3	0	9	4	12
2	BANFIELD	6	3	2	1	13	8	11
3	Morelia	6	1	2	3	4	8	5
4	Deportivo Cuenca	6	1	1	4	7	13	4

GROUP 7

CA VÉLEZ SÁRSFIELD – CRUZEIRO EC 2-0 (1-0)
Estadio José Amalfitani, Buenos Aires, 10.02.2010
Referee: Martín Emilio VÁZQUEZ Broquetas (URU), Attendance: 11.100
CA VÉLEZ SÁRSFIELD: Marcelo Germán MONTOYA, Sebastián Enrique DOMÍNGUEZ, Pablo Martín LIMA Olid (64 Alejandro Ariel CABRAL), Nicolás Hernán Gonzalo OTAMENDI, Leandro Daniel SOMOZA, Víctor Eduardo ZAPATA, Fabián Andrés CUBERO, Maximiliano Nicolás MORALEZ, Nicolás Alejandro CABRERA (63 Juan Manuel MARTÍNEZ), Santiago Martín SILVA Olivera (84 Rolando David ZÁRATE Riga), Hernán Rodrigo LÓPEZ Mora. DT: Ricardo Alberto GARECA Nardi
CRUZEIRO EC: Deivison Lopes Maciel "FÁBIO", JONATHAN Cícero Moreira, LEANDRO Fabiano da SILVA e Silva, DIEGO RENÁN de Lima Ferreira (39 THIAGO HELENO Henrique Ferreira), Carlos Gilberto Nascimento da Silva e Silva "GIL", GILBERTO da Silva Melo, Antônio Marcos da Silva Filho "MARQUINHOS PARANÁ", HENRIQUE Pacheco de Lima, ELICARLOS Souza Santos, KLÉBER Giacomace de Souza Freitas (67 WELLINGTON "PAULISTA" Pereira do Nascimento), THIAGO RIBEIRO Cardoso (52 PEDRO KEN Morimoto Moreira). DT: ADÍLSON Dias BATISTA
Sent off: Gilberto (2), Gil (37)
Goals: Santiago Martín SILVA Olivera (5), Juan Manuel MARTÍNEZ (77).

CSD COLO COLO SANTIAGO – CLUB DEPORTIVO ITALIA 1-0 (0-0)
Estadio Monumental David Arellano, Santiago, 16.02.2010
Referee: Víctor Hugo CARRILLO Casanova (PER), Attendance: 10.840
CSD COLO COLO SANTIAGO: Francisco Javier PRIETO Caroca, Andrés SCOTTI Ponce de Léon, Pablo Cezar MAGALHAES Lobos (46 José Pedro FUENZALIDA Gana), Roberto Andrés CERECEDA Guajardo, Sebastián TORO Hormazábal, Macnelly TORRES Berrio (90+2 Diego Alejandro OLATE Jería), Charles Mariano ARÁNGUIZ Sandoval, Rodrigo David MELÉNDEZ Araya, Rodrigo Javier MILLAR Carvajal, Esteban Efraín PAREDES Quintanilla, Cristian Venancio BOGADO Morinigo (81 Claudio Fernando GRAF). DT: Hugo Daniel TOCALLI
CLUB DEPORTIVO ITALIA: José Carlos FERNÁNDEZ González, David Andrew McINTOSH Parra, Marcelo Omar MAIDANA, Carlos Javier LÓPEZ, Gabriel José URDANETA Rángel, Evelio de Jesús HERNÁNDEZ Guedez, Rafael LOBO (82 Diomar DÍAZ), Leopoldo Rafael JIMÉNEZ, Gianfranco DI JULIO (74 Cristian Félix CÁSSERES), Cristian Alfonso CÁSSERES Cásseres, Richard BLANCO (55 Amir BUELVAS Salsa). DT: Eduardo SARAGÓ
Goal: Esteban Efraín PAREDES Quintanilla (58).

CLUB DEPORTIVO ITALIA – CA VÉLEZ SÁRSFIELD 0-1 (0-0)
Estadio Olímpico de la UCV, Caracas, 23.02.2010
Referee: Samuel Rolando HARO Inca (ECU), Attendance: 1.351
CLUB DEPORTIVO ITALIA: José Carlos FERNÁNDEZ González, David Andrew McINTOSH Parra, Marcelo Omar MAIDANA, Carlos Javier LÓPEZ, Gabriel José URDANETA Rángel, Evelio de Jesús HERNÁNDEZ Guedez (64 Cristian Félix CÁSSERES), Rafael LOBO, Leopoldo Rafael JIMÉNEZ, Gianfranco DI JULIO (78 Diomar DÍAZ), Emerson Mariano PANIGUTTI (71 Richard BLANCO), Cristian Alfonso CÁSSERES Cásseres. DT: Eduardo SARAGÓ
CA VÉLEZ SÁRSFIELD: Marcelo Germán MONTOYA, Sebastián Enrique DOMÍNGUEZ, Pablo Martín LIMA Olid, Nicolás Hernán Gonzalo OTAMENDI, Leandro Daniel SOMOZA, Víctor Eduardo ZAPATA, Fabián Andrés CUBERO, Maximiliano Nicolás MORALEZ (87 Alejandro Ariel CABRAL), Nicolás Alejandro CABRERA (83 Ricardo Gastón DÍAZ), Santiago Martín SILVA Olivera (72 Juan Manuel MARTÍNEZ), Hernán Rodrigo LÓPEZ Mora. DT: Ricardo Alberto GARECA Nardi
Goal: Hernán Rodrigo LÓPEZ Mora (54).

CRUZEIRO EC – CSD COLO COLO SANTIAGO 4-1 (1-1)
Estádio Governador Magalhães Pinto (Mineirão), Belo Horizonte, 24.02.2010
Referee: Óscar Julián RUÍZ Acosta (COL), Attendance: 32.927
CRUZEIRO EC: Deivison Lopes Maciel "FÁBIO", JONATHAN Cícero Moreira, THIAGO HELENO Henrique Ferreira, LEANDRO Fabiano da SILVA e Silva, DIEGO RENÁN de Lima Ferreira, Antônio Marcos da Silva Filho "MARQUINHOS PARANÁ", HENRIQUE Pacheco de Lima (83 BERNARDO Vieira de Souza), ELICARLOS Souza Santos (25 PEDRO KEN Morimoto Moreira), ROGER Galera Flores (55 WELLINGTON "PAULISTA" Pereira do Nascimento), KLÉBER Giacomace de Souza Freitas, THIAGO RIBEIRO Cardoso. DT: ADÍLSON Dias BATISTA
CSD COLO COLO SANTIAGO: Francisco Javier PRIETO Caroca, Andrés SCOTTI Ponce de Léon, Roberto Andrés CERECEDA Guajardo, Diego Alejandro OLATE Jería, Sebastián TORO Hormazábal, Macnelly TORRES Berrio (59 Pablo Cezar MAGALHAES Lobos), Charles Mariano ARÁNGUIZ Sandoval, Rodrigo David MELÉNDEZ Araya, Rodrigo Javier MILLAR Carvajal, Ezequiel Rodrigo MIRALLES, Esteban Efraín PAREDES Quintanilla (72 Héctor Arturo SANHUEZA Medel). DT: Hugo Daniel TOCALLI
Sent off: Olate (57), Cereceda (67)
Goals: THIAGO RIBEIRO Cardoso (7), KLÉBER Giacomace de Souza Freitas (62 pen, 72 pen), PEDRO KEN Morimoto Moreira (69) / Esteban Efraín PAREDES Quintanilla (37).

CLUB DEPORTIVO ITALIA – CRUZEIRO EC 2-2 (1-1)
Estadio Olímpico de la UCV, Caracas, 11.03.2010
Referee: Carlos Alfredo VERA Rodríguez (ECU), Attendance: 212
CLUB DEPORTIVO ITALIA: Alan LIEBESKIND, David Andrew McINTOSH Parra, Daniel DÍEZ (87 Rafael LOBO), Marcelo Omar MAIDANA, Carlos Javier LÓPEZ, Gabriel José URDANETA Rángel, Diomar DÍAZ (67 Cristian Félix CÁSSERES), Bladimir Alejandro MORALES Duarte, Alain Giancarlo GIROLETTI Nardali, Emerson Mariano PANIGUTTI (77 Cristian Alfonso CÁSSERES Cásseres), Richard BLANCO. DT: Eduardo SARAGÓ
CRUZEIRO EC: Deivison Lopes Maciel "FÁBIO", JONATHAN Cícero Moreira, THIAGO HELENO Henrique Ferreira, LEANDRO Fabiano da SILVA e Silva, DIEGO RENÁN de Lima Ferreira (64 Carlos Gilberto Nascimento da Silva e Silva "GIL"), Antônio Marcos da Silva Filho "MARQUINHOS PARANÁ", HENRIQUE Pacheco de Lima, PEDRO KEN Morimoto Moreira, ROGER Galera Flores (74 ELIANDRO dos Santos Gonzaga), KLÉBER Giacomace de Souza Freitas, THIAGO RIBEIRO Cardoso (90 BERNARDO Vieira de Souza). DT: ADÍLSON Dias BATISTA
Sent off: Lobo (88) / Kléber (86)
Goals: Richard BLANCO (11), David Andrew McINTOSH Parra (66) /
KLÉBER Giacomace de Souza Freitas (27, 50).

CSD COLO COLO SANTIAGO – CA VÉLEZ SÁRSFIELD 1-1 (0-0)
Estadio Monumental David Arellano, Santiago, 16.03.2010
Referee: Carlos Arecio AMARILLA Demarqui (PAR), Attendance: 11.204
CSD COLO COLO SANTIAGO: Francisco Javier PRIETO Caroca, Andrés SCOTTI Ponce de Léon, Miguel Augusto RIFFO Garay, Pablo Cezar MAGALHAES Lobos, Sebastián TORO Hormazábal, Héctor Arturo SANHUEZA Medel (46 Macnelly TORRES Berrio), Charles Mariano ARÁNGUIZ Sandoval, Rodrigo David MELÉNDEZ Araya (82 José Pedro FUENZALIDA Gana), Rodrigo Javier MILLAR Carvajal, Ezequiel Rodrigo MIRALLES, Esteban Efraín PAREDES Quintanilla. DT: Hugo Daniel TOCALLI
CA VÉLEZ SÁRSFIELD: Marcelo Germán MONTOYA, Sebastián Enrique DOMÍNGUEZ, Ricardo Gastón DÍAZ (63 Franco RAZZOTTI), Nicolás Hernán Gonzalo OTAMENDI, Leandro Daniel SOMOZA, Víctor Eduardo ZAPATA, Fabián Andrés CUBERO, Maximiliano Nicolás MORALEZ (85 Rolando David ZÁRATE Riga), Emiliano Ramiro PAPA, Santiago Martín SILVA Olivera, Hernán Rodrigo LÓPEZ Mora (68 Juan Manuel MARTÍNEZ). DT: Ricardo Alberto GARECA Nardi
Sent off: Zapata (59)
Goals: Esteban Efraín PAREDES Quintanilla (57) / Santiago Martín SILVA Olivera (90+3).

CRUZEIRO EC – CLUB DEPORTIVO ITALIA 2-0 (1-0)
Estádio Governador Magalhães Pinto (Mineirão), Belo Horizonte, 24.03.2010
Referee: Antonio Javier ARIAS Alvarenga (PAR), Attendance: 17.237
CRUZEIRO EC: Deivison Lopes Maciel "FÁBIO", JONATHAN Cícero Moreira, THIAGO HELENO Henrique Ferreira, LEANDRO Fabiano da SILVA e Silva, DIEGO RENÁN de Lima Ferreira, GILBERTO da Silva Melo (68 PEDRO KEN Morimoto Moreira), Fábio Alves Félix "FABINHO", Antônio Marcos da Silva Filho "MARQUINHOS PARANÁ" (87 ELIANDRO dos Santos Gonzaga), HENRIQUE Pacheco de Lima, WELLINGTON "PAULISTA" Pereira do Nascimento, THIAGO RIBEIRO Cardoso (87 FABRÍCIO de Sousa). DT: ADÍLSON Dias BATISTA
CLUB DEPORTIVO ITALIA: José Carlos FERNÁNDEZ González, David Andrew McINTOSH Parra, Daniel DÍEZ (82 Evelio de Jesús HERNÁNDEZ Guedez), Marcelo Omar MAIDANA, Carlos Javier LÓPEZ, Gabriel José URDANETA Rángel, Diomar DÍAZ (72 Cristian Félix CÁSSERES), Leopoldo Rafael JIMÉNEZ, Alain Giancarlo GIROLETTI Nardali, Emerson Mariano PANIGUTTI (66 Cristian Alfonso CÁSSERES Cásseres), Richard BLANCO. DT: Eduardo SARAGÓ
Goals: Fábio Alves Félix "FABINHO" (6), PEDRO KEN Morimoto Moreira (70).

CA VÉLEZ SÁRSFIELD – CSD COLO COLO SANTIAGO 2-1 (2-1)
Estadio José Amalfitani, Buenos Aires, 25.03.2010
Referee: Roberto Carlos SILVERA Calcerrad a (URU), Attendance: 9.325
CA VÉLEZ SÁRSFIELD: Marcelo Germán MONTOYA, Sebastián Enrique DOMÍNGUEZ, Ricardo Gastón DÍAZ, Nicolás Hernán Gonzalo OTAMENDI, Leandro Daniel SOMOZA (75 Franco RAZZOTTI), Alejandro Ariel CABRAL, Fabián Andrés CUBERO, Maximiliano Nicolás MORALEZ (83 Juan Manuel MARTÍNEZ), Emiliano Ramiro PAPA, Santiago Martín SILVA Olivera, Hernán Rodrigo LÓPEZ Mora (90+2 Nicolás Alejandro CABRERA). DT: Ricardo Alberto GARECA Nardi
CSD COLO COLO SANTIAGO: Francisco Javier PRIETO Caroca, Andrés SCOTTI Ponce de Léon, Miguel Augusto RIFFO Garay, Roberto Andrés CERECEDA Guajardo, Sebastián TORO Hormazábal (80 Claudio Fernando GRAF), Macnelly TORRES Berrio, Charles Mariano ARÁNGUIZ Sandoval (61 José Pedro FUENZALIDA Gana), Rodrigo David MELÉNDEZ Araya, Rodrigo Javier MILLAR Carvajal, Ezequiel Rodrigo MIRALLES, Esteban Efraín PAREDES Quintanilla. DT: Hugo Daniel TOCALLI
Sent off: Millar (87)
Goals: Hernán Rodrigo LÓPEZ Mora (13), Santiago Martín SILVA Olivera (29) / Ezequiel Rodrigo MIRALLES (8).

CRUZEIRO EC – CA VÉLEZ SÁRSFIELD 3-0 (1-0)
Estádio Governador Magalhães Pinto (Mineirão), Belo Horizonte, 31.03.2010
Referee: Wilmar Alexander ROLDÁN Pérez (COL), Attendance: 43.374
CRUZEIRO EC: Deivison Lopes Maciel "FÁBIO", JONATHAN Cícero Moreira, THIAGO HELENO Henrique Ferreira (34 Carlos Gilberto Nascimento da Silva e Silva "GIL"), LEANDRO Fabiano da SILVA e Silva, DIEGO RENÁN de Lima Ferreira, GILBERTO da Silva Melo (69 FABRÍCIO de Sousa), Fábio Alves Félix "FABINHO", Antônio Marcos da Silva Filho "MARQUINHOS PARANÁ", HENRIQUE Pacheco de Lima, KLÉBER Giacomace de Souza Freitas, THIAGO RIBEIRO Cardoso (77 WELLINGTON "PAULISTA" Pereira do Nascimento). DT: ADÍLSON Dias BATISTA
CA VÉLEZ SÁRSFIELD: Marcelo Germán MONTOYA, Sebastián Enrique DOMÍNGUEZ, Ricardo Gastón DÍAZ (52 Pablo Martín LIMA Olid), Nicolás Hernán Gonzalo OTAMENDI, Leandro Daniel SOMOZA, Víctor Eduardo ZAPATA, Fabián Andrés CUBERO, Maximiliano Nicolás MORALEZ (76 Nicolás Alejandro CABRERA), Emiliano Ramiro PAPA, Santiago Martín SILVA Olivera, Hernán Rodrigo LÓPEZ Mora (58 Juan Manuel MARTÍNEZ). DT: Ricardo Alberto GARECA Nardi
Sent off: Somoza (82)
Goals: THIAGO RIBEIRO Cardoso (33), KLÉBER Giacomace de Souza Freitas (49, 54).

CLUB DEPORTIVO ITALIA – CSD COLO COLO SANTIAGO 2-3 (1-2)
Estadio Olímpico de la UCV, Caracas, 6.04.2010
Referee: Marco Antonio RODRÍGUEZ Moreno (MEX), Attendance: 207
CLUB DEPORTIVO ITALIA: José Carlos FERNÁNDEZ González, David Andrew McINTOSH Parra, Marcelo Omar MAIDANA, Carlos Javier LÓPEZ, Gabriel José URDANETA Rángel, Rafael LOBO (60 Richard BLANCO), Bladimir Alejandro MORALES Duarte (67 Diomar DÍAZ), Alain Giancarlo GIROLETTI Nardali, Emerson Mariano PANIGUTTI, Cristian Alfonso CÁSSERES Cásseres (81 Evelio de Jesús HERNÁNDEZ Guedez), Cristian Félix CÁSSERES. DT: Eduardo SARAGÓ
CSD COLO COLO SANTIAGO: Francisco Javier PRIETO Caroca, Andrés SCOTTI Ponce de Léon, Pablo Cezar MAGALHAES Lobos, Roberto Andrés CERECEDA Guajardo, Sebastián TORO Hormazábal, Macnelly TORRES Berrio, José Pedro FUENZALIDA Gana (84 Miguel Augusto RIFFO Garay) , Charles Mariano ARÁNGUIZ Sandoval, Rodrigo David MELÉNDEZ Araya (52 Héctor Arturo SANHUEZA Medel), Ezequiel Rodrigo MIRALLES, Cristian Venancio BOGADO Morinigo. DT: Hugo Daniel TOCALLI
Goals: Emerson Mariano PANIGUTTI (15), Richard BLANCO (86 penalty) /
Cristian Venancio BOGADO Morinigo (26), Ezequiel Rodrigo MIRALLES (38, 57).

CSD COLO COLO SANTIAGO – CRUZEIRO EC 1-1 (0-0)
Estadio Monumental David Arellano, Santiago, 15.04.2010
Referee: Carlos Manuel TORRES Nuñez (PAR), Attendance: 8.402
CSD COLO COLO SANTIAGO: Francisco Javier PRIETO Caroca, Andrés SCOTTI Ponce de Léon, Pablo Cezar MAGALHAES Lobos (46 José Pedro FUENZALIDA Gana), Roberto Andrés CERECEDA Guajardo (66 Matías Lionel QUIROGA), Sebastián TORO Hormazábal, Macnelly TORRES Berrio, Charles Mariano ARÁNGUIZ Sandoval (90+1 Claudio Fernando GRAF), Rodrigo David MELÉNDEZ Araya, Rodrigo Javier MILLAR Carvajal, Ezequiel Rodrigo MIRALLES, Cristian Venancio BOGADO Morinigo. DT: Hugo Daniel TOCALLI
CRUZEIRO EC: Deivison Lopes Maciel "FÁBIO", JONATHAN Cícero Moreira, LEANDRO Fabiano da SILVA e Silva, DIEGO RENÁN de Lima Ferreira (65 THIAGO HELENO Henrique Ferreira), Carlos Gilberto Nascimento da Silva e Silva "GIL", GILBERTO da Silva Melo, Fábio Alves Félix "FABINHO" (46 FABRÍCIO de Sousa), Antônio Marcos da Silva Filho "MARQUINHOS PARANÁ", HENRIQUE Pacheco de Lima, WELLINGTON "PAULISTA" Pereira do Nascimento (74 ROGER Galera Flores), THIAGO RIBEIRO Cardoso. DT: ADÍLSON Dias BATISTA
Sent off: Scotti (80)
Goals: Rodrigo Javier MILLAR Carvajal (61) / THIAGO RIBEIRO Cardoso (57).

CA VÉLEZ SÁRSFIELD – CLUB DEPORTIVO ITALIA 4-0 (1-0)
Estadio José Amalfitani, Buenos Aires, 15.04.2010
Referee: Darío Agustín UBRIACO Mederos (URU), Attendance: 5.408
CA VÉLEZ SÁRSFIELD: Marcelo Germán MONTOYA, Sebastián Enrique DOMÍNGUEZ (63 Omar Fernando TOBIO), Ricardo Gastón DÍAZ, Nicolás Hernán Gonzalo OTAMENDI, Leandro CORONEL (77 Alejandro Ariel CABRAL), Víctor Eduardo ZAPATA, Fabián Andrés CUBERO, Maximiliano Nicolás MORALEZ, Emiliano Ramiro PAPA, Juan Manuel MARTÍNEZ, Hernán Rodrigo LÓPEZ Mora. DT: Ricardo Alberto GARECA Nardi
CLUB DEPORTIVO ITALIA: Alan LIEBESKIND, Daniel DÍEZ, Marcelo Omar MAIDANA, Norberto RIASCOS, Carlos Javier LÓPEZ, Diomar DÍAZ, Evelio de Jesús HERNÁNDEZ Guedez (70 Cristian Félix CÁSSERES), Bladimir Alejandro MORALES Duarte, Gianfranco DI JULIO, Emerson Mariano PANIGUTTI (43 Amir BUELVAS Salsa), Cristian Alfonso CÁSSERES Cásseres (77 Yhonny SALCEDO). DT: Eduardo SARAGÓ
Goals: Víctor Eduardo ZAPATA (42), Hernán Rodrigo LÓPEZ Mora (48 penalty, 83),
Emiliano Ramiro PAPA (73).

1	VÉLEZ SARSFIELD	6	4	1	1	10	5	13
2	CRUZEIRO	6	3	2	1	12	6	11
3	Colo Colo	6	2	2	2	8	10	8
4	Deportivo Italia	6	0	1	5	4	13	1

GROUP 8

CF UNIVERSIDAD DE CHILE – CARACAS FC 1-0 (1-0)
Estadio Sausalito, Viña del Mar, 18.02.2010
Referee: Georges BUCKLEY de Meritens (PER), Attendance: 10.091
CF UNIVERSIDAD DE CHILE: Estéban Néstor CONDE Quintana, Matías Nicolás RODRÍGUEZ, Rafael Andrés OLARRA Guerrero, José Raúl CONTRERAS Arrau, Mauricio Bernardo VICTORINO Dansilio, Wálter Damián MONTILLO (56 Diego Gabriel RIVAROLA Popon), Marco Andrés ESTRADA Quinteros, Felipe Ignatio SEYMOUR Dobud, Álvaro FERNÁNDEZ Gay (83 Marcelo Alfonso DÍAZ Rojas), Gabriel Alejandro VARGAS Venegas (56 Edson Raúl PUCH Cortez), Juan Manuel OLIVERA López. DT: Gerardo PELUSO
CARACAS FC: Renny Vicente VEGA Hernández, José Manuel REY Cortegoso, Franklin José LUCENA Peña (72 Samir VALOYES Nebollán), Giovanny Michael ROMERO Armenio, Alejandro Enrique CICHERO Konarek, Gabriel Alejandro CICHERO Konarek, Alejandro Abraham GUERRA Morales, Édgar Hernán JIMÉNEZ González, Darío Damián FIGUEROA (80 Bremer Alfredo PIÑANGO Arévalo), Rafael Ernesto CASTELLÍN García, Jesús Javier GÓMEZ Mercado (62 Rodrigo PRIETO Aubert). DT: Noel SANVICENTE Bethelmy
Goal: Juan Manuel OLIVERA López (2 penalty).

CR FLAMENGO – CD UNIVERSIDAD CATÓLICA 2-0 (1-0)
Estádio Jornalista Mário Filho (Maracaña), Río de Janeiro, 24.02.2010
Referee: Carlos Arecio AMARILLA Demarqui (PAR), Attendance: 30.930
CR FLAMENGO: MARCELO LOMBA do Nascimento, ÁLVARO Luiz Maior de Aquino, Leonardo da Silva "LÉO" MOURA (76 EVERTON José Modesto SILVA), JUAN Maldonado Jaimez Júnior Duarte, FABRÍCIO Silva Dornellas, José KLÉBERSON Pereira, Rafael Ferreira Francisco "TORÓ", WILLIANS Domingos Fernandes, ADRIANO Leite Ribeiro, VÁGNER "LOVE" Silva de Souza (86 Dejan PETKOVIC), VINÍCIUS PACHECO dos Santos (58 FERNANDO Gomes de Jesus). DT: Jorge Luís ANDRADE da Silva
CD UNIVERSIDAD CATÓLICA: Paulo Andrés GARCÉS Contreras, Ismael Ignacio FUENTES Castro, Waldo Alonso PONCE Carrizo, Hans MARTÍNEZ Cabrera, David Andrés HENRÍQUEZ Espinoza (70 Leonel Jonathan MENA Gutiérrez), Damián Rodrigo DÍAZ, Rodrigo Alejandro TOLOZA Vilches (67 Rodrigo Martín MANNARA), Rodrigo Ignatio VALENZUELA Avilés, Francisco Andrés SILVA Gajardo, Milovan Petar MIROSEVIC Albornoz, Juan José MORALES (55 Pablo Andrés VRANJICÁN). DT: Marco Antonio FIGUEROA Montero
Sent off: Willians (3) / Mirosevic (42)
Goals: Leonardo da Silva "LÉO" MOURA (10), ADRIANO Leite Ribeiro (58).

CD UNIVERSIDAD CATÓLICA – CF UNIVERSIDAD DE CHILE 2-2 (1-1)
Estadio Bicentenario Francisco Sánchez Rumoroso, Coquimbo, 9.03.2010
Referee: Claudio Alfredo PUGA Briones (CHI), Attendance: 11.667
CD UNIVERSIDAD CATÓLICA: Paulo Andrés GARCÉS Contreras, Ismael Ignacio FUENTES Castro, Waldo Alonso PONCE Carrizo, Diego ROSENDE Lagos, Hans MARTÍNEZ Cabrera, David Andrés HENRÍQUEZ Espinoza, Damián Rodrigo DÍAZ, Rodrigo Alejandro TOLOZA Vilches (90+1 Adán Jonathan VERGARA Villagra), Francisco Andrés SILVA Gajardo, Matías Martín RUBIO Kostner (84 Francisco PIZARRO Cortés), Pablo Andrés VRANJICÁN (74 Juan José MORALES). DT: Marco Antonio FIGUEROA Montero
CF UNIVERSIDAD DE CHILE: Estéban Néstor CONDE Quintana, Matías Nicolás RODRÍGUEZ, Rafael Andrés OLARRA Guerrero, José Raúl CONTRERAS Arrau, Mauricio Bernardo VICTORINO Dansilio, Wálter Damián MONTILLO, Marco Andrés ESTRADA Quinteros (77 Manuel Rolando ITURRA Urrutía), Felipe Ignatio SEYMOUR Dobud (85 Álvaro FERNÁNDEZ Gay), Edson Raúl PUCH Cortez, Eduardo Jesús VARGAS Rojas (73 Diego Gabriel RIVAROLA Popon), Juan Manuel OLIVERA López. DT: Gerardo PELUSO
Goals: Matías Martín RUBIO Kostner (21), Francisco Andrés SILVA Gajardo (70) /
Juan Manuel OLIVERA López (19), Edson Raúl PUCH Cortez (90+2).

CARACAS FC – CR FLAMENGO 1-3 (0-1)
Estadio Olímpico de la UCV, Caracas, 10.03.2010
Referee: Wilmar Alexander ROLDÁN Pérez (COL), Attendance: 19.400
CARACAS FC: Renny Vicente VEGA Hernández, Franklin José LUCENA Peña, Jaime Andrés BUSTAMANTE Suárez, Giovanny Michael ROMERO Armenio (56 Rodrigo PRIETO Aubert), Alejandro Enrique CICHERO Konarek, Gabriel Alejandro CICHERO Konarek, Alejandro Abraham GUERRA Morales, Édgar Hernán JIMÉNEZ González, Rafael Ernesto CASTELLÍN García (77 Fernando Luís ARISTEGUIETA de Luca) , Jesús Javier GÓMEZ Mercado (79 Alexander David GONZÁLEZ Sibulo), Samir VALOYES Nebollán. DT: Noel SANVICENTE Bethelmy
CR FLAMENGO: BRUNO Fernandes das Dores de Souza, ÁLVARO Luiz Maior de Aquino, Leonardo da Silva "LÉO" MOURA, JUAN Maldonado Jaimez Júnior Duarte, FABRÍCIO Silva Dornellas, José KLÉBERSON Pereira, Rafael Ferreira Francisco "TORÓ", Dejan PETKOVIC (59 RONALDO Simões ANGELIM), FERNANDO Gomes de Jesus (53 RODRIGO Oliveira da Silva ALVIM), VÁGNER "LOVE" Silva de Souza, VINÍCIUS PACHECO dos Santos (83 Gonzalo Antonio FIERRO Caniullán). DT: Jorge Luís ANDRADE da Silva
Sent off: Toró (53)
Goals: Rafael Ernesto CASTELLÍN García (65) /
VÁGNER "LOVE" Silva de Souza (36 penalty, 75), RODRIGO Oliveira da Silva ALVIM (90+3).

CARACAS FC – CD UNIVERSIDAD CATÓLICA 0-0
Estadio Olímpico de la UCV, Caracas, 17.03.2010
Referee: Mauricio Rafael MORALES Ovalle (MEX), Attendance: 15.500
CARACAS FC: Renny Vicente VEGA Hernández, Franklin José LUCENA Peña, Jaime Andrés BUSTAMANTE Suárez, Giovanny Michael ROMERO Armenio (79 Pablo Jesus CAMACHO), Alejandro Enrique CICHERO Konarek, Gabriel Alejandro CICHERO Konarek, Édgar Hernán JIMÉNEZ González, Darío Damián FIGUEROA (56 Samir VALOYES Nebollán), Rafael Ernesto CASTELLÍN García, Jesús Javier GÓMEZ Mercado, Rodrigo PRIETO Aubert (56 Alejandro Abraham GUERRA Morales). DT: Noel SANVICENTE Bethelmy
CD UNIVERSIDAD CATÓLICA: Paulo Andrés GARCÉS Contreras, Ismael Ignacio FUENTES Castro (46 Jorge ORMEÑO Guerra), Waldo Alonso PONCE Carrizo, Diego ROSENDE Lagos (72 Rodrigo Ignatio VALENZUELA Avilés), Hans MARTÍNEZ Cabrera, David Andrés HENRÍQUEZ Espinoza, Damián Rodrigo DÍAZ (46 Matías Martín RUBIO Kostner), Rodrigo Alejandro TOLOZA Vilches, Francisco Andrés SILVA Gajardo, Milovan Petar MIROSEVIC Albornoz, Pablo Andrés VRANJICÁN. DT: Marco Antonio FIGUEROA Montero

CF UNIVERSIDAD DE CHILE – CR FLAMENGO 2-1 (1-0)
Estadio Monumental David Arellano, Santiago, 17.03.2010
Referee: Jorge Luis LARRIONDA Pietrafesa (URU), Attendance: 20.936
CF UNIVERSIDAD DE CHILE: Estéban Néstor CONDE Quintana, Matías Nicolás RODRÍGUEZ, Rafael Andrés OLARRA Guerrero, José Raúl CONTRERAS Arrau, Mauricio Bernardo VICTORINO Dansilio, Wálter Damián MONTILLO, Marco Andrés ESTRADA Quinteros (52 Nelson Alejandro PINTO Martínez), Felipe Ignatio SEYMOUR Dobud, Edson Raúl PUCH Cortez, Eduardo Jesús VARGAS Rojas (68 Álvaro FERNÁNDEZ Gay), Juan Manuel OLIVERA López (86 Diego Gabriel RIVAROLA Popon). DT: Gerardo PELUSO
CR FLAMENGO: BRUNO Fernandes das Dores de Souza, ÁLVARO Luiz Maior de Aquino, Leonardo da Silva "LÉO" MOURA (78 EVERTON José Modesto SILVA), JUAN Maldonado Jaimez Júnior Duarte, RODRIGO Oliveira da Silva ALVIM, FABRÍCIO Silva Dornellas, José KLÉBERSON Pereira (60 Gonzalo Antonio FIERRO Caniullán), WILLIANS Domingos Fernandes, ADRIANO Leite Ribeiro, VÁGNER "LOVE" Silva de Souza, VINÍCIUS PACHECO dos Santos (67 Dejan PETKOVIC). DT: Jorge Luís ANDRADE da Silva
Goals: Eduardo Jesús VARGAS Rojas (42), Felipe Ignatio SEYMOUR Dobud (55) /
RODRIGO Oliveira da Silva ALVIM (51).

CD UNIVERSIDAD CATÓLICA – CARACAS FC 1-1 (0-0)
Estadio San Carlos de Apoquindo, Santiago, 24.03.2010
Referee: Néstor Fabian PITANA (ARG), Attendance: 9.103
CD UNIVERSIDAD CATÓLICA: Paulo Andrés GARCÉS Contreras, Ismael Ignacio FUENTES Castro, Waldo Alonso PONCE Carrizo, David Andrés HENRÍQUEZ Espinoza, Damián Rodrigo DÍAZ (46 Hans MARTÍNEZ Cabrera), Rodrigo Alejandro TOLOZA Vilches (56 Fernando Andrés MENESES Cornejo), Rodrigo Ignatio VALENZUELA Avilés (67 Pablo Andrés VRANJICÁN), Francisco Andrés SILVA Gajardo, Milovan Petar MIROSEVIC Albornoz, Juan José MORALES, Matías Martín RUBIO Kostner. DT: Marco Antonio FIGUEROA Montero
CARACAS FC: Renny Vicente VEGA Hernández, Jaime Andrés BUSTAMANTE Suárez, Alejandro Enrique CICHERO Konarek, Pablo Jesus CAMACHO, Gabriel Alejandro CICHERO Konarek, Alejandro Abraham GUERRA Morales (74 César Iván GONZÁLEZ), Édgar Hernán JIMÉNEZ González, Bremer Alfredo PIÑANGO Arévalo, Darío Damián FIGUEROA (83 Samir VALOYES Nebollán), Rafael Ernesto CASTELLÍN García (89 Rodrigo PRIETO Aubert), Jesús Javier GÓMEZ Mercado. DT: Noel SANVICENTE Bethelmy
Goals: Juan José MORALES (82) / Jaime Andrés BUSTAMANTE Suárez (50).

CR FLAMENGO – CF UNIVERSIDAD DE CHILE 2-2 (0-1)
Estádio Jornalista Mário Filho (Maracaña), Río de Janeiro, 8.04.2010
Referee: Roberto Carlos SILVERA Calcerrada (URU), Attendance: 20.330
CR FLAMENGO: BRUNO Fernandes das Dores de Souza, ÁLVARO Luiz Maior de Aquino, Leonardo da Silva "LÉO" MOURA, JUAN Maldonado Jaimez Júnior Duarte, RONALDO Simões ANGELIM, José KLÉBERSON Pereira (46 BRUNO "MEZENGA" Ferreira Mombra Rosa), Rafael Ferreira Francisco "TORÓ", MICHAEL Anderson Pereira da Silva (86 Claudio Andrés del Tránsito MALDONADO Rivera), WILLIANS Domingos Fernandes, VÁGNER "LOVE" Silva de Souza, VINÍCIUS PACHECO dos Santos (59 Dejan PETKOVIC). DT: Jorge Luís ANDRADE da Silva
CF UNIVERSIDAD DE CHILE: Estéban Néstor CONDE Quintana, Matías Nicolás RODRÍGUEZ, Rafael Andrés OLARRA Guerrero, José Raúl CONTRERAS Arrau, José Manuel ROJAS Bahamondes, Mauricio Bernardo VICTORINO Dansilio, Manuel Rolando ITURRA Urrutía, Wálter Damián MONTILLO (90+3 Nelson Alejandro PINTO Martínez), Felipe Ignatio SEYMOUR Dobud, Edson Raúl PUCH Cortez (69 Eduardo Jesús VARGAS Rojas), Juan Manuel OLIVERA López (78 Diego Gabriel RIVAROLA Popon). DT: Gerardo PELUSO
Goals: MICHAEL Anderson Pereira da Silva (68), Leonardo da Silva "LÉO" MOURA (83) / Wálter Damián MONTILLO (43), Matías Nicolás RODRÍGUEZ (90+2).

CARACAS FC – CF UNIVERSIDAD DE CHILE 1-3 (0-3)
Estadio Olímpico de la UCV, Caracas, 13.04.2010
Referee: Jorge Joaquín ANTEQUERA Castedo (BOL), Attendance: 6.353
CARACAS FC: Renny Vicente VEGA Hernández, Jaime Andrés BUSTAMANTE Suárez, Alejandro Enrique CICHERO Konarek, Pablo Jesus CAMACHO, Gabriel Alejandro CICHERO Konarek, Alejandro Abraham GUERRA Morales, Édgar Hernán JIMÉNEZ González, Bremer Alfredo PIÑANGO Arévalo (46 Franklin José LUCENA Peña), Jesús Javier GÓMEZ Mercado (74 César Iván GONZÁLEZ), Rodrigo PRIETO Aubert (46 Darío Damián FIGUEROA), Samir VALOYES Nebollán. DT: Ceferino BENCOMO
CF UNIVERSIDAD DE CHILE: Miguel Angel PINTO Jérez, Matías Nicolás RODRÍGUEZ, Rafael Andrés OLARRA Guerrero, José Raúl CONTRERAS Arrau, José Manuel ROJAS Bahamondes, Mauricio Bernardo VICTORINO Dansilio, Manuel Rolando ITURRA Urrutía, Wálter Damián MONTILLO (87 Marco Andrés ESTRADA Quinteros), Felipe Ignatio SEYMOUR Dobud, Edson Raúl PUCH Cortez (9 Eduardo Jesús VARGAS Rojas, 75 Diego Gabriel RIVAROLA Popon), Juan Manuel OLIVERA López. DT: Gerardo PELUSO
Sent off: Guerra (67)
Goals: César Iván GONZÁLEZ (76) / Mauricio Bernardo VICTORINO Dansilio (18), Juan Manuel OLIVERA López (32 penalty), Matías Nicolás RODRÍGUEZ (35).

CD UNIVERSIDAD CATÓLICA – CR FLAMENGO 2-0 (2-0)
Estadio San Carlos de Apoquindo, Santiago, 14.04.2010
Referee: Sergio Fabián PEZZOTTA (ARG), Attendance: 7.709
CD UNIVERSIDAD CATÓLICA: Paulo Andrés GARCÉS Contreras, Ismael Ignacio FUENTES Castro, Waldo Alonso PONCE Carrizo (81 Diego ROSENDE Lagos), Hans MARTÍNEZ Cabrera (67 Fernando Andrés MENESES Cornejo), David Andrés HENRÍQUEZ Espinoza, Damián Rodrigo DÍAZ, Jorge ORMEÑO Guerra (75 Matías Martín RUBIO Kostner), Rodrigo Ignatio VALENZUELA Avilés, Francisco Andrés SILVA Gajardo, Milovan Petar MIROSEVIC Albornoz, Juan José MORALES. DT: Marco Antonio FIGUEROA Montero
CR FLAMENGO: BRUNO Fernandes das Dores de Souza, ÁLVARO Luiz Maior de Aquino (24 FABRÍCIO Silva Dornellas), Leonardo da Silva "LÉO" MOURA, JUAN Maldonado Jaimez Júnior Duarte, RONALDO Simões ANGELIM, Rafael Ferreira Francisco "TORÓ", Dejan PETKOVIC (46 Gonzalo Antonio FIERRO Caniullán), Claudio Andrés del Tránsito MALDONADO Rivera, WILLIANS Domingos Fernandes (46 VINÍCIUS PACHECO dos Santos), VÁGNER "LOVE" Silva de Souza, BRUNO "MEZENGA" Ferreira Mombra Rosa. DT: Jorge Luís ANDRADE da Silva
Goals: Damián Rodrigo DÍAZ (2), Francisco Andrés SILVA Gajardo (45).

CF UNIVERSIDAD DE CHILE – CD UNIVERSIDAD CATÓLICA 0-0
Estadio Monumental David Arellano, Santiago, 21.04.2010
Referee: Pablo Antonio POZO Quinteros (CHI), Attendance: 9.286
CF UNIVERSIDAD DE CHILE: Miguel Angel PINTO Jérez, Juan Claudio GONZÁLEZ Calderón, Marcelo Alfonso DÍAZ Rojas, Mauricio Antonio ARIAS González (90+1 Juan Manuel OLIVERA López), Juan René ABARCA Fuentes, Manuel Rolando ITURRA Urrutía (46 Felipe Ignatio SEYMOUR Dobud), Nelson Alejandro PINTO Martínez, Álvaro FERNÁNDEZ Gay, José Luis SILVA Araya (68 Wálter Damián MONTILLO), Gabriel Alejandro VARGAS Venegas, Diego Gabriel RIVAROLA Popon. DT: Gerardo PELUSO
CD UNIVERSIDAD CATÓLICA: Paulo Andrés GARCÉS Contreras, Ismael Ignacio FUENTES Castro, Leonel Jonathan MENA Gutiérrez, Hans MARTÍNEZ Cabrera (46 Diego ROSENDE Lagos), Damián Rodrigo DÍAZ, Jorge ORMEÑO Guerra, Rodrigo Ignatio VALENZUELA Avilés, Francisco Andrés SILVA Gajardo, Fernando Andrés MENESES Cornejo (46 Pablo Andrés VRANJICÁN), Milovan Petar MIROSEVIC Albornoz, Juan José MORALES (72 Ángel Rodrigo CARREÑO Ballesteros). DT: Marco Antonio FIGUEROA Montero Sent off: Díaz (89)

CR FLAMENGO – CARACAS FC 3-2 (2-1)
Estádio Jornalista Mário Filho (Maracaña), Río de Janeiro, 21.04.2010
Referee: Jorge Luis LARRIONDA Pietrafesa (URU), Attendance: 34.106
CR FLAMENGO: BRUNO Fernandes das Dores de Souza, Leonardo da Silva "LÉO" MOURA, JUAN Maldonado Jaimez Júnior Duarte, RONALDO Simões ANGELIM, DAVID Braz de Oliveira Filho, MICHAEL Anderson Pereira da Silva (79 Gonzalo Antonio FIERRO Caniullán), Claudio Andrés del Tránsito MALDONADO Rivera (85 José KLÉBERSON Pereira), WILLIANS Domingos Fernandes, ADRIANO Leite Ribeiro, VÁGNER "LOVE" Silva de Souza, VINÍCIUS PACHECO dos Santos (68 Dejan PETKOVIC). DT: Jorge Luís ANDRADE da Silva
CARACAS FC: Javier Eduardo TOYO Bárcenas, Franklin José LUCENA Peña, Jaime Andrés BUSTAMANTE Suárez, Giovanny Michael ROMERO Armenio, Alejandro Enrique CICHERO Konarek, Henry Leonardo BAUTISTA Blanco, Édgar Hernán JIMÉNEZ González, Darío Damián FIGUEROA, César Iván GONZÁLEZ (40 Jesús Javier GÓMEZ Mercado), Rafael Ernesto CASTELLÍN García (74 Fernando Luís ARISTEGUIETA de Luca), Samir VALOYES Nebollán (61 Alexander David GONZÁLEZ Sibulo). DT: Ceferino BENCOMO
Goals: RONALDO Simões ANGELIM (17), MICHAEL Anderson Pereira da Silva (19), DAVID Braz de Oliveira Filho (75) / Rafael Ernesto CASTELLÍN García (14), Jesús Javier GÓMEZ Mercado (67).

1	UNIVERSIDAD DE CHILE	6	3	3	0	10	6	12
2	FLAMENGO	6	3	1	2	11	9	10
3	Universidad Católica	6	1	4	1	5	5	7
4	Caracas	6	0	2	4	5	11	2

ROUND OF 16

CD "Chivas" Guadalajara SA and San Luis FC (who were forced to withdraw from the tournament during the previous season due to the influenza outbreak in Mexico) automatically entered the quarter-finals without needing to play any qualifying matches.

SAN LUIS FC – CA ESTUDIANTES DE LA PLATA 0-1 (0-1)
Estadio Alfonso Lastras Ramírez, San Luis Potosí, 27.04.2010
Referee: Juan Ernesto SOTO Arevalo (VEN), Attendance: 5.666
SAN LUIS FC: Carlos Alberto TREJO Sánchez, Pablo César AGUILAR Benítez, Óscar Yaroslav MASCORRO Ábrego, Diego Alfonso MARTÍNEZ Balderas, Braulio LUNA Guzmán, Ignacio TORRES Olvera, Noé MAYA Vilches (46 Diego Javier DE LA TORRE Muciño), Juan Pablo RODRÍGUEZ Conde, Guillermo RANGEL Álvarez (72 Rodolfo SALINAS Ortiz), Blas Antonio PÉREZ Ortega (63 Víctor Hugo LOJERO Alexanderson), Alfredo David MORENO. DT: Marcos Ignacio "Nacho" AMBRIZ Espinoza
CA ESTUDIANTES DE LA PLATA: Agustín Ignacio ORIÓN, Christian Ariel CELLAY, Clemente Juan RODRÍGUEZ, Federico FERNÁNDEZ, Faustino Marcos Alberto ROJO (76 Raúl Alejandro IBERBIA), Marcelo Adrián CARRUSCA (70 Germán David RÉ), Leandro Damián BENÍTEZ, Matías Ariel SÁNCHEZ, Maximiliano Ezequiel NÚÑEZ, Leandro GONZÁLEZ, Gastón Nicolás FERNÁNDEZ (64 Enzo Nicolás PÉREZ). DT: Alejandro Javier 4 SABELLA
Sent off: Rodríguez (69)
Goal: Leandro GONZÁLEZ (25).

CA ESTUDIANTES DE LA PLATA – SAN LUIS FC 3-1 (1-1)
Estadio Centenario Dr. José Luis Meiszner, Quilmes, 5.05.2010
Referee: Víctor Hugo CARRILLO Casanova (PER), Attendance: 9.359
CA ESTUDIANTES DE LA PLATA: Agustín Ignacio ORIÓN, Marcos Alberto ANGELERI, Leandro DESÁBATO, Federico FERNÁNDEZ, Faustino Marcos Alberto ROJO (79 Germán David RÉ), Marcelo Adrián CARRUSCA (35 José Ernesto SOSA), Juan Sebastián VERÓN (67 Matías Ariel SÁNCHEZ), Leandro Damián BENÍTEZ, Maximiliano Ezequiel NÚÑEZ, Mauro BOSELLI, Leandro GONZÁLEZ. DT: Alejandro Javier 4 SABELLA
SAN LUIS FC: Carlos Alberto TREJO Sánchez, Pablo César AGUILAR Benítez, Óscar Yaroslav MASCORRO Ábrego, Edwin William HERNÁNDEZ Herrera, Gonzalo PINEDA Reyes, César Eduardo GONZÁLEZ Amais, Jesús Alejandro PALACIOS Olague, Braulio LUNA Guzmán, Diego Javier DE LA TORRE Muciño (75 Juan Pablo RODRÍGUEZ Conde), Ignacio TORRES Olvera (64 Blas Antonio PÉREZ Ortega), Alfredo David MORENO.
Goals: Leandro GONZÁLEZ (4), Leandro Damián BENÍTEZ (51, 55) /
Diego Javier DE LA TORRE Muciño (7).

CD "CHIVAS" GUADALAJARA SA – CA VÉLEZ SÁRSFIELD 3-0 (1-0)
Estadio Jalisco, Guadalajara, 27.04.2010
Referee: Óscar Julián RUÍZ Acosta (COL), Attendance: 8.322
CD GUADALAJARA: Liborio Vicente SÁNCHEZ Ledezma, Édgar Eduardo MEJÍA Viruete (66 Patricio Gabriel ARAÚJO Vázquez), Héctor REYNOSO López, Omar Alejandro ESPARZA Morales, Mario Humberto DE LUNA Saucedo, Miguel Ángel PONCE Briseño, Christian Alejandro PÉREZ Vázquez (80 Xavier Iván BÁEZ Gamiño), Édgar Iván SOLÍS Castillón, Omar BRAVO Tordecillas, Omar ARELLANO Riverón, Marco Jhonfal FABIÁN de la Mora (66 Ulises Alejandro DÁVILA Plascencia). DT: José Luis REAL Casillas
CA VÉLEZ SÁRSFIELD: Marcelo Germán MONTOYA, Sebastián Enrique DOMÍNGUEZ, Ricardo Gastón DÍAZ, Nicolás Hernán Gonzalo OTAMENDI, Leandro Daniel SOMOZA, Víctor Eduardo ZAPATA, Fabián Andrés CUBERO (81 Iván Gonzalo BELLA), Maximiliano Nicolás MORALEZ, Emiliano Ramiro PAPA (46 Marco Natanel TORSIGLIERI), Juan Manuel MARTÍNEZ, Hernán Rodrigo LÓPEZ Mora (80 Rolando David ZÁRATE Riga). DT: Ricardo Alberto GARECA Nardi
Sent off: Montoya (90)
Goals: Omar BRAVO Tordecillas (25, 79), Héctor REYNOSO López (90+2).

CA VÉLEZ SÁRSFIELD – CD "CHIVAS" GUADALAJARA SA 2-0 (1-0)
Estadio José Amalfitani, Buenos Aires, 4.05.2010
Referee: Wilson Luiz SENEME (BRA), Attendance: 10.055
CA VÉLEZ SÁRSFIELD: Marcelo Alberto BAROVERO, Sebastián Enrique DOMÍNGUEZ, Ricardo Gastón DÍAZ (56 Juan Manuel MARTÍNEZ), Nicolás Hernán Gonzalo OTAMENDI, Leandro Daniel SOMOZA, Víctor Eduardo ZAPATA (79 Rolando David ZÁRATE Riga), Fabián Andrés CUBERO, Maximiliano Nicolás MORALEZ (69 R icardo Gabriel ÁLVAREZ), Emiliano Ramiro PAPA, Santiago Martín SILVA Olivera, Hernán Rodrigo LÓPEZ Mora. DT: Ricardo Alberto GARECA Nardi
CD GUADALAJARA SA: Liborio Vicente SÁNCHEZ Ledezma, Édgar Eduardo MEJÍA Viruete, Héctor REYNOSO López, Omar Alejandro ESPARZA Morales, Mario Humberto DE LUNA Saucedo, Miguel Ángel PONCE Briseño, Christian Alejandro PÉREZ Vázquez, Édgar Iván SOLÍS Castillón, Jorge ENRÍQUEZ García (80 Patricio Gabriel ARAÚJO Vázquez), Omar BRAVO Tordecillas (76 Xavier Iván BÁEZ Gamiño), Omar ARELLANO Riverón (63 Ulises Alejandro DÁVILA Plascencia). DT: José Luis REAL Casillas
Goals: Santiago Martín SILVA Olivera (3), Rolando David ZÁRATE Riga (89).

UNIVERSITARIO DE DEPORTES – SÃO PAULO FC 0-0
Estadio Monumental, Lima, 28.04.2010
Referee: Saúl Esteban LAVERNI (ARG), Attendance: 37.034
UNIVERSITARIO DE DEPORTES: Luis Ricardo LLONTOP Godeau, Carlos Alberto GALVÁN, Rodolfo ESPINOZA Díaz, Renzo REVOREDO Zuazo, Giancarlo CARMONA Maldonado (84 Miguel Ángel TORRES Quintana), Rainer TORRES Salas, Jesús RABANAL Dávila, Antonio Emiliano GONZÁLEZ Canchari (46 Luis Alberto HERNÁNDEZ Díaz), Jorge Johan VÁZQUEZ Rosales (61 Raúl RUIDÍAZ), Víctor Enrique PÍRIZ Álvez, Piero Fernando ALVA Niezen. DT: Juan Máximo REYNOSO Guzmán
SÃO PAULO FC: ROGÉRIO Rodrigo CENI, Cícero João de Cezare "CICINHO" (37 JEAN Raphael Vanderlei de Moreira), João MIRANDA de Souza Filho, ALEX Sandro da SILVA, JORGE WÁGNER Goes Conceição, RODRIGO Ribeiro SOUTO, RICHARLYSON Barbosa Felisbino, Anderson HERNANES de Carvalho Andrade Lima, MARLOS Romero Bonfim (68 JÚNIOR CÉSAR Eduardo Machado), WASHINGTON Stecanela Cerqueira (84 RENATO Assís da SILVA), DAGOBERTO Pelentier. DT: Raymundo RICARDO GOMES
Sent off: Richarlyson (65)

SÃO PAULO FC – UNIVERSITARIO DE DEPORTES 0-0; 3-1 penalties
Estádio Cícero Pompeu de Toledo (Morumbi), São Paulo, 4.05.2010
Referee: Carlos Manuel TORRES Nuñez (PAR), Attendance: 8.402
SÃO PAULO FC: ROGÉRIO Rodrigo CENI, Cícero João de Cezare "CICINHO" (74 JEAN Raphael Vanderlei de Moreira), João MIRANDA de Souza Filho, JÚNIOR CÉSAR Eduardo Machado, ALEX Sandro da SILVA, JORGE WÁGNER Goes Conceição (46 WASHINGTON Stecanela Cerqueira), RODRIGO Ribeiro SOUTO, Anderson HERNANES de Carvalho Andrade Lima, MARLOS Romero Bonfim, DAGOBERTO Pelentie, Luiz Fernando Pereira de Silva "FERNANDINHO" (90 Marcelo dos Santos "MARCELINHO PARAÍBA"). DT: Raymundo RICARDO GOMES
UNIVERSITARIO DE DEPORTES: Luis Ricardo LLONTOP Godeau, Carlos Alberto GALVÁN, Rodolfo ESPINOZA Díaz, Renzo REVOREDO Zuazo, Giancarlo CARMONA Maldonado, Rainer TORRES Salas (78 Luis Alberto RAMÍREZ Lucay), Jesús RABANAL Dávila, Luis Alberto HERNÁNDEZ Díaz, Jorge Johan VÁZQUEZ Rosales (73 Miguel Ángel TORRES Quintana), Víctor Enrique PÍRIZ Álvez (46 Alberto Gianfranco LABARTHE Tome), Piero Fernando ALVA Niezen. DT: Juan Máximo REYNOSO Guzmán
Penalties: * ROGÉRIO Rodrigo CENI, 0-1 Luis Alberto RAMÍREZ Lucay, 1-1 Anderson HERNANES de Carvalho Andrade Lima, * Piero Fernando ALVA Niezen, 2-1 Marcelo dos Santos "MARCELINHO PARAÍBA", Carlos Alberto GALVÁN, 3-1 DAGOBERTO Pelentie, Alberto Gianfranco LABARTHE Tome

CR FLAMENGO – SC CORINTHIANS PAULISTA 1-0 (0-0)
Estádio Jornalista Mário Filho (Maracaña), Río de Janeiro, 28.04.2010
Referee: Carlos Arecio AMARILLA Demarqui (PAR), Attendance: 72.442
CR FLAMENGO: BRUNO Fernandes das Dores de Souza, Leonardo da Silva "LÉO" MOURA, JUAN Maldonado Jaimez Júnior Duarte, RONALDO Simões ANGELIM, DAVID Braz de Oliveira Filho, RÔMULO Noronha, MICHAEL Anderson Pereira da Silva, Claudio Andrés del Tránsito MALDONADO Rivera (77 Rafael Ferreira Francisco "TORÓ"), WILLIANS Domingos Fernandes (85 Gonzalo Antonio FIERRO Caniullán), ADRIANO Leite Ribeiro, VÁGNER "LOVE" Silva de Souza (81 VINÍCIUS PACHECO dos Santos). DT: ROGÉRIO Moraes LOURENÇO
SC CORINTHIANS PAULISTA: JÚLIO CÉSAR de Souza Santos, ROBERTO CARLOS da Silva, Anderson Sebastião Cardoso "CHICÃO", WILLIAM Machado de Oliveira, DANILO Gabriel de Andrade (67 JORGE HENRIQUE de Souza), ELÍAS Mendes Trinidade, MOACIR Costa da Silva, RALF de Souza Teles, JUCILEI da Silva, RONALDO Luis Nazário de Lima (83 Rodrigo de SOUZA Cardoso), Bruno Ferreira Bonfim "DENTINHO" (66 Pedro IARLEY Lima Dantas). DT: Luiz Antonio "MANO" Venker MENEZES
Sent off: Michael (37)
Goal: ADRIANO Leite Ribeiro (66 penalty).

SC CORINTHIANS PAULISTA – CR FLAMENGO 2-1 (2-0)
Estádio Municipal Paulo Machado de Carvalho (Pacaembú), São Paulo, 5.05.2010
Referee: Roberto Carlos SILVERA Calcerrada (URU), Attendance: 35.561
SC CORINTHIANS PAULISTA: Luiz FELIPE Ventura dos Santos, ROBERTO CARLOS da Silva, Anderson Sebastião Cardoso "CHICÃO", WILLIAM Machado de Oliveira, ALESSANDRO Mori Nunes (78 José Paulo Bezerra Maciel Junior "PAULINHO"), DANILO Gabriel de Andrade, ELÍAS Mendes Trinidade (69 JUCILEI da Silva), RALF de Souza Teles, RONALDO Luis Nazário de Lima, JORGE HENRIQUE de Souza (67 Pedro IARLEY Lima Dantas), Bruno Ferreira Bonfim "DENTINHO".DT: Luiz Antonio "MANO" Venker MENEZES
CR FLAMENGO: BRUNO Fernandes das Dores de Souza, Leonardo da Silva "LÉO" MOURA, JUAN Maldonado Jaimez Júnior Duarte, RONALDO Simões ANGELIM, DAVID Braz de Oliveira Filho, RÔMULO Noronha, Claudio Andrés del Tránsito MALDONADO Rivera (87 Rafael Ferreira Francisco "TORÓ"), WILLIANS Domingos Fernandes, ADRIANO Leite Ribeiro, VÁGNER "LOVE" Silva de Souza (78 Gonzalo Antonio FIERRO Caniullán), VINÍCIUS PACHECO dos Santos (46 José KLÉBERSON Pereira). DT: ROGÉRIO Moraes LOURENÇO
Goals: DAVID Braz de Oliveira Filho (28 own goal), RONALDO Luis Nazário de Lima (39) / VÁGNER "LOVE" Silva de Souza (49).

CA BANFIELD – SC INTERNACIONAL 3-1 (0-0)
Estadio Florencio Solá, Banfield, 28.04.2010
Referee: Jorge Luis LARRIONDA Pietrafesa (URU), Attendance: 6.794
CA BANFIELD: Cristian David LUCCHETTI, Jonathan Ramón MAIDANA, Santiago Andrés LADINO, Víctor Rubén LÓPEZ, Roberto Miguel BATTIÓN, Julio Eduardo BARRAZA, Wálter Daniel ERVITI, Marcelo Nildo QUINTEROS, James David RODRÍGUEZ Rubio (86 Mauro Javier DOS SANTOS), Rubén Darío RAMÍREZ, Sebastián Bruno FERNÁNDEZ Miglierina (90+4 Federico Javier SARDELLA). DT: Julio César FALCIONI
SC INTERNACIONAL: Roberto Carlos ABBONDANZIERI, Gonzalo SORONDO Amaro, Fabián Guedes "BOLÍVAR", FABIANO ELLER dos Santos, Claudinei Cardoso Félix da Silva "NEI", KLÉBER de Carvalho Correa, Andrés Nicolás D'ALESSANDRO (89 TAISON Barcellos Freda), Pablo Horacio GUIÑAZÚ, André Luiz Tavares "ANDREZINHO" (89 EVERTON Santos da Costa), SANDRO Guimaraes Cordeiro Ranieri, ALECSANDRO Barbosa Felisbino (79 WALTER Henrique da Silva). DT: Jorge Daniel FOSATTI Lurachi
Sent off: Barraza (84) / Kléber (58)
Goals: James David RODRÍGUEZ Rubio (47), Roberto Miguel BATTIÓN (59), Sebastián Bruno FERNÁNDEZ Miglierina (81) / KLÉBER de Carvalho Correa (50).

SC INTERNACIONAL – CA BANFIELD 2-0 (1-0)
Estádio José Pinheiro Borda (Beira-Rio), Porto Alegre, 6.05.2010
Referee: Wilmar Alexander ROLDÁN Pérez (COL), Attendance: 34.643
SC INTERNACIONAL: Roberto Carlos ABBONDANZIERI, Gonzalo SORONDO Amaro, Fabián Guedes "BOLÍVAR", FABIANO ELLER dos Santos, Claudinei Cardoso Félix da Silva "NEI", Andrés Nicolás D'ALESSANDRO (90+3 GLAYDSON Marcelino Freire), Pablo Horacio GUIÑAZÚ, André Luiz Tavares "ANDREZINHO" (70 GIULIANO Victor de Paula), SANDRO Guimaraes Cordeiro Ranieri, ALECSANDRO Barbosa Felisbino, WALTER Henrique da Silva (88 EVERTON Santos da Costa). DT: Jorge Daniel FOSATTI Lurachi
CA BANFIELD: Cristian David LUCCHETTI, Jonathan Ramón MAIDANA, Santiago Andrés LADINO (90 Mauro Javier DOS SANTOS), Víctor Rubén LÓPEZ, Walter Marcelo BUSTAMANTE (81 Maximiliano LASO), Roberto Miguel BATTIÓN, Wálter Daniel ERVITI, Marcelo Nildo QUINTEROS (74 Mathias Adolfo CARDACCIO Alaguich), James David RODRÍGUEZ Rubio, Rubén Darío RAMÍREZ, Sebastián Bruno FERNÁNDEZ Miglierina. DT: Julio César FALCIONI
Sent off: Rodríguez (82)
Goals: ALECSANDRO Barbosa Felisbino (41), WALTER Henrique da Silva (57).

CRUZEIRO EC – CLUB NACIONAL MONTEVIDEO 3-1 (3-0)
Estádio Governador Magalhães Pinto (Mineirão), Belo Horizonte, 29.04.2010
Referee: Héctor Wálter BALDASSI (ARG), Attendance: 32.254
CRUZEIRO EC: Deivison Lopes Maciel "FÁBIO", JONATHAN Cícero Moreira, LEANDRO Fabiano da SILVA e Silva, DIEGO RENÁN de Lima Ferreira, Carlos Gilberto Nascimento da Silva e Silva "GIL", GILBERTO da Silva Melo (75 Joffre David GUERRÓN Méndez), Antônio Marcos da Silva Filho "MARQUINHOS PARANÁ", HENRIQUE Pacheco de Lima, FABRÍCIO de Sousa (46 ELICARLOS Souza Santos), KLÉBER Giacomace de Souza Freitas, THIAGO RIBEIRO Cardoso. DT: ADÍLSON Dias BATISTA
CLUB NACIONAL MONTEVIDEO: Rodrigo Martín MUÑOZ Salomón, Alejandro Daniel LEMBO Betancor, Christian Washington NÚÑEZ Medina, Sebastián COATES Nion, Gustavo Antonio VARELA Rodríguez (39 Diego Daniel VERA Méndez), Álvaro Rafael GONZÁLEZ Luengo, Ángel Alejandro MORALES Santos (69 Gonzalo GODOY), Óscar Javier MORALES Albornoz (81 Mauricio Ernesto PEREYRA Antonini), Raúl Freddy FERRO Olivera, Maximiliano Matías CALZADA Fuentes, Mario Ignacio REGUEIRO Pintos. DT: Eduardo Mario ACEVEDO Cardozo
Goals: THIAGO RIBEIRO Cardoso (7, 22, 42) / Mario Ignacio REGUEIRO Pintos (51).

CLUB NACIONAL MONTEVIDEO – CRUZEIRO EC 0-3 (0-1)
Estadio Gran Parque Central, Montevideo, 5.05.2010
Referee: Federico José BELIGOY (ARG), Attendance: 13.919
CLUB NACIONAL MONTEVIDEO: Rodrigo Martín MUÑOZ Salomón, Alejandro Daniel LEMBO Betancor, Christian Washington NÚÑEZ Medina (63 Mauricio Ernesto PEREYRA Antonini), Sebastián COATES Nion, Gustavo Antonio VARELA Rodríguez, Álvaro Rafael GONZÁLEZ Luengo (83 Gonzalo GODOY), Ángel Alejandro MORALES Santos, Óscar Javier MORALES Albornoz, Raúl Freddy FERRO Olivera, Maximiliano Matías CALZADA Fuentes (46 Diego Daniel VERA Méndez), Mario Ignacio REGUEIRO Pintos. DT: Eduardo Mario ACEVEDO Cardozo
CRUZEIRO EC: Deivison Lopes Maciel "FÁBIO", JONATHAN Cícero Moreira, LEANDRO Fabiano da SILVA e Silva, DIEGO RENÁN de Lima Ferreira, Carlos Gilberto Nascimento da Silva e Silva "GIL", GILBERTO da Silva Melo, Antônio Marcos da Silva Filho "MARQUINHOS PARANÁ", HENRIQUE Pacheco de Lima, FABRÍCIO de Sousa (71 PEDRO KEN Morimoto Moreira), KLÉBER Giacomace de Souza Freitas (57 THIAGO HELENO Henrique Ferreira), THIAGO RIBEIRO Cardoso (82 WELLINGTON "PAULISTA" Pereira do Nascimento). DT: ADÍLSON Dias BATISTA
Sent off: Coates (54), Varela (70) / Leandro Silva (53)
Goals: THIAGO RIBEIRO Cardoso (30), DIEGO RENÁN de Lima Ferreira (48), GILBERTO da Silva Melo (81).

CLUB ALIANZA LIMA – CF UNIVERSIDAD DE CHILE 0-1 (0-0)
Estadio Alejandro Villanueva, Lima, 29.04.2010
Referee: Carlos Eugênio SIMÓN (BRA), Attendance: 29.247
CLUB ALIANZA LIMA: George Patrick FORSYTH Somer, Carlos Javier SOLÍS Alvarado, Amilton Jair PRADO Barron, Héctor Vidal SOSA Gaona, Édgar VILLAMARÍN Arguedas, Édgar Daniel GONZÁLEZ Brítez, Henry Edson QUINTEROS Sánchez (59 Johnnier Esteiner MONTAÑO Bolaño), Jean Carlos TRAGODARA Gálvez, Joel Melchor SÁNCHEZ Alegría (75 Alexander Gustavo SÁNCHEZ Reyes), José Carlos FERNÁNDEZ Piedra (60 Claudio Matías VELÁSQUEZ), Wilmer Alexander AGUIRRE Vasquez. DT: Gustavo Adolfo COSTAS
CF UNIVERSIDAD DE CHILE: Miguel Angel PINTO Jérez, Matías Nicolás RODRÍGUEZ, Rafael Andrés OLARRA Guerrero, José Raúl CONTRERAS Arrau (68 Álvaro FERNÁNDEZ Gay), José Manuel ROJAS Bahamondes, Mauricio Bernardo VICTORINO Dansilio, Manuel Rolando ITURRA Urrutía, Wálter Damián MONTILLO, Felipe Ignatio SEYMOUR Dobud (84 Nelson Alejandro PINTO Martínez), Eduardo Jesús VARGAS Rojas, Juan Manuel OLIVERA López (73 Diego Gabriel RIVAROLA Popon). DT: Gerardo PELUSO
Goal: Diego Gabriel RIVAROLA Popon (86).

CF UNIVERSIDAD DE CHILE – CLUB ALIANZA LIMA 2-2 (0-1)
Estadio Monumental David Arellano, Santiago, 6.05.2010
Referee: Carlos Alfredo VERA Rodríguez (ECU), Attendance: 28.663
CF UNIVERSIDAD DE CHILE: Miguel Angel PINTO Jérez, Matías Nicolás RODRÍGUEZ, Rafael Andrés OLARRA Guerrero, José Raúl CONTRERAS Arrau (46 Edson Raúl PUCH Cortez), José Manuel ROJAS Bahamondes, Mauricio Bernardo VICTORINO Dansilio, Manuel Rolando ITURRA Urrutía, Wálter Damián MONTILLO, Felipe Ignatio SEYMOUR Dobud, Eduardo Jesús VARGAS Rojas (77 Álvaro FERNÁNDEZ Gay), Juan Manuel OLIVERA López (85 Diego Gabriel RIVAROLA Popon). DT: Gerardo PELUSO).
CLUB ALIANZA LIMA: George Patrick FORSYTH Somer, Carlos Javier SOLÍS Alvarado, Amilton Jair PRADO Barron, Héctor Vidal SOSA Gaona, Édgar VILLAMARÍN Arguedas (46 Wálter Ricardo VÍLCHEZ Soto), Édgar Daniel GONZÁLEZ Brítez, Henry Edson QUINTEROS Sánchez (53 Óscar Cristopher VÍLCHEZ Soto), Jean Carlos TRAGODARA Gálvez (71 Johnnier Esteiner MONTAÑO Bolaño), Joel Melchor SÁNCHEZ Alegría, José Carlos FERNÁNDEZ Piedra, Wilmer Alexander AGUIRRE Vasquez. DT: Gustavo Adolfo COSTAS
Goals: Eduardo Jesús VARGAS Rojas (63), Felipe Ignatio SEYMOUR Dobud (90+2) / José Carlos FERNÁNDEZ Piedra (24, 87).

CD ONCE CALDAS – CLUB LIBERTAD ASUNCIÓN 0-0
Estadio Palogrande, Manizales, 29.04.2010
Referee: Sálvio Spínosa FAGUNDES Filho (BRA), Attendance: 10.981
CD ONCE CALDAS: Luis Enrique MARTÍNEZ Rodríguez, Oswaldo Augusto VIZCARRONDO Araujo, Alexis Héctor HENRÍQUEZ Charales, Luis Alberto NUÑEZ Charales, José Iván VÉLEZ Castillo, Diego Armando AMAYA Solano (66 Sebastián HERNÁNDEZ Mejía), John Jairo VALENCIA Ortiz, Jaime Alberto CASTRILLÓN Vásquez (55 Danny Manuel SANTOYA Otero), Diego Alejandro ARIAS Hincapié, Dayro Mauricio MORENO Galindo, Fernando URIBE Himcapie. DT: Juan Carlos OSORIO Arbelaez
CLUB LIBERTAD ASUNCIÓN: Bernardo David MEDINA, Pedro Alcides SARABIA Achucarro, Arnaldo Andrés VERA Chamorro, Adalberto ROMÁN Benítez, Ismael BENEGAS, Sergio Daniel AQUINO, Víctor Javier CÁCERES Centurión, Miguel Ángel Ramón SAMUDIO (81 Omar Héber POUSO Osores), Víctor Hugo AYALA Núñez (74 Édgar Arnulfo ROBLES Coronel), Pablo César VELÁZQUEZ Centurión (39 Roberto Carlos GAMARRA Acosta), Rodolfo Vicente GAMARRA Varela. DT: Gregorio Elso PÉREZ Perdigón

CLUB LIBERTAD ASUNCIÓN – CD ONCE CALDAS 2-1 (0-0)
Estadio Defensores del Chaco, Asunción, 6.05.2010
Referee: Sergio Fabián Pezzotta (ARG), Attendance: 2.000
CLUB LIBERTAD ASUNCIÓN: Bernardo David MEDINA, Pedro Alcides SARABIA Achucarro, Arnaldo Andrés VERA Chamorro, Adalberto ROMÁN Benítez, Ismael BENEGAS (64 Aldo David OLMEDO Román), Sergio Daniel AQUINO, Víctor Javier CÁCERES Centurión, Miguel Ángel Ramón SAMUDIO (57 Manuel José MACIEL Fernández),Víctor Hugo AYALA Núñez, Pablo César VELÁZQUEZ Centurión (64 Roberto Carlos GAMARRA Acosta), Rodolfo Vicente GAMARRA Varela. DT: Gregorio Elso PÉREZ Perdigón
CD ONCE CALDAS: Luis Enrique MARTÍNEZ Rodríguez, Oswaldo Augusto VIZCARRONDO Araujo, Alexis Héctor HENRÍQUEZ Charales, Luis Alberto NUÑEZ Charales, José Iván VÉLEZ Castillo, Carlos JOHNSON Carpio, Dayron Alexander PÉREZ Calle (60 Diego Armando AMAYA Solano), John Jairo VALENCIA Ortiz (65 Jaime Alberto CASTRILLÓN Vásquez), Diego Alejandro ARIAS Hincapié, Dayro Mauricio MORENO Galindo, Fernando URIBE Himcapie (70 Danny Manuel SANTOYA Otero). DT: Juan Carlos OSORIO Arbelaez
Goals: Roberto Carlos GAMARRA Acosta (73 penalty, 89) / Dayro Mauricio MORENO Galindo (55).

QUARTER-FINALS

CD "CHIVAS" GUADALAJARA – CLUB LIBERTAD ASUNCIÓN 3-0 (2-0)
Estadio Jalisco, Guadalajara, 11.05.2010
Referee: Pablo Antonio POZO Quinteros (CHI), Attendance: 15.011
CD GUADALAJARA: Liborio Vicente SÁNCHEZ Ledezma, Héctor REYNOSO López, Patricio Gabriel ARAÚJO Vázquez, Mario Humberto DE LUNA Saucedo, Christian Alejandro PÉREZ Vázquez, Xavier Iván BÁEZ Gamiño, Julio César NAVA García (70 Édgar Iván SOLÍS Castillón), Abraham CORONADO Tafoya (65 Omar Alejandro ESPARZA Morales), Omar BRAVO Tordecillas, Omar ARELLANO Riverón (18 Ricardo Michel VÁZQUEZ Gallien), Marco Jhonfai FABIÁN de la Mora. DT: José Luis REAL Casillas
CLUB LIBERTAD ASUNCIÓN: Bernardo David MEDINA, Pedro Alcides SARABIA Achucarro, Arnaldo Andrés VERA Chamorro, Adalberto ROMÁN Benítez, Aldo David OLMEDO Román, Sergio Daniel AQUINO, Víctor Javier CÁCERES Centurión, Miguel Ángel Ramón SAMUDIO (72 Manuel José MACIEL Fernández), Víctor Hugo AYALA Núñez (46 Pablo César VELÁZQUEZ Centurión), Roberto Carlos GAMARRA Acosta (46 Jorge Luis MOREIRA Ferreira), Rodolfo Vicente GAMARRA Varela. DT: Gregorio Elso PÉREZ Perdigón
Goals: Omar BRAVO Tordecillas (9, 80), Ricardo Michel VÁZQUEZ Gallien (30)

CLUB LIBERTAD ASUNCIÓN – CD "CHIVAS" GUADALAJARA 2-0 (1-0)
Estadio Defensores del Chaco, Asunción, 18.05.2010
Referee: Héctor Wálter Baldassi (ARG), Attendance: 260
CLUB LIBERTAD ASUNCIÓN: Bernardo David MEDINA, Pedro Alcides SARABIA Achucarro, Arnaldo Andrés VERA Chamorro, Adalberto ROMÁN Benítez, Sergio Daniel AQUINO, Víctor Javier CÁCERES Centurión, Miguel Ángel Ramón SAMUDIO (40 Manuel José MACIEL Fernández), Wilson Omar PITTONI Rodríguez (59 Roberto Carlos GAMARRA Acosta), Jorge Luis MOREIRA Ferreira, Pablo César VELÁZQUEZ Centurión, Rodolfo Vicente GAMARRA Varela (62 José Ariel NÚÑEZ Portelli). DT: Gregorio Elso PÉREZ Perdigón
CD GUADALAJARA SA: Liborio Vicente SÁNCHEZ Ledezma, Héctor REYNOSO López, Omar Alejandro ESPARZA Morales, Patricio Gabriel ARAÚJO Vázquez, Mario Humberto DE LUNA Saucedo, Christian Alejandro PÉREZ Vázquez, Xavier Iván BÁEZ Gamiño, Édgar Iván SOLÍS Castillón (73 Miguel Ángel PONCE Briseño), Jorge ENRÍQUEZ García (66 Édgar Eduardo MEJÍA Viruete), Omar BRAVO Tordecillas, Omar ARELLANO Riverón (56 Ulises Alejandro DÁVILA Plascencia). DT: José Luis REAL Casillas
Goals: Adalberto ROMÁN Benítez (20), Manuel José MACIEL Fernández (68).

CR FLAMENGO – CF UNIVERSIDAD DE CHILE 2-3 (1-2)
Estádio Jornalista Mário Filho (Maracaña), Río de Janeiro, 12.05.2010
Referee: Carlos Arecio AMARILLA Demarqui (PAR), Attendance: 68.153
CR FLAMENGO: BRUNO Fernandes das Dores de Souza, Leonardo da Silva "LÉO" MOURA, JUAN Maldonado Jaimez Júnior Duarte, RONALDO Simões ANGELIM, DAVID Braz de Oliveira Filho, José KLÉBERSON Pereira (73 DÊNIS MARQUES do Nascimento), RÔMULO Noronha (21 MICHAEL Anderson Pereira da Silva), Claudio Andrés del Tránsito MALDONADO Rivera (46 Dejan PETKOVIC), WILLIANS Domingos Fernandes, ADRIANO Leite Ribeiro, VÁGNER "LOVE" Silva de Souza. DT: ROGÉRIO Moraes LOURENÇO
CF UNIVERSIDAD DE CHILE: Miguel Angel PINTO Jérez, Matías Nicolás RODRÍGUEZ, Rafael Andrés OLARRA Guerrero, José Manuel ROJAS Bahamondes, Mauricio Bernardo VICTORINO Dansilio, Manuel Rolando ITURRA Urrutía, Wálter Damián MONTILLO (82 Edson Raúl PUCH Cortez), Felipe Ignatio SEYMOUR Dobud, Álvaro FERNÁNDEZ Gay, Eduardo Jesús VARGAS Rojas (46 Nelson Alejandro PINTO Martínez), Juan Manuel OLIVERA López (75 Diego Gabriel RIVAROLA Popon). DT: Gerardo PELUSO
Sent off: Iturra (45)
Goals: ADRIANO Leite Ribeiro (39), JUAN Maldonado Jaimez Júnior Duarte (88) /
Mauricio Bernardo VICTORINO Dansilio (4), Rafael Andrés OLARRA Guerrero (24),
Álvaro FERNÁNDEZ Gay (47).

CF UNIVERSIDAD DE CHILE – CR FLAMENGO 1-2 (0-1)
Estadio Santa Laura-Universidad SEK, Santiago, 20.05.2010
Referee: Roberto Carlos SILVERA Calcerrada (URU), Attendance: 14.450
CF UNIVERSIDAD DE CHILE: Miguel Angel PINTO Jérez, Matías Nicolás RODRÍGUEZ, Rafael Andrés OLARRA Guerrero, José Manuel ROJAS Bahamondes, Mauricio Bernardo VICTORINO Dansilio, Nelson Alejandro PINTO Martínez, Wálter Damián MONTILLO (80 José Raúl CONTRERAS Arrau), Felipe Ignatio SEYMOUR Dobud, Álvaro FERNÁNDEZ Gay, Eduardo Jesús VARGAS Rojas (55 Edson Raúl PUCH Cortez), Juan Manuel OLIVERA López (85 Diego Gabriel RIVAROLA Popon). DT: Gerardo PELUSO
CR FLAMENGO: BRUNO Fernandes das Dores de Souza, Leonardo da Silva "LÉO" MOURA, JUAN Maldonado Jaimez Júnior Duarte, RONALDO Simões ANGELIM, DAVID Braz de Oliveira Filho, José KLÉBERSON Pereira (86 BRUNO "MEZENGA" Ferreira Mombra Rosa), Rafael Ferreira Francisco "TORÓ" (79 VINÍCIUS PACHECO dos Santos), MICHAEL Anderson Pereira da Silva (46 Dejan PETKOVIC), WILLIANS Domingos Fernandes, ADRIANO Leite Ribeiro, VÁGNER "LOVE" Silva de Souza. DT: ROGÉRIO Moraes LOURENÇO
Sent off: Willians (89), Vágner 'Love' (90+5)
Goals: Wálter Damián MONTILLO (73) /
VÁGNER "LOVE" Silva de Souza (45), ADRIANO Leite Ribeiro (78).

CRUZEIRO EC – SÃO PAULO FC 0-2 (0-1)
Estádio Governador Magalhães Pinto (Mineirão), Belo Horizonte, 12.05.2010
Referee: Óscar Julián RUÍZ Acosta (COL), Attendance: 48.602
CRUZEIRO EC: Deivison Lopes Maciel "FÁBIO", JONATHAN Cícero Moreira, THIAGO HELENO Henrique Ferreira, DIEGO RENÁN de Lima Ferreira (55 Joffre David GUERRÓN Méndez), Carlos Gilberto Nascimento da Silva e Silva "GIL", GILBERTO da Silva Melo (78 ROGER Galera Flores), Antônio Marcos da Silva Filho "MARQUINHOS PARANÁ", HENRIQUE Pacheco de Lima, FABRÍCIO de Sousa (62 FÁBIO dos SANTOS Barbosa), KLÉBER Giacomace de Souza Freitas, THIAGO RIBEIRO Cardoso. DT: ADÍLSON Dias BATISTA
SÃO PAULO FC: ROGÉRIO Rodrigo CENI, Cícero João de Cezare "CICINHO" (81 JEAN Raphael Vanderlei de Moreira), JÚNIOR CÉSAR Eduardo Machado (79 JORGE WÁGNER Goes Conceição), ALEX Sandro da SILVA, Alexandre Luiz Reame "XANDÃO", RODRIGO Ribeiro SOUTO, RICHARLYSON Barbosa Felisbino, Anderson HERNANES de Carvalho Andrade Lima, MARLOS Romero Bonfim, Fernando Lúcio da Costa "FERNANDÃO" (79 WASHINGTON Stecanela Cerqueira), DAGOBERTO Pelentie. DT: Raymundo RICARDO GOMES
Goals: DAGOBERTO Pelentie (23), Anderson HERNANES de Carvalho Andrade Lima (65).

SÃO PAULO FC – CRUZEIRO EC 2-0 (1-0)
Estádio Cícero Pompeu de Toledo (Morumbi), São Paulo, 19.05.2010
Referee: Jorge Luis LARRIONDA Pietrafesa (URU), Attendance: 52.196
SÃO PAULO FC: ROGÉRIO Rodrigo CENI, Cícero João de Cezare "CICINHO", João MIRANDA de Souza Filho (86 Alexandre Luiz Reame "XANDÃO"), JÚNIOR CÉSAR Eduardo Machado, ALEX Sandro da SILVA, RODRIGO Ribeiro SOUTO, RICHARLYSON Barbosa Felisbino (83 JEAN Raphael Vanderlei de Moreira), Anderson HERNANES de Carvalho Andrade Lima, MARLOS Romero Bonfim, Fernando Lúcio da Costa "FERNANDÃO", DAGOBERTO Pelentie (76 Luiz Fernando Pereira da Silva "FERNANDINHO"). DT: Raymundo RICARDO GOMES
CRUZEIRO EC: Deivison Lopes Maciel "FÁBIO", JONATHAN Cícero Moreira (28 THIAGO HELENO Henrique Ferreira), LEONARDO Fabiano da SILVA e Silva, DIEGO RENÁN de Lima Ferreira (58 ELICARLOS Souza Santos), Carlos Gilberto Nascimento da Silva e Silva "GIL", GILBERTO da Silva Melo, Antônio Marcos da Silva Filho "MARQUINHOS PARANÁ", HENRIQUE Pacheco de Lima, FABRÍCIO de Sousa (46 WELLINGTON "PAULISTA" Pereira do Nascimento), KLÉBER Giacomace de Souza Freitas, THIAGO RIBEIRO Cardoso. DT: ADÍLSON Dias BATISTA
Sent off: Kléber (2)
Goals: Anderson HERNANES de Carvalho Andrade Lima (24), DAGOBERTO Pelentie (53).

SC INTERNACIONAL – CA ESTUDIANTES DE LA PLATA 1-0 (0-0)
Estádio José Pinheiro Borda (Beira-Rio), Porto Alegre, 13.05.2010
Referee: Roberto Carlos SILVERA Calcerrada (URU), Attendance: 40.115
SC INTERNACIONAL: Roberto Carlos ABBONDANZIERI, Gonzalo SORONDO Amaro, Fabián Guedes "BOLÍVAR", Claudinei Cardoso Félix da Silva "NEI" (75 GLAYDSON Marcelino Freire), KLÉBER de Carvalho Correa, Andrés Nicolás D'ALESSANDRO (76 GIULIANO Victor de Paula), Pablo Horacio GUIÑAZÚ, André Luiz Tavares "ANDREZINHO", SANDRO Guimaraes Cordeiro Ranieri, ALECSANDRO Barbosa Felisbino, WALTER Henrique da Silva (64 TAISON Barcellos Freda). DT: Jorge Daniel FOSATTI Lurachi
CA ESTUDIANTES DE LA PLATA: Agustín Ignacio ORIÓN, Leandro DESÁBATO, Christian Ariel CELLAY, Germán David RÉ, Clemente Juan RODRÍGUEZ, Federico FERNÁNDEZ, Juan Sebastián VERÓN, Enzo Nicolás PÉREZ (85 Darío Gustavo STEFANATTO), José Ernesto SOSA (72 Leandro Damián BENÍTEZ), Matías Ariel SÁNCHEZ, Mauro BOSELLI. DT: Alejandro Javier SABELLA
Goal: Gonzalo SORONDO Amaro (88).

CA ESTUDIANTES DE LA PLATA – SC INTERNACIONAL 2-1 (2-0)
Estadio Centenario Dr. José Luis Meiszner, Quilmes, 20.05.2010
Referee: Óscar Julián RUÍZ Acosta (COL), Attendance: 14.500
CA ESTUDIANTES DE LA PLATA: Agustín Ignacio ORIÓN, Leandro DESÁBATO, Christian Ariel CELLAY, Germán David RÉ, Clemente Juan RODRÍGUEZ (89 Federico FERNÁNDEZ), Juan Sebastián VERÓN, Enzo Nicolás PÉREZ (81 Leandro Damián BENÍTEZ), José Ernesto SOSA, Matías Ariel SÁNCHEZ, Mauro BOSELLI, Leandro GONZÁLEZ (46 Marcos Alberto ANGELERI). DT: Alejandro Javier SABELLA
SC INTERNACIONAL: Roberto Carlos ABBONDANZIERI, Gonzalo SORONDO Amaro, Fabián Guedes "BOLÍVAR", FABIANO ELLER dos Santos, Claudinei Cardoso Félix da Silva "NEI" (68 WALTER Henrique da Silva), KLÉBER de Carvalho Correa, Andrés Nicolás D'ALESSANDRO (77 GIULIANO Victor de Paula), Pablo Horacio GUIÑAZÚ, André Luiz Tavares "ANDREZINHO", SANDRO Guimaraes Cordeiro Ranieri (85 Luis Eduardo Schmidt "EDÚ"), ALECSANDRO Barbosa Felisbino. DT: Jorge Daniel FOSATTI Lurachi
Goals: Leandro GONZÁLEZ (19), Enzo Nicolás PÉREZ (21) / GIULIANO Victor de Paula (88).

SEMI-FINALS

CD "CHIVAS" GUADALAJARA – CF UNIVERSIDAD DE CHILE 1-1 (0-0)
Estadio Azteca, Mexico City, 27.07.2010
Referee: Juan Ernesto SOTO Arevalo (VEN), Attendance: 52.035
CD GUADALAJARA: Luis Ernesto MICHEL Vergara, José Jonny MAGALLÓN Oliva, Édgar Eduardo MEJÍA Viruete, Héctor REYNOSO López, Omar Alejandro ESPARZA Morales, Miguel Ángel PONCE Briseño, Alberto MEDINA Briseño (70 Marco Jhonfai FABIÁN de la Mora), Xavier Iván BÁEZ Gamiño, Omar BRAVO Tordecillas, Adolfo BAUTISTA Herrera, Omar ARELLANO Riverón. DT: José Luis REAL Casillas
CF UNIVERSIDAD DE CHILE: Miguel Angel PINTO Jérez, Matías Nicolás RODRÍGUEZ, Rafael Andrés OLARRA Guerrero, José Raúl CONTRERAS Arrau (80 Ángel Orlando ROJAS Ortega), José Manuel ROJAS Bahamondes, Mauricio Bernardo VICTORINO Dansilio, Manuel Rolando ITURRA Urrutía, Wálter Damián MONTILLO, Felipe Ignatio SEYMOUR Dobud (86 Nelson Alejandro PINTO Martínez), Edson Raúl PUCH Cortez, Juan Manuel OLIVERA López (67 Diego Gabriel RIVAROLA Popon). DT: Gerardo PELUSO
Goals: Omar ARELLANO Riverón (52) / Rafael Andrés OLARRA Guerrero (47).

CF UNIVERSIDAD DE CHILE – CD "CHIVES" GUADALAJARA 0-2 (0-1)
Estadio Nacional Julio Martínez Prádanos, Santiago, 3.08.2010
Referee: Sergio Fabián Pezzotta (ARG), Attendance: 40.060
CF UNIVERSIDAD DE CHILE: Miguel Angel PINTO Jérez, Matías Nicolás RODRÍGUEZ, Rafael Andrés OLARRA Guerrero (74 Eduardo Jesús VARGAS Rojas), José Raúl CONTRERAS Arrau (46 Diego Gabriel RIVAROLA Popon), José Manuel ROJAS Bahamondes (63 Ángel Orlando ROJAS Ortega), Mauricio Bernardo VICTORINO Dansilio, Manuel Rolando ITURRA Urrutía, Wálter Damián MONTILLO, Felipe Ignatio SEYMOUR Dobud, Edson Raúl PUCH Cortez, Juan Manuel OLIVERA López. DT: Gerardo PELUSO
CD GUADALAJARA SA: Luis Ernesto MICHEL Vergara, José Jonny MAGALLÓN Oliva, Édgar Eduardo MEJÍA Viruete, Héctor REYNOSO López, Patricio Gabriel ARAÚJO Vázquez, Mario Humberto DE LUNA Saucedo, Miguel Ángel PONCE Briseño, Xavier Iván BÁEZ Gamiño, Omar BRAVO Tordecillas (90+1 Ricardo Michel VÁZQUEZ Gallien), Adolfo BAUTISTA Herrera (82 Ulises Alejandro DÁVILA Plascencia), Marco Jhonfai FABIÁN de la Mora (86 Dionicio Manuel ESCALANTE Moreno). DT: José Luis REAL Casillas
Goals: Xavier Iván BÁEZ Gamiño (22), José Jonny MAGALLÓN Oliva (55).

SC INTERNACIONAL – SÃO PAULO FC 1-0 (0-0)
Estádio José Pinheiro Borda (Beira-Rio), Porto Alegre, 28.07.2010
Referee: Héctor Wálter Baldassi (ARG), Attendance: 48.166
SC INTERNACIONAL: RENAN Brito Soares, Fabián Guedes "BOLÍVAR", Claudinei Cardoso Félix da Silva "NEI", KLÉBER de Carvalho Correa, Marcos Antônio de Lima "ÍNDIO", Andrés Nicolás D'ALESSANDRO, Pablo Horacio GUIÑAZÚ, André Luiz Tavares "ANDREZINHO" (64 GIULIANO Victor de Paula), SANDRO Guimaraes Cordeiro Ranieri, TAISON Barcellos Freda (86 RAFAEL Augusto SÓBIS do Nascimento), ALECSANDRO Barbosa Felisbino. DT: CELSO Juarez ROTH
SÃO PAULO FC: ROGÉRIO Rodrigo CENI, João MIRANDA de Souza Filho, JÚNIOR CÉSAR Eduardo Machado, ALEX Sandro da SILVA, RODRIGO Ribeiro SOUTO, RICHARLYSON Barbosa Felisbino (71 CLÉBER SANTANA Loureiro), Anderson HERNANES de Carvalho Andrade Lima, JEAN Raphael Vanderlei de Moreira, MARLOS Romero Bonfim (83 Luiz Fernando Pereira da Silva "FERNANDINHO"), Fernando Lúcio da Costa "FERNANDÃO", DAGOBERTO Pelentie (72 "RICARDO OLIVEIRA" Iomar do Nascimento). DT: Raymundo RICARDO GOMES
Goal: GIULIANO Victor de Paula (68).

SÃO PAULO FC – SC INTERNACIONAL 2-1 (1-0)
Estádio Cícero Pompeu de Toledo (Morumbi), São Paulo, 5.08.2010
Referee: Carlos Arecio AMARILLA Demarqui (PAR), Attendance: 62.129
SÃO PAULO FC: ROGÉRIO Rodrigo CENI, João MIRANDA de Souza Filho, JÚNIOR CÉSAR Eduardo Machado, ALEX Sandro da SILVA, RODRIGO Ribeiro SOUTO (87 Marcelo dos Santos "MARCELINHO PARAÍBA"), Anderson HERNANES de Carvalho Andrade Lima, CLÉBER SANTANA Loureiro (73 MARLOS Romero Bonfim), JEAN Raphael Vanderlei de Moreira, "RICARDO OLIVEIRA" Iomar do Nascimento, Fernando Lúcio da Costa "FERNANDÃO", DAGOBERTO Pelentie (81 Luiz Fernando Pereira da Silva "FERNANDINHO").
SC INTERNACIONAL: RENAN Brito Soares, Fabián Guedes "BOLÍVAR", Claudinei Cardoso Félix da Silva "NEI", KLÉBER de Carvalho Correa, Marcos Antônio de Lima "ÍNDIO", Andrés Nicolás D'ALESSANDRO (78 GIULIANO Victor de Paula), Paulo César Fonseca do Nascimento "TINGA", Pablo Horacio GUIÑAZÚ, SANDRO Guimaraes Cordeiro Ranieri, TAISON Barcellos Freda (89 WILSON TIAGO Mathías), ALECSANDRO Barbosa Felisbino. DT: CELSO Juarez ROTH
Sent off: Tinga (79)
Goals: ALEX Sandro da SILVA (30), "RICARDO OLIVEIRA" Iomar do Nascimento (54) / ALECSANDRO Barbosa Felisbino (52).

FINALS

CD "CHIVAS" GUADALAJARA – SC INTERNACIONAL 1-2 (1-0)
Estadio Omnilife, Zapopan, 11.08.2010
Referee: Héctor Wálter BALDASSI (ARG), Attendance: 30.870
CD GUADALAJARA: Luis Ernesto MICHEL Vergara, José Jonny MAGALLÓN Oliva, Édgar Eduardo MEJÍA Viruete, Héctor REYNOSO López, Mario Humberto DE LUNA Saucedo, Miguel Ángel PONCE Briseño, Xavier Iván BÁEZ Gamiño (86 Ulises Alejandro DÁVILA Plascencia), Omar BRAVO Tordecillas, Adolfo BAUTISTA Herrera, Omar ARELLANO Riverón (69 Patricio Gabriel ARAÚJO Vázquez), Marco Jhonfai FABIÁN de la Mora (79 Dionicio Manuel ESCALANTE Moreno). DT: José Luis REAL Casillas
SC INTERNACIONAL: RENAN Brito Soares, Fabián Guedes "BOLÍVAR", Claudinei Cardoso Félix da Silva "NEI", KLÉBER de Carvalho Correa, Marcos Antônio de Lima "ÍNDIO", Andrés Nicolás D'ALESSANDRO, Pablo Horacio GUIÑAZÚ, GIULIANO Victor de Paula, SANDRO Guimaraes Cordeiro Ranieri, TAISON Barcellos Freda (86 WILSON TIAGO Mathías), ALECSANDRO Barbosa Felisbino (34 EVERTON Santos da Costa, 72 RAFAEL Augusto SÓBIS do Nascimento).
Goals: Adolfo BAUTISTA Herrera (45+2) /
GIULIANO Victor de Paula (73), Fabián Guedes "BOLÍVAR" (76).

SC INTERNACIONAL – CD "CHIVAS" GUADALAJARA 3-2 (0-1)
Estádio José Pinheiro Borba (Beira-Rio), Porto Alegre, 18.08.2010
Referee: Óscar Julián RUÍZ Acosta (COL), Attendance: 56.000
SC INTERNACIONAL: RENAN Brito Soares, Fabián Guedes "BOLÍVAR", Claudinei Cardoso Félix da Silva "NEI", KLÉBER de Carvalho Correa, Marcos Antônio de Lima "ÍNDIO", Andrés Nicolás D'ALESSANDRO, Paulo César Fonseca do Nascimento "TINGA" (84 WILSON TIAGO Mathías), Pablo Horacio GUIÑAZÚ, SANDRO Guimaraes Cordeiro Ranieri, RAFAEL Augusto SÓBIS do Nascimento (72 LEANDRO DAMIÃO da Silva dos Santos), TAISON Barcellos Freda (65 GIULIANO Victor de Paula). DT: CELSO Juarez ROTH
CD GUADALAJARA: Luis Ernesto MICHEL Vergara, José Jonny MAGALLÓN Oliva, Héctor REYNOSO López, Patricio Gabriel ARAÚJO Vázquez, Mario Humberto DE LUNA Saucedo, Miguel Ángel PONCE Briseño (78 Dionicio Manuel ESCALANTE Moreno), Xavier Iván BÁEZ Gamiño (81 Ricardo Michel VÁZQUEZ Gallien), Omar BRAVO Tordecillas, Adolfo BAUTISTA Herrera, Omar ARELLANO Riverón, Marco Jhonfai FABIÁN de la Mora. DT: José Luis REAL Casillas
Sent off: Arellano (86)
Goals: RAFAEL Augusto SÓBIS do Nascimento (61), LEANDRO DAMIÃO da Silva dos Santos (76), GIULIANO Victor de Paula (89) /
Marco Jhonfai FABIÁN de la Mora (43), Omar BRAVO Tordecillas (90+2).

2011

FIRST STAGE

CA INDEPENDIENTE AVELLANEDA – SD QUITO 2-0 (0-0)
Estadio Libertadores de América, Avellaneda, 25.01.2011
Referee: Héber Roberto LOPES (BRA), Attendance: 16.844
CA INDEPENDIENTE AVELLANEDA: Hilario Bernardo NAVARRO, Carlos Javier MATHEU, Lucas Armando MAREQUE, Maximiliano Nicolás VELÁZQUEZ (20 Patricio Julián RODRÍGUEZ), Eduardo Nicolás TUZZIO, Julián Albert VELÁZQUEZ, Roberto Miguel BATTIÓN, Nicolás Alejandro CABRERA, Néstor Andrés SILVERA (83 Alberto Martín GÓMEZ), Matías Adrian DEFEDERICO (69 Cristian Alberto PELLERANO), Facundo Manuel PARRA. DT: Antonio R. MOHAMED Matijevich
SD QUITO: Marcelo Ramón ELIZAGA Ferrero, Pedro Luis ESTERILLA Delgado (81 Roberto Michael CASTRO Cadena), Mariano Florencio MINA Orobio, Luis Armando CHECA Villamar, Isaac Bryan MINA Arboleda, Segundo Alejandro CASTILLO, Luis Fernando SARITAMA Padilla, Michael Jackson QUIÑÓNEZ Cabeza (66 Gustavo Ariel RODAS), Alex Leonardo BOLAÑOS Reascos, Julio Maximiliano BEVACQUA (57 Luis Alberto PEREA Pérez), Juan Carlos PAREDES Reasco. DT: Luis Fabián BUSTOS
Goals: Matías Adrian DEFEDERICO (49), Patricio Julián RODRÍGUEZ (70).

SD QUITO – CA INDEPENDIENTE AVELLANEDA 1-0 (0-0)
Estadio Olímpico Atahualpa, Quito, 1.02.2011
Referee: Jorge Luis LARRIONDA Pietrafesa (URU), Attendance: 12.029
SD QUITO: Marcelo Ramón ELIZAGA Ferrero, Jayro Rolando CAMPOS Leon, Luis Armando CHECA Villamar, Isaac Bryan MINA Arboleda, Segundo Alejandro CASTILLO, Luis Fernando SARITAMA Padilla, Gustavo Ariel RODAS (62 Gonzalo Eduardo ROVIRA), Tilson Oswaldo MINDA Suscal (79 Ángel Gabriel ESCOBAR Arce), Julio Maximiliano BEVACQUA, Luis Alberto PEREA Pérez, Juan Carlos PAREDES Reasco (55 Michael Jackson QUIÑÓNEZ Cabeza). DT: Luis Fabián BUSTOS
CA INDEPENDIENTE AVELLANEDA: Hilario Bernardo NAVARRO, Carlos Javier MATHEU, Lucas Armando MAREQUE, Eduardo Nicolás TUZZIO, Julián Albert VELÁZQUEZ, Roberto Miguel BATTIÓN, Nicolás Alejandro CABRERA, Fernando Gabriel GODOY (68 Cristian Alberto PELLERANO), Néstor Andrés SILVERA, Matías Adrian DEFEDERICO (76 Patricio Julián RODRÍGUEZ), Facundo Manuel PARRA (65 Maximiliano Nicolás VELÁZQUEZ). DT: Antonio Ricardo MOHAMED Matijevich
Goal: Michael Jackson QUIÑÓNEZ Cabeza (56).

CLUB ALIANZA LIMA – CF JAGUARES DE CHIAPAS SA 0-2 (0-2)
Estadio Alejandro Villanueva, Lima, 26.01.2011
Referee: Néstor Fabian PITANA (ARG), Attendance: 28.285
CLUB ALIANZA LIMA: Salomón Alexis LIBMAN Pastor, Leandro Roberto FLEITAS, Christian Guillermo RAMOS Garagay, Paolo Giancarlo DE LA HAZA Urquiza, Édgar VILLAMARÍN Arguedas, Édgar Daniel GONZÁLEZ Britez, Henry Edson QUINTEROS Sanchez (46 César Junior VIZA Seminario), Alexander Gustavo SÁNCHEZ Reyes, Jean Carlos TRAGODARA Gálvez, Hernán Gastón PEIRONE (60 David Leonardo CASTRO Cortés), Roberto OVELAR Maldonado (35 Cristofer Augusto Jesús SOTO Gonzáles). DT: Gustavo Adolfo COSTAS Makeira
CF JAGUARES DE CHIAPAS SA: Gerardo Daniel RUÍZ Barragán, Óscar Francisco RAZO Ventura, Omar Alejandro FLORES Serrano, Miguel Ángel MARTÍNEZ, Christian de Jesús VALDÉZ Loaiza, Guillermo ROJAS Rumilla, Damián Alejandro MANSO, Luis Ricardo ESQUEDA Ornelas (74 Marvin Gabriel CABRERA Ibarra), Jorge Marcelo RODRÍGUEZ Núñez (79 Alan Miguel ZAMORA González), Jackson Arley MARTÍNEZ Valencia (8 Antonio Michael PEDROZA Whitham), Jorge Daniel HERNÁNDEZ Govea. DT: José Guadalupe CRUZ Núnez
Goals: Antonio Michael PEDROZA Whitham (41), Jorge Marcelo RODRÍGUEZ Núñez (45+1 pen).

CF JAGUARES DE CHIAPAS SA – CLUB ALIANZA LIMA 2-0 (0-0)
Estadio Zoque Víctor Manuel Reyna, Tuxtla Gutiérrez, 1.02.2011
Referee: José Hernando BUITRAGO Arango (COL), Attendance: 6.800
CF JAGUARES DE CHIAPAS SA: Gerardo Daniel RUÍZ Barragán, Ismael Ignacio FUENTES Castro, Marvin Gabriel CABRERA Ibarra (50 Christian de Jesús VALDÉZ Loaiza), Óscar Francisco RAZO Ventura, Miguel Ángel MARTÍNEZ, Guillermo ROJAS Rumilla, Damián Alejandro MANSO (64 Antonio SALAZAR Castillo), Jorge Marcelo RODRÍGUEZ Núñez, Alan Miguel ZAMORA González (57 Luis Ricardo ESQUEDA Ornelas), Antonio Michael PEDROZA Whitham, Jorge Daniel HERNÁNDEZ Govea. DT: José Guadalupe CRUZ Núnez
CLUB ALIANZA LIMA: Salomón Alexis LIBMAN Pastor, Leandro Roberto FLEITAS, Christian Guillermo RAMOS Garagay, Paolo Giancarlo DE LA HAZA Urquiza, Édgar VILLAMARÍN Arguedas, Édgar Daniel GONZÁLEZ Britez, Alexander Gustavo SÁNCHEZ Reyes, Luis Enrique TRUJILLO Ortiz, César Junior VIZA Seminario (46 Óscar Christopher VÍLCHEZ Soto), Jean Carlos TRAGODARA Gálvez (67 David Leonardo CASTRO Cortés), Hernán Gastón PEIRONE (83 Henry Edson QUINTEROS Sanchez). DT: Gustavo Adolfo COSTAS Makeira
Sent off: Villamarín (28)
Goals: Antonio Michael PEDROZA Whitham (68), Antonio SALAZAR Castillo (74).

CS CORINTHIANS PAULISTA – CC DEPORTES TOLIMA 0-0
Estádio Municipal Paulo Machado de Carvalho (Pacaembu), São Paulo, 26.01.2011
Referee: Enrique Roberto OSSES Zencovich (CHI), Attendance: 26.536
CS CORINTHIANS PAULISTA: JÚLIO CÉSAR de Souza Santos, ROBERTO CARLOS da Silva (73 MARCELO OLIVEIRA Ferreira), Anderson Sebastião Cardoso "CHICÃO", ALESSANDRO Mori Nunes, LEANDRO CASTAN da Silva, RALF de Souza Teles, BRUNO CÉSAR Zanaki (56 EDNO Roberto Cunha), JUCILEI da Silva, RONALDO Luís Nazário de Lima, JORGE HENRIQUE de Souza, Bruno Ferreira Bomfin "DETINHO" (79 DANILO Gabriel de Andrade). DT: Adenor Léonardo Bachi "TITE"
CC DEPORTES TOLIMA: Antony Domingo SILVA Cano, Gerardo Enrique VALLEJO Metaute, Félix Enrique NOGUERA Collante, Julián HURTADO Izquierdo, Yair ARRECHEA Amú, Elkin Antonio MURILLO Amor (85 Danny Manuel SANTOYA Otero), Rafael Arlex CASTILLO Galvis (67 Christian Camilo MARRUGO Rodríguez), Diego Ferney CHARÁ Zamora, Gustavo Adolfo BOLÍVAR Zapata, Jhon Fredy HURTADO, Wilder Andrés MEDINA Tamayo (77 Pablo Júnior GIMÉNEZ). DT: Hernán TORRES Oliveros

CC DEPORTES TOLIMA – CA CORINTHIANS PAULISTA 2-0 (0-0)
Estadio Manuel Murillo Toro, Ibagué, 2.02.2011
Referee: Roberto Carlos SILVERA Calcerrada (URU), Attendance: 15.014
CC DEPORTES TOLIMA: Antony Domingo SILVA Cano, Gerardo Enrique VALLEJO Metaute, Félix Enrique NOGUERA Collante, Julián HURTADO Izquierdo, Yair ARRECHEA Amú, Elkin Antonio MURILLO Amor (83 Marlon Javier PIEDRAHITA Londoño), Rafael Arlex CASTILLO Galvis (58 Danny Manuel SANTOYA Otero), Diego Ferney CHARÁ Zamora, Gustavo Adolfo BOLÍVAR Zapata, Jhon Fredy HURTADO, Wilder Andrés MEDINA Tamayo (89 Luis Alberto CLOSA González). DT: Hernán TORRES Oliveros
CS CORINTHIANS PAULISTA: JÚLIO CÉSAR de Souza Santos, FÁBIO SANTOS Romeu (80 EDNO Roberto Cunha), Anderson Sebastião Cardoso "CHICÃO", ALESSANDRO Mori Nunes, LEANDRO CASTAN da Silva, José Paulo Bezerra Maciel Júnior "PAULINHO" (70 DANILO Gabriel de Andrade), RALF de Souza Teles, JUCILEI da Silva, RONALDO Luís Nazário de Lima, JORGE HENRIQUE de Souza, Bruno Ferreira Bomfin "DETINHO" (70 Luís Alberto "Cachito" RAMÍREZ Lucay). DT: Adenor Léonardo Bachi "TITE"
Sent off: Ramírez (72)
Goals: Danny Manuel SANTOYA Otero (65), Wilder Andrés MEDINA Tamayo (77).

LIVERPOOL FC – GRÊMIO FOOT-BALL PORTO ALEGRENSE 2-2 (2-1)
Estadio Centenario, Montevideo, 26.01.2011
Referee: Carlos Manuel TORRES Nuñez (PAR), Attendance: 13.875
LIVERPOOL FC: Matías Fidel CASTRO Fuentes, Juan Daniel ÁLVEZ Ortiz, Hugo Fernando SOUZA Días, Maximiliano Felipe MONTERO Rodríguez, Jhonatan Daniel SOUZA MOTTA Montero, Mauricio Damián FELIPE Herrera, Hernán FIGUEREDO Alonzo (88 Christian SILVERA González), Carlos Germán MACCHI Vacelaire, Alfredo Nicolás GUEVARA (46 Johnatan BLANES Núñez), Emiliano ALFARO Toscano, Maureen Javier FRANCO Alonso (78 Elías Ricardo FIGUERA Silva). DT: Eduardo Jorge FAVARO Carbajal
GRÊMIO FOOT-BALL PORTO ALEGRENSE: VÍCTOR Leandro Bagy, RAFAEL MARQUES Pinto, GABRIEL Rodrigues dos Santos, LÚCIO Carlos Cajeiro Souza, VILSON Xavier de Menezes Júnior, Paulo Marcos de Jesús Ribeiro "PAULÃO", GÍLSON Gomes do Nascimento (81 DIEGO José CLEMENTINO), FÁBIO ROCHEMBACK, DOUGLAS dos Santos, ANDRÉ Luiz Barreto Silva LIMA (87 LINS Lima de Brito), Luiz Severo JÚNIOR "VIÇOSA" (59 VINÍCIUS PACHECO dos Santos). DT: RENATO "GAÚCHO" Portaluppi
Goals: Maureen Javier FRANCO Alonso (9), Carlos Germán MACCHI Vacelaire (25) / ANDRÉ Luiz Barreto Silva LIMA (6), DOUGLAS dos Santos (13).

GRÊMIO FOOT-BALL PORTO ALEGRENSE – LIVERPOOL FC 3-1 (1-1)
Estádio Olímpico Monumental, Porto Alegre, 2.02.2011
Referee: Sergio Fabián PEZZOTTA (ARG), Attendance: 31.426
GRÊMIO FOOT-BALL PORTO ALEGRENSE: VÍCTOR Leandro Bagy, RAFAEL MARQUES Pinto, GABRIEL Rodrigues dos Santos, LÚCIO Carlos Cajeiro Souza, BRUNO Bairros COLLAÇO, Paulo Marcos de Jesús Ribeiro "PAULÃO", FÁBIO ROCHEMBACK, ADÍLSON Warken (37 VINÍCIUS PACHECO dos Santos), DOUGLAS dos Santos, ANDRÉ Luiz Barreto Silva LIMA (86 DIEGO José CLEMENTINO), Luiz Severo JÚNIOR "VIÇOSA" (89 LINS Lima de Brito). DT: RENATO "GAÚCHO" Portaluppi
LIVERPOOL FC: Matías Fidel CASTRO Fuentes, Juan Daniel ÁLVEZ Ortiz, Hugo Fernando SOUZA Días, Maximiliano Felipe MONTERO Rodríguez (34 Hernán FIGUEREDO Alonzo), Fernando Martín BONJOUR, Jhonatan Daniel SOUZA MOTTA Montero, Mauricio Damián FELIPE Herrera (70 Johnatan BLANES Núñez), David Michael ACOSTA Márquez, Carlos Germán MACCHI Vacelaire (75 Renzo Daniel POZZI Palombo), Emiliano ALFARO Toscano, Maureen Javier FRANCO Alonso. DT: Eduardo Jorge FAVARO Carbajal
Sent off: Acosta (55)
Goals: ANDRÉ Luiz Barreto Silva LIMA (37), VINÍCIUS PACHECO dos Santos (57, 73) / Emiliano ALFARO Toscano (34).

CLUB CERRO PORTEÑO – DEPORTIVO PETARE FC 1-0 (0-0)
Estadio General Pablo Rojas, Asunción, 27.01.2011
Referee: Paulo César DE OLIVEIRA (BRA), Attendance: 15.663
CLUB CERRO PORTEÑO: Diego Daniel BARRETO Cáceres, Mariano Esteban UGLESSICH, Luís Carlos CARDOZO Espillaga, Lautaro Roque FORMICA, Iván Rodrigo PIRIS Leguizamón, César Iván BENÍTEZ León, Julio Daniel DOS SANTOS Rodríguez (78 Luís Enrique CÁCERES Centurión), Javier Alejandro VILLARREAL, Jorge Daniel NÚÑEZ Espínola (63 Jonathan FABBRO), Juan Manuel LUCERO (69 Diego MADRIGAL Rica), Roberto Antonio NANNI. DT: Javier Luis TORRENTE
DEPORTIVO PETARE FC: Alan José LIEBESKIND Díaz, David Andrew McINTOSH Parra, Marcelo Omar MAIDANA, Andrés Elionai SÁNCHEZ León, Rafael Antonio LOBO Espino, Evelio de Jesús HERNÁNDEZ Guedez (69 Alain Giancarlo GIROLLETI Nardali), Bladimir Alejandro MORALES Duarte, Gianfranco DI JULIO Bartolomeo (79 Yohnjer Iván GUERRERO Zambrano), Felix Mauel CÁSSERES, Alex SINISTERRA Villa (66 Ricard José BLANCO Delgado), Víctor Alfonso GUAZÁ Lucumí. DT: Eduardo SARAGÓ
Goal: Roberto Antonio NANNI (70).

DEPORTIVO PETARE FC – CLUB CERRO PORTEÑO 1-1 (1-1)
Estadio Olímpico de la UCV, Caracas, 3.02.2011
Referee: Carlos Alfredo VERA Rodríquez (ECU), Attendance: 2.897
DEPORTIVO PETARE FC: Alan José LIEBESKIND Díaz, David Andrew McINTOSH Parra, Marcelo Omar MAIDANA, Andrés Elionai SÁNCHEZ León, Rafael Antonio LOBO Espino (73 John Alexis CÓRDOBA Alvaláez), Evelio de Jesús HERNÁNDEZ Guedez, Bladimir Alejandro MORALES Duarte (64 Yohnjer Iván GUERRERO Zambrano), Alain Giancarlo GIROLLETI Nardali (86 Nolberto RIASCOS Segura), Felix Mauel CÁSSERES, Víctor Alfonso GUAZÁ Lucumí, Ricard José BLANCO Delgado. DT: Eduardo SARAGÓ
CLUB CERRO PORTEÑO: Diego Daniel BARRETO Cáceres, Mariano Esteban UGLESSICH, Luís Carlos CARDOZO Espillaga, Lautaro Roque FORMICA, Iván Rodrigo PIRIS Leguizamón, César Iván BENÍTEZ León, Julio Daniel DOS SANTOS Rodríguez (79 Rodrigo Ramon BURGOS), Javier Alejandro VILLARREAL, Jorge Daniel NÚÑEZ Espínola, Juan Manuel LUCERO (66 Jonathan FABBRO), Roberto Antonio NANNI (71 Fredy José BAREIRO Gamarra). DT: Javier Luis TORRENTE
Sent off: Córdoba (84)
Goals: Víctor Alfonso GUAZÁ Lucumí (13) / Roberto Antonio NANNI (34).

CLUB BOLÍVAR – UNIÓN ESPAÑOLA S.A.D.P. 0-1 (0-1)
Estadio Hernando Siles, La Paz, 27.01.2011
Referee: Víctor Hugo RIVERA Chavez (PER), Attendance: 20.433
CLUB BOLÍVAR: Marcos Ariel ARGÜELLO, Lorgio ÁLVAREZ Roca, Edemir RODRÍGUEZ Mercado (62 Ronald EGUINO Segovia), Ronald Tylor RIVERO Kuhn, Pablo Javier FRONTINI, Ronald Lázaro "Nacho" GARCÍA Justiniano, Walter Alberto FLORES Condarco (55 Alex Rodrigo DA ROSA Dorneles), Rudy Alejandro CARDOZO Fernández, Abdo REYES Cardozo (67 José MARCELO GÓMES), William FERREIRA Martinez, José "ZÉ" CARLOS da Silva Santos. DT: Guillermo Angel HOYOS
UNIÓN ESPAÑOLA S.A.D.P.: Rainer Klaus WIRTH Castro, Luis Pedro FIGUEROA Sepúlveda, Rafael Andrés OLARRA Guerrero, Fernando Patricio CORDERO Fonseca, Rodolfo Alejandro MADRID González, Leandro Javier DELGADO Plenkovich, Braulio Antonio LEAL Salvo, Gonzalo Andrés VILLAGRA Lira, Martín Ricardo LIGÜERA López (80 Esteban Eduardo GONZÁLEZ Herrera), Leonardo Esteban MONJE Valenzuela (84 Mario Antonio ARAVENA Bonilla), Sebastián Óscar JAIME (72 Diego Martín SCOTTI Ponce de León). DT: José Luis SIERRA Pando
Sent off: Zé Carlos (81)
Goal: Fernando Patricio CORDERO Fonseca (16).

UNIÓN ESPAÑOLA S.A.D.P. – CLUB BOLÍVAR 0-0
Estadio Santa Laura-Universidad SEK, Santiago, 3.02.2011
Referee: Carlos Arecio AMARILLA Demarqui (PAR), Attendance: 5.245
UNIÓN ESPAÑOLA S.A.D.P.: Rainer Klaus WIRTH Castro, Luis Pedro FIGUEROA Sepúlveda, Rafael Andrés OLARRA Guerrero, Fernando Patricio CORDERO Fonseca (65 Raúl Enrique ESTÉVEZ), Rodolfo Alejandro MADRID González, Leandro Javier DELGADO Plenkovich, Braulio Antonio LEAL Salvo, Gonzalo Andrés VILLAGRA Lira, Martín Ricardo LIGÜERA López, Leonardo Esteban MONJE Valenzuela, Sebastián Óscar JAIME (86 Kevin Andrew HARBOTTLE Carrasco). DT: José Luis SIERRA Pando
CLUB BOLÍVAR: Marcos Ariel ARGÜELLO, Lorgio ÁLVAREZ Roca, Edemir RODRÍGUEZ Mercado, Ronald Tylor RIVERO Kuhn, Pablo Javier FRONTINI, Ronald Lázaro "Nacho" GARCÍA Justiniano, Alex Rodrigo DA ROSA Dorneles (46 Rodrigo VARGAS Touchard),Walter Alberto FLORES Condarco, José MARCELO GÓMES (66 Juan Enrique BUSTILLOS Bozo), Rudy Alejandro CARDOZO Fernández, Abdo REYES Cardozo (27 Diego Gabriel RIVERO Cortéz). DT: Guillermo Angel HOYOS
Sent off: García (67)

SECOND PHASE

GROUP 1

SAN LUIS FC – CLUB LIBERTAD ASUNCIÓN 1-2 (1-1)
Estadio Alfonso Lastras Ramírez, San Luis Potosí, 15.02.2011
Referee: José Hernando BUITRAGO Arango (COL), Attendance: 12.198
SAN LUIS FC: Carlos Alberto TREJO Sánchez, Christian Emmanuel SÁNCHEZ Narváez (82 Jesús Antonio ISIJARA Rodríguez), Aníbal Samuel MATELLÁN, Juan Ezequiel CUEVAS, Ignacio TORRES Olvera, Carlos Alberto HURTADO Arteaga, Sergio Amaury PONCE Villegas, Michael Antonio ARROYO Mina (67 Víctor Hugo LOJERO Alexanderson), Noé MAYA Vilches (78 Othoniel ARCE Jaramillo), Wilmer Alexander AGUIRRE Vazquez, Juan Manuel CAVALLO. DT: Marcos Ignacio AMBRIZ Espinoza
CLUB LIBERTAD ASUNCIÓN: Tobías Antonio VARGAS Insfrán, Carlos BONET Cacéres, Pedro Paulo PORTOCARRERO Angulo, Arnaldo Andrés VERA Chamorro, Sergio Daniel AQUINO, Víctor Javier CÁCERES Centurión, Miguel Ángel Ramon SAMUDIO, Jorge Daniel GONZÁLEZ Marquet (42 Juan Rodrigo ROJAS Ovelar), Nicolás PAVLOVICH, Manuel José MACIEL Fernández (56 Ángel Reinaldo ORUÉ Echeverría), Rodolfo Vicente GAMARRA Varela (46 Omar Heber POUSO Osores). DT: Gregorio Elso PÉREZ Perdigón
Sent off: Torres (84)
Goals: Juan Manuel CAVALLO (38) /
Nicolás PAVLOVICH (18), Sergio Daniel AQUINO (54 penalty).

CD ONCE CALDAS – CD UNIVERSIDAD SAN MARTÍN DE PORRES 0-3 (0-2)
Estadio Palogrande, Manizales, 16.02.2011
Referee: Sergio Fabián PEZZOTTA (ARG), Attendance: 7.689
CD ONCE CALDAS: Luis Enrique MARTÍNEZ Rodríguez, Alexis Héctor HENRÍQUEZ Charales, Luis Alberto NÚÑEZ Charales (58 John Fredy PAJOY Ortíz), Elkin Darío CALLE Grajales (73 Yedinson PALACIOS León), Diego Armando AMAYA Solano, Mario Alejandro GONZÁLEZ Castro, Félix Andrés MICOLTA Micolta, Alexander MEJÍA Sabalsa, Claudio Matías MIRABAJE Correa (46 Carlos Andrés RAMÍREZ Aguirre), Dayro Mauricio MORENO Galindo, Carlos Mario CARBONERO Mancilla. DT: Juan Carlos OSORIO Arbeláez
CD UNIVERSIDAD SAN MARTÍN DE PORRES: Ricardo Daniel FARRO Caballero, Guillermo Alejandro GUIZASOLA La Rosa, Orlando CONTRERAS Collantes, Adán Adolfo BALBÍN Silva, Aldo Sebastián CORZO Chávez, Julio César MOREYRA, Ronald QUINTEROS Sánchez, John Christopher HINOSTROZA Guzmán, Carlos Osvaldo FERNÁNDEZ Maldonando (88 Walter Milciades FRETES Bogar), Héber Alberto ARRIOLA Ruiz Díaz, Germán Ariel ALEMANNO (71 Alberto Gianfranco LABARTHE Tome). DT: Aníbal RUÍZ Leites
Goals: Héber Alberto ARRIOLA Ruiz Díaz (37, 59), 0-2 Germán Ariel ALEMANNO (41)

CD UNIVERSIDAD SAN MARTÍN DE PORRES – SAN LUIS FC 2-0 (0-0)
Estadio Miguel Grau del Callao, Callao, 22.02.2011
Referee: Wilson Luiz SENEME (BRA), Attendance: 6.000
CD UNIVERSIDAD SAN MARTÍN DE PORRES: Ricardo Daniel FARRO Caballero, Guillermo Alejandro GUIZASOLA La Rosa, Orlando CONTRERAS Collantes, Adán Adolfo BALBÍN Silva, Aldo Sebastián CORZO Chávez, Julio César MOREYRA, Ronald QUINTEROS Sánchez, John Christopher HINOSTROZA Guzmán, Carlos Osvaldo FERNÁNDEZ Maldonando (72 Carlos Ariel MARINELLI), Héber Alberto ARRIOLA Ruiz Díaz (55 Christian Alberto CUEVA Bravo), Germán Ariel ALEMANNO (73 Alberto Gianfranco LABARTHE Tome). DT: Aníbal RUÍZ Leites
SAN LUIS FC: Carlos Alberto TREJO Sánchez, Osmar MARES Martínez, Luis Omar HERNÁNDEZ Hernández, Aníbal Samuel MATELLÁN, Jaime CORREA Cordoba, Juan Ezequiel CUEVAS (75 Víctor Hugo LOJERO Alexanderson), Sergio Amaury PONCE Villegas, Noé MAYA Vilches, Wilmer Alexander AGUIRRE Vazquez (66 Juan Carlos MEDINA Alonso), Juan Manuel CAVALLO, Othoniel ARCE Jaramillo (55 Michael Antonio ARROYO Mina). DT: Marcos Ignacio AMBRIZ Espinoza
Goals: Alberto Gianfranco LABARTHE Tome (84), Carlos Ariel MARINELLI (89).

CD ONCE CALDAS – CLUB LIBERTAD ASUNCIÓN 1-1 (1-0)
Estadio Palogrande, Manizales, 22.02.2011
Referee: Saúl Esteban LAVERNI (ARG), Attendance: 6.226
CD ONCE CALDAS: Luis Enrique MARTÍNEZ Rodríguez, Alexis Héctor HENRÍQUEZ Charales, Luis Alberto NÚÑEZ Charales (78 Jefferson CUERO Castro), Elkin Darío CALLE Grajales, Diego Armando AMAYA Solano, Carlos Andrés RAMÍREZ Aguirre, Félix Andrés MICOLTA Micolta (66 John Fredy PAJOY Ortíz), Alexander MEJÍA Sabalsa, Hárrison Steve HENAO Hurtado (81 Diego Alejandro ARANGO Montoya), Dayro Mauricio MORENO Galindo, Carlos Mario CARBONERO Mancilla. DT: Juan Carlos OSORIO Arbeláez
CLUB LIBERTAD ASUNCIÓN: Tobías Antonio VARGAS Insfrán, Carlos BONET Cacéres, Pedro Paulo PORTOCARRERO Angulo, Sergio Daniel AQUINO, Omar Heber POUSO Osores (58 Rodolfo Vicente GAMARRA Varela), Víctor Javier CÁCERES Centurión, Miguel Ángel Ramon SAMUDIO, Juan Rodrigo ROJAS Ovelar (58 Víctor Hugo AYALA Núñez), Ignacio CANUTO, Nicolás PAVLOVICH, Manuel José MACIEL Fernández (70 José Ariel NÚÑEZ Portelli). DT: Gregorio Elso PÉREZ Perdigón
Goals: Dayro Mauricio MORENO Galindo (28) / Víctor Hugo AYALA Núñez (90+4).

SAN LUIS FC – CD ONCE CALDAS 1-1 (1-1)
Estadio Alfonso Lastras Ramírez, San Luis Potosí, 2.03.2011
Referee: Jorge Joaquín ANTEQUERA Castedo (BOL), Attendance: 6.522
SAN LUIS FC: César Amado LOZANO Figueroa, Osmar MARES Martínez, Luis Omar HERNÁNDEZ Hernández, Aníbal Samuel MATELLÁN, Juan Ezequiel CUEVAS (81 Carlos Alberto HURTADO Arteaga), Sergio Amaury PONCE Villegas, Michael Antonio ARROYO Mina, Isai ARREDONDO Fainsod (71 Víctor Hugo LOJERO Alexanderson), Noé MAYA Vilches, Juan Manuel CAVALLO (65 Juan Carlos MEDINA Alonso), Othoniel ARCE Jaramillo. DT: Marcos Ignacio AMBRIZ Espinoza
CD ONCE CALDAS: Luis Enrique MARTÍNEZ Rodríguez, Alexis Héctor HENRÍQUEZ Charales, Luis Alberto NÚÑEZ Charales, Elkin Darío CALLE Grajales, Diego Armando AMAYA Solano, Alexander MEJÍA Sabalsa, Claudio Matías MIRABAJE Correa (56 Félix Andrés MICOLTA Micolta), Hárrison Steve HENAO Hurtado (71 Mario Alejandro GONZÁLEZ Castro), Dayro Mauricio MORENO Galindo, Wason Libardo RENTERÍA Cuesta (87 Diego Alejandro ARANGO Montoya), Carlos Mario CARBONERO Mancilla. DT: Juan Carlos OSORIO Arbeláez
Goals: Michael Antonio ARROYO Mina (17) / Wason Libardo RENTERÍA Cuesta (2).

CLUB LIBERTAD ASUNCIÓN – CD UNIVERSIDAD SAN MARTÍN DE PORRES 5-1 (3-1)
Estadio Dr. Nicolás Léoz, Asunción, 8.03.2011
Referee: Roberto Carlos SILVERA Calcerrada (URU), Attendance: 2.317
CLUB LIBERTAD ASUNCIÓN: Tobías Antonio VARGAS Insfrán, Carlos BONET Cacéres (88 Nelson David ROMERO Cárdenas), Pedro Paulo PORTOCARRERO Angulo, Sergio Daniel AQUINO, Víctor Javier CÁCERES Centurión, Miguel Ángel Ramon SAMUDIO, Juan Rodrigo ROJAS Ovelar (73 Omar Heber POUSO Osores), Ignacio CANUTO, Víctor Hugo AYALA Núñez, Manuel José MACIEL Fernández (67 Rodolfo Vicente GAMARRA Varela), Ángel Reinaldo ORUÉ Echeverría. DT: Gregorio Elso PÉREZ Perdigón
CD UNIVERSIDAD SAN MARTÍN DE PORRES: Ricardo Daniel FARRO Caballero, Guillermo Alejandro GUIZASOLA La Rosa, Orlando CONTRERAS Collantes, Adán Adolfo BALBÍN Silva (43 Walter Milciades FRETES Bogar), Aldo Sebastián CORZO Chávez, Julio César MOREYRA, Ronald QUINTEROS Sánchez (61 Christian Alberto CUEVA Bravo), John Christopher HINOSTROZA Guzmán, Carlos Osvaldo FERNÁNDEZ Maldonando (46 Carlos Ariel MARINELLI), Héber Alberto ARRIOLA Ruiz Díaz, Germán Ariel ALEMANNO. DT: Aníbal RUÍZ Leites
Goals: Juan Rodrigo ROJAS Ovelar (14), Ángel Reinaldo ORUÉ Echeverría (18), Manuel José MACIEL Fernández (28), Víctor Hugo AYALA Núñez (50), Omar Heber POUSO Osores (84) / Germán Ariel ALEMANNO (4).

CD UNIVERSISAD SAN MARTÍN DE PORRES – CLUB LIBERTAD ASUNCIÓN 0-1 (0-1)
Estadio Miguel Grau del Callao, Callao, 15.03.2011
Referee: Héber Roberto LOPES (BRA), Attendance: 1.414
CD UNIVERSIDAD SAN MARTÍN DE PORRES: Ricardo Daniel FARRO Caballero, Guillermo Alejandro GUIZASOLA La Rosa, Orlando CONTRERAS Collantes, Adán Adolfo BALBÍN Silva, Aldo Sebastián CORZO Chávez, Julio César MOREYRA, Ronald QUINTEROS Sánchez (73 Alberto Gianfranco LABARTHE Tome), John Christopher HINOSTROZA Guzmán, Christian Alberto CUEVA Bravo (89 Diego Fernando NADAYA), Héber Alberto ARRIOLA Ruiz Díaz (59 Carlos Ariel MARINELLI), Germán Ariel ALEMANNO. DT: Aníbal RUÍZ Leites
CLUB LIBERTAD ASUNCIÓN: Tobías Antonio VARGAS Insfrán, Carlos BONET Cacéres, Pedro Paulo PORTOCARRERO Angulo, Sergio Daniel AQUINO, Víctor Javier CÁCERES Centurión, Miguel Ángel Ramon SAMUDIO, Juan Rodrigo ROJAS Ovelar (69 Omar Heber POUSO Osores), Ignacio CANUTO, Víctor Hugo AYALA Núñez (61 Jorge Daniel GONZÁLEZ Marquet), Nicolás PAVLOVICH (72 Rodolfo Vicente GAMARRA Varela), Manuel José MACIEL Fernández. DT: Gregorio Elso PÉREZ Perdigón
Sent off: Moreyra (24)
Goal: Sergio Daniel AQUINO (23 penalty).

CD ONCE CALDAS – SAN LUIS FC 1-1 (0-0)
Estadio Palogrande, Manizales, 15.03.2011
Referee: Omar Andres PONCE Manzo (ECU), Attendance: 6.906
CD ONCE CALDAS: Luis Enrique MARTÍNEZ Rodríguez, Alexis Héctor HENRÍQUEZ Charales, Luis Alberto NÚÑEZ Charales, Elkin Darío CALLE Grajales, Óliver Antonio FULA Perea, Mario Alejandro GONZÁLEZ Castro (84Arnulfo VALENTIERRA Cuero), Félix Andrés MICOLTA Micolta (62 Claudio Matías MIRABAJE Correa), Alexander MEJÍA Sabalsa (80 Hárrison Steve HENAO Hurtado), Dayro Mauricio MORENO Galindo, Wason Libardo RENTERÍA Cuesta, Carlos Mario CARBONERO Mancilla. DT: Juan Carlos OSORIO Arbeláez
SAN LUIS FC: Carlos Alberto TREJO Sánchez, Juan Carlos MEDINA Alonso, Luis Omar HERNÁNDEZ Hernández, Gabriel Rojo DE LA VEGA Piccolo, Juan Ezequiel CUEVAS (84 Jesús Antonio ISIJARA Rodríguez), Ignacio TORRES Olvera, Sergio Amaury PONCE Villegas, Michael Antonio ARROYO Mina, Noé MAYA Vilches, Víctor Hugo LOJERO Alexanderson, Juan Manuel CAVALLO (62 Isai ARREDONDO Fainsod). DT: Marcos Ignacio AMBRIZ Espinoza
Sent off: Henríquez (88) / Ponce (88)
Goals: Luis Alberto NÚÑEZ Charales (78) / Juan Carlos MEDINA Alonso (90+3).

CLUB LIBERTAD ASUNCIÓN – CD ONCE CALDAS 2-2 (1-2)
Estadio Dr. Nicolás Léoz, Asunción, 22.03.2011
Referee: Líber Tabare PRUDENTE González (URU), Attendance: 1.240
CLUB LIBERTAD ASUNCIÓN: Tobías Antonio VARGAS Insfrán, Carlos BONET Cacéres, Pedro Paulo PORTOCARRERO Angulo (81 Ángel Reinaldo ORUÉ Echeverría), Sergio Daniel AQUINO, Víctor Javier CÁCERES Centurión, Miguel Ángel Ramon SAMUDIO (81 Víctor Hugo AYALA Núñez), Jorge Daniel GONZÁLEZ Marquet (62 Manuel José MACIEL Fernández), Juan Rodrigo ROJAS Ovelar, Ignacio CANUTO, Nicolás PAVLOVICH, Rodolfo Vicente GAMARRA Varela. DT: Gregorio Elso PÉREZ Perdigón
CD ONCE CALDAS: Luis Enrique MARTÍNEZ Rodríguez, Luis Alberto NÚÑEZ Charales, Elkin Darío CALLE Grajales, Diego Armando AMAYA Solano, Carlos Andrés RAMÍREZ Aguirre, Óliver Antonio FULA Perea, Mario Alejandro GONZÁLEZ Castro (55 Hárrison Steve HENAO Hurtado), Alexander MEJÍA Sabalsa, Dayro Mauricio MORENO Galindo, Wason Libardo RENTERÍA Cuesta (81 Claudio Matías MIRABAJE Correa), Carlos Mario CARBONERO Mancilla (72 Félix Andrés MICOLTA Micolta). DT: Juan Carlos OSORIO Arbeláez
Goals: Nicolás PAVLOVICH (15, 90+2) / Wason Libardo RENTERÍA Cuesta (11, 17).

SAN LUIS FC – CD UNIVERSIDAD SAN MARTÍN DE PORRES 3-1 (2-0)
Estadio Alfonso Lastras Ramírez, San Luis Potosí, 22.03.2011
Referee: Diego Hernán ABAL (ARG), Attendance: 2.750
SAN LUIS FC: César Amado LOZANO Figueroa, Juan Carlos MEDINA Alonso (80 Carlos Alberto HURTADO Arteaga), Osmar MARES Martínez, Luis Omar HERNÁNDEZ Hernández, Aníbal Samuel MATELLÁN, Jaime CORREA Cordoba, Juan Ezequiel CUEVAS (70 Víctor Hugo LOJERO Alexanderson), Ignacio TORRES Olvera, Michael Antonio ARROYO Mina, Noé MAYA Vilches, Wilmer Alexander AGUIRRE Vazquez (89 Juan Manuel CAVALLO). DT: M.I. AMBRIZ Espinoza
CD UNIVERSIDAD SAN MARTÍN DE PORRES: Ricardo Daniel FARRO Caballero, Guillermo Alejandro GUIZASOLA La Rosa, Orlando CONTRERAS Collantes, Adán Adolfo BALBÍN Silva (46 Antony Belkier MOLINA Rubio), Aldo Sebastián CORZO Chávez, Carlos Ariel MARINELLI, Walter Milciades FRETES Bogar (46 Christian Alberto CUEVA Bravo), Ronald QUINTEROS Sánchez, John Christopher HINOSTROZA Guzmán, Carlos Osvaldo FERNÁNDEZ Maldonando, Germán Ariel ALEMANNO. DT: Aníbal RUÍZ Leites Sent off: Quinteros (78)
Goals: Juan Carlos MEDINA Alonso (2), Michael Antonio ARROYO Mina (13, 74) / Ronald QUINTEROS Sánchez (60).

CLUB LIBERTAD ASUNCIÓN – SAN LUIS FC 2-0 (2-0)
Estadio Dr. Nicolás Léoz, Asunción, 19.04.2011
Referee: Sálvio Spinola FAGUNDES Filho (BRA), Attendance: 474
CLUB LIBERTAD ASUNCIÓN: Tobías Antonio VARGAS Insfrán, Carlos BONET Cacéres, Pedro Paulo PORTOCARRERO Angulo, Sergio Daniel AQUINO (19 Víctor Hugo AYALA Núñez), Víctor Javier CÁCERES Centurión (41 Omar Heber POUSO Osores), Miguel Ángel Ramon SAMUDIO, Jorge Daniel GONZÁLEZ Marquet, Juan Rodrigo ROJAS Ovelar (65 Rodolfo Vicente GAMARRA Varela), Ignacio CANUTO, Nicolás PAVLOVICH, José Ariel NÚÑEZ Portelli. DT: Gregorio Elso PÉREZ Perdigón
SAN LUIS FC: César Amado LOZANO Figueroa, Juan Carlos MEDINA Alonso (86 Noé MAYA Vilches), Christian Emmanuel SÁNCHEZ Narváez, Osmar MARES Martínez, Aníbal Samuel MATELLÁN, Jaime CORREA Cordoba (54 Daniel ALCÁNTAR García), Juan Ezequiel CUEVAS (82 Juan Manuel CAVALLO),Sergio Amaury PONCE Villegas, Michael Antonio ARROYO Mina, Isai ARREDONDO Fainsod, Wilmer Alexander AGUIRRE Vazquez. DT: Marcos I. AMBRIZ Espinoza
Goals: Jorge Daniel GONZÁLEZ Marquet (10), Nicolás PAVLOVICH (16).

CD UNIVERSIDAD SAN MARTÍN DE PORRES – CD ONCE CALDAS 0-2 (0-1)
Estadio Miguel Grau del Callao, Callao, 19.04.2011
Referee: Enrique Roberto OSSES Zencovich (CHI), Attendance: 1.904
CD UNIVERSIDAD SAN MARTÍN DE PORRES: Ricardo Daniel FARRO Caballero, Guillermo Alejandro GUIZASOLA La Rosa (73 Diego Fernando NADAYA), Orlando CONTRERAS Collantes, Adán Adolfo BALBÍN Silva, Aldo Sebastián CORZO Chávez, Julio César MOREYRA, John Christopher HINOSTROZA Guzmán, Carlos Osvaldo FERNÁNDEZ Maldonando, Christian Alberto CUEVA Bravo, Héber Alberto ARRIOLA Ruiz Díaz (46 Alberto Gianfranco LABARTHE Tome), Germán Ariel ALEMANNO (86 Benjamín UBIERNA Barandiarán). DT: Aníbal RUÍZ Leites
CD ONCE CALDAS: Luis Enrique MARTÍNEZ Rodríguez, Alexis Héctor HENRÍQUEZ Charales, Luis Alberto NÚÑEZ Charales, Elkin Darío CALLE Grajales, Diego Armando AMAYA Solano, Alexander MEJÍA Sabalsa, Claudio Matías MIRABAJE Correa (78 Mario Alejandro GONZÁLEZ Castro), Hárrison Steve HENAO Hurtado, Dayro Mauricio MORENO Galindo, Wason Libardo RENTERÍA Cuesta (90 Óliver Antonio FULA Perea), Carlos Mario CARBONERO Mancilla (85 Félix Andrés MICOLTA Micolta). DT: Juan Carlos OSORIO Arbeláez
Sent off: Balbín (81), Contreras (90)
Goals: Wason Libardo RENTERÍA Cuesta (16), Claudio Matías MIRABAJE Correa (76).

1	LIBERTAD	6	4	2	0	13	5	14
2	ONCE CALDAS	6	1	4	1	7	8	7
3	Universidad San Martín	6	2	0	4	7	11	6
4	San Luís FC	6	1	2	3	6	9	5

GROUP 2

CSD LEÓN DE HUÁNUCO – CPD JUNIOR 1-2 (0-1)
Estadio Heraclio Tapia León, Huánuco, 17.02.2011
Referee: Paulo César DE OLIVEIRA (BRA), Attendance: 11.115
CSD LEÓN DE HUÁNUCO: Juan Ángel FLORES Ascencio, Roller CAMBINDO Ibarra, Luís Felipe CARDOZA Zúñiga, Jorge Martín ARAUJO Paredes (90 Jorge Alfredo LEIVA Urbano), Jair Edson CÉSPEDES Zegarra, José Harrison OTÁLVARO Arce (78 Carlos Roberto ELÍAS Galliani), Jean Franco FERRARI Chiabra, Carlos Alberto ZEGARRA Zamora, Éver Gustavo CHÁVEZ Hernández (46 Víctor Manuel PEÑA Espinoza), Carlos Alberto OREJUELE Pita, Orlando Edmundo RODRÍGUEZ Llorente. DT: Franco Enrique NAVARRO Monteiro
CPD JUNIOR: Mário Sebastián VIERA Galain, César Augusto FAWCETT Lébolo, Sérgio Andrés OTÁLVARO Botero (56 Juan David VALENCIA Hinestroza), ANSELMO de Almeida Machado, Harold MACÍAS Cabrera, Jhon Eduis VIÁFARA Mina (62 Brayner Yesid GARCÍA Leal), Giovanni HERNÁNDEZ Soto, José Antonio AMAYA Pardo, Jossymar Andrés GÓMEZ Pereira, Luis Alfonso PÁEZ Restrepo, Carlos Arturo BACCA Ahumada (77 Julian BARAHONA Angulo). DT: Óscar Héctor QUINTABANI Faggionali
Sent off: Amaya (79)
Goals: Carlos Roberto ELÍAS Galliani (86) /
Jhon Eduis VIAFÁRA Mina (23), Carlos Arturo BACCA Ahumada (65).

GRÊMIO FOOT-BALL PORTO ALEGRENSE – CD ORIENTE PETROLERO 3-0 (1-0)
Estádio Olímpico Monumental, Porto Alegre, 17.02.2011
Referee: Líber Tabare PRUDENTE González (URU), Attendance: 32.791
GRÊMIO FOOT-BALL PORTO ALEGRENSE: VÍCTOR Leandro Bagy, RODOLFO Dantas Bispo, GABRIEL Rodrigues dos Santos, LÚCIO Carlos Cajeiro Souza (84 MAYLSON Barbosa Teixeira), Paulo Marcos de Jesús Ribeiro "PAULÃO", GÍLSON Gomes do Nascimento, FÁBIO ROCHEMBACK, CARLOS ALBERTO Gomes de Jesús (77 ADÍLSON Warken), DOUGLAS dos Santos, ANDRÉ Luiz Barreto Silva LIMA (73 Damián Ariel ESCUDERO), Humberlito BORGES Teixeira. DT: RENATO "GAÚCHO" Portaluppi
CD ORIENTE PETROLERO: Hugo SUÁREZ Vaca, Alejandro Javier SCHIAPPARELLI (35 Alejandro MELEÁN Villarroel), Luis Alberto GUTIÉRREZ Herrera, Miguel Ángel HOYOS Guzmán, Gustavo Martín CAAMAÑO, Diego TERRAZAS Pérez (57 Marcelo Eduardo AGUIRRE Biscaldi), Joselito VACA Velasco, Jhasmany CAMPOS Davalos (70 Alcides PEÑA Jimenez), Mauricio SAUCEDO Guardia, Fernando Javier SAUCEDO Pereyra, Juan Carlos ARCE Justiniano. DT: Ariel Rubén CUFFARO Russo
Goals: DOUGLAS dos Santos (43 penalty, 70), GÍLSON Gomes do Nascimento (48)

CSD LEÓN DE HUÁNUCO – CD ORIENTE PETROLERO 1-0 (1-0)
Estadio Heraclio Tapia León, Huánuco, 23.02.2011
Referee: Marlon Giovanny ESCALANTE Alvarez (VEN), Attendance: 5.964
CSD LEÓN DE HUÁNUCO: Juan Ángel FLORES Ascencio, Roller CAMBINDO Ibarra (69 Jorge Martín ARAUJO Paredes), Luís Felipe CARDOZA Zúñiga, Gianfranco Roberto ESPINOZA Andrade, Jair Edson CÉSPEDES Zegarra, Jean Franco FERRARI Chiabra, Carlos Alberto ZEGARRA Zamora, Carlos Roberto ELÍAS Galliani (61 José Harrison OTÁLVARO Arce), Víctor Manuel PEÑA Espinoza, Carlos Alberto OREJUELE Pita (86 Guillermo Sandro SALAS Suarez), Juan Diego GONZÁLEZ-VIGIL Bentin. DT: Franco Enrique NAVARRO Monteiro
CD ORIENTE PETROLERO: Hugo SUÁREZ Vaca, Luis Alberto GUTIÉRREZ Herrera, Miguel Ángel HOYOS Guzmán, Gustavo Martín CAAMAÑO (84 Fernando Javier SAUCEDO Pereyra), Diego TERRAZAS Pérez (74 Alcides PEÑA Jimenez), Alejandro MELEÁN Villarroel, Joselito VACA Velasco, Jhasmany CAMPOS Davalos, Mauricio SAUCEDO Guardia, Marcelo Eduardo AGUIRRE Biscaldi, Juan Carlos ARCE Justiniano (84 Nicolás Santiago FERNÁNDEZ). DT: Ariel Rubén CUFFARO Russo
Sent off: Gutiérrez (90)
Goal: Carlos Alberto ZEGARRA Zamora (36).

CPD JUNIOR – GRÊMIO FOOT-BALL PORTO ALEGRENSE 2-1 (1-1)
Estadio Metropolitano Roberto Meléndez, Barranquilla, 24.02.2011
Referee: Marco Antonio RODRÍGUEZ Moreno (MEX), Attendance: 20.348
CPD JUNIOR: Carlos Andrés RODRÍGUEZ Ibarra, César Augusto FAWCETT Lébolo, ANSELMO de Almeida Machado, Harold MACÍAS Cabrera, Jhon Eduis VIÁFARA Mina, Giovanni HERNÁNDEZ Soto, Brayner Yesid GARCÍA Leal, Jossymar Andrés GÓMEZ Pereira, Luis Alfonso PÁEZ Restrepo (80 Juan David VALENCIA Hinestroza), Víctor Javier CORTÉS (60 Sherman Andrés CÁRDENAS Estupiñan, 88 Julian BARAHONA Angulo), Carlos Arturo BACCA Ahumada. DT: Óscar Héctor QUINTABANI Faggionali
GRÊMIO FOOT-BALL PORTO ALEGRENSE: VÍCTOR Leandro Bagy, RODOLFO Dantas Bispo, GABRIEL Rodrigues dos Santos, Paulo Marcos de Jesús Ribeiro "PAULÃO", GÍLSON Gomes do Nascimento, FÁBIO ROCHEMBACK, CARLOS ALBERTO Gomes de Jesús (36 BRUNO Bairros COLLAÇO), ADÍLSON Warken, DOUGLAS dos Santos, ANDRÉ Luiz Barreto Silva LIMA (78 Luiz Severo JÚNIOR "VIÇOSA"), Humberlito BORGES Teixeira (88 VINÍCIUS PACHEDO dos Santos). DT: RENATO "GAÚCHO" Portaluppi
Goals: Giovanni HERNÁNDEZ Soto (28), Jhon Eduis VIÁFARA Mina (74) /
Humberlito BORGES Teixeira (4).

GRÊMIO FOOT-BALL PORTO ALEGRENSE – CSD LEÓN DE HUÁNUCO 2-0 (1-0)
Estádio Olímpico Monumental, Porto Alegre, 3.03.2011
Referee: Enrique Roberto OSSES Zencovich (CHI), Attendance: 26.455
GRÊMIO FOOT-BALL PORTO ALEGRENSE: VÍCTOR Leandro Bagy, RODOLFO Dantas Bispo (89 MÁRIO Figueira FERNANDES), RAFAEL MARQUES Pinto, GABRIEL Rodrigues dos Santos, GÍLSON Gomes do Nascimento, FÁBIO ROCHEMBACK, CARLOS ALBERTO Gomes de Jesús (75 BRUNO Bairros COLLAÇO), ADÍLSON Warken, DOUGLAS dos Santos, ANDRÉ Luiz Barreto Silva LIMA (82 Damián Ariel ESCUDERO), Humberlito BORGES Teixeira. DT: RENATO "GAÚCHO" Portaluppi
CSD LEÓN DE HUÁNUCO: Juan Ángel FLORES Ascencio, Luís Felipe CARDOZA Zúñiga, Guillermo Sandro SALAS Suarez, Gianfranco Roberto ESPINOZA Andrade, Jorge Martín ARAUJO Paredes, Jair Edson CÉSPEDES Zegarra, Jean Franco FERRARI Chiabra (85 Miguel Ángel CEVASCO Abad), Carlos Alberto ZEGARRA Zamora, Carlos Roberto ELÍAS Galliani (70 José Harrison OTÁLVARO Arce), Carlos Alberto OREJUELE Pita, Juan Diego GONZÁLEZ-VIGIL Bentin (64 Orlando Edmundo RODRÍGUEZ Llorente). DT: Franco Enrique NAVARRO Monteiro
Goals: ANDRÉ Luiz Barreto Silva LIMA (41), Humberlito BORGES Teixeira (54 penalty).

CD ORIENTE PETROLERO – CPD JUNIOR 1-2 (0-1)
Estadio Ramón Tahuichi Aguilera Costas, Santa Cruz, 9.03.2011
Referee: Gabriel Norberto FAVALE (ARG), Attendance: 10.668
CD ORIENTE PETROLERO: Hugo SUÁREZ Vaca, Alejandro Javier SCHIAPPARELLI, Miguel Ángel HOYOS Guzmán, Gustavo Martín CAAMAÑO, Diego TERRAZAS Pérez (56 Alcides PEÑA Jimenez), Alejandro MELEÁN Villarroel (74 Fernando Javier SAUCEDO Pereyra), Joselito VACA Velasco, Jhasmany CAMPOS Davalos, Mauricio SAUCEDO Guardia (68 Nicolás Santiago FERNÁNDEZ), Marcelo Eduardo AGUIRRE Biscaldi, Juan Carlos ARCE Justiniano. DT: Ariel Rubén CUFFARO Russo
CPD JUNIOR: Carlos Andrés RODRÍGUEZ Ibarra, César Augusto FAWCETT Lébolo, Juan David VALENCIA Hinestroza, ANSELMO de Almeida Machado, Harold MACÍAS Cabrera, Jhon Eduis VIÁFARA Mina, Giovanni HERNÁNDEZ Soto (85 Sherman Andrés CÁRDENAS Estupiñan), Brayner Yesid GARCÍA Leal, Jossymar Andrés GÓMEZ Pereira, Luis Alfonso PÁEZ Restrepo (80 Carlos Arturo BACCA Ahumada), Víctor Javier CORTÉS (88 Vladimir Javier HERNÁNDEZ Rivero). DT: Óscar Héctor QUINTABANI Faggionali
Goals: Juan Carlos ARCE Justiniano (90+1) /
Víctor Javier CORTÉS (27), Luis Alfonso PÁEZ Restrepo (46).

CSD LEÓN DE HUÁNUCO – GRÊMIO FOOT-BALL PORTO ALEGRENSE 1-1 (1-0)
Estadio Heraclio Tapia León, Huánuco, 17.03.2011
Referee: Roberto GARCÍA Orozco (MEX), Attendance: 9.684
CSD LEÓN DE HUÁNUCO: Juan Ángel FLORES Ascencio, Roller CAMBINDO Ibarra, Luís Felipe CARDOZA Zúñiga, Guillermo Sandro SALAS Suarez, Gianfranco Roberto ESPINOZA Andrade, Jair Edson CÉSPEDES Zegarra (67 Víctor Manuel PEÑA Espinoza), Jean Franco FERRARI Chiabra, Carlos Alberto ZEGARRA Zamora, Carlos Roberto ELÍAS Galliani (78 José Harrison OTÁLVARO Arce), Carlos Alberto OREJUELE Pita (83 Orlando Edmundo RODRÍGUEZ Llorente), Juan Diego GONZÁLEZ-VIGIL Bentin. DT: Franco Enrique NAVARRO Monteiro
GRÊMIO FOOT-BALL PORTO ALEGRENSE: VÍCTOR Leandro Bagy, RODOLFO Dantas Bispo, RAFAEL MARQUES Pinto, GABRIEL Rodrigues dos Santos, LÚCIO Carlos Cajeiro Souza, GÍLSON Gomes do Nascimento, FÁBIO ROCHEMBACK, CARLOS ALBERTO Gomes de Jesús (72 BRUNO Bairros COLLAÇO), DOUGLAS dos Santos, FERNANDO Lucas Martins (35 Luiz Severo JÚNIOR "VIÇOSA"), Humberlito BORGES Teixeira (83 DIEGO José CLEMENTINO). DT: RENATO "GAÚCHO" Portaluppi
Goals: Carlos Roberto ELÍAS Galliani (43) / CARLOS ALBERTO Gomes de Jesús (54).

CPD JUNIOR – CD ORIENTE PETROLERO 2-1 (0-0)
Estadio Metropolitano Roberto Meléndez, Barranquilla, 17.03.2011
Referee: Juan Ernesto SOTO Arevalo (VEN), Attendance: 13.155
CPD JUNIOR: Carlos Andrés RODRÍGUEZ Ibarra, César Augusto FAWCETT Lébolo, ANSELMO de Almeida Machado, Harold MACÍAS Cabrera, Jhon Eduis VIÁFARA Mina, Giovanni HERNÁNDEZ Soto, Sherman Andrés CÁRDENAS Estupiñan, Brayner Yesid GARCÍA Leal, Jossymar Andrés GÓMEZ Pereira (46 Jáider José ROMERO Romero), Luis Alfonso PÁEZ Restrepo (46 Carlos Arturo BACCA Ahumada), Víctor Javier CORTÉS (83 Juan David VALENCIA Hinestroza). DT: Óscar Héctor QUINTABANI Faggionali
CD ORIENTE PETROLERO: Hugo SUÁREZ Vaca (84 Michael ETULAIN Castro), Alejandro Javier SCHIAPPARELLI, Luis Alberto GUTIÉRREZ Herrera, Miguel Ángel HOYOS Guzmán, Gustavo Martín CAAMAÑO, Alejandro MELEÁN Villarroel, Joselito VACA Velasco, Jhasmany CAMPOS Davalos, Mauricio SAUCEDO Guardia (29 Alcides PEÑA Jimenez), Marcelo Eduardo AGUIRRE Biscaldi, Juan Carlos ARCE Justiniano (42 Nicolás Santiago FERNÁNDEZ). DT: Ariel Rubén CUFFARO Russo
Sent off: Aguirre (57)
Goals: Carlos Arturo BACCA Ahumada (64, 72 penalty) / Jhasmany CAMPOS Davalos (48).

CD ORIENTE PETROLERO – CSD LEÓN DE HUÁNUCO 2-0 (1-0)
Estadio Ramón Tahuichi Aguilera Costas, Santa Cruz, 24.03.2011
Referee: Alfredo Stalin INTRIAGO Ortega (ECU), Attendance: 2.020
CD ORIENTE PETROLERO: Michael ETULAIN Castro, Alejandro Javier SCHIAPPARELLI, Luis Alberto GUTIÉRREZ Herrera, Miguel Ángel HOYOS Guzmán, Gustavo Martín CAAMAÑO, Alejandro MELEÁN Villarroel, Joselito VACA Velasco, Jhasmany CAMPOS Davalos (84 Wálter VEIZAGA Argote), Fernando Javier SAUCEDO Pereyra (88 Diego TERRAZAS Pérez), Alcides PEÑA Jimenez, Nicolás Santiago FERNÁNDEZ (73 Juan Carlos ARCE Justiniano). DT: Ariel Rubén CUFFARO Russo
CSD LEÓN DE HUÁNUCO: Juan Ángel FLORES Ascencio, Luís Felipe CARDOZA Zúñiga, Guillermo Sandro SALAS Suarez, Gianfranco Roberto ESPINOZA Andrade, Jorge Martín ARAUJO Paredes, Jair Edson CÉSPEDES Zegarra (76 Víctor Manuel PEÑA Espinoza), José Harrison OTÁLVARO Arce, Jean Franco FERRARI Chiabra, Carlos Alberto ZEGARRA Zamora, Carlos Alberto OREJUELE Pita, Juan Diego GONZÁLEZ-VIGIL Bentin (90 Jorge Aldredo LEIVA Urbano). DT: Franco Enrique NAVARRO Monteiro
Goals: Alcides PEÑA Jimenez (16), Jhasmany CAMPOS Davalos (77).

GRÊMIO FOOT-BALL PORTO ALEGRENSE – CPD JUNIOR 2-0 (1-0)
Estádio Olímpico Monumental, Porto Alegre, 7.04.2011
Referee: Héctor Wálter BALDASSI (ARG), Attendance: 28.798
GRÊMIO FOOT-BALL PORTO ALEGRENSE: VÍCTOR Leandro Bagy, RODOLFO Dantas Bispo, RAFAEL MARQUES Pinto, GABRIEL Rodrigues dos Santos, LÚCIO Carlos Cajeiro Souza (81 FERNANDO Lucas Martins), BRUNO Bairros COLLAÇO, FÁBIO ROCHEMBACK (69 VINÍCIUS PACHEDO dos Santos), ADÍLSON Warken, Damián Ariel ESCUDERO (76 DIEGO José CLEMENTINO), DOUGLAS dos Santos, Humberlito BORGES Teixeira. DT: RENATO "GAÚCHO"
CPD JUNIOR: Mário Sebastián VIERA Galain, César Augusto FAWCETT Lébolo, Jáider José ROMERO Romero, Sérgio Andrés OTÁLVARO Botero, Juan David VALENCIA Hinestroza, ANSELMO de Almeida Machado, Harold MACÍAS Cabrera (44 José Antonio AMAYA Pardo), Giovanni HERNÁNDEZ Soto (80 Víctor Javier CORTÉS), Julian BARAHONA Angulo, Sherman Andrés CÁRDENAS Estupiñan, Carlos Arturo BACCA Ahumada (87 Wainer Javier CADENA Rueda). DT: Óscar Héctor QUINTABANI Faggionali Sent off: Romero (67)
Goals: LÚCIO Carlos Cajeiro Souza (33), Humberlito BORGES Teixeira (60).

CD ORIENTE PETROLERO – GRÊMIO FOOT-BALL PORTO ALEGRENSE 3-0 (0-0)
Estadio Ramón Tahuichi Aguilera Costas, Santa Cruz, 14.04.2011
Referee: Omar Andres PONCE Manzo (ECU), Attendance: 3.360
CD ORIENTE PETROLERO: Michael ETULAIN Castro, Alejandro Javier SCHIAPPARELLI, Luis Alberto GUTIÉRREZ Herrera, Miguel Ángel HOYOS Guzmán, Gustavo Martín CAAMAÑO, Diego TERRAZAS Pérez, Marcelo Eduardo AGUIRRE Biscaldi, Fernando Javier SAUCEDO Pereyra, Juan Carlos ARCE Justiniano (81 Alejandro MELEÁN Villarroel), Wálter VEIZAGA Argote (65 Jhasmany CAMPOS Davalos), Nicolás Santiago FERNÁNDEZ (66 Alcides PEÑA Jimenez). DT: Ariel Rubén CUFFARO Russo
GRÊMIO FOOT-BALL PORTO ALEGRENSE: VÍCTOR Leandro Bagy, RODOLFO Dantas Bispo, RAFAEL MARQUES Pinto, GABRIEL Rodrigues dos Santos, LÚCIO Carlos Cajeiro Souza, MÁRIO Figueira FERNANDES (57 DIEGO José CLEMENTINO), BRUNO Bairros COLLAÇO (31 FERNANDO Lucas Martins), FÁBIO ROCHEMBACK, ADÍLSON Warken (57 VINÍCIUS PACHEDO dos Santos), Damián Ariel ESCUDERO, Humberlito BORGES Teixeira. DT: RENATO "GAÚCHO" Portaluppi Sent off: Rodolfo (85)
Goals: Nicolás Santiago FERNÁNDEZ (50), Fernando Javier SAUCEDO Pereyra (75), Juan Carlos ARCE Justiniano (79).

CPD JUNIOR – CSD LEÓN DE HUÁNUCO 1-1 (0-0)
Estadio Metropolitano Roberto Meléndez, Barranquilla, 14.04.2011
Referee: Carlos Alfredo VERA Rodríguez (ECU), Attendance: 7.626
CPD JUNIOR: Mário Sebastián VIERA Galain, Jhon Alexander VALENCIA Hinestroza, Sérgio Andrés OTÁLVARO Botero, Juan David VALENCIA Hinestroza, ANSELMO de Almeida Machado, Julian BARAHONA Angulo (46 César Augusto FAWCETT Lébolo), Sherman Andrés CÁRDENAS Estupiñan (46 Giovanni HERNÁNDEZ Soto), Brayner Yesid GARCÍA Leal, Jossymar Andrés GÓMEZ Pereira, Luis Alfonso PÁEZ Restrepo, Víctor Javier CORTÉS (62 Carlos Arturo BACCA Ahumada). DT: Óscar Héctor QUINTABANI Faggionali
CSD LEÓN DE HUÁNUCO: Sebastián Leonel CUERDO, Roller CAMBINDO Ibarra, Luís Felipe CARDOZA Zúñiga (83 Éver Gustavo CHÁVEZ Hernández), Guillermo Sandro SALAS Suarez, Gianfranco Roberto ESPINOZA Andrade, José Harrison OTÁLVARO Arce (69 Orlando Edmundo RODRÍGUEZ Llorente), Jean Franco FERRARI Chiabra, Carlos Alberto ZEGARRA Zamora, Víctor Manuel PEÑA Espinoza, Carlos Alberto OREJUELE Pita (73 Jair Edson CÉSPEDES Zegarra), Juan Diego GONZÁLEZ-VIGIL Bentin. DT: Franco Enrique NAVARRO Monteiro
Goals: Jossymar Andrés GÓMEZ Pereira (75) / Orlando Edmundo RODRÍGUEZ Llorente (84).

1	JUNIOR	6	4	1	1	9	7	13
2	GRÊMIO	6	3	1	2	9	6	10
3	Oriente Petrolero	6	2	0	4	7	8	6
4	León de Huánuco	6	1	2	3	4	8	5

GROUP 3

FLUMINENSE FC – AA ARGENTINOS JUNIORS 2-2 (0-1)
Estádio Olímpico João Havelange (Engenhão), Rio de Janeiro, 9.02.2011
Referee: Carlos Manuel TORRES Nuñez (PAR), Attendance: 15.939
FLUMINENSE FC: DIEGO CAVALIERI, ANDRÉ LUIS García (73 Marco Antônio de Mattos Filho "MARQUINHO"), Carlos Andrade Souza "CARLINHOS", MARIANO Ferreira Filho, Welington Pereira Rodrigues "GUM", Rodrigo Oliveira de Bittencourt "DIGUINHO", Willamis de SOUZA Silva (88 Edwin Armando VALENCIA Rodríguez), Edimo Ferreira Campos "EDINHO", Darío Leonardo CONCA, WILLIANS dos Santos Santana (46 Rodrigo Batista da Cruz "RODRIGUINHO"), RAFAEL Martiniano de Miranda MOURA. DT: Muricy RAMALHO
AA ARGENTINOS JUNIORS: Nicolás Gastón NAVARRO, Gonzalo Sebastián PRÓSPERI, Sergio Daniel ESCUDERO (90 Nicolás BERARDO), Santiago Juan GENTILETTI , Miguel Ángel TORRÉN, Juan Alberto SABIA, Juan Ignacio MERCIER, Germán Rodrigo BASUALDO (85 Mauro Ezequiel BOGADO), Franco NIELL, Santiago Gabriel SALCEDO González, Gustavo Andrés OBERMAN (63 Pedro Pablo HERNÁNDEZ). DT: Pedro Antonio TROGLIO
Goals: RAFAEL Martiniano de Miranda MOURA (57, 73) / Franco NIELL (44, 70).

CD AMÉRICA SA – CLUB NACIONAL MONTEVIDEO 2-0 (1-0)
Estadio Guillermo Cañedo (Estadio Azteca), Mexico City, 15.02.2011
Referee: Óscar Julián RUÍZ Acosta (COL), Attendance: 18.049
CD AMÉRICA SA: Francisco Guillermo OCHOA Magaña, Aquivaldo MOSQUERA Romaña, Juan Carlos VALENZUELA Hernández, Oscar Adrián ROJAS Castillón, Miguel Arturo LAYÚN Prado, Pavel PARDO Segura, ROSINEI Adolfo, Daniel Gastón MONTENEGRO (78 Diego Antonio REYES Rosales), Andrés Nicolás "Nico" OLIVERA (58 Ángel Eduardo REYNA Martínez),Vicente Martín SÁNCHEZ Bragunde (71 Antonio LÓPEZ Ojeda), Vicente José Matías VUOSO. DT: Carlos Enzo REINOSO Valdenegro
CLUB NACIONAL MONTEVIDEO: Leonardo Fabián BURIÁN Castro, Daniel Alejandro LEMBO Betancor, Christian Washington NÚÑEZ Medina, Flavio Armando CÓRDOBA Rodríguez, GABRIEL MARQUES de Andrade Pinto, Matías Julio CABRERA Acevedo, Facundo Julián PÍRIZ González (60 Maximiliano Matías CALZADA Fuentes), Robert Mario FLORES Bistolfi, Richard Aníbal PORTA Cabdelaresi (46 Nicolás Ignacio VIGNERI Cetrullo), Tabaré Uruguay VIUDEZ Mora, Santiago Damian GARCÍA Correa (63 Bruno FORNAROLI Mezza). DT: Juan Ramón CARRASCO Torres
Goals: Vicente Martín SÁNCHEZ Bragunde (3), Vicente José Matías VUOSO (48).

FLUMINENSE FC – CLUB NACIONAL MONTEVIDEO 0-0
Estádio Olímpico João Havelange (Engenhão), Rio de Janeiro, 23.02.2011
Referee: Carlos Arecio AMARILLA Demarqui (PAR), Attendance: 10.017
FLUMINENSE FC: RICARDO Ferreira BERNA, LEANDRO da Fonseca EUZÉBIO, Carlos Andrade Souza "CARLINHOS", MARIANO Ferreira Filho, Wellington Pereira Rodrigues "GUM", Rodrigo Júnior Paulo Silva "DIGÃO" (73 Clemenson de ARAÚJO Soares), Rodrigo Oliveira de Bittencourt "DIGUINHO", Edwin Armando VALENCIA Rodríguez (60 Vinícius Silva Soares "TARTÁ"), Darío Leonardo CONCA, Marco Antônio de Mattos Filho "MARQUINHO" (81 Willamis de SOUZA Silva), RAFAEL Martiniano de Miranda MOURA. DT: Muricy RAMALHO
CLUB NACIONAL MONTEVIDEO: Leonardo Fabián BURIÁN Castro, Daniel Alejandro LEMBO Betancor, Christian Washington NÚÑEZ Medina, Sebastián COATES Nión, GABRIEL MARQUES de Andrade Pinto, Matías Julio CABRERA Acevedo (56 Maximiliano Matías CALZADA Fuentes), Mauricio Ernesto PEREYRA Antonini, Facundo Julián PÍRIZ González, Nicolás Ignacio VIGNERI Cetrullo, Bruno FORNAROLI Mezza (61 Santiago Damian GARCÍA Correa), Tabaré Uruguay VIUDEZ Mora (72 Flavio Armando CÓRDOBA Rodríguez). DT: Juan Ramón CARRASCO Torres

AA ARGENTINOS JUNIORS – CD AMÉRICA SA 3-1 (1-1)
Estadio Diego Armando Maradona, Buenos Aires, 24.02.2011
Referee: Víctor Hugo CARRILLO Casanova (PER), Attendance: 4.373
AA ARGENTINOS JUNIORS: Nicolás Gastón NAVARRO, Gonzalo Sebastián PRÓSPERI, Sergio Daniel ESCUDERO (82 Nicolás BERARDO), Santiago Juan GENTILETTI , Miguel Ángel TORRÉN (46 Cristian Nicolás SÁNCHEZ PRETTE), Juan Alberto SABIA, Germán Rodrigo BASUALDO, Pedro Pablo HERNÁNDEZ (46 Mauro Ezequiel BOGADO), Franco NIELL, Santiago Gabriel SALCEDO González, Gustavo Andrés OBERMAN. DT: Pedro Antonio TROGLIO
CD AMÉRICA SA: Francisco Guillermo OCHOA Magaña, Juan Carlos VALENZUELA Hernández, Diego Alberto CERVANTES Chávez, Oscar Adrián ROJAS Castillón, Miguel Arturo LAYÚN Prado, Diego Antonio REYES Rosales (80 Daniel Omar MÁRQUEZ Palacios), Pavel PARDO Segura, ROSINEI Adolfo (76 Ángel Eduardo REYNA Martínez), Daniel Gastón MONTENEGRO, Andrés Nicolás "Nico" OLIVERA (68 Vicente Martín SÁNCHEZ Bragunde), Vicente José Matías VUOSO. DT: Carlos Enzo REINOSO Valdenegro
Goals: Santiago Gabriel SALCEDO González (45 penalty, 73), Cristian N. SÁNCHEZ PRETTE (90+3) / Daniel Gastón MONTENEGRO (27).

CLUB NACIONAL MONTEVIDEO – AA ARGENTINOS JUNIORS 0-1 (0-1)
Estadio Gran Parque Central, Montevideo, 2.03.2011
Referee: Antonio Javier ARIAS Alvarenga (PAR), Attendance: 8.991
CLUB NACIONAL MONTEVIDEO: Leonardo Fabián BURIÁN Castro, Daniel Alejandro LEMBO Betancor, Christian Washington NÚÑEZ Medina, Sebastián COATES Nión, GABRIEL MARQUES de Andrade Pinto (83 Richard Aníbal PORTA Candelaresi), Matías Julio CABRERA Acevedo (45 Tabaré Uruguay VIUDEZ Mora), Mauricio Ernesto PEREYRA Antonini, Facundo Julián PÍRIZ González, Walter Horacio PERALTA Saracho, Bruno FORNAROLI Mezza (70 Jonathan Sebastián CHARQUERO López), Santiago Damian GARCÍA Correa. DT: Juan Ramón CARRASCO Torres
AA ARGENTINOS JUNIORS: Nicolás Gastón NAVARRO, Gonzalo Sebastián PRÓSPERI, Sergio Daniel ESCUDERO, Santiago Juan GENTILETTI , Miguel Ángel TORRÉN, Juan Alberto SABIA, Matías Alejandro LABA, Pedro Pablo HERNÁNDEZ (62 Mauro Ezequiel BOGADO), Franco NIELL (68 Ciro Pablo RIUS), Santiago Gabriel SALCEDO González, Gustavo Andrés OBERMAN (83 Cristian Nicolás SÁNCHEZ PRETTE). DT: Pedro Antonio TROGLIO
Goal: Franco NIELL (21).

CD AMÉRICA SA – FLUMINENSE FC 1-0 (0-0)
Estadio Guillermo Cañedo (Estadio Azteca), Mexico City, 2.03.2011
Referee: Wilmar Alexander ROLDÁN Pérez (COL), Attendance: 22.099
CD AMÉRICA SA: Francisco Guillermo OCHOA Magaña, Aquivaldo MOSQUERA Romaña, Juan Carlos VALENZUELA Hernández, Oscar Adrián ROJAS Castillón, Miguel Arturo LAYÚN Prado (63 Daniel Omar MÁRQUEZ Palacios), Pavel PARDO Segura (55 Ángel Eduardo REYNA Martínez), ROSINEI Adolfo, Daniel Gastón MONTENEGRO, Andrés Nicolás "Nico" OLIVERA (70 José Joaquín MARTÍNEZ Valadez), Vicente Martín SÁNCHEZ Bragunde, Vicente José Matías VUOSO. DT: Carlos Enzo REINOSO Valdenegro
FLUMINENSE FC: RICARDO Ferreira BERNA, LEANDRO da Fonseca EUZÉBIO, Carlos Andrade Souza "CARLINHOS", MARIANO Ferreira Filho, Wellington Pereira Rodrigues "GUM", Rodrigo Júnior Paulo Silva "DIGÃO" (82 Willamis de SOUZA Silva), Rodrigo Oliveira de Bittencourt "DIGUINHO", Edwin Armando VALENCIA Rodríguez (62 Edimo Ferreira Campos "EDINHO"), Vinícius Silva Soares "TARTÁ", Darío Leonardo CONCA (74 Clemenson de ARAÚJO Soares), RAFAEL Martiniano de Miranda MOURA. DT: Muricy RAMALHO
Goal: Daniel Omar MÁRQUEZ Palacios (70).

AA ARGENTINOS JUNIORS – CLUB NACIONAL MONTEVIDEO 0-1 (0-1)
Estadio Diego Armando Maradona, Buenos Aires, 15.03.2011
Referee: Enrique Roberto OSSES Zencovich (CHI), Attendance: 6.834
AA ARGENTINOS JUNIORS: Nicolás Gastón NAVARRO, Gonzalo Sebastián PRÓSPERI, Sergio Daniel ESCUDERO, Santiago Juan GENTILETTI , Juan Alberto SABIA, Cristian Nicolás SÁNCHEZ PRETTE (68 Nicolás BLANDI), Nicolás BERARDO (37 Emilio Exequiel HERNÁNDEZ Hernández), Mauro Ezequiel BOGADO (57 Ciro Pablo RIUS), Matías Alejandro LABA, Franco NIELL, Santiago Gabriel SALCEDO González. DT: Pedro Antonio TROGLIO
CLUB NACIONAL MONTEVIDEO: Leonardo Fabián BURIÁN Castro, JÁDSON VIERA Castro, Gonzalo Damián GODOY Silva, Christian Washington NÚÑEZ Medina, Sebastián COATES Nión, Matías Julio CABRERA Acevedo, Facundo Julián PÍRIZ González, Robert Mario FLORES Bistolfi (56 Marcelo Daniel GALLARDO), Richard Aníbal PORTA Candelaresi (64 Maximiliano Matías CALZADA Fuentes), Tabaré Uruguay VIUDEZ Mora (69 Mauricio Ernesto PEREYRA Antonini), Santiago Damian GARCÍA Correa. DT: Juan Ramón CARRASCO Torres
Goal: Santiago Damian GARCÍA Correa (33).

FLUMINENSE FC – CD AMÉRICA SA 3-2 (1-1)
Estádio Olímpico João Havelange (Engenhão), Rio de Janeiro, 23.03.2011
Referee: Antonio Javier ARIAS Alvarenga (PAR), Attendance: 13.158
FLUMINENSE FC: RICARDO Ferreira BERNA, JÚLIO CÉSAR Coelho de Moraes Júnior (75 Clemenson de ARAÚJO Soares), MARIANO Ferreira Filho (52 Anderson Luis de Souza "DECO"), Wellington Pereira Rodrigues "GUM", Rodrigo Júnior Paulo Silva "DIGÃO", Rodrigo Oliveira de Bittencourt "DIGUINHO", Willamis de SOUZA Silva, Edwin Armando VALENCIA Rodríguez, Darío Leonardo CONCA, Frederico Chaves Guedes "FRED", Márcio Psssos de Albuquerque "EMERSON" (69 RAFAEL Martiniano de Miranda MOURA). DT: RONALDO TORRES
CD AMÉRICA SA: Armando NAVARRETE García, Juan Carlos VALENZUELA Hernández, Diego Alberto CERVANTES Chávez, Oscar Adrián ROJAS Castillón, Miguel Arturo LAYÚN Prado, Pavel PARDO Segura, ROSINEI Adolfo (89 Daniel Omar MÁRQUEZ Palacios), Daniel Gastón MONTENEGRO, Andrés Nicolás "Nico" OLIVERA (46 Ángel Eduardo REYNA Martínez), Vicente Martín SÁNCHEZ Bragunde, Vicente José Matías VUOSO (83 Enrique Alejandro ESQUEDA Tirado). DT: Carlos Enzo REINOSO Valdenegro
Goals: Wellington Pereira Rodrigues "GUM" (20), Clemenson de ARAÚJO Soares (79), Anderson Luis de Souza "DECO" (86) / Vicente Martín SÁNCHEZ Bragunde (14, 71).

CLUB NACIONAL MONTEVIDEO – FLUMINENSE FC 2-0 (0-0)
Estadio Centenario, Montevideo, 6.04.2011
Referee: Óscar Julián RUÍZ Acosta (COL), Attendance: 44.952
CLUB NACIONAL MONTEVIDEO: Rodrigo Martín MUÑÓZ Salomón, JÁDSON VIERA Castro, Gonzalo Damián GODOY Silva, Sebastián COATES Nión, GABRIEL MARQUES de Andrade Pinto, Matías Julio CABRERA Acevedo (70 Maximiliano Matías CALZADA Fuentes), Mauricio Ernesto PEREYRA Antonini (53 Marcelo Daniel GALLARDO), Facundo Julián PÍRIZ González, Jonathan Sebastián CHARQUERO López (53 Carlos Eduardo Dutra de Oliveira "CARLÃO"), Tabaré Uruguay VIUDEZ Mora, Santiago Damian GARCÍA Correa. DT: Juan Ramón CARRASCO Torres
FLUMINENSE FC: RICARDO Ferreira BERNA, JÚLIO CÉSAR Coelho de Moraes Júnior (70 Clemenson de ARAÚJO Soares), MARIANO Ferreira Filho, Wellington Pereira Rodrigues "GUM", Rodrigo Oliveira de Bittencourt "DIGUINHO" (78 RAFAEL Martiniano de Miranda MOURA), Willamis de SOUZA Silva (55 Anderson Luis de Souza "DECO"), Edimo Ferreira Campos "EDINHO", Edwin Armando VALENCIA Rodríguez, Darío Leonardo CONCA, Frederico Chaves Guedes "FRED", Márcio Psssos de Albuquerque "EMERSON". DT: ENDERSON Alves MOREIRA
Sent off: Gallardo (85)
Goals: Santiago Damian GARCÍA Correa (50, 66).

CD AMÉRICA SA – AA ARGENTINOS JUNIORS 2-1 (0-0)
Estadio Guillermo Cañedo (Estadio Azteca), Mexico City, 6.04.2011
Referee: Carlos Arecio AMARILLA Demarqui (PAR), Attendance: 19.451
CD AMÉRICA SA: Francisco Guillermo OCHOA Magaña, Aquivaldo MOSQUERA Romaña, Juan Carlos VALENZUELA Hernández, Diego Alberto CERVANTES Chávez, Oscar Adrián ROJAS Castillón, Pavel PARDO Segura (81 Daniel Omar MÁRQUEZ Palacios), ROSINEI Adolfo, Daniel Gastón MONTENEGRO, Andrés Nicolás "Nico" OLIVERA (46 Ángel Eduardo REYNA Martínez), Vicente Martín SÁNCHEZ Bragunde, Enrique Alejandro ESQUEDA Tirado (46 Vicente José Matías VUOSO). DT: Carlos Enzo REINOSO Valdenegro
AA ARGENTINOS JUNIORS: Nicolás Gastón NAVARRO, Gonzalo Sebastián PRÓSPERI, Santiago Juan GENTILETTI , Miguel Ángel TORRÉN, Juan Alberto SABIA, Nicolás BERARDO, Juan Ignacio MERCIER, Matías Alejandro LABA (78 Germán Rodrigo BASUALDO), Franco NIELL (74 Mauro Ezequiel BOGADO), Santiago Gabriel SALCEDO González, Ciro Pablo RIUS (67 Gustavo Andrés OBERMAN). DT: Pedro Antonio TROGLIO
Goals: Vicente José Matías VUOSO (72), Daniel Omar MÁRQUEZ Palacios (82) / Franco NIELL (48).

CLUB NACIONAL MONTEVIDEO – CD AMÉRICA SA 0-0
Estadio Centenario, Montevideo, 20.04.2011
Referee: Víctor Hugo CARRILLO Casanova (PER), Attendance: 45.779
CLUB NACIONAL MONTEVIDEO: Rodrigo Martín MUÑÓZ Salomón, JÁDSON VIERA Castro, Gonzalo Damián GODOY Silva, Sebastián COATES Nión, GABRIEL MARQUES de Andrade Pinto, Mauricio Ernesto PEREYRA Antonini (61 Matías Julio CABRERA Acevedo), Facundo Julián PÍRIZ González, Bruno FORNAROLI Mezza (70 Carlos Eduardo Dutra de Oliveira "CARLÃO"), Jonathan Sebastián CHARQUERO López (75 ANDERSON SILVA de França), Tabaré Uruguay VIUDEZ Mora, Santiago Damian GARCÍA Correa. DT: Juan Ramón CARRASCO Torres
CD AMÉRICA SA: Francisco Guillermo OCHOA Magaña, Aquivaldo MOSQUERA Romaña, Juan Carlos VALENZUELA Hernández, Diego Alberto CERVANTES Chávez, Oscar Adrián ROJAS Castillón, Diego Antonio REYES Rosales, ROSINEI Adolfo, Daniel Gastón MONTENEGRO (82 Pavel PARDO Segura), Andrés Nicolás "Nico" OLIVERA (69 Vicente José Matías VUOSO), Vicente Martín SÁNCHEZ Bragunde (81 Daniel Omar MÁRQUEZ Palacios), Ángel Eduardo REYNA Martínez. DT: Carlos Enzo REINOSO Valdenegro

AA ARGENTINOS JUNIORS – FLUMINENSE FC 2-4 (1-2)
Estadio Diego Armando Maradona, Buenos Aires, 20.04.2011
Referee: Wilmar Alexander ROLDÁN Pérez (COL), Attendance: 5.706
AA ARGENTINOS JUNIORS: Nicolás Gastón NAVARRO, Gonzalo Sebastián PRÓSPERI, Sergio Daniel ESCUDERO, Santiago Juan GENTILETTI (75 Cristian Nicolás SÁNCHEZ PRETTE), Miguel Ángel TORRÉN (46 Gustavo Andrés OBERMAN), Juan Alberto SABIA, Juan Ignacio MERCIER, Germán Rodrigo BASUALDO (61 Matías Alejandro LABA), Franco NIELL, Santiago Gabriel SALCEDO González, Ciro Pablo RIUS. DT: Pedro Antonio TROGLIO
FLUMINENSE FC: RICARDO Ferreira BERNA, JÚLIO CÉSAR Coelho de Moraes Júnior (81 Vinícius Silva Soares "TARTÁ"), MARIANO Ferreira Filho, Wellington Pereira Rodrigues "GUM", Rodrigo Oliveira de Bittencourt "DIGUINHO" (87 Clemenson de ARAÚJO Soares), Edimo Ferreira Campos "EDINHO", Edwin Armando VALENCIA Rodríguez, Darío Leonardo CONCA, Marco Antônio de Mattos Filho "MARQUINHO", Frederico Chaves Guedes "FRED", RAFAEL Martiniano de Miranda MOURA (90 FERNANDO "BOB" Paixão da Silva). DT: ENDERSON Alves MOREIRA
Goals: Santiago Gabriel SALCEDO González (25 penalty), Gustavo Andrés OBERMAN (54) / JÚLIO CÉSAR Coelho de Moraes Júnior (17), Frederico Chaves Guedes "FRED" (40, 88 penalty), RAFAEL Martiniano de Miranda MOURA (68)

1	AMÉRICA	6	3	1	2	8	7	10
2	FLUMINENSE	6	2	2	2	9	9	8
3	Nacional	6	2	2	2	3	3	8
4	Argentinos Juniors	6	2	1	3	9	10	7

GROUP 4

CA VÉLEZ SARSFIELD – CARACAS FC 3-0 (1-0)
Estadio José Amalfitani, Buenos Aires, 15.02.2011
Referee: Enrique Roberto OSSES Zencovich (CHI), Attendance: 7.351
CA VÉLEZ SARSFIELD: Marcelo Alberto BAROVERO, Sebastián Enrique DOMÍNGUEZ, Emiliano Ramiro PAPA, Fernando Omar TOBIO, Franco RAZZOTTI Viretto, Fabián Alberto CUBERO, Maximiliano Nicolás MORALEZ (79 Iván Gonzalo BELLA), Arturo David RAMÍREZ (71 Augusto Matías FERNÁNDEZ), Héctor Miguel CANTEROS, Guillermo Luis FRANCO Farcuarson (7 Maximiliano Jorge GIUSTI), Juan Manuel MARTÍNEZ. DT: Ricardo Alberto GARECA
CARACAS FC: David GONZÁLEZ, Giovanny Michael ROMERO Armenio, Julio César MACHADO Cesario, Rohel Antonio BRICEÑO Carpio, Alexander David GONZÁLEZ Sibulo (85 Rómulo OTERO Vásquez), Franklin José LUCENA Peña, Edgar Hernán JIMÉNEZ González, Louis Angelo PEÑA Puentes, Nelson Alberto BARAHONA Collins (71 César Iván GONZÁLEZ Torres), Juan GUERRA, Edwards Yesid JIMÉNEZ Gómez (65 Luis Carlos CABEZAS Mairongo). DT: Ceferino BENCOMO
Sent off: Peña (12)
Goals: Maximiliano Nicolás MORALEZ (44), Arturo David RAMÍREZ (59),
Juan Manuel MARTÍNEZ (83 penalty).

UNIÓN ESPAÑOLA S.A.D.P. – CD UNIVERSIDAD CATÓLICA 2-2 (0-0)
Estadio Santa Laura-Universidad SEK, Santiago, 16.02.2011
Referee: Claudio Alfredo PUGA Briones (CHI), Attendance: 10.660
UNIÓN ESPAÑOLA S.A.D.P.: Eduardo Eugenio LOBOS Landaeta, Luis Pedro FIGUEROA Sepúlveda, Rafael Andrés OLARRA Guerrero (61 Giovanny Patricio ESPINOZA Pavon), Rodolfo Alejandro MADRID González, Leandro Javier DELGADO Plenkovich, Braulio Antonio LEAL Salvo, Gonzalo Andrés VILLAGRA Lira, Martín Ricardo LIGÜERA López (80 José Eduardo PÉREZ Ferrada), Raúl Enrique ESTÉVEZ (80 Kevin Andrew HARBOTTLE Carrasco), Leonardo Esteban MONJE Valenzuela, Sebastián Óscar JAIME. DT: José Luis SIERRA Pando
CD UNIVERSIDAD CATÓLICA: Cristopher Benjamín TOSELLI Ríos, Alfonso Cristián PAROT Rojas, David Andrés HENRÍQUEZ Espinoza, Juan Eduardo ELUCHANS, Jorge Andrés ORMEÑO Guerra, Rodrigo Ignacio VALENZUELA Avilés, Francisco Andrés SILVA Gajardo, Fernando Andrés MENESES Cornejo (84 Diego Alexis OPAZO González), Marcelo CAÑETE (58 José Luis VILLANUEVA Ahumada), Lucas David PRATTO (75 Tomás COSTA), Roberto Carlos GUTIÉRREZ Gamboa. DT: Juan Antonio PIZZI Torroja
Goals: Leonardo Esteban MONJE Valenzuela (47), Braulio Antonio LEAL Salvo (90+2 penalty) / Lucas David PRATTO (66), Fernando Andrés MENESES Cornejo (71).

CA VÉLEZ SARSFIELD – CD UNIVERSIDAD CATÓLICA 3-4 (3-1)
Estadio José Amalfitani, Buenos Aires, 3.03.2011
Referee: Carlos Manuel TORRES Nuñez (PAR), Attendance: 8.954
CA VÉLEZ SARSFIELD: Marcelo Alberto BAROVERO, Sebastián Enrique DOMÍNGUEZ, Emiliano Ramiro PAPA, Fernando ORTIZ, Franco RAZZOTTI Viretto, Víctor Eduardo ZAPATA, Fabián Alberto CUBERO, Maximiliano Nicolás MORALEZ (54 Fernando Omar TOBIO), Augusto Matías FERNÁNDEZ, Juan Manuel MARTÍNEZ (78 Ricardo Gastón DÍAZ), Maximiliano Jorge GIUSTI (46 Santiago Martín SILVA Olivera). DT: Ricardo Alberto GARECA
CD UNIVERSIDAD CATÓLICA: Cristopher Benjamín TOSELLI Ríos, Hans Alexis MARTÍNEZ Cabrera, Alfonso Cristián PAROT Rojas (64 Francisco Javier PIZARRO Cartes), David Andrés HENRÍQUEZ Espinoza, Juan Eduardo ELUCHANS, Jorge Andrés ORMEÑO Guerra, Fernando Andrés MENESES Cornejo (78 Marcelo CAÑETE), Tomás COSTA, Felipe Alejandro GUTIÉRREZ Leiva, Lucas David PRATTO, Roberto Carlos GUTIÉRREZ Gamboa (80 Pablo Ignacio CALANDRIA). DT: Juan Antonio PIZZI Torroja
Sent off: Ortiz (52)
Goals: Fernando ORTIZ (20), Augusto Matías FERNÁNDEZ (21), Emiliano Ramiro PAPA (45+1) / Lucas David PRATTO (1, 87), Tomás COSTA (73), Francisco Javier PIZARRO Cartes (90+1).

CARACAS FC – UNIÓN ESPAÑOLA S.A.D.P. 2-0 (1-0)
Estádio Olímpico de la UCV, Caracas, 3.03.2011
Referee: Carlos Alfredo VERA Rodríguez (ECU), Attendance: 10.120
CARACAS FC: Renny Vicente VEGA Hernández, Giovanny Michael ROMERO Armenio, Julio César MACHADO Cesario, Rohel Antonio BRICEÑO Carpio (80 Edder Alfonso PÉREZ Consuegra), Alexander David GONZÁLEZ Sibulo, Franklin José LUCENA Peña, Edgar Hernán JIMÉNEZ González, Nelson Alberto BARAHONA Collins, Juan GUERRA, Luis Carlos CABEZAS Mairongo (86 Daniel FEBLES), Josef Alexander MARTÍNEZ (75 Edwards Yesid JIMÉNEZ Gómez). DT: Ceferino BENCOMO
UNIÓN ESPAÑOLA S.A.D.P.: Eduardo Eugenio LOBOS Landaeta, Rafael Andrés OLARRA Guerrero (57 Giovanny Patricio ESPINOZA Pavon), Fernando Patricio CORDERO Fonseca, Esteban Eduardo GONZÁLEZ Herrera, Leandro Javier DELGADO Plenkovich, Braulio Antonio LEAL Salvo, Gonzalo Andrés VILLAGRA Lira (72 José Eduardo PÉREZ Ferrada), Martín Ricardo LIGÜERA López, Raúl Enrique ESTÉVEZ, Leonardo Esteban MONJE Valenzuela, Sebastián Óscar JAIME (80 Kevin Andrew HARBOTTLE Carrasco). DT: José Luis SIERRA Pando
Goals: Edgar Hernán JIMÉNEZ González (39 penalty), Nelson Alberto BARAHONA Collins (53).

CD UNIVERSIDAD CATÓLICA – CARACAS FC 1-3 (0-0)
Estadio San Carlos de Apoquindo, Santiago, 9.03.2011
Referee: Raúl OROSCO Delgadillo (BOL), Attendance: 13.491
CD UNIVERSIDAD CATÓLICA: Cristopher Benjamín TOSELLI Ríos, Hans Alexis MARTÍNEZ Cabrera, Alfonso Cristián PAROT Rojas (54 Marcelo CAÑETE), David Andrés HENRÍQUEZ Espinoza, Juan Eduardo ELUCHANS, Jorge Andrés ORMEÑO Guerra, Fernando Andrés MENESES Cornejo, Tomás COSTA, Felipe Alejandro GUTIÉRREZ Leiva (61 Roberto Carlos GUTIÉRREZ Gamboa), Lucas David PRATTO, Pablo Ignacio CALANDRIA (81 José Luis VILLANUEVA Ahumada). DT: Juan Antonio PIZZI Torroja
CARACAS FC: Renny Vicente VEGA Hernández, Giovanny Michael ROMERO Armenio, Julio César MACHADO Cesario, Rohel Antonio BRICEÑO Carpio, Alexander David GONZÁLEZ Sibulo (71 César Iván GONZÁLEZ Torres), Franklin José LUCENA Peña, Edgar Hernán JIMÉNEZ González, Louis Angelo PEÑA Puentes (80 Josef Alexander MARTÍNEZ), Nelson Alberto BARAHONA Collins, Juan GUERRA, Luis Carlos CABEZAS Mairongo (88 Daniel FEBLES). DT: Ceferino BENCOMO
Sent off: Martínez (69)
Goals: Pablo Ignacio CALANDRIA (53) / Luis Carlos CABEZAS Mairongo (46, 49),
Nelson Alberto BARAHONA Collins (48).

UNIÓN ESPAÑOLA S.A.D.P. – CA VÉLEZ SARSFIELD 2-1 (2-0)
Estadio Santa Laura-Universidad SEK, Santiago, 10.03.2011
Referee: Wilson Luiz SENEME (BRA), Attendance: 6.209
UNIÓN ESPAÑOLA S.A.D.P.: Eduardo Eugenio LOBOS Landaeta, Luis Pedro FIGUEROA Sepúlveda, Rafael Andrés OLARRA Guerrero, Fernando Patricio CORDERO Fonseca, Leandro Javier DELGADO Plenkovich, Braulio Antonio LEAL Salvo, Gonzalo Andrés VILLAGRA Lira, Martín Ricardo LIGÜERA López (71 Kevin Andrew HARBOTTLE Carrasco), Raúl Enrique ESTÉVEZ (87 José Eduardo PÉREZ Ferrada), Leonardo Esteban MONJE Valenzuela (70 Diego Martín SCOTTI Ponce de León), Sebastián Óscar JAIME. DT: José Luis SIERRA Pando
CA VÉLEZ SARSFIELD: Marcelo Alberto BAROVERO, Sebastián Enrique DOMÍNGUEZ, Emiliano Ramiro PAPA, Ricardo Gastón DÍAZ (46 Arturo David RAMÍREZ), Fernando Omar TOBIO, Franco RAZZOTTI Viretto (84 Héctor Miguel CANTEROS), Víctor Eduardo ZAPATA (64 Ricardo Gabriel ÁLVAREZ), Fabián Alberto CUBERO, Maximiliano Nicolás MORALEZ, Santiago Martín SILVA Olivera, Juan Manuel MARTÍNEZ. DT: Ricardo Alberto GARECA
Goals: Martín Ricardo LIGÜERA López (3), Braulio Antonio LEAL Salvo (25) /
Arturo David RAMÍREZ (68).

CARACAS FC – CD UNIVERSIDAD CATÓLICA 0-2 (0-0)
Estádio Olímpico de la UCV, Caracas, 22.03.2011
Referee: Paul Enrique DELGADILLO Haro (MEX), Attendance: 18.232
CARACAS FC: Renny Vicente VEGA Hernández, Giovanny Michael ROMERO Armenio (69 Edwards Yesid JIMÉNEZ Gómez), Julio César MACHADO Cesario, Rohel Antonio BRICEÑO Carpio, Alexander David GONZÁLEZ Sibulo, Franklin José LUCENA Peña, Edgar Hernán JIMÉNEZ González, Louis Angelo PEÑA Puentes (76 César Iván GONZÁLEZ Torres)), Nelson Alberto BARAHONA Collins, Juan GUERRA, Luis Carlos CABEZAS Mairongo (65 Josef Alexander MARTÍNEZ). DT: Ceferino BENCOMO
CD UNIVERSIDAD CATÓLICA: Paulo Andrés GARCÉS Contreras, Alfonso Cristián PAROT Rojas, David Andrés HENRÍQUEZ Espinoza, Juan Eduardo ELUCHANS, Jorge Andrés ORMEÑO Guerra, Francisco Andrés SILVA Gajardo, Fernando Andrés MENESES Cornejo (68 Francisco Javier PIZARRO Cartes), Tomás COSTA, Marcelo CAÑETE (74 Adán Jonathan VERGARA Villagrá), Lucas David PRATTO, José Luis VILLANUEVA Ahumada (80 Roberto Carlos GUTIÉRREZ Gamboa). DT: Juan Antonio PIZZI Torroja
Sent off: Barahona (88)
Goals: José Luis VILLANUEVA Ahumada (48), Lucas David PRATTO (84).

CA VÉLEZ SARSFIELD – UNIÓN ESPAÑOLA S.A.D.P. 2-1 (1-1)
Estadio José Amalfitani, Buenos Aires, 24.03.2011
Referee: Sálvio Spínola FAGUNDES Filho (BRA), Attendance: 5.913
CA VÉLEZ SARSFIELD: Marcelo Alberto BAROVERO, Sebastián Enrique DOMÍNGUEZ, Emiliano Ramiro PAPA, Fernando ORTIZ, Víctor Eduardo ZAPATA, Fabián Alberto CUBERO (64 Ricardo Gastón DÍAZ), Maximiliano Nicolás MORALEZ (85 Iván Gonzalo BELLA), Arturo David RAMÍREZ (46 Augusto Matías FERNÁNDEZ), Héctor Miguel CANTEROS, Santiago Martín SILVA Olivera, Juan Manuel MARTÍNEZ. DT: Ricardo Alberto GARECA
UNIÓN ESPAÑOLA S.A.D.P.: Eduardo Eugenio LOBOS Landaeta, Luis Pedro FIGUEROA Sepúlveda, Rafael Andrés OLARRA Guerrero, Fernando Patricio CORDERO Fonseca, Leandro Javier DELGADO Plenkovich, Braulio Antonio LEAL Salvo, Gonzalo Andrés VILLAGRA Lira, Martín Ricardo LIGÜERA López (76 José Eduardo PÉREZ Ferrada), Raúl Enrique ESTÉVEZ, Leonardo Esteban MONJE Valenzuela (76 Kevin Andrew HARBOTTLE Carrasco), Sebastián Óscar JAIME. DT: José Luis SIERRA Pando
Goals: Emiliano Ramiro PAPA (23), Santiago Martín SILVA Olivera (68) /
Leandro Javier DELGADO Plenkovich (33).

UNIÓN ESPAÑOLA S.A.D.P. – CARACAS FC 1-2 (1-1)
Estadio Santa Laura-Universidad SEK, Santiago, 6.04.2011
Referee: LEANDRO Pedro VUADEN (BRA), Attendance: 5.411
UNIÓN ESPAÑOLA S.A.D.P.: Eduardo Eugenio LOBOS Landaeta, Luis Pedro FIGUEROA Sepúlveda (72 Esteban Eduardo GONZÁLEZ Herrera), Rafael Andrés OLARRA Guerrero, Fernando Patricio CORDERO Fonseca, Leandro Javier DELGADO Plenkovich, Braulio Antonio LEAL Salvo, Gonzalo Andrés VILLAGRA Lira, Martín Ricardo LIGÜERA López, Raúl Enrique ESTÉVEZ, Leonardo Esteban MONJE Valenzuela (71 Kevin Andrew HARBOTTLE Carrasco), Sebastián Óscar JAIME. DT: José Luis SIERRA Pando
CARACAS FC: Renny Vicente VEGA Hernández, Giovanny Michael ROMERO Armenio, Julio César MACHADO Cesario, Rohel Antonio BRICEÑO Carpio, Alexander David GONZÁLEZ Sibulo, Franklin José LUCENA Peña, Edgar Hernán JIMÉNEZ González, Louis Angelo PEÑA Puentes (82 Josef Alexander MARTÍNEZ), Juan GUERRA, Edwards Yesid JIMÉNEZ Gómez (63 César Iván GONZÁLEZ Torres), Luis Carlos CABEZAS Mairongo. DT: Ceferino BENCOMO
Goals: Sebastián Óscar JAIME (2) /
Louis Angelo PEÑA Puentes (33), Josef Alexander MARTÍNEZ (83).

CD UNIVERSIDAD CATÓLICA – CA VÉLEZ SARSFIELD 0-0
Estadio San Carlos de Apoquindo, Santiago, 7.04.2011
Referee: Jorge Luis LARRIONDA Pietrafesa (URU), Attendance: 11.143
CD UNIVERSIDAD CATÓLICA: Paulo Andrés GARCÉS Contreras, Hans Alexis MARTÍNEZ Cabrera, Adán Jonathan VERGARA Villagrá (90 Roberto Carlos GUTIÉRREZ Gamboa), David Andrés HENRÍQUEZ Espinoza, Juan Eduardo ELUCHANS, Jorge Andrés ORMEÑO Guerra, Francisco Andrés SILVA Gajardo (75 Francisco Javier PIZARRO Cartes), Fernando Andrés MENESES Cornejo, Felipe Alejandro GUTIÉRREZ Leiva (56 José Luis VILLANUEVA Ahumada), Marcelo CAÑETE, Lucas David PRATTO. DT: Juan Antonio PIZZI Torroja
CA VÉLEZ SARSFIELD: Marcelo Alberto BAROVERO, Sebastián Enrique DOMÍNGUEZ, Emiliano Ramiro PAPA, Fernando ORTIZ, Víctor Eduardo ZAPATA (85 Maximiliano Jorge GIUSTI), Fabián Alberto CUBERO , Maximiliano Nicolás MORALEZ (79 Iván Gonzalo BELLA), Augusto Matías FERNÁNDEZ, Héctor Miguel CANTEROS, Santiago Martín SILVA Olivera, Juan Manuel MARTÍNEZ (68 Ricardo Gabriel ÁLVAREZ). DT: Ricardo Alberto GARECA
Sent off: Augusto Fernández (66)

CD UNIVERSIDAD CATÓLICA – UNIÓN ESPAÑOLA S.A.D.P. 2-1 (0-0)
Estadio San Carlos de Apoquindo, Santiago, 14.04.2011
Referee: Jorge Luis OSORIO Reyes (CHI), Attendance: 10.118
CD UNIVERSIDAD CATÓLICA: Paulo Andrés GARCÉS Contreras, Hans Alexis MARTÍNEZ Cabrera, David Andrés HENRÍQUEZ Espinoza, Juan Eduardo ELUCHANS, Jorge Andrés ORMEÑO Guerra, Rodrigo Ignacio VALENZUELA Avilés, Francisco Andrés SILVA Gajardo (68 Tomás COSTA), Fernando Andrés MENESES Cornejo (82 Felipe Alejandro GUTIÉRREZ Leiva), Marcelo CAÑETE, Lucas David PRATTO, Pablo Ignacio CALANDRIA (71 José Luis VILLANUEVA Ahumada). DT: Juan Antonio PIZZI Torroja
UNIÓN ESPAÑOLA S.A.D.P.: Eduardo Eugenio LOBOS Landaeta, Giovanny Patricio ESPINOZA Pavon, Fernando Patricio CORDERO Fonseca, Esteban Eduardo GONZÁLEZ Herrera, Rodolfo Alejandro MADRID González, Leandro Javier DELGADO Plenkovich (76 Francisco ALARCÓN Cruz), Gonzalo Andrés VILLAGRA Lira (65 Martín Ricardo LIGÜERA López), Diego Martín SCOTTI Ponce de León, Mario Antonio ARAVENA Bonilla, José Eduardo PÉREZ Ferrada, Kevin Andrew HARBOTTLE Carrasco (75 Nahuel DONADELL Álvarez). DT: José Luis SIERRA Pando
Goals: Pablo Ignacio CALANDRIA (48), Marcelo CAÑETE (78) /
Kevin Andrew HARBOTTLE Carrasco (47).

CARACAS FC – CA VÉLEZ SARSFIELD 0-3 (0-1)
Estádio Olímpico de la UCV, Caracas, 14.04.2011
Referee: José Hernando BUITRAGO Arango (COL), Attendance: 17.824
CARACAS FC: Renny Vicente VEGA Hernández, Giovanny Michael ROMERO Armenio (62 Alexander David GONZÁLEZ Sibulo), Julio César MACHADO Cesario, Rohel Antonio BRICEÑO Carpio, Franklin José LUCENA Peña, Louis Angelo PEÑA Puentes (62 César Iván GONZÁLEZ Torres), Nelson Alberto BARAHONA Collins, Juan GUERRA, Edwards Yesid JIMÉNEZ Gómez, Luis Carlos CABEZAS Mairongo, Josef Alexander MARTÍNEZ (69 Edgar Hernán JIMÉNEZ González). DT: Ceferino BENCOMO
CA VÉLEZ SARSFIELD: Marcelo Alberto BAROVERO, Sebastián Enrique DOMÍNGUEZ, Emiliano Ramiro PAPA, Fernando ORTIZ, Víctor Eduardo ZAPATA, Fabián Alberto CUBERO (58 Ricardo Gastón DÍAZ), Maximiliano Nicolás MORALEZ (71 Fernando Omar TOBIO), Héctor Miguel CANTEROS, Ricardo Gabriel ÁLVAREZ (79 Iván Gonzalo BELLA), Santiago Martín SILVA Olivera, Juan Manuel MARTÍNEZ. DT: Ricardo Alberto GARECA
Sent off: Díaz (85)
Goals: Maximiliano Nicolás MORALEZ (21), Santiago Martín SILVA Olivera (47,55)

1	UNIVERSIDAD CATÓLICA	6	3	2	1	11	9	11
2	VÉLEZ SARSFIELD	6	3	1	2	12	7	10
3	Caracas FC	6	3	0	3	7	10	9
4	Unión Española	6	1	1	4	7	11	4

GROUP 5

DEPORTIVO TÁCHIRA FC – SANTOS FC 0-0
Estadio Polideportivo de Pueblo Nuevo, San Cristóbal, 15.02.2011
Referee: Carlos Alfredo VERA Rodríguez (ECU), Attendance: 30.226
DEPORTIVO TÁCHIRA FC: Manuel Alejandro SANHOUSE Contreras, Enrique Andrés ROUGA Rossi, Wálter José MORENO Arco, José Jesús YÉGÜEZ Salgado, Gerzon Armando CHACÓN Varela, Pedro Alfonso FERNÁNDEZ Camacho, Sebastián HERNÁNDEZ Mejía (76 Yonathan Alexander DEL VALLE Rodríguez), Jorge Francisco CASANOVA Canchila (56 José Mauricio PARRA Perdomo), Diego Alejandro GUERRERO Corredor, Sergio Darío HERRERA Month, Edgar Fernando PÉREZ Greco. DT: Jorge Luis PINTO Afanador
SANTOS FC: RAFAEL Cabral Barbosa, Eduardo Luís Abonízio de Souza "EDU DRACENA", Severino dos Ramos DURVAL da Silva, Leonardo Lourenço Bastos "LÉO" (77 ALEX SANDRO Lobo Silva), Marcos Rogério Ricci Lopes "PARÁ" (73 ADRIANO Bispo dos Santos), DANILO Luiz da Silva, ELANO Ralph Blumer, Marcos AROUCA da Silva, RODRIGO Pereira POSSEBON, DIOGO Luis Santo (64 José "ZÉ" EDUARDO Bischofe de Almeida), NEYMAR da Silva Santos Júnior. DT: Adílson Dias BATISTA

CLUB CERRO PORTEÑO – CSD COLO COLO SANTIAGO 5-2 (2-1)
Estadio General Pablo Rojas, Asunción, 17.02.2011
Referee: Héber Roberto LOPES (BRA), Attendance: 14.597
CLUB CERRO PORTEÑO: Diego Daniel BARRETO Cáceres, Pedro Juan BENÍTEZ Dominguez, Lautaro Roque FORMICA, Iván Rodrigo PIRIS Leguizamón, Diego VIERA (76 César Iván BENÍTEZ León), Julio Daniel DOS SANTOS Rodríguez (46 Juan Manuel ITURBE Arévalo), Luís Enrique CÁCERES Centurión, Rodrigo Ramon BURGOS, Jonathan FABBRO (64 Fredy José BAREIRO Gamarra), Iván Arturo TORRES Riveros, Roberto Antonio NANNI. DT: Blas Marcelo CRISTALDO
CSD COLO COLO SANTIAGO: Juan Guillermo CASTILLO Iriarte, Andrés SCOTTI Ponce de León, Álvaro Andrés ORMEÑO Salazar, Paulo Cezar MAGALHAES Lobos, Sebastián Patricio TORO Hormazábal, José Domingo SALCEDO González (75 Mario Antonio SALGADO Jiménez), Marco Antonio MEDEL de la Fuente, Cristóbal Andrés JORQUERA Torres, Rodrigo Javier MILLAR Carvajal, Ezequiel Nicolás MIRALLES Sabugo, Esteban Efraín PAREDES Quintanilla. DT: Luis PÉREZ Muñóz
Goals: Roberto Antonio NANNI (1, 68 penalty), Julio Daniel DOS SANTOS Rodríguez (6), Juan Manuel ITURBE Arévalo (46, 85) /
Cristóbal Andrés JORQUERA Torres (12), Esteban Efraín PAREDES Quintanilla (73).

DEPORTIVO TÁCHIRA FC – CSD COLO COLO SANTIAGO 2-4 (0-2)
Estadio Polideportivo de Pueblo Nuevo, San Cristóbal, 1.03.2011
Referee: Omar Andres PONCE Manzo (ECU), Attendance: 15.323
DEPORTIVO TÁCHIRA FC: Manuel Alejandro SANHOUSE Contreras, Enrique Andrés ROUGA Rossi, Wálter José MORENO Arco, José Jesús YÉGÜEZ Salgado, Gerzon Armando CHACÓN Varela, Pedro Alfonso FERNÁNDEZ Camacho, Sebastián HERNÁNDEZ Mejía, Diego Alejandro GUERRERO Corredor (80 Jorge Francisco CASANOVA Canchila), Sergio Darío HERRERA Month, Yonathan Alexander DEL VALLE Rodríguez (54 Julio Brian GUTIÉRREZ González), Edgar Fernando PÉREZ Greco (46 José Mauricio PARRA Perdomo). DT: Jorge Luis PINTO Afanador
CSD COLO COLO SANTIAGO: Juan Guillermo CASTILLO Iriarte, Andrés SCOTTI Ponce de León, Nelson David CABRERA Báez, José Luis CABIÓN Dianta (46 Paulo Cezar MAGALHAES Lobos), José Domingo SALCEDO González, Luis Antonio PAVEZ Contreras, Cristóbal Andrés JORQUERA Torres (70 Lucas Daniel WÍLCHEZ), Rodrigo Javier MILLAR Carvajal, Patricio Andrés JEREZ Díaz, Ezequiel Nicolás MIRALLES Sabugo (80 Mario Antonio SALGADO Jiménez), Esteban Efraín PAREDES Quintanilla. DT: Américo Rubén GALLEGO
Goals: Julio Brian GUTIÉRREZ González (86, 87) / Ezequiel Nicolás MIRALLES Sabugo (20, 45+1), Esteban Efraín PAREDES Quintanilla (70), Lucas Daniel WÍLCHEZ (82).

SANTOS FC – CLUB CERRO PORTEÑO 1-1 (0-0)
Estádio Urbano Caldeira (Vila Belmiro), São Paulo, 2.03.2011
Referee: Héctor Wálter BALDASSI (ARG), Attendance: 6.735
SANTOS FC: RAFAEL Cabral Barbosa, Eduardo Luís Abonízio de Souza "EDU DRACENA", JONATHAN Cícero Moreira, Severino dos Ramos DURVAL da Silva, Leonardo Lourenço Bastos "LÉO", DANILO Luiz da Silva, ELANO Ralph Blumer, RODRIGO Pereira POSSEBON (59 ADRIANO Bispo dos Santos), José "ZÉ" EDUARDO Bischofe de Almeida (84 KEIRRISON de Souza Carneiro), DIOGO Luis Santo (75 ALEX SANDRO Lobo Silva), NEYMAR da Silva Santos Júnior. DT: MARCELO Martelote
CLUB CERRO PORTEÑO: Diego Daniel BARRETO Cáceres, Luís Carlos CARDOZO Espillaga (81 Fredy José BAREIRO Gamarra), Pedro Juan BENÍTEZ Dominguez, Lautaro Roque FORMICA (56 Iván Arturo TORRES Riveros), Iván Rodrigo PIRIS Leguizamón, César Iván BENÍTEZ León, Luís Enrique CÁCERES Centurión (71 Julio Daniel DOS SANTOS Rodríguez), Rodrigo Ramon BURGOS, Jorge Daniel NÚÑEZ Espínola, Roberto Antonio NANNI, Juan Manuel ITURBE Arévalo. DT: Blas Marcelo CRISTALDO
Goals: ELANO Ralph Blumer (54 penalty) / Roberto Antonio NANNI (90+1 penalty).

CLUB CERRO PORTEÑO – DEPORTIVO TÁCHIRA FC 1-1 (1-0)
Estadio General Pablo Rojas, Asunción, 10.03.2011
Referee: Darío Agustín UBRIACO Mederos (URU), Attendance: 15.499
CLUB CERRO PORTEÑO: Diego Daniel BARRETO Cáceres, Mariano Esteban UGLESSICH, Pedro Juan BENÍTEZ Dominguez, Iván Rodrigo PIRIS Leguizamón, César Iván BENÍTEZ León, Julio Daniel DOS SANTOS Rodríguez (70 Juan Manuel LUCERO), Luís Enrique CÁCERES Centurión (78 Jorge Daniel NÚÑEZ Espínola), Rodrigo Ramon BURGOS, Iván Arturo TORRES Riveros, Roberto Antonio NANNI, Juan Manuel ITURBE Arévalo (83 Jonathan FABBRO). DT: Leonardo Rubén ASTRADA
DEPORTIVO TÁCHIRA FC: Manuel Alejandro SANHOUSE Contreras, Enrique Andrés ROUGA Rossi, Wálter José MORENO Arco, José Jesús YÉGÜEZ Salgado (65 Layneker Evelio ZAFRA Martínez), Gerzon Armando CHACÓN Varela, Wilker ÁNGEL, Pedro Alfonso FERNÁNDEZ Camacho, Sebastián HERNÁNDEZ Mejía, Diego Alejandro GUERRERO Corredor (80 Jorge Francisco CASANOVA Canchila), Sergio Darío HERRERA Month, Edgar Fernando PÉREZ Greco (66 Julio Brian GUTIÉRREZ González). DT: Jorge Luis PINTO Afanador
Goals: Roberto Antonio NANNI (27) / Sergio Darío HERRERA Month (61).

CSD COLO COLO SANTIAGO – SANTOS FC 3-2 (3-1)
Estadio Monumental David Arellano, Santiago, 16.03.2011
Referee: Sergio Fabián PEZZOTTA (ARG), Attendance: 26.343
CSD COLO COLO SANTIAGO: Juan Guillermo CASTILLO Iriarte, Andrés SCOTTI Ponce de León, Luis Arturo MENA Irarrázabal (55 Luis Antonio PAVEZ Contreras), Nelson David CABRERA Báez, José Luis CABIÓN Dianta (46 Álvaro Andrés ORMEÑO Salazar), José Domingo SALCEDO González (67 Lucas Daniel WÍLCHEZ), José Pedro FUENZALIDA Gana, Cristóbal Andrés JORQUERA Torres, Patricio Andrés JEREZ Díaz, Ezequiel Nicolás MIRALLES Sabugo, Esteban Efraín PAREDES Quintanilla. DT: Américo Rubén GALLEGO
SANTOS FC: RAFAEL Cabral Barbosa, Eduardo Luís Abonízio de Souza "EDU DRACENA", Severino dos Ramos DURVAL da Silva, Leonardo Lourenço Bastos "LÉO" (33 RODRIGO Pereira POSSEBON), Marcos Rogério Ricci Lopes "PARÁ", DANILO Luiz da Silva, ELANO Ralph Blumer, ADRIANO Bispo dos Santos, Paulo Henrique Chagas de Lima "P.H. GANSO" (84 KEIRRISON de Souza Carneiro), José "ZÉ" EDUARDO Bischofe de Almeida (77 MAIKON Fernando Souza LEITE), NEYMAR da Silva Santos Júnior. DT: MARCELO Martelote
Goals: Esteban Efraín PAREDES Quintanilla (26), Ezequiel Nicolás MIRALLES Sabugo (34), Andrés SCOTTI Ponce de León (42) / ELANO Ralph Blumer (4), NEYMAR da Silva Santos Júnior (48).

DEPORTIVO TÁCHIRA FC – CLUB CERRO PORTEÑO 0-2 (0-1)
Estadio Polideportivo de Pueblo Nuevo, San Cristóbal, 6.04.2011
Referee: Sergio Fabián PEZZOTTA (ARG), Attendance: 3.587
DEPORTIVO TÁCHIRA FC: Manuel Alejandro SANHOUSE Contreras, Enrique Andrés ROUGA Rossi, Wálter José MORENO Arco, José Jesús YÉGÜEZ Salgado, Gerzon Armando CHACÓN Varela, Pedro Alfonso FERNÁNDEZ Camacho, Diego Alejandro GUERRERO Corredor (73 Jorge Francisco CASANOVA Canchila), José Mauricio PARRA Perdomo (58 Sebastián HERNÁNDEZ Mejía), Julio Brian GUTIÉRREZ González, Sergio Darío HERRERA Month, Edgar Fernando PÉREZ Greco (67 Yonathan Alexander DEL VALLE Rodríguez). DT: Jorge Luis PINTO Afanador
CLUB CERRO PORTEÑO: Diego Daniel BARRETO Cáceres, Luís Carlos CARDOZO Espillaga, Pedro Juan BENÍTEZ Dominguez, Lautaro Roque FORMICA, Iván Rodrigo PIRIS Leguizamón, Javier Alejandro VILLARREAL, Rodrigo Ramon BURGOS (83 Mariano Esteban UGLESSICH), Jonathan FABBRO (46 Julio Daniel DOS SANTOS Rodríguez), Iván Arturo TORRES Riveros (80 Diego MADRIGAL Rica), Jorge ROJAS, Roberto Antonio NANNI. DT: Leonardo Rubén ASTRADA
Goals: Roberto Antonio NANNI (20), Iván Arturo TORRES Riveros (65).

SANTOS FC – CSD COLO COLO SANTIAGO 3-2 (2-0)
Estádio Urbano Caldeira (Vila Belmiro), São Paulo, 6.04.2011
Referee: Roberto Carlos SILVERA Calcerrada, Attendance: 11.871
SANTOS FC: RAFAEL Cabral Barbosa, Eduardo Luís Abonízio de Souza "EDU DRACENA", Severino dos Ramos DURVAL da Silva, Leonardo Lourenço Bastos "LÉO", Marcos Rogério Ricci Lopes "PARÁ" (84 BRUNO Henrique Fortunato AGUIAR), DANILO Luiz da Silva, ELANO Ralph Blumer (78 MAIKON Fernando Souza LEITE), ADRIANO Bispo dos Santos, Paulo Henrique Chagas de Lima "P.H. GANSO" (65 ALEX SANDRO Lobo Silva), José "ZÉ" EDUARDO Bischofe de Almeida, NEYMAR da Silva Santos Júnior. DT: MARCELO Martelote
CSD COLO COLO SANTIAGO: Juan Guillermo CASTILLO Iriarte, Andrés SCOTTI Ponce de León, Paulo Cezar MAGALHAES Lobos, Luis Arturo MENA Irarrázabal (46 José Luis CABIÓN Dianta), Nelson David CABRERA Báez, Lucas Daniel WÍLCHEZ, José Domingo SALCEDO González (63 Daúd Jared GAZALE Álvarez), José Pedro FUENZALIDA Gana (69 Diego Iván RUBIO Köstner), Cristóbal Andrés JORQUERA Torres, Patricio Andrés JEREZ Díaz, Ezequiel Nicolás MIRALLES Sabugo. DT: Américo Rubén GALLEGO
Sent off: Neymar (52), Zé Eduardo (56), Elano (90) / Scotti (56), Jorquera (90)
Goals: ELANO Ralph Blumer (33), DANILO Luiz da Silva (35), NEYMAR da Silva Santos Júnior (51) / Patricio Andrés JEREZ Díaz (81), Diego Iván RUBIO Köstner (86).

CSD COLO COLO SANTIAGO – DEPORTIVO TÁCHIRA FC 2-1 (2-1)
Estadio Monumental David Arellano, Santiago, 12.04.2011
Referee: Héctor Wálter BALDASSI (ARG), Attendance: 17.632
CSD COLO COLO SANTIAGO: Juan Guillermo CASTILLO Iriarte, Paulo Cezar MAGALHAES Lobos, Luis Arturo MENA Irarrázabal, Nelson David CABRERA Báez, Lucas Daniel WÍLCHEZ, José Domingo SALCEDO González (64 José Luis CABIÓN Dianta), José Pedro FUENZALIDA Gana, Rodrigo Javier MILLAR Carvajal (75 Álvaro Andrés ORMEÑO Salazar), Patricio Andrés JEREZ Díaz, Esteban Efraín PAREDES Quintanilla, Diego Iván RUBIO Köstner (61 Ezequiel Nicolás MIRALLES Sabugo). DT: Américo Rubén GALLEGO
DEPORTIVO TÁCHIRA FC: Manuel Alejandro SANHOUSE Contreras, Enrique Andrés ROUGA Rossi, Wálter José MORENO Arco, Layneker Evelio ZAFRA Martínez, José Jesús YÉGÜEZ Salgado (72 José Mauricio PARRA Perdomo), Gerzon Armando CHACÓN Varela, Pedro Alfonso FERNÁNDEZ Camacho, Diego Alejandro GUERRERO Corredor, Julio Brian GUTIÉRREZ González (67 Yonathan Alexander DEL VALLE Rodríguez), Sergio Darío HERRERA Month, Edgar Fernando PÉREZ Greco (55 Sebastián HERNÁNDEZ Mejía). DT: Jorge Luis PINTO Afanador
Goals: Diego Iván RUBIO Köstner (6, 22) / Edgar Fernando PÉREZ Greco (4).

CLUB CERRO PORTEÑO – SANTOS FC 1-2 (0-1)
Estadio General Pablo Rojas, Asunción, 14.04.2011
Referee: Martín Emilio VÁZQUEZ Broquetas (URU), Attendance: 12.940
CLUB CERRO PORTEÑO: Diego Daniel BARRETO Cáceres, Luís Carlos CARDOZO Espillaga, Pedro Juan BENÍTEZ Dominguez, Lautaro Roque FORMICA (65 Juan Manuel ITURBE Arévalo), Iván Rodrigo PIRIS Leguizamón, Javier Alejandro VILLARREAL, Rodrigo Ramon BURGOS, Jonathan FABBRO, Iván Arturo TORRES Riveros (46 Juan Manuel LUCERO), Jorge ROJAS (46 Jorge Daniel NÚÑEZ Espínola), Roberto Antonio NANNI. DT: Leonardo Rubén ASTRADA
SANTOS FC: RAFAEL Cabral Barbosa, Eduardo Luís Abonízio de Souza "EDU DRACENA", JONATHAN Cícero Moreira, Severino dos Ramos DURVAL da Silva, Leonardo Lourenço Bastos "LÉO", DANILO Luiz da Silva, Marcos AROUCA da Silva (84 Marcos Rogério Ricci Lopes "PARÁ"), ADRIANO Bispo dos Santos, Paulo Henrique Chagas de Lima "P.H. GANSO", KEIRRISON de Souza Carneiro (76 ALEX SANDRO Lobo Silva), DIOGO Luis Santo (32 MAIKON Fernando Souza LEITE). DT: Muricy RAMALHO
Goals: Pedro Juan BENÍTEZ Dominguez (90+3) /
DANILO Luiz da Silva (11), MAIKON Fernando Souza LEITE (47).

CSD COLO COLO SANTIAGO – CLUB CERRO PORTEÑO 2-3 (2-1)
Estadio Monumental David Arellano, Santiago, 20.04.2011
Referee: Jorge Luis LARRIONDA Pietrafesa (URU), Attendance: 19.816
CSD COLO COLO SANTIAGO: Francisco Javier PRIETO Caroca, Andrés SCOTTI Ponce de León, Paulo Cezar MAGALHAES Lobos, Luis Arturo MENA Irarrázabal (54 Rodrigo Javier MILLAR Carvajal), Nelson David CABRERA Báez, José Luis CABIÓN Dianta, Lucas Daniel WÍLCHEZ (55 José Pedro FUENZALIDA Gana, 63 Álvaro Andrés ORMEÑO Salazar), José Domingo SALCEDO González, Cristóbal Andrés JORQUERA Torres, Ezequiel Nicolás MIRALLES Sabugo, Esteban Efraín PAREDES Quintanilla. DT: Américo Rubén GALLEGO
CLUB CERRO PORTEÑO: Diego Daniel BARRETO Cáceres, Luís Carlos CARDOZO Espillaga (57 Mariano Esteban UGLESSICH), Pedro Juan BENÍTEZ Dominguez, Iván Rodrigo PIRIS Leguizamón, César Iván BENÍTEZ León, Javier Alejandro VILLARREAL, Jonathan FABBRO, Jorge Daniel NÚÑEZ Espínola (84 Fredy José BAREIRO Gamarra), Iván Arturo TORRES Riveros, Juan Manuel LUCERO (73 Juan Manuel ITURBE Arévalo), Roberto Antonio NANNI. DT: Leonardo Rubén ASTRADA
Goals: Cristóbal Andrés JORQUERA Torres (4), Esteban Efraín PAREDES Quintanilla (20) /
Jonathan FABBRO (42, 76), Iván Rodrigo PIRIS Leguizamón (47).

SANTOS FC – DEPORTIVO TÁCHIRA FC 3-1 (2-0)
Estádio Municipal Paulo Machado de Carvalho (Pacaembú), São Paulo, 20.04.2011
Referee: Néstor Fabian PITANA (ARG), Attendance: 37.701
SANTOS FC: RAFAEL Cabral Barbosa, Eduardo Luís Abonízio de Souza "EDU DRACENA", JONATHAN Cícero Moreira, Severino dos Ramos DURVAL da Silva, Leonardo Lourenço Bastos "LÉO", DANILO Luiz da Silva, ELANO Ralph Blumer (79 ADRIANO Bispo dos Santos), Marcos AROUCA da Silva, Paulo Henrique Chagas de Lima "P.H. GANSO" (90 Marcos Rogério Ricci Lopes "PARÁ"), José "ZÉ" EDUARDO Bischofe de Almeida (74 MAIKON Fernando Souza LEITE), NEYMAR da Silva Santos Júnior. DT: Muricy RAMALHO
DEPORTIVO TÁCHIRA FC: Manuel Alejandro SANHOUSE Contreras, Enrique Andrés ROUGA Rossi, Wálter José MORENO Arco, Layneker Evelio ZAFRA Martínez, José Jesús YÉGÜEZ Salgado, Gerzon Armando CHACÓN Varela, Pedro Alfonso FERNÁNDEZ Camacho, Sebastián HERNÁNDEZ Mejía (59 Julio Brian GUTIÉRREZ González), Diego Alejandro GUERRERO Corredor (78 Yonathan Alexander DEL VALLE Rodríguez), Sergio Darío HERRERA Month, Edgar Fernando PÉREZ Greco (74 José Mauricio PARRA Perdomo). DT: Jorge Luis PINTO Afanador
Goals: NEYMAR da Silva Santos Júnior (4), JONATHAN Cícero Moreira (13),
DANILO Luiz da Silva (72) / Gerzon Armando CHACÓN Varela (69).

1	CERRO PORTEÑO	6	3	2	1	13	8	11
2	SANTOS FC	6	3	2	1	11	8	11
3	Colo Colo	6	3	0	3	15	16	9
4	Deportivo Táchíra	6	0	2	4	5	12	2

GROUP 6

CS EMELEC – SC INTERNACIONAL 1-1 (0-0)
Estadio George Capwell, Guayaquil, 16.02.2011
Referee: Néstor Fabian PITANA (ARG), Attendance: 13.589
CS EMELEC: Javier Hernán KLIMOWICZ Laganá, Gabriel Eduardo ACHILIER Zurita, Óscar Dalmiro BAGÜÍ Angulo, Julio Marcelo FLEITAS Silveira (76 Carlos Andrés QUIÑÓNEZ Valencia), Édison Vicente MÉNDEZ Méndez, Miguel David QUIRÓZ Villón (83 Leandro Gabriel TORRES), Fernando Augusto GIMÉNEZ Solis, Pedro Ángel QUIÑÓNEZ Rodríguez (72 Polo Raúl WILA Cangá), Cristian Matías MENÉNDEZ, Ángel Israel MENA Delgado, Eial STRAHMAN. DT: Omar Andrés ASAD
SC INTERNACIONAL: LAURO Júnior Batista da Cruz, Gonzalo SORONDO Amaro, Claudinei Cardoso Féliz da Silva "NEI", KLÉBER de Carvalho Correa, Marcos Antônio de Lima "ÍNDIO", Andrés Nicolás D'ALESSANDRO, José "ZÉ" ROBERTO de Oliveira (78 Fernando Ezequiel CAVENAGHI), Pablo Horacio GUIÑAZÚ, Mario Áriel BOLATTI (81 RODRIGO Baldasso da Costa), WILSON Tiago MATÍAS, LEANDRO DAMIÃO da Silva dos Santos. DT: CELSO Juarez ROTH
Goals: Fernando Augusto GIMÉNEZ Solis (90+5) / Mario Áriel BOLATTI (79).

CF JAGUARES DE CHIAPAS SA – CLUB JORGE WILSTERMANN 2-0 (0-0)
Estadio Zoque Víctor Manuel Reyna, Tuxtla Gutiérrez, 16.02.2011
Referee: Juan Ernesto SOTO Arevalo (VEN), Attendance: 6.345
CF JAGUARES DE CHIAPAS SA: Jorge VILLALPANDO Romo, Ismael Ignacio FUENTES Castro (64 Óscar Francisco RAZO Ventura), Marvin Gabriel CABRERA Ibarra, Omar Alejandro FLORES Serrano, Miguel Ángel MARTÍNEZ, Christian de Jesús VALDÉZ Loaiza, Damián Alejandro MANSO (46 Édgar Bismarck ANDRADE Rentería), Luis Ricardo ESQUEDA Ornelas, Alan Miguel ZAMORA González (46 Guillermo ROJAS Rumilla), Antonio SALAZAR Castillo, Jorge Daniel HERNÁNDEZ Govea. DT: José Guadalupe CRUZ Núnez
CLUB JORGE WILSTERMANN: MAURO MACHADO da Silva, Luis Eduardo ZAPATA Zapata (46 Víctor Hugo MELGAR Bejarano), Lucas Ezequiel FERNÁNDEZ, Juan Ignacio BROWN, Jusselío Donizete da Silva "CELINHO", Ramiro RODRÍGUEZ Rendón, Juan Carlos OJEDA, Ezequiel Gregorio ABREGÚ, Luis Gabriel GARCÍA Uribe (69 Nicolás MOSQUERA Pardo), Cristhian MACHADO Pinto, Jesús Daniel TOSCANINI Correa (58 FABIO "MINEIRO" Lima de Campos). DT: Marcelo NEVELEFF
Goals: Miguel Ángel MARTÍNEZ (66), Luis Ricardo ESQUEDA Ornelas (78).

CS EMELEC – CLUB JORGE WILSTERMANN 1-0 (1-0)
Estadio George Capwell, Guayaquil, 22.02.2011
Referee: Jorge Luis OSORIO Reyes (CHI), Attendance: 11.679
CS EMELEC: Javier Hernán KLIMOWICZ Laganá, Gabriel Eduardo ACHILIER Zurita, Óscar Dalmiro BAGÜÍ Angulo, Polo Raúl WILA Cangá, Édison Vicente MÉNDEZ Méndez, Miguel David QUIRÓZ Villón (64 Carlos Andrés QUIÑÓNEZ Valencia),Fernando Augusto GIMÉNEZ Solis (77 Marcos Jackson CAICEDO Caicedo), Cristian Matías MENÉNDEZ, Eduardo Javier MORANTE Rosas, Ángel Israel MENA Delgado, Eial STRAHMAN (71 Leandro Gabriel TORRES).
CLUB JORGE WILSTERMANN: MAURO MACHADO da Silva, Lucas Ezequiel FERNÁNDEZ, Juan Ignacio BROWN, Jusselío Donizete da Silva "CELINHO", Juan Carlos OJEDA, Víctor Hugo MELGAR Bejarano, Iani Martín VERÓN (46 Oliver Cristhian FERNÁNDEZ Ocaña), Ezequiel Gregorio ABREGÚ, Luis Gabriel GARCÍA Uribe, Cristhian MACHADO Pinto, Jesús Daniel TOSCANINI Correa (72 FABIO "MINEIRO" Lima de Campos). DT: Marcelo NEVELEFF
Goal: Eduardo Javier MORANTE Rosas (33).

SC INTERNACIONAL – CF JAGUARES DE CHIAPAS SA 4-0 (2-0)
Estádio José Pinheiro Borda (Beira-Rio), Porto Alegre, 23.02.2011
Referee: Roberto Carlos SILVERA Calcerrada (URU), Attendance: 26.337
SC INTERNACIONAL: LAURO Júnior Batista da Cruz, Gonzalo SORONDO Amaro, Claudinei Cardoso Féliz da Silva "NEI", KLÉBER de Carvalho Correa, Marcos Antônio de Lima "ÍNDIO", José "ZÉ" ROBERTO de Oliveira (85 André Luiz Tavares "ANDREZINHO"), Pablo Horacio GUIÑAZÚ, Mario Áriel BOLATTI, WILSON Tiago MATÍAS, Fernando Ezequiel CAVENAGHI (83 ALECSANDRO Barbosa Felisbino), LEANDRO DAMIÃO da Silva dos Santos (81 OSCAR dos Santos Emboaba Júnior). DT: CELSO Juarez ROTH
CF JAGUARES DE CHIAPAS SA: Jorge VILLALPANDO Romo, Ismael Ignacio FUENTES Castro (28 Omar Alejandro FLORES Serrano), Marvin Gabriel CABRERA Ibarra, Hugo SÁNCHEZ Guerrero, Miguel Ángel MARTÍNEZ, Francisco Javier TORRES Zamores (62 Antonio SALAZAR Castillo), Guillermo ROJAS Rumilla, Damián Alejandro MANSO (72 Alan Miguel ZAMORA González), Jorge Marcelo RODRÍGUEZ Núñez, Julio Daniel FRÍAS Adame, Jorge Daniel HERNÁNDEZ Govea. DT: José Guadalupe CRUZ Núnez
Sent off: Marcelo Rodríguez (90)
Goals: Mario Áriel BOLATTI (19, 43), LEANDRO DAMIÃO da Silva dos Santos (65), OSCAR dos Santos Emboaba Júnior (90+1).

CF JAGUARES DE CHIAPAS SA – CS EMELEC 2-1 (1-0)
Estadio Zoque Víctor Manuel Reyna, Tuxtla Gutiérrez, 8.03.2011
Referee: Marlon Giovanny ESCALANTE Alvarez (VEN), Attendance: 5.832
CF JAGUARES DE CHIAPAS SA: Jorge VILLALPANDO Romo, Ismael Ignacio FUENTES Castro, Óscar Francisco RAZO Ventura, Miguel Ángel MARTÍNEZ, Christian de Jesús VALDÉZ Loaiza, Francisco Javier TORRES Zamores (88 Édgar Bismarck ANDRADE Rentería), Guillermo ROJAS Rumilla, Damián Alejandro MANSO (82 Hugo SÁNCHEZ Guerrero), Luis Ricardo ESQUEDA Ornelas, Julio Daniel FRÍAS Adame (12 Antonio SALAZAR Castillo), Jorge Daniel HERNÁNDEZ Govea. DT: José Guadalupe CRUZ Núnez
CS EMELEC: Javier Hernán KLIMOWICZ Laganá, Gabriel Eduardo ACHILIER Zurita, Carlos Andrés QUIÑÓNEZ Valencia, Édison Vicente MÉNDEZ Méndez, Leandro Gabriel TORRES (65 Enner Remberto VALENCIA Lastra), Fernando Augusto GIMÉNEZ Solis, Pedro Ángel QUIÑÓNEZ Rodríguez, José Luis QUIÑÓNEZ Quiñónez (81 Fernando Vicente GAIBOR Orellana), Cristian Matías MENÉNDEZ, Ángel Israel MENA Delgado, Eial STRAHMAN (70 Armando Nevil ANGULO Mina). DT: Omar Andrés ASAD
Goals: Francisco Javier TORRES Zamores (43 penalty), Antonio SALAZAR Castillo (66) / Cristian Matías MENÉNDEZ (69).

CLUB JORGE WILSTERMANN – SC INTERNACIONAL 1-4 (1-3)
Estadio Félix Capriles, Cochabamba, 16.03.2011
Referee: Enrique Patricio CÁCERES Villafañe (PAR), Attendance: 19.532
CLUB JORGE WILSTERMANN: MAURO MACHADO da Silva, Lucas Ezequiel FERNÁNDEZ, Juan Ignacio BROWN, Jusselío Donizete da Silva "CELINHO", Juan Carlos OJEDA (62 Nicolás MOSQUERA Pardo), Oliver Cristhian FERNÁNDEZ Ocaña (56 FABIO "MINEIRO" Lima de Campos), Víctor Hugo MELGAR Bejarano (46 Amílcar Alvaro SÁNCHEZ Guzmán), Ezequiel Gregorio ABREGÚ, Luis Gabriel GARCÍA Uribe, Cristhian MACHADO Pinto, Jesús Daniel TOSCANINI Correa. DT: Marcelo NEVELEFF
SC INTERNACIONAL: LAURO Júnior Batista da Cruz, Gonzalo SORONDO Amaro, RODRIGO Baldasso da Costa, Claudinei Cardoso Féliz da Silva "NEI", KLÉBER de Carvalho Correa, Paulo César Fonseca do Nascimento "TINGA" (46 WILSON Tiago MATÍAS), José "ZÉ" ROBERTO de Oliveira, Pablo Horacio GUIÑAZÚ, Mario Áriel BOLATTI, OSCAR dos Santos Emboaba Júnior (68 André Luiz Tavares "ANDREZINHO"), LEANDRO DAMIÃO da Silva dos Santos (66 Fernando Ezequiel CAVENAGHI). DT: CELSO Juarez ROTH
Goals: Juan Ignacio BROWN (8, 16 own goal) / LEANDRO DAMIÃO da Silva dos Santos (18), José "ZÉ" ROBERTO de Oliveira (24), KLÉBER de Carvalho Correa (80).

CS EMELEC – CF JAGUARES DE CHIAPAS SA 1-0 (0-0)
Estadio George Capwell, Guayaquil, 16.03.2011
Referee: Víctor Hugo CARRILLO Casanova (PER), Attendance: 11.831
CS EMELEC: Javier Hernán KLIMOWICZ Laganá, Gabriel Eduardo ACHILIER Zurita, Óscar Dalmiro BAGÜÍ Angulo, Julio Marcelo FLEITAS Silveira, Carlos Andrés QUIÑÓNEZ Valencia, Miguel David QUIRÓZ Villón (88 Fernando Vicente GAIBOR Orellana), Fernando Augusto GIMÉNEZ Solis, Pedro Ángel QUIÑÓNEZ Rodríguez, Cristian Matías MENÉNDEZ, Wálter Ramiro IZA Garcia (69 José Luis QUIÑÓNEZ Quiñónez), Ángel Israel MENA Delgado (80 Enner Remberto VALENCIA Lastra). DT: Omar Andrés ASAD
CF JAGUARES DE CHIAPAS SA: Jorge VILLALPANDO Romo, Marvin Gabriel CABRERA Ibarra (68 Damián Alejandro MANSO), Hugo SÁNCHEZ Guerrero, Óscar Francisco RAZO Ventura, Omar Alejandro FLORES Serrano, Miguel Ángel MARTÍNEZ, Christian de Jesús VALDÉZ Loaiza, Luis Ricardo ESQUEDA Ornelas (60 Antonio Michael PEDROZA Whitham), Jorge Marcelo RODRÍGUEZ Núñez, Antonio SALAZAR Castillo, Jorge Daniel HERNÁNDEZ Govea (51 Francisco Javier TORRES Zamores). DT: José Guadalupe CRUZ Núnez
Goal: Miguel David QUIRÓZ Villón (53 penalty).

SC INTERNACIONAL – CLUB JORGE WILSTERMANN 3-0 (1-0)
Estádio José Pinheiro Borda (Beira-Rio), Porto Alegre, 31.03.2011
Referee: Darío Agustín UBRIACO Mederos (URU), Attendance: 28.085
SC INTERNACIONAL: LAURO Júnior Batista da Cruz, Fabián Guedes "BOLÍVAR", Claudinei Cardoso Féliz da Silva "NEI", KLÉBER de Carvalho Correa, Marcos Antônio de Lima "ÍNDIO" (77 RODRIGO Baldasso da Costa), Andrés Nicolás D'ALESSANDRO, José "ZÉ" ROBERTO de Oliveira (73 RAFAEL Augusto SÓBIS do Nascimento), Pablo Horacio GUIÑAZÚ, WILSON Tiago MATÍAS, OSCAR dos Santos Emboaba Júnior (82 André Luiz Tavares "ANDREZINHO"), LEANDRO DAMIÃO da Silva dos Santos. DT: CELSO Juarez ROTH
CLUB JORGE WILSTERMANN: MAURO MACHADO da Silva, Luis Eduardo ZAPATA Zapata, Marcelo Antonio CARBALLO Cadima, Lucas Ezequiel FERNÁNDEZ, Juan Ignacio BROWN, Jusselío Donizete da Silva "CELINHO", Ramiro RODRÍGUEZ Rendón, Ezequiel Gregorio ABREGÚ (68 Juan Carlos OJEDA), Luis Gabriel GARCÍA Uribe (46 Amílcar Alvaro SÁNCHEZ Guzmán), Cristhian MACHADO Pinto (60 Jesús Daniel TOSCANINI Correa), FABIO "MINEIRO" Lima de Campos. DT: Marcelo NEVELEFF
Sent off: Fernández (69)
Goals: OSCAR dos Santos Emboaba Júnior (18), Andrés Nicolás D'ALESSANDRO (56), José "ZÉ" ROBERTO de Oliveira (72).

CF JAGUARES DE CHIAPAS SA – SC INTERNACIONAL 1-0 (0-0)
Estadio Zoque Víctor Manuel Reyna, Tuxtla Gutiérrez, 6.04.2011
Referee: Wilmar Alexander ROLDÁN Pérez (COL), Attendance: 7.553
CF JAGUARES DE CHIAPAS SA: Fabián Israel VILLASEÑOR López, Óscar Francisco RAZO Ventura, Jaime DURÁN Gomez, Omar Alejandro FLORES Serrano, Miguel Ángel MARTÍNEZ, Francisco Javier TORRES Zamores (46 Damián Alejandro MANSO), Édgar Bismarck ANDRADE Rentería, José Híber RUIZ Nataren (66 Christian de Jesús VALDÉZ Loaiza), Jorge Marcelo RODRÍGUEZ Núñez, Alan Miguel ZAMORA Gonzalez (46 Antonio SALAZAR Castillo), Jorge Daniel HERNÁNDEZ Govea. DT: José Guadalupe CRUZ Núnez
SC INTERNACIONAL: LAURO Júnior Batista da Cruz, Fabián Guedes "BOLÍVAR", Claudinei Cardoso Féliz da Silva "NEI", KLÉBER de Carvalho Correa, Marcos Antônio de Lima "ÍNDIO", Andrés Nicolás D'ALESSANDRO, José "ZÉ" ROBERTO de Oliveira (70 André Luiz Tavares "ANDREZINHO"), Pablo Horacio GUIÑAZÚ, Mario Áriel BOLATTI (74 WILSON Tiago MATÍAS), OSCAR dos Santos Emboaba Júnior (59 RAFAEL Augusto SÓBIS do Nascimento), LEANDRO DAMIÃO da Silva dos Santos. DT: CELSO Juarez ROTH
Goal: Antonio SALAZAR Castillo (54).

CLUB JORGE WILSTERMANN – CS EMELEC 0-0
Estadio Félix Capriles, Cochabamba, 7.04.2011
Referee: Marlon Giovanny ESCALANTE Alvarez (VEN), Attendance: 1.171
CLUB JORGE WILSTERMANN: MAURO MACHADO da Silva, Juan Ignacio BROWN, Jusselío Donizete da Silva "CELINHO" (82 Marcelo Antonio CARBALLO Cadima), Sergio Daniel GARZÓN Garzón, Diego Didier BENGOLEA Vargas (60 Juan Carlos OJEDA), Ramiro RODRÍGUEZ Rendón, Víctor Hugo MELGAR Bejarano (55 Ezequiel Gregorio ABREGÚ), Luis Gabriel GARCÍA Uribe, Cristhian MACHADO Pinto, Jesús Daniel TOSCANINI Correa, FABIO "MINEIRO" Lima de Campos. DT: Marcelo NEVELEFF
CS EMELEC: Wilmer Fabian ZUMBA Ramirez, Gabriel Eduardo ACHILIER Zurita, Óscar Dalmiro BAGÜÍ Angulo, Carlos Andrés QUIÑÓNEZ Valencia, Miguel David QUIRÓZ Villón, Fernando Augusto GIMÉNEZ Solis (75 Armando Nevil ANGULO Mina), Pedro Ángel QUIÑÓNEZ Rodríguez, José Luis QUIÑÓNEZ Quiñónez, Cristian Matías MENÉNDEZ, Wálter Ramiro IZA Garcia (69 Marcos Jackson CAICEDO Caicedo), Ángel Israel MENA Delgado (61 Enner Remberto VALENCIA Lastra). DT: Omar Andrés ASAD

CLUB JORGE WILSTERMANN – CF JAGUARES DE CHIAPAS SA 2-1 (0-1)
Estadio Félix Capriles, Cochabamba, 19.04.2011
Referee: Julio Cesar QUINTANA Rodriguez (PAR), Attendance: 1.510
CLUB JORGE WILSTERMANN: MAURO MACHADO da Silva, Lucas Ezequiel FERNÁNDEZ, Juan Ignacio BROWN, Jusselío Donizete da Silva "CELINHO", Diego Didier BENGOLEA Vargas (60 Jesús Daniel TOSCANINI Correa), Ramiro RODRÍGUEZ Rendón, Juan Carlos OJEDA, Nicolas (Nicky) TORRES, Iani Martín VERÓN (60 Ezequiel Gregorio ABREGÚ), Nicolás MOSQUERA Pardo (78 Luis Gabriel GARCÍA Uribe), FABIO "MINEIRO" Lima de Campos. DT: Marcelo NEVELEFF
CF JAGUARES DE CHIAPAS SA: Jorge VILLALPANDO Romo, Ismael Ignacio FUENTES Castro, Óscar Francisco RAZO Ventura, Jaime DURÁN Gomez (86 Diego Mauricio CASTELLANOS Sánchez), Francisco Javier TORRES Zamores, Guillermo ROJAS Rumilla (82 Jesús Roberto CHÁVEZ Guzmán), José Híber RUIZ Nataren, Luis Ricardo ESQUEDA Ornelas, Alan Miguel ZAMORA Gonzalez, Antonio Michael PEDROZA Whitham, Julio Daniel FRÍAS Adame. DT: José Guadalupe CRUZ Núnez
Sent off: Frías (50)
Goals: FABIO "MINEIRO" Lima de Campos (76), Nicolas TORRES (81) / Julio D. FRÍAS Adame (7).

SC INTERNACIONAL – CS EMELEC 2-0 (0-0)
Estádio José Pinheiro Borda (Beira-Rio), Porto Alegre, 19.04.2011
Referee: Óscar Julián RUÍZ Acosta (COL), Attendance: 36.175
SC INTERNACIONAL: RENAN Brito Soares, Fabián Guedes "BOLÍVAR", RODRIGO Baldasso da Costa, Claudinei Cardoso Féliz da Silva "NEI", KLÉBER de Carvalho Correa, Andrés Nicolás D'ALESSANDRO, Pablo Horacio GUIÑAZÚ, Mario Áriel BOLATTI, André Luiz Tavares "ANDREZINHO", RAFAEL Augusto SÓBIS do Nascimento (79 Fernando Ezequiel CAVENAGHI), LEANDRO DAMIÃO da Silva dos Santos (86 José "ZÉ" ROBERTO de Oliveira). DT: Paulo Roberto FALCÃO
CS EMELEC: Javier Hernán KLIMOWICZ Laganá, Gabriel Eduardo ACHILIER Zurita, Óscar Dalmiro BAGÜÍ Angulo, Carlos Andrés QUIÑÓNEZ Valencia (63 Enner Remberto VALENCIA Lastra), Miguel David QUIRÓZ Villón, Fernando Augusto GIMÉNEZ Solis, Pedro Ángel QUIÑÓNEZ Rodríguez, José Luis QUIÑÓNEZ Quiñónez, Cristian Matías MENÉNDEZ, Fernando Vicente GAIBOR Orellana (85 Eial STRAHMAN), Wálter Ramiro IZA Garcia (73 Marcos Jackson CAICEDO Caicedo). DT: Omar Andrés ASAD
Goals: RAFAEL Augusto SÓBIS do Nascimento (51), LEANDRO DAMIÃO da Silva dos Santos (84).

1	INTERNACIONAL	6	4	1	1	14	3	13
2	JAGUARES	6	3	0	3	6	8	9
3	Emelec	6	2	2	2	4	5	8
4	Jorge Wilstermann	6	1	1	4	3	11	4

GROUP 7

CC DEPORTES TOLIMA – CLUB GUARANÍ ASUNCIÓN 1-0 (0-0)
Estadio Manuel Murillo Toro, Ibagué, 15.02.2011
Referee: Omar Andres PONCE Manzo (ECU), Attendance: 8.021
CC DEPORTES TOLIMA: Antony Domingo SILVA Cano, Gerardo Enrique VALLEJO Metaute, Félix Enrique NOGUERA Collante, Julián HURTADO Izquierdo, Yair ARRECHEA Amú, Elkin Antonio MURILLO Amor (76 Christian Camilo MARRUGO Rodríguez), Rafael Arlex CASTILLO Galvis (59 Pablo Júnior GIMÉNEZ), Diego Ferney CHARÁ Zamora, Gustavo Adolfo BOLÍVAR Zapata, Jhon Fredy HURTADO (46 Danny Manuel SANTOYA Otero), Wilder Andrés MEDINA Tamayo. DT: Hernán TORRES Oliveros
CLUB GUARANÍ ASUNCIÓN: Pablo Fernando AURRECOCHEA Medina, Héctor Federico CARBALLO, Elvis Israel MARECOS, Eduardo Javier FILIPPINI, Francisco Joel BENÍTEZ, Pedro Julian CHÁVEZ Ruiz (58 Osvaldo HOBECKER García), Ángel Antonio ORTIZ Cabrera, Miguel Ángel PANIAGUA Rivarola, Jorge Darío MENDOZA Torres, Pablo Nicolás CABALLERO (67 Fabio ESCOBAR Benítez), Julián Alfonso BENÍTEZ. DT: Carlos Horacio COMPAGNUCCI
Goal: Danny Manuel SANTOYA Otero (83).

CRUZEIRO EC – CA ESTUDIANTES DE LA PLATA 5-0 (3-0)
Estádio Joaquim Henrique Nogueira (Arena do Jacaré), Sete Lagoas, 16.02.2011
Referee: Carlos Arecio AMARILLA Demarqui (PAR), Attendance: 10.955
CRUZEIRO EC: FÁBIO Deivison Lopes Maciel, Mauricio Bernardo VICTORINO Dansilio, PABLO de Barros Paulino, Carlos Gilberto Nascimento da Silva e Silva "GIL", GILBERT da Silva Melo (67 DIEGO RENÁN de Lima Ferreira), Antônio Marcos da Silva Filho "MARQUINHOS PARANÁ", HENRIQUE Pacheco de Lima, Walter Damián MONTILLO, ROGER Galera Flores (70 Eduardo Pereira Rodrigues "DUDU"), WALLYSON Ricardo Maciel Monteiro, WELLINGTON "PAULISTA" Pereira do Nascimento (77 THIAGO RIBEIRO Cardoso). DT: Alexis Stival "CUCA" Beluda
CA ESTUDIANTES DE LA PLATA: Agustín Ignacio ORIÓN, Leandro DESÁBATO, Nelson Fabián BENÍTEZ, Germán David RÉ, Gabriel Iván MERCADO, Federico FERNÁNDEZ, Juan Sebastián VERÓN, Rodrigo BRAÑA, Leandro Damián BENÍTEZ (58 Maximiliano Ezequiel NÚÑEZ), Enzo Nicolás PÉREZ, Gastón Nicolás FERNÁNDEZ (80 Hernán Rodrigo LÓPEZ Mora). DT: Manuel Eduardo BERIZZO
Goals: WALLYSON Ricardo Maciel Monteiro (1, 82), ROGER Galera Flores (17), Walter Damián MONTILLO (38, 58).

CRUZEIRO EC – CLUB GUARANÍ ASUNCIÓN 4-0 (1-0)
Estádio Joaquim Henrique Nogueira (Arena do Jacaré), Sete Lagoas, 22.02.2011
Referee: Raúl OROSCO Delgadillo (BOL), Attendance: 12.067
CRUZEIRO EC: FÁBIO Deivison Lopes Maciel, Mauricio Bernardo VICTORINO Dansilio, PABLO de Barros Paulino, DIEGO RENÁN de Lima Ferreira, Carlos Gilberto Nascimento da Silva e Silva "GIL", Antônio Marcos da Silva Filho "MARQUINHOS PARANÁ", HENRIQUE Pacheco de Lima, Walter Damián MONTILLO, ROGER Galera Flores (75 THIAGO RIBEIRO Cardoso), WALLYSON Ricardo Maciel Monteiro (81 Eduardo Pereira Rodrigues "DUDU"), WELLINGTON "PAULISTA" Pereira do Nascimento (62 Ernesto Antonio FARIÁS). DT: Alexis Stival "CUCA" Beluda
CLUB GUARANÍ ASUNCIÓN: Pablo Fernando AURRECOCHEA Medina, Ignacio "Nacho" ITHURRALDE Sáez (73 Pedro Julian CHÁVEZ Ruiz, 79 Tomás Javier BARTOMÉUS Viveros), Héctor Federico CARBALLO, Elvis Israel MARECOS, Eduardo Javier FILIPPINI, Francisco Joel BENÍTEZ, Ángel Antonio ORTIZ Cabrera, Miguel Ángel PANIAGUA Rivarola, Jorge Darío MENDOZA Torres (58 Osvaldo HOBECKER García), Julián Alfonso BENÍTEZ, Fabio ESCOBAR Benítez. DT: Carlos Horacio COMPAGNUCCI
Goals: WALLYSON Ricardo Maciel Monteiro (29, 63), Ernesto Antonio FARIÁS (85), THIAGO RIBEIRO Cardoso (88).

CA ESTUDIANTES DE LA PLATA – CC DEPORTES TOLIMA 1-0 (1-0)
Estadio Ciudad de La Plata, La Plata, 23.02.2011
Referee: Darío Agustín UBRIACO Mederos (URU), Attendance: 29.034
CA ESTUDIANTES DE LA PLATA: Agustín Ignacio ORIÓN, Facundo Sebastián RONCAGLIA, Leandro DESÁBATO, Gabriel Iván MERCADO, Federico FERNÁNDEZ, Pablo César BARRIENTOS (70 Leandro Damián BENÍTEZ), Juan Sebastián VERÓN, Rodrigo BRAÑA, Enzo Nicolás PÉREZ (51 Maximiliano Ezequiel NÚÑEZ), Leandro GONZÁLEZ, Gastón Nicolás FERNÁNDEZ (84 Nelson Fabián BENÍTEZ). DT: Manuel Eduardo BERIZZO
CC DEPORTES TOLIMA: Antony Domingo SILVA Cano, Gerardo Enrique VALLEJO Metaute, Félix Enrique NOGUERA Collante, Julián HURTADO Izquierdo, Yair ARRECHEA Amú, Elkin Antonio MURILLO Amor (55 Danny Manuel SANTOYA Otero), Rafael Arlex CASTILLO Galvis (46 Christian Camilo MARRUGO Rodríguez), Diego Ferney CHARÁ Zamora, Gustavo Adolfo BOLÍVAR Zapata, Jhon Fredy HURTADO (75 Wílmer PARRA Cadena), Wilder Andrés MEDINA Tamayo. DT: Hernán TORRES Oliveros
Goal: Pablo César BARRIENTOS (44).

CC DEPORTES TOLIMA – CRUZEIRO EC 0-0
Estadio Manuel Murillo Toro, Ibagué, 2.03.2011
Referee: Jorge Luis LARRIONDA Pietrafesa (URU), Attendance: 11.233
CC DEPORTES TOLIMA: Antony Domingo SILVA Cano, Félix Enrique NOGUERA Collante, Julián HURTADO Izquierdo, Yair ARRECHEA Amú, Elkin Antonio MURILLO Amor (60 Wílmer PARRA Cadena), Diego Ferney CHARÁ Zamora, Christian Camilo MARRUGO Rodríguez, Gustavo Adolfo BOLÍVAR Zapata, Hamilton Alexander ACUÑA Rubiano, Danny Manuel SANTOYA Otero, Wilder Andrés MEDINA Tamayo. DT: Hernán TORRES Oliveros
CRUZEIRO EC: FÁBIO Deivison Lopes Maciel, Mauricio Bernardo VICTORINO Dansilio, PABLO de Barros Paulino, DIEGO RENÁN de Lima Ferreira (79 LEANDRO Luchese GUERREIRO), Carlos Gilberto Nascimento da Silva e Silva "GIL", Antônio Marcos da Silva Filho "MARQUINHOS PARANÁ", HENRIQUE Pacheco de Lima, Walter Damián MONTILLO, ROGER Galera Flores (70 Eduardo Pereira Rodrigues "DUDU"), WALLYSON Ricardo Maciel Monteiro, WELLINGTON "PAULISTA" Pereira do Nascimento (61 THIAGO RIBEIRO Cardoso). DT: Alexis Stival "CUCA" Beluda

CLUB GUARANÍ ASUNCIÓN – CA ESTUDIANTES DE LA PLATA 1-2 (1-0)
Estadio Defensores del Chaco, Asunción, 9.03.2011
Referee: Víctor Hugo CARRILLO Casanova (PER), Attendance: 1.078
CLUB GUARANÍ ASUNCIÓN: Pablo Fernando AURRECOCHEA Medina, Héctor Federico CARBALLO, Elvis Israel MARECOS, Eduardo Javier FILIPPINI, Francisco Joel BENÍTEZ, Miguel Ángel PANIAGUA Rivarola, Juan José AGUILAR Orzusa (46 Cristian Gustavo SOSA), Jorge Darío MENDOZA Torres, Luis DE LA CRUZ (55 Fabio ESCOBAR Benítez), Pablo Nicolás CABALLERO (75 Luis Armando OVELAR Maldonado), Julián Alfonso BENÍTEZ. DT: Félix Darío LEÓN
CA ESTUDIANTES DE LA PLATA: Agustín Ignacio ORIÓN, Facundo Sebastián RONCAGLIA, Leandro DESÁBATO, Gabriel Iván MERCADO, Federico FERNÁNDEZ, Raúl Alejandro IBERBIA, Pablo César BARRIENTOS (90 Nelson Fabián BENÍTEZ), Rodrigo BRAÑA, Leandro Damián BENÍTEZ, Enzo Nicolás PÉREZ (74 Matías Ariel SÁNCHEZ), Leandro GONZÁLEZ (80 Hernán Rodrigo LÓPEZ Mora). DT: Manuel Eduardo BERIZZO
Goals: Pablo Nicolás CABALLERO (43 penalty) /
Pablo César BARRIENTOS (50), Leandro GONZÁLEZ (53).

CRUZEIRO EC – CC DEPORTES TOLIMA 6-1 (2-0)
Estádio Joaquim Henrique Nogueira (Arena do Jacaré), Sete Lagoas, 16.03.2011
Referee: Carlos Alfredo VERA Rodríguez (ECU), Attendance: 8.198
CRUZEIRO EC: FÁBIO Deivison Lopes Maciel, Mauricio Bernardo VICTORINO Dansilio, PABLO de Barros Paulino, DIEGO RENÁN de Lima Ferreira (77 GILBERT da Silva Melo), Carlos Gilberto Nascimento da Silva e Silva "GIL", Antônio Marcos da Silva Filho "MARQUINHOS PARANÁ", HENRIQUE Pacheco de Lima, Walter Damián MONTILLO (80 LEANDRO Luchese GUERREIRO), ROGER Galera Flores, WALLYSON Ricardo Maciel Monteiro, WELLINGTON "PAULISTA" Pereira do Nascimento (67 THIAGO RIBEIRO Cardoso). DT: Alexis Stival "CUCA" Beluda
CC DEPORTES TOLIMA: Antony Domingo SILVA Cano, Gerardo Enrique VALLEJO Metaute, Félix Enrique NOGUERA Collante (74 Hamilton Alexander ACUÑA Rubiano), Wílmer DÍAZ Lucumí, Julián HURTADO Izquierdo, Elkin Antonio MURILLO Amor, Rafael Arlex CASTILLO Galvis (57 Danny Manuel SANTOYA Otero), Diego Ferney CHARÁ Zamora, Christian Camilo MARRUGO Rodríguez, Gustavo Adolfo BOLÍVAR Zapata, Wilder Andrés MEDINA Tamayo (75 Wílmer PARRA Cadena). DT: Hernán TORRES Oliveros
Sent off: Hurtado (87)
Goals: Walter Damián MONTILLO (3), WALLYSON Ricardo Maciel Monteiro (31), ROGER Galera Flores (61, 70 penalty), GILBERT da Silva Melo (88), THIAGO RIBEIRO Cardoso (90+1) / Christian Camilo MARRUGO Rodríguez (68)

CA ESTUDIANTES DE LA PLATA – CLUB GUARANÍ ASUNCIÓN 5-1 (3-0)
Estadio Ciudad de La Plata, La Plata, 17.03.2011
Referee: Martín Emilio VÁZQUEZ Broquetas (URU), Attendance: 13.318
CA ESTUDIANTES DE LA PLATA: Agustín Ignacio ORIÓN, Facundo Sebastián RONCAGLIA, Leandro DESÁBATO, Gabriel Iván MERCADO, Federico FERNÁNDEZ, Raúl Alejandro IBERBIA, Juan Sebastián VERÓN (85 Matías Ariel SÁNCHEZ), Rodrigo BRAÑA, Enzo Nicolás PÉREZ (64 Pablo César BARRIENTOS), Leandro GONZÁLEZ, Hernán Rodrigo LÓPEZ Mora (73 Maximiliano Ezequiel NÚÑEZ). DT: Manuel Eduardo BERIZZO
CLUB GUARANÍ ASUNCIÓN: Pablo Fernando AURRECOCHEA Medina, Ignacio "Nacho" ITHURRALDE Sáez (28 Francisco Joel BENÍTEZ), Héctor Federico CARBALLO, Elvis Israel MARECOS, Eduardo Javier FILIPPINI, Tomás Javier BARTOMÉUS Viveros (68 Cristian Gustavo SOSA), Osvaldo HOBECKER García, Miguel Ángel PANIAGUA Rivarola, Jorge Darío MENDOZA Torres, Julián Alfonso BENÍTEZ, Luis Armando OVELAR Maldonado (70 Fabio ESCOBAR Benítez). DT: Félix Darío LEÓN
Sent off: Roncaglia (51)
Goals: Hernán Rodrigo LÓPEZ Mora (1, 18, 58), Leandro GONZÁLEZ (24, 81) / Julián Alfonso BENÍTEZ (79).

CC DEPORTES TOLIMA – CA ESTUDIANTES DE LA PLATA 1-1 (1-1)
Estadio Manuel Murillo Toro, Ibagué, 30.03.2011
Referee: Víctor Hugo RIVERA Chavez (PER), Attendance: 7.797
CC DEPORTES TOLIMA: Antony Domingo SILVA Cano, Gerardo Enrique VALLEJO Metaute, Félix Enrique NOGUERA Collante (88 Roberto Carlos GAMARRA Acosta), Wílmer DÍAZ Lucumí, Yair ARRECHEA Amú, Elkin Antonio MURILLO Amor (58 Danny Manuel SANTOYA Otero), Diego Ferney CHARÁ Zamora, Christian Camilo MARRUGO Rodríguez (80 Luis Alberto CLOSA González), Gustavo Adolfo BOLÍVAR Zapata, Wilder Andrés MEDINA Tamayo, Wílmer PARRA Cadena. DT: Hernán TORRES Oliveros
CA ESTUDIANTES DE LA PLATA: Agustín Ignacio ORIÓN, Leandro DESÁBATO, Nelson Fabián BENÍTEZ, Gabriel Iván MERCADO, Federico FERNÁNDEZ, Raúl Alejandro IBERBIA, Juan Sebastián VERÓN, Leandro Damán BENÍTEZ, Enzo Nicolás PÉREZ, Leandro GONZÁLEZ (67 Pablo César BARRIENTOS), Hernán Rodrigo LÓPEZ Mora (89 Darío Gustavo STEFANATTO). DT: Manuel Eduardo BERIZZO
Goals: Félix Enrique NOGUERA Collante (30 penalty) / Federico FERNÁNDEZ (23).

CLUB GUARANÍ ASUNCIÓN – CRUZEIRO EC 0-2 (0-1)
Estadio Defensores del Chaco, Asunción, 30.03.2011
Referee: Enrique Roberto OSSES Zencovich (CHI), Attendance: 119
CLUB GUARANÍ ASUNCIÓN: Joel Alberto SILVA Estigarribia, Ignacio "Nacho" ITHURRALDE Sáez (78 Héctor Federico CARBALLO), Elvis Israel MARECOS, Eduardo Javier FILIPPINI, Francisco Joel BENÍTEZ, Miguel Ángel PANIAGUA Rivarola, Cristian Gustavo SOSA, Jorge Darío MENDOZA Torres (66 Osvaldo HOBECKER García), Luis DE LA CRUZ, Julián Alfonso BENÍTEZ, Luis Armando OVELAR Maldonado (66 Fabio ESCOBAR Benítez). DT: Félix Darío LEÓN
CRUZEIRO EC: FÁBIO Deivison Lopes Maciel, Mauricio Bernardo VICTORINO Dansilio, PABLO de Barros Paulino, Carlos Gilberto Nascimento da Silva e Silva "GIL", GILBERT da Silva Melo, Antônio Marcos da Silva Filho "MARQUINHOS PARANÁ", HENRIQUE Pacheco de Lima, Walter Damián MONTILLO, ROGER Galera Flores (67 Francisco EVERTON de Almeida Andrade), WALLYSON Ricardo Maciel Monteiro (81 WELLINGTON "PAULISTA" Pereira do Nascimento), THIAGO RIBEIRO Cardoso (66 José Maria ORTIGOZA Ortiz). DT: Alexis Stival "CUCA" Beluda
Goals: THIAGO RIBEIRO Cardoso (15), José Maria ORTIGOZA Ortiz (90+2).

CLUB GUARANÍ ASUNCIÓN – CC DEPORTES TOLIMA 0-2 (0-0)
Estadio Defensores del Chaco, Asunción, 13.04.2011
Referee: Jorge Joaquín ANTEQUERA Castedo (BOL), Attendance: 200
CLUB GUARANÍ ASUNCIÓN: Pablo Fernando AURRECOCHEA Medina, Héctor Federico CARBALLO, Tomás Javier BARTOMÉUS Viveros, MICAEL Jordane MODINGER (59 Ignacio "Nacho" ITHURRALDE Sáez), Osvaldo HOBECKER García, Ángel Antonio ORTIZ Cabrera, Miguel Ángel PANIAGUA Rivarola, Cristian Gustavo SOSA, Fabián STARK (65 Julián Alfonso BENÍTEZ), Fabio ESCOBAR Benítez (59 Pablo Nicolás CABALLERO), Luis Armando OVELAR Maldonado. DT: Félix Darío LEÓN
CC DEPORTES TOLIMA: Antony Domingo SILVA Cano, Marlon Javier PIEDRAHITA Londoño, Julián HURTADO Izquierdo, Yair ARRECHEA Amú, Christian Camilo MARRUGO Rodríguez, Luis Alberto CLOSA González, Mike CAMPAZ, Jhon Fredy HURTADO, Hamilton Alexander ACUÑA Rubiano, Danny Manuel SANTOYA Otero (76 Wílmer PARRA Cadena), Roberto Carlos GAMARRA Acosta (56 Pablo Júnior GIMÉNEZ). DT: Hernán TORRES Oliveros
Goals: Danny Manuel SANTOYA Otero (48), Luis Alberto CLOSA González (68).

CA ESTUDIANTES DE LA PLATA – CRUZEIRO EC 0-3 (0-2)
Estadio Ciudad de La Plata, La Plata, 13.04.2011
Referee: Roberto Carlos SILVERA Calcerrada (URU), Attendance: 14.828
CA ESTUDIANTES DE LA PLATA: Agustín Ignacio ORIÓN, Facundo Sebastián RONCAGLIA, Nelson Fabián BENÍTEZ, Germán David RÉ, Gabriel Iván MERCADO (46 Federico FERNÁNDEZ), Gabriel Martín PEÑALBA, Pablo César BARRIENTOS, Darío Gustavo STEFANATTO (77 Leandro Damán BENÍTEZ), Maximiliano Ezequiel NÚÑEZ, Juan Pablo PEREYRA, Gastón Nicolás FERNÁNDEZ (62 Leandro GONZÁLEZ). DT: Manuel Eduardo BERIZZO
CRUZEIRO EC: FÁBIO Deivison Lopes Maciel, Mauricio Bernardo VICTORINO Dansilio, PABLO de Barros Paulino, Carlos Gilberto Nascimento da Silva e Silva "GIL", GILBERT da Silva Melo, Antônio Marcos da Silva Filho "MARQUINHOS PARANÁ", LEANDRO Luchese GUERREIRO, HENRIQUE Pacheco de Lima, ROGER Galera Flores (77 Francisco EVERTON de Almeida Andrade), WALLYSON Ricardo Maciel Monteiro (87 José Maria ORTIGOZA Ortiz), THIAGO RIBEIRO Cardoso (77 Ernesto Antonio FARÍAS). DT: Alexis Stival "CUCA" Beluda
Goals: THIAGO RIBEIRO Cardoso (10), WALLYSON Ricardo Maciel Monteiro (45+1), GILBERT da Silva Melo (82).

1	CRUZEIRO	6	5	1	0	20	1	16
2	ESTUDIANTES LA PLATA	6	3	1	2	9	11	10
3	Deportes Tolíma	6	2	2	2	5	8	8
4	Guaraní	6	0	0	6	2	16	0

GROUP 8

CD GODOY CRUZ ANTONIO TOMBA – L.D.U. DE QUITO 2-1 (1-0)
Estadio Malvinas Argentinas, Mendoza, 17.02.2011
Referee: Martín Emilio VÁZQUEZ Broquetas (URU), Attendance: 19.524
CD GODOY CRUZ ANTONIO TOMBA: Sebastián Alberto TORRICO, Leonardo Germán SIGALI, Nicolás Gabriel SÁNCHEZ, Roberto Emilio RUSSO (46 Emir FACCIOLI), Zelmar GARCÍA, Diego Nicolás VILLAR, Nicolás Andrés OLMEDO, Ariel Mauricio ROJAS, Carlos Andrés SÁNCHEZ Arcosa, Rubén Darío RAMÍREZ (90 Mariano Martín DONDA), Pablo MIRANDA (59 Álvaro Damián NAVARRO Bica). DT: Jorge Orosmán DA SILVA Echeverrito
L.D.U.: Alexander DOMÍNGUEZ Carabalí, Jorge Daniel GUAGUA Tamayo, Ulises Hernán DE LA CRUZ Bernardo, José Luis VALENCIA Murillo (38 Paúl Vicente AMBROSI Zambrano), Néicer REASCO Yano, Diego Armando CALDERÓN Espinoza, Patricio Javier URRUTIA Espinoza (46 Fernando Roberto HIDALGO Maldonado), Enrique Daniel VERA Torres, William Francisco ARAUJO Ogonaga (67 Miler Alejandro BOLAÑOS Reasco), Carlos Ariel LUNA, Luis Alberto BOLAÑOS León. DT: Edgardo BAUZA
Sent off: Hidalgo (90)
Goals: Carlos Andrés SÁNCHEZ Arcosa (16), Nicolás Gabriel SÁNCHEZ (59) /
Néicer REASCO Yano (53).

CA INDEPENDIENTE AVELLANEDA – CA PEÑAROL MONTEVIDEO 3-0 (0-0)
Estadio Libertadores de América, Avellaneda, 24.02.2011
Referee: Sálvio Spínola FAGUNDES Filho (BRA), Attendance: 21.354
CA INDEPENDIENTE AVELLANEDA: Hilario Bernardo NAVARRO, Maximiliano Nicolás VELÁZQUEZ, Eduardo Nicolás TUZZIO, Leonel GALEANO, Julián Albert VELÁZQUEZ, Leandro GRACIÁN (63 Roberto Miguel BATTIÓN), Patricio Julián RODRÍGUEZ, Cristian Alberto PELLERANO, Nicolás Alejandro CABRERA, Matías Adrian DEFEDERICO (72 Leonel Jorge NÚÑEZ), Facundo Manuel PARRA (66 Néstor Andrés SILVERA). DT: Antonio Ricardo MOHAMED Matijevich
CA PEÑAROL MONTEVIDEO: Héctor Fsabián CARINI Hernández, Octavio Darío RODRÍGUEZ Peña, Carlos Adrián VALDÉZ Suarez (46 Alejandro Damián GONZÁLEZ Hernández), Guillermo Daniel RODRÍGUEZ Pérez, Matías CORUJO Díaz, Luis Bernardo AGUIAR Burgos, Nicolás Andrés FREITAS Silva, Antonio PACHECO D'Agosti, Jonathan Matías URRETAVISCAYA da Luz (81 Fabián Larry ESTOYANOFF Poggio), Nicolás Mario DOMINGO, Juan Manuel OLIVERA López (66 Alejandro MARTINUCCIO). DT: Diego Vicente AGUIRRE Camblor
Goals: Facundo Manuel PARRA (46), Cristian Alberto PELLERANO (70),
Néstor Andrés SILVERA (85).

CD GODOY CRUZ ANTONIO TOMBA – CA PEÑAROL MONTEVIDEO 1-3 (1-2)
Estadio Malvinas Argentinas, Mendoza, 1.03.2011
Referee: Paulo César DE OLIVEIRA (BRA), Attendance: 12.946
CD GODOY CRUZ ANTONIO TOMBA: Sebastián Alberto TORRICO, Leonardo Germán SIGALI, Nicolás Gabriel SÁNCHEZ, Roberto Emilio RUSSO, Zelmar GARCÍA (46 Álvaro Damián NAVARRO Bica), Diego Nicolás VILLAR, Nicolás Andrés OLMEDO, Ariel Mauricio ROJAS (70 Mariano Martín DONDA), Carlos Andrés SÁNCHEZ Arcosa, Rubén Darío RAMÍREZ, Fabricio Damián NÚÑEZ Lozano (70 Gabriel MOYANO). DT: Jorge Orosmán DA SILVA Echeverrito
CA PEÑAROL MONTEVIDEO: Carlos Sebastián SOSA Silva, Octavio Darío RODRÍGUEZ Peña, Carlos Adrián VALDÉZ Suarez (81 Édison Eliazer TORRES Martínez), Guillermo Daniel RODRÍGUEZ Pérez, Matías CORUJO Díaz, Alejandro Damián GONZÁLEZ Hernández, Luis Bernardo AGUIAR Burgos, Nicolás Andrés FREITAS Silva, Henry Matías MIER Codina (70 Emiliano ALBÍN Antognazza), Juan Manuel OLIVERA López (88 Mauro GUEVGEOZIAN Crespa), Alejandro MARTINUCCIO. DT: Diego Vicente AGUIRRE Camblor
Goals: Rubén Darío RAMÍREZ (30) /
Juan Manuel OLIVERA López (1, 41), Luis Bernardo AGUIAR Burgos (67).

L.D.U. DE QUITO – CA INDEPENDIENTE AVELLANEDA 3-0 (1-0)
Estadio de Liga Deportiva Universitaria (La Casa Blanca), Quito, 3.03.2011
Referee: Óscar Julián RUÍZ Acosta (COL), Attendance: 13.768
L.D.U.: Alexander DOMÍNGUEZ Carabalí, Paúl Vicente AMBROSI Zambrano, Jorge Daniel GUAGUA Tamayo, Ulises Hernán DE LA CRUZ Bernardo, Néicer REASCO Yano, Diego Armando CALDERÓN Espinoza, Banner Geovanny CAICEDO Quiñonez, Ezequiel "Equi" GONZÁLEZ (62 Patricio Javier URRUTIA Espinoza), Enrique Daniel VERA Torres (73 William Francisco ARAUJO Ogonaga), Miler Alejandro BOLAÑOS Reasco, Hernán BARCOS (80 Carlos Ariel LUNA). DT: Edgardo BAUZA
CA INDEPENDIENTE AVELLANEDA: Adrián José GABBARINI, Carlos Javier MATHEU, Lucas Armando MAREQUE, Maximiliano Nicolás VELÁZQUEZ, José Iván VÉLEZ Castillo, Leonel GALEANO, Hernán Daniel FREDES (72 Cristian Alberto PELLERANO), Leandro GRACIÁN (62 Patricio Julián RODRÍGUEZ), Fernando Gabriel GODOY, Facundo Manuel PARRA (62 Néstor Andrés SILVERA), Leonel Jorge NÚÑEZ. DT: Antonio Ricardo MOHAMED Matijevich
Goals: Paúl Vicente AMBROSI Zambrano (10), Miler Alejandro BOLAÑOS Reasco (52), Patricio Javier URRUTIA Espinoza (78).

CA PEÑAROL MONTEVIDEO – L.D.U. DE QUITO 1-0 (0-0)
Estadio Centenario, Montevideo, 9.03.2011
Referee: Víctor Hugo RIVERA Chavez (PER), Attendance: 42.455
CA PEÑAROL MONTEVIDEO: Carlos Sebastián SOSA Silva, Octavio Darío RODRÍGUEZ Peña, Carlos Adrián VALDÉZ Suarez, Matías CORUJO Díaz, Alejandro Damián GONZÁLEZ Hernández, Luis Bernardo AGUIAR Burgos, Nicolás Andrés FREITAS Silva, Antonio PACHECO D'Agosti (76 Alejandro MARTINUCCIO), Jonathan Matías URRETAVISCAYA da Luz (90 Emiliano ALBÍN Antognazza), Henry Matías MIER Codina (59 Fabián Larry ESTOYANOFF Poggio), Juan Manuel OLIVERA López. DT: Diego Vicente AGUIRRE Camblor
L.D.U.: Alexander DOMÍNGUEZ Carabalí, Paúl Vicente AMBROSI Zambrano (70 José Luis VALENCIA Murillo), Jorge Daniel GUAGUA Tamayo, Ulises Hernán DE LA CRUZ Bernardo, Néicer REASCO Yano, Diego Armando CALDERÓN Espinoza, Banner Geovanny CAICEDO Quiñonez, Ezequiel "Equi" GONZÁLEZ (86 Patricio Javier URRUTIA Espinoza), Enrique Daniel VERA Torres, Fernando Roberto HIDALGO Maldonado (64 Carlos Ariel LUNA), Hernán BARCOS. DT: Edgardo BAUZA
Goal: Luis Bernardo AGUIAR Burgos (57).

CA INDEPENDIENTE AVELLANEDA – CD GODOY CRUZ ANTONIO TOMBA 1-3 (1-2)
Estadio Libertadores de América, Avellaneda, 10.03.2011
Referee: Patricio Hernán LOUSTAU (ARG), Attendance: 10.625
CA INDEPENDIENTE AVELLANEDA: Hilario Bernardo NAVARRO, Lucas Armando MAREQUE, Eduardo Nicolás TUZZIO, José Iván VÉLEZ Castillo, Leonel GALEANO, Hernán Daniel FREDES (58 Matías Adrian DEFEDERICO), Leandro GRACIÁN, Patricio Julián RODRÍGUEZ, Fernando Gabriel GODOY, Facundo Manuel PARRA, Jairo Fernando CASTILLO Cortés (58 Leonel Jorge NÚÑEZ). DT: Antonio Ricardo MOHAMED Matijevich
CD GODOY CRUZ ANTONIO TOMBA: Sebastián Alberto TORRICO, Leonardo Germán SIGALI, Nicolás Gabriel SÁNCHEZ, Roberto Emilio RUSSO, Zelmar GARCÍA, Diego Nicolás VILLAR, Israel Alejandro DAMONTE, Nicolás Andrés OLMEDO, Ariel Mauricio ROJAS (90 Pablo MIRANDA), Carlos Andrés SÁNCHEZ Arcosa, Rubén Darío RAMÍREZ (79 Álvaro Damián NAVARRO Bica). DT: Jorge Orosmán DA SILVA Echeverrito
Goals: Facundo Manuel PARRA (15) /
Hernán Daniel FREDES (28 *own goal*), Ariel Mauricio ROJAS (32), Rubén Darío RAMÍREZ (56).

L.D.U. DE QUITO – CA PEÑAROL MONTEVIDEO 5-0 (2-0)
Estadio de Liga Deportiva Universitaria (La Casa Blanca), Quito, 17.03.2011
Referee: Wilmar Alexander ROLDÁN Pérez (COL), Attendance: 15.329
L.D.U.: Alexander DOMÍNGUEZ Carabalí, Paúl Vicente AMBROSI Zambrano, Jorge Daniel GUAGUA Tamayo, Ulises Hernán DE LA CRUZ Bernardo, Néicer REASCO Yano, Diego Armando CALDERÓN Espinoza, Banner Geovanny CAICEDO Quiñonez, Ezequiel "Equi" GONZÁLEZ (69 William Francisco ARAUJO Ogonaga), Enrique Daniel VERA Torres (66 Fernando Roberto HIDALGO Maldonado), Hernán BARCOS, Carlos Ariel LUNA (24 Walter Richard CALDERÓN Carcelen). DT: Edgardo BAUZA
CA PEÑAROL MONTEVIDEO: Carlos Sebastián SOSA Silva, Octavio Darío RODRÍGUEZ Peña, Carlos Adrián VALDÉZ Suarez, Matías CORUJO Díaz, Alejandro Damián GONZÁLEZ Hernández, Emiliano ALBÍN Antognazza, Luis Bernardo AGUIAR Burgos, Nicolás Andrés FREITAS Silva (69 Nicolás Mario DOMINGO), Henry Matías MIER Codina (59 Fabián Larry ESTOYANOFF Poggio), Mauro GUEVGEOZIAN Crespa (59 Juan Manuel OLIVERA López), Alejandro MARTINUCCIO. DT: Diego Vicente AGUIRRE Camblor
Goals: Carlos Ariel LUNA (22), Walter Richard CALDERÓN Carcelen (45+1, 78),
Carlos Adrián VALDÉZ Suarez (58 *own goal*), Hernán BARCOS (63)

CD GODOY CRUZ ANTONIO TOMBA – CA INDEPENDIENTE AVELLANEDA 1-1 (1-1)
Estadio Malvinas Argentinas, Mendoza, 23.03.2011
Referee: Héctor Wálter BALDASSI (ARG), Attendance: 11.819
CD GODOY CRUZ ANTONIO TOMBA: Sebastián Alberto TORRICO, Leonardo Germán SIGALI, Nicolás Gabriel SÁNCHEZ, Roberto Emilio RUSSO, Zelmar GARCÍA, Diego Nicolás VILLAR, Israel Alejandro DAMONTE, Nicolás Andrés OLMEDO, Carlos Andrés SÁNCHEZ Arcosa, Rubén Darío RAMÍREZ, Fabricio Damián NÚÑEZ Lozano (73 Mariano Martín DONDA). DT: Jorge Orosmán DA SILVA Echeverrito
CA INDEPENDIENTE AVELLANEDA: Hilario Bernardo NAVARRO, Carlos Javier MATHEU, Maximiliano Nicolás VELÁZQUEZ, Eduardo Nicolás TUZZIO, Leonel GALEANO, Leandro GRACIÁN (55 Hernán Daniel FREDES), Nicolás Alejandro CABRERA, Federico Andrés MANCUELLO (76 Patricio Julián RODRÍGUEZ), Fernando Gabriel GODOY, Néstor Andrés SILVERA, Matías Adrian DEFEDERICO (50 Facundo Manuel PARRA). DT: Antonio Ricardo MOHAMED Matijevich
Goals: Rubén Darío RAMÍREZ (33) / Matías Adrian DEFEDERICO (1).

CA PEÑAROL MONTEVIDEO – CD GODOY CRUZ ANTONIO TOMBA 2-1 (1-0)
Estadio Centenario, Montevideo, 31.03.2011
Referee: Héber Roberto LOPES (BRA), Attendance: 43.179
CA PEÑAROL MONTEVIDEO: Carlos Sebastián SOSA Silva, Octavio Darío RODRÍGUEZ Peña, Carlos Adrián VALDÉZ Suarez, Matías CORUJO Díaz, Alejandro Damián GONZÁLEZ Hernández, Nicolás Andrés FREITAS Silva, Antonio PACHECO D'Agosti (74 Emiliano ALBÍN Antognazza), Jonathan Matías URRETAVISCAYA da Luz, Henry Matías MIER Codina (66 Fabián Larry ESTOYANOFF Poggio), Nicolás Mario DOMINGO, Juan Manuel OLIVERA López (90 Diego Martín ALONSO López). DT: Diego Vicente AGUIRRE Camblor
CD GODOY CRUZ ANTONIO TOMBA: Sebastián Alberto TORRICO, Leonardo Germán SIGALI, Nicolás Gabriel SÁNCHEZ, Roberto Emilio RUSSO, Zelmar GARCÍA, Diego Nicolás VILLAR (78 Fabricio Damián NÚÑEZ Lozano), Mariano Martín DONDA, Israel Alejandro DAMONTE (72 Álvaro Damián NAVARRO Bica), Nicolás Andrés OLMEDO, Carlos Andrés SÁNCHEZ Arcosa (60 Ariel Mauricio ROJAS), Rubén Darío RAMÍREZ. DT: Jorge Orosmán DA SILVA Echeverrito
Goals: Juan Manuel OLIVERA López (42), Nicolás Andrés FREITAS Silva (70) /
Octavio Darío RODRÍGUEZ Peña (57 *own goal*).

CA INDEPENDIENTE AVELLANEDA – L.D.U. DE QUITO 1-1 (1-0)
Estadio Libertadores de América, Avellaneda, 5.04.2011
Referee: Carlos Manuel TORRES Nuñez (PAR), Attendance: 13.270
CA INDEPENDIENTE AVELLANEDA: Walter Fabián ASSMANN, Lucas Armando MAREQUE, Eduardo Nicolás TUZZIO (79 Hernán Daniel FREDES), Leonel GALEANO, Julián Albert VELÁZQUEZ, Roberto Miguel BATTIÓN, Patricio Julián RODRÍGUEZ (70 Facundo Manuel PARRA), Fernando Gabriel GODOY (71 Leandro GRACIÁN), Jorge Iván PÉREZ, Néstor Andrés SILVERA, Leonel Jorge NÚÑEZ. DT: Antonio Ricardo MOHAMED Matijevich
L.D.U.: Alexander DOMÍNGUEZ Carabalí, Paúl Vicente AMBROSI Zambrano, Jorge Daniel GUAGUA Tamayo, Ulises Hernán DE LA CRUZ Bernardo, Néicer REASCO Yano, Diego Armando CALDERÓN Espinoza, Banner Geovanny CAICEDO Quiñonez, Ezequiel "Equi" GONZÁLEZ (77 Walter Richard CALDERÓN Carcelen), Enrique Daniel VERA Torres, Hernán BARCOS (87 Patricio Javier URRUTIA Espinoza), Luis Alberto BOLAÑOS León (68 William Francisco ARAUJO Ogonaga). DT: Edgardo BAUZA
Goals: Leonel Jorge NÚÑEZ (23 penalty) / Julián Albert VELÁZQUEZ (57 *own goal*).

CA PEÑAROL MONTEVIDEO – CA INDEPENDIENTE AVELLANEDA 0-1 (0-1)
Estadio Centenario, Montevideo, 12.04.2011
Referee: Antonio Javier ARIAS Alvarenga (PAR), Attendance: 51.989
CA PEÑAROL MONTEVIDEO: Carlos Sebastián SOSA Silva, Octavio Darío RODRÍGUEZ Peña, Carlos Adrián VALDÉZ Suarez, Matías CORUJO Díaz, Alejandro Damián GONZÁLEZ Hernández, Luis Bernardo AGUIAR Burgos, Antonio PACHECO D'Agosti (58 Diego Martín ALONSO López), Jonathan Matías URRETAVISCAYA da Luz (23 Fabián Larry ESTOYANOFF Poggio), Henry Matías MIER Codina (57 Alejandro MARTINUCCIO), Nicolás Mario DOMINGO, Juan Manuel OLIVERA López. DT: Diego Vicente AGUIRRE Camblor
CA INDEPENDIENTE AVELLANEDA: Walter Fabián ASSMANN, Carlos Javier MATHEU, Maximiliano Nicolás VELÁZQUEZ, José Iván VÉLEZ Castillo, Julián Albert VELÁZQUEZ, Roberto Miguel BATTIÓN, Leandro GRACIÁN, Federico Andrés MANCUELLO (76 Jorge Iván PÉREZ), Fernando Gabriel GODOY (75 Hernán Daniel FREDES), Facundo Manuel PARRA, Jairo Fernando CASTILLO Cortés (46 Patricio Julián RODRÍGUEZ). DT: Antonio Ricardo MOHAMED Matijevich
Sent off: Olivera (84) / Assmann (84)
Goal: Facundo Manuel PARRA (33).

L.D.U. DE QUITO – CD GODOY CRUZ ANTONIO TOMBA 2-0 (0-0)
Estadio de Liga Deportiva Universitaria (La Casa Blanca), Quito, 12.04.2011
Referee: Paulo César DE OLIVEIRA (BRA), Attendance: 15.516
L.D.U.: Alexander DOMÍNGUEZ Carabalí, Paúl Vicente AMBROSI Zambrano, Jorge Daniel GUAGUA Tamayo, Ulises Hernán DE LA CRUZ Bernardo (82 Patricio Javier URRUTIA Espinoza), Néicer REASCO Yano, Diego Armando CALDERÓN Espinoza, Banner Geovanny CAICEDO Quiñonez, Ezequiel "Equi" GONZÁLEZ, Enrique Daniel VERA Torres (71 William Francisco ARAUJO Ogonaga), Hernán BARCOS, Luis Alberto BOLAÑOS León (76 Fernando Roberto HIDALGO Maldonado). DT: Edgardo BAUZA
CD GODOY CRUZ ANTONIO TOMBA: Sebastián Alberto TORRICO, Leonardo Germán SIGALI, Nicolás Gabriel SÁNCHEZ, Roberto Emilio RUSSO, Zelmar GARCÍA, Juan Carlos FALCÓN, Diego Nicolás VILLAR (71 Mariano Martín DONDA), Israel Alejandro DAMONTE, Ariel Mauricio ROJAS (64 Fabricio Damián NÚÑEZ Lozano), Carlos Andrés SÁNCHEZ Arcosa, Álvaro Damián NAVARRO Bica (65 Rodrigo Javier SALINAS). DT: Jorge Orosmán DA SILVA Echeverrito
Sent off: Carlos Sánchez (62)
Goals: Luis Alberto BOLAÑOS León (47), Hernán BARCOS (58).

1	LIGA de QUITO	6	3	1	2	12	4	10
2	PEÑAROL	6	3	0	3	6	11	9
3	Independiente	6	2	2	2	7	8	8
4	Godoy Cruz	6	2	1	3	8	10	7

ROUND OF 16

GRÊMIO FOOT-BALL PORTO ALEGRENSE – CD UNIVERSIDAD CATÓLICA 1-2 (0-1)
Estádio Olímpico Monumental, Porto Alegre, 26.04.2011
Referee: Néstor Fabian PITANA (ARG), Attendance: 31.559
GRÊMIO FOOT-BALL PORTO ALEGRENSE: MARCELO Grohe, RAFAEL MARQUES Pinto, GABRIEL Rodrigues dos Santos, NEUTON Sérgio Picolli, GÍLSON Gomes do Nascimento (90 Damián Ariel ESCUDERO), FÁBIO ROCHEMBACK, ADÍLSON Warken, DOUGLAS dos Santos, WILLIAN "MAGRÃO" Henrique Antunes (46 LINS Lima de Brito), Humberlito BORGES Teixeira, Weverson LEANDRO Oliveira Moura (78 CARLOS ALBERTO Gomes de Jesús). DT: RENATO "GAÚCHO" Portaluppi
CD UNIVERSIDAD CATÓLICA: Paulo Andrés GARCÉS Contreras, Hans Alexis MARTÍNEZ Cabrera, David Andrés HENRÍQUEZ Espinoza, Juan Eduardo ELUCHANS, Jorge Andrés ORMEÑO Guerra, Rodrigo Ignacio VALENZUELA Avilés, Francisco Andrés SILVA Gajardo (64 Felipe Alejandro GUTIÉRREZ Leiva), Fernando Andrés MENESES Cornejo, Tomás COSTA (83 Gonzalo Alfredo SEPÚLVEDA Domínguez), Marcelo CAÑETE (76 José Luis VILLANUEVA Ahumada), Lucas David PRATTO. DT: Juan Antonio PIZZI Torroja
Sent off: Borges (35)
Goals: DOUGLAS dos Santos (58) / Lucas David PRATTO (28, 73).

CD UNIVERSIDAD CATÓLICA – GRÊMIO FOOT-BALL PORTO ALEGRENSE 1-0 (0-0)
Estadio San Carlos de Apoquindo, Santiago, 4.05.2011
Referee: Carlos Arecio AMARILLA Demarqui (PAR), Attendance: 13.502
CD UNIVERSIDAD CATÓLICA: Paulo Andrés GARCÉS Contreras, Hans Alexis MARTÍNEZ Cabrera, David Andrés HENRÍQUEZ Espinoza, Juan Eduardo ELUCHANS, Jorge Andrés ORMEÑO Guerra, Rodrigo Ignacio VALENZUELA Avilés, Francisco Andrés SILVA Gajardo, Fernando Andrés MENESES Cornejo, Tomás COSTA (53 Milovan Petar MIROSEVIC Albornoz), Marcelo CAÑETE (72 Felipe Alejandro GUTIÉRREZ Leiva), Lucas David PRATTO (90 Roberto Carlos GUTIÉRREZ Gamboa). DT: Juan Antonio PIZZI Torroja
GRÊMIO FOOT-BALL PORTO ALEGRENSE: MARCELO Grohe, RODOLFO Dantas Bispo, RAFAEL MARQUES Pinto (63 Weverson LEANDRO Oliveira Moura), VILSON Xavier de Menezes Júnior, MÁRIO Figueira FERNANDES (84 VINÍCIUS PACHECO dos Santos), GÍLSON Gomes do Nascimento, ADÍLSON Warken, DOUGLAS dos Santos, FERNANDO Lucas Martins, LINS Lima de Brito (79 Damián Ariel ESCUDERO), Luiz Severo JÚNIOR "VIÇOSA". DT: RENATO "GAÚCHO" Portaluppi
Goal: Milovan Petar MIROSEVIC Albornoz (85).

CA VÉLEZ SÁRSFIELD – L.D.U. DE QUITO 3-0 (2-0)
Estadio José Amalfitani, Buenos Aires, 26.04.2011
Referee: Carlos Arecio AMARILLA Demarqui (PAR), Attendance: 7.134
CA VÉLEZ SARSFIELD: Marcelo Alberto BAROVERO, Sebastián Enrique DOMÍNGUEZ, Emiliano Ramiro PAPA, Fernando ORTIZ, Franco RAZZOTTI Viretto (72 Arturo David RAMÍREZ), Víctor Eduardo ZAPATA (44 Ricardo Gabriel ÁLVAREZ), Fabián Alberto CUBERO, Maximiliano Nicolás MORALEZ, Augusto Matías FERNÁNDEZ, Santiago Martín SILVA Olivera, Juan Manuel MARTÍNEZ (87 Agustín VULETICH). DT: Ricardo Alberto GARECA
L.D.U.: Alexander DOMÍNGUEZ Carabalí, Jorge Daniel GUAGUA Tamayo, Ulises Hernán DE LA CRUZ Bernardo (82 Patricio Javier URRUTIA Espinoza), José Luis VALENCIA Murillo, Néicer REASCO Yano, Norberto Carlos ARAUJO López, Diego Armando CALDERÓN Espinoza, Enrique Daniel VERA Torres, Fernando Roberto HIDALGO Maldonado, Hernán BARCOS (78 Walter Richard CALDERÓN Carcelen), Luis Alberto BOLAÑOS León. DT: Edgardo BAUZA
Sent off: Bolaños (54), Reasco (69)
Goals: Augusto Matías FERNÁNDEZ (7, 10), Sebastián Enrique DOMÍNGUEZ (54).

L.D.U. DE QUITO – CA VÉLEZ SÁRSFIELD 0-2 (0-1)
Estadio de Liga Deportiva Universitaria (La Casa Blanca), Quito, 5.05.2011
Referee: Wilmar Alexander ROLDÁN Pérez (COL), Attendance: 19.158
L.D.U.: Alexander DOMÍNGUEZ Carabalí, Jorge Daniel GUAGUA Tamayo, Ulises Hernán DE LA CRUZ Bernardo, Norberto Carlos ARAUJO López (66 Patricio Javier URRUTIA Espinoza), Diego Armando CALDERÓN Espinoza, Enrique Daniel VERA Torres, Fernando Roberto HIDALGO Maldonado, Miler Alejandro BOLAÑOS Reasco, Marlon Javier GANCHOZO Santana (46 José Francisco CEVALLOS Enriquez), Hernán BARCOS, Walter Richard CALDERÓN Carcelen (60 José Luis VALENCIA Murillo). DT: Edgardo BAUZA
CA VÉLEZ SARSFIELD: Marcelo Alberto BAROVERO, Sebastián Enrique DOMÍNGUEZ, Emiliano Ramiro PAPA, Fernando ORTIZ, Franco RAZZOTTI Viretto, Fabián Alberto CUBERO, Maximiliano Nicolás MORALEZ (44 Arturo David RAMÍREZ), Augusto Matías FERNÁNDEZ, Héctor Miguel CANTEROS, Ricardo Gabriel ÁLVAREZ (68 Iván Gonzalo BELLA), Juan Manuel MARTÍNEZ (79 Agustín VULETICH). DT: Ricardo Alberto GARECA
Sent off: Guagua (88)
Goals: Ricardo Gabriel ÁLVAREZ (45+10), Iván Gonzalo BELLA (80).

CF JAGUARES DE CHIAPAS SA – CPD JUNIOR 1-1 (0-1)
Estadio Zoque Víctor Manuel Reyna, Tuxtla Gutiérrez, 27.04.2011
Referee: Omar Andres PONCE Manzo (ECU), Attendance: 5.071
CF JAGUARES DE CHIAPAS SA: Jorge VILLALPANDO Romo, Ismael Ignacio FUENTES Castro, Marvin Gabriel CABRERA Ibarra (23 Alan Miguel ZAMORA Gonzalez), Óscar Francisco RAZO Ventura, Miguel Ángel MARTÍNEZ, Christian de Jesús VALDÉZ Loaiza, Damián Alejandro MANSO (53 Édgar Bismarck ANDRADE Rentería), Luis Ricardo ESQUEDA Ornelas (76 Jorge Marcelo RODRÍGUEZ Núñez), Antonio SALAZAR Castillo, Jackson Arley MARTÍNEZ Valencia, Jorge Daniel HERNÁNDEZ Govea. DT: José Guadalupe CRUZ Núnez
CPD JUNIOR: Mário Sebastián VIERA Galain, César Augusto FAWCETT Lébolo, Jhon Alexander VALENCIA Hinestroza, Harold MACÍAS Cabrera, Jhon Eduis VIAFÁRA Mina, Giovanni HERNÁNDEZ Soto (89 Wainer Javier CADENA Rueda), Brayner Yesid GARCÍA Leal, Jossymar Andrés GÓMEZ Pereira, Luis Alfonso PÁEZ Restrepo (46 Julian BARAHONA Angulo), Luis Carlos RUÍZ Morales (64 Víctor Javier CORTÉS), Carlos Arturo BACCA Ahumada. DT: Óscar Héctor QUINTABANI Faggionali
Goals: Jackson Arley MARTÍNEZ Valencia (57) / Luis Alfonso PÁEZ Restrepo (6).

CPD JUNIOR – CF JAGUARES DE CHIAPAS SA 3-3 (1-1)
Estadio Metropolitano Roberto Meléndez, Barranquilla, 5.05.2011
Referee: Héber Roberto LOPES (BRA), Attendance: 17.371
CPD JUNIOR: Mário Sebastián VIERA Galain, César Augusto FAWCETT Lébolo, Jhon Alexander VALENCIA Hinestroza, Juan David VALENCIA Hinestroza (69 Víctor Javier CORTÉS), ANSELMO de Almeida Machado, Jhon Eduis VIAFÁRA Mina, Giovanni HERNÁNDEZ Soto, Brayner Yesid GARCÍA Leal, Jossymar Andrés GÓMEZ Pereira (82 José Antonio AMAYA Pardo), Luis Alfonso PÁEZ Restrepo, Carlos Arturo BACCA Ahumada. DT: Óscar Héctor QUINTABANI Faggionali
CF JAGUARES DE CHIAPAS SA: Jorge VILLALPANDO Romo (75 Fabián Israel VILLASEÑOR López), Ismael Ignacio FUENTES Castro, Óscar Francisco RAZO Ventura (80 Julio Daniel FRÍAS Adame), Miguel Ángel MARTÍNEZ, Christian de Jesús VALDÉZ Loaiza, Édgar Bismarck ANDRADE Rentería, Jorge Marcelo RODRÍGUEZ Núñez, Alan Miguel ZAMORA Gonzalez (69 Luis Ricardo ESQUEDA Ornelas), Antonio SALAZAR Castillo, Jackson Arley MARTÍNEZ Valencia, Jorge Daniel HERNÁNDEZ Govea. DT: José Guadalupe CRUZ Núnez
Sent off: Fawcett (76) / Martínez (78)
Goals: Juan David VALENCIA Hinestroza (35), Luis Alfonso PÁEZ Restrepo (50 penalty),
Carlos Arturo BACCA Ahumada (72) /
Jackson Arley MARTÍNEZ Valencia (39, 63), Édgar Bismarck ANDRADE Rentería (86).

CA ESTUDIANTES DE LA PLATA – CLUB CERRO PORTEÑO 0-0
Estadio Ciudad de La Plata, La Plata, 27.04.2011
Referee: Sálvio Spínola FAGUNDES Filho (BRA), Attendance: 15.815
CA ESTUDIANTES DE LA PLATA: Agustín Ignacio ORIÓN, Facundo Sebastián RONCAGLIA, Leandro DESÁBATO, Germán David RÉ, Federico FERNÁNDEZ, Pablo César BARRIENTOS (88 Leandro GONZÁLEZ), Juan Sebastián VERÓN (84 Leandro Damán BENÍTEZ), Rodrigo BRAÑA, Enzo Nicolás PÉREZ, Gastón Nicolás FERNÁNDEZ, Hernán Rodrigo LÓPEZ Mora. DT: Manuel Eduardo BERIZZO
CLUB CERRO PORTEÑO: Diego Daniel BARRETO Cáceres, Luís Carlos CARDOZO Espillaga, Pedro Juan BENÍTEZ Dominguez, Iván Rodrigo PIRIS Leguizamón, César Iván BENÍTEZ León, Javier Alejandro VILLARREAL, Rodrigo Ramon BURGOS, Jonathan FABBRO (88 Mariano Esteban UGLESSICH), Jorge Daniel NÚÑEZ Espínola, Iván Arturo TORRES Riveros (77 Luís Enrique CÁCERES Centurión), Roberto Antonio NANNI. DT: Leonardo Rubén ASTRADA
Sent off: Burgos (86)

CLUB CERRO PORTEÑO – CA ESTUDIANTES DE LA PLATA 0-0; 5-3 penalties
Estadio General Pablo Rojas, Asunción, 5.05.2011
Referee: Óscar Julián RUÍZ Acosta (COL), Attendance: 20.408
CLUB CERRO PORTEÑO: Diego Daniel BARRETO Cáceres, Luís Carlos CARDOZO Espillaga, Pedro Juan BENÍTEZ Dominguez, Iván Rodrigo PIRIS Leguizamón, César Iván BENÍTEZ León, Javier Alejandro VILLARREAL, Luís Enrique CÁCERES Centurión, Jonathan FABBRO, Jorge Daniel NÚÑEZ Espínola (66 Juan Manuel ITURBE Arévalo), Iván Arturo TORRES Riveros (85 Julio Daniel DOS SANTOS Rodrígues), Roberto Antonio NANNI. DT: Leonardo Rubén ASTRADA
CA ESTUDIANTES DE LA PLATA: Agustín Ignacio ORIÓN, Facundo Sebastián RONCAGLIA, Leandro DESÁBATO, Germán David RÉ, Federico FERNÁNDEZ, Raúl Alejandro IBERBIA, Rodrigo BRAÑA, Leandro Damán BENÍTEZ, Enzo Nicolás PÉREZ, Gastón Nicolás FERNÁNDEZ (75 Juan Pablo PEREYRA), Hernán Rodrigo LÓPEZ Mora. DT: Manuel Eduardo BERIZZO
Penalties: 1-0 Julio Daniel DOS SANTOS Rodrígues, 1-1 Leandro Damán BENÍTEZ, 2-1 Jonathan FABBRO, 2-2 Hernán Rodrigo LÓPEZ Mora, 3-2 Roberto Antonio NANNI, 3-3 Juan Pablo PEREYRA, 4-3 Luís Enrique CÁCERES Centurión, * Facundo Sebastián RONCAGLIA, 5-3 Javier Alejandro VILLARREAL

CD ONCE CALDAS – CRUZEIRO EC 1-2 (0-0)
Estadio Palogrande, Manizales, 27.04.2011
Referee: Víctor Hugo CARRILLO Casanova (PER), Attendance: 13.286
CD ONCE CALDAS: Luis Enrique MARTÍNEZ Rodríguez, Alexis Héctor HENRÍQUEZ Charales, Luis Alberto NÚÑEZ Charales, Elkin Darío CALLE Grajales (78 John Fredy PAJOY Ortíz), Diego Armando AMAYA Solano, Alexander MEJÍA Sabalsa, Claudio Matías MIRABAJE Correa (54 Félix Andrés MICOLTA Micolta), Hárrison Steve HENAO Hurtado (69 Mario Alejandro GONZÁLEZ Castro), Dayro Mauricio MORENO Galindo, Wason Libardo RENTERÍA Cuesta, Carlos Mario CARBONERO Mancilla. DT: Juan Carlos OSORIO Arbeláez
CRUZEIRO EC: FÁBIO Deivison Lopes Maciel, Mauricio Bernardo VICTORINO Dansilio, Carlos Gilberto Nascimento da Silva e Silva "GIL", GILBERT da Silva Melo (82 Cicero VITOR dos Santos Junior), Antônio Marcos da Silva Filho "MARQUINHOS PARANÁ", LEANDRO Luchese GUERREIRO, HENRIQUE Pacheco de Lima, Walter Damián MONTILLO, ROGER Galera Flores (46 Francisco EVERTON de Almeida Andrade), Evaeverson Lemos da Silva BRANDÃO (67 José Maria ORTIGOZA Ortiz), WALLYSON Ricardo Maciel Monteiro. DT: Alexis Stival "CUCA" Beluda
Goals: Luis Alberto NÚÑEZ Charales (88) /
WALLYSON Ricardo Maciel Monteiro (72), José Maria ORTIGOZA Ortiz (83).

CRUZEIRO EC – CD ONCE CALDAS 0-2 (0-0)
Estádio Joaquim Henrique Nogueira (Arena do Jacaré), Sete Lagoas, 4.05.2011
Referee: Antonio Javier ARIAS Alvarenga (PAR), Attendance: 14.972
CRUZEIRO EC: FÁBIO Deivison Lopes Maciel, Mauricio Bernardo VICTORINO Dansilio, PABLO de Barros Paulino, Carlos Gilberto Nascimento da Silva e Silva "GIL", GILBERT da Silva Melo, Antônio Marcos da Silva Filho "MARQUINHOS PARANÁ", HENRIQUE Pacheco de Lima (75 ANDRÉ Felippe Seixas DIAS), Walter Damián MONTILLO, ROGER Galera Flores, Ernesto Antonio FARÍAS (37 Francisco EVERTON de Almeida Andrade), José Maria ORTIGOZA Ortiz (67 Eduardo Pereira Rodrigues "DUDU"). DT: Alexis Stival "CUCA" Beluda
CD ONCE CALDAS: Luis Enrique MARTÍNEZ Rodríguez, Alexis Héctor HENRÍQUEZ Charales, Luis Alberto NÚÑEZ Charales, Elkin Darío CALLE Grajales, Diego Armando AMAYA Solano, Alexander MEJÍA Sabalsa, Claudio Matías MIRABAJE Correa (66 Jefferson CUERO Castro), Hárrison Steve HENAO Hurtado (55 John Fredy PAJOY Ortíz), Dayro Mauricio MORENO Galindo (85 Félix Andrés MICOLTA Micolta), Wason Libardo RENTERÍA Cuesta, Carlos Mario CARBONERO Mancilla. DT: Juan Carlos OSORIO Arbeláez
Sent off: Roger (31) / Carbonero (56)
Goals: Diego Armando AMAYA Solano (66), Dayro Mauricio MORENO Galindo (71).

SANTOS FC – CD AMÉRICA SA 1-0 (0-0)
Estádio Úrbano Caldeira (Vila Belmiro), Santos, 27.04.2011
Referee: Jorge Luis LARRIONDA Pietrafesa (URU), Attendance: 11.417
SANTOS FC: RAFAEL Cabral Barbosa, Eduardo Luís Abonízio de Souza "EDU DRACENA", JONATHAN Cícero Moreira, Severino dos Ramos DURVAL da Silva, Leonardo Lourenço Bastos "LÉO", DANILO Luiz da Silva, ELANO Ralph Blumer (90 ADRIANO Bispo dos Santos), Marcos AROUCA da Silva, Paulo Henrique Chagas de Lima "P.H. GANSO", José "ZÉ" EDUARDO Bischofe de Almeida (82 ALAN PATRICK Lourenço), NEYMAR da Silva Santos Júnior. DT: Muricy RAMALHO
CD AMÉRICA SA: Francisco Guillermo OCHOA Magaña, Aquivaldo MOSQUERA Romaña, Juan Carlos VALENZUELA Hernández, Diego Alberto CERVANTES Chávez (44 Miguel Arturo LAYÚN Prado), Oscar Adrián ROJAS Castillón, Diego Antonio REYES Rosales, ROSINEI Adolfo, Andrés Nicolás "Nico" OLIVERA (64 Vicente Martín SÁNCHEZ Bragunde), José Joaquín MARTÍNEZ Valadez, Vicente José Matías VUOSO (52 Ángel Eduardo REYNA Martínez), Daniel Omar MÁRQUEZ Palacios. DT: Carlos Enzo REINOSO Valdenegro
Sent off: Layún (90)
Goal: Paulo Henrique Chagas de Lima "P.H. GANSO" (38).

CD AMÉRICA SA – SANTOS FC 0-0
Estadio La Corregidora, Santiago de Querétaro, 3.05.2011
Referee: Carlos Alfredo VERA Rodríguez (ECU), Attendance: 32.673
CD AMÉRICA SA: Francisco Guillermo OCHOA Magaña, Aquivaldo MOSQUERA Romaña, Juan Carlos VALENZUELA Hernández, Oscar Adrián ROJAS Castillón, Patricio Enrique TREVIÑO Tripp, Diego Antonio REYES Rosales, Pavel PARDO Segura (51 Ángel Eduardo REYNA Martínez), ROSINEI Adolfo, Daniel Gastón MONTENEGRO (73 Lugiani Iván GALLARDO Rodríguez), Vicente Martín SÁNCHEZ Bragunde (54 Enrique Alajandro ESQUEDA Tirado), Vicente José Matías VUOSO. DT: Carlos Enzo REINOSO Valdenegro
SANTOS FC: RAFAEL Cabral Barbosa, Eduardo Luís Abonízio de Souza "EDU DRACENA" (85 ALEX SANDRO Lobo Silva), JONATHAN Cícero Moreira, Severino dos Ramos DURVAL da Silva, Leonardo Lourenço Bastos "LÉO", DANILO Luiz da Silva, Marcos AROUCA da Silva (57 RODRIGO Pereira POSSEBON), ADRIANO Bispo dos Santos, Paulo Henrique Chagas de Lima "P.H. GANSO", José "ZÉ" EDUARDO Bischofe de Almeida (63 BRUNO Henrique Fortunato AGUIAR), NEYMAR da Silva Santos Júnior. DT: Muricy RAMALHO

CA PEÑAROL MONTEVIDEO – SC INTERNACIONAL 1-1 (1-0)
Estadio Centenario, Montevideo, 28.04.2011
Referee: Carlos Manuel TORRES Nuñez (PAR), Attendance: 43.472
CA PEÑAROL MONTEVIDEO: Carlos Sebastián SOSA Silva, Octavio Darío RODRÍGUEZ Peña, Carlos Adrián VALDÉZ Suarez, Guillermo Daniel RODRÍGUEZ Pérez, Matías CORUJO Díaz, Alejandro Damián GONZÁLEZ Hernández, Luis Bernardo AGUIAR Burgos, Nicolás Andrés FREITAS Silva, Antonio PACHECO D'Agosti (79 Diego Martín ALONSO López), Henry Matías MIER Codina (70 Fabián Larry ESTOYANOFF Poggio), Alejandro MARTINUCCIO. DT: Diego Vicente AGUIRRE Camblor
SC INTERNACIONAL: RENAN Brito Soares, Fabián Guedes "BOLÍVAR", RODRIGO Baldasso da Costa, Claudinei Cardoso Féliz da Silva "NEI", KLÉBER de Carvalho Correa, Andrés Nicolás D'ALESSANDRO, Pablo Horacio GUIÑAZÚ, Mario Áriel BOLATTI, André Luiz Tavares "ANDREZINHO" (79 Paulo César Fonseca do Nascimento "TINGA"), RAFAEL Augusto SÓBIS do Nascimento (46 OSCAR dos Santos Emboaba Júnior), LEANDRO DAMIÃO da Silva dos Santos. DT: Paulo Roberto FALCÃO
Goals: Matías CORUJO Díaz (36) / LEANDRO DAMIÃO da Silva dos Santos (64).

SC INTERNACIONAL – CA PEÑAROL MONTEVIDEO 1-2 (1-0)
Estádio José Pinheiro Borda (Beira-Rio), Porto Alegre, 4.05.2011
Referee: Enrique Roberto OSSES Zencovich (CHI), Attendance: 42.863
SC INTERNACIONAL: RENAN Brito Soares, Fabián Guedes "BOLÍVAR", RODRIGO Baldasso da Costa, Claudinei Cardoso Féliz da Silva "NEI" (73 RAFAEL Augusto SÓBIS do Nascimento), KLÉBER de Carvalho Correa, Andrés Nicolás D'ALESSANDRO, Pablo Horacio GUIÑAZÚ, Mario Áriel BOLATTI, André Luiz Tavares "ANDREZINHO" (59 RICARDO GOULART Pereira), OSCAR dos Santos Emboaba Júnior (59 Paulo César Fonseca do Nascimento "TINGA"), LEANDRO DAMIÃO da Silva dos Santos. DT: Paulo Roberto FALCÃO
CA PEÑAROL MONTEVIDEO: Carlos Sebastián SOSA Silva, Octavio Darío RODRÍGUEZ Peña, Carlos Adrián VALDÉZ Suarez (72 Emiliano ALBÍN Antognazza), Guillermo Daniel RODRÍGUEZ Pérez, Matías CORUJO Díaz, Alejandro Damián GONZÁLEZ Hernández, Luis Bernardo AGUIAR Burgos, Nicolás Andrés FREITAS Silva, Henry Matías MIER Codina (80 Nicolás Mario DOMINGO), Juan Manuel OLIVERA López, Alejandro MARTINUCCIO (90 Édison Eliazer TORRES Martínez). DT: Diego Vicente AGUIRRE Camblor
Goals: OSCAR dos Santos Emboaba Júnior (1) /
Alejandro MARTINUCCIO (46), Juan Manuel OLIVERA López (50).

FLUMINENSE FC – CLUB LIBERTAD ASUNCIÓN 3-1 (1-0)
Estádio OlímpicoJoão Havelange (Engenhão), Rio de Janeiro, 28.04.2011
Referee: Sergio Fabián Pezzotta (ARG), Attendance: 25.378
FLUMINENSE FC: RICARDO Ferreira BERNA, JÚLIO CÉSAR Coelho de Moraes Júnior (40 FERNANDO "BOB" Paixão da Silva, 72 Clemenson de ARAÚJO Soares), MARIANO Ferreira Filho, Wellington Pereira Rodrigues "GUM", Rodrigo Oliveira de Bittencourt "DIGUINHO", Edimo Ferreira Campos "EDINHO", Edwin Armando VALENCIA Rodríguez, Darío Leonardo CONCA, Marco Antônio de Mattos Filho "MARQUINHO", Frederico Chaves Guedes "FRED", RAFAEL Martiniano de Miranda MOURA (87 DIOGO Antunes de Oliveira). DT: ENDERSON Alves MOREIRA
CLUB LIBERTAD ASUNCIÓN: Tobías Antonio VARGAS Insfrán, Carlos BONET Cacéres, Pedro Paulo PORTOCARRERO Angulo, Víctor Javier CÁCERES Centurión, Miguel Ángel Ramon SAMUDIO, Juan Rodrigo ROJAS Ovelar (83 Jorge Luís MOREIRA Ferreira), Ignacio CANUTO, Víctor Hugo AYALA Núñez, Nicolás PAVLOVICH (64 Ángel Reinaldo ORUÉ Echeverría), José Ariel NÚÑEZ Portelli (59 Manuel José MACIEL Fernández), Rodolfo Vicente GAMARRA Varela. DT: Gregorio Elso PÉREZ Perdigón
Goals: RAFAEL Martiniano de Miranda MOURA (3), Marco Antônio de Mattos Filho "MARQUINHO" (71), Darío Leonardo CONCA (74) / Rodolfo Vicente GAMARRA Varela (59).

CLUB LIBERTAD ASUNCIÓN – FLUMINENSE FC 3-0 (0-0)
Estadio Defensores del Chaco, Asunción, 4.05.2011
Referee: Roberto Carlos SILVERA Calcerrada (URU), Attendance: 2.699
CLUB LIBERTAD ASUNCIÓN: Tobías Antonio VARGAS Insfrán, Carlos BONET Cacéres, Pedro Paulo PORTOCARRERO Angulo, Sergio Daniel AQUINO (83 Ángel Reinaldo ORUÉ Echeverría), Víctor Javier CÁCERES Centurión, Miguel Ángel Ramon SAMUDIO, Ignacio CANUTO, Víctor Hugo AYALA Núñez (55 Juan Rodrigo ROJAS Ovelar), Nicolás PAVLOVICH, Manuel José MACIEL Fernández, Rodolfo Vicente GAMARRA Varela (74 José Ariel NÚÑEZ Portelli). DT: Gregorio Elso PÉREZ Perdigón
FLUMINENSE FC: RICARDO Ferreira BERNA, JÚLIO CÉSAR Coelho de Moraes Júnior, MARIANO Ferreira Filho, Wellington Pereira Rodrigues "GUM", Rodrigo Oliveira de Bittencourt "DIGUINHO" (88 Rodrigo Batista da Cruz "RODRIGUINHO"), Edimo Ferreira Campos "EDINHO", Edwin Armando VALENCIA Rodríguez (17 DIOGO Antunes de Oliveira), Darío Leonardo CONCA, Marco Antônio de Mattos Filho "MARQUINHO", Frederico Chaves Guedes "FRED", RAFAEL Martiniano de Miranda MOURA (73 Clemenson de ARAÚJO Soares). DT: ENDERSON Alves MOREIRA Sent off: Mariano (90)
Goals: Juan Rodrigo ROJAS Ovelar (57), Miguel Ángel Ramon SAMUDIO (85), José Ariel NÚÑEZ Portelli (90+1).

QUARTER-FINALS

CA PEÑAROL MONTEVIDEO – CD UNIVERSIDAD CATÓLICA 2-0 (1-0)
Estadio Centenario, Montevideo, 11.05.2011
Referee: Héctor Wálter BALDASSI (ARG), Attendance: 46.550
CA PEÑAROL MONTEVIDEO: Carlos Sebastián SOSA Silva, Octavio Darío RODRÍGUEZ Peña, Guillermo Daniel RODRÍGUEZ Pérez, Matías CORUJO Díaz, Alejandro Damián GONZÁLEZ Hernández, Luis Bernardo AGUIAR Burgos, Nicolás Andrés FREITAS Silva, Jonathan Matías URRETAVISCAYA da Luz (78 Fabián Larry ESTOYANOFF Poggio), Henry Matías MIER Codina (62 Emiliano ALBÍN Antognazza), Juan Manuel OLIVERA López (86 Diego Martín ALONSO López), Alejandro MARTINUCCIO. DT: Diego Vicente AGUIRRE Camblor
CD UNIVERSIDAD CATÓLICA: Paulo Andrés GARCÉS Contreras, Hans Alexis MARTÍNEZ Cabrera, Alfonso Cristián PAROT Rojas, Juan Eduardo ELUCHANS, Jorge Andrés ORMEÑO Guerra, Rodrigo Ignacio VALENZUELA Avilés, Francisco Andrés SILVA Gajardo (58 Felipe Alejandro GUTIÉRREZ Leiva), Fernando Andrés MENESES Cornejo (84 Francesco Javier PIZARRO Cartes), Tomás COSTA, Marcelo CAÑETE (75 Pablo Ignacio CALANDRIA), Lucas David PRATTO. DT: Juan Antonio PIZZI Torroja
Goals: Juan Manuel OLIVERA López (36), Alejandro MARTINUCCIO (90+3).

CD UNIVERSIDAD CATÓLICA – CA PEÑAROL MONTEVIDEO 2-1 (1-0)
Estadio San Carlos de Apoquindo, Santiago, 19.05.2011
Referee: Héber Roberto LOPES (BRA), Attendance: 12.942
CD UNIVERSIDAD CATÓLICA: Paulo Andrés GARCÉS Contreras, Hans Alexis MARTÍNEZ Cabrera, Alfonso Cristián PAROT Rojas, Juan Eduardo ELUCHANS, Jorge Andrés ORMEÑO Guerra, Rodrigo Ignacio VALENZUELA Avilés, Fernando Andrés MENESES Cornejo (78 Marcelo CAÑETE), Milovan Petar MIROSEVIC Albornoz, Tomás COSTA (51 Francisco Andrés SILVA Gajardo), Lucas David PRATTO, José Luis VILLANUEVA Ahumada (62 Roberto Carlos GUTIÉRREZ Gamboa). DT: Juan Antonio PIZZI Torroja
CA PEÑAROL MONTEVIDEO: Carlos Sebastián SOSA Silva, Octavio Darío RODRÍGUEZ Peña, Carlos Adrián VALDÉZ Suarez, Guillermo Daniel RODRÍGUEZ Pérez, Matías CORUJO Díaz, Alejandro Damián GONZÁLEZ Hernández, Luis Bernardo AGUIAR Burgos, Nicolás Andrés FREITAS Silva, Henry Matías MIER Codina (67 Fabián Larry ESTOYANOFF Poggio), Juan Manuel OLIVERA López (89 Diego Martín ALONSO López), Alejandro MARTINUCCIO. DT: Diego Vicente AGUIRRE Camblor
Goals: Fernando Andrés MENESES Cornejo (18), Roberto Carlos GUTIÉRREZ Gamboa (69) / Fabián Larry ESTOYANOFF Poggio (85).

CD ONCE CALDAS – SANTOS FC 0-1 (0-1)
Estadio Palogrande, Manizales, 11.05.2011
Referee: Juan Ernesto SOTO Arevalo (VEN), Attendance: 23.984
CD ONCE CALDAS: Luis Enrique MARTÍNEZ Rodríguez, Alexis Héctor HENRÍQUEZ Charales, Luis Alberto NÚÑEZ Charales, Elkin Darío CALLE Grajales, Diego Armando AMAYA Solano, Alexander MEJÍA Sabalsa, Claudio Matías MIRABAJE Correa (62 Yedinson PALACIOS León), Hárrison Steve HENAO Hurtado, Dayro Mauricio MORENO Galindo, Wason Libardo RENTERÍA Cuesta, John Fredy PAJOY Ortíz (53 Mario Alejandro GONZÁLEZ Castro). DT: Juan Carlos OSORIO Arbeláez
SANTOS FC: RAFAEL Cabral Barbosa, Eduardo Luís Abonízio de Souza "EDU DRACENA", JONATHAN Cícero Moreira, Severino dos Ramos DURVAL da Silva, Leonardo Lourenço Bastos "LÉO" (58 ALEX SANDRO Lobo Silva), DANILO Luiz da Silva, ELANO Ralph Blumer (90 BRUNO Henrique Fortunato AGUIAR), ADRIANO Bispo dos Santos, ALAN PATRICK Lourenço (74 FELIPE ANDERSON Pereira Gomes), José "ZÉ" EDUARDO Bischofe de Almeida, NEYMAR da Silva Santos Júnior. DT: Muricy RAMALHO
Sent off: Calle (59)
Goal: ALAN PATRICK Lourenço (42).

SANTOS FC – CD ONCE CALDAS 1-1 (1-1)
Estádio Municipal Paulo Machado de Carvalho (Pacaembú), São Paulo, 18.05.2011
Referee: Enrique Roberto OSSES Zencovich (CHI), Attendance: 35.135
SANTOS FC: RAFAEL Cabral Barbosa, Eduardo Luís Abonízio de Souza "EDU DRACENA", Severino dos Ramos DURVAL da Silva, Leonardo Lourenço Bastos "LÉO" (80 ALEX SANDRO Lobo Silva), DANILO Luiz da Silva, ELANO Ralph Blumer, Marcos AROUCA da Silva, ADRIANO Bispo dos Santos, ALAN PATRICK Lourenço (24 Marcos Rogério Ricci Lopes "PARÁ"), José "ZÉ" EDUARDO Bischofe de Almeida (68 KEIRRISON de Souza Carneiro), NEYMAR da Silva Santos Júnior. DT: Muricy RAMALHO
CD ONCE CALDAS: Luis Enrique MARTÍNEZ Rodríguez, Alexis Héctor HENRÍQUEZ Charales, Luis Alberto NÚÑEZ Charales, Yedinson PALACIOS León, Diego Armando AMAYA Solano, Jefferson CUERO Castro (76 John Fredy PAJOY Ortíz), Alexander MEJÍA Sabalsa, Claudio Matías MIRABAJE Correa (65 Hárrison Steve HENAO Hurtado), Dayro Mauricio MORENO Galindo, Wason Libardo RENTERÍA Cuesta, Carlos Mario CARBONERO Mancilla. DT: Juan Carlos OSORIO Arbeláez
Goals: NEYMAR da Silva Santos Júnior (11) / Wason Libardo RENTERÍA Cuesta (29).

CA VÉLEZ SÁRSFIELD – CLUB LIBERTAD ASUNCIÓN 3-0 (1-0)
Estadio Alberto J.Armando, Buenos Aires, 12.05.2011
Referee: Wilson Luiz SENEME (BRA), Attendance: 9.086
CA VÉLEZ SARSFIELD: Marcelo Alberto BAROVERO, Sebastián Enrique DOMÍNGUEZ, Emiliano Ramiro PAPA, Fernando ORTIZ, Franco RAZZOTTI Viretto, Víctor Eduardo ZAPATA, Fabián Alberto CUBERO, Maximiliano Nicolás MORALEZ (83 Ricardo Gastón DÍAZ), Augusto Matías FERNÁNDEZ (71 Iván Gonzalo BELLA), Arturo David RAMÍREZ (62 Ricardo Gabriel ÁLVAREZ), Juan Manuel MARTÍNEZ. DT: Ricardo Alberto GARECA
CLUB LIBERTAD ASUNCIÓN: Tobías Antonio VARGAS Insfrán, Carlos BONET Cacéres, Pedro Paulo PORTOCARRERO Angulo, Sergio Daniel AQUINO, Víctor Javier CÁCERES Centurión, Miguel Ángel Ramon SAMUDIO, Ignacio CANUTO, Víctor Hugo AYALA Núñez (46 Juan Rodrigo ROJAS Ovelar), Nicolás PAVLOVICH (84 Ángel Reinaldo ORUÉ Echeverría), Manuel José MACIEL Fernández (68 José Ariel NÚÑEZ Portelli), Rodolfo Vicente GAMARRA Varela. DT: Gregorio Elso PÉREZ Perdigón
Goals: Maximiliano Nicolás MORALEZ (20), Juan Manuel MARTÍNEZ (75 penalty, 80).

CLUB LIBERTAD ASUNCIÓN – CA VÉLEZ SÁRSFIELD 2-4 (1-1)
Estadio Defensores del Chaco, Asunción, 18.05.2011
Referee: Sálvio Spínola FAGUNDES Filho (BRA), Attendance: 2.300
CLUB LIBERTAD ASUNCIÓN: Tobías Antonio VARGAS Insfrán, Carlos BONET Cacéres (50 Víctor Hugo AYALA Núñez), Arnaldo Andrés VERA Chamorro, Sergio Daniel AQUINO, Víctor Javier CÁCERES Centurión, Miguel Ángel Ramon SAMUDIO, Juan Rodrigo ROJAS Ovelar, Ignacio CANUTO, Nicolás PAVLOVICH (46 Ángel Reinaldo ORUÉ Echeverría), Manuel José MACIEL Fernández (71 José Ariel NÚÑEZ Portelli), Rodolfo Vicente GAMARRA Varela. DT: Gregorio Elso PÉREZ Perdigón
CA VÉLEZ SARSFIELD: Marcelo Alberto BAROVERO, Sebastián Enrique DOMÍNGUEZ, Emiliano Ramiro PAPA, Fernando ORTIZ, Franco RAZZOTTI Viretto, Víctor Eduardo ZAPATA, Fabián Alberto CUBERO, Maximiliano Nicolás MORALEZ (76 Arturo David RAMÍREZ), Augusto Matías FERNÁNDEZ, Ricardo Gabriel ÁLVAREZ (83 Iván Gonzalo BELLA), Santiago Martín SILVA Olivera (64 Guillermo Luis FRANCO Farcuarson). DT: Ricardo Alberto GARECA
Goals: Juan Rodrigo ROJAS Ovelar (44), Manuel José MACIEL Fernández (50) / Maximiliano Nicolás MORALEZ (45, 66), Guillermo Luis FRANCO Farcuarson (86 penalty), Augusto Matías FERNÁNDEZ (87).

CF JAGUARES DE CHIAPAS SA – CLUB CERRO PORTEÑO 1-1 (0-0)
Estadio Zoque Víctor Manuel Reyna, Tuxtla Gutiérrez, 12.05.2011
Referee: Sergio Fabián PEZZOTTA (ARG), Attendance: 14.022
CF JAGUARES DE CHIAPAS SA: Fabián Israel VILLASEÑOR López, Ismael Ignacio FUENTES Castro, Óscar Francisco RAZO Ventura, Miguel Ángel MARTÍNEZ, Christian de Jesús VALDÉZ Loaiza, Édgar Bismarck ANDRADE Rentería, Luis Ricardo ESQUEDA Ornelas, Jorge Marcelo RODRÍGUEZ Núñez (67 Guillermo ROJAS Rumilla), Alan Miguel ZAMORA Gonzalez (46 Antonio Michael PEDROZA Whitham), Antonio SALAZAR Castillo (79 Julio Daniel FRÍAS Adame), Jorge Daniel HERNÁNDEZ Govea. DT: José Guadalupe CRUZ Núnez
CLUB CERRO PORTEÑO: Diego Daniel BARRETO Cáceres, Mariano Esteban UGLESSICH, Pedro Juan BENÍTEZ Dominguez, Iván Rodrigo PIRIS Leguizamón, César Iván BENÍTEZ León, Javier Alejandro VILLARREAL, Luís Enrique CÁCERES Centurión, Jonathan FABBRO (80 Rodrigo Ramon BURGOS), Iván Arturo TORRES Riveros, Juan Manuel LUCERO (62 Juan Manuel ITURBE Arévalo), Roberto Antonio NANNI (72 Fredy José BAREIRO Gamarra). DT: Leonardo Rubén ASTRADA
Goals: Antonio Michael PEDROZA Whitham (90+1) / Jonathan FABBRO (72).

CLUB CERRO PORTEÑO – CF JAGUARES DE CHAIPAS SA 1-0 (0-0)
Estadio General Pablo Rojas, Asunción, 19.05.2011
Referee: Darío Agustín UBRIACO Mederos (URU), Attendance: 24.178
CLUB CERRO PORTEÑO: Diego Daniel BARRETO Cáceres, Mariano Esteban UGLESSICH, Pedro Juan BENÍTEZ Dominguez, Iván Rodrigo PIRIS Leguizamón, César Iván BENÍTEZ León, Javier Alejandro VILLARREAL, Luís Enrique CÁCERES Centurión (70 Jorge Daniel NÚÑEZ Espínola), Jonathan FABBRO, Iván Arturo TORRES Riveros, Juan Manuel LUCERO (73 Julio Daniel DOS SANTOS Rodríguez), Roberto Antonio NANNI (63 Fredy José BAREIRO Gamarra). DT: Leonardo Rubén ASTRADA
CF JAGUARES DE CHIAPAS SA: Fabián Israel VILLASEÑOR López, Ismael Ignacio FUENTES Castro, Óscar Francisco RAZO Ventura, Miguel Ángel MARTÍNEZ, Christian de Jesús VALDÉZ Loaiza, Édgar Bismarck ANDRADE Rentería (56 Alan Miguel ZAMORA Gonzalez), Luis Ricardo ESQUEDA Ornelas, Jorge Marcelo RODRÍGUEZ Núñez, Jackson Arley MARTÍNEZ Valencia, Antonio Michael PEDROZA Whitham (62 Antonio SALAZAR Castillo), Jorge Daniel HERNÁNDEZ Govea (80 Guillermo ROJAS Rumilla). DT: José Guadalupe CRUZ Núnez
Sent off: Fuentes (82)
Goal: Pedro Juan BENÍTEZ Dominguez (72).

SEMI-FINALS

SANTOS FC – CLUB CERRO PORTEÑO 1-0 (1-0)
Estádio Municipal Paulo Machado de Carvalho (Pacaembú), São Paulo 25.05.2011
Referee: Jorge Luis LARRIONDA Pietrafesa (URU), Attendance: 31.434
SANTOS FC: RAFAEL Cabral Barbosa, Eduardo Luís Abonízio de Souza "EDU DRACENA", Severino dos Ramos DURVAL da Silva, Leonardo Lourenço Bastos "LÉO" (81 ALEX SANDRO Lobo Silva), Marcos Rogério Ricci Lopes "PARÁ", DANILO Luiz da Silva, ELANO Ralph Blumer (88 ALAN PATRICK Lourenço), Marcos AROUCA da Silva, ADRIANO Bispo dos Santos, José "ZÉ" EDUARDO Bischofe de Almeida (81 MAIKON Fernando Souza LEITE), NEYMAR da Silva Santos Júnior. DT: Muricy RAMALHO
CLUB CERRO PORTEÑO: Diego Daniel BARRETO Cáceres, Mariano Esteban UGLESSICH, Pedro Juan BENÍTEZ Dominguez, Iván Rodrigo PIRIS Leguizamón, César Iván BENÍTEZ León, Julio Daniel DOS SANTOS Rodríguez, Javier Alejandro VILLARREAL (85 Rodrigo Ramon BURGOS), Luís Enrique CÁCERES Centurión, Jonathan FABBRO, Iván Arturo TORRES Riveros (65 Jorge Daniel NÚÑEZ Espínola), Fredy José BAREIRO Gamarra (74 Roberto Antonio NANNI). DT: Leonardo Rubén ASTRADA
Goal: Eduardo Luís Abonízio de Souza "EDU DRACENA" (43).

CLUB CERRO PORTEÑO – SANTOS FC 3-3 (1-3)
Estadio General Pablo Rojas, Asunción, 1.06.2011
Referee: Wilmar Alexander ROLDÁN Pérez (COL), Attendance: 32.000
CLUB CERRO PORTEÑO: Diego Daniel BARRETO Cáceres, Mariano Esteban UGLESSICH, Pedro Juan BENÍTEZ Dominguez, Iván Rodrigo PIRIS Leguizamón, César Iván BENÍTEZ León, Julio Daniel DOS SANTOS Rodríguez, Luís Enrique CÁCERES Centurión, Rodrigo Ramon BURGOS (41 Juan Manuel LUCERO), Jonathan FABBRO, Iván Arturo TORRES Riveros (10 Juan Manuel ITURBE Arévalo), Fredy José BAREIRO Gamarra (66 Roberto Antonio NANNI). DT: Leonardo Rubén ASTRADA
SANTOS FC: RAFAEL Cabral Barbosa, Eduardo Luís Abonízio de Souza "EDU DRACENA", JONATHAN Cícero Moreira (26 Marcos Rogério Ricci Lopes "PARÁ"), Severino dos Ramos DURVAL da Silva, DANILO Luiz da Silva, ALEX SANDRO Lobo Silva, ELANO Ralph Blumer (70 RODRIGO Pereira POSSEBON), Marcos AROUCA da Silva, ADRIANO Bispo dos Santos, José "ZÉ" EDUARDO Bischofe de Almeida (73 MAIKON Fernando Souza LEITE), NEYMAR da Silva Santos Júnior. DT: Muricy RAMALHO
Sent off: Edu Dracena (90)
Goals: César Iván BENÍTEZ León (31), Juan Manuel LUCERO (60), Jonathan FABBRO (81) / José "ZÉ" EDUARDO Bischofe de Almeida (2), Diego Daniel BARRETO Cáceres (28 *own goal*), NEYMAR da Silva Santos Júnior (45+2).

CA PEÑAROL MONTEVIDEO – CA VÉLEZ SÁRSFIELD 1-0 (1-0)
Estadio Centenario, Montevideo, 26.05.2011
Referee: Carlos Arecio AMARILLA Demarqui (PAR), Attendance: 52.904
CA PEÑAROL MONTEVIDEO: Carlos Sebastián SOSA Silva, Octavio Darío RODRÍGUEZ Peña, Carlos Adrián VALDÉZ Suarez, Guillermo Daniel RODRÍGUEZ Pérez, Matías CORUJO Díaz (57 Fabián Larry ESTOYANOFF Poggio), Alejandro Damián GONZÁLEZ Hernández, Luis Bernardo AGUIAR Burgos, Nicolás Andrés FREITAS Silva, Henry Matías MIER Codina (76 Emiliano ALBÍN Antognazza), Juan Manuel OLIVERA López (83 Diego Martín ALONSO López), Alejandro MARTINUCCIO. DT: Diego Vicente AGUIRRE Camblor
CA VÉLEZ SARSFIELD: Marcelo Alberto BAROVERO, Sebastián Enrique DOMÍNGUEZ, Emiliano Ramiro PAPA, Fernando ORTIZ, Franco RAZZOTTI Viretto, Víctor Eduardo ZAPATA, Fabián Alberto CUBERO, Augusto Matías FERNÁNDEZ (81 Iván Gonzalo BELLA), Ricardo Gabriel ÁLVAREZ, Santiago Martín SILVA Olivera (86 Guillermo Luis FRANCO Farcuarson), Juan Manuel MARTÍNEZ (75 Arturo David RAMÍREZ). DT: Ricardo Alberto GARECA
Goal: Octavio Darío RODRÍGUEZ Peña (44).

CA VÉLEZ SÁRSFIELD – CA PEÑAROL MONTEVIDEO 2-1 (1-1)
Estadio José Amalfitani, Buenos Aires, 2.06.2011
Referee: Enrique Roberto OSSES Zencovich (CHI), Attendance: 45.000
CA VÉLEZ SARSFIELD: Marcelo Alberto BAROVERO, Sebastián Enrique DOMÍNGUEZ, Emiliano Ramiro PAPA, Fernando ORTIZ, Víctor Eduardo ZAPATA (88 Arturo David RAMÍREZ), Fabián Alberto CUBERO (14 Fernando Omar TOBIO), Maximiliano Nicolás MORALEZ (61 Ricardo Gabriel ÁLVAREZ), Augusto Matías FERNÁNDEZ, Héctor Miguel CANTEROS, Santiago Martín SILVA Olivera, Juan Manuel MARTÍNEZ. DT: Ricardo Alberto GARECA
CA PEÑAROL MONTEVIDEO: Carlos Sebastián SOSA Silva, Octavio Darío RODRÍGUEZ Peña, Carlos Adrián VALDÉZ Suarez, Guillermo Daniel RODRÍGUEZ Pérez, Matías CORUJO Díaz, Alejandro Damián GONZÁLEZ Hernández, Luis Bernardo AGUIAR Burgos, Nicolás Andrés FREITAS Silva, Henry Matías MIER Codina (70 Fabián Larry ESTOYANOFF Poggio), Juan Manuel OLIVERA López, Alejandro MARTINUCCIO (83 Emiliano ALBÍN Antognazza). DT: Diego Vicente AGUIRRE Camblor
Sent off: Ortiz (69)
Goals: Fernando Omar TOBIO (45+1), Santiago Martín SILVA Olivera (66) /
Henry Matías MIER Codina (33).

FINALS

CA PEÑAROL MONTEVIDEO – SANTOS FC 0-0
Estadio Centenario, Montevideo, 15.06.2011
Referee: Carlos Arecio AMARILLA Demarqui (PAR), Attendance: 60.000
CA PEÑAROL MONTEVIDEO: Carlos Sebastián SOSA Silva, Octavio Darío RODRÍGUEZ Peña, Carlos Adrián VALDÉZ Suarez, Guillermo Daniel RODRÍGUEZ Pérez, Matías CORUJO Díaz (67 Antonio PACHECO D'Agosti), Alejandro Damián GONZÁLEZ Hernández, Luis Bernardo AGUIAR Burgos, Nicolás Andrés FREITAS Silva, Henry Matías MIER Codina (56 Fabián Larry ESTOYANOFF Poggio), Juan Manuel OLIVERA López (82 Diego Martín ALONSO López), Alejandro MARTINUCCIO. DT: Diego Vicente AGUIRRE Camblor
SANTOS FC: RAFAEL Cabral Barbosa, Severino dos Ramos DURVAL da Silva, Marcos Rogério Ricci Lopes "PARÁ", BRUNO RODRIGO Fenelon Palomo, DANILO Luiz da Silva, ALEX SANDRO Lobo Silva, ELANO Ralph Blumer (79 ALAN PATRICK Lourenço), Marcos AROUCA da Silva, ADRIANO Bispo dos Santos, José "ZÉ" EDUARDO Bischofe de Almeida (89 BRUNO Henrique Fortunato AGUIAR), NEYMAR da Silva Santos Júnior. DT: Muricy RAMALHO

SANTOS FC – CA PEÑAROL MONTEVIDEO 2-1 (0-0)
Estádio Municipal Paulo Machado de Carvalho (Pacaembú), São Paulo, 22.06.2011
Referee: Sergio Fabián PEZZOTTA (ARG), Attendance: 37.952
SANTOS FC: RAFAEL Cabral Barbosa, Eduardo Luís Abonízio de Souza "EDU DRACENA", Severino dos Ramos DURVAL da Silva, Leonardo Lourenço Bastos "LÉO" (68 ALEX SANDRO Lobo Silva), DANILO Luiz da Silva, ELANO Ralph Blumer, Marcos AROUCA da Silva, ADRIANO Bispo dos Santos, Paulo Henrique Chagas de Lima "P.H. GANSO" (86 Marcos Rogério Ricci Lopes "PARÁ"), José "ZÉ" EDUARDO Bischofe de Almeida, NEYMAR da Silva Santos Júnior. DT: Muricy RAMALHO
CA PEÑAROL MONTEVIDEO: Carlos Sebastián SOSA Silva, Octavio Darío RODRÍGUEZ Peña, Carlos Adrián VALDÉZ Suarez, Guillermo Daniel RODRÍGUEZ Pérez, Matías CORUJO Díaz, Alejandro Damián GONZÁLEZ Hernández (38 Emiliano ALBÍN Antognazza, 79 Fabián Larry ESTOYANOFF Poggio), Luis Bernardo AGUIAR Burgos, Nicolás Andrés FREITAS Silva, Henry Matías MIER Codina (63 Jonathan Matías URRETAVISCAYA da Luz), Juan Manuel OLIVERA López, Alejandro MARTINUCCIO. DT: Diego Vicente AGUIRRE Camblor
Goals: NEYMAR da Silva Santos Júnior (46), DANILO Luiz da Silva (68) /
Severino dos Ramos DURVAL da Silva (79 *own goal*).